THE TAIWAN POLITICAL MIRACLE

Essays on Political Development, Elections and Foreign Relations

John F. Copper

East Asia Research Institute
and
University Press of America, Inc.
Lanham • New York • Oxford

Copyright © 1997 by
East Asia Research Institute

University Press of America,® Inc.
4720 Boston Way
Lanham, Maryland 20706

12 Hid's Copse Rd.
Cummor Hill, Oxford OX2 9JJ

Copublished by arrangement with the East Asia Research Institute

Library of Congress Cataloging-in-Publication Data

Copper, John Franklin.
The Taiwan political miracle: essays on political development,
elections and foreign relations / by John F. Copper.
p.   cm.
Includes index.
l. Political culture--Taiwan. 2. Elections--Taiwan. 3. Taiwan--
Politics and government-1945- I. Title.
JQ1536.C67 1997 306.2'095124'9--dc21   96-25161 CIP

ISBN 0-7618-0112-X (cloth: alk. ppr.)

To Richard L. Walker

Scholar and Statesman

Mentor and Friend

Table of Contents

Section III   Essays on Foreign Policy and Diplomacy

About the Author

Foreword

For decades many in the academic community dismissed Taiwan's economic development as the result of American economic aid. Even after Taiwan experienced rapid economic growth for several years most scholars still failed to recognize Taiwan's experience was worthy of emulation. Time has demonstrated the error of that view. Taiwan's rapid economic growth is now almost everywhere recognized as "miraculous." Moreover, it is now axiomatic that Taiwan's economic success is instructive for other countries. So impressive has been its economic success that even the communist leadership in the People's Republic of China has used the Taiwan model to modernize its economy. In fact, doing as Taiwan did, in large measure, explains China's recent rapid economic growth.

If few scholars early on took note of Taiwan's economic development experience, even fewer recognized that Taiwan had a political development experience worth studying. Patently Taiwan has more to teach us than simply how to industrialize a densely populated and resource-poor small island. What Taiwan has done politically is perhaps more impressive and worthy of emulation than its economic accomplishments. It is a nation that has made the transition from autocracy to democracy quickly and without setback or violence. It has also accomplished that feat in some unique ways and in the face of formidable obstacles.

In The *Taiwan Political Miracle*, Professor Copper helps us appreciate Taiwan's fantastic political modernization. Copper tells us that the political accomplishments of the Republic of China have been every bit as spectacular as its economic development. He informs us that the implications of its political development are as salient as those of Taiwan's economic growth and industrialization. He advises us that political change in Taiwan was not as easily accomplished as its economic development and that Taiwan's transition to democracy makes it likely the world's foremost political development experiment.

Obviously the story of the democratization of Taiwan deserves to be told, and told well. Professor Copper tells it well. Dr. Copper is the West's most prolific writer on Taiwan and one of the most foremost scholars dealing with the politics of the Republic of China.

Finally, *The Taiwan Political Miracle* is not just a story of one nation's political change to democracy, but an analysis of the events and processes that accompanied that and made it possible. It is a book that I recommend to anyone interested in the democratization process in this unique nation where it happened so fast yet so smoothly. This book should be read by anyone with an interest in this "miracle" country.

A. James Gregor
August 1996

Preface

Much has been written about the "Taiwan miracle"—referring, of course, to the extremely successful, widely praised and often emulated economic development of Republic of China's (the country's official title). In fact, that Taiwan is an economic success story is axiomatic.

Less, however, has been written about Taiwan's political development, which in the past dozen or so years has been even more dramatic in many ways. Taiwan is, in my opinion, as worthy of praise for its political modernization as for its economic miracle. In just three to four decades, the Republic of China's polity has been transformed from an authoritarian, closed system to a democracy. It did this without a contributing colonial experience and while living under the threat of invasion.

The process went something like this: In the early 1950s the Nationalist Party, or Kuomintang (KMT), launched a party reform and an anti-corruption campaign to reform itself and change the government. Meanwhile it undertook land reform that made democracy grow in rural Taiwan. In the 1960s, the political system was modernized in other important ways. Opposition politics began to emerge. So did interest groups. In the 1970s, the ruling party, which was composed mostly of Chinese that moved to Taiwan from the mainland in 1949, began to recruit locally-born Chinese or Taiwanese in a kind of "affirmative action" program. Nationalist Party leaders got rid of much of Taiwan's oppressive bureaucracy and reformed the system in some creative ways while making government officials sensitive to public demands and responsive to a modern and dynamic economy.

Political change during this time was in large part both necessitated and energized by rapid economic development. As the economy grew and matured, the free flow of information was essential to continued economic expansion. The modernization of Taiwan's polity thus became a sine qua non to sustain its miracle growth. U.S. pressure also helped bring about political change. So did Taiwan's forward-looking top officials.

In 1987, martial law was ended. At this juncture, the rest of the world took note of Taiwan's democratization. This was considered a watershed event. This change, however, was more formality than substance—though it did encourage opposition politicians to be more assertive and was followed by important changes in Taiwan's legal system.

These and other advances were possible because Taiwan's political leadership saw the need for change. It was an enlightened leadership. Those responsible for economic development possessed a kind of genius for managing the economy and fostering growth. But they also understood the relationship between economic and political modernization. Chiang Ching-kuo possessed this same kind of genius for political change. So does Lee Teng-hui.

In 1980, the nation held its first competitive national election—following years of local democratic elections. In 1986, after the formation of the Democratic Progressive Party (DPP), Taiwan held the first two-party election ever held in a Chinese nation. It was also one of the earliest and perhaps the first meaningful two-party election in any country that was not prepared for democracy during a colonial experience.

In December 1989, the opposition Democratic Progressive Party "won" a national election, at least according to reports in every major Taiwan newspaper. It set back or "defeated" (though it did not win a majority of seats in the Legislative Yuan) the Nationalist Party, which had suffered from internal confusion after President Chiang Ching-Kuo's death in 1988 and subsequent factional strife. Pundits at the time spoke of a two-party system having taken root.

Meanwhile, the Nationalist Party changed its own rules and democratized. The ruling party did this notwithstanding the fact that many political parties in Western democracies are not run according to democratic principles because they don't need to be; democracy can work without this. Party leaders, however, saw this step as necessary; if the nation were to democratize, they reckoned, the party had to also, and did.

In 1991, the ruling Nationalist Party persuaded or forced "elder parliamentarians" in all of the elected bodies of the government to retire. The National Assembly subsequently picked by the elect-orate was thus a "new" one. Some U.S. political observers noted at that time that this was something the United States needed to do and was proof that Taiwan's political system was thoroughly reformed and the nation was now a democracy. Constitutional revision followed. In 1992, a new Legislative Yuan was elected. In 1994, the governor of Taiwan and the mayors of its metropolitan cities, Taipei and Kaohsiung, were elected in another important election.

The Republic of China, however, suffered serious diplomatic setbacks in the 1970s and 1980s. During the Cold War, Taipei aligned with the West. It claimed jurisdiction over all of China and represented all Chinese people in the world community for more than two decades after Mao established the People's Republic of China, which ruled the mainland. Nevertheless, it lost the China seat in the United Nations in 1971 and was "expelled" (perhaps the wrong word, since Taipei did not use the veto to try to prevent what happened as it might have) from this world body. It subsequently lost official diplomatic ties with most nations of the world—including the United States in 1979.

Yet Taiwan did not despair. It gained such confidence about its political modernization process during the 1980s that it promoted itself as a model for Chinese leaders in Beijing to consider following. Its leaders spoke of the "Taiwan experience"—meaning its political modernization as well as economic development. Taiwan then began investing in and trading with the mainland, building extensive economic links across the Taiwan Strait. Taiwan, in fact, seemed destined to affect the future of the mainland both economically and politically rather than simply succumbing to absorption.

In 1989, Taipei dropped its claim to rule all of China. In 1991, it ended the state of war with Beijing. It subsequently negotiated with Chinese representatives from Beijing, thereby acknowledging that the Cold War had ended and that the two Chinese governments were in the same Pacific Rim economic bloc (one of three that dominated world politics). But, it also realized that it was still threatened militarily by Beijing; in fact, that threat had become larger as Beijing now had to worry less about enemies on its borders and had increased its military spending by huge amounts.

Yet, whether Taiwan is to unify with China in the near future remains uncertain. It is still growing apart politically, but it is quickly integrating with the mainland economically. Most of Taiwan's citizens favor the status quo is since a solution to the question of unification or separation can probably not be found immediately. In fact, in this case time may solve a problem that could provoke a crisis and possibly war.

The following essays represent a considerable span of time, though they were all written during a period when political change in Taiwan was remarkable both for its pace and for its impact on Taiwan's polity. During this time Taiwan became a paradigm for success in political modernization. Internal political reform was the most salient part of the modernization process. Elections likewise played an essential role. Finally, an effective foreign policy facilitated the process and vice versa. Students of the process of political development can and should learn much from Taiwan's experiences. I hope the following chapters will contribute to this learning process.

During the period covered in this book, both attitudes and language have changed. Rather than try to be consistent, I have generally left terms as they were at the time; thus the reader will see Teng Hsiao-p'ing and Deng Xiaoping and Peking and Beijing which refer to the same person and place, respectively. Some editing has been done, however, to afford stylistic consistency.

Finally, I am indebted to too many people to mention here—for their ideas, encouragement, and help. I alone, however, take the blame for any errors of either commission or omission and for not always understanding events fully or seeing the future clearly.

John F. Copper
August 1996

Acknowledgements

The author wishes to acknowledge and express thanks to the original publishers of the article/chapters in this book. The following journals or publishers are recognized:

Part I

1. Hungdah Chiu and Shao-chuan Leng, eds, *China: Seventy Years Since the Hsin Hai Revolution* (Charlottesville, VA: University of Virginia Press, 1984)

2. Hungdah Chiu, ed., *Survey of Recent Developments in China (Mainland and Taiwan), 1985–86* (Baltimore: University of Maryland School of Law, 1987)

3. *Current History*, April 1986

4. *Asian Thought and Society*, January 1988

5. *Journal of Northeast Asian Studies*, Summer 1988

6. *Backgrounder*, Asian Studies Center, The Heritage Foundation, July 14, 1987

7. *Asian Background Papers* , 1988

8. *Midsouth Political Science Journal*, Spring 1992

9. Cynthia Chenault, ed., *Modernizing East Asia: Economic and Cultural Dimensions of Political Change* (New York: St. John's University Press, 1989)

10. *Journal of Chinese Studies*, October 1994

Part II

1. John F. Copper with George P. Chen, *Taiwan's Elections: Political Development and Democratization in the Republic of China* (Baltimore: University of Maryland School of Law, 1984)

2. John F. Copper with George P. Chen, *Taiwan's Elections: Political Development and Democratization in the Republic of China* (Baltimore: University of Maryland School of Law, 1984)

3. *Asian Thought and Society*, July 1987

4. *Journal of Northeast Asian Studies*, Winter 1990

5. *Journal of Northeast Asian Studies*,

6. *World Affairs*, Fall 1992

7. *Asian Affairs*, Spring 1995

8. *Asian Affairs*, Spring 1989

9. Cecilia S. Chang, ed., *The Republic of China on Taiwan, 1949-1988* (New York: St. John's University Press, 1991)

10. *World Affairs*, Winter 1993

Part III

1. *Orbis*, Summer 1977

2. *Asian Quarterly*, Number 3, 1972

3. *Asian Affairs*, May-June 1979

4. *Journal of Northeast Asian Studies*, December 1982

5. *The American Asian Review*, Winter 1992

6. *Asian Perspective*, Spring-Summer 1983

7. *Journal of East Asian Affairs*, Winter/Spring 1992

8. Jung Hyun Shin, Tai-huan Kwak and Edward A. Olsen, eds., *Northeast Asian Security and Peace: Toward the 1990s* (Seoul: Kyung Kee University Press, 1989)

9. King-yu Chang, ed., *ROC-US Relations Under the Taiwan Relations Act: Practice and Prospects* (Taipei: Institute of International Relations, 1988)

10. *Journal of East Asian Affairs*, Winter/Spring 1995

Section I
Politics and Political Change

Introduction

This section is comprised of essays on various aspects of Taiwan's domestic politics that relate to and explain its political development. The chapters in this section cover a considerable period of time, from three or four decades ago to the present time. The focus is on the process of democratic change—excluding elections, political parties, and party competition—which are covered in Section II.

That Taiwan, or the Republic of China, has democratized is now known to most observers. When that democratization process started and why it happened is less clear. The degree to which Taiwan's policy has modernized from an authoritarian system to a democracy is, likewise, still the topic of some debate.

I believe that some of the preconditions for democracy can be found in the island's history. Its population was cosmopolitan centuries ago, Taiwan having had numerous contacts with other countries, including Western democracies, through trade and colonization. A bureaucratic system was not transplanted from China by immigrants from the mainland and did not evolve to any extent in Taiwan. Neither did a rigid class system take root in Taiwan to the degree one might think given the fact that Chinese culture was brought to the island by the early Chinese migrants. Most immigrants disdained the class barriers in Chinese society and organized their social systems differently.

When the government of the Republic of China and the Nationalist Party or Kuomintang (KMT), moved to Taiwan in 1949, they facilitated political change. The Nationalist's defeat at the hands of Mao and the Chinese Communist Party had taught them a bitter lesson, but in some respects also a good lesson. When they arrived in Taiwan, KMT leaders realized that they had to have the support of the people on Taiwan at least to some degree. Winning public support meant getting rid of corruption, working hard, and doing a good job of leading and managing public administration. Aware of these things, they reformed the government and the ruling party.

The Nationalist Chinese also took a constitution with them to Taiwan. The island had not been ruled constitutionally before. Although many of the individual and civil rights in the constitution were canceled by the Temporary Provisions, top Republic of China leaders never expressed any desire to establish a nondemocratic form of government. Democracy was simply to be delayed or implemented slowly because the people were not ready and the nation lived under threat. How sincere was their desire to build a democratic system? This question was frequently asked. In fact, opposition politicians often called on KMT leaders to fulfill their promises to build democracy. It is worthy of note and may go far in explaining Taiwan's political modernization, that top KMT officials never once said they would not. Thus, there was always in Taiwan's future a plan for a democratic system.

That the United States provided for Taiwan's security was also critical. With the outbreak of the Korean War, President Truman sent the Seventh Fleet to the Taiwan Strait to block a then-imminent invasion by Mao's army. After that, the United States continued to protect Taiwan from attack by the People's Republic of China. This safe and secure environment made political change in the direction of democracy feasible. U.S. efforts, of course, were made easier by the fact that Taiwan is an island with ocean barriers to invasion. This feature may also have helped Taiwan establish a democratic system of government. Democracies historically most often evolved in island countries or in countries that had secure borders due to geography.

The next major step in political modernization, and the first in terms of an official plan for transforming the island to a democracy (though its main aim were economic and social change), was land reform. The land reform program, launched in the early 1950s, destroyed the feudal economic and political systems in rural Taiwan. The political sociology in Taiwan's countryside changed dramatically, as did the workings of rural politics. Although not widely acclaimed at the time, the program was patently instrumental in bringing grassroots democracy Taiwan. This is particularly important if one gives credence to the argument that democracy in Taiwan grew from "the bottom up," or started in local government and moved from there to national politics—even though the central government and the Nationalist Party must be given credit for laying the groundwork.

Taiwan's economic development was also a major factor behind its political development. Growth started in the agricultural sector. Next came the industrial sector. Industrialization brought further prosperity and fostered urbanization and the growth of the middle class; both were closely related to the process of democratization. One must keep in mind, incidently, that economic development based on hard work and good planning often facilitates the growth of democracy. Economic growth built on foreign assistance or selling natural resources usually does not facilitate a democratic transition. Another important variable was that

Taiwan's economic growth benefited all; in other words, there was growth with equity. Economic growth stimulated by trade also helped. Commerce, especially with Western democracies, has fostered, in many nations, an understanding of the relationship between capitalist economic development and a democratic system. One would so describe Taiwan's economic development. Of course, the business community's realization that continued economic prosperity depended upon the free flow of information, which only democratic systems provide for, was another significant factor, especially in a subsequent stage of the development process. In addition, the populace of Taiwan understood the link and so did the country's political leaders.

Specific efforts by the government and the KMT to build popular support and alleviate ethnic tension (between early migrants or Taiwanese and later immigrants, meaning after World War II arrivals, or Mainland Chinese) was also relevant to constructing a democratic system. Mainland Chinese dominated the national government (though not local governments) and the ruling party in the early years. In the 1970s, this situation began to change, especially as Chiang Ching-kuo increased his authority in both the KMT and the government. Taiwanese were encouraged to join the Nationalist Party and to seek government jobs. Soon Taiwan's political leadership became a fairly equitable mixture of ethnic groups; this change was necessary if democracy was to prevail, especially mass democracy.

Democratization in Taiwan was also, as historical events or trends of significance often are, impacted by one special individual. In Taiwan's case, this person was Chiang Ching-kuo. His father, Chiang Kai-shek, launched Taiwan's land reform and started its economic miracle, both of which were instrumental in creating an environment conducive to political change. Local democracy as well worked for the first time under his leadership. But it was Chiang Ching-kuo who implemented political change of the democratic type in national politics. Under his stewardship democracy became real. Lee Teng-hui also deserves much credit for the Taiwan political miracle. Lee preserved the progress Chiang Ching-kuo started and pushed the democratization process to an advanced stage.

Getting rid of corruption and preventing the growth of elite bureaucracies was likewise important to the process of democratization. As premier Chiang Ching-kuo adopted anti-corruption and administrative streamlining policies. Government employees at all levels became or were forced to be responsive to public demands. The business community supported the president, realizing that economic growth, especially of an advanced economy, required an enlightened and responsive political system run by competent and able leaders.

Elections, too, played a role. So big was their contribution that, as noted above, I have devoted Section II to their impact together with the evolution of a competitive party system. Elections, however, came only after the foundation for meaningful change had to be laid. In other words, preconditions for democracy had to be in place; otherwise, elections would not have had the impact they did.

Legislative decisions also evoked democracy. They have not been noticed very much, but they were crucial. An active judiciary was also important and infrequently praised. Similarly the success of democracy in local government mentioned above needed access and its leaders mobility (which they did) to have a positive influence on the national government.

The abolition of martial law in 1987 was viewed by most observers as a watershed event in Taiwan's democratization. In fact, most observers give much more importance to this event than to other democratic changes made at this time or even the many instances of progress that preceded or accompanied it. This event, competes with the formation of the Democratic Progressive Party in 1988 in the eyes of most observers as the turning point in Taiwan's successful political modernization.

Chapter 1 looks at the Republic of China's political system: how it was designed, how it works, where political power resides, and so on. The author notes that the blueprint for the nation's political system in its constitution was democracy. In the past, however, many questioned whether the Republic of China would ever really become a democracy. Later, opposition politicians, often complained that democratization was too slow. In retrospect, however, going slow and engineering democracy in stages and with caution, as the father of the Republic of China, Sun Yat-sen, had recommended, was the best approach.

In Chapter 2, I examine some of the impediments to political change at a critical juncture in Taiwan's recent history. Could the democratization process have been reversed? Certainly this possibility needs to be contemplated, even if in retrospect.

In the third chapter, I discuss national politics and the 1986 election. This election and others are discussed in depth in Section II. But since this was a crisis period, and was (and is still) seen by many observers and students of Taiwan politics as a turning point, this analysis is vital to understanding the course of political change in Taiwan.

In the fourth chapter, Chiang Ching-kuo's role in transforming Taiwan's political system from an authoritarian one to a democratic one is the central theme. CCK, as he is called by many, played a special role in Taiwan's democratization. Some say he was democratic at heart. Others say he simply understood the times and the type of political system that was needed as Taiwan's economy became more advanced and more a part of the global economy. Some say he built democracy in a dictatorial manner—that he created democracy by edict. The latter statement is certainly true, but this may have been the best way or even the only way to accomplish that task. In any case, this individual deserves special attention when talking about political modernization in Taiwan, since certainly that process would have been much slower had it not been for him.

Chapter 5 concerns the ending of martial law. Terminating martial law, or the emergency decree, as it was called in Taiwan, is seen by many observers, especially from abroad, as *the* major event in the democratization process. But is that so? Was terminating martial law that important? A second opinion is perhaps needed. Clearly there were those in Taiwan who thought that telling the foreign press how important martial law had been and how it had been an impediment to democracy would convince the world that Taiwan had changed.

Chapter 6 looks at democratization in Taiwan as a challenge to U.S. Taiwan policy. The United States espouses a one-China policy, which means that Taiwan is inseparable from China and presumable is part of the People's Republic of China. But, as Taiwan becomes a democracy—which the United States has encouraged—its citizens should presumably have some say about not only who its leaders are but also the future of the island—and their choice may be to remain separate from China and independent.

Chapter 7 is about Taiwan's so-called "undemocratic" elective bodies of government. The National Assembly, the Legislative Yuan and the Control Yuan were so labeled because they were composed of many delegates representing districts on the China mainland and never stood for election in Taiwan. Were they a major impediment to democracy before the early 1990s when the system was changed? Certainly. Though this was not true to the extent generally assumed. And, maybe because of such impediments to democracy, which dictated that the pace of democratization not be too hasty, their existence helped make the process successful.

The eighth chapter in this section is the author's analysis of the role of political parties in the democratization process. I look at Taiwan as an authoritarian system rather than a totalitarian polity while observing that such democratic changes did not occur in the People's Republic of China. Taiwan is a model for political change in Beijing, as it should be. Yet, though culturally Chinese, Taiwan is unique in many ways. This chapter addresses what differences were, and are, important.

Chapters 9 and 10 examine two KMT party congresses: one in 1988, the other in 1993. If Taiwan's political system is to democratize, some have asked, isn't change within the ruling party necessary? In other words, because the ruling party, plays such an important role in the decision-making process, doesn't it have to democratize to make the polity democratic. Even though many political parties in Western democracies do not function democratically, the population in Taiwan, as well as most party members, said yes. The evidence in these two chapters shows that it has democratized and that this process has been critical to the evolution of the Taiwan political miracle.

Chapter One
Political Development
in the Republic of China, 1949–1981

Political development in the Republic of China (ROC) has been as impressive as it has been extensive. The ROC is clearly among the rapidly changing and developing nations of the world in this respect. Yet political development in Taiwan generally has gone unnoticed. The Republic of China is not regarded seriously as a model by many students of political change. Many writers who have not studied Taiwan even deny that political modernization has occurred there. Before proceeding to assess this modernization process, I shall suggest some reasons for this misunderstanding.

First of all, there is a lack of visible political change in the Republic of China. Unlike many developing nations, Taiwan has not written a new constitution in recent years. Nor has the Constitution been revised, altered, or amended in any significant way. Similarly, the structure of government is almost the same as it was more than three decades ago. Even within the main branches of the government in Taiwan, there have been no major organizational changes that have attracted much notice.

Nor have there been any changes in the nation's ideology. Sun Yat-sen's Three Principles of the People have not been revised, updated, criticized, or even discussed seriously by many scholars or citizens in the Republic of China or elsewhere. Sun's ideology is simply too broad and common-sensical to arouse much controversy. Today, Taiwan's political elites embrace an eclectic mix of ideologies ranging from Sun Yat-sen's teachings and Confucianism to some Western theories, while others disregard ideology altogether due to pragmatic constraints or a simple lack of interest. In general, the government in Taiwan has not found ideology very useful in maintaining political control or in fostering economic or political development.

This kind of secularism reflects political sophistication, but does not attract much attention or study. Conversely, Maoist ideology in the People's Republic of China (PRC), which is not in most respects secular and is, therefore, by definition less "modern," has attracted considerable attention overseas—both in its past propagation and now in its refutation. It is ironic, but true, that in the ROC this lack of interest in ideology should suggest to some the absence of political modernization when in fact it reflects its success.

Taiwan's policy also gives the appearance of rigid conservatism. The emphasis on preserving Chinese culture, the age of high officials, resistance to changing policies that are antiquated, and the repetition of slogans coined decades earlier all suggest stubborn resistance to change. In reality, however, this resistance is both superficial and a means of hiding or perhaps easing some of the shock of the rapid modernization Taiwan has experienced.

Second, few Western scholars find the Republic of China an interesting subject of study. It is regarded as a small nation, and its claim to represent all of China is not taken very seriously. In contrast, the People's Republic of China is a large nation that many Western scholars perceive will change the course of history. In the past, it was the enemy of the West, and therefore, attracted attention and warranted the efforts of the scholar. Now it is seen as a friend or ally that can offset the growing threat of the Soviet Union. So, again there is much interest. Moreover, vast social and political changes have been seen to characterize the PRC and not the ROC. This is an erroneous view; nevertheless, it is a popular one and has affected the work of scholars.

Since the admission of the PRC into the United Nations in 1971 and Washington's derecognition of the ROC in 1979, this view has been even more common. Relatively speaking, even less scholarly energy is now being devoted to the ROC—even though it is a place where economic, social, and political changes have taken place, all of which can be investigated easily.

A related problem, and perhaps an explanation for the situation just described, is that there are not many sociologists in the Republic of China, especially Western-trained sociologists, who can translate economic development into social change or relate social change to economic growth. There are still fewer who are able to relate social change to new political interests and demands and anticipate the consequent need for political development. Finally, there are few political scientists in Taiwan who are specialists in political development.

Third, the Republic of China is a pariah state. It is seen as a right-wing dictatorship by many liberal scholars and the media in most Western nations because of the government's circumventing the Constitution and its maintaining a legal state of war (with the PRC). It is also viewed as a one-party, U.S.-client, garrison state.

In some cases these images are the result of ignorance; in other cases they are generalizations representing a liberal bias. In any event, the view has been widely propagated that the government of Taiwan has sought to avoid political change and has done so successfully. It is difficult to understand how such mis-understandings can persist. Taiwan is highly penetrated by Western ideas and quite cosmopolitan, and economic and social change there have transpired at a rate that few other countries can match. Nevertheless, they do persist.

Fourth, some years ago it was assumed that economic and political develop-ment were inextricably tied: that economic development would only take place where there was a minimum level of political development, and that as economic development proceeded it would produce political modernization. This view is less accepted now, though it certainly has not been repudiated. In Taiwan's case most observers realize that economic development has been very successful, but few realize that it has produced vast and significant political change. In fact, some writers speak of a gap, even a "revolutionary gap," referring to an alleged lack of congruency between the high level of economic development and a lower level of political development in Taiwan. Because of this "gap," a potential revolutionary or unstable situation is said to exist.

In this connection, it is also noteworthy that with the advent of environ-mentalism economic growth is now less admired in the West. In fact, there is widespread sentiment among liberal thinkers that economic growth is evil, or at least undesirable. Others are jealous of Taiwan's success, which is indeed embar-rassing to Western leaders whose citizens want more economic prosperity and in recent years have not had their desires fulfilled. Also, the Republic of China's political leadership has been immensely competent in promoting economic growth without allowing increases in crime and social problems thought in the West to be a natural by-product of economic success—again causing resentment.

Similarly Taiwan no longer is seen as a poor country deserving of help and sympathy and, therefore, as a nation that should be given the "right" to some economic development. It is seen by others as catching up too fast and thus a threat. Hence, many criticize the Republic of China for ignoring political devel-opment and urge that it be given more attention and that economic growth be given less emphasis.

Fifth, the Japanese success story has awed Westerners to the point that its economic and political systems (seen as intimately tied together, though for some reason the same is not seen as true in Taiwan's case) have been the subject of greater interest and study. Also, inasmuch as Japan's political system, at least in form (though clearly not so much in substance), is more Western than that of Taiwan or other developing countries, it is seen as a better model. Hence, although Japan is often seen as a threat to the West, it is a "Western" threat, and its political system is viewed as a genuinely democratic one.

This view, of course, ignores the fact that Taiwan's economic development in recent years has been faster than Japan's, even though Taiwan, like Japan, has no natural resources, is overpopulated, and does not even have much land for agriculture. Thus, economic and political development are indeed inextricably tied, since Taiwan's development cannot be attributed to the fortune of resources or to luck. Furthermore, Taiwan has not had the benefit of buying U.S. technology at cheap prices or the advantage of low defense budgets. Also ignored is the fact that Taiwan's political culture shares much in common with that of Japan and there are many similarities in the two countries' political modernization processes.

In this chapter, I attempt to transcend these mind-sets and other obstacles to assessing objectively Taiwan's success in political modernization. I shall undertake an objective analysis of Taiwan's political development, first by examining its economic growth and the social change this has produced, and then by describing the political change that has inevitably followed. Political modernization, especially when defined as efficiency of government, which was a necessary condition before a high level of economic growth was possible, will also be discussed as a factor that made economic progress possible. Next, I provide a detailed look at the political structure of the government of the Republic of China. Here change has been subtle, and, contrary to some views, the sometimes rigid political system has not impeded modernization. Rather, like the United States, which has changed its constitution only infrequently, Taiwan has adapted to new situations and needs in extra-constitutional or informal ways. Governmental performance and political participation will also be assessed. Here the modernization process is obvious. Taiwan's political participation has increased markedly. In fact, progress in these two realms has been no less than startling. Finally, I draw conclusions concerning the value of the Republic of China's political development experience and the nation's future in light of its political modernization.

Economic Development and Social Change

Most scholars agree that economic development propels social change and, in turn, social change necessitates and fosters political modernization. Taiwan is clearly a nation that has experienced economic development. But it has not experienced just economic development; it has seen economic growth of the kind that inevitably produces social and political change.

In 1949, when the government of the Republic of China moved to Taiwan, the gross national product (GNP) of Taiwan and the Pescadore Islands was about $95 million with a per capita income of around $100 annually, making Taiwan an underdeveloped or less developed area in economic terms.[1] Economic development followed in the early 1950s, and from 1952 through 1977 Taiwan experienced, by global standards, a phenomenal growth of 815 percent in GNP. The only Asian nation to surpass Taiwan's record was Japan. From 1970 to 1976, Taiwan's annual growth of GNP was 12.8 percent—higher than that of Japan.[2]

As a result of this success, Taiwan is now referred to as a "newly industrialized nation" or "near developed nation." Taiwan, along with South Korea, Hong Kong, and Singapore (which are called facetiously the "Gang of Four"), is regarded as a model of economic development. Many, in fact, regard the Republic of China as the most outstanding of the "Gang" inasmuch as Hong Kong and Singapore are too small and in many ways too unique to be models and South Korea has experienced many fluctuations in its economic growth that Taiwan has not had.[3]

Some explain the ROC's economic growth as the product of coincidence or luck. But the circumstances belie this view. Taiwan experienced this growth in spite of virtually no natural resources, a very dense population (the densest of any nation in the world except Bangladesh and some very small countries), a heavy defense burden (which Japan did not have), and an economy originally based on agriculture. In addition, some geographers put Taiwan in a zone of unfavorable climate for maximum human energy and accomplishment. The Republic of China did have the advantage of U.S. economic assistance, but most other nations that received large quantities of U.S. financial help at the time did not develop. Thus, Taiwan's admirable economic accomplishments must have been the result in large part of effective planning, much of which came from the government sector.

Clearly this was the case. First was the land reform program, which increased agricultural productivity. These reforms made it possible to feed the island's population while releasing workers to the industrial sector, which was in the process of rapid growth. From 1953 to 1977, agricultural productivity rose at an annual rate of 4.4 percent, or at a rate about 2 percent higher than population growth.[4] And this occurred without a significant increase in the amount of land under cultivation, which means that effective land use and new farming methods, both of which required governmental planning, explain the increases. Currently Taiwan is about 90 percent self-sufficient in food production.

Next came government-induced industrialization through a strategy of import substitution. This was followed by an export-oriented growth plan, which was implemented by encouraging and assisting export industries, thereby tying the nation's economy to increases in world trade. During this time there was also a transition from small industry to heavy industry and from labor-intensive to capital-intensive production.[5] At present, Taiwan is experiencing another transition, to knowledge-intensive production. All of this required detailed and extensive planning by the government and government help to business—though the economy remained a free and open one.[6] It is apparent that this planning was for the most part prescient.

While per capita income lagged somewhat behind economic growth measured in GNP figures, owing to a high rate of investment (again largely government induced) and large population increases, average incomes of citizens of the Republic of China tripled between 1951 and 1975.[7] By 1977, the average per capita income in Taiwan had reached $1,079, and by 1980 it was $2,000.[8] The 1981 figure was $2,400.[9]

Per capita income growth engendered a rising standard of living and a consumer society. For example, from 1952 to 1980 average calorie intake increased from 2,078 daily to 2,820, with the protein part of the diet increasing from 49 grams to 79 grams daily; clothing expenditures rose from $7 per capita annually to $46; living space increased from 12.6 square feet (in 1955) per person to 28.2 square feet; electricity consumption increased from 24 kilowatt hours per person to 432; illiteracy declined from 42.1 percent to 10.3 percent; higher education rose from 0.12 percent to 1.5 percent of the population; and the life span lengthened from 58.6 years to 70.7 years.[10]

In Taiwan at the present time, one person in four owns a motorcycle, one in twenty-three an auto, and there is an average of one black-and-white television per person.[11] According to one scholar, Taiwan is in the process of becoming a full-fledged consumer society in twenty-five years, doing what it took Japan one hundred years to accomplish and most Western nations two hundred years.[12]

The standard of living in Taiwan has improved as a result of economic growth in a number of other ways. Cholera has been virtually eliminated, and the incidence of dysentery, polio, rabies, and smallpox are rare. Tuberculosis, which was once one of the leading causes of death in Taiwan, is not as prevalent as in Western countries.[13] The number of physicians now approximates that in the most modern Western countries.

In addition, there is a very low level of unemployment and virtually no poverty—which even Western countries cannot boast of now. Unemployment has generally ranged at slightly over 1 percent of the work force—a figure that translates into those changing jobs and little or no more.

Meanwhile, social welfare programs, workers' insurance programs, recreation areas, and travel opportunities have been made available to the general population. In 1980, the government passed legislation providing for funds amounting to $27.7 million for loans to factory workers to buy homes, $870 million for public housing and roads, and $20.3 million for assistance to the poor, while projecting a need for $1.2 billion for social security and welfare for the next decade.[14] Also reflecting Taiwan's affluence, visitors to scenic areas in Taiwan have been increasing at a rate of over 5 percent per year, making the rate of visits by its citizens nearly two per capita per year.[15] Likewise, visits to foreign countries have increased at a very rapid rate, giving Taiwan's citizenry the opportunity to see other parts of the world.

The effect of equitable economic growth upon social change and political modernization (just as important as a high level of economic growth and consumerism) has been the product of a leveling of income. Income disparity in Taiwan is now less than in the United States or Japan, signifying that all of the population has participated in economic development.[16] Thus, the social and political development that inevitably follows economic development should naturally be greater in the Republic of China than in other countries because economic development has had an impact on a larger portion of the population.

Economic growth and political development in Taiwan are also closely related because economic development plans have been and remain based upon effective government and private-sector planning, and hard work, as well as ingenuity, on the part of the population. In contrast, a number of countries have grown affluent because of their raw materials and their ability to sell these in the world market. Another important factor in Taiwan's development experience is that its rapid economic growth was built upon foreign trade and investment. Now it is based upon a highly educated and skilled labor force that is being geared to higher levels of knowledge and technology. This means that the nation has been for some years and remains highly permeated by foreign ideas and influence. This, of course, has made the populace of the Republic of China very worldly or cosmopolitan.

Reflecting the magnitude of Taiwan's ties with other nations and the international community, its foreign trade accounts for around 50 percent of its GNP.[17] That of Japan—a nation generally perceived to be highly dependent upon international trade—is 10 percent. As a consequence, Taiwan's business leaders have had to learn how to market their products in foreign markets while investors (who make up a high proportion of the population owing to the high level of savings) pay attention to foreign business news and the economic situation of their trading partners abroad, not to mention international business and politics generally.

All of this has given rise to changing attitudes among the population of Taiwan. Sociological studies reveal that traditional values have weakened, that there are increasing demands upon government, and that the population desires greater participation in political decisions. In fact, Taiwan has experienced nearly all of the problems of a materialist culture: social problems, crime, cynicism, and the like. However, the negative example of many Western countries, a conscious and planned effort to deal with such problems (largely through prevention), and the stress on stability in Chinese society have all dampened or offset such trends.

There are some other reasons why the Republic of China has adjusted to economic growth and the resultant social change quite efficiently and without the instability that many think is present in other countries developing as rapidly. One is simply the potency of Chinese culture—which absorbs some of the jolt of change. A similar situation can be seen in Japan and some other Asian countries. This strong cultural influence has not only cushioned the shock of rapid change but also has tempered it. More important still, it has engendered considerable caution concerning wholesale westernization.

A second reason that Taiwan has not experienced many of the problems associated with modernization seen in the West is the fact that the Republic of China, like Israel and South Africa, is a pariah nation. Yet Taiwan's populace is convinced that its government's views are correct and that it has a right to continue to exist as an independent nation-state. This confidence has made Taiwan's populace more immune to outside influence and more determined to make the process of political change a stable and orderly one. The fact that the nation is locked in struggle (technically it is war) with the People's Republic of China has had the same effect. Thus, there is a certain level of insecurity in Taiwan that translates into consciously and studiously avoiding political change that might be disruptive. This attitude is reinforced by the fear of the political chaos and anarchy that the Chinese have long experienced when political control faltered (typically occurring together with the failure to maintain public water control projects and usually resulting in disastrous floods followed by mass starvation).

Finally, dissent in Taiwan to a large extent focuses on the question of Taiwan's independence and the ultimate political role to be played by the Taiwanese (Chinese whose ancestors were born on Taiwan, as opposed to the Chinese who came after World War II). Thus, there is less dissent against a materialist culture or change in the abstract than there would be otherwise. The problem of the political role to be played by the Taiwanese, however, is being resolved automatically because differences between the two groups are eroding with time and the weakening of social barriers. Also, the hard core of the movement for independence is fragmented, is only active abroad, and has to some extent lost touch with the modernization process in Taiwan.

The Political Structure and Modernization

The structure and functioning of government in the Republic of China are seen by most observers to have changed very little since the government moved to Taiwan in 1949. However, as already noted, a political system can change without altering its basic structure. Similarly, political systems can evolve without this process being visible. Taiwan's political system, in fact, has changed in some very important ways.

In terms of its organization, the government of the Republic of China is a mixed Western and Chinese system. The three branches of government (yuan)— executive, legislative, and judicial—are supplemented by an Examination Yuan and a Control Yuan, which were important organs of government in Imperial China. In addition to the five yuans, there is a National Assembly and an Office of the President and Vice President at the top of the government hierarchy. Another locus of political power is the Nationalist Party, or Kuomintang (KMT).[18] Still another is the military.

Three branches of government—the Executive Yuan, the Legislative Yuan, and the Judicial Yuan—perform functions similar to their counterparts in Western systems. However, they are not as independent, nor are they as effective, except for the Executive Yuan. The other two yuans are less important: The Examination Yuan handles matters of administration relating to examinations for hiring government employees, making appointments, evaluating performance, and deciding salary and pension issues. The Control Yuan has the power of impeachment, censure, and audit.

The National Assembly—for which there is no exact Western counterpart, since the legislative branch of government performs all or most its functions in parliamentary systems—is constitutionally the highest organ of government. Its main duties are to elect the president and vice president, act on impeachment procedures, amend the Constitution, and ratify constitutional amendments proposed by the Legislative Yuan. In reality, the National Assembly does not have much power for several reasons: it is not representative (with the Republic of China claiming jurisdiction over all of China, and the National Assembly retaining representatives of provinces on the mainland); it meets only once every six years in regular session (just before the expiration of the term of office of the president); and its function of electing the president and vice president are in reality done by the KMT.

The National Assembly, the Legislative Yuan, and the Control Yuan—all of which are elected, though not completely democratically because of the problem of representation of provinces in the People's Republic—together carry out functions similar to those of a Western parliament.[19] Powers, however, are dispersed and are subject, in terms of actual use, to approval by the KMT and the president.

The president, who in theory is selected by the National Assembly, is actually picked by the ruling party—the KMT. According to the Constitution, he has the authority of head of state given to similar officials in Western presidential and parliamentary systems. His prerogatives, however, are broader and more extensive because of the KMT's extraordinary political power and the "Temporary Provisions of the Constitution," which give him the authority to declare martial law and the ability to bypass normal constitutional and legal procedures in various ways.

The Executive Yuan also carries out executive functions of government, which it shares with the Office of the Presidency. Under normal circumstances, the president is clearly supreme and dictates policy to the Executive Yuan. The Executive Yuan is headed by the premier, who has at times been an important figure and who in one instance was groomed for the presidency. The system has sometimes functioned as a dual executive system, where executive authority has switched back and forth from the presidency to the premiership.

Two centers of political power outside the government are the party (the KMT) and the military. As in Western political systems, many decisions, especially those of an ideological nature and those relating to general and long-range planning, are made in party circles. The difference between the ROC and most Western systems is that there is, for all intents and purposes, only one political party and thus little party competition. However, this may be in the process of change.

The military has not played a very active role in politics in Taiwan. In fact, after more than three decades of having political influence similar to that of Western military forces, it may be expected that it will never assume the power or prerogatives of its counterpart in military dictatorships. The military does play a more important political role in Taiwan than might otherwise be the case, however, because of its size and the fact it would be expected to assume an active political role more quickly than in Western systems in the event of political instability or a succession crisis. This special "state of readiness" is due primarily to the perceived threat of political instability among both military leaders and the populace.

In terms of its level of development and the effect of modernization, the political system in the ROC shows a high degree of specialization and secularization. In fact, the structure of the ROC system reflects more specialization than Western systems because it has more branches of government. Also, more checks and balances are built into the system. This structure comes from the Chinese traditional political system and the fact that the founder of the system, Sun Yat-sen, feared factionalism and favored a more complicated system that balanced authority.

The ROC's political system is both presidential and parliamentary in character. It is presidential in that the president is elected separately, albeit indirectly, and has more political power than is usual for prime ministers in parliamentary systems. It is parliamentary in that legislative and executive functions are, in working terms, not so clearly separated and because the president is, by definition, the head of the majority party.

The relationship between the central and provincial government suggests the system is both a unitary and a federal one. It is federal in formal structure and unitary in operation, though it also must be described as a dual system wherein the central government and the provincial or other local governments often perform identical functions. This kind of dual system at first sight would appear repetitive and inefficient. Because of the role played by the central government and the KMT as mediator vis-à-vis local factional politics, however, there is, in fact, not as much duplication of function as might be expected.[20]

One reason the ROC's policy has not moved toward further specialization nor increased its sub-organs and agencies, is the fact that the system was originally designed to rule all of China and was created with broad governing functions in mind. Ruling Taiwan then, only three-hundredths the size of mainland China, did not require organizational additions or changes to accommodate a growing complex nation. Similarly, the ROC possessed a large reservoir of administrative and bureaucratic talent when it moved to Taiwan in 1949. This meant that the recruiting and personnel training functions of government required less emphasis.

Another reason that change in the structure of government was less necessary than otherwise would be the case (and clearly has been the case in other countries that have experienced the level of economic growth Taiwan has) is the fact that provisions for political representation, mass participation, democracy, and civil rights were already written into the Constitution—no doubt to a greater degree than the citizenry was ready to demand or exercise. The Constitution was written in a milieu of considerable idealism and optimism regarding the establishment of a democratic system of government with mass participation. When the government moved to Taiwan, many of the Constitution's democratic principles were truncated by the Temporary Provisions giving Taiwan a system of government that was less democratic.

Thus, as economic development proceeded apace during the 1960s, it carried with it extensive social change (though not as extensive as in as some other countries experiencing similar demands upon their systems for more mass participation and democracy). These demands, however, did not take the form of writing a new constitution or formalizing in constitutional or other legal forms, various civil and human rights. Rather, demands centered upon the actual implementation of the Constitution and a more conscientious application of Sun's Three Principles of the People.

The demand for the implementation of democracy was also dampened by an external threat (or at least a perceived one that was real to most of the population), and there was a singular preoccupation with economic growth. Through the 1960s and 1970s most citizens perceived Taiwan to be on the threshold of becoming a developed nation, and they wanted to ensure that it reached that goal. In the 1970s the oil crisis and the threat of resource shortages caused public attention to continue to focus on the goal of economic freedoms that usually accompany economic growth at its mid or final stages. Subsequently, trade problems, international inflation, and Taiwan's lack of resources tended to perpetuate this situation.

Still another reason there was little demand for structural change in the government was the implementation of democracy at the local level—in many respects to a degree equal to or even beyond that present in Western democracies. Voter awareness, turnout, and interest in local elections (and local politics in general) were, and remain, very high.[21] Thus, like Japan, but not for the same reasons (a greater interest in local elections in Japan stems from sectionalism caused by geography and the Japanese identification with the "home place"), Taiwan has experienced more interest in local politics generally than in national politics. There has also been more preoccupation, in terms of political modernization, with reforming local government, including enhancing citizen participation and political freedoms.

In this connection, the KMT's role as mediator in local politics between and among local factions has been crucial. Thus, the ruling party could allow democracy to develop, usually without feeling any threat to its own prerogatives or political practices, and has been worked for many years with the central government to control local political factions or play one off against another.[22]

Notwithstanding the fact that the political structure of the ROC has changed very little (and there are good reasons that it did not), there have been some changes worthy of mention. The most important is the creation of a Joint Commission on Rural Reconstruction (JCRR) soon after the Nationalists moved to Taiwan. It managed one of the most successful land reform programs ever undertaken by any nation. The U.S.-ROC Joint Commission for Rural Reconstruction still functions to help farmers maintain agricultural productivity while performing a variety of other tasks. When the ROC ruled the mainland, governmental organs were established to implement land reform, but they were not effective and by 1949 were hardly functioning. Thus, the JCRR was really a new governmental organ established in Taiwan.

New organs of government have also been created within the Ministry of Economic Affairs. It is here that the political infrastructure has been augmented the most. Early on, new agencies were created to implement rapid economic growth and to engineer liaisons between government and the business community. This took the form of direct government involvement and a new role for government to plan, manage, and oversee the "Ten Projects" and later the "Twelve Projects." Similarly, the government has maintained direct control and oversight responsibilities (also requiring new agencies or the restructuring and expansion of existing agencies) for the export-processing zones and several industrial and science parks.

Some structural changes or reforms have also been made in the heart of the infrastructure of the system, though these are not extensive. In December 1978, following derecognition of Taiwan by the United States, the KMT's Central Committee established a "working committee" to propose reforms in government. Subsequently, the high courts and the district courts were moved from the Executive Yuan to the Judicial Yuan. This change separated prosecutors and judges into different branches of the government so that the system of checks and balances could work more effectively. It also made it possible for the Executive Yuan to feel more free to investigate the behavior of judges.[23]

At the same time, police offense laws were rewritten and the KMT was reorganized at the top to make it more flexible and efficient. These latter changes were substantial, though they did not directly affect the structure of the government very much.

Following the death of President Chiang Kai-shek in 1975, Vice President Yen Chia-kan became president. Chiang Kai-shek's son Chiang Ching-kuo, however, held the mantle of political authority in the country from his position as premier, or head of the Executive Yuan. Chiang Ching-kuo was not formally elected president until 1978. Thus, the country managed a smooth succession without the transfer of actual political power by formal constitutional means and without a violation of the Constitution or a change in the political structure. This was an unusual way to handle the transfer of political power; yet considering the high incidence of violence and political turmoil in most Third World countries and even developed Communist nations during a time of political succession it was to be lauded.

Governmental Performance

Although political change or modernization in the Republic of China has not taken the form of alterations to the government's organization chart, significant change has taken place. To duly note these changes, one must assess which branches or organs of government are most efficient and whether increases in efficiency, on the one hand, and growth of power and prerogatives, on the other hand, are parallel. It is also necessary to analyze the extent to which efficiency and power gained by various branches and organs of government are based upon needs for political change, specialization, problem solving, and the requirement for mass participation in politics that are the product of economic development and social change.

Similarly, an examination of where the government has demonstrated a high level of performance is a sine qua non to measuring political modernization. In other words, which sections of government have been effective in problem solving? And has the government, overall, proved its capabilities in ways that demonstrate that political modernization has occurred? Here, both specific and unique problems the government has faced in recent years, as well as its ability to modernize in standard or usual ways, need to be assessed.

One branch of government, the Executive Yuan, has significantly increased its contacts with the business community and various interest groups in recent years.[24] The Executive Yuan and its ministries have also increased contacts with the provincial and local government to facilitate various types of coordination between the central and local governments. It is only natural, then, to assume that the Executive Yuan is also at least in part responsible for the effectiveness of government policies as well as the growth of democracy and mass participation at the local level.

One of the reasons that the Executive Yuan has been outstanding in terms of its efficiency and its problem solving ability is the fact that for a number of years it was led by Chiang Ching-kuo—the driving force behind political modernization in Taiwan. Alternatively, one might argue the reverse: that

Chiang Ching-kuo sought the premiership because the Executive Yuan was the branch of government most geared toward problem solving, particularly of the kind that Taiwan needed, and that this branch of government was the most capable of being improved under his leadership. In any event, it has been the Executive Yuan that has been the center of action in terms of problem solving, planning, and policy making.[25]

The eight ministries of the Executive Yuan—Interior, Foreign Affairs, National Defense, Finance, Education, Justice, Economic Affairs, and Communications—have all been active sections of government in terms of managing the yuan's work load, dealing with important issues, and maintaining contacts with the people. They have all attracted talent, especially younger people with higher levels of education and proven abilities in business or elsewhere. It is also here where the technocrats are to be found.

Not only is the Executive Yuan the seat of authority for policy making and problem solving in the realms usually considered important relative to the administrative functions of government and reflected in the names of the ministries, but it also performs other important functions. In particular, it maintains liaisons with important sectors of the business and financial communities. For example, the Government Information Office, which oversees the media; the Council for Economic Planning and Development, which coordinates economic and finance work; the Research, Development, and Evaluations Commission, which oversees and evaluates academic as well as economic and other kinds of research; the National Science Council, which is involved in technological research and its applications in science; the Atomic Energy Council; the Central Bank of China; and the Council for Agricultural Planning and Development, are all part of the Executive Yuan.[26]

In short, most of the government work that involves planning, problem solving, and contact with the population, as well as maintaining coordination between national, provincial and local governments, is handled by the ministries or commissions of the Executive Yuan. As reflected in efforts at the top to improve efficiency, the amount of work load versus the number of employees, and the ability to keep in touch with progress in the economy, science, and other areas, the Executive Yuan has performed at a high level of efficiency.[27]

The parallel between efficiency and task performance, on one hand, and political power and authority, on the other, is verified by the Executive Yuan's direct line to the president. The president relies upon the Executive Yuan for information and advice for implementing policies made in his office. Premiers and vice premiers have always had a close working relationship with the president. Likewise, the Executive Yuan constitutionally has the power to override the Legislative Yuan, control the budget, and oversee, and to a large extent control, local government—powers that have been enhanced or increased through use and performance. It is more and more clear to all government officials in Taiwan, whether at the national level or in provincial or local government, that real political authority lies in the Executive Yuan (along with the president and the KMT).

The Executive Yuan has also effectively dealt with increased public demands for more government actions and greater public participation in the decision-making process. Although it is not an elective branch of government and is thus not responsive to the public through the election process, it nevertheless may be seen as a very democratic organ of government in the sense of reacting to citizens' demands, public opinion polls, complaints, and the like. In fact, it responds to the needs and desires of the people better than any other branch of government. For example, more than any other branch of government, it ignores nonsecular and ideological issues and thus is less influenced by ideologies and personal relationships. It has done the most to rid the system of corruption and to improve the morale and effectiveness of government employees. Several years ago, Chiang Ching-kuo even had published in daily newspapers the addresses and telephone numbers of government organs responsible for handling certain public demands as well as offices that would hear citizens' complaints when the government did not respond.[28] Most agree that Chiang Ching-kuo's strategy for dealing with increased public demands for more responsive government has worked.

Of the specific issues or problems where the government's performance can be judged, land reform, economic growth planning, taxation, education, social welfare, energy, and dealing with the losses of representation in the United Nations and diplomatic recognition by the United States are probably the best to measure the government's quality of response.

When the Nationalists took jurisdiction of Taiwan in 1945, they realized the problems of unequal land distribution on the island and the existence of many tenant farmers. Having learned a lesson from the loss of the mainland in 1949, and being able to better focus on these problems in Taiwan, they undertook a land reform program that has been regarded by many as one of the most success-ful in the world. When the program started, 39 percent of the farmers in Taiwan were tenants and 25 percent were partial tillers; due to the land reforms, 78 percent became tillers of their own land.[29] This improvement led to increases in agricultural output during every year up to the mid-1970s—even though there was a simultaneous movement of labor to the cities to work in the newly built factories.

Since distributing farmland to the farmers, the government has maintained stability in the agricultural sector through price controls, loans, and other mechanisms. The agricultural sector of Taiwan's economy is highly efficient and productive because land ownership is by law tied to the use of the land. Farm incomes are nearly equal to city incomes, and there is an even distribution of income in rural areas.[30]

In short, government action increased productivity and raised the standard of living in rural areas. This made possible a more significant shift of labor to industry than would otherwise have been possible and thus encouraged faster growth in the industrial sector. At the same time it promoted democracy and political development in the rural areas by breaking the bonds between farmers and landowners and by substituting farm organizations and local government operations for tenant-landlord ties.

Meanwhile, in the 1950s, the government announced plans for import-substitution-based economic growth (i.e., to manufacture products to replace the same or similar items that were formerly imported) and set up organizations to utilize U.S. economic assistance. Both actions were very successful. Although the import-substitution policy was soon outdated and had to be replaced, it did work well in the short run. The efforts to find and attract outside financial help were successful, and by the early 1960s Taiwan was ready to be weaned from economic aid.[31] The government, taking into account the success of economic development to that point and the need to export in order to build larger and more efficient industries, began a plan of export-led economic growth. This involved considerable infrastructure analysis on the part of government planning agencies to decide which industries could export successfully (essentially some of the same things the Japanese government did that boasted economic growth there). Simultaneously the government sought to help the business community export.

The government kept a low profile and always maintained the economy was a free one. While Taiwan's economy is certainly, in relative terms, a free one, this should not be interpreted to mean that economic growth occurred automatically or simply because of a dynamic business community, which Taiwan indeed has. There was considerable government planning and a very close relationship between government and the business community. In short, the government has been too modest about taking credit for planning for and engineering Taiwan's extremely successful economic growth.

Another area where the government deserves recognition is in taxation. Almost all underdeveloped countries lack an effective system of taxation, especially on individual incomes. They rely upon tariffs and other duties and taxes on specific goods and upon business. The establishment of an income tax system is a mark of political modernization since it requires a sophisticated bureaucracy to make it work. Such a system was established during the 1960s in Taiwan and has been working well since then.[32] In fact, in terms of its taxation system, the ROC may well be seen as a fully developed country.

The taxation system has ensured that government could expand in terms of adding responsibilities and functions to maintain control over an increasingly complex society. It also has fostered and maintained income equality, though, as already mentioned, income equalization occurred primarily because of the dynamic growth of the economy, which caused shortages of labor. And, if there is a future downturn in the economy, the new tax system will likely make it possible for income equality, along with an equal distribution of buying power, to be maintained, and may help guard against precipitous drops in domestic demands for consumer goods.

Another sphere where government performance can be judged is in education. Over the past thirty years momentous progress has been made in improving educational opportunities in Taiwan, raising the level of literacy and helping to meet the demands of industry and a modern nation.

Early emphasis was upon increasing literacy, teaching the national language, and generally increasing the level of education. Energy and attention were also devoted to broadening educational opportunities, especially in the countryside, and to equality in education. These efforts produced laudable success: The number of schools increased from 1,504 in 1949 to 4,950 in 1979, while the number of students increased during the same period from 1,055,000 to 4,750,000.[33] A mandatory six years of schooling was enforced, followed by adding middle school in 1968. High school (for a total of twelve years of education) will be required soon. As a result, illiteracy was reduced to an almost imperceptible level among Taiwan's youth.

In recent years more attention has been devoted to higher education, technical training, libraries and research facilities, and informal mass education. College enrollment has in the past two decades increased markedly, to the point of putting Taiwan in the category of a developed country according to its level of higher education. Demonstrating better government performance in this realm than many other countries, including even the developed Western countries, Taiwan has not had a problem of unemployment among the highly educated because of accurate assessments of future needs and effective controls on the kinds of education provided and the fields of study or degrees encouraged. In fact, the ROC government deserves high marks for this accomplishment at a time when a large number of Western governments, including the United States, have failed as witnessed by the glut of highly educated people in certain fields.

Still another area where the government has demonstrated astute planning is in social welfare. Although there has been and remains a strong feeling among the population against social welfare because of the success record of the capitalist, free-market growth model and the strong work ethic in Taiwan, the government has nevertheless instituted a number of social welfare programs. At first the emphasis was on the handicapped. The government's goals were to provide work training and work opportunities. More recently, the government has focused disability insurance, aid to workers who want to purchase houses or apartments, and health care.

The government has astutely avoided social programs that in many countries have contributed to larger unemployment, dependency upon the government, and general laziness. It has also eschewed burdensome taxes to pay for a costly social benefits program by designing social help programs to encourage better work habits, home ownership, higher health standards, and the like.

Two other problems—the energy crisis and diplomatic setbacks (the loss of the U.N. seat and U.S. recognition)—unlike those already mentioned, required improvisational planning rather than decision-making based upon projections and long-range planning. Here, the ROC government also has demonstrated a high level of performance.

When the oil crisis occurred in 1973, Taiwan was very dependent upon external sources of energy, relying upon petroleum for about three-fourths of its energy while importing nearly all of that from OPEC nations. Taiwan's industrialization and its economic growth both were founded upon the increasing use of imported energy. Thus, when OPEC increased prices steeply, Taiwan's economy suffered a severe jolt. Inflation resulted, threatening continued economic growth and even economic stability. In less than a year, however, government actions brought inflation down to an acceptable level and got economic growth back on track.[34] Of the rapidly developing nations that were dependent upon imported oil for their industrial and economic growth, Taiwan's adjustment to the new situation was outstanding—perhaps the most effective among the rapidly developing countries. Effective government actions and leadership must be given credit.

In 1971 and 1978, the government of the Republic of China suffered two diplomatic setbacks of proportions known to few other nations. First was the loss of its United Nations seat and what amounted to an expulsion from the world body. Second was derecognition by the only major nation with which it had diplomatic ties and its most important friend, ally, and trading partner. Both caused a loss of credibility for the government and severe shocks to the nation's economic and political stability. However, in both cases, the government managed to weather both crises quite well. This was done by taking swift and decisive actions to maintain economic stability in the face of a near panic situation (especially in the latter crisis) and by compensating for these diplomatic defeats with economic successes. Clearly, the government's credibility for engineering economic growth and dealing with domestic problems to a large extent offset its diplomatic defeats. This, together with the effective management of political communications to prevent panic and mass defeatism and despair, made it possible to get through these crises with relative ease.

Although it is difficult to say how other governments might have reacted in a similar situation, the ROC clearly deserves praise for the way it handled these situations. There is no denying that the government took appropriate and effective action to solve the problems it confronted on the world stage.

Mass Participation

The last index to be discussed in seeking to measure and evaluate political development in the Republic of China is the level of public participation in government. This concept may be taken to reflect the level of democracy attained, although democracy here means both democracy as a Western concept and as a Third World idea that is not colored by its Western origins. Again, it is assumed that economic development fosters social change, including the desire to participate more directly in political decisions that affect both the individual and the society, and that the government must either respond to those desires in a positive way by creating the means whereby public demands can be heard and responded to or else seek to repress them.

The realms where mass participation in Taiwan can be most easily and accurately examined are civic and professional organizations, the political "parties" (meaning the KMT and the nonparty organizations that compete with the KMT), and elections. In Taiwan, unlike in the United States and some other Western democracies, local government affords an efficient means of translating public demands into policy alternatives. In contrast, public opinion polls have not caught on in Taiwan and are generally regarded by government and the public alike as less than accurate measurements of public desires and needs. With this in mind, the combination of mechanisms used to promote mass participation in Taiwan must be seen as unique.

Because of the importance of the family in Chinese tradition, individuals tend to express their demands to smaller or lower units of government than in nations where the role of the family was never as important as in Taiwan.

Localism or provincialism is also an influencing factor; during the course of the development of feudalism in Taiwan, the local fiefdom demanded individual loyalty and in return met demands and provided services. Thus, Chinese tend to look to smaller and closer organizations and not necessarily governmental ones to express their expectations and needs.[35] The Japanese rule of Taiwan for fifty years before the end of World War II tended to reinforce this tendency—though this same situation exists in Japan for different reasons (geography more than the importance of the family).

In Taiwan it is relatively easy to join one or a number of social or professional organizations, and it is almost equally simple to start such an organization. The number of persons participating in local civic and professional organizations exceeds 3 million, or more than 20 percent of the population. Membership in national civic and professional organizations is around three-quarters of a million.[36]

The most important of these two types of groups is the professional organization, and the largest category of professional organization is the agricultural group. Labor organizations, "free professional" groups, and fishermen's organizations follow in terms of size. For many individuals in these professions, the local organization constitutes their most important direct line of communication to both local and national government. They identify strongly with their group and make demands upon government as a member of the group.

These large professional groups as well as smaller, more specialized ones constitute the equivalent of Western lobbies or interest groups in terms of their relationship with government. Government and the ruling Nationalist Party are generally very sympathetic and responsive to their demands because of the importance of such groups and the fact that many elected politicians rely upon such organizations for electoral support. Many non-elected officials likewise are very responsive to these organizations because of the efforts made by Chiang Ching-kuo as vice premier and president to make government more sensitive to public demands. By strengthening and encouraging these organizations, most professional groups now know how to make their needs and dissatisfactions known to the president or someone else in high office who is close to the president.

Social or civic organizations are generally smaller and less important in winning citizens' loyalty. Thus, they are usually not as powerful in influencing government officials or the decision-making process. However, they are usually regarded as better barometers of social problems than are the professional organizations and for this reason are able to influence the media and officials who are concerned more specifically with social problems. They are also able to bring to bear considerable influence relating to political issues that transcend the vested interests of professional groups.

In any case, civic and professional organizations play a more important role in terms of mass participation in the political processes than comparable organizations in most Western countries. Their impact is particularly more noticeable in local government. (Labor unions are, of course, an exception when a comparison is made with Western countries.) Professional and civic organizations are also growing in numbers and membership; in the 1970s the number of such organizations increased by 60 to 70 percent.[37]

More national in character than the civic and professional organizations, and better able to carry on the process of conveying public desires and demands to the national government, is the party, or KMT. The KMT has nearly 2 million members, or about 11 percent of the population of Taiwan.[38] Thus, it must be regarded as a mass party; its membership is larger than almost all Communist parties or Western parties, unless party membership is defined by voter registration lists, which reflect only vague party support or voting tendencies in Western democratic systems.

The party fulfills a number of functions that relate to mass participation in politics, such as maintaining close ties with civic and professional organizations (in some cases sponsoring or creating them), fielding candidates in local and national elections, balancing factions in local politics, and even adjudicating various kinds of disputes at the local level.

Inasmuch as the party is responsible for planning and policy making at the top (with and through the Executive Yuan), it is the avenue whereby the citizen often tries to impact the decision-making process. This can be done by presenting one's case to a party member or by joining the party. It can be done by any group, organized or otherwise. The party is, in fact, active in soliciting opinions and views with the purpose of increasing the size of the party, winning elections, and preserving citizen loyalty to party objectives and to the nation.[39]

Although the KMT is frequently criticized as being led by octogenarians and resistant to change or to allowing mass input in the decision-making process, this is true only in a narrow sense. It is clearly not true about the leadership of Chiang Ching-kuo. Nor is this charge borne out by the representative nature of the party's membership: 20 percent women, 65 percent under age forty, and 65 to 70 percent Taiwanese. Moreover, eighty-five percent of the new members are Taiwanese, which is more than their share of the population.[40] So the party, which is already an important medium for transmitting mass feelings and needs, seems destined to be even more important in this realm in the future, notwithstanding the age problem at a certain level in the party.

There are two other political parties in Taiwan that play a role in interpreting citizen opinions and demands, but they are small in size and importance in comparison to the KMT. They are minor parties and will probably remain that in the foreseeable future. However, there is a growing number of influential nonparty or "without party" officials, however. Many of them have been elected to public office, and in a collective, though not in a very cohesive, sense, provide competition to the KMT. They also afford alternative lines of political communications. This has been especially true in recent years as a result of more competitive elections. Independent politicians likewise afford more choices in elections and often provide a challenge for KMT candidates.[41]

As the populace plays a more important role in making political decisions in the future, one might anticipate an increase in competition between the KMT and nonparty politicians—a situation constituting, in a sense, a two-party system. Alternately, many of the nonparty candidates will be absorbed by the KMT. As the KMT increases in size and broadens its political ideology, and as competition to satisfy public demands becomes more prevalent within the party, factions will likely develop in the KMT something like those in the Liberal Democratic Party in Japan. If this happens, faction competition will mirror competing private and public demands.

Finally, mass participation in politics in the ROC has been enhanced by elections. Meaningful elections were not permitted in Taiwan during the period of Japanese rule from 1895 to 1945 (although there were assemblies in each prefecture, county, and town after 1935). Competitive elections—the first in Taiwan's history—were first held in 1950 for county and city offices, including mayors, magistrates, and city councils. These were real elections and brought virtually all citizens into the political decision-making process in a significant way. And this has remained true since 1950. Reflecting the attitudes of the populace toward local elections is the high level of knowledge of candidates by voters and the percentage of voter turnout.[42] Voters are no doubt encouraged by the fact that many officials voted into office in these elections have risen to higher positions in government at the provincial or national level.

In 1959, the Provincial Assembly was created. Its members at first were chosen by the city and county councils. Later, however, the Provincial Assembly became an elected body. Since then, the process of choosing representatives to this body has also constituted an important exercise in mass participation. And again, the attitudes of the voters and the voter turnout reflect confidence in the electoral process.

At the national level, the voting process has been less significant in terms of reflecting public desires and demands, but the trends are nevertheless very

positive. The three elective bodies in the national government—the National
Assembly, the Legislative Yuan, and the Control Yuan—were all transferred
from the mainland when the Nationalists fled to Taiwan in 1949. Subsequently,
because no elections could be held on the mainland, attrition reduced the size of
these bodies and some vacancies were filled by appointment. In 1969 and 1972
special elections were held in Taiwan to add elected representatives to these
bodies and to give Taiwan Province added representatives in the national government. In the two elections, fifteen and fifty-three members, respectively, were
added to the National Assembly, eleven and fifty-three to the Legislative Yuan,
and two and fifteen to the Control Yuan.[43] Although these numbers are relatively small in comparison to the total size of these organs of government, the
elections did indicate a new and positive trend.

In December 1980 another election was held to increase local representation
in the National Assembly and the Legislative Yuan. This time ninety-seven and
seventy-six seats, respectively, were popularly elected, representing over 7
percent of the delegates of the former and just over 23 percent of the size of the
latter.[44] Of the candidates chosen in this election, 55 percent of the Legislative
Yuan candidates were picked by the general electorate and 17 percent by women's
groups and professional organizations; the rest were candidates representing overseas Chinese and thus were not chosen through direct election processes. Seventy
percent of the candidates for National Assembly seats were picked by the general
electorate and thirty percent by women's and professional groups.

Subsequent elections were held in November 1981, January and June 1982,
and December 1983, giving additional significance to the voting process. In all
of these elections voter turnout was high and irregularities were at a minimum.
In short, elections have become a more important process in the ROC's political
system with the passage of time. Moreover, they have been regularized so that
the electorate can anticipate political participation. Finally, enthusiasm for and
participation in the election processes have been high.

Conclusions

The conclusion is inescapable that political development has transpired in
the ROC despite little noticeable change in the political structure or the Constitution. Leaders in Taiwan tend to play down their role in economic decisions,
seek to maintain a low profile, and consistently speak of a free economy. They
have been, nevertheless, intimately involved in planning the economy, supply-

ing a favorable political climate for economic growth, and maintaining close ties with the business community.

In several realms, the efficient role of government is very apparent even upon very superficial investigation. The land reform program, initiated soon after the Nationalists retreated from the mainland, was a very successful effort in government planning. Subsequent government efforts to help rural Taiwan have greatly improved agricultural productivity upgrading considerably farmers' standards of living.

The astute planning of industrial growth is another realm where the government proved itself. Economists almost unanimously agree that the strategy of import substitution was successful and that the shift to export-led growth was done with a brilliant sense of timing and effectiveness. Similarly, the government made efficient use of U.S. economic assistance at a time when few other nations did. Clearly these accomplishments cannot be written off to chance or to cultural or other factors. Planning produced these successes.

The government must also be credited with erasing class barriers and fostering economic and social equality, first through the land reform program and rent reduction, and later through government efforts to locate labor-intensive industries and various other special programs in the poorer areas of the country. Other general measures taken by the government helped to eliminate unemployment, which also fostered the remarkable level of economic and social equity.

Continued progress in education, labor and social mobility, and the growth of successful industries, will probably ensure that Taiwan will succeed in the next step of its development: the transition to a knowledge-intensive economy. Currently, the ROC government is laying the foundation for such a change.

Despite the government's preoccupation with economic development, it has also made successful efforts to reduce ethnic tensions, control the birth rate, and keep crime under control. Social problems such as divorce and juvenile delinquency have grown only slowly notwithstanding the magnitude of economic and social change in the country, reflecting government efforts to check these problems before they become serious.

Likewise, the ROC government has been successful in attracting foreign investment and in weathering the storms of the loss of representation in the United Nations and its affiliate organizations and diplomatic recognition. It has performed well in spite of these adversities and remains to this day quite competitive in holding the loyalties of the overseas Chinese. In fact, Taiwan has done so well that in the course of trying to resolve the "Taiwan question" the PRC has been obliged to admit to the ROC's successes and even speak of Taiwan as a model.

This should make all observers wonder why the political system on Taiwan has not been the subject of more study and its experience applied to the problems of other underdeveloped countries. For Third World nations, the Taiwan experience is, in many ways, more relevant than Japan's. Taiwan has accomplished nearly what Japan has—all in the post–World War II period. Japan started its political modernization more than a century ago. Also, Taiwan's experience is more meaningful in that it occurred in a shorter span of time, and because its culture and politics remain less influenced by the West. Finally, like most Third World countries, Taiwan is small and has no hope of someday becoming a world power.

Two other contrasts with Japan are also significant: Taiwan had no feudal period in its recent past and, therefore, had less in common with Western political systems; in addition, social and economic equality in Taiwan have resulted from economic growth and government efforts, not from a foreign occupation.

Still another factor may have considerable relevance: Taiwan's experience is probably more valid than Japan's because of the fact that just two or three decades ago Taiwan's bureaucracy was rife with corruption and self-serving individuals. This was not true of Japan. Thus, in another respect, Taiwan's political past, which it has overcome, is more like that of most Third World nations. Moreover, Taiwan had to train, almost from scratch, a new class of technocrats and, at the same time, make them honest and responsible.

Nevertheless, there are some striking similarities between Taiwan's political experience and Japan's. In both there is a one-party or one-party-dominant system. This has facilitated long-range planning and social stability. Also, in both systems politicians maintain contacts with the population and control demands to alleviate social change that might lead to unrealistic expectations on the part of the public. Planning is done by an elite group of bureaucrats whose morale is high and whose commitment to the future is clear. This system gives Taiwan an obvious advantage over most Western systems, suggesting that its experience may even be instructive to Western countries that are now experiencing low growth and paralysis in government.

This is not to say that Taiwan's polity is problem-free. However, it does bring to question the notion of a "revolutionary gap" caused by rapid strides in economic development without commensurate progress in political modernization. Some have spoken of the Kaohsiung riots in 1979 as evidence of such circumstances. This view, however, ignores the riots in Japan in 1960 over the Security Treaty and youth problems during the rest of the 1960s and 1970s. It also ignores riots and unrest in the United States, Western Europe and Hong Kong during the same period. Did those suggest places "ripe for revolution"?

The ROC government may, in fact, be judged coping with the side effects of economic and social change more astutely than Japan, Hong Kong, or South Korea, inasmuch as Taiwan has a problem of regional differences between Taiwanese and mainlanders and an independence movement abroad, which the others do not. Some would say that Taiwan has the advantage of an external threat, perceived or real. It is a nation that has suffered from discrimination at the hands of the United Nations and the international community and is, therefore, more united. Yet these are as much problems the government has had to deal with as they are advantages in terms of keeping the populace pre-occupied with issues that call for unity and obedience to political authority.

In terms of performance in problem solving, the ROC government must obviously be applauded. It has solved a number of very difficult problems in a short period of time and in spite of many handicaps. However, it has not been ostentatious. In fact, promoting Taiwan as a model would suggest that more subtle and less spectacular accomplishments should be given more credit and the showy efforts of many nations, including most Communist ones, less credit. In addition, other countries should place more emphasis on education and training, maintaining good morale and the coordination of efforts in the bureaucracy, not to mention the relationship between planners and the politicians in their efforts to build an efficient political system.

Another lesson of the Taiwan experience is that mass participation in politics is more meaningful when it reflects the political culture and relates to important public concerns. The populace of Taiwan has expressed a strong desire to participate in decisions affecting the economy as well as social legislation. Citizens are less interested in participation in purely political issues. They do not like to demonstrate or criticize their leaders in public. Their greater interest in local problems, as opposed to national affairs, is another facet of Taiwan politics. Many people believe good government and problem solving have to start at the bottom.

In conclusion, it needs to be said that there are few models of political development that are not in the mold of Western democracies or Communist systems. Along with Singapore and South Korea, which also have experienced rapid economic growth built upon effective government planning and where rapid social and political changes have been the rule (albeit molded by cultural and other factors), Taiwan is one of the best or most successful of the developing nations. Obviously Taiwan can serve as a prototype of political change and modernization for other nations.

Endnotes

1. See Anthony Y.C. Koo, "Economic Development of Taiwan," in Paul K.T. Sih, ed., *Taiwan in Modern Times* (New York: St. John's University Press, 1973), pp. 397–433, for an account of Taiwan's early economic development.

2. Jan S. Prybyla, "Economic Development in Taiwan," in Hungdah Chiu, ed., *China and the Taiwan Issue* (New York: Praeger, 1979), p. 82.

3. See Herman Kahn, *World Economic Development: 1979 and Beyond* (Boulder, CO: Westview Press, 1979), for further details on this view.

4. Prybyla, "Economic Development in Taiwan," p. 85.

5. See Chi-ming Hou, "Institutional Innovations, Technological Change, and Agricultural Growth in Taiwan," in Yuan-li Wu and Kung-chia Yeh, eds., *Growth, Distribution, and Social Change: Essays on the Economy of the Republic of China,* Occasional Papers/Reprints Series in Contemporary Asian Studies, No. 3-1978 (Baltimore: University of Maryland School of Law, 1978), pp. 113–19.

6. For details on the role of government planning in economic growth, see Maurice Scott, "Foreign Trade," in Walter Galenson, ed., *Economic Growth and Structural Change in Taiwan* (Ithaca, NY: Cornell University Press, 1979), p. 314.

7. Prybyla, "Economic Development in Taiwan," p. 82.

8. Ian M.D. Little, "An Economic Renaissance," in Galenson, ed., *Economic Growth and Structural Change,* p. 448.

9. *Free China Weekly,* Aug. 2, 1981.

10. Ibid., July 26, 1981.

11. Ibid.

12. Kahn, *World Economic Development,* pp. 378–79.

13. *Free China Weekly*, Aug. 2, 1981.

14. See John F. Copper, "Taiwan in 1980: Entering a New Decade," *Asian Survey* 21, No. 1 (Jan. 1981): 55, for further details on this point.

15. *Free China Weekly*, July 26, 1981.

16. For details on this issue, see Yuan-li Wu, "Income Distribution in the Process of Economic Growth in Taiwan," in Wu and Yeh, eds., *Growth, Distribution, and Social Change*, pp. 67–112.

17. Kung-Chia Yeh, "Economic Growth: An Overview," in ibid., p. 30.

18. For background information on the ROC's political system, see Lih-wu Han, *Taiwan Today* (Taipei: Institute of International Relations, 1974).

19. See Ralph N. Clough, *Island China* (Cambridge: Harvard University Press, 1978), p. 36, for the figures on this point.

20. See Arthur J. Lerman, *Taiwan's Politics: The Provincial Assemblyman's World* (Washington, DC: University Press of America, 1978), chapter 3, for further elaboration on this point.

21. See ibid., chapter. 1 and 2, for further details.

22. Ibid., p. 62.

23. See Copper, "Taiwan in 1980," for further details.

24. I have made this same argument elsewhere. See "Political Development in Taiwan," in Chiu, ed., *China and the Taiwan Issue*, pp. 37–76.

25. Clough, *Island China*, p. 36.

26. *China Yearbook 1980* (Taipei: China Publishing Co., 1980), pp. 103–9.

27. Some statistics relating to the handling and paperwork seem very relevant to the streamlining efforts made by the Executive Yuan. From 1973 to 1978 documents processed in three days rose from 51 to 63 percent. The average time

needed to handle a memo fell during the same period from 5.66 to 4.31 days. During this same period, the Executive Yuan merged 263 government agencies and cut 5,287 employees. See Research, Development, and Evaluation Commission, Executive Yuan, *Annual Review of Government Administration, Republic of China, 1979–80* (Taipei, 1981), pp. 31, 39.

28. This practice has been maintained. The public is now very aware of the names of officials and their office addresses and telephone numbers where complaints about government performance can be directed. Many officials' performances are now judged in part by public reaction.

29. Yung Wei, "Modernization Process in Taiwan: An Allocative Analysis," *Asian Survey* 16, No. 3 (March 1976): pp. 249–69.

30. See Hou, "Institutional Innovations, Technological Change, and Agricultural Growth in Taiwan," pp. 115–19.

31. For further details on this point, see Neil H. Jacoby, *U.S. Aid to Taiwan: A Study of Foreign Aid, Self-Help, and Development* (New York: Praeger, 1966).

32. Clough, *Island China*, p. 76.

33. Theodore Hsi-en Chen, "The Educational System," in James C. Hsiung, ed., *Contemporary Republic of China: The Taiwan Experience, 1950–1980* (New York: Praeger, 1981), p. 66.

34. See Clough, *Island China*, p. 76.

35. For details on this point, see Richard H. Solomon, *Mao's Revolution and Chinese Political Structure* (Berkeley: University of California Press, 1971).

36. Research, Development, and Evaluation Commission, *Annual Review of Government Administration, Republic of China, 1978* (Taipei, 1979), p. 156.

37. Ibid.

38. This figure was provided in an interview with a high KMT official in the summer of 1981 in Taipei.

39. Clough, *Island China*, p. 37.

40. From an interview with a high KMT official in summer of 1981 in Taipei.

41. This has been a growing phenomenon in recent years but was more notice-able during the December 1980 election campaign. Some argue that it is a threat to the KMT; others argue that it is not.

42. Voter turnout in elections Taiwan's elections has consistently been high, in the range of 70 to 80 percent. In the 1964 election it was 76.8 percent. See Frederick H. Chaffee et al., *Area Handbook for the Republic of China* (Washington, DC: Government Printing Office, 1969), pp. 201–2, for further details on early elections.

43. Clough, *Island China*, p. 36.

44. See John F. Copper, "Taiwan's Recent Election: Progress Toward Democracy," *Asian Survey* 21, No. 10 (Oct. 1981): 1029–39, for further details.

Chapter Two
Challenges to Political Development
in Taiwan

The Republic of China is often cited as a model of development. It is a nation that has changed faster in the direction of democracy than perhaps any other in the world. Some say its political change stems from its rapid economic growth. Clearly Taiwan's experience supports the theory that economic development fosters political development or that the two must occur in tandem. The questions that need to be addressed then are: Could slower growth reverse or slow the political modernization process? And what is the current status of democratization in Taiwan? The context for asking these questions is that Taiwan's rapid economic and political development appear to be experiencing a bumpy road. Will the government, as some evidence suggests is the case, adopt sufficiently effective measures to deal with the problems that currently threaten the modernization process?

Economic Growth Challenges

Over the past two decades, Taiwan's economic growth (measured in annual increases in the gross national product, or GNP) has ranked it one of the top three or four nations in the world. Depending on what period of time is considered, Taiwan may be the world's fastest growing economy. Moreover, it has attained this rank despite the fact that it has virtually no natural resources, little arable land and three times the population density of Japan and nine times that of China. And, unlike Japan, Taiwan has sustained large military budgets during the time of its rapid growth.

Although it has been less noticeable and has trailed economic development chronologically, Taiwan has also experienced rapid political development. Its government has been stable, and there have been two smooth transfers of executive power at the top (something that happens rarely in developing countries).

Government efficiency has improved and corruption has been reduced to a level similar to that found in governments in Western Europe, Japan, and the United States.

During 1984 and 1985, however, serious new problems arose. In fact, Taiwan seemed to experience obstacles both to sustaining rapid economic growth and to further political modernization. Its leading economic indicators and its economic trends do not paint a rosy future. Progressive political change has been and is currently threatened by serious political issues, creating what some call a "crisis of confidence" in the nation's top leadership.

Some background to this "crisis" is instructive. Taiwan's economic growth was initially based on land reforms that increased farm production and released farm labor to man the textile factories and other light industries that were started in the 1950s. Land distribution was an important part of the land reforms. The government held sizable amounts of land it had confiscated from Japanese land-owners and the Japanese colonial government after World War II, which it could sell to landless peasants. Landlords took payment for the land in industrial bonds or used the money to invest in the fledgling industrial sector, which they also managed.[1]

In the second phase of economic development, Taiwan's growth was led by light industry using cheap and easily trained labor. Specialization in export products, which provided the foreign exchange to further modernize the economy, was also part of Taiwan's economic development plan.

The third phase involved a major shift from labor-intensive to capital-intensive industries, large infrastructure projects and the production of higher quality and specialty market goods. During this period, Taiwan "stole" some of Japan's industries that had become less competitive because of higher labor costs. Both exports and the growth of consumerism at this time propelled economic growth.

Taiwan successfully weathered the oil crisis of 1973-1974, although it suffered high inflation for approximately a year. It also sustained impressive economic growth during the global recession of the early 1980s. In 1984, the gross national product grew over 10 percent—one of the highest rates of economic growth in the world.[2]

In 1985, however, economic growth slipped. Also the economic indicators suggested that the rate of future growth might be far less rapid. Economic growth for 1985 was 4.9 percent. Foreign trade declined, in contrast to the usual double-digit increases; in October, trade was down 4 percent from the previous year. In August, the rate of unemployment reached 4.1 percent, the highest in many years. Domestic investment fell 5.7 percent from 1984. This was the fourth successive year of stagnant or declining domestic investment—always a bellwether of future economic development.[3]

Two "structural" causes apparently explain the downturn, and seemed to be more than temporary. First, the nation's economy may have passed the period of rapid growth suggesting that, like Japan, Taiwan may have to be content with good rather than outstanding growth as it assumes the status of a "developed" country. Second, Taiwan has for some time been "in transition," or shifting gears to a knowledge-intensive economy. Clearly, if the transition is successful, it will make Taiwan a developed country, where rapid growth is more difficult, long-range planning more important, and global competition keener.

Another reason for its recent economic difficulties is Taiwan's dependence on foreign trade. Taiwan's foreign trade as a ratio of its GNP (imports plus exports combined) is near 100 percent. For Japan—a nation generally regarded as trade dependent—trade as a ratio of the GNP is less than 30 percent.[4] And nearly half Taiwan's exports—over 48 percent in 1985—go to one country, the United States.[5] Exports have suffered recently because of a downturn in the U.S. economy and a consequent diminished demand in the United States for Taiwan's products.

Moreover, growing protectionist sentiment in the America may make this situation even worse in the future. Taiwan has a large trade surplus with the United States and Congress has frequently criticized and even singled out Taiwan for special retaliation. It is difficult for Taipei to counter this criticism for several reasons: its inability to reverse its sizable trade deficit with Japan; its non-competitiveness in the European Common Market because the New Taiwan dollar is pegged to the U.S. dollar; and its only moderate success in breaking into other markets.[6]

Another serious problem for Taiwan is the aftershocks of the Tenth Credit Cooperative scandal that broke in February 1985. This serious financial crisis caused a decline in public trust in the government and shook investor confidence. When the scandal broke, it was estimated that the group owned assets in more than 100 companies in Taiwan worth more than U.S.$3.5 billion. Tsai Chen-chou (head of Cathy Plastics), who controlled the group, was subsequently convicted on six counts of writing bad checks and sentenced to fifteen years in prison on each count. His conviction however, did not absolve several government agencies that should have prevented the mess and which were seen to have been grossly negligent. One-half billion dollars in bad loans, in the eyes of many observers, indicated poor government oversight and even raised questions about the financial structure of the country.

Minister of Economic Affairs (and former Minister of Finance) Hsu Li-teh and Finance Minister Loh Jen-kong resigned over the scandal. Many felt, however, that other government officials were equally responsible. In fact, critics pointed a finger at Prime Minster Yu Kuo-hua because he had been head of the Central Bank when many of the shaky transactions were initiated.

In addition to the Tenth Credit fiasco, during 1984 and 1985 Taiwan experienced four coal mine disasters that claimed 277 lives. In response, the government closed half of Taiwan's 130 coal mines—which were providing only 4 percent of the nation's energy needs and were highly (and not rationally) subsidized for national security reasons. In a related matter, there was a fire at one of Taiwan's nuclear power plants (though it caused no danger to the public). These incidents led to criticism of Taiwan's energy planning drawing attention to the fact there was an over-capacity of 37 percent in electricity production, yet plans had been made (though they were canceled) to build another nuclear power plant. Again, government oversight seemed to have gone awry.

Yet another problem was the situation in Hong Kong. In September 1984, China signed an agreement with the British government that would place Hong Kong under the sovereignty of the People's Republic of China in 1997. Inasmuch as Taiwan has sizable investments in Hong Kong and sends that territory 8 to 10 percent of its exports, some businessmen questioned the wisdom of the government's plan to restrict trade with Hong Kong. The government, however, feared that trade with Hong Kong would lead to a dependence on Beijing and that might become difficult politically for Taiwan.

Another problem that affected long-term investor confidence was the uncertainty of U.S. arms sales to Taiwan. In August 1982, in a joint communique with the People's Republic of China, the United States agreed to reduce arms sales to Taiwan with the goal of eventually ending such sales, in exchange for a pledge from Beijing to seek a "peaceful solution only to the 'Taiwan problem.'" During 1984 and 1985 the United States abided by its promise, even though Beijing denied that it had promised a peaceful solution only.

Late in 1985, some of the factors causing Taiwan's economic turndown seemed to be fading or changing in Taiwan's favor. The decline of America's thirst for Taiwan-made products seemed to be reversing. Then, because Taiwan's currency is tied to the U.S. dollar, a decrease in the value of the dollar also caused a decline in the price of Taiwan's exports, while the price of competing exports was rising. These trends indicated Taiwan should be better able to sell its products in Japan and in Europe, thereby reducing, to some degree the importance of the U.S. market.

To deal with specific complaints from the United States regarding the balance of trade deficit, Taipei sent another "buying mission" to the United States in late 1985 and took action to lower tariffs from a maximum of over 120 percent to 75 percent. At the same time, Taiwan significantly cut a surcharge tariff inaugurated in 1983 ranging from 20 percent to 5 percent, promising to drop it entirely in 1986. The government also planed to reduce Taiwan's actual overall tariff (total imports divided by customs charges) from a current 7.7 percent to 5 percent in the next five years.[7] (The overall U.S. tariff is 4 percent.) Actions were likewise taken to assuage another sore spot in U.S.–Taiwan relations: copyright and patent violations. Taipei passed stricter laws against violations—including the field of computer software—and began to enforce laws already in place. By year's end, the U.S. Congress and U.S. companies seemed to be placated.

The lessons learned from the Tenth Credit Cooperative collapse will probably prevent another such occurrence. In the course of parrying public criticism, government officials noted that there was relatively little government control over the economy. The majority obviously believes that the economy should remain as free as possible inasmuch as a free economy made Taiwan prosperous. The coal mine disasters could be considered a short-range problem. As for Hong Kong, the government seems to be taking the most appropriate tack: allowing debate on the subject while holding a final decision in abeyance.

The government moved to deal with the problem of declining capital investment before the year ended by increasing state enterprise investment by 10 percent and government capital investment by 13 percent (mostly in infrastructure). Although private capital accumulation accounts for nearly 60 percent of total capital investment in Taiwan, these actions seemed to help correct the problem at hand and restore private investor confidence. Overseas Chinese investment and investment from the United States and Japan (the largest sources of private investment) continued to flow in, being given favored treatment by the government. Government actions to stimulate the economy seemed to have another desired effect: by the last quarter of 1985, unemployment showed a 0.4 percent decline.[8]

Inflation remained at a very low level, presenting no immediate threat to the economy, and if other economic problems can be managed, economic growth will probably not falter. The Council for Economic Planning in Taipei predicted a 5.5 percent growth rate for 1986, a figure most thought was realistic.[9]

Political Development

After fifty years of Japanese colonial rule, Taiwan became a province of the Republic of China in 1945.[10] Although local Chinese or Taiwanese at first welcomed Nationalist Chinese rule, the first three or four years of Kuomintang control were a disaster. Gross incompetence in the top levels of government, disregard for effective rule or constitutionalism (because the Nationalists were at war with the Communists on the mainland), and hostile attitudes on the part of the Mainland Chinese, who held political power, toward the Taiwanese were the causes. In 1947, a revolt by Taiwanese against the Mainlander-run government was put down by brute military force with a significant loss of life.

The Chinese Nationalists, who were defeated on the mainland and fled to Taiwan to regroup in 1949, tried to alleviate the hatred and distrust felt by the Taiwanese. The former governor, who had been largely responsible for the 1947 "incident" was executed, and efforts were made to promote local democracy. In 1950, Taiwan had its first island-wide election.[11]

In subsequent years, however, democratization of the political system was generally limited to local government. There were several reasons for this: (1) The country was at war; (2) the Mainland Chinese, who controlled the government, did not trust the Taiwanese, nor did they want to surrender power; (3) the failure of democracy elsewhere in the Third World had created a negative precedent.

Nevertheless, the ruling elite was imbued with the political thinking of Sun Yat-sen, who had promised a democratic system. In addition, the Constitution that the Nationalists brought with them to Taiwan assumed a democratic system.

Thus, through the 1950s and 1960s, democratization proceeded at a slow, albeit continuous, pace. The government at the national level became more efficient; corruption and bureaucratization were in large part eliminated. Citizen participation in the political process increased and so did confidence in the government. The political modernization process was in some ways very unique. Local governments in Taiwan—which was dominated by the Taiwanese—were characterized by serious factionalism, which allowed the Nationalists to act as intermediaries and to manipulate local politics.[12] Mainland Chinese perceived that they had to build democracy in Taiwan. Taiwanese in contrast, felt that Mainland Chinese would not facilitate local democracy. In spite the differences of perspectives, democracy flourished locally in Taiwan. Elections at the top did not become important, and the system at the center, or national politics, remained authoritarian.

In 1972, when Chiang Ching-kuo became prime minister, more significant reforms were made at the top. Government agencies and bureaus were made more responsive to the public, and more important, an "affirmative action" kind of effort was made to bring more Taiwanese into the Kuomintang.[13] These changes occurred largely because of Chiang Ching-kuo's orders. Yet, they must be viewed in the context of a decade or more of successful economic growth, which gave the government enough confidence to risk democratization while eradicating ill feelings between Taiwanese and Mainland Chinese (since the two had co-operated to produce the economic miracle). Political change was also fostered by U.S. pressure and facilitated by the growing perception that the Nationalists had no chance of recovering the mainland from the Communists and that they had to remain in Taiwan indefinitely.

In 1980, Taiwan witnessed for the first time party competition (meaning the Kuomintang versus nonparty or independent candidates) in a national election. Competitive national elections subsequently became part of the operation of the political system which became significantly more democratic.[14]

During 1984 and 1985, however, a pall was cast over an otherwise increasingly democratic and an increasingly freer political system. The first problem was the incapacitation of Prime Minister Sun Yuan-suan after a stroke in February 1984. Sun, who ran the day-to-day operations of government, not only was a superb administrator but also understood the nation's problems as few others did. He perceived the need for both economic and political development and comprehended the relationship between the two. He was also highly regarded by both Taiwanese and Mainland Chinese. Sun was replaced by Yu Kuo-hua, who had built an excellent reputation for political savvy as an adviser to the president and as an economic planner as head of the Central Bank. But Yu, at least during his first months in office, did not show he had Sun Yuan-suan's ability or desire to engineer democratic change.

In April 1985, a serious political incident made many observers question exactly who was in charge and if political leaders were committed to reform. The government was linked to the killing of writer and businessman Henry Liu in California the previous October. It was soon disclosed that only one or two officials in military intelligence were responsible, and they had acted in direct disobedience of orders from the top. Nevertheless, many Western critics of Taiwan questioned in newspaper editorials and elsewhere how and why the writer had been murdered and whether President Chiang's health was a factor. To some, the murder proved that the military's influence in government was still strong and that democracy had not evolved as far as was thought. The incident clearly hurt the government's reputation both at home and abroad.[15]

This was followed by the Tenth Credit Cooperative fiasco described earlier and by the resignation of two ministers. The secretary general of the Kuomintang was also implicated and resigned. His replacement, Ma Su-lay, assumed less personal control over the management of foreign affairs, allowing other top party officials who had little contact with or understanding of foreigners, especially Americans, to influence foreign policy making.

The mine disasters already mentioned, several industrial accidents, poisoned wine that was marketed by the government's Wine and Tobacco Monopoly, and other unfortunate incidents further damaged the government's image. Rumors circulated about who would be the next foreign minister and the next prime minister, undermining the credibility of both, while concern over President Chiang Ching-kuo's health and likely successor contributed to what many called in mid-1985 a "crisis of confidence" in the government.

Foreign policy problems only made matters worse. Taipei seemed to lack confidence when responding to overtures from Beijing to negotiate or to Chinese leader Deng Xiaoping's veiled threats to use military force to "liberate" Taiwan. In late 1985, the Republic of China suffered the loss of formal diplomatic ties with two countries—Bolivia and in Nicaragua—adding further to the malaise. Taipei's continued membership in the Asian Development Bank also seemed to be less certain, the ADB being the last international organization of any importance where Taipei still has representation.

Before the November elections for the Taiwan Provincial Assembly, the Taipei and Kaohsiung city councils, and mayors and the magistrates, many political pundits were predicting that the Kuomintang would do poorly. Many citizens seemed to agree with vocal opposition politicians that there was a real "crisis" in the government. Critics said the process of democratization was being ignored or set back because the top leadership was unable to cope with the nation's problems and furthermore that the country lacked a sense of direction.

Judging from the results of provincial and local elections, however, the situation was not as serious as it was thought to be. A sizable majority of the voters apparently perceived that many of the Kuomintang's difficulties did not reflect incompetence or devolution in government. Furthermore, as in the past, independent "opposition" politicians afforded few intelligent alternatives and opposition leaders continued to fight among themselves. Voter turnout did not drop; in fact, it increased compared to the same elections held four years earlier and was higher than average—well above 70 percent. The Kuomintang held on to its majority, and the voters gave the ruling party essentially the same mandate in local politics that it had received in previous elections.[16]

After the election, the public cautiously applauded the Kuomintang for not abandoning the process of democratization and for running a fair and open campaign. Generally, the election was viewed as proof that democratization was still on track notwithstanding the political difficulties of the past year or two. Some, in fact, argued that the Kuomintang doing well in electoral competition while trying to resolve the problems just cited said something very positive about Taiwan's political leadership.

At almost the same time that Taiwan was holding elections, Sino-American relations were being questioned by the U.S. Senate, which was reviewing the nuclear agreement made by the Reagan administration to transfer nuclear technology to China. The debate was not very complimentary to Beijing's policies, which were branded by several Senate leaders as furthering nuclear proliferation. The apprehension created by the case of spy Larry Chin, who had been passing secrets to the People's Republic of China for thirty years, also made Taipei look trustworthy by comparison.

Just before the election, Vice President Lee Teng-hui was given Taiwan's highest civilian honor, prompting some speculation that he was in line for succession. This had a salutary effect on most Taiwanese, Lee being Taiwanese and highly respected for his education (a Cornell University Phd), his political experience (as governor of Taiwan and in a number of other top positions), and his personal leadership abilities and integrity.

There was also less talk about the president's health late in the year—either because he had become more active or, as some said, because his diabetes had improved with new medications. Immediately after the election, Kuomintang officials proposed that a provision be put into the election law specifically prohibiting politicians from making personal attacks on the president or his family, as had happened during the campaign. President Chiang replied publicly that he opposed such a law and stepped in personally to kill the proposal, catching the opposition off guard and surprising some critics abroad who opined that the personal affronts on President Chiang would result in some kind of retaliation.

Finally, President Chiang, in his New Year's address, cleared the air about the matter of succession that had evoked both rumors and serious concern about political development in Taiwan, with a speech that was widely applauded in Taiwan and abroad. He said that his successor would be chosen in a constitutional manner and that it was not possible that his successor would be a member of his family. "It cannot happen and it will not happen," he declared. The president also promised that there would never be a military government in Taiwan.

Conclusions

In terms of economic growth, Taiwan has come close to accomplishing in just over two decades what Western Europe and the United States did in 200 years. It has likewise experienced, albeit delayed or following economic growth, rapid political development.

The speed and magnitude of both economic and political change in Taiwan have caused problems for Taiwan. Yet, the fact that it has accomplished so much in such a short time and at considerable risk may make Taiwan a better model for the world's economically and politically underdeveloped nations notwithstanding the problems or bumps along the road to democracy.

Taiwan is certainly a more relevant model in the eyes of most Third World leaders than Western countries or Japan—because it was colonized and because it began to develop in the post-World War II period with little experience in either economic or political development. It also faced serious economic and political handicaps. Nor did it have the advantage of defense provided free of charge or access to U.S. technology as Japan did. Finally, it is not culturally Western, nor does it have a democratic tradition.

Until recently, Taiwan's impressive economic and political development seemed to prove that economic development directly fostered political development. Recent difficulties, economic and political, however, suggest that development in either realm reinforces the other. In other words, problem solving in one area reduces the seriousness of problems in the other, and progress in either helps the other.

Taiwan's economic and political success also says something about its future. Per capita income in Taiwan is approximately ten times what it is in China. That fact alone should tell observers that there is little support among Taiwan's populace for becoming a part of the People's Republic of China. Economic progress has also ameliorated ethnic differences.

Yet Taiwan's move toward democracy has accentuated ethnic problems, especially in elections. This has been particularly noticeable during election campaigns. Ethnic tensions have not been a serious problem in Taiwan, however, compared to other countries. In fact, ethnic differences have disappeared very quickly. This may be because a Taiwan national identity is forming. Certainly this is something to ponder.

What problems remain? Taiwan needs to reestablish itself in the global community. It has not yet decided how it should view Hong Kong's future. It is uncertain how or when to drop the pretense of claiming China in a way that doesn't unnecessarily provoke leaders in Beijing or arouse Taiwanese separatism at home. And Taipei must deal with a large trade imbalance with its two largest trading partners—a surplus with the United States and a deficit with Japan? Should Taiwan diversify its trade and if so how?

Neither the international community nor the United States—upon whom Taiwan stakes its future—doubts that Taiwan's economic and political development is impressive. Taiwan has recently become the eleventh largest trading nation in the world (larger than China, with one-sixtieth the territory). It has become the fifth largest trading partner of the United States, passing the United Kingdom. Public opinion polls reflect a high degree of confidence in the government and a strong desire to remain on the course of democratization, maintaining ties with the West and the rest of the world, but no desire to become part of a poor and Communist China.

Endnotes

1. For excellent background works on Taiwan's economic development, see Shirley W.Y. Kuo, Gustav Ranis, and John C.H. Fei, *The Taiwan Success Story: Rapid Growth and Improved Distribution in the Republic of China, 1952–1979* (Boulder, CO: Westview Press, 1981); Shirley W.Y. Kuo et al., *Growth with Equity: The Taiwan Case* (London: Oxford University Press, 1979); Yuan-li Wu and Kung-chia Yeh, eds., *Growth, Distribution and Social Change: Essays on the Republic of China* (Baltimore: University of Maryland School of Law, 1978).

2. *Asia 1985 Yearbook* (Hong Kong: Far Eastern Economic Review, Ltd., 1984), p. 7. The estimate was 11 percent. In 1984, Japan's growth rate was 5.3 percent, South Korea's was 7.5 percent, Singapore's was 8.0 percent, and Hong Kong's was 6.0 percent. Taiwan was clearly the leader.

3. These statistics are cited in Carl Goldstein, "Taiwan: Trade Growth Loses Steam," *Far Eastern Economic Review*, December 5, 1985, p. 72.

4. *Asia 1985 Yearbook*, pp. 8–9.

5. Carl Goldstein, "The Problem of Plenty," *Far Eastern Economic Review*, December 19, 1985, p. 100.

6. *Asia 1986 Yearbook* (Hong Kong: Far Eastern Economic Review, Ltd., 1985), pp. 245–46. Also see "Air Goes Out of Asia's Business Balloon," *U.S. News and World Report,* December 16, 1985, p. 49.

7. *Free China Journal* (Taipei), December 8–14, 1985.

8. See Goldstein, "Taiwan: Trade Growth."

9. Lee Kao-chao, "Economy on Course Despite International Recession," *Japan Times,* October 10, 1985, p. 17.

10. For background studies on Taiwan's political development, see John F. Copper, "Political Development in Taiwan," in Hungdah Chiu, ed., *China and the Taiwan Issue* (New York: Praeger, 1979), and John F. Copper, "Political Development in the Republic of China, 1949–1981," in Hungdah Chiu and Shao-chuan Leng, eds., *China: Seventy Years After the 1911 Hsin-Hai Revolution* (Charlottesville, VA: University of Virginia Press, 1984). For an excellent study of the relationship between economic and political development, see A. James Gregor and Maria Hsia Chang, *Ideology and Development: Sun Yat-sen and the Economic History of Taiwan* (Berkeley: Center for Chinese Studies, University of California, 1981).

11. See John F. Copper with George P. Chen, *Taiwan's Elections: Political Development and Democratization in the Republic of China* (Baltimore: University of Maryland School of Law, 1984).

12. Ibid., chapter 3.

13. Ralph N. Cough, *Island China* (Cambridge: Harvard University Press, 1978), pp. 62–64.

14. See John F. Copper, "Taiwan's Recent Election: Progress Toward a Democratic System," *Asian Survey,* October 1981.

15. Members of the U.S. Congress called for a reconsideration of U.S. arms sales to Taiwan, and the House Foreign Affairs Committee, Subcommittee on Asia and the Pacific, held hearings on the matter.

16. For further details, see John F. Copper, "Taiwan's 1985 Elections," *Asian-American Review* (forthcoming).

Chapter Three
Politics in Taiwan, 1985-1986:
Political Development and Elections

Simply put, the political situation in Taiwan during 1985-1986—both in terms of mood and tangible problems—went from bad to good. The year 1985—at least until near year's end—must be defined as a difficult time for Taipei. The government and the ruling Nationalist Party, or Kuomintang (KMT), were plagued by various troubles. In fact, taken collectively the problems were sufficiently serious that some referred to a "crisis of confidence" in government. Though the use of this term may have been exaggerated, and was certainly employed unfairly at times by the opposition as a campaign tactic to discredit the government, one could certainly sense a mood of frustration and discouragement in Taiwan. Moreover, several intractable issues seemed to defy solution, at least during the first part of the period.

This "down" period resulted from a number of factors—political (relating to domestic politics) as well as foreign policy and economic. The Henry Liu case (which will be explained below), a serious financial scandal, problems with the United States over arms purchases, and a lack of innovative policies to deal with overtures by Peking aimed at pressuring Taipei into negotiations leading to "reunification" were among the causes.[1]

In the summer of 1985, it appeared that the KMT was heading for a major defeat in the fall election. Some said that it was "overdue" because of KMT victories—a chain of them—in recent elections. Others predicted a defeat because many of the nation's difficulties were being blamed on the ruling KMT. In any case, by late summer 1985 the government and the ruling party were suffering from bad morale and there was less public confidence that the country was resolving its problems.

The situation improved in the fall of 1985. By election time, it appeared that the KMT would not suffer badly at the polls. Things seemed to once again be "under control." In fact, the KMT did as well in this election as it had been doing previously in terms of winning the support of the electorate. After the election, there was less talk about top officials who needed to resign or be dismissed. Other problems also seemed less serious.[2]

The government followed up its election victory with announcements that it would seek talks with opposition leaders on legalizing the *tang wai* or "outside the party"—that is, the opposition. Legal and other political reforms should be undertaken, the President said, including the substitution of national security laws for martial law. Meetings were held, proposals were tabled, and, seemingly, solutions reached.

The KMT meanwhile demonstrated that it was sincere about reform, meaning democratic political change and modernization, when in the spring of 1986 at its plenum meeting it appointed four new members to the Central Standing Committee of the party—notably half of them Taiwanese and all younger and better-educated than previously picked party stalwarts. Meanwhile, President Chiang Ching-kuo made a number of moves to prove that there was no succession "problem" and that neither his relatives nor the military would decide that issue. In other words, succession would be accomplished democratically.

In October 1986, President Chiang announced that martial law would be ended soon and that the ban on the formation of new parties would also be lifted. This announcement was praised by the Western media, usually unsympathetic toward Taiwan's allegedly "authoritarian" government. The U.S. State Department and Congress reacted in a similarly positive manner. In the meantime, the opposition, apparently not wanting to be upstaged and seeking to avoid being seen as a party that was the "creation of the KMT" or a product of a deal with KMT leaders, struck out on its own and announced the formation of the new Democratic Progressive Party. Though this action was technically illegal and was certainly done in defiance of the government, the president and other top KMT officials seemed unflappable. Their reaction was by any measure mild and controlled.

This was the prelude to a national election on December 6. The voice of the people (as reflected in public opinion polls taken at this time) said that Taiwan needed party competition in elections to make the system a democracy. But the electorate also sent a word of caution in their vote. Thus moderate opposition candidates did better at the polls than the more radical ones. Many incumbents lost, but experience still counted. Issues were important; ideology was not.

In short, 1985 and 1986 were eventful years politically in Taiwan. One might say that the manner in which numerous serious problems were resolved, the pace at which critical decisions to democratize were made, and the ability of both sides to compromise boded well for Taiwan's future.

Early and Mid-1985: "Crisis of Confidence"

In January 1985, it was reported that several top intelligence officials of the Taiwan government had been involved in—that is, that they had ordered—the murder of writer and businessman Henry Liu in San Francisco in October 1984. According to both U.S. and Taiwanese published reports, Liu had written a biography of President Chiang Ching-kuo that was uncomplimentary, thereby providing the motive; the actual murder was carried out by members of a Chinese gang. But such situations are seldom as simple as they seem at first, and this one was no exception .

In February 1985, Vice Admiral Wang Hsi-ling, head of the Defense Ministry's Intelligence Bureau, was indicted for masterminding the crime. Three members of the Bamboo Union Gang were subsequently convicted of perpetrating the crime. One of the gang members testified specifically in court that Wang had ordered Liu's murder. Wang was subsequently convicted and given a sentence of life in prison.

The incident caused considerable difficulty for the government and especially for the Kuomintang. A number of editorials in U.S. newspapers suggested that other government officials in Taipei were involved. Congressman Stephen Solarz, chairman of the House Foreign Affairs Sub-Committee on Asia and the Pacific, called for hearings on the case with the intent of demonstrating that the incident was "typical of Taipei's behavior," that is, its intimidation of Chinese in the United States.[3] He also sought to link the case to U.S. arms sales to Taiwan, arguing that such arms sales should be cut.

Further investigation, however, revealed that there was little or no logic in the original explanation of Liu's murder. His negative comments about President Chiang Ching-kuo had been written years earlier and were known or remembered by very few people at the time of his death. Furthermore, it was learned that Liu had served as an agent for Taiwan—providing Taipei with intelligence information about the People's Republic of China—and had only recently purveyed Taipei with some intimate details on Peking's military preparedness in South China. He had also served in an intelligence capacity for Peking and for the F.B.I. in the United States, making him a triple agent. Some said he was killed in retaliation for exposing some of Taiwan's agents resulting in their executions.[4] Finally, the gang member who testified that Wang had specifically ordered the murder changed his testimony during an appeal hearing.

In any event, the attempt to tie the case to arms sales failed, as did Mrs. Liu's demand that Admiral Wang and the gang members be extradited to the United States for punishment. (Congressman Gerald Solomon meanwhile had remarked during the hearings that if Mrs. Liu wanted her husband's killers out on parole in a few months, they should be brought to trial in the United States; in Taiwan they would be duly punished. This dampened any move to bring the accused to the United States.) But, the affair had other ramifications; most important, it underscored the fact that the United States did not have an extradition treaty with Taiwan (which allowed criminals from Taiwan to live in the United States) and that Taiwan remained an important issue in the United States notwithstanding a China policy that sought to ignore the "Taiwan issue."

Still, the case did considerable damage to Taiwan, in terms of public opinion, both at home and abroad. The government lost credibility locally, notwithstanding the fact that the decision to kill Liu was made by only one or two individuals without the knowledge or consent of the president or other high officials. Thus it seemed to reflect more a breakdown in the chain of command in the government in Taiwan than a pattern of behavior as some had said.

Following on the heels of the Liu case, Taiwan suffered its worst financial scandal ever. Runs began on two financial institutions controlled by the Tsai family, whose Cathay Group was the second largest business empire in the country (with 100 companies and assets of up to $3.6 billion). The Ministry of Finance took control of the Cathy Group, but not before creditors lost an estimated US$320 million.[5]

This time a host of officials in the top ranks of the government were implicated. The Cathay Group had operated under the control of the Ministry of Finance and officers of the group had close ties with other government ministries and bureaus. Finance Minister Loh Jen-kong immediately resigned, as did Tsiang Yen-si, secretary general of the KMT. Minister of Economic Affairs Hsu Li-teh (formerly minister of finance) also resigned. Rumors abounded that others should likewise step down, including Premier Yu Kuo-hua.

An Executive Yuan report in August named fifteen additional Ministry of Finance officials responsible for the collapse of the Cathay Group. They were demoted or received administrative punishment, or they were forced to resign. The government meanwhile revised regulations regarding such institutions to ensure that a similar event could not occur again in the future.[6] Fallout from the Cathay scandal was exacerbated by several other "incidents": a mine disaster resulting in several deaths—at the same site where a disaster had occurred the year before; the discovery of contaminated and poisonous wine produced by the government's Wine and Tobacco Monopoly; and a fire at one of Taiwan's nuclear power facilities. More fingers were pointed at the government as the responsible party, further undermining public confidence.

All of these events underscored the problem of succession, an issue the opposition found to offer opportunities. Tsiang Yen-si had been considered the top candidate to succeed President Chiang in the party. It was believed he could help maintain stability in the government during a succession crisis or while a new leadership was forming. Now it appeared Tsiang would play little of any role. Chiang's constitutional successor was Vice President Lee Teng-hui. Lee's stature was questioned, however, because of his relatively lower rank in the party and the fact that he had not been in office long. In addition, he had no experience in the military or the intelligence services. Rumors about Chiang's health, and claims by the opposition that Chiang was grooming his son to succeed him and that the military was waiting in the wings, made the situation even worse. Even though there was no real evidence to support either claim, uncertainty created by all of the above-mentioned problems made both believable to many people.

The economy was also some cause for alarm. Economic growth, measured by the increase in gross national product (GNP) in 1984, was over 10 percent. In 1985 it was less than half that. Foreign trade saw an almost unprecedented decline. In August, the rate of unemployment reached 4.1 percent —the highest it had been in many years. Domestic investment was also down from 1984.[7]

These problems seemed to be partly the product of the reality of a slower growth period (because Taiwan was already a "developed country" by many standards) and partly the result of an economy shifting gears to more capital and knowledge-intensive industries. Still, the Cathay scandal had a dampening effect on economic growth (at least by affecting investor confidence), as did a lower level of public trust in the government, concern about U.S. protectionism (the United States accounting for nearly half of Taiwan's exports) and the potential for a cessation of trade links with Hong Kong (because of an agreement between London and Peking in 1984 declaring that Hong Kong would become part of the People's Republic of China in 1997). The question of continued U.S. arms sales to Taiwan injected another element of uncertainty into the equation: If Taiwan was to remain a secure place for investment (for both domestic and foreign investors), it had to provide better national security.[8]

The 1985 Elections

Nationwide local elections scheduled for November 16, 1985, were considered by many outsiders through the summer of 1985 to be a litmus test for public confidence in both the government and the ruling Nationalist Party and for political stability in general in Taiwan. Voters were to elect twenty-one city mayors and county magistrates (five and sixteen, respectively), seventy-seven members of the Taiwan Provincial Assembly, and fifty-one members of the Taipei City Council. The opposition charged the government and the KMT with misgovernance and incompetence in office, as well as dishonest, authoritarian, and dictatorial practices. Some asserted that the KMT was no longer qualified to rule the country. KMT officials cited the party's past record, especially in creating the "Taiwan economic miracle," and played down most of these problems, subsuming them in the categories of bad luck or coincidence.[9]

The election was another test of a rapidly evolving democratic system in Taiwan whose credibility depended on party competition, or, more specifically, competition between the party (meaning the Kuomintang) and the *tang wai.* This election was particularly telling in terms of the working relationship between the two because of the political polarization in Taiwan caused by the issues cited above. Taiwan's image abroad—as a country evolving toward a Western-style, open, competitive and democratic polity—was also at stake.

In August, a core *tang wai* group of candidates met and formed what it called the "Candidates Aid Group." In doing so, the *tang wai* began acting like a political party and seemingly was committing an act that, according to the temporary provisions of the Constitution, was illegal (since the formation of new parties was therein banned). Both the government and the KMT had closed their eyes to *tang wai* actions during the national elections in 1980 and subsequent elections, and did so again. The Candidates Aid Group formulated a party platform and sought to find an acceptable way of choosing candidates and preventing *tang wai* politicians from competing with each other in ways that, in previous elections, had resulted in a waste of voting strength. They also sought to avoid a polarization between radicals and moderates within their ranks.[10]

Tang wai candidates, pretty much in unison, attacked the KMT on the issues mentioned earlier. It linked the succession question, the Henry Liu case, and other problems to falling economic performance. The *tang wai* related all of these issues to "excessive" KMT authority, penetration of the government by the KMT, and the need for more democracy. In addition, the opposition cited "serious" foreign policy failures and unfair election rules favoring KMT candidates.

Public opinion polls, however, suggested that major election issues in terms of public concern were traffic, crime, and other "practical" issues such as welfare and labor reform, tourism, education, administrative reform, water control, and the like.[11] The polls as well as the mood of KMT candidates just before the election, indicated that the "malaise" or "crisis of confidence" that troubled the KMT and the government had peaked sometime before the campaigning started. By campaign time, there was a slight trend toward public optimism. Many voters opined that the KMT was not to blame directly for many of the country's problems and that, even if the KMT were to blame, the opposition could do no better to rectify the situation.

During the last days of the campaign, *tang wai* supporters in Chungli turned over a car and threw rocks when one of their candidates lost by a very narrow margin. Near Taipei a candidate was almost stabbed. But neither the government nor the opposition tried to exacerbate tensions or take advantage of these incidents, instead deciding to resolve any problems in the courts or by appealing to the Election Commission when the election was over.[12] In short, the election went off without too many hitches.

The fact that voter turnout was higher than usual (in fact, it reversed a slow ten-year decline) suggested that public interest in the election and its issues was high. An overwhelming majority—71.7 percent of the electorate—voted, in spite of dreary weather in most of the country.

The division of the popular vote was close to the usual seventy to thirty split between the KMT and the opposition, though because a number of winning candidates could not be identified with either "party," this was to some extent a rough estimate. KMT candidates won 146 of the total 191 contested seats—or 76.8 percent. In the Provincial Assembly the KMT won 59 of 77 seats. In the local races the KMT performed well. The *tang wai* had targeted six areas for victory: four counties (Taipei, Hsinchu, Tainan, and Kaohsiung) and two cities (Hsinchu and Taichung). Of the six, it unequivocally won only in Kaohsiung County, though the main opposition party returned incumbents in Chiayi City, Yilan County and Changhua County.[13] In addition, the opposition experienced an unexpected victory in the Taipei City Council race where all eleven of its Candidates Aid Committee representatives won—resulting in a loss of three seats for the KMT.

Assessing the election in general terms, the KMT legitimately claimed victory because it had not done as badly as was expected just weeks before the election. The KMT also did well in some rural areas that are primarily Taiwanese and considered *tang wai* strongholds. The *tang wai* also claimed victory because it managed to remain more unified than in recent elections. In addition, the *tang wai* surprised the KMT and the population generally with its performance in the Taipei City Council race (a victory attributed to opposition charges of a "crisis of confidence" and the effects of the Cathay scandal, which were felt more intensely in Taipei than in any other areas of the country).

Just as important as who won was the fact that the election went off without any serious difficulties. Gentlemen's agreements between the KMT and the opposition held, and the *tang wai* became a more legitimate and perhaps loyal opposition. The KMT was clearly no longer a Mainland Chinese party; most of its candidates were Taiwanese (over 90 percent) and it won over half of the Taiwanese vote (though it had been doing this regularly). Clearly ethnic identity was less important. The explanation for this was that the KMT, seen as a conservative party, had more appeal in the rural areas that were predominantly Taiwanese, whereas the *tang wai*, being more progressive, had special appeal to some Mainland Chinese city dwellers. Observers also noted that Taiwanese businessmen were suspicious of *tang wai* candidates because of their anti-business, "socialist" attitudes. Ideology, how-ever, in most cases did not seem to attract voters; the same was true for sensationalism. These and other voting habits seemed to reflect a growing sophistication of the electorate—a good sign in terms of the continuing democratization of the political process in Taiwan.[14]

Just before the election, Vice President Lee Teng-hui was awarded Taiwan's highest civilian honor. The award gave him added prestige as a political leader and engendered speculation that he not only would be the formal successor, but also would wield considerable de facto power in the event of Chiang Ching-kuo's death or serious illness. Since Lee is Taiwanese, this event had an especially salutary effect on the Taiwanese population and this may have dampened their criticism of the government as the election approached. President Chiang's activities during the election, including timely statements on vital issues and problems, also helped. Clearly his visibility put to rest speculation that his health was deteriorating seriously.

Soon after the election was over, President Chiang personally acted to quell a controversy that arose during the election. During the campaign a *tang wai* candidate had charged the president with nepotism and had gone to considerable lengths to use this as a campaign issue. His campaign advertisements included a diagram of the President's family tree and pointed to relatives who might be in line for political office—even as his successor—after his demise. The Election Commission was about to press charges when President Chiang advised publicly against any such prosecution, saying in essence that he did not mind personal criticism.

In short, the absence of problems during the election, the fact that the KMT performed as well as it had in the past, a positive change in economic forecasts and a better public mood all seemed to reflect that Taiwan had passed through the "down period" and that things were back to normal again. Subsequent events supported this conclusion.

Post-election Political Change

In his New Year's address, President Chiang again moved to clear the air of rumors about the succession issue and his commitment to democracy. There was some suspicion (evoked mostly by comments in opposition magazines) that because of his age he had "turned reactionary" or that he was "surrounded by old hacks" in the party who sought to reverse the political modernization process.[15] In his speech, Chiang said that his successor would be chosen in a constitutional manner. He further declared that it was "not possible" that his successor would be a member of his family. "It cannot happen and will not happen," he emphasized. Chiang likewise declared that the military would play no role in the succession process or in a post-Chiang government. His assertions on both counts were credible, or were soon to be.

Chiang had already quieted rumors regarding the military's future role in the government when he demoted General Wang Sheng—head of military intelligence and psychological warfare and a contender for political power in the ruling party. Wang was assumed, from his party rank and close ties to the president over many years, to be the President's successor.[16] That he was considered to be in line for the presidency troubled many who had wanted to see the system continue to democratize and perceived Wang, because of his military background and his attitude toward democratic political change, to be someone who would not support that process. General Wang was demoted not only from his positions in the military, but also from those in the party. He was then sent abroad to be the Republic of China's ambassador to Paraguay.

Soon after his January speech, the president dispatched his son—about whom rumors had spread, mainly among unsophisticated political observers, to the effect that he also was in line for succession—to Singapore as the country's trade representative. That move underscored the veracity of his promise that a relative would not follow him as president or as head of the party.

Both decisions signaled that the "Chiang era" was coming to an end. More important, these decisions sent a message that the president was still very much in charge and further that he had not lost his enthusiasm for political change that would fulfill his promises of democracy.

In March, at the KMT's third plenary session of the Twelfth Central Committee, President Chiang announced the appointment of a twelve-member committee, headed by former President Yen Chia-kan, to study the "most urgent" problems faced by the Republic of China. The two most important were a review of national security matters, including the lifting of martial law, and regulations governing the formation of new civic organizations, including political parties.

A third issue, reorganizing the three elective branches of government, was also seen to have important implications. Discussions regarding the reorganization of the three elective bodies of government included adding representation from Taiwan while reducing the number of members representing districts on the mainland. This debate had a serious impact: Making the political system more representative of the territory governed by Taipei would make it more democratic. But it also gave the impression that the government was abandoning its one-China policy.[17] The decision to increase Taiwan's representation in the elective bodies of government was apparently intended to help leaders in Taiwan deal with Peking's efforts to force Taipei into negotiations regarding reunification as well as to support the political modernization process. Many said democracy meant reunification was less likely. Still others said it was unrealistic anyway.

Two other issues—martial law and the Temporary Provisions—were even more sensitive. Both were seen as obstacles to democratization and the two were linked by those who advocated reform even though they had separate origins. They were cited by the foreign media when pointing to authoritarianism in Taiwan.[18]

At this same meeting four new members were appointed to the Central Standing Committee of the KMT. Of the four, two were Taiwanese, while all four departing members were Mainland Chinese. This brought the percentage of Taiwanese in this high-level decision-making body to nearly 50 percent—not an insignificant change considering that after the first plenum of the Twelfth Central Committee meeting just five years earlier the ratio of Taiwanese to Mainland Chinese was only slightly more than 1:4.[19] Opposition politicians often pointed out that the Central Standing Committee was the real locus of decision-making power and Taiwanese were not well represented there. This charge was obviously no longer valid.

The Central Standing Committee also became younger. After the first plenum there were no members under fifty in this body. Now there were two in their forties. In addition, there were more representatives with higher education, especially graduate degrees from U.S. universities. The new appointments also conspicuously did not include anyone that might be defined as military. Finally, there was no relative of the president serving on the committee. This gave further weight to his promise of no military involvement and no nepotism in the post-Chiang government.

Although there was still no successor named and some critics assailed the party for not replacing one or two ministers they felt should be replaced, Vice President Lee Teng-hui's rank in the Central Standing Committee rose from ten to three. (He was fifteenth after the first plenum.) Clearly his star was rising and he looked more and more like Chiang's heir. Formally speaking, there was no question that Lee would become president in Chiang's absence. However, whether he could wield actual political power was another matter. Some argued that because Taiwan had become much more a pluralistic society in recent years and because the democratization process had reached the level that it had, less power should be centered in the presidency. Thus, a collective leadership or more checks and balances in the decision-making process, or both, seemed appropriate. Others suggested that it was impossible to find a successor who could match President Chiang's power and influence, given the fading of the autocratic structure of the past and the absence of a top leader with influence and support in the party, government, and military.

Just two months after this party meeting, the KMT opened a dialogue with *tang wai* leaders for the purpose of making the *tang wai* legal, or at least more legitimate. At nearly the same time, it was announced that the *tang wai* could have offices island-wide—in the form of the Tangwai Research Association for Public Policy (TRAPP)—which could operate other than during campaign periods. TRAPP thus became for all intents and purposes a national party organization for *tang wai*.[20] These moves seem to suggest that efforts to build a two-party system were about to succeed.

A New Party and the End of Martial Law

Although talks between the KMT and *tang wai* leaders (including several noted scholars and statesmen) formally broke down during the summer, behind-the-scenes negotiations continued. The theme of meetings within both the KMT and the *tang wai*, and indirectly between them, was the full and formal legalization of the *tang wai* as an opposition party. Naturally many KMT members opposed granting the *tang wai* legal status. Some argued Taiwan was not ready for more party competition in elections. Others said *tang wai* politicians were already creating political instability and weakening the unity and morale of the country. A more moderate view was that it was simply a wise precautionary move to keep them illegal, while simultaneously allowing them to operate as a de facto competing party.

Ironically some *tang wai* opposed any deal with the KMT and in essence opposed legalization, because it would undermine the unity of the *tang wai* (which some thought hinged on their illegal status). Other *tang wai* politicians perceived that their legalization, following discussions with the KMT, or even as a side effect of such dialogue, would give the impression of an inside deal that would sully the *tang wai*'s reputation as an opposition party; *tang wai*, in short, would be seen as an adjunct or outgrowth of the KMT. Most *tang wai* politicians and supporters certainly wanted to avoid creating this impression.

The final upshot was that, on September 28, 135 opposition leaders unilaterally announced the formation of the Democratic Progressive Party (DPP). Simultaneously they announced 20 candidates for Legislative Yuan seats and 22 candidates for National Assembly seats in the upcoming December 6 election. DPP spokespersons promised that the "party" would hold a "congress" on November 20 to decide on a platform and formal leadership.[21] At the same time, they said that no links would be formed with U.S.-based Taiwan Independence Movement groups.

That "sudden" announcement of the formation of the DPP followed street demonstrations in Taipei provoked by the sentencing of several well-known *tang wai* politicians on charges of libel and election irregularities. The punishments handed down seemed unduly severe and appeared timed so that they could not enter as a candidates in the December 6 election. KMT officials said they had not influenced the judicial process, which was independent of the ruling party and the other branches of the government. In any event, on September 14 several thousand "marchers" gathered near National Taiwan University and jammed the streets for a short time.[22]

Judging from the orderliness of the protest and the fact that KMT and *tang wai* negotiators had not really reached an impasse in their discussions aimed at legalizing the *tang wai*, the formation of the DPP hardly seemed the product of street demonstrations or mass "anger" about the sentencing of a *tang wai* candidate. Rather, the DPP sought to give the appearance of being established as the result of public protest and wanted to avoid being cast as a party born out of compromise or KMT "permission." After all, the DPP's base of support consisted mainly of an anti-KMT segment of the electorate; it could not claim the support of regional, class, professional, or interest groups. DPP leaders also saw the demonstrations as unifying the opposition and strengthening their cause.

Since the formation of the DPP technically was illegal, the minister of justice immediately filed charges against the DPP for violation of the Temporary Provisions. This indictment, however, turned out to be an empty one when President Chiang announced just days later that he would pursue legislation to abolish martial law and allow the formation of new political parties. Then, on October 7, in an interview with Katherine Graham, owner and head of the Board of Directors of the *Washington Post*, he declared specifically that martial law, in effect since 1949, would soon be lifted and that the ban on the formation of new political parties would be dropped. His conditions were that any new party renounce communism, swear allegiance to the Constitution, and forswear the Taiwanese Independence Movement and efforts to create two Chinas.[23]

Although the DPP did not want to agree to any conditions, the conditions were in no way onerous or unacceptable. First, communism had no appeal in Taiwan among any political faction or the electorate. Moreover, since the DPP organized itself for the purpose of winning seats in elected organs of government, it had no interest in refusing to renounce communism. Second, inasmuch as *tang wai* politicians had long complained that the government was undemocratic because it often circumvented the Constitution, it could hardly consider the second condition unacceptable. Third, in view of the fact the DPP had already denied links with the Taiwanese Independence Movement, the condition to forswear support for the movement did not seem troublesome either.

Unclear, however, was the advocacy of two Chinas. Many *tang wai* politicians argued that there were de facto two Chinas (or more) and believed it was already the policy of the government that Taiwan remain separate from China (even though officially denying it). Clearly an overwhelming portion of the populace (99 percent plus) opposed unification with the People's Republic of China (PRC). Thus, this issue was nettlesome and was destined to cause future problems.

The DPP was impressed by the fact that Chiang's announcement concerning the imminent end of martial law and the repeal of the ban on political parties was so well received in the United States and the Western media. The DPP could not deny it was a "momentous" move in changing Taiwan from an authoritarian dictatorship to a democratic republic, even though democratization was already well advanced. Most also perceived that the decision would make Beijing's overtures toward Taipei to negotiate "reunification" less credible while also making it less likely that the United States or other Western countries might support Beijing's efforts to pressure Taipei to the negotiating table. In short, the DPP could not help but interpret Chiang's promise as meaning that both democracy and local sovereignty were an inalienable part of Taiwan's future.

Both sides—the KMT and the DPP—also had to be persuaded by public opinion polls. Nearly two-thirds of those questioned by pollsters at this time replied that the formation of a new political party would help promote democracy in Taiwan. Over half said it would help reduce tension between KMT and the *tang wai*. Yet less than 40 percent saw it as helping to improve the investment climate or the economy, and about 40 percent opposed the formation of a new party for this and other reasons. Thirty percent voiced support for "an opposition party"—about the same percentage as had voted for *tang wai* candidates in recent elections.[24]

The public seemed to be ready for a new party—but with some reservations and caution. Martial law was seen (again according to polls taken at this time) as creating a bad image for the country, but it was not otherwise offensive. Notwithstanding the polls, judging from the public reaction to both moves, the populace supported President Chiang's initiatives.

The 1986 National Election

On November 21, campaigning began for the December 6 national election for the National Assembly and the Legislative Yuan. There were 169 candidates for 84 seats in the National Assembly, and 137 candidates for 73 seats in the Legislative Yuan. Of the 306 candidates, 179 were KMT; 44 were DPP. The rest were independents.

It was Taiwan's sixty-eighth major election in three decades. But many saw it as the most important. It was the first election in which the KMT competed with another political party. Though the DPP had yet to receive formal legal status, its leaders, the KMT and the public, regarded it as Taiwan's first real opposition party, as did the electorate.[25] In other words, formal party competition—which many viewed as the prerequisite for a truly democratic system—was born.

The campaign period lasted for fifteen days, with eight days allocated for individual campaigning and seven days for government-sponsored forums. Opposition candidates had complained of the short campaign period, but the Election Commission's contention that it was justified by Taiwan's frequent elections (compared to other nations), and public concerns to limit campaign spending and the disruption caused by election campaigns, prevailed. In any case, many opposition candidates started campaigning ahead of time by holding teas and other parties and by giving "educational or public information talks."[26]

Polls taken immediately before and during the campaign reflected overriding public concern over traffic, crime, and the environment. Most candidates, however, ignored these issues—apparently seeing them as less dramatic and not sufficiently good attention getters. Candidates ranked social welfare, economic freedom and growth, foreign relations, and national security as the nation's most important problems. On the "real" issues (as defined by voter polls), the candidates generally took similar or identical positions, though their proposed solutions differed somewhat.

The candidates split on other issues. KMT candidates generally espoused a more conservative position, supporting the government's record on economic growth and opportunity, while stressing political stability. They advocated incremental progress toward democracy, a cautious foreign policy, and a greater need for national security. DPP candidates railed for more press freedom and freedom of speech, fewer restrictions on campaigning (including spending), increased social welfare, and a more aggressive foreign policy that would get Taiwan back into some or many of the international organizations from which it had been expelled from during the 1970s and early 1980s (though they did explain exactly how this could be done).

The campaign was full of antics. A number of candidates started rumors against their opponents. Some accused other candidates publicly of moral (usually meaning sexual) impropriety, corruption and bribery, or even vote fraud. Several launched lawsuits against their opponents prior to or during the campaign. Numerous disruptions occurred during campaign speeches. Firecrackers were set off, car horns were honked, and the electricity was cut (in order to shut down the public address systems and lighting). Some of this was done by candidates' own workers to provide an excuse for their candidate to blame the opponents. Candidates also reportedly hired gang members to disrupt their opponents' campaigns and employed crowds to cheer their own speeches.[27]

Two or three Democratic Progressive Party female candidates regularly called themselves "Corazons"—referring to President Aquino in the Philippines. Some spoke directly of revolution. Others criticized the government, even referring to President Chiang Ching-kuo as a "pig." Most DPP candidates discussed self-determination and, implicit in such talk, a two-China policy and independence. Some even suggested that all Mainland Chinese (those who came to Taiwan after 1949) should "go home."[28]

KMT candidates deplored the "nasty" and ungentlemanly conduct of the DPP. They stressed the need for political stability and suggested that opposition candidates, if elected, would engender lawlessness and anarchy. They hit at the immaturity of many DPP candidates and their lack of experience and realism. They also criticized election "tricks"—used more frequently by DPP candidates.

Midway during the campaign, dissident Hsu Hsin-liang (who was formerly a county magistrate in Taiwan and in 1979 fled to the United States under charges of treason) tried to return to Taiwan. Several airlines in Japan refused to let him

on an aircraft, since he lacked a valid passport. Nevertheless, supporters went to
the airport when they thought he would arrive, seeing another opportunity to
unify the opposition party and attract attention to its cause.

Conflict broke out between the demonstrators and the police. In the resulting melee, police cars were damaged or burned and policemen and tourists were
hit with rocks and clubs. To most observers, it seemed that the demonstrators
initiated the violence. One reporter even videotaped a demonstrator pushing
police then putting animal blood or paint on his face and claiming he was
beaten. All of this was grist for KMT candidates, who claimed DPP candidates
were promoting violence.

The DPP publicly repudiated the violence that had occurred at the airport and
rebutted the charges that party members had initiated the conflict. Many
candidates, including the DPP's top leadership, stated that they did not support
Hsu and did not agree with his methods. Others simply stated that they felt the
government should not prevent his return.[29]

The bottom line seemed to be this: On the one hand, the election violence
seemed to give KMT candidates an advantage. On the other hand, perhaps
because of the newness of the party competition and the excitement of the campaign, it could not be turned into a very successful campaign issue by KMT
candidates. DPP leaders defused the issue by condemning the violence and
cautiously distancing themselves from Hsu. They also had videotapes of the
airport incident that showed the police using force against the demonstrators
without being provoked.

Meanwhile, election law violations occurred in large numbers during the
campaign. But this was less a cause for alarm than their frequency suggested at
this time. A large portion of the population perceived that the election codes had
to be rewritten and that minor violations, such as too many placards and flags,
didn't really matter. Some saw the campaign period as a temporary "free-for-all."
Some said the newness of two-party competition made violations of the rules
inevitable.

In any event, the DPP finished with 12 seats in the Legislative Yuan and 11
in the National Assembly, an increase of 5 and 8, respectively, over what the
tang wai had won in the preceding election. The KMT won 59 seats in the
Legislative Yuan, a decrease of 3, and 68 seats in the National Assembly, an
increase of 7. Two seats in the Legislative Yuan and 4 in the National Assembly
went to independents. The pro-KMT China Democratic Socialist Party won 1
seat in the National Assembly.[30]

The DPP claimed victory—certainly not an unreasonable claim. This new
party had done better than the "united" opposition in the previous national

election. The main reason: The DPP did not split as the *tang wai* had done in the past. Many of the largest vote-getters, including the top four in the Legislative Yuan race, were DPP candidates. The DPP also did well in Taipei and several other large cities, suggesting good performance in future elections since the big cities set voting trends.[31]

The KMT won a somewhat smaller portion of the popular vote, and in terms of numbers of victorious candidates, it really neither gained nor lost, losing three seats in the Legislative Yuan while gaining seven in the National Assembly.[32] The KMT did well considering the fact that the opposition was not factionalize as it had been in previous elections. In fact, many say its strength in both the National Assembly and the Legislative Yuan before the election was artificially high because of past opposition disunity and poor campaign planning (running competing candidates in many districts). Finally, it performed up to par in spite of running for the first time against a full-fledged opposition party.

After the election, pundits suggested that it was not a victory of one party or for issues, but a victory for the system. The electorate wanted party competition and got it, while at the same time sending a signal for moderation by voting for more moderate DPP candidates and more progressive KMT candidates. This outcome, they said, meant a two-party system was developing. Others suggested such a conclusion was premature and unjustified. They saw little evidence for a two-party system evolving, though it was clear Taiwan would no longer have a one-party system. Several experts said too much was being concluded from the election results. Winning candidates, they said, had charisma and local support. It was a conglomeration of local elections and reflected, they said, other things more than long-range political trends.

Clearly it seemed (at the end of 1986) too early to conclude much about election politics in Taiwan. Understood boundaries of acceptable and unacceptable campaign conduct, however, had become apparent. Restraint and the development of a loyal opposition could be seen, notwithstanding an election that on the surface seemed chaotic and disorderly. The fact that it was the third election (after 1980 and 1983) in which there was party competition, and the first for a formal opposition party recognized by both sides as well as the electorate, seems to suggest that democratization had gone a long way, and the election was both orderly and significant in view of these factors.

Conclusions

The years 1985 and 1986 will go down in Taiwan's political history as a period of rapid, if not historic, change. Political modernization proceeded at a rate faster than ever in Taiwan—perhaps faster than in any other nation in the world. Clearly, it seems no longer valid to speak of a "gap" between economic and political development in Taiwan—if, in fact, there ever was such a gap.

The difficulties Taiwan witnessed throughout most of 1985 and the way they were handled, like other aspects of Taiwan's recent history, suggest that the country thrives on challenge. Alternatively, Taiwan has had so much difficulty that perhaps it is simply able to cope better than other nations and better than most outside observers expect. One might apply the cliche "When the going gets tough, the tough get going" to Taiwan.

Taking another point of view, one could interpret the events of late 1986 (the formation of the Democratic Progressive Party, President Chiang Ching-kuo's announcements that martial law would be ended and the ban on new political parties lifted, and what appeared to be the formalization of a two-party system) as the culmination of a two- or three-decade long process of political modernization. Taiwan's political development model had always placed security first or at least as a precondition to democratization. That is why certain conditions had to be met before change could occur. This strategy certainly worked, if one assumes that the changes announced by President Chiang were not out of desperation but a natural consequence of long-term political change.

Still there are other opinions. Whereas Taiwan is obviously evolving toward a pluralistic system, one may doubt whether a two-party system is developing, in spite of the impressions conveyed by these events. The KMT certainly is accepting party competition, but most evidence suggests it is not losing voter support. Thus, it seems that Taiwan may be evolving toward a political system like Japan's: a system that has a dominant party with several opposition parties that do not seriously bid for control of the government.

If there was any desperation in recent decisions by Chiang Ching-kuo, and some say there was, it was to democratize in order to fend off foreign criticism of Taiwan and to improve Taiwan's image abroad. In the context of Peking's efforts to induce the United States and other Western countries to pressure Taipei to negotiate reunification, this effort is vitally important. Taipei apparently has other ideas about its future—namely maintaining the status quo, that is continued independence and sovereignty. To prevent Beijing's efforts from being successful, Taipei perceived that it had to demonstrate its worthiness. The way to do that was to democratize quickly and visibly.

Notwithstanding the shift to the right and the progressive changes in China over the past several years (though there have been reversals recently), Taiwan is still politically decades ahead of the People's Republic of China. Moreover, it is moving ahead so quickly that Beijing won't catch up soon, at least not in the foreseeable future. In this connection, many believe that Taiwan can not compete with Beijing militarily or economically, but can politically." Clearly democratization and unification are contradictions, at least for now. Moreover, Taipei wishes to make this known.

Endnotes

1. See James C. Hsiung, "Taiwan in 1985: Scandals and Setbacks," *Asian Survey*, No. 1 (January 1986), p. 93, for further details.

2. See John F. Copper, "Taiwan: New Challenges to Development," *Current History* 85, No. 510 (April 1986), p. 168.

3. Katherine Bishop, "Wisdom Says Asian Gang Arrests May Show Wider Plot in Murder," *New York Times*, September 20, 1985, Sect. IV, p. 16.

4. Dinah Lee, "California Murder Jars Taiwan Intelligence Agencies,"*Washington Post*, January 24, 1985, pp. A23–24.

5. See *Asia 1986 Yearbook* (Hong Kong: Far Eastern Economic Review, Ltd., 1985), pp. 242–43. Also see Hsiung, "Taiwan in 1985," and Copper, "Taiwan: New Challenges to Development."

6. Ibid.

7. See Copper, "Taiwan: New Challenges to Development," p. 168.

8. Ibid., pp. 168–69.

9. See John F. Copper, "Taiwan's 1985 Elections," *Asian Affairs* 13, No. 1 (Spring 1986), pp. 27–45, for further details.

10. Ibid., p. 30.

11. See *Free China Journal*, November 2 and 9, 1985.

12. Copper, "Taiwan's 1985 Elections," p. 36.

13. See Hsiung, "Taiwan in 1985," p. 99.

14. This seems to have developed several years earlier, but was a bit more pronounced at this time. For further details, see John F. Copper with George P. Chen, *Taiwan's Elections: Political Development and Democratization in the Republic of China* (Baltimore: University of Maryland Law School, 1984).

15. For an earlier version of this argument, see Parris H. Chang, "Taiwan in 1983: Setting the State for Power Transition," *Asian Survey* 23, No. 1 (January 1983), p. 38.

16. It is not entirely certain why Wang was demoted. Some said that he tried to become the successor. Others contend that it was simply because the president and others felt that a military leader should not be in line for succession to the presidency or the head of the party.

17. The average age of appointed National Assembly and Legislative Yuan delegates is 75. They have been dying at a rate of about one per month. Some argue that the simplest and less provocative (to Beijing) solution is simply not to replace them.

18. Martial law was declared in 1949 as the Nationalists fled to Taiwan during the Communist victory on the mainland. The "Temporary Provisions" had been added to the constitution earlier and applied in Taiwan. For details, see Thomas B. Gold, *State and Society in the Taiwan Miracle* (Armonk, NY: ME Sharpe, 1986), p. 54.

19. See Edwin A. Winckler, "After the Chiangs: The Coming Political Succession in Taiwan," in Richard C. Bush, ed., *China Briefing, 1982* (Boulder, Colorado: Westview Press, 1983), pp. 111–12, for further details on the old Central Standing Committee.

20. "Choosing Cautious Change," *Asiaweek*, April 13, 1986, pp. 18–19.

21. Paul Mooney, "Braving the KMT Ban," *Far Eastern Economic Review*, October 9, 1986, pp. 19–20.

22. "The Talking Stops," *Asiaweek*, June 22, 1986, p. 29.

23. Donald Sutherland, "Chiang Envisions Change for Taiwan," *Washington Post*, October 13, 1986, p. A18.

24. See, "Polls Show Widespread Concern Over New Political Developments," *Free China Journal*, October 13, 1986, p. 2.

25. The DPP drew up a charter before the election. It also announced party leaders and a slate of candidates. During the campaign it displayed the DPP flag and insignia. Newspapers in Taiwan referred to the DPP as a party, and in vote tallying listed the victorious candidates as KMT, DPP, and others.

26. For details on the campaign and the election, see John F. Copper, "Taiwan's 1986 National Election," (forthcoming).

27. Ibid.

28. Ibid.

29. The airport incident occurred shortly after several newspapers had published some of Hsu's writings advocating violence and killing as a way for the revolution to succeed.

30. For a list of winning candidates and further details on the election, see China *Post*, December 7, 1986, p. 1.

31. See Copper, "Taiwan's 1986 National Election."

32. According to the Election Committee the KMT won 67.5 percent of the popular vote, and the DPP 28.6 percent. Other sources put the figures at close to 65 percent and 25 percent. Figures vary on the KMT's popular vote in the previous election (from 70 to 73 percent).
     It is difficult to assess the popular vote by party because both the KMT and the *tang wai* had candidates run, and win, without party endorsement. In addition, independents may be one party or the other, but did not claim party affiliation.

See *Lien-ho Pao* (United Daily News), International edition, December 8, 1986, p. 1, and *Chung-yang Jih-pao* (Central Daily News), International edition, December 8, 1986, p. 1.

Chapter Four
Profile: Remembering Taiwan's President Chiang Ching-kuo

When Chiang Ching-kuo died January 13, 1988 of a heart attack, his leadership had received popularity ratings in the 70 to 80 percent range for years. There were clearly good reasons for this approval rating.

The Republic of China, or Taiwan, was the leading nation in the world measured by increases in the gross national product (GNP) over twenty years (the criterion most economists use to measure economic success). It had the highest rate of personal savings of any nation in the world, and its unemployment rate was the lowest in the world of nations keeping such figures. Its foreign reserves ranked it number one among developing countries. With a population of less than 20 million, Taiwan has recently become the eleventh largest trading nation in the world. In Taiwan, 80 percent of families now own their own homes. The country is the best among developing nations for the level of education of its citizens. Taiwan in recent years has also democratized more successfully than any other nation in the world. In short, its accomplishments are nothing less than miraculous.

Chiang Ching-kuo ruled Taiwan during a period when Taiwan made much of this progress and became the envy of the rest of the world. He was in a large part responsible for the Taiwan success story. CCK, as he fondly became known, was born in Chekiang province, a coastal province in south-central China, in 1910. His father was Chiang Kai-shek. His mother was a village girl whom his father had married through an arrangement made by his parents. CCK's education was entrusted to a paternal grandmother—a devout Buddhist. He saw very little of his father during his youth.

At the age of fifteen, the young Chiang was sent to the Soviet Union to attend the Sun Yat-sen University in Moscow. He spent twelve years in the Soviet Union. This experience was written with indelible ink on his brain. He joined the Communist Youth League. But Lenin died and CCK was caught up in the Stalin-Trotsky feud. Throughout this period, he increasingly grew disenchanted with communism. After a split between his father and Stalin, CCK was dealt with like many others in the Soviet Union at the time: He was sent to do forced labor on a farm and then to the mines in Siberia. But he survived, some say, because of the help of an orphaned Russian girl named Fiana, whom CCK later married. She, their two sons, and one daughter survive him.

After a "united front" was negotiated between Chiang Kai-shek's Nationalist Party and the Chinese Communists in 1936, Stalin decided to allow the young Chiang to return to China as a gesture of friendship. At home, his father gave him several jobs as a kind of test. He quickly proved his ability and loyalty. In the late 1940s he was entrusted with the task of stopping currency speculation and black marketing in Shanghai—an almost impossible assignment. But he was effective—so effective that he became known for his strict, unflinching honesty and a rare ability to handle difficult jobs.

In 1949, when the Nationalists were defeated by the Communists, CCK left for Taiwan with his father. There, he helped the party adjust to a new environment. His first important job, which he assumed in 1952, was to head the China Youth Corps. Chiang Ching-kuo had learned while in the Soviet Union the importance of youth for the future of the country and the fight against communism. The Communists were converting the youth; the Nationalists had to give the people an alternative. CCK remained in that position until 1973, though in the meantime he had taken a number of other important posts. He always felt the China Youth Corps to be of vital importance to the nation.

In 1954, he became the secretary general of the National Defense Council. In 1964, he was made vice minister of defense. In 1965, he became defense minister, a position he held until 1969. In 1969, he became vice premier, and in 1972, premier.

As premier, or head of the executive branch of the government, he launched a national anti-corruption drive. To prove he was serious, not just making noise or going through the motions, he jailed some high officials—even some of his relatives. Everyone took notice. He then mandated that government agencies that were a part of the executive branch of government respond to public demands. They had to advertise their duties. They had to answer complaints. Telephone numbers were published in the newspapers— including numbers citizens could call if they found government unresponsive, or even if officials were impolite.

CCK also ordered the government to recruit more native-born citizens or Taiwanese. The government was then staffed largely by Chinese who had come from the mainland in 1949 after the Nationalist exodus. Premier Chiang instituted what some have since called an "equal opportunity" employment program.

But he went further than that: He encouraged Taiwanese to apply for government jobs.

The government, as a result, became open to the citizens asking for action or information and to young people looking for a career. Moreover, government became efficient and honest. Now Taiwan is seldom troubled by bribery and corruption. If service delivered per dollar taken in through taxes is the criterion, Taiwan's government is less bureaucratic and more cost efficient than the U.S. government or the governments of most or all Western European countries.

In 1975, upon the death of his father, CCK became the head of the Nationalist Party. He held that job until his death in January 1988. As party leader, he instituted another program of "Taiwanization." The Nationalist Party, or Kuomintang (KMT), at that time had recruited few native-born Chinese, or Taiwanese, members. Party members were mostly Chinese who moved to Taiwan after World War II, particularly in 1949, from the mainland and who had joined the KMT much earlier. As a result of CCK's efforts, it is now around 80 percent Taiwanese—only slightly less than the percentage of Taiwanese in the general population. In some recent elections, the Kuomintang has fielded 90 percent Taiwanese candidates. In all elections more than half of Taiwanese have voted for the Kuomintang—debunking the notion that it is a Mainlander Chinese party. This more than anything anyone else has done has fostered national unity in Taiwan.

In 1978, CCK became president. When Chiang Kai-shek died in 1975, Vice President Yen Chia-kan had succeeded him. But President Yen declined to run for another term and CCK was the party's natural choice. In fact, there was no opposition. Chiang Ching-kuo had the experience and the ability to run the country. Its destiny was in his hands. And he took the job seriously.

That year, President Carter decided to grant diplomatic relations to Beijing and, in so doing, break with Taipei. CCK was awakened in the middle of the night and informed of the decision. It was a shocking blow. Taiwan felt hurt, betrayed. The stock market had to be closed. A national election was canceled. Chiang Ching-kuo had to rethink Taiwan's future after being jilted by its most important friend.

CCK decided that the United States was still a friend: The American people had a good image of Taiwan and supported Taipei, notwithstanding a new relationship between Washington and Beijing. Some suggested that the Soviet Union was a potential ally; this he didn't take seriously. Going nuclear was also a possibility; CCK, however, felt that Taiwan had to be a nation of peace even though it was threatened by Beijing. Deng Xiaoping refused to renounce the use of armed force against Taiwan and suggested he would invade if Taipei did not negotiate. CCK refused to do that; to him communism was not a part of Taiwan's future and the people did not want him to bargain away what they had worked so hard to attain. But he did offer negotiations.

In 1980, CCK rescheduled the election that was canceled in 1978. A new election law was written. He ordered the government to allow independent candidates to organize and, in effect, compete as an opposition party. It was the first competitive party election in the nation's history. Nevertheless, the Nationalist Party did well. It proved that the party under CCK's leadership had mass popular support based on its many accomplishments. Some had questioned whether the party and government had broad support; the election laid these questions to rest. Another election of the same kind in 1983, and intermittent but frequent elections there-after, were further proof.

Meanwhile, there arose speculation about President Chiang's health. He was diabetic and had other health problems. Nevertheless he was reelected president in 1984 for another six-year term. Soon he began to make preparations for his eventual demise. He promised that the military would not run any post-CCK government. Nor would any relative succeed him; the Chiang "dynasty" was ending. To keep his promise that neither the military nor any of his relatives would assume leadership, he had some want-to-be successors transferred to jobs outside of the country. In addition, he took other measures to ensure a proper succession.

Democracy, CCK knew, was the key to Taiwan's future. CCK's vice president, Lee Teng-hui, was a respected and well-educated Taiwanese—holding an American Ph.D. He represented the future. CCK groomed him for the Presidency.

In 1986, he promised that new political parties could form and that martial law would be terminated. Restrictions on press freedom, which had long since almost disappeared, would be formally ended. The Democratic Progressive Party (DPP), a new political party made up of *tang wai* ("outside the party") independents, formed almost immediately. The 1986 national election thus became a two-party election—the first in Chinese history and one of the first in an underdeveloped country without a contributing colonial experience.

In 1987, martial law was terminated— rather uneventfully, particularly in light of the problems democratization had caused in the nearby Philippines and in South Korea. CCK made the difference. As he had done before, and unlike many leaders elsewhere, he allowed the opposition to call him names, accuse him of nepotism, and even libel him. The public reacted negatively to this criticism and sent a signal to future political candidates that they had to be decent or the electorate would not give them support. This, as much as anything else, made the transition to democracy a smooth one.

Political leaders can never be certain what will happen after they die. In many countries they can only decide who will replace them temporarily; they cannot determine who will ultimately rule the country. Nor can they decide how the country will be ruled. In Taiwan it was different: the Constitution would decide. Taiwan was to be a democratic state. CCK made sure this would be the case. Thus, he left his mark permanently on Taiwan.

Chiang Ching-kuo will be remembered for accomplishments few men in history can match. He sustained the course of rapid economic development in Taiwan launched by his father. He continued the political modernization and democratization started by his father, but here he did so much that the accomplishments of Taiwan's political development are usually considered to redound to his credit alone. That Taiwan is now seen as a model by other world leaders, especially leaders of developing countries, both for its economic growth and for its political modernization of the democratic kind, is perceived to be his most important accomplishment.

CCK in most ways lived the life of an ordinary citizen. He eschewed big houses, fancy parties, and luxury. He was a man of the people; he worked hard and expected the same from others. He was a no-nonsense person. Most important, he loved his country and gave his life to his people. In the final analysis he lived the life of an ordinary person, but accomplished extraordinary things.

Chapter Five
Ending Martial Law In Taiwan:
Implications and Prospects

On July 15, 1987, martial law (or emergency decrees, depending upon one's perspective) in Taiwan ended after thirty-eight years. The decision was proclaimed an important one by the Western media. In Taiwan it was also viewed as a very salient event, though for different reasons. Clearly it had significant symbolic meaning, if not real importance, in terms of the nation's politics.

Taiwan had been under what is termed martial law rule in the West since 1949, a few months before the Nationalist Chinese were defeated by the Communists and fled to the island redoubt. If it was genuinely martial law, this was the longest stint of martial law rule in any country's recent history. Even if the constitutional processes were only circumvented in part by "emergency decrees," ending those decrees was an important decision and was certain to inaugurate a period of more strict constitutionalism.

The views in Taiwan about what actually transpired and the implications of the decision can be separated into pro-government and anti–government views. Within each there are at least two disparate perceptions.[1]

One pro-government view is that Taiwan never had martial law. The Chinese term *chieh yen fa,* which literally means "stringent measures law," was not really martial law.[2] It was mistranslated into English. The term should have been rendered as "emergency law" or "emergency decrees." Advocates of this view note the difficulties involved in accurately translating Chinese. They also point out that Taiwan has had no curfew and that civilian rule had prevailed. In addition, they contend there was no danger in Taiwan resulting from political instability, chaos, or revolution; nor were there restrictions on individual freedom of movement as in countries under martial law.

They also argue that most of Taiwan's population was not conscious of the emergency decrees, which they would have been had there really been martial law in force. Similarly, they point to opinion polls taken in recent years that reflect public support for keeping the emergency decrees and surveys that indicate that an overwhelming majority of the masses did not perceive any inconvenience or restrictions to their freedoms because of the decrees.

Others espousing a pro-government view, wanting to make as much as possible out of the decision to abandon martial law, readily admit that the country was under martial law, or something like it, and that it was indeed the product of an authoritarian system.[3] But they are quick to point out that democratization has changed this, and that is the reason why martial law was terminated.

They seek to emphasize the progress made in political development in Taiwan and the democratization of the political system. Hence, they promote the view that getting rid of martial law was a watershed event. Some holding this position admit in private that they necessarily exaggerate the significance of martial law, but they argue that the Western media has used martial law to convey a negative perception about Taiwan for so long that ending it should be seen as having far-reaching consequences. They also stress the importance of the decision in order to change the widely held view of Taiwan's political system being autocratic and give the country some good publicity. A Government Information Agency spokesman noted that martial law is one of the few things foreigners know about Taiwan and that changing that image will make a big difference.

The most popular opposing view—taken generally by the newly formed Democratic Progressive Party (DPP)—is that martial law was not abolished; it was simply replaced by a new State Security Law and things will remain the same in terms of the absence of democratization.[4] They have dubbed the State Security Law "old wine in a new bottle." In other words, according to the DPP, nothing has changed.

Their objective is to counter the impression that Taiwan has become democratic and suggest that their failure to do better in elections and to operate successfully within the confines of a democratic system is due to the fact Taiwan is still authoritarian. They want to convey the view that democracy has yet to arrive and that support for the DPP is the way to realize democratic processes.

A second and very different view is espoused by other opposition politicians and activists: that abolishing martial law really does make a difference.[5] In fact, they claim that lifting martial law (and it really was martial law in their view) amounts to opening Pandora's box. It will, in short, create a situation like those in the Philippines and Korea, namely, mass political protest and perhaps even revolution.

In consonance with their political objectives, these members of the opposition propound that lifting oppressive controls will lead to an outpouring of protest against the government, and that they will lead and benefit from this protest. This view is espoused by the more radical opposition, especially those opposition politicians left out of leadership positions in the DPP.

This chapter assesses martial law in terms of the impact it had on politics in Taiwan when it was in force, the State Security Law which replaced it, and the termination of martial law in the context of political development in Taiwan. Conclusions will focus on reconciling the different views and the prospects for Taiwan without martial law or emergency decrees.

Taiwan Under Martial Law

Martial law was proclaimed in May 1949 by the Peace Preservation Command of the Army of the Republic of China. Nationalist military forces were doing poorly in the war against the Communists on the mainland, and plans were already being made to retreat to Taiwan. It was naturally feared that their retreat would be followed by a Communist invasion of Taiwan; therefore, the island had to be put under military rule. Martial law was also seen as necessary in view of a revolt against Nationalist Chinese rule in 1947 by native Taiwanese and subsequent friction between the Nationalists and the Taiwanese population.

Martial law, however, may have been proclaimed for reasons unrelated to these obvious ones. According to some observers, Chiang Kai-shek's eldest son, Chiang Ching-kuo, sought to strengthen his hold over the Nationalist intelligence community, and because he had the loyalty of the Garrison Command and the Intelligence Bureau, he wanted to install martial law to widen the prerogatives and powers of these organs of government.[6]

In any event, the Taiwan Garrison Command was given the authority to control the press, including applying censorship when necessary, and it, like the Bureau of Intelligence, benefited from martial law provisions made legal under the previously passed "Temporary Provisions (of the Constitution) Effective During the Period of Communist Rebellion." The Temporary Provisions gave the president the authority to take emergency measures not subject to procedural restrictions of the Legislative Yuan. Declaring martial law was among the most important emergency powers delegated.

The declaration of martial law clearly enhanced the government's powers. Its provisions not only gave the government control over the press but also banned strikes and the formation of new political parties. Furthermore, martial law permitted the government to circumscribe other civic and political organizations and to limit political protest. Some even interpreted martial law as outlawing rumor-mongering. Clearly martial law had the effect of diluting or negating provisions in the Constitution that extended or protected basic political and civil rights. It also gave the military or military-related organizations, especially the intelligence agencies, powers not granted to them under the Constitution.

Under martial law rule, those "endangering the nation" could be arrested and executed or sentenced to more than ten years in prison. Due process, after the fashion of Western law, was weakened. Military courts could be used to try civilians for treason (endangering the nation), and trials and appeals were handled quickly and without the encumbrances of legal procedures used in civilian courts.

In 1950, however, after the immediate peril of an invasion by Communist Chinese forces passed and there no longer seemed to be serious local opposition to Nationalist rule, the government issued a decree prohibiting unauthorized arrests of individuals suspected of a crime. Arresting officers had to have a warrant and follow proper arrest procedures. This same decree, or order, also stated that the "person and property of the individual should not be infringed upon" notwithstanding martial law.[7]

In three revisions of martial law rule during the period from 1951 through 1953, civilian authorities and the courts were given exclusive jurisdiction over all civilian cases except treason. In addition, criminal suspects had to be sent to civilian courts for prosecution or released within 24 hours. Similarly, suspects could not be routinely held in jail pending legal procedures. Subsequently, criminal suspects were given the right to legal counsel, even if they could not afford a lawyer. In short, martial law provisions were ameliorated or weakened.[8] Some argued that, because of these orders and revisions, martial law became in essence a set of national security laws, which many other countries of the world had in force and which did not interfere with the practice of civil liberties.

Critics, however, pointed out that martial law rule still prevented opposition political parties from forming and thus precluded competitive free elections and democracy. They also argued that martial law hampered the development of a free press, labor organizations, and much more. They even contended that martial law protected corruption in government and the stock market, facilitated the construction of nuclear power plants in violation of sensible safety precautions and public opinion, allowed foreign companies unreasonable "tax holidays," and prevented free political debate, since discussing (i.e., advocating) Communism was prohibited. They also criticized martial law because it restricted freedom of travel.[9] (It allowed for the arrest of those who traveled to China and made exit permits difficult to obtain for some people.)

The most extreme critics assailed martial law as institutionalizing the debasing of human rights. They pointed out that under martial law dissidents were arrested and held without trial and even tortured and that quick trials and executions were used to control anti-government elements and to intimidate the population.[10] In short, Taiwan had a bad human rights record and martial law was the cause.

Other opponents argued that even if martial law had little legal impact, it had a considerable psychological effect. It symbolized authoritarianism and impeded political modernization and democratization. It projected an unfavorable image, because, even if martial law had been weakened or transformed into something else, this was not widely known abroad.

In recent years, only a handful of criminal cases came under the rubric of treason, and civilians were rarely tried in military courts; consequently, the legal aspects of martial law did not excite much attention or opposition. Many even argued that it promoted social stability and therefore facilitated economic growth. Most of Taiwan's population perceived that it had at least one good side: It helped prevent crime. (In fact, it was implemented at various times in response to upsurges in the crime rate.) There was also support for martial law (or at least less opposition to it) because of periodic threats against Taiwan by the People's Republic of China and the not infrequent arrest of Communist agents in Taiwan.

In other words, martial law over the years became a less than contentious issue. It had the support of government officials, except for a few younger and more progressive leaders who saw it as sullying Taiwan's image abroad or perceived that it eventually must be terminated to make way for democratic institutions. For the most part, those who opposed martial law saw opportunities to operate within the confines of the system while they viewed a frontal assault to abolish martial law as unnecessary and unlikely to succeed. Many, including Nationalist Party leaders, believed that it was both possible and preferable to democratize the system from the bottom up (meaning local government first) and in other ways not affected by the strictures of martial.

However, martial law became a very heated issue after December 1979 when anti-government demonstrators marching in protest of the government on Human Rights Day became embroiled in a direct confrontation with police in Kaohsiung—the largest city in southern Taiwan. Nearly 200 police were injured (though most not seriously), and the melee turned public opinion against the anti-government opposition. Seeing a shift in public feeling and wanting to suppress the opposition, the government indicted the "Kaohsiung Incident's" leaders on charges of treason and tried them in military courts under martial law provisions. Several well-known defendants were given stiff prison sentences.[11]

Even though the trials were open to the public and the population had changed its view of the demonstrators (initially seeing their protest as justified, but later seeing it as a danger to political stability), the use of martial law provisions and the severe sentences meted out both angered and unified the opposition. It likewise evoked criticism from the Western media.

The use of martial law in this instance and the prison sentences handed down to members of the opposition also polarized Taiwan politically. And this occurred at a time when the government was trying to regain its credibility after the severance of diplomatic ties with the United States (which had moved its embassy to Beijing in early 1979 and the termination of an important (to Taipei) defense treaty with Taiwan. Not only did Taipei lose face and see its diplomatic strength undermined, it was confronted with a campaign by Beijing to have Western nations pressure Taipei into negotiations leading to its reunification with China. One of Taipei's options in dealing with the situation was to democratize in hopes of winning support from the international community for its claim to sovereignty.

During the subsequent preparations for the 1980 national election, an occasion when the opposition was allowed to participate (i.e., to campaign openly and freely), abolishing martial law became one of the planks of the antigovernment platform. In fact, it became a very controvertible and frequently debated issue. Though the opposition could not argue that martial law was unpopular, anti-Nationalist Party candidates did make a case that it impeded democracy and gave Taiwan a bad reputation abroad.[12]

In the meantime, in early 1979, the thirtieth anniversary of establishing martial law, the U.S. Congress held hearings on the subject. Democratic Congressman Stephen Solarz sent a letter to other members of congress comparing Taiwan with Poland. Republicans condemned the Solarz letter as an invidious comparison; nevertheless, Taiwan got the kind of publicity it did not want.

In 1982, the issue came up again in Congress. Liberal members of Congress condemned the Taiwan government for human rights violations and other undemocratic (i.e., authoritarian) practices.[13] A compromise was reached and a motion passed urging "democratic progress" and an end to martial law. Taiwan's friends in the United States could not support or defend martial law.

In early 1986, President Chiang Ching-kuo appointed a special committee to investigate "special problems," one of which was martial law. A few months later, in an interview with Katherine Graham of the *Washington Post*, he promised that martial law would be rescinded.[14] At that juncture it appeared that the end of martial law was certain and would happen soon.

Taiwan's State Security Law

When President Chiang Ching-kuo's pledged to abolish martial law he assumed that national security legislation would be written to retain some of the needed provisions in the martial law decrees. Thus, drafting of a State Security Law began soon after the president announced the end of martial law. The job of writing new legislation belonged to the Executive Yuan.

Premier Yu Kuo-hua, as head of the Executive Yuan, contacted constitutional experts, lawyers, and various scholars both in Taiwan and abroad. Security laws in several Western countries were examined and used as models. By January 1987 a draft of the new State Security Law was completed and made ready to present to the Legislative Yuan for debate. Three committees of the Legislative Yuan—Home Affairs, Judicial Administration, and National Defense—went over the draft, adding new provisions and altering old ones. Plenum sessions of the Legislative Yuan were then convened to debate the revised draft. The debate process lasted until June.[15]

Even before the committees finished their work on the draft, opposition legislators together with their party workers railed against the legislation. They demanded that martial law decrees be rescinded and that no security law be considered. They assailed the draft law as a "means to keep martial law in actuality, while dismissing it in name." They charged that it was unnecessary and a duplication of other laws. They also argued that the new law was not in accord with the spirit of democracy and the exercise of civil and political rights.

Concerning specific issues in the draft legislation, DPP leaders especially found fault with the provisions that set guidelines for the formation of new civic organizations (which included political parties). Since the DPP was not yet technically legal, it did not want to accept prior conditions before formally becoming a party. In particular, the DPP opposed legal constraints or limits on political party activities and specific functions of parties. The DPP likewise disputed the final draft wording that disallowed appeals of sentences meted out in the past under martial law.

The issue of new civic organizations, and discussions about the possibility of writing separate legislation on the matter of national security, eventually faded somewhat. Debate over the main provisions of the new State Security Law took priority. Also, because conditions for the formation of new parties were cited in the draft law but no punishments were mentioned, it was not possible for the opposition to charge that the law was unduly harsh. The second complaint, that it did not allow appeals of previous sentences, became less controversial when the president ordered a review of all cases of civilians held in military prisons.

DPP activists, however, were still not satisfied. They continued to complain that many political prisoners convicted under martial law remained in jail and that this constituted a serious human rights concern. The government replied that there were no political prisoners in Taiwan; all those mentioned by the opposition had been charged and convicted of offenses that are crimes in other countries. Amnesty International at the time identified what it called "political prisoners of conscience"—but counted less than twenty.[16]

The DPP boycotted several Legislative Yuan sessions that discussed the new State Security Law and on several occasions called public meetings to debate the draft bill and the related issues. It also organized protest demonstrations. In late March, DPP leaders encouraged students from National Taiwan University to stage a sit-in at the Legislative Yuan building.[17] Not many students participated, however, and the police ignored the event. The DPP subsequently organized other demonstrations and protests both inside and around the Legislative Yuan building.

In April, DPP activists began to organize a mass protest rally to demonstrate opposition to the State Security Law. The rally was to be held in front of the Presidential Palace. This plan provoked a political controversy because the vicinity of the Presidential Palace was by law off-limits to demonstrations. The rally, scheduled for April 19, was subsequently canceled and the crisis—which some anticipated as another Kaohsiung Incident—passed.[18] Meanwhile, the DPP continued to attract media attention with its opposition to the continuation of martial law, as well as provisions in State Security Law. Both issues seemed to be good grist for the DPP, which sought confrontation with the government and the ruling Nationalist Party and hoped to attract new party members. The DPP was also experiencing factionalism and was being challenged by other opposition politicians' efforts to form other new political parties. The government's tack was to remain cool and play down the controversy. Its response to the DPP was that martial law would be terminated when the State Security Law was in place.

In May, the DPP organized another provocative rally and protest march. Attracting between 1,000 and 5,000 participants and onlookers, DPP leaders gathered near the Presidential Palace. The government considered the rally illegal but chose not to use strong measures to break it up. Police and security personnel instead blocked the street leading to the Presidential Palace and played music on loudspeakers to drown out DPP speeches. The crowd that had gathered soon dissipated because of rain.[19]

In June the new State Security Law passed after a third reading in the Legislative Yuan. DPP members boycotted that session. But, their boycott reflected opposition to the law, not their exclusion from the process. In fact, DPP legislative members participated actively in revising six of the law's ten articles (the four that they did not influence were the articles of the bill that were not controversial), thus playing a central role in the legislative process.[20]

For this reason, some members of the ruling Nationalist Party had, in fact, complained about the disproportionate weight of DPP input, in view of the DPP's small numbers. One noted that a party that won less than half of the vote gained by either Walter Mondale or George McGovern in the United States should not have so much say or be taken so seriously. Still, many ruling party leaders felt the DPP should have a voice and that their participation would preclude their opposition later.

After the new State Security Law was passed by the Legislative Yuan and subsequently pronounced as law by the president, the DPP continued to express complaints about two articles of the ten-part law. They most strongly opposed Article 2, which states that the exercise of the rights of assembly and association should not "violate the Constitution, advocate communism or the division of the national territory."

Though the DPP and other opposition leaders had long advocated fully implementing the Constitution, they perceived that mention of the Constitution in this context might possibly enable to the government to place limits on various kinds of protest. Since there is no support for communism in Taiwan, this part of Article 2 was not at issue, or at least not meaningfully so. Some opposition politicians, however, complained that the article might be interpreted to prohibit advocating contacts with the People's Republic of China (PRC) or discussing anything about the PRC in public. This they opposed.

Division of the national territory was the most controversial issue. The DPP regarded self-determination, which some equated with advocacy of territorial division or Taiwan independence, as reasonable. They also felt it had popular support. Furthermore, it had been an important DPP plank in the 1986 election. DPP leaders had long used the issue of self-determination to attract attention, to argue for further democratization (referring to their efforts to make the elective bodies of government represent only Taiwan), and to criticize the ruling party's policy regarding returning to the mainland. The government and the Nationalist Party saw the opposition's position as a disguised means of advocating Taiwan's independence.

The DPP also objected to Article 9, which states that those convicted under martial law are not entitled to a retrial. Its leaders pointed out that martial law provisions contained rules for retrial and that without these provisions, those convicted under martial law could never have their civil right restored. They called for a general amnesty as a means of dealing with the problem. Nationalist

Party leaders responded that this solution would undermine the legal system and encourage crime.

Regarding the remaining provisions of the new State Security Law, opposition politicians generally charged that they were not needed and did not contribute to democracy. The opposition referred to Article 1, which describes the purpose of the law ("to maintain national security") as unnecessary. Supporters argued that since the law replaced a number of other laws, it had to have a general purpose provision. Articles 3 and 4, which transfer control over entry and exit into and out of Taiwan to civilian authorities, reminded the opposition of the case involving Hsu Hsin-liang. Hsu, a dissident living in the United States, tried to return to Taiwan before the December 1986 election. His entry was blocked, even though he was a citizen of the Republic of China, because he did not have a valid passport or visa. DPP leaders felt that he was not allowed to come home at the time for political reasons. Supporters of the provision asserted that the control of entry and exit is the sovereign right of all nations and that Taiwan could not be secure without it.

Article 5 authorizes the Ministry of Defense to designate certain areas for military bases or zones. Articles 6 and 7 provide penalties for violations of Articles 3, 4, and 5—ostensibly needed since separate legislation was not anticipated to delineate punishments. Articles 8 and 9 bar the use of military courts to try civilians. Article 10 provides for the writing of legal provisions for the enforcement of the other sections of the law and provisions for bringing the security laws into force. The opposition did not strenuously oppose any of these provisions, though it went on record saying they were unnecessary.[21]

After the State Security Law was officially announced, public opinion surveys were taken that measured public support for the new law. According to a poll taken by one of Taiwan's leading newspapers, 60 percent of the population favored the new legislation; 3 percent opposed it.[22] Another poll showed 68 percent for and 11 percent opposed.[23] The new law clearly had the support of the majority of the public. In fact, opposition was even lower than the polls suggest because many who had opposed the law instead favored keeping martial law. Still, a sizable portion of those who opposed martial law also opposed the new State Security Law—40 percent, according to one poll.[24]

The Effects of Ending Martial Law

The termination of martial law will have a number of effects, both direct and indirect. It will impact Taiwan's legal system, the political party system, freedom of the press, the role of the military, strikes, and political protest. There will also be a number of side effects in areas such as the economy, political development, civil and political liberties, and human rights.

The most obvious and immediate impact of martial law will be the end of the use of military courts to try civilians and the use of military law outside the military in general. In short, the legal system will become purely a civilian one. The use of military prisons will be limited to the incarceration of soldiers on active duty who violate military law.

This aspect of the State Security Law will not inaugurate a new or vastly changed legal system in Taiwan; it will not even change legal practice very much. But it will have a major psychological effect, in that there will no longer be an element of intimidation in legal proceedings. Treason and endangering the security of the nation will also be more narrowly defined. It will have one other important extra-legal impact. It will reduce the credibility of charges that the opposition is not free to challenge the ruling party, for it is entitled to do so under a now unencumbered or fully operational Constitution.[25]

The end of martial law will probably also mean that Taiwan's civil law system, patterned after the countries of continental Europe, will evolve more in the direction of the U.S. system. It will certainly mean that the legal system plays a greater role in the future—a truly independent role. Some say it will mark the transition from rule by man to rule by law.

Legislators will have to write a number of new laws to replace at least thirty martial law decrees or ordinances.[26] Thus, a spate of legislation can be expected, although much of it will be in the form of administrative decrees or regulations, since many of the provisions in martial law fell into this category. New laws will also have to be written to clarify or implement the State Security Law.

The day that martial law ended President Chiang ordered that the sentences of 237 civilians convicted of crimes under martial law be cut in half. Of the 237, 144 were already out on parole or probation; 23 were released from jail immediately. The others had their sentences reduced; life sentences were pared to fifteen years for the prisoners in this group.[27] The only prisoners kept in jail were those convicted of treason more than once or those also convicted of terrorism or the use of firearms. And they were moved to civilian jails.

The role of the military in Taiwan will be affected in some ways by the abolition of martial law. The military will be relieved of customs responsibilities, press control duties, and jurisdiction over public protests and demonstrations. Special civilian police (i.e., customs police) will take over customs responsibilities immediately. The responsibility for controlling demonstrations, protest, and civil disobedience will go to city or county police. The Taiwan

Garrison Command will no longer deal with the press; the Government Information Office, a civilian organ of government, will assume that role.

The military will also have much less influence politically in Taiwan in the future. The military's weight in politics has been declining over the past two or three decades. President Chiang's pronouncement in early 1986 that the military would play no role in deciding the next president contributed even further to that decline. Already there is evidence that because martial law has ended, the National Security Council, which represents the military, will be less frequently the organ of government for making high-level executive decisions.[28]

New political parties will form as a result of ending martial law. In fact this has already happened. Although new legislation is yet to be written regulating civic organizations, including political parties, the ban on forming new parties has been dropped. In early July, just before martial law was abolished, the Chinese Liberty Party formed from a group of 300 anti-DPP activists; in September a former National Assembly member announced the birth of the Democratic Freedom Party.[29] Other parties have organized since then.

The DPP will be made a fully legal party as a result of the decision. It had been, for all intents and purposes, a legitimate opposition party from the time it formed in September 1986. It was referred to as a political party by the press and most voters during the December 1986 election. However, it now has an even more formal status. Shortly after the end of martial law was announced, the DPP began to set up an island-wide network of local branches.[30] Most expect it to expand its functions to include those performed by most Western political parties.

It is uncertain, however, whether its new legitimate status will help the DPP. The party has had difficulties recruiting, with only 1,500 members at last count.[31] Compared to the Nationalist Party, nearly 2.5 million members strong, the DPP it is in essence a minor party. Some even suggest that legalizing the DPP will have a negative result, since it is a protest party. Others disagree.

It is also uncertain whether lifting the ban on new parties will evoke the development of a new political party system. For a while at least, it will probably create a rather fluid situation in terms of the nation's party system. Ending martial law formalizes the end of the one-party system. But whether a two-party system is evolving—as it appeared during the December 1986 election campaign—is difficult to say.[32] If the DPP grows in coming months and years, this may well be the case. The appearance of other parties, however, suggests a multi-party system. Many say a one-party dominant system like Japan's is most likely, at least in the short run.

The end of martial law also means fewer and less stringent controls over the press. The Government Information Office, because of its size and make-up, will certainly not control the press as rigidly or as strictly as the Taiwan Garrison Command did. In fact, for a while it will probably not be able to regulate the media very well because of the large burden given to it so quickly and because it is understaffed.

Press freedom overall, however, will not be impacted in a major way by the end of martial law. The press in Taiwan had already become very competitive, and press freedom had been widened considerably in recent years. In fact, many observers say that the biggest concern regarding an independent and free media in Taiwan is the fierce and sometimes bitter competition between newspapers and the resulting disincentive for the media to abide by either press laws or ethical standards.[33] New laws regulating the press can be anticipated, but whether they will be effective is quite another matter.

Martial law banned rallies and demonstrations, and its disappearance will certainly result in more public protest of various kinds. Rallies, marches, and political demonstrations no doubt will also be more lively and vociferous. In the wake of the announcement ending martial law, the minister of interior announced that the police will not withhold permission for rallies or demonstrations unless public order and security are threatened. Hence, local police systems will have to issue permits and laws, and local ordinances will have to be written to control marches, parades, rallies, and other forms of political demonstrations and protest. This change will inevitably mean that the police forces of Taiwan's major cities will have to be enlarged and trained to take over this function.

Many observers have noted that there was already a serious hiatus in the law and in terms of police practice in the area of controlling public group expression and that something had to be done anyway. Although martial law officially banned marches and street demonstrations, that ban was being ignored. There were 347 protest demonstrations recorded in Taiwan in the first five months of 1987.[34] Most were disruptive of social order, at minimum traffic control. Clearly martial law was not working.

Finally, though strikes were not prohibited under martial law, labor unions were weak and not allowed to organize easily because of martial law. This will also change. Legislation will probably be written in coming months to legalize strikes, though walkouts may remain banned.[35] In any event, new labor legislation is needed and can be expected.

Yet, one should not expect large numbers of strikes or disruptive labor activities. Labor is not well organized in Taiwan, not only because unions are disadvantaged and their functions have been preempted by the KMT, but also because of the nature of Taiwan's economy: Taiwan has a larger portion of family and small businesses than other countries at a similar stage of development. In addition, wages have risen rapidly as a result of very low unemployment (in early 1988 the lowest in the world among nations publishing unemployment figures) and Taiwan's "miracle growth" economy.

The end of martial law has also had some indirect effects. Coinciding with the end of martial law the government announced the lifting of the ban imposed on books and other publications printed in the PRC and ruled that, except for blatant propaganda, such materials could now be imported and sold to the public. It was also announced that restrictions on Taiwan's citizens traveling to Hong Kong (from where they frequently go to the PRC) would be discontinued and that visits to the PRC. by Taiwan's citizens will be permitted. Athletic contests and the exchange of cultural groups with the mainland were also mentioned.[36]

These changes reflect the development of some important attitudes that favor democracy as well as confidence that Taiwan has experienced such economic and political development that communism is no longer attractive to Taiwan's populace and is therefore not much of a threat. They also indicate that Taipei's "three no's" policy toward the PRC is being diluted and that Taiwan is adopting a more positive and confident foreign policy.

Some people in Taiwan have even expressed a concern that ending martial law may result in too much freedom, laxness about regulations and social responsibilities, and an end to the work ethic. Linking martial law to a period of miracle economic growth, they calculate that Taiwan's economic development—upon which social change and political modernization were built—may come to an end with the end of martial law. In a sense, this may be a superstition; yet it is true that Taiwan's economic growth was partly built on the maintenance of national security and law enforcement, which suppressed ethnic tensions and other centrifugal tendencies.

It is also noteworthy that there has been tremendous external pressure on Taiwan, particularly from the United States, to do something about its large trade surplus. This problem has evoked several pieces of new legislation and a major revaluation of the nation's currency just as martial law was ending. If they cause an economic downturn, many people may blame a bad economy on the termination of martial law.

Conclusions

The view that Taiwan was not under martial law has some substance. Clearly Taiwan has not been under military rule since 1949. Most of the conditions one would associate with martial law were not in evidence after 1950.

Furthermore, throughout its recent history, compared to other nations Taiwan has had a more stable government and its public safety was much less threatened. If Taiwan had martial law, it certainly was not like martial law in other countries. Moreover, most people living in Taiwan were not aware of the martial law or did not object to it.

Martial law did affect the way the legal system worked, however, and gave the military influence in politics it was not entitled to have under the Constitution. Likewise, martial law did, for at least psychological reasons, impede the development of democracy—though not very much in recent years.

The case can and no doubt will be made that the decision was important in the evolution of the system from an authoritarian to a democratic one. Future historians will no doubt look for a turning point in the development of democracy in Taiwan, and it is likely that 1987 will be seen as that. In at least one sense they will be right: If martial law had a psychologically oppressive effect, abolishing it certainly erased it.

Conversely, political development has been in evidence in Taiwan for a number of years. Some see the process beginning in the early 1970s when then Premier Chiang Ching-kuo ordered the government to recruit Taiwanese and end corruption; he reformed the system so that it was responsive to public demands and the needs of a modern economy. The 1980 election, which witnessed party competition for the first time, or the 1986 election, which many observers labeled a two-party race—the first ever held in any China and one of the first outside of a colonial experience—can be cited as important events in Taiwan's political modernization and democratization process. Thus, it is not rational to say that political reform in Taiwan originated in July 1987.

The argument that the new State Security Law supplanted martial law in form, if not in spirit, is accurate for a number of reasons. It certainly embodied some of the provisions in martial law. It had to; many of the provisions of martial law needed to be retained for national security reasons. Yet it is not accurate to say that the State Security Law will impede democratization in the way martial law did in the 1950s and 1960s. In particular, it will not have the psychological effect martial law had. Clearly, it is not correct to say that it represents an effort to preserve an authoritarian or one-party political system. It is similar to national security legislation in a number of Western democracies; in fact, a comparison shows that the punishments for almost all violations is considerably lighter in Taiwan under the new law than in the United States or other Western democracies.[37]

The termination of martial law could precipitate anti-government protest, maybe even widespread demonstrations and rallies, especially in view of problems in the Philippines and South Korea, which many have long felt might spread to Taiwan. Some argue that it was problems there that created pressure on Taiwan to abolish martial law. Clearly protest is contagious. Unprecedented rallies and street demonstrations did accompany the end of martial law rule in Taiwan.

There are marked differences between Taiwan and either the Philippines or South Korea, however. There is also evidence of a backlash against the protest surrounding the State Security Law. On one occasion during the debate of the State Security Law, DPP protesters caused a traffic jam and blocked an ambulance from getting to a hospital; consequently, a heart attack victim died on the street. DPP leaders—seeing a change in public attitudes—apologized. Just before the end of martial law was announced, the DPP canceled planned street marches, realizing that the population did not want chaos during the Lions International Club meeting in Taipei or during the period of college entrance examinations. At the same time, it was reported that the DPP was experiencing difficulties in its recruitment efforts, some said because the protest at this time did not enlist the sympathy its leaders had hoped for.

Whether ending martial law will promote democracy and usher in the beginning of an era as many observers have suggested, is also debatable. Some pundits have argued that it was undemocratic to get rid of it, since it had the support of the public. Others note that efforts to end martial law were successful because the authority and prestige of President Chiang Ching-kuo transcend the rules and constraints of democracy. Most of those who have adamantly opposed martial law admit that it could not have been dispensed with at the time it was had it not been for the personal (and authoritarian) decision of the president. It is thus ironic that martial law ended the way it did.

Nevertheless, the end of martial law can be expected to foster democratic processes in manifold ways. The most important have been previously discussed. There is, however, a also down side. There have been unprecedented fistfights and disruption in Legislative Yuan sessions recently. This is the dark side of democracy at work. Likewise, the abolition of martial law may cause economic slowdown; indeed this perception has become widespread. Whether it will engender a movement to restore it, however, is doubtful.

There will no doubt be an expansion of civil and political liberties. The end of martial law will make the political system more free and open. But here there is also a negative impact: Many expect the crime rate to increase. It already has, and it will probably get worse.

Taiwan's legal system will be strengthened by the termination of martial law. At present, this does not appear to present a problem since the judicial branch of government is considerably weaker than the executive or legislative branches. It would be unfortunate in the eyes of most of Taiwan's citizens, however, if lawsuits became as frequent and as costly and disruptive as in the United States.

The end of martial law creates still another dilemma. It was said that it was possible (to some people necessary) to end martial law because social and political modernization and a better-educated populace had created a climate in which communism no longer has any appeal. The end of martial law has also been viewed as a turning point in the transition of Taiwan's polity to a democratic one. Unification with the People's Republic of China is now certainly less likely unless it is to be accomplished by military force. For this reason, not to mention the fact that Beijing ostensibly supported martial law in the past, the decision to end it was not an auspicious event for PRC leaders. The case can certainly be made—and has been—that Beijing did not want martial law ended. [38] Similarly, ending martial law presents a dilemma for policy makers in the United States. Those that have most strongly condemned martial law in Taiwan and have been most vociferous in their demands that it end are generally also advocates of better U.S. relations with Beijing. The fact that Taiwan has ended martial law thus makes Taiwan more democratic and public opinion more relevant to determining Taiwan's future. Hence, ending martial law is a possible source of trouble in U.S.-China relations.

Terminating martial law in Taiwan will have a major impact on the future of the country in terms of its political modernization, its image abroad, and its citizens' perceptions of their nation and its political system. It no doubt will be seen by future historians as an important event.

Endnotes

1. The following categories of views are based on discussions with a number of people in Taiwan during the summer of 1987.

2. This view is espoused by more conservative government officials and is the "official" position taken by the Nationalist Party.

3. This perspective is taken by more progressive officials in the government, especially in those agencies dealing with the foreign media. Many, however, agree in part with the view that Taiwan was never really under martial law.

4. This is the "official" view of the Democratic Progressive Party. It is a position that members of the DPP pushed during the debate over the State Security Law.

5. This is the position taken by more radical members of the DPP as well as non–DPP opposition.

6. See Richard C. Kagan, "Martial Law in Taiwan," *Bulletin of Concerned Asian Scholars,* July–September 1982, pp. 48–54.

7. Lih-wu Han, *Taiwan Today* (Taipei: Cheng Chung Book Company, 1986), p. 34.

8. Ibid.

9. See Kagan, "Martial Law in Taiwan," pp. 48–54.

10. Over the years, a number of public opinion polls have been taken asking citizens if they are bothered or inconvenienced by martial law and if they want to abolish it. These polls have generally reflected strong public support for keeping martial law. See, for example, *China Post,* December 2, 1983. Cited here is a poll taken by the Republic of China Opinion Polling Association that recorded that more than 80 percent of the population perceived that martial law did not inconvenience them.

11. For an elaboration of this view, see John F. Copper with George P. Chen, *Taiwan's Elections: Political Development and Democratization in the Republic of China* (Baltimore: University of Maryland School of Law, 1984), pp. 61–63.

12. Ibid., p. 118.

13. See "Martial Law on Taiwan and United States Foreign Policy Interests," Hearings Before the Subcommittee of Asia and Pacific Affairs, House of Representatives, Ninety–Seventh Congress (Washington, DC: U.S. Government Printing Office, 1982).

14. See Daniel Southerland, "Taiwan President to Propose End to Island's Martial Law," *Washington Post,* October 8, 1986, p. 6.

15. See "Legislative Yuan OK's State Security Law," *China News* (Taipei), June 24, 1987, p. 8.

16. See *Amnesty International Report 1987* (London: Amnesty International Publications, 1987), p. 269. The report refers to nineteen political prisoners arrested between 1975 and 1980. Another source estimates the number of political prisoners in Taiwan at fifty. See "Taiwan: The Dawn of a New Era," *Asiaweek*, July 19, 1987, p. 28.

17. See "Security Law Screened Amidst Protest," *Asian Bulletin*, May 1987, p. 28.

18. See *China Post*, March 31, 1987, p. 12, for details on the objectives and plans for the demonstration.

19. For details, see texts of AFP broadcast from Hong Kong May 19 and China News Agency broadcast from Taipei May 20, both in *Foreign Broadcasting Information Service*, May 20, 1987, pp. VI–V3.

20. During the committee debate on the State Security Law, DPP legislators took the floor 167 times (which equaled 49.1 percent of the times legislators took the podium). During the second reading of the bill DPP legislators had the floor 35.1 percent of the time. See "New Law to Protect the Rights of All the People in the ROC," *New China Journal*, July 27, 1987, p. 2.

21. See Terry Emerson, "New Law not so Different from U.S. Law in Many Respects," *Free China Journal*, July 27, 1987, p. 2.

22. "Most Believe Lifting of Martial Law Will Have Little Effect on Daily Life," *China News*, July 7, 1987, p. 3. This poll was done by the *China Times*.

23. "Survey Shows Most Support Enactment of Security Law," *China News* (Taipei), June 24, 1987, p. 2. The latter poll was taken by the World College of Journalism.

24. See "Most Believe Lifting of Martial Law Will Have Little Effect on Daily Life."

25. The opposition charges that 8,000 people have been imprisoned on sedition charges in the past, although they admit that the number has been very small in recent years. See Carl Goldstein, "Retaining the Edge," *Far Eastern Economic Review*, July 9, 1987, p. 24.

26. For a list of these, see *United Daily News* (in Chinese), International Edition, June 24, 1987, p. 1. Also see "16 Administrative Decrees to be Abolished Soon," *China News*, June 24, 1987, p. 8.

27. Daniel Southerland, "After 38 Years, Taiwan Lifts Martial Law; Prisoners Freed," *Washington Post*, July 15, 1987, p. 1.

28. See Carl Goldstein, "Oiling the Old Machine," *Far Eastern Economic Review*, September 3, 1987, pp. 14–15.

29. See various stories in China *Post*, July 12, 1987, p. 8. Also see "Taiwan gets 4th Political Party,"*Washington Times*, September 7, 1987, p. A6. There were also reports before this that a Labor party might form.

30. See Carl Goldstein, "New Look for Old Guard," *Far Eastern Economic Review*, September 3, 1987, p. 14.

31. See "Stirrings of Democracy," *Newsweek* (International Edition), June 8, 1987, p. 9.

32. See John F. Copper, "Taiwan's 1986 National Election: Pushing Democracy Ahead," *Asian Thought and Society*, July 1987, pp. 132–33.

33. It is common knowledge in Taiwan that most newspapers frequently violate laws regulating the press and that there is intense competition among newspapers for readers. Because of this, most will seldom agree not to print news in order to please government officials.

34. Thom F.P. Meng, "Making Government Work for All," *Free China Journal*, July 27, 1987, p. 2.

35. "Taiwan to Lift Ban of Strikes," *Journal of Commerce* (New York), July 7, 1987, p. 5A.

36. See "Taipei's Bold Gambit," *Asiaweek,* September 6, 1987, pp. 24–26.

37. See Emmerson, "New Law not so Different from U.S. Law."

38. See Kagan, "Martial Law in Taiwan."

Chapter Six
Democracy in Taiwan Challenges
U.S.-China Policy

The Republic of China (ROC) has long been recognized as a valuable strategic ally by the United States. Since moving to Taiwan in 1949, the government of the Republic of China has repeatedly offered the use of the island's facilities to U.S. forces in time of war. This offer remains in effect today. Taiwan's location, only ninety miles from the coast of mainland Asia, makes its air bases and port facilities among the most geopolitically important in the world.

In addition to its strategic value to the United States, the ROC has proved to be one of the most attractive models of how free enterprise unleashes potential economic growth. Nations throughout the Third World, particularly in Latin America, look to Taiwan as a model for their own economic development. The ROC's promotion of free trade also has served U.S. economic interests admirably.

More recently, the ROC has demonstrated that it may also become a model for developing countries that seek to become democracies. This has very special meaning to the United States, which has long encouraged democratic political development in Taiwan. Not only is spreading democracy an American ideological goal, which applies particularly to Taiwan because of the "Free China-Communist China" dichotomy, but greater democracy on Taiwan could lead to greater internal stability on the island and hence contribute to the goal of peace in East Asia.

The ROC has indeed witnessed rapid political change over the past decade. Island-wide elections in December 1986 saw competition between two political parties—the first ever in any Chinese nation. This election was the outcome of ROC President Chiang Ching-kuo's promise in September to end martial law and terminate the ban on political parties. ROC and foreign observers alike applauded these decisions and the election as proof that the political system is becoming more democratic.

Democracy in Taiwan, however, is almost certain to cause problems for the United States in its relations with the People's Republic of China (PRC). Beijing has asked, cajoled, and pressured Washington to force Taipei to negotiate reunification. The United States can hardly do this in view of the fact that the vast majority of the 19 million people on Taiwan have little sympathy with the mainland Communist government and do not want to be ruled by Beijing. Moreover, as citizens of the ROC gain a stronger political voice, which will inevitably happen as Taiwan becomes even more democratic, their determination not to become part of the mainland will make reunification even more difficult. This poses a challenge for U.S. policy makers who want to encourage democracy on Taiwan and at the same time maintain friendly relations with the PRC. These objectives, in the final analysis, are clearly contradictory.

U.S.-China Policy and Taiwan

Since the normalization of relations between the United States and the PRC began in the early 1970s, U.S.-China policy has been vague regarding the so-called "Taiwan issue," or the legal status of Taiwan. Washington has been deliberately ambiguous about whether it considers Taiwan to be part of the territory of the People's Republic of China. Though Beijing has been very sensitive about this issue, it has not prevented U.S.-PRC relations from improving dramatically during the past four U.S. administrations. Their rapprochement was built upon mutual security concerns, namely the Soviet threat.

In the Shanghai Communique, signed at the end of President Richard Nixon's visit to the PRC in February 1972, the United States stated that it "does not challenge" Beijing's position that "there is but one China and Taiwan is a part of China." This statement was interpreted by most to mean that, although Washington did not agree with the PRC's assertions about Taiwan or its claim that Taiwan constitutes its territory, the Nixon administration, for strategic reasons, did not want the Taiwan issue to impede better relations between the two countries.

In the December 15, 1978 Normalization Agreement signed with the PRC, the Carter administration, however, went a step further. It recognized Beijing "as the sole legal government of China." Still, President Carter said nothing specific about or in support of the PRC's legal claim to Taiwan.

To ensure that the shift in diplomatic recognition would not adversely affect Taiwan's international status and that President Carter's actions would not be interpreted as implying U.S. recognition or support of Beijing's territorial claim to Taiwan, the U.S. Congress in April 1979 passed the Taiwan Relations Act (TRA). The TRA treated Taiwan as a sovereign nation-state in all but name (referring to the "people of Taiwan" rather than the "Republic of China"). Taipei's diplomats were given diplomatic privileges in the United States, and the ROC, vis. Taiwan, was allowed the use of U.S. courts.

The TRA also declared that any threat of the use of force against Taiwan, including boycotts or embargoes, would be considered of "grave concern to the United States." Observers took this to mean that the United States assumed responsibility for Taiwan's security and sought to preserve a peaceful climate wherein the ROC could continue its economic and political development—even though this would widen the gulf between China and Taiwan.

Improved relations with the PRC during the Nixon, Ford, and Carter administrations were built upon two important assumptions: (1) that the PRC shared a common interest with the United States in countering the threat caused by the massive buildup of Soviet forces throughout the world and particularly in Asia; and (2) that the United States could maintain ties with Taipei and at the same time improve relations with Beijing.

These assumptions have proven correct. For example, since the 1979 Normalization Agreement that established formal United States-People's Republic of China relations to 1986, U.S. trade with the ROC has increased from $9 billion to $26.7 billion. Moreover, Washington continues to sell large quantities of defensive arms to Taipei. Since 1979 these sales have totaled more than $5 billion.

At the same time that steps have been taken to ensure Taiwan's prosperity and security, the United States has expressed a keen interest in seeing the ROC become more open and democratic. This concern was not only written into the TRA but has been the subject of American pressure on Taiwan and even hearings in the U.S. Congress. Meanwhile, relations dramatically improved between the United States and the People's Republic of China on several fronts: security cooperation, trade, technology transfer, investments, and cultural and educational exchanges. Thus Washington pursued a "two-front" policy of improving relations with the PRC while maintaining cordial and important ties with the ROC.

Although the United States since in began the pursuit of rapprochement with Beijing in 1972 has refused to recognize PRC sovereignty over Taiwan and its 19 million inhabitants, Chinese leaders have nevertheless proposed unification talks to Taipei on a number of occasions. Most of these offers have been friendly ones—at least from Beijing's perspective. The PRC has even made specific offers, such as promising to let Taiwan keep its political and economic systems and even its military under the "one country, two systems" formula—a policy that sets forth the basic principles whereby China will resume sovereignty over both Hong Kong and Macao at the end of the next decade and which Chinese leaders say apply to the "Taiwan problem." Significantly, however, Beijing has made threats to use military force against the ROC if its government refuses to negotiate. This, of course, makes Beijing's proposals appear less than friendly and causes its policy toward Taipei to lose credibility.

Anyway, as far as the ROC is concerned, Beijing has promised nothing Taipei does not already have. Furthermore, public opinion polls on Taiwan reveal that more than 99 percent of the population does not want to live under Communist rule. Both the ROC government and its citizens, in fact, see other serious disadvantages in unifying with the mainland. High among their concerns are the deterioration in their standard of living and personal freedoms. The ROC's per capita income is nearly ten times that of the PRC, and Beijing's record on human rights in the past two decades is one of the worst in the world.

The ROC as an Economic and Political Model

U.S. interests throughout the world are served by the success of the ROC as both an economic and political development model to the Third World. The ROC has, in fact, become one of the globe's great economic success stories, largely because of its adoption of the free-enterprise system. Increasingly over the last few years, it has also become a model of building democracy.

At the end of World War II, the annual per capita income in Taiwan and on the mainland were nearly the same—about $50. In 1949, when the Communists took control of the mainland and the Nationalists fled to Taiwan, the situation had changed very little. Today the ROC's per capita income approaches $3,500; the PRC's is roughly $400. And the ROC has made this progress despite formidable handicaps. For example, Taiwan has a population density nine times that of the main-land; it has virtually no natural resources; and it lacks diplomatic relations with most nations of the world.

The ROC's economic growth has been built on both free market principles and astute planning. Land reform during the early 1950s was followed by a policy of export-led growth. A generally free internal market and government policies that encouraged foreign trade made the ROC the leading nation in the world in economic growth over the past two decades. Taiwan has grown faster than Japan or South Korea and many times faster than the United States and Western Europe.

Compared to the rapid growth of its economy, the pace of ROC political modernization was slow during the 1950s and 1960s. By the early 1970s, however, it had sped up considerably. President Chiang Ching-kuo (then premier) ordered government offices to accept suggestions and complaints from the public. According to opinion polls at that time, the Executive Yuan, the executive branch of the government, was more responsive to public demands than elected legislative organs of government. Democratization was energized by internal reform.

The ruling Kuomintang (KMT) party and the government also began a program to promote equal representation of all ethnic groups in both major centers of political power. Individuals born in Taiwan (so-called Taiwanese), who compose 85 percent of the island's population, were given preferential treatment in government employment and party membership.

Meanwhile, restrictions were lifted on foreign travel and on the sale of books, magazines, and newspapers. Tourism was encouraged. The number of business peoples' contacts abroad increased dramatically, and an awareness of economic and political developments in other countries was encouraged.

Today the ROC is highly cosmopolitan and pluralist. The portion of its citizens travelling abroad is higher than in the United States. Opinion polls show a very high level of public awareness of international affairs in Taiwan in comparison to most other countries.

Prosperity has meanwhile fostered the growth of a large middle class. According to recent opinion polls, most of the ROC's population regards itself as members of this class. Educational opportunities have expanded to the extent that the ROC is now, according to the United Nations, the leading developing country in the world in terms of its citizens' level of education.

Meanwhile, because of rapid economic and political modernization, ethnic differences now play a much diminished role in ROC politics. According to public opinion surveys, ethnic identification or defining oneself as a member of a particular ethnic group, is rapidly disappearing among Mainland Chinese (those who came to Taiwan after 1945) and native-born Taiwanese (Chinese living on the island before 1945). Some 90 percent of KMT candidates in recent elections have been Taiwanese.

As the ROC has prospered economically and has become more open, there has been a corresponding increase in demands from the population for more democracy. This process has accelerated over the past few years. And the ruling party and the government have delivered.

In 1985, President Chiang Ching-kuo, son of the late Nationalist leader Chiang Kai-shek, publicly promised that none of his relatives would succeed him. This announcement was necessary, he thought, to quell reports that one of his sons was accumulating political power in preparation for making a bid to become his successor. Other speculation pointed to the military as a likely locus of power in the post-Chiang era. Chiang also addressed this worry by declaring that the military would not rule Taiwan. Making this promise credible, he had demoted and transferred abroad a leading military leader contending for presidential power. The likely successor to Chiang is ROC Vice President Lee Teng-hui, a Taiwanese.

As noted earlier, economic and political development have made Taiwan an attractive model to Third World nations. The poignancy of this can not be lost in the United States. The promotion of free enterprise and democracy abroad are basic American principles not to mention long-term U.S. objectives. Hence, U.S. interests are furthered by Taiwan's accomplishments, and it is in U.S. national interest to see that continued progress is made on the island. However, to repeat, this contradicts better U.S.–PRC relations given Beijing's policies toward Taiwan.

Elections in the ROC

Taiwan held its first island-wide election in 1950, only one year after the Nationalist government moved from the mainland. Since then, nearly seventy major elections have been held at regular intervals. Few nations have had more frequent elections than the ROC. These elections have also become increasingly more open and competitive over time.

In 1980, the ROC held its first national election with non-KMT candidates competing with the ruling Nationalist Party. Non-KMT independents organized a political group known as *tang wai* (meaning "outside the party"), drafted and publicized their own platform, supported candidates for office, raised campaign funds, and helped each other campaign. The government accepted their participation in the election, even though the formation of new political parties was illegal at the time.

During the campaign preceding this election for 205 seats in the National Assembly, Legislative Yuan, and Control Yuan, there was a fairly open debate on the issues. *Tang wai* candidates accused the KMT of maintaining a one-party system and not allowing democracy to develop. They also charged the government with misrule, incompetence, and mismanagement of foreign policy (particularly relations with the United States). KMT candidates countered by charging the *tang wai* with unrealistic policies that could reverse the ROC's economic and political progress. The voters had a clear choice; 70 percent of them went for the KMT.

In 1983, there was a national election for seventy-one seats in the Legislative Yuan. Again the electorate had a clear choice between the KMT and the *tang wai*. On important issues the lines were drawn. During this election, party competition was accepted as the norm and the public viewed the contest between the two much as voters view opposing political parties in Western democracies, even though the *tang wai*, formally speaking, was still yet-to-be a legal political party.

Several months before the December 1986 election for the Legislative Yuan and National Assembly, the government announced that the *tang wai* could maintain offices throughout the island to serve as campaign headquarters. This concession enabled the *tang wai* to establish an national party organization. President Chiang also announced the formation of a twelve–member committee composed of representatives of both the KMT and the *tang wai* to discuss political reforms, including putting an end to both martial law and the ban against the formation of new political parties.

The discussions, however, soon reached an impasse. A court ruling in a libel case and the resultant jailing of several *tang wai* politicians led to indefinite delays. Finally, a number of *tang wai* leaders met in September and announced they had formed the Democratic Progressive Party (DPP). The move was technically illegal, but President Chiang took no action against DPP leaders or new party members. After all, the *tang wai* had been, in practice, a political party. The DPP then announced a slate of candidates for the December 6 election. The government did not try to stop its efforts.

During the campaign, Democratic Progressive Party candidates carried their former *tang wai* party flag and identified themselves as members of the DPP. Their campaign platform called for expanded political freedoms, more party competition, less restrictive election laws, and national "self-determination." This last plank was very controversial. It suggested the people of Taiwan should decide their own future, but it was widely understood to mean that they could choose to be independent from the mainland. In other words, self-determination meant independence. The KMT and the ROC government had insisted on a one-China policy and eventual reunification with the mainland—a position also supported by the ruling Communist Party in the PRC. It was likewise U.S. policy—that is United States China policy as enunciated by the executive branch of government (but not the Congress).

In the December election campaign, both the KMT and the DPP moderated their views as a result of public pressure and a more sophisticated electorate.

Some KMT members welcomed the DPP's challenge, saying that it would bring democracy to the political system and force the KMT to do better. Most DPP candidates stressed that they would play the role of a loyal opposition. Advocating an independent Taiwan was often used by the DPP to gain attention, but it was not defined clearly and most DPP leaders stopped short of translating their words into specific actions or policies.

In the elections, the DPP won 21 percent of the popular vote and 23 seats in the Legislative Yuan and National Assembly. Thus it performed much better than the *tang wai* had in the past. The KMT won just under 70 percent of the popular vote, giving it 127 seats in both elective bodies.

More important, perhaps, than the numbers, the election demonstrated that two-party competition could work in the ROC and that a democratic system was evolving. To some extent, the process worked because of U.S. encouragement and the perception in the ROC that building a democratic system would improve the country's status in the international community.

The End of Martial Law

Another step in the ROC's political evolution was President Chiang's decision to lift the martial law that had been imposed in 1949 as allowed under the Temporary Provision of the Constitution. Under martial law, civilians were often tried in military courts and given severe sentences for crimes deemed to endanger the security of the nation. The foreign press consistently criticized Taipei for maintaining martial law in the face of the island's apparent stability and prosperity.

The truth is, however, that martial law was never fully enforced on the island. In August 1950, martial law provisions were weakened when the government banned arrests without warrants and blocked martial law decrees from being used to infringe on an individual's person or property. Over the following three years, martial law provisions were revised again, restoring to civilian courts exclusive jurisdiction in all cases except those involving treason. Public defenders were provided for all defendants who could not afford to hire an attorney and all curfews were lifted. The military assumed fewer duties relating to internal security and concentrated instead on national defense.

Though public opinion polls in the 1970s revealed that few in Taiwan considered martial law even an inconvenience, those favoring political modernization and democracy argued that martial law should be abolished because it was psychologically intimidating and sometimes used by police to suppress the exercise of political freedoms and civil rights. They also observed that it gave the ROC a bad image abroad.

Meanwhile, after debate on this issue in May 1983, the U.S. Congress passed a series of non-binding resolutions criticizing the ROC's martial law and urging continued "democratic progress." Reformist members of the KMT and a number of top government officials in Taipei made the same recommendation. Subsequently the *tang wai* and some independent opposition politicians took up the issue, making it a major rallying point against the government.

Many top KMT leaders and high government officials, however, wanted to retain martial law because of continued military and other threats posed by Beijing. PRC leaders, after all, had promised to invade Taiwan should Taipei refuse to negotiate reunification. A significant segment of the population thus felt that martial law was needed. Many even thought it facilitated the democratic process because it maintained stability during a period of rapid economic and social change.

Nevertheless, in early 1986 President Chiang announced that discussions would be held on how to lift martial law. He declared that martial law damaged the ROC's image abroad and probably impeded ROC democratization. Therefore, he announced that martial law would be abolished once national security legislation had been enacted to provide a legal basis for maintaining the nation's internal security. The Legislative Yuan currently is debating a national security law, some version of which will be adopted soon.

The United States responded to this decision favorably. The Western media lauded it as a watershed event in the nation's efforts to democratize. This in turn made public opinion in the U.S. more positive about Taiwan. The United States government also took note and applauded Taiwan's democratic progress. Again, however, this conflicted, or would, with improving U.S.-PRC relations.

Conclusions

The ROC has and continues to support United States interests in a number of ways. Among them the following are the most important:

1. The ROC has, and continues to help the United States in its strategic and military efforts to contain Communism in Asia. It was an American ally in both the Korean and Vietnam wars and offered the use of its excellent air and seaport facilities to the United States during these conflicts. These bases were, and are still available in the event of a confrontation with the Soviet Union.

2. The ROC's economic success serves as proof that free enterprise and a market economy provide the best strategy for growth for developing countries. This Taiwan learned from the United States. It was implemented with American help. The United States hopes that other countries throughout the world will follow Taiwan's example.

3. The ROC's steady progress toward democracy has made it a political model for the Third World. Democracy in Taiwan is also proof that capitalism and a free market economy and successful economic growth are ingredients to political modernization that leads to democracy. Again this is a major tenet of U.S. political philosophy.

But, good things have their limits and sometimes their downsides. Although democracy in the ROC serves U.S. political interests, contributes to regional peace and stability, and is satisfying to Americans (since it proves the validity of the American experience and the advantages of the American system of government), U.S. policy makers must nevertheless recognize that democracy in Taiwan may make China's unification more unlikely. Thus, Washington's (meaning the White House and the Department of State) one-China policy, which is seen by many as fundamental to its good relations with Beijing, is brought into question. Citizens of the ROC do not want to forfeit their economic prosperity and political freedom to join the Communist mainland. And the United States can hardly force them to do so.

Perhaps time will resolve this problem. Yet, Beijing may grow more impatient with the ROC in the future and step up pressure on Washington to help bring the two Chinese sides together. Should this occur, the United States must stand fast. America must continue to applaud and support Taiwan's economic and political development successes, even though they may impede unification. Taiwan must be given a right to choose; it deserves that. The one-China ideal, therefore, must be seen as that, an ideal, or as a future goal, not a policy that the United States will force upon Taiwan.

Chapter Seven
Taiwan's "Undemocratic" Elective Bodies of Government

Taiwan's political system has been criticized at home and abroad for being undemocratic because its elective bodies of government—the National Assembly, the Legislative Yuan, and the Control Yuan—represent China (where Taipei cannot hold elections) as well as Taiwan. Members of those bodies of government who represent the Chinese provinces on the mainland in these bodies were not elected by voters on the island of Taiwan and have been locked in place since 1949. Taiwan's population is "over-represented" in the elective bodies of government; still critics claim that for democracy to prevail China should not be represented at all.

If one sees the Republic of China as a separate nation and wishes to promote democracy in that country, then it is perhaps impeccably logical that all of the elected representatives to the above-mentioned bodies should represent Taiwan only. In fact, hardly anyone cannot be persuaded to some extent by this argument.

Political systems, however, like political events, are never as simple as they appear. There is almost always another angle or point of view about politics. Thus, let me offer a second opinion concerning the accusation that Taiwan's elective bodies of government are not democratic because they represent something other than Taiwan.

The first argument, and perhaps the most compelling, against changing the system is that China's strongman, Deng Xiaoping, has stated repeatedly that he will use military force to resolve the "Taiwan question" if Taipei declares independence. We need recall that in 1979 Deng warned everyone who would listen, in the United States and around the world, that he would "teach Vietnam a lesson" for its invasion and occupation of nearby Kampuchea. He was not bluffing; he launched a war against Vietnam a few weeks later that was very costly to both Vietnam and China in lives and money.

If Deng decides to use military force against Taiwan, the losses would be much higher. Some estimate that 2 million people would be killed. The damage to property and to Taiwan's economy would be equally staggering. If other countries get involved, and there is good reason to believe they would, the conflict could become global in nature and could even involve nuclear weapons. China is, after all, a nuclear power.

The question then arises: Is changing the system worth the risk? The old representatives in Taiwan's elected bodies of government are going to die soon anyway and will probably not be replaced. At least not many of them will be replaced. And probably none of their replacements will not be replaced. Thus, "democratizing" the system by changing it only speeds up an otherwise inevitable process. Since Deng may be provoked to do what he said he would by a sudden change in Taiwan's political system, it is probably safer to wait for the delegates to die. If the ROC decides not to replace these delegates, it is doubtful that Deng can construe this action, or lack of action, as provocative.

A second reason for not changing the system overnight is based on a lesson we can glean from history. As Japan evolved toward a democratic system in the early part of this century, there were large numbers of "elder statesmen" in the Japanese parliament. They also were not elected. They were there because they were wise and respected, and they provided a great deal of stability at a time when Japan was experiencing rapid social and political change. In the 1930s many of these "un-elected" elder statesmen were forced out of politics by Japan's "young turks," some of whom wanted faster change and purer democracy (of course, others simply desired a power shift in their favor and shrouded it in democratic verbiage). In any event, Japanese politics became more unstable. The image of the parliament deteriorated, and with that, democracy failed. The final result was militarism and World War II. Had the old, un-elected elder statesmen not been pushed out, events might have been different.

A third reason for not removing the elder representatives, appointed (or elected a long time ago) from the National Assembly, the Legislative Yuan, and the Control Yuan, is that they are not beholden to special interests. Therefore they represent and protect the national interest better than the younger elected representatives. In fact, because of them Taiwan is partially protected from the plague of special interests. Hopefully it can be in the future, but there is no plan on the drawing board for this. This is particularly important because of the speed of economic and political development. (In this connection, it is worth remembering that Taiwan achieved economic growth with equity because of bills or legislation—such as the "land to the tiller" program, labor insurance laws, and so on—that were passed by the elder representatives who were unobstructed by special-interest politics.)

A related point to ponder is that as democracy has developed in many countries, big money individuals and groups have preyed upon the system and the population through elected officials. After all, elected officials must campaign and campaigning requires money. Taiwan's democratization has, as most observers well know, involved money politics. Money buys influence. And there doesn't seem to be any good remedy for that. Keeping the elder parliamentarians will help, even if only temporarily.

In short, even though the older members of the elected bodies of government do not represent districts, professional groups, or other entities in Taiwan, they keep these decision-making bodies aware of the greater good of the society and the country. Thus they provide a needed (at least at the time) service.

Fourth, two of Taiwan's elected bodies of government are too large to debate political issues effectively: the National Assembly and the Legislative Yuan. While this does not make much difference in the case of the former, since it is not really a deliberative body, it does in the case of the Legislative Yuan. The latter is too big for effective, free debate. A deliberative body of one hundred or fewer members is better. A study of other democratic systems makes this clear.

If the members of the Legislative Yuan that do not represent Taiwan were suddenly dismissed, there would be considerable (perhaps irresistible) pressure for them to be replaced by elected representatives. There are numerous politicians waiting in the wings who would like more seats to be opened up in the legislative branch of government so they could campaign for one.

If the members of the Legislative Yuan, who do not represent Taiwan are not replaced after their deaths, however, the Legislative Yuan will decrease in size and become a more effective lawmaking body of government. It will debate and deliberate the issues more efficiently and in a way the public can understand and appreciate. In addition, the prestige of the elected representatives of this body will increase as will public respect for them and the body itself.

All in all, the second opinion on whether to try to reform the system quickly or let reform happen over time seems to favor a more gradual approach. It is safer and, in at least three respects, more logical.

Chapter Eight
Totalitarianism, Authoritarianism, and the Pursuit of Democracy

One of the most serious questions asked by students of politics almost everywhere in the world in recent years is: Why do certain countries or political systems evolve into democracies more easily than others? This is also a question that is of great interest to political observers and to laymen.

Answering this question is difficult. Therefore, an assessment of the reasons—since there are so many and all are complex—must focus on the most relevant variables, namely the political party structures of the respective political systems. A one-party system is typically (almost as a rule) not democratic, and is in many ways resistant to the development of democracy.[1] In other words, democratizing countries must shed or change their one-party systems. This is patently easier for some countries or political systems than for others. Therefore, the question must be posed: Why can some one-party systems give way to competitive party systems while others do not or cannot?

The ability, or willingness, of dominant or monopolistic parties to allow other parties to form, or exist if they have formed, and thus to tolerate competition and consequently the possibility of their own demise, depends upon a number of factors. Theoretical factors include whether that nation is Communist or non-Communist (meaning traditional authoritarian) and the nature and degree to which an ideology (especially an anti-democratic one) is essential to the workings of the system. One may also cite the degree of authoritarianism or totalitarianism in the said nation (if indeed there can be a degree of totalitarianism). Both of these dichotomies are controversial among political thinkers.

Also of considerable relevance to the ability of nations or political systems to evolve into democracy are conditions such as the security of the said system; the level, speed, and kind of economic development; problems of social change; and qualities of the political leadership. In this chapter, the author will consider those factors as well as issues of political culture, the democratization process, and of course, "ideological" matters relating to the development or non-development of political party competition.[2]

It should be self-evident that the two nations (assuming for the purposes of this chapter that Taiwan is a nation-state) under consideration make for a very interesting and in many ways "advantageous" comparison, inasmuch as they are populated by people who speak a common language and have a common culture. This enables one to exclude a number of variables, especially historical , as well as early cultural factors, and focus on "newer" factors. In fact, it may be argued that the two Chinas provide an instructive contrast, showing the advantages and shortcomings of two very different political systems vis-à-vis the democratizing process.

Differences in Polities and Party Systems

The polities, and to a lesser extent the party systems, of the People's Republic of China and the Republic of China share the same origins. They evolved from 2,000 or 3,000 years of Chinese history and came, more recently, from a revolution in the early part of this century—1911 to be precise—that overthrew the Qing Dynasty and with it the imperial bureaucratic system that had prevailed for two millennia. There are some major differences, however, between the two. These disparities are of considerable interest and relevance in terms of explaining the later development of party competition and democracy.[3]

The Nationalist Party and the government it established trace their origins directly to Sun Yat-sen's revolution and his political philosophy. This revolution was a democratic one, at least in form and intent. Philosophically, and in terms of the central role given to a political party, it was patterned after Western models of political change and political modernization of a democratic kind (though in many Western nations the formal development of parties followed democratic revolution). Though Sun became disappointed with the West for not supporting his efforts, he never abandoned Western political thought or Western democracy. He also knew democracy had to be delayed in its implementation in China because the Chinese people were not ready for it. Sun himself developed a political ideology, but that ideology (perhaps better described as merely a collection of political ideas) was not as systematic or as powerful and uncompromising as communism, at least as it took root in China a decade later.[4]

Following Sun's demise, Chiang Kai-shek assumed the mantle of power and supported the revolutionary cause. However, Chiang was not so much a democrat; rather, he was a pragmatist and a military leader. His ultimate goal was to unite China and make it a strong nation. Chiang was somewhat anti-Western in his perception of China's problems, as can be seen in his book *China's Destiny*. Still, he was pro-Western in his political thinking and came to depend upon ties with the West—notably through his wife and advisors. He also became anti-Communist (after the Chinese Communists made an attempt on his life and Chiang began to see them as enemies and traitors).

Chiang's political party, the Nationalist Party or Kuomintang (KMT), was structured after Leninist organizational patterns and may be called a Leninist party. However, it was not so clearly an elite party (as the Chinese Communist Party, or CCP) and was somewhat more tolerant of other political parties and party competition. The Nationalist Party's ideology was Sun's Three Principles of the People, but they were not of such overriding importance as the basic tenets of communism were to the CCP. The Nationalist Party was democratic in its outlook (though not in its style of rule for some time), unlike the CCP's view of democracy which requires the destruction of capitalism to put it into operation and advocated a dictatorship of the proletariat.[5]

Similarly, the KMT was not so determined to control the economy through central planning. In fact, its economic development scheme was very different: It used the free market and avoided too much central control (though one could argue that central control was not really feasible when the Nationalists controlled China anyway). Nor was the KMT and its police force interested in controlling the population beyond maintaining law and order and precluding the development of an opposition that might threaten the party and the government. From the very outset of its rule of China, the CCP endeavored to use its political authority to control the population in more than just a negative or punitive sense. It also sought to create a new society and used movements and campaigns to change the individual psychologically.

China, under the KMT from 1928 to 1949, was an authoritarian system. Since then, under communism, China has been a totalitarian system. There are big differences, especially noticeable in the realms of completeness or thoroughness of political control sought and attained by the two regimes and the degree to which the parties have accepted and now allow (in the case of Taiwan) political thinking and actions not exactly like their own.

When the Nationalist government moved to Taiwan in 1949, it encountered some significant changes in the political culture milieu in which it had to operate. China's was a bureaucratic political culture based, according to the well-known scholar Karl Wittfogel, on the control of water—or, as he says, a "hydraulic culture." In China, feudalism (a decentralized system politically and economically) was relegated to the status of historical record two centuries before

Christ. Taiwan, in contrast, did not develop a hydraulic culture; there are no rivers in Taiwan that damage agriculture and kill millions when they flood. Moreover, Taiwan is fragmented by mountains, making central government more difficult, and was ruled by Japan for fifty years from 1895–1945—a nation that had just recently (in the late 1860s) evolved out of feudalism and that retained many of the political characteristics of a post-feudal country.[6] To many students of Asian political development, this feudal heritage (from which Western democracies evolved) explains why Japan adjusted to the West quickly and efficiently while China did not. It may also explain Taiwan's recent success in democratization.

Taiwan was also historically quite cosmopolitan; it had ties with other nations and civilizations in the area. China was not cosmopolitan; it had been isolationist for centuries and remained so under communism. Similarly, Taiwan had a history of being ruled by foreign countries: Holland, China (though the term "colonization" may not be appropriate here), and Japan. It was also more eclectic in terms of religious thought. And, through trade with other countries in the area, it laid the groundwork for the development of capitalism may have been laid.[7] China, in contrast, was less influenced by foreign religious ideas (or at least more slowly, as in the case of Buddhism) and did not trade very much, considering itself self-sufficient economically or an autarky. Thus, China did not experience capitalism until much later.

After 1950, Taiwan had the advantage in terms of democratic political development because it was basically secure. When the Korean War started, the United States put the Seventh Fleet in the Taiwan Strait, precluding an invasion of Taiwan by Mao's forces. Taiwan also felt safe since, being an island, it could not be invaded easily, and it was generally less vulnerable to espionage, sabotage, and the like. (One should recall in this connection that democracy first evolved in England—a secure, island country. Then it grew in the United States, which was shielded from invasion by two oceans and bordered by weak countries.) In contrast to Taiwan, China was threatened (or so it perceived) by U.S. "imperialist" forces in Korea and elsewhere on China's periphery from 1950 on. It was also menaced by insecure boundaries: hostile Soviet forces on their long mutual border (incidentally the longest anywhere in the world) beginning in the late 1950s or early 1960s, and very insecure boundaries elsewhere. China, in fact, borders more countries with unnatural frontiers and has had more border disputes than any other nation in the world. It can be argued that the justification for its totalitarian political system lies to a considerable degree in China's physical insecurity, as witnessed by the nature of its various mobilization campaigns, the size of its standing military and militias, and tight social control that were all rationalized by external threats.[8]

In the early 1950s, both Chinas undertook land reform. In each, the political impact was deep and long-lasting. In Taiwan's case, land reform destroyed feudal society in the rural part of the country. It gave land to the farmers and provided them a stake in the political system. It increased agricultural productivity, thereby fostering urbanization (which will be discussed below) with its accompanying political impact. It is no coincidence that local elections and democracy in local politics began at this time.[9] In China, by way of contrast, land reform accentuated class differences—coinciding with a political purge of the landlord class, scapegoating, and policies of persecution of an enemy class by the Chinese Communist Party. It failed in most respects to create political awareness in terms of building a political community or in terms of individuals attaining a stake in the nation or the political process. Nor did it increase agricultural productivity. In short, the effect of land reform in China was not the creation of a civic culture or the dilution of authoritarian tendencies, but rather increased tension in the society, class struggle, and the continued need for centralized political control.[10]

It is also instructive to compare economic development in the two countries and its relationship to political change. Taiwan took off economically in the late 1960s and, over the next two-plus decades, had the fastest growing economy in the world. Economic growth based on a free market and foreign trade created a large middle class and a population aware of political systems and political change abroad. Growth with equity was particularly important in creating an interest in politics, voting, political change, political parties, and so on. The business community meanwhile became more politically influential, realizing that a free flow of information was essential to sustain rapid economic growth. Entrepreneurs thus provided the impetus for expanding civil and political freedoms. In other words, capitalism engendered democratic freedoms.[11] In China, economic growth was slow after the first few years or following a period of economic rehabilitation. In fact, through the late 1950s, 1960s, and even into the 1970s, the rate of expansion of China's economy fell below the world's average. Economic equality prevented a regression to class politics of the old style; yet the system's attraction to central planning created a new elite ruling class while it limited political change that economic development could have otherwise produced, particularly change of a democratic sort.

Social change that occurred during this same period can be seen as related to economic change; again, the situations in the two Chinas are very different. Land reform, higher productivity in the agricultural sector, and industrialization all engendered rapid urbanization in Taiwan—the fastest of any nation in the world during the 1960s and 1970s. Social mobility was tremendous. People learned about politics elsewhere in the world, especially in the Western democracies with whom they traded and visited. City political machines developed and new publications sprouted, resulting in a highly educated populace. The political interest groups that developed performed the functions of "interest aggregation and articulation" (to use the terms of political development theorists Gabriel A. Almond and Bingham Powell, Jr.). These things did not happen in China. There, political movements were launched to support the party (or one of its factions); most were not intended to produce genuine political participation, but rather forced participation. As these were started and halted capriciously, participants became cynical. Meanwhile, China's population remained 80 percent rural. Few people learned much about the rest of the world as few read foreign publications or traveled. In fact, in the 1970s, most people in China had not been 100 miles from their birthplace.

Recent Democratic Change in China and Taiwan

The recent drive toward political modernization in each of the two Chinas began at almost the same time. Perhaps one can identify the year 1978 as the watershed year for both. That year, Deng Xiaoping consolidated power in China and quickly began to put various reforms into practice. He oversaw the writing of a new constitution in February. Late in the year, "Democracy Wall" was launched, reflecting efforts by Deng to enlist public participation in political decision making and a new, or at least revised, practice of free speech.[12] At the same time, Taiwan was about to hold a significant national election that was to increase the number of the locally elected representatives (most were still representing areas in China) to the National Assembly and the Legislative Yuan. The election was canceled because the United States broke diplomatic relations with Taipei and moved its embassy to Beijing—thereby seriously undermining the credibility of the government and evoking public insecurity. Otherwise, 1978 might have been a turning point in the democratic political development of Taiwan.

One may argue that what happened after 1978 in the two Chinas was a product or result of earlier developments and that success or failure (and it failed in China and succeeded in Taiwan) was determined by previous conditions, developments, and events. Still, what transpired during the next ten years was important and instructive.

In 1979, the public demanded democracy in Taiwan in response to the loss of legitimacy (though this may be too strong a word) suffered by the Nationalist Party and the government after U.S. de-recognition. Democracy was seen as necessary to the nation's survival inasmuch as Taiwan needed to win support from the United States and the global community to fend off efforts by China to force negotiations that would, it was perceived, end Taiwan's sovereignty. Democracy and self-determination became almost synonymous. An opposition formed that advocated quick democratic reform and looked to Western democratic systems as its model. The opposition had the support of the Western media in these efforts, and its members knew this. (The Western media had long been a harsh critic of the government and ruling party.)[13]

The advocates of democracy became more radical. They began to push reform and independence for Taiwan and even challenged the right of the government and the Nationalist Party to rule. This kind of activity ended with the Kaohsiung Incident in December 1979, when a major protest demonstration turned violent. Exactly who provoked the violence is not quite clear, but a number of police were injured. In any case, the incident turned public opinion against the radical reformers and the government put their leaders in prison following trials a few months later.

The chain of events (the public support for reform and its change of heart when the protest turned violent) was cause for sober rethinking on the part of both sides during mid-1980. Both showed willingness to compromise, and in that context a new election law was written and preparations were made for a competitive national election in December. Scholars, including many from abroad, participated in rewriting the election law. Compromises or gentlemen's agreements were made behind the scenes. The most important were promises made by government to allow free speech during the campaign and permit an open and free election—if the opposition would not advocate overthrowing the government or try to proclaim independence.

The December 1980 election, though still a supplementary one (many seats still represented districts in China and therefore were not elective), was unprecedented in terms of the openness, the lively campaign, and the competition. The Nationalist Party vied with *tang wai* (meaning "outside the party") candidates who acted together with a platform and group objectives and which behaved like a political party (though forming new parties remained illegal). Voters were astonished by candidates' criticisms of the government, ruling party, and top leaders of both. This election, to many observers, was a turning point. Taiwan now had democracy, many said. Others contended that it was an "election holiday," a show to impress the United States and the Western media.[14]

In 1983, after another national election that was at least as open and competitive as the election in 1980, no one spoke of the 1980 election as an "election holiday." Competitive national elections had become institutionalized.

In December 1986, Taiwan held the first two-party competitive election ever held in a Chinese nation. Earlier that year *tang wai* politicians had met and established the Democratic Progressive Party, a true opposition party. (Two small parties had run candidates in previous elections but were not really competing with the Nationalist Party.) After this election, observers said that Taiwan no longer had a one-party system.[15]

In 1987, Taiwan terminated martial law. Protest marches and demonstrations increased. In early 1988, President Chiang Ching-kuo died and Lee Teng-hui became president. He was the country's first locally born—that is, Taiwanese—president, something that the critics of Taiwan's "authoritarian government" said would never happen. The government had been led up to this time by Chinese who fled to Taiwan with Chiang Kai-shek in 1949 and who constituted only 15 percent of Taiwan's population. At the same time, a new press law went into effect, allowing new newspapers to publish and old ones to print larger papers (which they could not do before). Later that year the Nationalist Party held its Thirteenth Congress and adopted democratic rules for party business, something many parties in Western democracies have yet to do.

In December 1989, Taiwan held another national election. This time, according to virtually every newspaper in the country, the opposition party won. Though the Democratic Progressive Party did not get more votes or have more of its candidates elected, its performance improved so much over past elections that it put a sufficient number of representatives in the Legislative Yuan to propose legislation. And it won executive positions in enough counties that it had jurisdiction over 40 percent of the population—including Taipei County, the seat of the national government. Some said this election had brought true democracy to Taiwan.[16] Whether or not Taiwan is now a democracy is debatable. Nevertheless, the rapid and remarkable progress it has made in that direction is clear.

This has not been so in China. There, democracy made some progress between 1978 and 1988. But this improvement was temporary, or at best it was set back in 1989. Why? There appear to be a number of explanations.

Some observers note that the Chinese people spoke out for democracy in April 1976 after Zhou Enlai's death. There were also massive public rallies in favor of political reforms. But this public outcry had little impact. Deng, who was then the party's strongest advocate for democracy, was purged. After Mao's death in the fall, a power struggle ensued. Mao's successor was decided by force.

The Gang of Four (Mao's closest supporters) lost. Deng made a gradual comeback over the next two years, and there seemed to be new hope of democratic reform. Deng encouraged democratic discussions and used "Democracy Wall" to his advantage—to catch his opponents off guard and to disgrace Mao and the party Left.[17]

Because of the factional nature of Chinese politics in Beijing, pro-democracy movements for the most part became factional struggles. Various factions advocated democracy, but they had different definitions. None defined democracy as it was defined in the West. To the Maoists and the Left, it meant egalitarianism. To the Right, it meant promoting economic development. Debate ensued about pluralist democracy, but most saw it as causing confusion and therefore as dangerous. Many said that democracy did not mean people influencing the government, but rather government acting in the interest of the people (which could hardly be distinguished from benevolent autocracy).[18]

Deng, however, was more an advocate of democracy in the Western sense than the Left. He argued that democracy (meaning private ownership, the opportunity to travel, and the right to better oneself economically) was necessary if the free market was to work. People had to be allowed to speak freely, to move freely, and to have money and invest. The rightist reformers sought to get the party cadres out of the management of the factories. In the rural areas, they promoted private plots and individual ownership—in opposition to Marx and Mao. Deng sought to transfer political power from the party to the government and from Beijing to provincial and local governments. He even went so far as to propose competitive elections with more than one candidate for each position in government.

But several times Deng was compelled move back to the left politically rather than push democratic reform further. He did this in 1983 and 1986. He did it again in June 1989, when the student-led Democracy Movement threatened to promote radical political change. The events of May and June 1989, in fact, strengthened the party Left. Why? In the context of serious unrest, insecurity, and what leftist leaders warned was the possibility of anarchy and even the breakup of China, the party left could play upon xenophobia and fear among party leaders and the population. What followed can be easily understood with this situation in mind: The military, using tanks and machine guns, cleared Tiananmen Square of the demonstrators, killing a large number, and ended the democracy campaign.[19]

Several things are noticeably different about China's "democratic experiment" as compared to Taiwan's. China was penetrated by Western ideas and thinking only to a very small extent. Democracy was debated in the Communist context. It was over-idealized and distorted by the rightist reformers. True democratic thinking and debate never really got started in China. Discussions about democracy were limited to intellectuals and elites. The masses got involved in a meaningful way only in the economic side of reform. And because of the anti-intellectual feeling in China created by communism, intellectual debate did not gain credibility. Deng at first (for a while after 1978) supported the intellectuals, but when he was labeled an ultraconservative for trying to reinstitute the imperial system, he allowed their standard of living, prestige, and influence to fall. Perhaps Deng did not like them anyway.

Taiwan, unlike China, was very penetrated by Western influence by the late 1970s. The ruling party or government could not dilute or alter democratic debate very much. There was too much information to control. Too many people had been abroad. Too many could simply call or write people in other countries to learn about democracy. In China, few students who studied abroad had returned. Thus, China had not been penetrated sufficiently by Western ideas. The other conditions just mentioned were absent. China did not need the free flow of information to such an extent.

Another factor was the Western media, which had been very critical of the government of Taiwan, some say ultra-critical. In contrast, it had been an apologist for the government of China. Most reporters liked Mao. The media generally ignored China's abominable human rights record. It gave China the benefit of the doubt. The U.S. government acted in a similar way. Hence, China was never under the kind of pressure to change that Taiwan was.

Taiwan had been the subject of media criticism for many years. In the case of the United States Taiwan was the focus of official government criticism, particularly by the Congress. After 1979, this was in a sense "legalized" in the Taiwan Relations Act. This law, passed by Congress, restored Taiwan's sovereignty but demanded democracy and a better human rights condition in return.[20] Opposition politicians in Taiwan were encouraged by this and became more active. Competitive elections and a competitive party system followed. Meanwhile, the U.S. government put U.S.-China relations in a special category; a "China Card" would help the United States offset the growing Soviet military threat. China's authoritarianism thus was not a matter of overriding concern.

Conclusions

In this essay, two sorts of variables relating to the success or failure of democratic movements in the two Chinas were identified: older and newer—with newer factors conditioned by the older. The evidence, in fact, seems to indicate that democracy is a long-range process, or at least it requires the laying of a foundation. In short, Sun Yat-sen appears to have been right in saying that the Chinese people must be trained and educated before democracy could work.

It is also easy to argue from the two Chinas' experience with democracy that ideology and the type of political system a nation espouses affect its ability to democratize. Communism is an anti-Western belief system. In many ways, Mao made it even more anti-Western. It would perforce then seem that this polity was a rejection of democracy, or at a minimum, a negative response to democracy. Mao, in fact, said as much. In contrast, this anti-Western sentiment was never present in the government or the Nationalist Party of Taiwan, at least not to the point that it constituted a refutation of democracy. Democracy was delayed, yes; but it was never repudiated in Taiwan.

Similarly, a political system that strives to attain complete control is antithetical to the development of democracy. The people must be given choices and they must be allowed information to make choices. If their time is taken by campaigns and movements, and sources of knowledge and information are limited, they cannot make rational (i.e., democratic) choices. Similarly, if they are pushed to spy on each other in an atomization process that fosters mutual alienation, a sense of community does not develop. This happened in China; it did not happen in Taiwan.

Geography and history are also important variables. The geographical factor, which had facilitated bureaucratic rule in China, disappeared once the Nationalists went to Taiwan. In China, Marxism reinforced China's bureaucratic tradition—as even Mao admitted. The political culture in Taiwan was also different because of its geographical differences from China. Furthermore, the Nationalists emphasized different aspects of Chinese history than did the Communists. They wanted to preserve China's humanist tradition, which Mao wanted to destroy. The Nationalists did not endeavor to preserve China's bureaucratic tradition; perhaps the Communists did not want to either, but they did.

Taiwan was also in a secure place from the 1950s on. It hardly seems a coincidence that Washington's decision to place the Seventh Fleet in the Taiwan Strait (thereby shielding Taiwan from invasion) was followed shortly after by Taiwan's first island-wide election. It is likewise noteworthy that the Taiwan Relations Act guaranteed Taiwan's security in very broad terms, and Taiwan's first competitive national election was held the next year, marking the beginning of the most meaningful period of democratization in Taiwan's history. China in contrast has been insecure, and its political leadership has reflected that. It demonstrated that vividly in June 1989 when it crushed the democracy movement and massacred students in Tiananmen Square. The hard-liners who made the fateful decisions declared that anarchy was threatening China. They conveyed the idea (and most Chinese understand this very clearly) that they needed to do what they did because chaos could lead to the breakup of China from within or invasion from without because of weakness and lack of unity. Thus, the strongman approach was needed, and, in that context, democracy was dangerous.

The democratization of Taiwan and the absence (or failure) of it in China seem also to reflect the level and kind of economic development in the two Chinas. Western scholars have argued this for years. But the evidence never seemed so clear or the cases so revealing until recent years. In Taiwan, democracy followed economic development. From the mid-1960s and into the 1980s, Taiwan developed economically faster than any other country in the world. It developed politically (democratized) faster in the 1980s than any other country in the world. The type of economic development also seems relevant: free market principles, export-led expansion, and growth with equity.

In China, economic growth was slow after the period of post-war recovery and democratization did not germinate. China experienced rapid economic growth from 1978 to 1988—and this clearly gave rise to democratic "urges." But economic growth occurred too suddenly. Alternatively, it was the wrong kind of growth. It was capitalist growth in a Communist political system which created serious economic inequality, to which China was hardly accustomed (though it was present in China's past), among other problems. Thus, it engendered popular resentment rather than fostering the growth of a middle class.

Social change in Taiwan followed land reform, urbanization, industrialization, prosperity (evenly distributed), consumerism, and an industrialization of the economy. This change was quite natural, not contrived. Social change in China was led by the Chinese Communist Party, and it was not in the direction of democracy. It was, in reality, very superficial and meaningless social change, save for the suffering it caused.

Another factor that relates to the growth of a democratic culture: Taiwan was quite cosmopolitan from early in its history. Later it became a highly penetrated country (especially by the Western democracies). China was not cosmopolitan. It was isolated historically and in recent times—until 1978. Under Mao, China practiced isolationism in the name of self-reliance. Related to this, Taiwan experienced considerable international pressure to improve its human rights record and to put into practice the democratic rights in its constitution. The American connection afforded this pressure. In fact, it is fair to say that Taiwan is one of the few countries to have had a competitive, two-party election without a Western democratic mother country to oversee it, though, the U.S. role was very similar to that of a democratic mother country. China was not pressured. In fact, its human rights abuses were ignored like no other country in the world. It was not asked to reform as Sino-American relations became more meaningful because, to many, communism was a reformed or progressive system. To others in the United States, China was important for strategic reasons, and interference in China's domestic affairs or even criticism of China was hence not welcomed.

The evolution of political parties followed these developments. In Taiwan, the Nationalist Party was conditioned not to allow competition, but it did not seek to attain total control over the society. This situation gave way to the KMT allowing some, only nominal at first, competition, and, as conditions changed and outside pressure influenced Taiwan more, to accepting real party competition. The Nationalist Party's success in engineering rapid economic growth and social progress gave it the confidence to allow a challenge to the one-party system. In China, the Communist Party sought to gain unlimited authority and control from the outset. China, being a large country, and certainly one difficult to rule, lacking modern means of transportation and communications to a large extent, continued to strive for greater and greater control. Frustration gave rise to power struggles; so did the lack of open debate on issues and the closing of the decision making process from public view. China's poor record in economic development further caused a lack of confidence within the ranks of the Chinese Communist Party.

Political party competition played a vital role in the democratization process in Taiwan. In contrast, an effort to allow party competition in China under Deng was viewed as a ploy. The party left saw it as a means to weaken its strength. Thus it caused the factional struggle in the party to escalate. Even the rightist reformers in the Chinese Communist Party to a considerable degree saw competition as a threat to the authority of the party; thus the left backlash in the spring of 1989 had support on the right.

In final summation, the two Chinas present very good evidence of the factors that lead to or prevent democratization. The comparison, because of the cultural similarities, helps demonstrate the verity of the causative factors cited in a way that looking at other countries, even in large numbers, would not demonstrate. Thus, the two Chinas provide an unusual model for arguing the relevance of certain variables in political party development and their importance in the democratization process.

Endnotes

1. Gabriel A. Almond and G. Bingham Powell, Jr., *Comparative Politics: System, Process, and Policy* (Boston: Little, Brown, 1978), pp. 220–224.

2. For a theoretical discussion of these issues, see Gabriel A. Almond and Sidney Verba, eds., *The Civic Culture Revisited* (Boston: Little, Brown, 1980) Robert Alford, *Party and Society* (Chicago: Rand McNally, 1963), Robert A. Dahl, *Polyarchy: Participation and Opposition* (New Haven: Yale University Press, 1971), Maurice Duverger, *Political Parties* (New York: John Wiley & Sons, 1955), Joseph La Palombara and Myron Weiner, *Political Parties and Political Development* (Princeton: Princeton University Press, 1966), Anthony Kubek, *Modernizing China: A Comparative Analysis of the Two Chinas*, (Washington DC: Regnery Gateway, 1987).

3. Immanuel C. Y. Hsu, *The Rise of Modern China* (New York: Oxford University Press), chapter 20.

4. James, A. Gregor, *Ideology and Development: Sun Yat–sen and the Economic History of Taiwan.* (Berkeley, CA: Institute of East Asian Studies, 1981).

5. Ralph N. Clough, *Island China* (Cambridge: Harvard University Press, 1978), chapter 2.

6. John F. Copper, Taiwan: *Nation-State or Province?* (Boulder, CO: Westview, 1990), pp. 53–55.

7. Ibid.

8. Arthur Huck, *The Security of China* (New York: Columbia University Press, 1970).

9. Copper, *Taiwan: Nation-State or Province?* pp. 42–43.

10. Stephen W. Mosher, *Broken Earth: The Rural Chinese* (New York: Free Press, 1983).

11. See John F. Copper, *A Quiet Revolution: Political Development in the Republic of China* (Lanham MD: University Press of America, 1988), chapters 2 and 3.

12. See Andrew J. Nathan, *China's Crisis* (New York: Columbia University Press, 1990), and Andrew J. Nathan, *Chinese Democracy* (New York: Alfred A. Knopf, 1985).

13. John F. Copper and George P. Chen, *Taiwan's Elections: Political Development and Democratization in the Republic of China* (Baltimore: University of Maryland Law School, 1984), chapter 3.

14. Ibid, chapter 5.

15. Copper, *Taiwan: Nation-State or Province?* chapter 3.

16. Ibid, chapter 5.

17. Nathan, *China's Crisis*, chapter 2.

18. Ibid.

19. Chu-yuan Cheng, *Behind the Tiananmen Massacre: Social, Political and Economic Ferment in China* (Boulder, CO: Westview, 1990), chapter 3.

20. John F. Copper, *China Diplomacy: The Washington, Taipei, Beijing Triangle* (Boulder, CO: Westview, 1991), chapter 3.

Chapter Nine
The KMT's 13th Party Congress: Democratizing the Party

The Nationalist Party, or Kuomintang (KMT), held its 13th Party Congress from July 7 to 13, 1988. More than 10,000 people attended the opening ceremony, including 1,209 party delegates. There were more than a thousand foreign dignitaries present, representing fifty-seven nations. KMT leaders invited representatives of foreign political parties for the first time. Closed circuit television provided a close-up view of the main speakers to all in the Lin Kuo Stadium where the meeting started. In addition to the pomp and ceremony, Taiwan's ruling party also undertook serious reform that many felt was necessary if the party were to keep pace with the rapid democratization the nation had experience in the past decade.

The venue of the Congress changed the next day. Just outside Taipei in Yangmingshan, substantive meetings began. A new party chairman, Central Committee and the Central Committee Standing Committee were elected. A new Party Advisory Committee was appointed. The ruling party amended its charter and adopted a new platform. Major decisions were made in the form of resolutions and policies.

The KMT had not had a congress for seven years. Much had happened in the interim. The nation's economy had continued to grow at a frantic rate; in fact, so much so that the Republic of China (ROC) was on the verge of becoming a developed country. In addition, Taiwan was the envy of the world for its huge foreign exchange surplus. Significant political change had occurred: a two-party election for the first time in Chinese history, the lifting of martial law (or the Emergency Decree), new regulations allowing the importation of books and magazines from the People's Republic of China and even visits there, and much more. Other reforms had been promised, including ending the ban on new parties and reform of the elected bodies of government. Most important of all, in January, the party's leader (and president of the Republic of China), Chiang Ching-kuo, died.

Vice President Lee Teng-hui became president after Chiang Ching-kuo's death. He was subsequently chosen acting chairman of the KMT. At this congress he was officially elected chairman. This and other events, particularly the composition of the party's new Central Standing Committee, signaled a transfer of power to the native-born Chinese, or Taiwanese. Party rules were also changed. Official party goals were altered.

Even longtime critics of the ROC declared that the meeting was a turning point in the democratization of Taiwan. Others said party democratization was in overdue since reforms had made the polity democratic everywhere else. Certainly, the 13th Party Congress may be regarded by future historians as an important watershed in the nation's political development process and the push toward democracy. In fact, Taiwan may be extending the idea of democracy to include party rules and procedures, internal decision-making processes, the selection of party leaders, and more. Many Western democracies have not done this.

In the following pages I will examine the precursory events, especially political developments, leading up to the 13th Party Congress; the changes made in rules and the party's platform and policies; and the composition of the party's leadership after the congress. I will attempt to demonstrate that this meeting was indeed a historic event and that it will have a major impact on the nation's political future.

Prelude to the 13th Party Congress

The Kuomintang traces its history to several revolutionary organizations founded by Sun Yat-sen and his supporters before and after the turn of the century. The most important were the Hsing Chung Hui (Society for the Rebuilding of China) and the Tung Meng Hui (Society for the Common Cause) established in 1894 (in Honolulu) and 1905 (in Tokyo), respectively.

Because of the KMT's origins and the composition of its base of support plus its opposition to efforts to reestablish monarchy after the fall of the Manchu government, party leaders perceived it as a revolutionary organization rather than a "democratic party." This was also confirmed by Sun's belief that China was not yet ready for democracy. He advocated a period of "tutelage," meaning that the nation was to have an authoritarian system before a democratic government could be realized.[1] From 1937 to 1945, the revolutionary style and structure of the KMT were strongly supported by its leaders and members in order to wage war effectively against Japan and, subsequently, to continue the struggle against the Chinese Communists.

That the KMT did not later welcome party competition mirrored its revolutionary origins as well as the influence of Soviet advisers and the Leninist model of party organization. This attitude persisted after the Nationalists were defeated and fled to Taiwan, because KMT leaders viewed the struggle with the Communists as continuing after 1949. They also faced a less than receptive local population that they perceived had to be taught to become "anti-Communist fighters." Also, the military's influence in the party was strong.

Though Taiwan had a one-party system which the KMT dominated, it was not a totalitarian system. Party careerists did not usually rise quickly, and there was some separation of powers in practice between the party and the government. Policies in the realms of economic planning, military strategy, and foreign affairs tended to be made outside the party hierarchy. Finally, the KMT was more a mass party than a Communist-style elite party. Of the adult population, 20 percent (or one-third of adult males) were members; this diluted the prestige of the Party when compared to elite parties.[2]

The KMT, moreover, actively pursued party reform after moving to Taiwan. KMT leaders admitted responsibility for the defeat by the Communists. They perceived that their survival, as well as that of the country, depended upon broad public support, constitutionalism, and democracy. Thus, repairing and changing the party was rather easy. In addition, most of the less loyal and corrupt party members had already defected or sought refuge elsewhere.

A year after moving to Taiwan, the KMT oversaw the first island-wide election in Taiwan. It also launched a land reform program that led directly to the demise of the feudal social and political system in rural Taiwan and set in motion democratic trends in local politics. Economic growth that benefited all segments of the society was set as the primary goal of economic development plans.

Most KMT leaders, however, did not accept direct challenges to their authority. They did not allow new political parties to form. Independent politicians who became popular were regarded as a threat. Similarly, the party maintained control over the media and used the police and intelligence network to maintain control. The political system was described by most outside observers as an authoritarian one. Moreover, the KMT was for all intents and purposes an exclusivist party that few Taiwanese joined; it was led by and composed largely of mainland Chinese.

By the early 1970s, however, the KMT began to change radically—going far beyond the reforms instituted after relocating to Taiwan. The party needed to respond to economic development, which had produced a large and growing middle class, rapid urbanization, vast social change, and external pressures to democratize. Taipei also needed global support to maintain its legitimacy in the international community. This was particularly true after the United States broke diplomatic relations with Taipei in 1979. Finally, the United States wanted Taiwan to democratize in order to justify continued friendly and close ties, and Taipei responded in a positive way.[3]

Since Taiwan's economic development strategy had been founded on free enterprise and a free market, for it to continue to work, or work more efficiently, the political system had to be decentralized. The government and the KMT also had to allow greater political freedoms and liberties. Economic expansion was likewise led by trade—mostly with Western, capitalist democracies. Economic growth, in fact, had already had the effect of spreading democratic ideals and linking continued economic success to increased political liberties and less government control. The penetration of Taiwan by foreign, especially Western, political thought and information similarly increased demands for democracy.

The party's initial response to the need for political modernization was to get rid of corruption in the party and government. After Chiang Ching-kuo became premier in 1972, this became a stated goal of the Party. CCK, as he was fondly known, ordered a crackdown on corruption in the government and jailed violators—even some of his own relatives. He also launched an "affirmative action" program to bring native-born Chinese, or Taiwanese, into the party. The KMT, in fact, began aggressively recruiting Taiwanese, and soon it became a party representing the whole population rather than a party of refugees.[4]

By the late 1970s, the KMT was widely perceived as a party that was actively promoting democratic political development. It continued to decentralize power. Corruption was no longer a serious problem (about the same as in most Western democracies). Likewise, the KMT became a party that represented different political views (with traditionalistic and progressive factions becoming evident) and virtually all segments of the population of Taiwan. In local politics the party continued to promote democracy by mediating factional struggle and promoting Sun Yat-sen's political philosophy and constitutionalism, and this gave the party genuine local bases of support throughout the island.[5]

In 1980, the KMT promoted the first competitive election at the national level in Taiwan. Party and government officials had, in advance, met with opposition leaders to work out differences on election rules and fairness. In the months leading up to the election, the KMT allowed independent politicians to organize. Independent opposition politicians became for all intents and purposes a political party—known as the *tang wai*, or "outside the party." Observers of the election called it open and free, and unprecedented. They also said it resembled Western democratic elections. *Tang wai* candidates criticized the KMT and the government. They assailed the one-party system and KMT "monopoly" pre-rogatives. They demanded more democracy. The campaign was full of antics. But all of this contributed to the feeling of democracy at work.[6]

Some thought December 1980 was an "election holiday" and that the performance would not be repeated; they said it was for show. They were wrong. In 1983 another national election (minus the National Assembly election) was just as competitive and free. Then, in 1985, nationwide local elections followed the democratic pattern and style already established. Party (or more accurately, KMT versus *tang wai*) competition again characterized the campaigning.[7]

In March 1986 President Chiang Ching-kuo announced that the ban on political parties would be dropped and martial law lifted. Six months later the *tang wai* became a party, taking the name Democratic Progressive Party (DPP). The 1986 election thus was a two-party election. It was the first such election ever held among Chinese people in any China—including the People's Republic of China, Hong Kong, and Singapore.[8]

The next year, in mid-1987, martial law was abolished. The new State Security Law that replaced it further reduced the role of the military in politics (which had been in decline for some time). The new law also enhanced press freedom and changed Taiwan's legal system in some important ways. Most important was the psychological impact of ending martial law, which had sym-bolized the authoritarian politics of the past. Terminating it, to many, signaled a new era of democratic politics.[9]

Other reforms followed. Citizens of the Republic of China were subse-quently allowed to purchase goods, including publications, from the People's Republic of China. They were even allowed to visit there—which they did in large numbers. Trade contracts were initiated with the Eastern European Com-munist countries. Taipei became more active in international organizations. A new foreign aid program was proposed—which some thought would help preclude Taiwan's diplomatic isolation. Actions were taken to liberalize trade and lower tariffs.

By 1988, then, the KMT had overseen major efforts to transform the polity of the Republic of China from an authoritarian to a democratic one. Yet, it seemed that the party itself had fallen behind in this process. The KMT was far from democratic in its rules and procedures for conducting party business. It did not select its leaders in a democratic fashion. It could be argued that political parties need not be democratic for democracy to work. This is the case in many democracies. But Taiwan had a dominant party, and probably would have for some years. Thus, for democracy to work better, the majority ruling party had to institute democratic changes within. Reform was also essential for the KMT to maintain its credibility and to set guidelines for continuing the democratization of the political system. At least this was the view of progressives in the party.

Nationalist Party Reform

Soon after the KMT and the Nationalist government moved to Taiwan, internal Party reform was given top priority. This led to ridding the party of lazy, disloyal, and corrupt officials and those who were simply careerists in the bad sense of the word. Reform of various other kinds followed. In the 1970s, reform continued, consisting of improving party efficiency, eliminating corruption that remained, and "Taiwanizing" the party membership. Still, the KMT's organization and decision-making process (democratic centralism) did not change. Party rules also remained fundamentally the same. The locus of power in the party clearly was unaffected by reform. The KMT penetrated and controlled the government. Chiang Kai-shek was both president and head of the party.

This remained the case after Chiang Ching-kuo assumed the presidency in 1978, though there had been a three-year hiatus when this situation did not technically prevail. Critics not only spoke of a monopoly or concentration of power, a situation wherein the party and the government were inseparable, and all important decisions were made in the party (as in Communist countries), but also of a "Chiang Dynasty."[10]

CCK, however, was determined that "real" democracy would be his legacy. In 1986 he vowed to prevent any of his relatives from assuming power—and sent his son Chiang Hsiao-wu to Singapore to be sure that he was not present during a succession crisis. He also moved to ensure that the military could not grasp power following his demise or during a debilitating ailment. He transferred military leaders frequently; some he sent to embassy posts abroad. He brought back a confidant and reformist, Lee Huan, and put him in control of party business (as secretary general of the KMT).[11]

In the wake of CCK's death in January 1988, "progressives" or "reformists" in the KMT gain influence. CCK had laid the groundwork. He had stood for reform, and after his death, owing to the tremendous respect that both party members and the population had for him, his reformist goals could not be repudiated. The "old guard" party officials similarly did not want to be seen as blocking reform, since they could then be blamed for any loss in popular support for the KMT and specifically for a decline in electoral support in the coming 1989 Legislative Yuan election.

There was, however, an attempt by the hardliners to maintain a "balance" in the party leadership and to prevent reform from going too far. After CCK's death, some top Party leaders moved to block President Lee Teng-hui's assumption of the party chairmanship. They argued for a postponement of a decision on this matter until the party congress. Some proposed that the chairmanship should rotate. Deputy Secretary General of the KMT James Soong, however, asserted that not choosing a real party chairman immediately would send the wrong signals abroad and would be a cause of political instability and economic uncertainty at a critical juncture. His proposal, supported by the premier and other KMT leaders, to elect President Lee the acting chairman won.[12]

Meanwhile, party rules were changed so that delegates to the Thirteenth Party Congress would be chosen by U.S.-style primaries and caucuses. As it turned out, 60 percent of the delegates to the 13th Party Congress were chosen by these democratic methods. Hence, the composition of the congress, unlike previous congresses, was different, as was the delegates' perceptions about their charge and role at the congress.[13]

After the opening ceremony of the 13th Party Congress, the primary task of the first plenary session was to elect a party chairman. President Lee Teng-hui, acting chairman of the KMT, was the obvious choice. He was voted party chairman by acclamation. Several delegates protested this kind of election, suggesting that a secret ballot should be used instead. Eight delegates didn't support Lee's candidacy with their votes, though they told the press later that they wanted him to be party chairman. They didn't like the less than democratic procedure for picking the chairman. Their actions were unprecedented and seemed to reflect an uncompromising mood in radically democratizing party rules.[14]

Later, when it came time to select the Central Committee, Party Chairman Lee Teng-hui submitted a list of 180 names. Delegates subsequently submitted their own list of 180 names—including most, but not all, of the candidates recommended by the chairman. In the final voting, thirty-three candidates nominated by the Chairman were not elected, notwithstanding the fact that—reflecting the mood of reform—the Chairman's list had included many new names (in fact, less than half members of the previous Central Committee) of which a number were young, progressive candidates.[15] In addition, a ranking of new Central Committee members based on the number of votes they received was made public. This ranking was significantly different from the order of candidates on the list submitted by the party chairman.

In several cases the discrepancy reflected an apparent effort by the delegates to embarrass or undermine the positions of certain officials. Most obvious was Premier Yu Kuo-hua, who was ranked thirty-fifth by popular vote. He was portrayed by progressives as being reactionary and an opponent of reform. Shen Chang-huan, secretary general of the Presidential Office, was another. There were several more. Some interpreted the withholding of support to be a call for their resignations. Others said it was the reformist mood of the meeting and meant nothing more than that.[16]

The importance of vote-getting, because of the ranking in the Central Committee by the number of votes won, was of such importance that candidates spent considerable time and effort lobbying delegates—even to the degree of talking with them, passing out cards and resumes, and requesting support during speeches or business meetings. One KMT member complained that the meeting had "turned into a market."[17]

The old guard pushed a proposal to choose a vice chairman of the party. CCK's only brother, Chiang Wei-kuo, chairman of the National Security Council, was advanced for that job. Some observers said this was intended to offset "reformer" Lee Teng-hui's influence. Both the intent and what then transpired are unclear. In any event, it was decided that the party would not have a vice chairman. In the event of the death or incapacitation of the party chairman, an acting chairman would be elected. Probably the decision not to have a vice chairman was influenced by the mood of the congress, its drive toward democracy, and the end of the "Chiang Dynasty" (notwithstanding the mood of respect shown for CCK).[18]

Party rules and procedures, in spite of the mood of the congress, which overwhelmingly favored party reform, cannot be said to have been completely or radically altered, however. In some important respects procedural rules were not changed. Elsewhere compromises were made.

The procedures for picking the Central Committee's Standing Committee, the real decision-making body of the party, were not altered. Some observers opined that compromises made earlier ensured the timely resignation of the older members of the Central Standing Committee and favored ethnic Taiwanese in the composition of this body. In exchange, changes in the procedures for picking the Central Standing Committee were not made and some other reforms were not discussed. Others offered alternative explanations. Some said that the democratization of the party had gone far enough and that the reformists had already accomplished essentially what they hoped for and consequently they did not want to push their agenda further.[19]

The party's Advisory Council was given somewhat increased powers as a trade-off for inducing older, less reform-minded members of the Central Standing Committee to retire and join the Advisory Council. It now has a more formal role in decision making. It can block controversial decisions if a solid majority of its members oppose certain policies or actions.[20]

Lastly, the issue of reforming the elected bodies of government (the National Assembly, the Legislative Yuan, and the Control Yuan) to make them represent Taiwan only, and the proposal to change the mayoral appointments of Taipei and Kaohsiung cities to elective offices, were not discussed seriously. President Lee had promised in February that he would act on both of these issues. Apparently some, or many, of those advocating quick democratization wanted to let him have a free rein and act outside the environment of heated debate.[21] Alternatively, debate about this issue may have faltered because many delegates were too busy rallying support for their own higher ranking in the Central Committee. Clearly "progressive" delegates were busy with other matters and had reached compromises behind the scenes.

New Personnel

A long-time observer of Taiwan's politics commented at the time of the congress that the most important changes made at that meeting involved people, not politics.[22] The foreign press concurred with this opinion. This also seems a reasonable view, if, as suggested above, compromises were made on issues in order to get more progressives and more Taiwanese into important positions in the party.

The most important personnel change was, of course, Lee Teng-hui. Lee is Taiwanese and was viewed as a progressive. He was also considered competent and qualified and the right person for the job. He was popular. Even the main opposition party, the Democratic Progressive Party, publicly applauded the appointment of President Lee to head the KMT, as well as most other personnel changes at the congress.[23]

Many said the election of President Lee Teng-hui to the post of party chairman was a foregone conclusion. Shortly after he became president, an *Independence Evening Post* poll showed over 93 percent of the public supported him as head of state.[24] In the January Central Standing Committee meeting, he was unanimously elected acting chairman. Inasmuch as this maneuvering took place before the party congress—party reformers dominating that meeting—he was seen by nearly all party members as the person who would become the party's standard bearer. In short, there was no serious contending candidate.

Yet many observers had predicted that a Taiwanese would never be either president or chairman of the Party. Holding both positions was seen as out of the question. Just months earlier, political pundits had predicted a "balance of power" between Taiwanese and Mainland Chinese with one in the presidency and the other controlling the party. It was certainly not anticipated, even by insiders, that a Taiwanese, or even one person, would hold both positions.[25]

Lee's popularity and his success in "consolidating" political power can be explained both by his personal leadership abilities and the pressure to localize or "Taiwanize" the political system. Lee had an excellent background: education in Japan and the United States (including a Ph.D. degree from Cornell University), work on land reform, experience in local politics, and loyalty to the party. He was highly respected both when he was governor of Taiwan and as vice president. He was trusted by both Taiwanese and top KMT officials (except for a few). He was the man of the hour when Chiang Ching-Kuo died. Also very much in his favor was the fact that there was fear of centrifugal tendencies and political instability in the wake of CCK's death.[26]

Lee was viewed by most party members as a reformist, as a leader who would promote economic development and bridge the gap between Taiwanese and Mainland Chinese and between other groups in the society. He was seen as a supporter of both business and labor. He had a good image with the press and abroad. Most of all, he was thought of as CCK's successor.

The election of Lee to the party chairmanship after he had become President had another effect; it offset recent policies that favored closer ties with the mainland. In other words, Lee, a Taiwanese president, reflected what some in Beijing had long feared—that Taiwanese would eventually gain control of the political system and forge a permanent separation from China. Yet policy decisions coming out of the congress sent the opposite signal. In other words, there was a balance in terms of what the congress did. (This point will be discussed in the next section.)

The subsequent election of the party Central Committee is also revealing, both in terms of those receiving high ranking and the data on the composition of the body. Party Secretary Lee Huan, a well-known reformist, received the largest number of votes. Former Premier Sun Yuan-suan, renowned for his progressive policies that promoted democracy, received the second highest number. Sun, who was still partly paralyzed from a stroke in 1985, received support almost solely because of his reformist image. Few thought he would be an active leader again. Deputy Secretary General James Soong, who with courage (some say daring) had advocated that President Lee be voted acting chairman of the party in January, came in third.[27] He was also considered a reformist.

Lin Yang-kang, president of the Judicial Yuan, and Wu Poh-hsiung, minister of interior, received the fourth and fifth largest votes, respectively. Both are Taiwanese. Both have been touted for higher positions.

Also ranking among the top ten vote getters were (in order) John Chang, vice minister of foreign affairs; Chiu Chuang-huan, governor of Taiwan Province; Li Tchong-koei, director of the China Youth Corps; Frederick Chien, then director of the Coordination Council for North American Affairs (Taiwan's "embassy" in Washington); and Huang Tsun-chiu, president of the Control Yuan.[28]

John Chang, one of CCK's sons, was ranked sixth. His twin brother ranked eleventh. Another of CCK's sons (this one carrying his name) ranked fifteenth. CCK's eldest legitimate son withdrew his name and was not elected to the Central Committee, although some had speculated that he would make a bid for a high position in the wake of his father's death. He returned from his post in Singapore for the Congress, but his presence was low-keyed. Li Tchong-koei, number eight, became the highest ranking female in the new Central Committee. Some said the victories Vice Foreign Minister John Chang and Frederick Chien (the eighth top vote getter), both of whom outranked the foreign minister, indicated pending personal shifts (which subsequently took place).

These rankings show a balance between Taiwanese and Mainlanders and between younger and older party leaders. Yet all of the top ten vote getters were either progressives or Taiwanese; no old guard Mainland Chinese party member received a high vote count.

A number of newly elected Central Committee members received a noticeably higher or lower number of votes than anticipated. Lee Huan, secretary general of the party, won 92 percent of delegates' support.[29] His popularity was widely known, but it turned out to be even more than expected. President Lee had nominated Shieh Tung-min, a Taiwanese and former vice president, for the number one slot. But Shieh's vote count was low, mainly because he was not seen as a progressive or as a dynamic, effective leader. Former Premier Sun's support was unexpectedly high because of the very high regard most held for him. James Soong, seventeenth on President Lee's list, ranked higher than expected. Lin Yang-kang's vote was similarly higher than most foresaw, as was that of party election strategist John Kuan, who ranked twelfth. Kuan had risen to fame after the 1980 election, which the KMT won handily, notwithstanding open competition with independent candidates. His stock had fallen after the 1986 election because the KMT did not do so well. According to many observers, Shaw Yu-ming, director of the Government Information Office, who had recently returned to Taiwan (after a prolonged stay in the United States), also

scored well. Although Shaw was often the subject of public criticism and controversy because of his position dealing with the media, he received more votes
than most had expected—ranking fifty-two in delegate votes.[30]

Premier Yu Kuo-hua, who ranked thirty-five in delegate votes, was embarrassed. He was number three on the chairman's list and was the highest government official the president had named. There was considerable speculation at the
time that this low ranking would prompt Yu's resignation, or that he would not
be reappointed. Others said that he was targeted by the reformists and made a
scapegoat because he was disliked by the opposition, but that his job performance was good. (He had overseen Taiwan's miracle economic growth and its
democratization as head of the Executive Yuan for four years.) Shen Chang-huan,
presidential secretary general, ranked only fifty-first, leading some to think his
political career was ending, particularly considering that his job depends upon the
whim of the new president. He was sixth on President Lee's list and was seen as
vital to maintaining continuity during the transition to President Lee's leadership.[31]

The average age of the new Central Committee is now 58.7, compared to
69.8 for the retiring body. This is a marked difference. Two new Central Committee members are forty years old. Seventy-one member were holdovers from
the 12th Party Congress in 1981; 109 or 60.5 percent were elected for the first
time. Nearly one-fourth of the members now hold Ph.D. degrees; 40 percent are
university graduates.[32]

Sixty-seven members are government officials from the executive branch,
eighteen are party leaders, and fourteen are from the military—all slightly higher
figures than on President Lee's list. Forty-two are from elected bodies of government and thirty are from the Legislative Yuan—the same number President Lee
had recommended. Eleven women were elected (one less than on President Lee's
list); three of them represent the media. Sixty-nine, or 38.3 percent, of the new
Central Committee is Taiwanese, compared to 41.7 percent on Lee's list and 20
percent of the old Central Committee.[33]

Even more revealing in terms of the party's leadership is the Standing
Committee of the Central Committee. It was picked the last day of the congress.
This powerful body, which nearly all observers of Taiwan politics say is the
nation's core decision-making body, was nominated by President Lee. The nominations were approved by the Central Committee in what most regarded as a pro
forma manner—not democratically. Hence democratization of the party rules did
not reach this level.

The new makeup of the Central Standing Committee, however, suggests the
reformists prevailed even at this level. The new top party decision-making body

was made younger and "Taiwanized." Before President Lee's nominations were announced, twelve members of the previous Central Standing Committee retired. (Ten of these were appointed to the Central Advisory Committee.) Twelve new younger appointments reduced the average age of this body considerably: The mean age of those retiring was over seventy-seven, compared to a mean of just over sixty for those added. Five of the newly appointed members hail from Taiwan, as opposed to only three retirees. This puts sixteen Taiwan-born party members on the Central Standing Committee—giving Taiwanese a majority.[34]

Critics of the KMT have often charged that the party is a Mainland Chinese party and does not represent the Taiwanese majority. The new composition of the Central Standing Committee plainly refutes this charge. Actually, the process of Taiwanizing the system has been going on for some time. In 1973, Taiwanese were 14 percent of the Central Standing Committee. In 1976, they were 18 percent; in 1979, 33 percent; in 1984, 39 percent; and in 1986, 45 percent.[35] Some observers even charged that President Lee intentionally made the body a majority of Taiwanese in order to give the impression of localizing the party and to help the KMT in the 1989 election.[36] Some say the move was a calculated signal to the United States and the People's Republic of China that Taiwan wanted to retain its sovereignty and did not choose to negotiate reunification. Others suggested it was one of the compromises made behind the scenes. In any event, it was a watershed.

The ranking of members of the Central Standing Committee, as in the past, seems to reflect age and length of service in the party more than anything else. Shieh Tung-min (eighty-two), the former vice president, was ranked first. Li Kwoh-ting (seventy-nine), former minister of economic affairs and the genius behind Taiwan's economic development, was ranked second. Nieh Wen-ya (age eighty-four), president of the Legislative Yuan, was ranked third. Yu Kuo-hua (seventy-five), was ranked fourth; and Lee Huan (seventy-one) was fifth. Ranking on the Central Standing Committee was obviously not based on ranking in the Central Committee: The first four (in order on the Central Standing Committee) ranked thirteenth, thirty-first, fiftieth, and thirty-fifth on the Central Committee. Twelve of the thirty-one members of the new Central Standing Committee, including five of the newly elected Taiwanese, would not have been chosen to this elite group based on their ranking in the Central Committee.[37]

The new Central Standing Committee for the first time has a female member: Shirley Kuo, deputy governor of the Central Bank and well-known economist. She is also Taiwanese. A representative of labor was also included for the first time: Hsieh Shen-shan, president of the Chinese Federation of Labor. Hsieh is also a member of the Legislative Yuan. Two KMT legislators identified as liaison with the opposition parties (and who have had close ties with the Democratic Progressive Party) were included. No member of the Chiang family was nominated, even though three received high billing in the Central Committee.[38]

The representation of the military on the Central Standing Committee dropped from four to three. General Hau Pei-tsun was ranked tenth. General Hsu Li-lung, head of the Vocational Assistance Commission for Retired Servicemen, was added. The media lost all three of their representatives on this elite body; all three (heads of the *United Daily News*, the *China Times* and the Central News Agency) retired and not one was replaced by a media leader. However, this loss of media representation was probably coincidence; also, it was offset by the fact that the media increased their representation in the Central Committee.[39]

The makeup of the new Central Standing Committee, with three members under age fifty and thirteen under sixty, gives some indication of the status of the young "rising stars" who have been talked about for some time. They are mostly U.S.-educated talent that returned to Taiwan a decade or two ago to take a position in the government or party. Chen Li-an, Lien Chan, Kao Yu-jen, and Wu Poh-hsiung were already members of the Central Standing Committee. They were joined by the more well known James Soong, Frederick Chien, Sih Chi-yang, Shirley Kuo and Su Nan-cheng. The composition of the new Central Standing Committee also evoked speculation about new cabinet members; but that issue was resolved soon after the 13th Party Congress.

New Party Policies

Policy decisions emanating from the 13th Party Congress may be categorized as follows: limiting and defining reform (which was the theme of the congress); adding to or revising economic, social, educational, cultural, and other policies; and balancing the "localizing" of the party with an affirmative or liberal mainland policy, while clarifying that policy with some new tenets of national defense policy.

In the realm of political reform, a resolution passed at the fourth plenary session of the congress on July 10 stated that to "continue the drive for democracy" is a major task of "glorifying the Three Principles of the People."[40] It went on to say that the party aimed "to speed up political reform and uphold the spirit of party politics." But it also mentioned the rule of law and constitutional democracy. In short, there was to be continued political modernization, but within the context of stability and law.

The party platform spoke of making the elected bodies of government fully representative, but it did not set any deadline or say how this was to be done. The stated goal, as with improving local government, was "strengthening the system" and "continuing the constitutional process."[41] The same document spoke of enforcing the rule of law and fostering social stability, establishing a clean and capable government, and promoting national unity.

In view of the rapid rate of democratization and the pro-reform mood of the congress, including an emphasis on "localization" of the system, party leaders apparently assumed that it was not wise to be too specific. They believed that democratization had to be tempered with greater respect for the law in order to prevent democracy from devolving into mob rule. Party leaders no doubt had fresh in their minds the mass, violent street demonstrations in May.[42] They also deemed it unwise to set a date for turning the elected bodies of government into organs representing solely Taiwan. This was too intimately associated with a two China Policy (or a one-Taiwan, one-China arrangement) to many in Taiwan as well as abroad.

Thus, although the changes in rules, which were written into the party Constitution, emphasized democratization both in the party and the government, and it was also the prevailing feeling of the Congress that the political modernization process had to go forward in the direction of democracy, no recipe to accomplish this could be agreed upon. It was going to happen; but, the process had to be a step-by-step one that considered many special circumstances. For these reasons, political reform constituted the first chapter of the party platform, but less was said about it than other issues.

In the realm of economic, social, educational, cultural and other policies, the party platform cited infrastructure improvement and sounder financial management—apparently as a signal to the business community that economic growth should continue and that the nation had to make the leap to capital- and knowledge-intensive industries. The privatization of public enterprises (a major demand of the opposition because of the KMT's ownership of numerous public enterprises), land policy, energy, and balanced foreign trade were all mentioned. All were problems that sorely needed government action. Specific policy proposals, however, were vague. One was the promise to enact a Fair Transaction Law. Another was to accelerate the building of mass transportation systems to relieve traffic congestion (the number one problem according to polls conducted in the capital city).[43]

A party resolution also cited the "equitable distribution of wealth" as a party goal.[44] Inasmuch as the nation has one of the most equitable income distribution levels in the world, this seemed odd to some observers. The distribution of wealth is, however, different. Many citizens have faced difficulties in recent years because of rapidly rising property values that have made it difficult to afford housing. Unearned income has also been a sensitive issue. Thus the party seemed determined to take action against what it calls "privilege and monopoly."

A substantive chapter in the party platform was devoted to education, though expressed mostly in general terms. Increasing government spending, upgrading teachers, and promoting sports as well as moral and citizenship education were cited. The only specific, however, was a promise to extend the number of years of compulsory education.[45] Chapters were also devoted to each of the following: Chinese culture and modern ethics; social well-being; environmental protection; labor welfare; farmer's welfare and protecting women's rights.[46]

The platform specifically cited establishing a Ministry of Cultural Affairs, improving mass communications, and strengthening freedom of the press (while enhancing journalistic self-restraint). Party leaders viewed "cultural problems" (broadly defined to include social issues) as serious and perceived that the country had the funds to at least improve the quality of art and literature and mass communications, and should do so. Meanwhile, it was thought this support would help promote democratic values.

In the realms of social development and environmental protection, parts of the party platform seemed a response to strong public demands for action on these matters. The platform contained promises of more funding for public health, social services, leisure, consumer protection, and pollution control. Specifics, however, were lacking. Regarding labor, farmers, and women, the platform pledged to revise the Labor Union Law and improve labor welfare and safety. It also promised import controls on agricultural products (a very heated issue inasmuch as food imports had led to protest demonstrations in recent months), price stabilization, and better administration. On women's rights, the party vowed to uphold equality as promised in the Constitution and protection against abuse of women. (With divorce rising at a faster rate than in any other country in the world and abuse a serious problem, demands for action were strong.) The platform even promised to revise the Criminal Code to deal with violence toward women.[47]

Of the three general areas cited above, the Party's mainland policy was the biggest attention-getter. The Platform speaks of promoting economic liberalization on the mainland, formulating a comprehensive mainland trade policy, and promoting understanding across the Taiwan Strait. It also boasts of supporting political democratization on the mainland and publicizing the Taiwan experience.

These ideas were stated in vague terms in this party document, however, and could be interpreted in different ways.[48]

Subsequent resolutions and statements made by party leaders indicate that mainland trade and investment will be allowed (perhaps "encouraged" is the right word) to increase. One party leader noted that trade and investment would be made formally legal, but he was vague about the limits or restrictions that would be included.[49] Mail and other exchanges, including sports meetings and travel across the Taiwan Strait, would also be sanctioned.

The party was plainly responding to public opinion favoring the freedom to have commercial and other contacts with the mainland. There were also strong feelings of apprehension. Businessmen generally wanted more freedom to take advantage of new business opportunities. They did not want to be shut out, and they did not want to be beaten in the race by others. Opposition leaders, however, still worried that the KMT was colluding with Beijing and promoting ties with the mainland in order to prevent full democracy and self-determination in Taiwan, or at least they made statements to that effect at that time.[50]

KMT leaders were also in a dilemma: They had to respond to Beijing's progressive policies and reform, which were getting considerable publicity abroad, yet they did not want to laud the policies of their adversaries. The platform thus contained statements critical of communism and pessimistic about reform in the People's Republic of China. Boasting of the Three Principles of the People as the solution to China's problems seemed to be a rational (though to many not realistic) mainland policy.[51]

The party's mainland policy seemed geared to promote more economic and people-to-people ties and a friendlier policy to offset the effects of reform, democracy, and localization, all of which suggest that Taiwan's separation from China is a growing reality. Though underscoring Taipei's openness and success in both economic development and political modernization, the mainland policy disguises Taipei's desires to remain sovereign and to avoid ties at the government level or negotiations that might lead to reunification talks. The party platform speaks of helping "mainland compatriots" attain property and land rights and political liberties and of the failure of communism to provide these rights.[52] The assumption is that a "pluralistic society" on the mainland is coming only in the distant future, so far away that Taipei need not worry about it, or that reform in the People's Republic of China would make military action against Taiwan less likely, and thus that reunification may eventually be something to consider (or at least to keep as an option to prevent localization from going too far too fast).

The open mainland policy was also balanced (read "contradicted") by several foreign policy statements. For example, the platform states that in the "spirit of independence" the nation seeks to "elevate the level of, and make a breakthrough in" foreign relations—so as to establish or resume the nation's diplomatic ties. The platform also mentions a more forward diplomacy in sustaining ties with international organizations and supporting anti-communism among the Overseas Chinese.[53] This policy does not seem to reflect a goal of better relations with Beijing aimed at reunification.

Nor do the declarations in the platform regarding national defense. Mention is made of "exposing the Chinese Communists' united front scheme and threats of force." The platform further talks about developing defense technology and specifically "major weapons systems."[54] The fact that Taiwan's former defense minister presided over the meeting on mainland policy seems, at least to this writer, revealing. So were the announcements (especially their timing) concerning Taiwan's building a fighter plane that would outperform any other one built in Asia (and would be ready to display at the end of the year) and the revelation that Taiwan would produce its own submarines within six months.[55]

Conclusions

The changes in rules, new personnel, and policies emanating from the KMT's Thirteenth Party Congress all attest to the fact that reform and democratization had impacted the party prior to July 1988, and both greatly influenced events and decisions made at the Thirteenth Party Congress. Moreover, it seems this influence is likely to continue. One might even say that the old guard in the party will never again set policy or alone make decisions.

If this turns out to be true, Taiwan has passed a major turning point in its democratization process. One may even say that Taiwan has in some respects gone beyond some Western democratic nations. In terms of the procedural rules and the means of picking delegates in the KMT, democracy has certainly proceeded further than in many democratic parties in the West.

Because Taiwan is a one-party-dominant system and no doubt will remain so in the foreseeable future, doing these things was a very important development. The fact is that the ruling party in Taiwan's fast evolving (toward democracy) system will now operate by more democratic rules and this will likely help change the polity of the Republic of China. It may also mean that the KMT lasts longer and rules more effectively as the dominant political party.

Otherwise, the two most salient accomplishments of the 13th Party Congress were: (1) making the Party leadership Taiwanese, and (2) agreeing upon new party policies. Some say that both occurred because of President Lee Teng-hui's leadership. Others argue the party had evolved toward democratic change already and it was CCK's legacy that explains the accomplishments of the congress. Still others say it was the natural consequence of years of national economic, social, and political development. Some say both leadership and policy changes were intended as signals to Beijing and/or Washington. Clearly, there were foreign policy goals involved. In any event, the implications transcend national politics in Taiwan.

Taipei's international status was no doubt improved because the system is more democratic and its leadership now Taiwanese—representing the majority of the nation's population. Although the issue of self-determination was hardly mentioned at the congress (and when it was, it was condemned), Taiwan's national sovereignty was highlighted—particularly by implication. Many in the KMT now feel the international community or an international organization (perhaps in the plural) must help decide Taiwan's future. Who in the international community can argue against allowing a democratic nation that is led by the majority decide its own future?

But to reiterate, democratization (signaling separation) was balanced or offset by the new mainland policies that came out of the congress. The latter policies suggested improved links with China rather than further separation. This also was a "big step." And it has been followed up with specific policy actions and even more new policies.

The congress in some senses served as a platform for the KMT to boast of its accomplishments. The act of offering various kinds of help to Beijing was certainly that. Decisions made at the meetings reflected an understanding, and an acceptance, of the fact that the bipolar nature of the world is changing. They are in consonance with U.S. China policy—which seeks to downplay the "Taiwan issue." They are also a calculated response to Beijing's "open" policies and the favorable media attention Beijing has garnered from its reforms (which by Taiwan's standards are hardly meaningful).

Clearly, the more Taiwan talks about its accomplishments, the worse Beijing looks. The KMT's reformist mood and its brandishing of its accomplishments at the Thirteenth Party Congress could not but make the People's Republic of China look bad, or at least look a decade or two behind. The ruling parties in the two Chinas are both changing, but the KMT is ahead and is reforming faster. By comparison the Chinese Communist Party is not democratic. In fact, there seem to be permanent or innate obstacles to its further democratization in China. Relatively, continued reform seemed easy for the KMT.

Reform, however, did not prevail completely at the congress. Compromises were made. The reformists picked Taiwanization and changes in the rules for picking delegates and members of the Central Committee as their major objectives. They did not make a great effort to change the means of selecting the Central Standing Committee. One may say their approach was one of starting reform at the "grass roots" or in a way that it can seep to the top. But it seems to be the best way to begin, or to ensure that reform will not be reversed. It also respects age and position, both important to Chinese culture. And it obviates open struggle that might induce political instability.

Some issues remained unresolved by the congress. The most important was the membership of the elected bodies of government. Approximately 70 to 80 percent of these representatives were chosen in the distant past, not picked by the Taiwan electorate. This makes the political system less than democratic in an important way. Yet the old elected delegates are being phased out by attrition rather quickly. Many felt that fair representation and democracy could better be accomplished gradually than through quick reform. This was considered a safer and less brash and would not provoke Beijing (or Washington). Many KMT leaders also opined that this problem had to be resolved through party-government negotiations and had to involve opposition party leaders. Therefore, it should be left out of KMT business.

The issue of whether the KMT is a revolutionary party or a democratic one was also decided in favor of the former. This decision rationalized its undemocratic rules. Some say it still does. Yet the rules were dramatically changed. Some delegates at the congress voiced the opinion that if Taiwan is to serve as a model for all of China, the Party must remain a revolutionary party. This is so for appearance's sake. Yet the KMT is hardly a revolutionary party anymore in most respects. In any event, although this was the decision reached, it was clear the KMT has became much more democratic in its procedures and clearly in its mood.

One may conclude, both from the mood of the Thirteenth Party Congress and substantive decisions, that Chiang Ching-kuo's influence was still strong. The reforms he wanted were in large part realized before he died. Other changes were attained by the leaders and delegates of this congress. The mood of the congress was as it might have been had he been present. Clearly he has left a mark. One might say it was "his congress." Looking at the congress from the vantage point of months later, one can see that it had a beneficial impact on party morale, cohesion, and decision-making effectiveness. The policies made at the congress generally have been carried out or are being set to be implemented. This goes for both domestic policies and foreign policies. Mainland policy, for example, has followed guidelines set at the congress. In short, based on observations made of the congress, its immediate aftermath, and events since, one can now say that it was a watershed event in Taiwan's political development.

Endnotes

1. For details on the history of the KMT, see Immanuel C.Y. Hsu, *The Rise of Modern China* (London: Oxford University Press, 1970), Parts IV and V.

2. Edwin A. Winckler, "After the Chiangs: The Coming Political Succession on Taiwan," in Richard C. Bush, ed., *China Briefing, 1982* (Boulder, CO: Westview Press, 1983), pp. 113–15, and Hung-mao Tien, "Taiwan in 1986: Reforms Under Adversity," in John S. Major and Anthony J. Kame, eds., *China Briefing, 1987* (Boulder, CO: Westview Press, 1987), pp. 136–38.

3. For details see John F. Copper, *A Silent Revolution: Political Development in the Republic of China* (Lanham, MD: University Press of America, 1988).

4. See Harmon Zeigler, *Pluralism, Corporation and Confucianism: Political Association and Conflict Regulation in the United States, Europe and Taiwan* (Philadelphia: Temple University Press, 1988), p. 136.

5. See A. James Gregor and Maria Hsia Chang, *The Republic of China and U.S. Policy* (Washington, DC: Ethics and Public Policy Center, 1983), pp. 66–68. It is worthy of note that more than 50 percent of the Taiwanese vote, which has often been identified with opposition to the KMT, went to KMT candidates in elections.

6. See John F. Copper with George P. Chen, *Taiwan's Elections: Political Development and Democratization in the Republic of China* (Baltimore: University of Maryland Law School, 1984).

7. See ibid. Also see John F. Copper, "Taiwan's 1985 Elections," *Asian Affairs*, Spring 1986.

8. See John F. Copper, "Taiwan's 1986 National Election: Pushing Democracy Ahead," *Asian Thought and Society*, July 1987.

9. See John F. Copper, "Ending Martial Law in Taiwan: Prospects and Implications," *Journal of Northeast Asian Studies,* Summer 1988, for views about ending martial law.

10. For a recent such analysis, See Parris H. Chang, "Taiwan in 1983: Setting the Stage for Power Transition," *Asian Survey,* January 1984.

11. For details see Tien, "Taiwan in 1986," and John F. Copper, "Taiwan in 1986: Back on Top Again," *Asian Survey,* January 1987.

12. For details, see *Far Eastern Economic Review,* February 7, 1988.

13. See Shim Jae Hoon, "Out with the Old, in with the New," *Far Eastern Economic Review,* June 23, 1988, p. 30, and "KMT Primaries Underway," *Free China Journal,* May 23, 1988, p. 1. Voting was held on May 14 with 1.6 million of the KMT's 2.4 million members eligible to vote.

14. Susan Chira, "Taiwan President Will Also Head Party," *New York Times* (International), July 9, 1988, p. 3.

15. See "More diverse leadership named to standing c'tee," *China Post,* July 15, 1988, p. 1 and "Facts and figures on Central C'tee nominees," *China Post,* July 11, 1988, p. 12.

16. "KMT Elects New Central C'tee: Premier Yu Gets Low Berth," *China News,* July 13, 1988, p. 1. It is worthy of note that both have since resigned from their positions. Probably neither will play a central role in Taiwan politics again.

17. "In First, KMT leaders nominated democratically," *China Post,* July 12, 1988, p. 1.

18. See "Lee spearheads injection of fresh blood into KMT," *China Post,* July 11, 1988, p. 1, and Susan Tifft, "New Mandate for a Native Son," *Time,* July 18, 1988, p. 19.

19. I was in Taipei at the time of the Thirteenth Party Congress; this view is based on talks with a number of officials, scholars, and observers.

20. "Lee appoints 10 elders to advisory C'tee care," *China Post,* July 14, 1988, p. 16.

21. "Taiwan's Kuomintang faces sweeping changes," *Washington Times*, July 6, 1988, p. A7. It appears now that the advocates of reforming the electoral bodies of government chose to make this an issue at a later time. Some now see it as an election issue.

22. Susan Chira, "Taiwan President Will Also Head Party," *New York Times*, July 9, 1988, p. 3. Writer refers to Antonio Chang, a local publisher.

23. Ibid.

24. Cited in *Japan Times,* January 28, 1988, p. 1.

25. See, for example, Winckler, "After the Chiangs," and Tien, "Taiwan in 1986." The *Far Eastern Economic Review* predicted at the time of CCK's death that Lee would not become president. See Carl Goldstein, "President Lee unlikely to win party leadership," *Far Eastern Economic Review*, January 28, 1988, pp. 22–24. In June an author, writing in that same magazine, referred to him as "like a figurehead." See Shim Jae Hoon, "After the dynasty, a local mandarin," *Far Eastern Economic Review*, June 23, 1988, p. 29.

26. See "Local Man on the Job," *Asiaweek,* January 29, 1988, p. 18.

27. See "KMT Elects New Central C'tee: Premier Yu Gets Low Berth," *China News*, July 13, 1988, p. 1.

28. "Lee spearheads injection of fresh blood into KMT," and "KMT's New Central Committee," *China News,* July 14, 1988, p. 6.

29. See "Pres. Lee Announces List of 180 Nominees for Next KMT Central Committee," *China News,* July 11, 1988, p. 1.

30. Some of the above is based on opinions stated by KMT members at the time to the author.

31. "Pres. Lee Announces List of 180 Nominees."

32. "Facts and Figures on Central C'tee Nominees," *China Post* and "KMT's New Central Committee."

33. Ibid.

34. "KMT's New Leaders Younger, Better-Educated: Native Sons Gain Ascendancy," *China News,* July 15, 1988, p. 1.

35. See Tien, "Taiwan in 1986."

36. Some observers noted that several of the Taiwanese appointed to the Central Standing Committee did not have high rankings (by popularity) in the Central Committee. Others noted that Shirley Kuo, Taiwanese and female, was nominated to the Central Standing Committee in favor of Li Tchong-koei, the highest-ranking female on the Central Committee.

37. See "Facts about the new Standing Committee," *China Post*, July 15, 1988, p. 12.

38. Some observers noted that CCK's sons were popular, but because of the feeling that the "Chiang Dynasty" should end there was opposition to them being appointed to the Central Standing Committee. In this connection, it is worthy of note that Wego Chiang, CCK's brother, remains popular even though the move to make him acting chairman of the party did not have much support. It is also worth mentioning that CCK's teachings have been added to those of Sun Yat-sen and Chiang Kai-shek as "party doctrine."

39. See "More diverse leadership named to standing c'tee." The fact that one "representative" of the media wanted to step down put pressure on the others.

40. Press release issued by the Government Information Office, Taipei, dated July 10, 1988.

41. "Platform of the Kuomintang of China," April 11, 1988 (Source: Government Information Office, Taipei).

42. This was a riot started by protesting farmers and was labeled the worst in forty years. Three hundred and eight-two policemen were injured. Some observers felt the riot involved much more than protesting farmers, and because of the

criminal element involved, the government had to take a tough policy. See Shim Jae Hoon, "Strains of success," *Far Eastern Economic Review*, July 2, 1988, p. 16.

43. See "Platform of the Kuomintang of China."

44. See Press release issued by the Government Information Office, Taipei, dated July 10, 1988.

45. See "Platform of the Kuomintang of China."

46. Ibid.

47. Ibid.

48. Ibid.

49. See press release issued by the Government Information Office, Taipei, dated July 8, 1988, and accompanying "Resolution on Kuomintang's Current Policy."

50. It is worthy of note that Yao Chia-wen, head of the Democratic Progressive Party, accused the government of secret negotiations with Beijing while the KMT 13th Congress was in session. See Kyoto News Service release of July 8, 1988.

51. See "Platform of the Kuomintang of China."

52. Ibid.

53. Ibid.

54. Ibid.

55. For further details, see "Gen. Hau Reports on Mil. Preparedness," *China News*, July 1988, p. 4.

Chapter Ten
The KMT's 14th Party Congress:
Toward Unity or Disunity?

Taiwan's Nationalist Party, or Kuomintang (KMT), held its 14th Party Congress at the Convention Center of Taipei's World Trade Center from August 16 to 22, 1993. Those who attended understood it was a critical meeting for the ruling party. The excitement and tension at the congress also reflected the widespread view that the party was facing numerous crises and was at a crossroads in many ways.

The congress was overdue. More than five years had elapsed since the 13th Congress, held in July 1988.[1] More important than the distance in time since the last meeting, democratic change in government and throughout the political system had not been matched by changes in the KMT's structure, decision-making processes, or leadership. Taiwan had become a democratic, pluralized society. The Legislative Yuan had greatly expanded its political power and influence in the course of democratization and both the Legislative Yuan and the National Assembly were now fully elected; yet few changes had been made in the ruling style or personnel in the top hierarchy of the ruling party.[2]

Both party members and the media questioned the KMT's future. With a ninety-nine-year history, the second oldest political party in Asia (after the Congress Party in India) and the longest ruling party anywhere in the world, the KMT, some felt, had not kept pace with global changes that had occurred over the past four years and was on the wrong side of the curve in terms of historical change. Observers compared the KMT's situation to that of Japan's Liberal Democratic Party, which had just fallen from power—many KMT leaders having often seen the LDP as their model.

Internal factionalism was serious. In fact, the party had appeared to be on the verge of a split for some time, with fighting between two blocs or factions escalating during the debate on constitutional reform in 1992 and leading up to the Legislative Yuan election in December. Centrifugal tendencies also caused several delays in scheduling the congress. The most divisive matter was the

161

transfer of national leadership from the recent immigrant Chinese or Mainland Chinese to the "native" Taiwanese. The Non-Mainstream faction that represented Mainland Chinese sought to protect its influence and interests; Taiwanese, represented by the Mainstream faction, wanted to reform and dominate the party.

Several noted Non-Mainstream KMT legislators left the KMT and formed a competing political party. President Lee's leadership was brought into question by the remaining Non-Mainstream faction before the congress started. Fights broke out during the congress. There was intense, and in some ways bitter, competition for seats on the Central Committee and the Central Standing Committee. Several groups formed to trade votes, undermining the party's leadership and its control of votes. There were also serious charges of buying votes.

Much was accomplished at the congress. Yet at the end of the week-long session few seemed certain it was enough to reverse the party's decline. Whether decisions made at the congress would suffice to reform the KMT and would have a positive effect on the party's image and popularity (especially at the polls) was not known. Also, whether the KMT was more or less unified was likewise a matter of speculation. What did seem unquestioned was the watershed nature of the meeting in terms of the KMT's future.

Backdrop to the Congress

The KMT's 14th Party Congress was considered long overdue, not only because Taiwan had experienced significant political change since the last congress, but also because the ruling party's style of governance and decision making were out of sync with democratic changes that the party itself had promoted in the government. The KMT, which had long ago infiltrated the government after the fashion of a Leninist party, had not adjusted to the nation's democratization by loosening its control over government organs or by reorganizing and democratizing itself.

Also, the KMT was trying to deal with an election defeat, feuds among its top leadership, factionalism, charges of corruption, sagging public opinion polls, and the prospect of losing future elections and possibly even its mandate to lead the country. How these problems affected the KMT in the months leading up to the 14th Congress are instructive in terms of understanding events at the congress and decisions made at that meeting.

First, about the election. Although the KMT did not lose its majority in the nation's lawmaking body, the Legislative Yuan, in the December 1992 election it performed poorly, dropping nearly 20 percent in the popular vote column to

53 percent, the lowest in any recent election. It also lost seats in the lawmaking branch of government, whereas the opposition Democratic Progressive Party (DPP) made sizable gains.[3]

In February 1993, the ruling party suffered a minor, but jolting, defeat in a by-election for the Penghu County chief. The KMT had regarded Penghu (the Pescadore Islands) as a stronghold because the KMT had 27,000 registered members there compared to the opposition DPP's 30. The loss was considered a serious matter by party leaders.[4] Former premier Yu Kuo-hua cited the "internal rift" in the party and the "immobility of the party mechanism."[5] President Lee apologized for the defeat before the party's Central Committee.

In March, the KMT ordered a review of its disappointing performance in the December election. The final report cited a number of errors: poor candidates, "uncreative" campaign literature, lack of party discipline, and intra-party squabbling (over the land value tax, the stock transaction tax, and a one-China versus a one-China and one-Taiwan policy). The party's Department of Organizational Affairs responded with a detailed plan for reform of the party apparatus.[6]

Questions about the nation's political system constituted another serious matter, exacerbated by a power struggle between President Lee Teng-hui and Premier Hau Pei-tsun. The powers assigned in the Constitution to their respective offices constituted the central focus of needed systemic changes. More specifically, some questioned whether the premier—who is appointed by the President, but cannot, according to the Constitution, be dismissed by him—should resign along with the cabinet when a new legislative session begins. An extraordinary session of top KMT leaders was held in January to decide this issue, and it was affirmed that Premier Hau should step down.[7] He did, but this did not end the controversy.

Reflecting the personal nature of the struggle between President Lee and Premier Hau and the ethnic division it represented, street demonstrations followed, culminating on January 10, 1993, with 10,000 protestors publicly supporting Premier Hau. Subsequently it was reported that 300,000 signatures had been collected calling for Hau to remain in office.[8] Later demonstrations for Hau turned violent. Protestors expressed strong sentiments against President Lee, accusing him of being a dictator and a supporter of Taiwan's independence. These events engendered a backlash and more than fifty KMT Mainstream National Assembly members joined DPP delegates in a motion in that body that accused Hau of blocking democratic reform.[9] The gulf between native-born Taiwanese, represented by President Lee, and Mainland Chinese, led by Hau, in the party widened.

On January 27, President Lee addressed a KMT Central Committee meeting and called for party unity. He declared that the party's biggest problem was that it did not have "mutual trust."[10] As a concession, or to ameliorate hostile feelings within and outside the party, President Lee put the former premier in charge of a special policy guidance task force that would prepare the agenda for the 14th Congress to be held in the summer. Hau thus became convener of the Central Policy Guidance Group, which was given a status higher than the Central Committee.[11] This position appeared to give Hau added clout and authority to promote policies of the Non-Mainstream faction.

Meanwhile the KMT leadership ordered local party units to conduct various policy reviews to speed up reform. Soong Chu-yu, secretary general of the KMT, proposed that more members of the Legislative Yuan be selected to the Central Committee to mirror the new importance of the legislative branch of government in the context of democratization.[12] However, there was considerable opposition to this idea in the ranks and among officials in other branches of government. Particularly strong opposition came from Hau's Non-Mainstream faction, whose members regarded this as an attempt to stack the committee with Lee supporters.

In March, KMT leaders announced that the party would conduct a detailed, nationwide opinion survey and would use the results to formulate future policies.[13] A few days later, an independent poll reflected a drastic plunge in popular support for the KMT. KMT National Assembly representative Chang Yi-hsi, who founded the polling organization, said the KMT was "mired in a crisis."[14] According to the poll, 34 percent of respondents believed the KMT would cease being the ruling party in three years.[15]

At the end of March, Hsu Shui-teh was sworn in as the new secretary general of the KMT replacing Soong Chu-yu. Hsu, who had just returned from Japan as Taiwan's unofficial head diplomat there, drew further attention to the parallels being drawn in the media and by political observers between the KMT's problems and those of the Japanese ruling party, the Liberal Democratic Party, which was about to fall from power. Some critics noted that both had been in office too long and had not adjusted to new "democratic realities" either in their own countries or throughout the world. Outgoing Secretary General Soong, whose performance in his job had been very good, though controversial, and who had been the brunt of criticism when feuds in the party became a problem and when other KMT difficulties arose, had long wanted to leave the position. His departure drew further attention to the serious nature of the KMT's on-going internal problems.

In May, members of the New KMT Alliance, which was part of the Non-Mainstream faction, disclosed a plan to form a new party called the New Alliance Nationalist Party. About thirty young and mostly second-generation Mainlanders announced the shocking news. At the time they also called Secretary General Soong's proposal (to increase the number of delegates to the congress) "an effort to ensure President Lee's reelection as Party Chairman."[16]

Although they did not at this time actually break from the KMT and start a new political party, the split between the New KMT Alliance and the Mainstream faction of the party did not heal. Bitterness over various issues escalated, a number of them relating to questions that were to be addressed and hopefully resolved at the up-coming congress.

In July, "vote distribution" plans by so-called vote-rationing coalitions led by KMT leaders in the Legislative Yuan and elsewhere became an issue that further exacerbated tensions between the New KMT Alliance and the Mainstream faction. Members of various party groups traded votes in order to increase their representation on the new KMT Central Committee.[17] At this juncture, on August 2, Jaw Shao-kong, a popular legislator and member of the New KMT Alliance, reiterated the group's intention to form a new party. Then, the New KMT Alliance set up a local branch office in Panchiao and publicized plans to recruit 50,000 members to join a new political party and hold "another 14th Congress."[18] At the same time, Yok Mu-ming, a member of the alliance and a Legislative Yuan member, told the press that President Lee was "only paying lip service to unification to appease us." Another Legislative Yuan member, in a letter to the public, asserted, "Taiwan is our only base. If we lose this ground the KMT will wither and die."[19]

The next day, President Lee, in a speech at a KMT meeting, called for various groups in the KMT to work together. New KMT Alliance leaders, however, refused to cooperate. One offered the opinion that the KMT would lose elections in the next three years and by 1996 would "ask for our cooperation." John Kuan, the strategist behind a number of KMT election victories and a member of the alliance, said that the New KMT Alliance would get 20 percent of the vote in the upcoming election in northern Taiwan, 15 percent in central Taiwan, and 10 percent in the south. He further stated that the alliance would dominate election politics in the north. Yok Mu-ming told the press that the KMT was "as corrupt as the LDP" (in Japan). Chairman of the Democratic Progressive Party, Hsu Hsin-liang, in response to the breakaway Alliance, said the DPP would "govern in about three years."[20]

On August 10, seven members of the New KMT Alliance announced the formation of the Chinese New Party (CNP). All were legislators or former legislators, and some had been big vote-getters in recent elections. The CNP's platform supported direct presidential elections, Sun Yat-sen's ideals, voluntary service in lieu of military service, and equal protection of human rights. Party leaders spoke of a "Great Chinese Common Market" and called for direct flights and navigation to China. CNP leaders accused the KMT of corruption and the DPP of being "too immature to lead." Party leaders announced a political rally on August 22, to occur when the KMT's 14th Congress was still in session.[21]

In summation, on the eve of the long–awaited 14th KMT Congress, the party that had ruled Taiwan since 1945 and that could justifiably take credit for its miracle economic growth, and more recently its successful strides toward democracy, seemed less a confident and victorious party than a troubled and divided one. Could this trend be changed at the congress? That was the question in the minds of delegates as well as observers.

Events at the Congress

The congress opened on the morning of August 16. More than 2,000 delegates arrived, including 180 from overseas and 50 representing (mainland) China. It was the largest party congress ever—twice as large as the 13th Congress in 1988 and ten times the size of the 1952 congress.[22]

President Lee Teng-hui, acting as chairman of the KMT, gave the opening address to formally launch the meeting. In his speech he cited the changes in the world that had brought about an end of the Cold War. These changes, he said, had fostered freedom and democracy. President Lee also praised the party and directed attention to its accomplishments. He pointed out that Taiwan had terminated the Period of Mobilization (or the state of war against Beijing) and the Temporary Provisions of the Constitution (which canceled many rights granted in the Constitution and gave the president extraordinary powers), amended the Constitution, and established a plan for reunification. He underscored Taiwan's economic development, noting that in forty years the per capita income had increased from $100 per year to more than $10,000.[23]

Early in his speech, he mentioned party reform. He declared that the KMT "had actively started to reform"—indicating that this was a central matter to be discussed at the congress and that reform had not been sufficient or in keeping with reform in the government. He chided Beijing for its hostile attitude toward Taipei and blamed its leaders for the tension across the Taiwan Strait. He referred, for the first time, to the Chinese New Party—commenting that "diversity in society had resulted in divergence of political ideals."[24]

The second day of the congress, confrontation broke out between Mainstream and Non-Mainstream factions. The voting rights of 700 ex officio delegates, the right to speak at the congress, and the appointment of vice chairmen were the central issues in the debate. Non-Mainstream delegates threatened to walk out over the issue of vice chairmen, charging that the vice chairmanships had already been promised by President Lee. The issue was put to a vote and failed to get the necessary two–thirds majority to pass (falling short by 91 votes, with 1,007 out of 1,684 delegates present at the time voting for it). After lunch, President Lee intervened, giving a passionate speech calling for unity and a vote in favor of having vice chairmen. A second vote resulted in a unanimous vote for the vice chairmen; a crisis was averted.[25]

Foreign Minister Frederick Chien also spoke the second day of the congress. He called for the unification of China while emphasizing Taiwan's right to play a bigger role in international affairs—a role that should be welcomed, he said, given the fact of the collapse of communism in East Europe and the Soviet Union and because economic power was replacing ideology and military power in international relations. Chien pointed out that the Republic of China had 90 representatives in 60 countries with which it has no formal ties and has joined 11 government-to-government international organizations and 795 non-governmental bodies.[26] The foreign minister's speech was clearly intended to support President Lee's efforts to promote Taipei's participation in the United Nations and blame Beijing for strained relations and lack of progress toward unification.

Premier Lien Chan's administrative report, presented the same day, also underscored the Republic of China's right to participate in the United Nations and Beijing's hostile attitude that threatened relations and kept unification "stagnant in the first stage." He declared that Beijing should recognize the Republic of China as an "equal political entity," adding that Taiwan would reduce its armed forces below 400,000 but make qualitative improvements.[27]

The third day of the congress, President Lee was reelected chairman with 1,686 votes (of 2,043) or 82.5 percent of the votes cast. It was the first time a party chairman had been elected by secret ballot. According to most observers this victory showed that Lee had strong support in the party and reflected party unity. Nevertheless, 357 delegates defaced their ballots in protest of Lee's leadership.[28]

The congress also approved Lee's nomination of four vice chairmen: Vice President Li Yuan-tzu, former premier Hau Pei–tsun, Judicial Yuan President Lin Yang-kang, and Premier Lien Chan. No ranking was given to the vice chairmen, though Vice President Li was made chairman of the group.

President Lee nominated 210 delegates to serve on the Central Committee; 159 others gained delegate endorsements. This made for a total of 369 candidates for 210 seats on the Central Committee. Lee's list comprised four categories: party members with seniority (with former premier Yu Kuo-hua listed first, followed by Lee Huan, Tsiang Yien-si, and others); most of the members of the 13th Congress's Central Committee; government officials; and those with "high social prestige." The average age of those nominated was 55.5, or four years less than that of the 13th Congress's Central Committee. Master's degrees were held by 119—16.5 percent more than in the 13th Congress. "People's representatives" (meaning elected officials from the Legislative Yuan, city councilors, and others) numbered 61, or 29 percent, with the Legislative Yuan delegates getting 32 nominations, compared to 55 for non-elected government officials. There were 20 females nominated, or 9.5 percent of the group.[29] It is worthy of note that the list of nominees included no military officers. Presidential spokesman Raymond Tai said that there was a "national consensus" to leave the military out of government, and the KMT's efforts to realize "military neutralization" reflected this view.[30]

On August 19, the Congress elected, by secret ballot, 210 party members to serve on the new Central Committee. Of President Lee's nominations, 152, or 72.4 percent, were chosen (compared to 81.6 percent in 1988), whereas 58 of the 159 candidates nominated by delegates won. Lee's nominees, however, included 8 of the top 10 by the number of votes. Interior Minister Wu Poh-hsiung was first, followed by Soong Chu-yu and Chang Hsiao-yen, head of the party's Overseas Chinese Affairs Commission.[31]

In total, 71 candidates were nominated from the elected bodies of the national government—the National Assembly and the Legislative Yuan. Fifty-nine won seats on the new Central Committee.[32] Appropriately, the KMT at this time declared that the party was a democratic party, not a revolutionary one—something that party leaders as well as rank and file had discussed and debated for some years.[33]

Before the week ended, President Lee nominated 15 members to serve on the party's Central Standing Committee.[34] Of those, 4 represented the government, but only 1 was from the Legislative Yuan. Legislator Kao Yu-jen forthwith threatened to form a "political union" in the Legislative Yuan if the party did not give Legislative Yuan members at least 6 seats on the Central Standing Committee. Also, a feud broke out between the Mainstream and Non-Mainstream factions over the method of balloting for these positions, with the former favoring a multiple ballot of 16 votes and the latter wanting a one-quarter multiple vote for 4 members. Meanwhile, two more KMT delegates to the congress left

to join the Chinese New Party. Last but not least, the party revised its constitution and issued a manifesto calling for world peace and prosperity.[35]

On the following Monday the Central Committee met and chose a new
Central Standing Committee. The 15 candidates picked by President Lee were
approved, plus 14 of 16 nominated by the party. Jeanne Li, appointed the first
ever female deputy secretary general before the balloting, won a seat, as did Sung
Shih-hsuan, former director of the party's Department of Organizational Affairs.
Neither had been nominated. The Central Committee also voted to meet annually
and reelect the Central Standing Committee.[36]

President Lee gave a closing address summarizing the meeting, calling again
for party unity, the unification of China, and support for the Republic of
China's bid for international status. Showing special concern about party unity,
he said: "No other parties can weaken our foundation unless we destruct our-
selves."[37]

Results of the 14th Congress

The results and accomplishments of the KMT's 14th Party Congress may
be subsumed into the categories of reform, new people, and party unity. In all of
these realms the party can speak of major accomplishments; yet in some important ways, little or no change was made.

In the area of reform, a fundamental change was made to define the nature
and role of the KMT as a democratic party. The party had, for ninety-nine years,
defined itself as a revolutionary party. President Lee, in commenting on the
change, said the new definition "complied with the tides of time and the opinions
of most Party members."[38] There was concern, however, that this move meant
the party was abandoning its concern about China, and that it reflected the "localization" of the party.

A revised party platform was passed, as well as plans for the growth of the
party and the development of the nation. Finally, a new set of guidelines on the
current political mission of the Party was approved.

Regarding the decision-making process of the party's main organs, a number
of important changes were made. It was decided that the party congress would be
held every two years (instead of every four), though delegates are still elected for
a four-year term. Also, the party congress in the future will be made up of 1,400
delegates elected by local chapters, in addition to 700 ex officio delegates com-
prising Central Committee members, Legislative Yuan and National Assembly
members, provincial and city council members, and heads of local government

and KMT chapters. Previously the party congress was attended by 1,059 delegates elected by local party chapters, plus 150 members of the Central Committee named as ex officio delegates. Although these changes were made in advance of the congress, they had to be formalized.

The new Central Committee consists of 210 full members and 105 alternates, all chosen by the delegates to the party congress. The last Central Committee was made of up 180 members and 90 alternates chosen from among party delegates. Allowing Central Committee members to be picked from non-delegates made the new Central Committee more broadly based and better able to reflect the people's interests and democracy.

President Lee nominated 210 candidates; 159 others became candidates by obtaining the endorsement of at least 8 party delegates. Of President Lee's nominees, 152 won seats—or 72.4 percent; 58 won seats on their own. Each delegate was allowed to vote for 105 candidates.[39] In the course of voting, there was intense competition among the candidates and many employed tactics such as joining vote-trading groups and engaging in bribery. Party leaders found it a nearly impossible task to prevent these activities. Some argued at the time that the democratization of the process had led to corruption.

The new Central Standing Committee is composed of 31 members, 15 of which were appointed by the party chairman. New rules allowed the chairman to pick 10 to 15, while 16 at minimum are elected by the Central Committee. Previously, the party chairman nominated all 31 members, after which they were approved by acclamation. The new Central Committee will meet annually; in the past it had only sometimes done so.

Delegates to the congress also chose 48 new members to the Central Advisory Committee; this number, together with the 138 nominated by President Lee and the members already serving on the committee, gave that body a total of 347 members. The Central Advisory Committee met on August 22 and decided that it would hold quarterly meetings in the future and that it would look into allegations of vote buying. This body, composed of "elder statesmen" party members and considered passive to orders from the party center, seemed to have become a much more active organ of the KMT.

The party chairman at this congress was elected for the first time by secret ballot. Before the party chairman was chosen by acclamation. The chairman was also limited to two, four-year terms. Previously the top leader of the party was essentially chosen for life. In addition, as noted above, four vice chairmen were picked by the chairman and approved by the congress. Before this there were no vice chairmen.

Some questions arose about changes in the party's charter that affected its top organs. For example, if the party congress is to meet every two years instead of every four years and its delegates are to serve for four years, what do they do during the off-year meetings? If the party congress becomes active in making party policy then what is the purpose of having a Central Committee? Eliminating the Central Committee was suggested as a way of getting rid of an unnecessary, controversial, and corrupt election.[40]

Examining the make-up of the new Central Committee and Central Standing Committee is also revealing because it allows one to assess the nature and degree of party reform achieved at the 14th Congress. Likewise, looking at the names of some of the individuals who were promoted—or not—is telling.

The new Central Committee is composed of 32 members of the Legislative Yuan and 34 members of the National Assembly for a total of more than 30 percent elected officials. This is more than triple the number in the previous Central Committee. Nearly all other Central Committee members are from other branches of government (chiefly the executive branch) or the party itself. Business is not represented well. In fact, 4 of 16 businessmen nominated by President Lee were not elected.[41] No military officers were elected since none was nominated. The biggest vote getters for Central Committee seats were from the executive branch of government and the party. Minister of Interior Wu Poh-hsiung ranked the highest in votes.

The new Central Committee is considerably younger than the previous one. Women are represented much better: Nineteen, or nearly twice the number in the 13th Congress, were elected. Professional groups and the disadvantaged did not fare so well: Only six were elected to represent labor, fishermen, and the handicapped.[42] About one-fifth of the new Central Committee are Non-Mainstream faction members; the rest are allies or supporters of President Lee.

The new Central Standing Committee contains 19 new members, including 15 of the 16 elected members. Thirty percent are considered "people's representatives" (from elected bodies of government), 45 percent are from other government organs and 25 percent are veteran party members or from business. Four from the 13th Congress were not reelected. Two that the party recommended were not elected.[43]

The new Central Standing Committee is younger and is considered more reform minded than the old one. Eighteen members are Taiwanese—three more than before. No member of the new Central Standing Committee holds a post in the military or the Ministry of Justice.[44] Almost half of the old Central Standing Committee held no government post; 75 percent of the members of the new one are government officials.

The main complaint about the new Central Standing Committee was that it under-represented the Legislative Yuan. Kao Yu-jen, head of the Public Opinion Society, a legislative group, said that the election of the new Central Standing Committee would have "repercussions" in the Legislative Yuan. Another complaint was that some of the seats had been bought; so, the last day of the congress Justice Minister Ma Ying-jeou called on the Central Advisory Committee to investigate the charges.[45]

Conclusions

KMT leaders and delegates to the 14th Party Congress grappled with a host of problems and controversial issues facing the ruling party that collectively threatened to split the party and jeopardize or even end its rule of the country. The KMT reformed. It democratized itself. It brought in new blood. In short, much was accomplished.

But was it enough? The reforms did not go far enough to make the party as democratic as the government it controls or enable it to keep pace with the reforms it has promoted elsewhere in Taiwan's political system. The Central Standing Committee still has 15 members who are the chairman's appointees (of 31). Moreover, most of its members have not been chosen to any political office by the electorate. Members of the Legislative Yuan were very unhappy about their serious under-representation in this powerful party organ. And they no doubt will cause difficulties for the party's leadership in the future.

Nevertheless, the pitfalls of democratization were also quite visible at the congress, vote trading and vote buying being the most important. This was a serious problem, and it was not resolved at the congress. Although it must be viewed as a blemish on the party's reputation, it represents more democracy in the party and was perhaps inevitable. Had the party center maintained better control and not made the concessions it did to majority rule and democratic procedures, these problems would not have happened, at least not to the degree that they did. But could the party center hold on to rules and procedures of the past?

President Lee improved his control over the party as a result of the congress. More of his supporters assumed positions in the Central Committee and the Central Standing Committee. He can probably count four-fifths of the Central Committee as supporters. Only three party leaders, former premier Hau, former party head Lee Huan and legislator John Kuan, can be viewed as strong critics of Lee on the Central Standing Committee.

Yet President Lee, in the future, will probably encounter stronger opposition in the Legislative Yuan as a result of reforms made during this congress. Elected KMT officials were disappointed in what happened at this congress and will no doubt vent those feelings in the future—making party discipline, not to mention getting legislation through that body, much more difficult. However, this situation was perhaps unavoidable given the Legislative Yuan's newly gained political clout resulting from the nation's rapid democratization.

Although democratization in the KMT helped President Lee put his people in positions of authority, at the same time it weakened the party's top leadership and its hold over party members. Thus, while Lee has more control over the party by virtue of the numbers, but new rules will make it more difficult for him to lead the party.

President Lee also made some progress in building party unity. His last-minute rescue effort of the vice chairmanships prevented a party split. It also showed that he had the influence to dramatically change the vote on this issue. Yet it was a concession that may cause him difficulties in the future. It gave two of his rivals, Hau Pei-tsun and Lin Yang-kang, added influence in the party. The fact that the most hostile members of the New KMT Alliance left to form a new political party just before the congress opened also helped Lee build unity. But it was at a cost; the Chinese New Party, because it came from the KMT, may present a challenge to the KMT in ways the opposition DPP has not been able to.

The party has new blood. It is much more representative of a pluralistic nation than before. Its leaders are younger, more energetic, and more forward looking. The party is now more Taiwanese; perhaps it can even be said that it is a Taiwan party now. But its members are not more loyal to the party and discipline and perhaps fragmentation will be much bigger problems in the future.

What remains to be seen is whether the reforms were sufficient to dampen public criticism of the party, raise its opinion ratings, and help it win elections. Some observers questioned whether the changes and new faces might simply cause more problems. Clearly much was done at the congress. The KMT will not be the same for it. Whether the ruling party can make a turnaround and continue to rule Taiwan as it has for forty-four years is another matter.

Endnotes

1. For details on the previous party congress, see John F. Copper, "The Kuomintang's 13th Party Congress: Reform, Renovation, New Blood, New Politics," in Cynthia L. Chennault, ed., *Modernizing East Asia: Economic and Cultural Dimensions of Political Change* (New York: St. John's University Press, 1989), pp. 59–83. Also see Jurgen Domes, "The 13th Party Congress of the Kuomintang: Towards Political Competition?" *China Quarterly,* June 1987, pp. 349–99.

2. For an analysis of Taiwan's transition to full or non-supplemental elections, see John F. Copper, *Taiwan's 1991 and 1992 Non-Supplemental Elections* (Lanham, MD: University Press of America, 1994).

3. For details, see John F. Copper, "Taiwan's 1992 Legislative Yuan Election," *World Affairs,* Fall 1992.

4. China News Agency broadcast on March 4, 1993, cited in *Foreign Broadcasting Information Service–China* (hereafter *FBIS*), March 4, 1993, p. 38.

5. Ibid.

6. "KMT Reviews 'Dismal Performance' in Election, " China News Agency, cited in *FBIS,* March 10, 1993, pp. 76–77.

7. "Kuomintang Leaders Meet on Cabinet Resignations," Kyoto News Service, cited in *FBIS*, January 19, 1993, p. 75.

8. "Premier Hau Resigns over Political Feuds," *Asian Bulletin,* March 1993, pp. 21–22.

9. Ibid.

10. Ibid.

11. "Kuomintang Policy Guidance Group to Begin Work," China Broadcasting Corporation, cited in *FBIS,* February 9, 1993, p. 69.

12. "Official Says KMT to Accelerate Party Reform," China News Agency, cited in *FBIS*, March 2, 1993, p. 72.

13. "KMT Plans Nationwide Opinion Poll," China News Agency, cited in *FBIS*, March 5, 1993, p. 75.

14. "Poll Shows Many Feel Kuomintang Facing Crisis," China News Agency, cited in *FBIS*, March 8, 1993, p. 81.

15. Ibid.

16. "Rebels in Kuomintang To Form New Party," Kyoto News Service, cited in *FBIS*, May 20, 1993, p. 54.

17. See R. L. Chen, "Legislator lashes against vote plan," *China Post* (International Edition), July 30, 1993, p. 1.

18. "Group sets up Panchiao branch office," *China Post* (International Edition), August 3, 1993, p. 4.

19. Annie Huang, "KMT Identity Crisis: Unclear Future for Island," *China Post* (International Edition), August 3, 1993, p. 1.

20. R. L. Chen, "A hope for no party separation," *China Post* (International Edition), August 4, 1993, p. 1.

21. Patricia Kuo, "KMT rebels form party," *China Post* (International Edition), August 11, 1993, p. 1.

22. "CNA Reviews KMT Congress," China News Agency, August 16, 1993, cited in *FBIS*, August 17, 1993, pp. 50–51.

23. "Li Teng-hui Addresses KMT Congress Opening," China Broadcasting Corporation, August 16, 1993, cited in *FBIS*, August 17, 1993.

24. Ibid.

25. "Li Teng-hui Appeals for Unity," China News Agency, August 17, 1993, cited in *FBIS*, August 18, 1993, p. 54.

26. "Foreign Minister Gives Speech," China News Agency, August 17, 1993, cited in *FBIS*, August 18, 1993, p. 54.

27. R. L. Chen, "Premier upholds unification stance,"*China Post* (International Edition), August 18, 1993, p. 4.

28. Jeremy Mark, "Taiwan Party Re-Elects Lee in Show of Unity," *Asian Wall Street Journal,* August 20, 1993, p. 1.

29. Patricia Kuo, "Central Committee to be picked today,"*China Post* (International Edition), August 19, 1993, p. 1.

30. "No Military Men on Committee," China News Agency, August 18, 1993, cited in *FBIS*, August 19, 1993, p. 41.

31. "New Central Committee Members," China News Agency, August 19, 1993, cited in *FBIS*, August 20, 1993, p. 57.

32. R. L. Chen, "KMT elects new breed,"*China Post* (International Edition), August 20, 1993, p. 1.

33. For further details, see *China Post* (International Edition), August 20, 1993, p. 1.

34. "14th KMT Congress Continues; Elections Held," China News Agency, August 20, 1993, cited in *FBIS*, August 23, 1993, p. 67.

35. See R. L. Chen, "Lee bids to stave off rift,"*China Post* (International Edition), August 23, 1993, for further details on the above mentioned events.

36. "Standing Committee Elected," China News Agency, August 23, 1993, cited in *FBIS*, August 23, 1993, p. 67.

37. "Li Teng-hui Gives Speech," China News Agency, August 23, 1993, cited in *FBIS*, August 23, 1993, p. 68.

38. "KMT Chairman Lee addresses end of Congress,"*China Post* (International Edition), August 23, 1993, p. 4.

39. See "New Central Committee Members," p. 57.

40. "The KMT Central Committee: Is it still a necessity?" (editorial) *China Post* (International Edition), August 20, 1993, p. 2.

41. R. L. Chen, "KMT elects new breed,"*China Post* (International Edition), August 20, 1993, p. 1.

42. Susan Yu, "'New generation' joints KMT leadership core," *Free China Journal,* August 27, 1993, p. 1.

43. Patricia Kuo, "KMT adds 16 to core,"*China Post* (International Edition), August 24, 1993, p. 1.

44. Susan Yu, "'New generation' joints KMT leadership core," p. 2.

45. Ibid.

Section II
Elections and Party Competition

Introduction

The chapters in this section assess Taiwan's major elections and the evolution of party politics and party competition that made those elections meaningful. They focus on the period from 1980 to 1994 and span a time-frame from the onset of competitive elections to Taiwan's emergence as a full-fledged democracy. That portion of Taiwan's democratization said to result from electoral politics (if one can reasonably make such an allocation) is attributable mainly to national plenary elections, though elections for Taiwan's governor and its metropolitan mayors were also very important. The chapters on political parties and party competition, of course, consider events before 1980.

The importance of elections and the role of political parties in a nation's political modernization and democratization process is axiomatic. In Taiwan, the media, scholars, and citizens alike have considered both very essential to the country's successful transition to democracy. Certainly elections have been the most noticed part of the democratic process and provide the best evidence that democratization has occurred and that the democratic processes are working.

There are several reasons why elections have played such a central role in Taiwan's political modernization. Elections are an essential part of the polity of the Republic of China as it was designed by the Constitution. Likewise, they are an basic ingredient of the nation's political thought or ideology, which comes primarily from Sun Yat-sen's writings and teachings. Finally, elections constitute the selection process for picking most government officials and help to legitimize the political system.

The history of elections becoming a vital part of the political process in Taiwan parallels the nation's economic growth. As Taiwan prospered, giving rise to urbanization and a middle class, interest groups formed. Soon they perceived that they had to pursue their goals in politics. Early on, they found they could either work with the ruling Nationalist Party, or Kuomintang (KMT), and the government (which, in the past, to a considerable degree was controlled by the KMT), or with independent politicians. Independent candidates, however, at first did not constitute a real opposition and had little political influence. Legal opposition parties were not a meaningful alternative.

181

But this situation soon changed. With rapid urbanization, city "political" organizations began to develop. Likewise, as the economy became more dependent upon trade, the need for democracy became more critical since most of Taiwan's trade partners were Western democracies and they supported political change of the democratic kind. In addition, as economic development became hostage to the flow of knowledge, a more open democratic system became a must. Of course, in this context new political parties and competitive elections became a demand that the government and the ruling party could not refuse.

Actually, Taiwan had elections beginning in the 1930s. While still a colony of Japan, the colonial government held elections for assemblies in the prefectures, counties, and towns. This followed several years of agitation by residents of the island for home rule. These elections, however, were not very meaningful inasmuch as half or more of the delegates to these bodies were appointed by the Japanese government.

In the 1950s, Taiwan witnessed meaningful local elections soon after the United States sent the Seventh Fleet to the Taiwan Strait to block an invasion from the mainland. The U.S. afforded Taiwan a secure and safe environment for electoral politics. Although the government was at this time quite authoritarian, it viewed local politics as faction ridden and undemocratic and hence perceived that it was not threatened by local political change and, moreover, that it had to train local politicians in constitutionalism and democracy.

In 1951, Taiwan had its first island-wide election in the form of a contest to pick representatives to the Taiwan Provincial Assembly. The Provincial Assembly had some important functions, though its powers were generally circumscribed by the central government and the body was to a considerable degree controlled by the ruling Nationalist Party. Consequently, this event did not constitute a significant national election in terms of democratization.

This situation remained through the rest of the 1950s and through the 1960s and 1970s, though there was a plethora of evidence of political modernization in the functional sense. There were regular local elections that were generally democratic and fair. Voters were knowledgeable about the issues and candidates, and voter turnout was high. Elected officials were able to rise in the system and sometimes into national politics.

Meaningful national elections were delayed because the country was at war. Or so it was said. But most citizens generally felt that democracy had to be realized slowly and in stages. There was still another reason: Delegates to the national elected bodies of government could not be chosen by the people of China, since most of China (the mainland) was controlled by the Chinese Communist Party. Changing the status quo would be tantamount to declaring a two-

China policy. To the critics these reasons were but rationalizations for holding democratic elections for local offices but not for national ones and for keeping the political system an authoritarian one.

Still, some progress was made. In 1969, Taiwan held its first supplemental election. Seats were added to the National Assembly and the Legislative Yuan to give Taiwan's populace greater representation in these bodies. Thenceforth, the National Assembly and the Legislative Yuan no longer represented all of China's population evenly. Taiwan was over-represented. Additional supplemental elections were held in 1972 and 1975.

A bigger supplemental election was scheduled for 1978, but it was canceled when the United States broke diplomatic relations with the Republic of China and established formal relations with the People's Republic of China. Otherwise, 1978 may have been a turning point in Taiwan's electoral politics.

Still, the need for competitive national elections remained. In fact, the system was modernizing without significant election politics. Thus, despite the insecure situation, something had to be done. Taiwan's economy required a more open and competitive electoral system. Taipei was under pressure from the United States and the international community to prove it was a democracy and worthy of their support. In the context of diplomatic failures, a loss of the government's credibility, and pressure by Beijing to negotiate unification on its terms, Taiwan needed to act quickly. Its leaders calculated that democracy was the key and that only competitive national elections would prove that democratization was in progress. That proof was supplied in 1980.

The first chapter in this section is about Taiwan's first competitive national election. In my view, it was its most significant election; certainly it was the most exciting. It set various precedents that were followed later. Agreements were made between the opposition and the ruling Nationalist Party, and there was a new election law written in advance of the election. These things made the process work. That the election was as democratic as it was prompted some citizens and observers to think that it was a one-time event staged to please the United States and the international community and thus that it was less than genuine.

A similar election held three years later is the topic of Chapter 2. It afforded proof that national competitive elections were now a permanent part of Taiwan's political landscape. This election, like the 1980 election, gave the Nationalist Party and the government confidence that competitive elections would not lead to violence or chaos and that the ruling party could win in open electoral contests. At this time the Nationalist Party was still an authoritarian party not accustomed to competition, and many of its leaders, not to mention rank and file members, did not welcome any challenge; yet it had ruled well, especially in terms of engineering economic growth, and many understood that it had broad public support.

In 1986, Taiwan had its first two-party election. In fact, this was the first two-party election ever in a Chinese nation. The Democratic Progressive Party (DPP) was formed in September by independent politicians who had earlier joined forces to become a proto-political party called the *tang wai*, which literally means "outside the party" (the party referring to the KMT). They had begun organizing in previous campaigns; now they constituted a genuine political party and ran a party campaign. The election thus was one of true party competition. Chapter 3 is an analysis of this watershed election.

Chapter 4 assesses the next Legislative Yuan election in 1989. Although the DPP had made the previous election a genuinely competitive two-party one, it had not performed very well—neither as well as expected nor well enough to be considered a serious challenge to the ruling party. The 1989 election was different. The DPP did well enough that all of the major newspapers proclaimed it a winner in the election and pundits predicted that it could become in the party in power in a few years.

In 1991, Taiwan witnessed its first non-supplemental election. Previous elections had not been plenary elections because many elected officials had been frozen in office after the government fled to Taiwan in 1949. This changed with the "elder parliamentarians" stepping down before December 1991, making possible the election of a new National Assembly. This election, which is the subject of Chapter 5, silenced the critics of Taiwan's political system who said it was unrepresentative of Taiwan and therefore undemocratic. It was also an important election because the DPP put the issue of independence in its platform and made it an election issue—for which they were repudiated by the voters. Finally, the ruling Nationalist Party did well, dampening some speculation after the 1989 election that it would lose power—as was happening with ruling parties in democracies throughout the world.

Chapter 6 contains an assessment of the following year's election of delegates to Legislative Yuan—which was also a non-supplemental election. The Legislative Yuan, the lawmaking organ of government, is more important than the National Assembly (which at that time elected the president and vice president and amended the Constitution, among other duties). This election was therefore considered more significant in terms of the democratization process than the 1991 election. Moreover, the DPP won, giving rise to more sanguine views again about the evolution of a two-party system. There also seemed to be a trend visible: Looking at a string of recent elections there was a cyclic pattern of KMT and DPP victories. An alternative explanation is that the DPP regarded this election as more important than the 1991 election and had learned from its defeat in that election and that independence was not a good election issue. Afterward, with a new Legislative Yuan, particularly one composed of many activists, Taiwan's national lawmaking body henceforth began to play a new political role. It subsequently contributed more to the democratization process, although at times, antics, grandstanding, and violence seemed to bring this ideal into question.

In Chapter 7 the reader will find an analysis of the 1994 election of the governor of Taiwan and the mayors of Taipei and Kaohsiung, Taiwan's biggest and most important cities. The governor had not been elected before and the mayors of these cities had not been chosen by the electorate for some years. Though technically it was not a national election, the parties had to compete in large districts and debate national issues. The ruling Kuomintang won the governorship and the mayorship of Kaohsiung; the DPP won the Taipei mayorship. A third party, the New Party (a breakaway from the KMT) won a significant number of seats on the Taipei city council. Some observers called this election Taiwan's first three-party election and noted that ethnic politics were center stage during to the campaign but did not decide the election. This election was also said to be a predictor of the Legislative Yuan election in 1995 and the first direct presidential election in 1996.

Chapter 8 is about the evolution and role of political parties in Taiwan. It takes note of that political parties have not played a really significant role in the democratization process in most developing countries recently and that party competition is generally something that is taught to a colony by a mother country. Taiwan is different. The history of political parties in Taiwan and the circumstances surrounding the appearance of the Democratic Progressive Party in 1986 and other parties are discussed in detail in this chapter.

In Chapter 9, the focus is on the development of both opposition politics and opposition political parties. Although for many years there had been nominal opposition parties in Taiwan, opposition politics really began with independents and the *tang wai* in the 1960s and 1970s. Indeed, this happened while the formation of new political parties was illegal. With the first competitive election in 1980, the *tang wai* became a kind of weak political organization with the characteristics of a political party. It became a political party in 1986, and, after successfully competing in the 1989 election against the ruling KMT, many began to speculate that Taiwan had a two-party system. This remains a commonly held view.

Chapter 10 is about minor parties or third parties in Taiwan. Most observers of Taiwan politics are convinced that there are only two viable political parties.

Yet the nation has many other political parties. Thus, Taiwan is technically a multiparty system. What role these parties have played and may play in the future is the subject of analysis in the final chapter of Section II.

Chapter One
Taiwan's 1980 Watershed Election

The election of delegates to the National Assembly, the Legislative Yuan and the Control Yuan (the three elective bodies of government in the Republic of China or sometimes collectively called the parliament) in 1980 marked the beginning of competitive national elections in Taiwan. Being the first such election it was the most exciting and set precedents for subsequent campaigns and elections. It was an election that happened because of Taiwan's dire need for democratization—both for domestic and inter-national reasons. Compromise made the election possible. A victory for the ruling Nationalist Party or Kuomintang (KMT) gave its leaders confidence and no doubt encouraged them to allow more such competitive elections.

Prior to 1969 there had been no general election of delegates to any of the Republic of China's elective branches of government. Supplemental elections were subsequently held in 1973 and 1975, but these elections added only a small number of representatives to the elected bodies of government. Nor were these elections competitive; competition took place primarily within the ruling Nationalist Party or Kuomintang (KMT), though a few independents ran in most elections. In fact, the KMT did not face any genuine competition at the polls until the local elections of 1977. However, neither this election nor any other prior to 1980 truly set any real precedent for future elections in terms of a transition to competitive party elections.

Furthermore, the 1977 election was not a national election and too little was at stake. Plus the violence that broke out in the city of Chungli during these elections made many worry that competitive campaigning might not be compatible with political development of a non-destabilizing nature. In fact, during 1978 and 1979 there was a strong current of opposition within the government and the KMT to increasing the number of seats contested in future elections or allowing candidates more latitude to campaign.[1]

Despite this, the Republic of China's top leadership—Chiang Ching-kuo and his close associates—planned a national election for 1978 that might have introduced competition into electoral politics in Taiwan at the national level. More seats in the elective bodies of the national government were to be filled by the electorate. Restrictions on campaigning were lifted. In fact, this might have been a watershed event in terms of creating mass participatory democracy in Taiwan. As it turned out, just days before the election, President Carter announced that he had decided to de-recognize the Republic of China and transfer formal diplomatic ties to the People's Republic of China. Because the United States was Taipei's only military ally and the most important country with which it had diplomatic ties, the decision was a shock for Taipei. As a consequence, the election was postponed indefinitely. It was rescheduled in 1980.

The Political Context of the Election

Following the loss of formal ties with the United States, "diehard" elements in the KMT and government strengthened their position as well as their resolve to suppress movements supporting democratization, independent or non-party candidates, and competitive elections. As a result, in the following months there occurred a wave of suppression of free publishing and free speech and a general clampdown on dissent that in any way challenged the government. In fact, anything that might be construed as a threat to the nation's security was viewed with suspicion by the government, and for a time a significant portion of the population agreed.[2]

This situation, however, did not last long. Progressive elements fought back, arguing that diplomatic defeat increased the need for genuine participatory democracy. Only in this way, they contended, could Taiwan convince other countries that it was truly a nation-state deserving to remain sovereign that should not be "sold" to the People's Republic of China (which had already made its intent known to incorporate Taiwan). Progressive forces similarly asserted that Taiwan must also push ahead with plans to democratize the system in order to maintain a good image in the United States—a nation that still remained a friend despite establishing diplomatic relations with Beijing.[3]

In the spring of 1979 Congress passed the Taiwan Relations Act, which in essence gave Taiwan nation-state status under U.S. law. Of equal importance was the fact that despite the breaking of diplomatic links, the United States did not sever trade and other ties, which, as a matter of fact, continued to grow. Thus, notwithstanding de-recognition, the United States still held the key to Taiwan's security and to its future in general. This was evidence that favored the progressives, who looked to the United States as a model for political development and democratization. Moderate forces in the government and much of the population were swayed by the progressives' admonitions.

In the spring and summer of 1979, progressive forces once again began to organize. For a variety of reasons, including the perception that the government's credibility had been utterly destroyed by U.S. de-recognition and that the situation for Taiwan was desperate, the movement quickly escalated its demands. Moreover, radical activists got control of (at least were leading the charge, so to speak) the progressive movement, including some revolutionaries who compared Taiwan's situation with Iran's. Opportunists also joined the movement seeing a chance for themselves to gain political influence. Some with criminal records participated.[4]

Government indecision on some major policy matters and a specific decision at the top to allow greater press freedom also stimulated activism. This relaxation in enforcing press control laws encouraged opposition groups and even individuals to publish anti-government statements that would not have heretofore been allowed. Precisely why press freedom was expanded so much at this time is not certain. Perhaps Chiang Ching-kuo felt that it was necessary in order to fully assess the nation's predicament. Perhaps he wanted to promote the kind of rapid political change that was necessitated by events, particularly his "Taiwanization" program which evoked calls for more reform; Chiang may have perceived that public debate on vital issues would help him outmaneuver party hacks and diehards in the government who wanted a permanent crackdown on protests and censorship of a genuinely regressive sort. In other words, compromise with those resisting change was difficult or impossible at this juncture and the president seemed to have perceived that he had to ride out the storm.[5]

During the summer and fall, progressive forces became more organized and politically even more active. As this happened, rightist opposition—made up in large part of veterans and veterans' groups—grew, resulting in several violent conflicts between "opposition" groups and "loyalists." Rightist forces were outnumbered, yet they were well organized and had the support of many government and KMT officials, including police organizations.

In December 1979, tension between progressives (joined by opportunist and criminal elements) and pro-government forces (joined by reactionary veterans and other rightist organizations) turned into violence during a mass demonstration commemorating Human Rights Day in the southern city of Kaohsiung. The demonstrators—after being cordoned off from onlookers and surrounded by police, who feared loss of crowd control—attacked the police.

It is uncertain whether the demonstrators reacted in fright or according to plan. The fact they carried clubs and other weapons indicated to some observers that they planned a confrontation with authorities. There remain many unknowns about the incident. It is clear, however, that local gangs infiltrated the ranks of the demonstrators, perhaps at the behest of the police (to make a police crackdown justified) or acting on their own (in order to take revenge on police who had recently cracked down on gang activities and had displaced certain underground organizations). It is also certain that news of the incident reached President Chiang. Prior to the outbreak of violence he ordered the release of detainees (who ostensibly had been beaten while in police custody) and police restraint, probably against the wishes of local authorities. In any event, a number of policemen (183 according to the official count, which was probably inaccurate or exaggerated because it included such things as scratches and broken fingernails) were injured. But, only one demonstrator was hurt.[6]

Subsequently, government authorities arrested leaders of the Formosa Magazine group that had organized and led the demonstration. In the spring, open trials were held and eight defendants were given prison sentences ranging from twelve years to life. The defendants were allowed attorneys and the right to speak for themselves at the trial, and both the local and foreign media were allowed to report freely on the case. According to a number of foreign observers, the government did not present a very convincing case on issues concerning democratic principles or political freedoms or on issues that related to the future of the nation.[7]

Nevertheless, the "Kaohsiung Incident," as it was now called, turned public opinion against the progressives. Before the incident, a large segment of the public sympathized with the anti-KMT, anti-government opposition, at least in principle. In fact, many felt that criticism of the government was healthy and that some drastic steps needed to be taken to deal with Taiwan's eroding diplomatic isolation following the loss of U.S. recognition. Most felt that one answer was a more democratic system that would justify support by the international community for Taiwan's continued autonomy and the Republic of China's sovereignty.

After the incident, public opinion changed dramatically. The demonstrators were now seen as promoting violence that threatened economic development and the nation's well-being. In fact, the public's sudden reversal of attitude surprised many foreign observers in Taiwan who did not realize that the Chinese view of violence (which is considered much more a threat to social harmony and therefore dangerous) differs considerably from the Western perspective, while political stability is viewed by Chinese as a sine qua non of the nation's survival. A general feeling of insecurity in Taiwan regarding the nation's economic success, which had been attained so quickly, compounded the public's sense of fear. The populace generally espoused the view that Taiwan's economic "miracle" was fragile and it could be lost if care was not taken to preserve the conditions that contributed to it—including, and perhaps most important of all, political stability. It was also widely believed that the People's Republic of China would quickly exploit any problems on Taiwan and was, in fact, looking for an excuse to intervene with military force. To the population of Taiwan that would mean an end to the political freedoms they had gained up to that point (which everyone knew far exceeded those provided by the government of the PRC) not to mention possibly their lives.[8]

Pre-Election Compromises

By May, progressive forces in the government and opposition groups began to work on formulating a modus vivendi. This took the form of writing new election laws and planning a campaign and an election for the end of 1980. The mood was one of seriousness: The nation's future was at stake and agreements and understandings needed to be hammered out. A democratic election had to be held and managed smoothly.

New election laws had been debated in government circles and by scholars and the press for some time. Issues simply had to be prioritized and the debate organized. In early 1980 the government, calling on scholars and the populace to participate, sponsored special meetings and debates. Government officials took part; legal and constitutional scholars were invited from abroad; and the press was asked to report on the discussions in order to engage public participation. The final result, officially adopted on May 14, 1980, was the new "Public Officials Election and Recall Law."[9]

The new set of regulations, or the new "Election and Recall Law, " as it was called, contained 113 articles and was widely viewed as a marked improvement over the previous set of election laws. This was particularly true in terms of making the system more democratic. The rights of candidates and restrictions on campaigning were made clear and specific. The new set of laws provided for much greater freedom in campaigning and electioneering. The new laws did not contain provisions allowing for additional parties, however. This left the opposition with the choice of joining one of the existing political parties (which to the overwhelming majority was not a real choice at all) or remaining a loosely organized group of independent, or *tang wai* (meaning "outside the party" or KMT) candidates with no official organization. Most opposition candidates accepted this as a "rule of the game," some noting that they could not compete very well as a group anyway, owing to the vastly superior organizational and financial capabilities of the KMT, plus the fact that opposition politicians were not united. Opposition candidates, it should be noted, came from various local factions that below the surface, and sometimes openly, disagreed adamantly and sometimes violently on many issues of importance.

Independent politicians, however, in unison openly criticized two provisions in the Election and Recall Law. These were (1) a provision that specified that handbills and other written materials for dissemination during the campaign be required to have a stamp bearing the printer's name and address, and (2) the fact that the campaign was divided into two parts: candidate-sponsored meetings and Election Commission-sponsored meetings, with the latter occupying the last few days of the campaign. (As will be seen in subsequent pages, steps have been taken to deal with these complaints.) [10] Some other provisions of the election law drew specific, though less animated, complaints.

On the positive side, the election laws took the supervision of elections away from the more partisan sphere of government, placing it in the hands of a relatively independent Central Election Commission. Also, since the election laws tightened procedures and proper conduct was defined much more clearly, there was less chance of the government, the KMT, non-party candidates, or anyone else committing irregularities. This meant less chance for election tampering, fewer opportunities for cheating by candidates, and a generally improved voting process.

In addition to the formal laws and regulations promulgated, there were also gentlemen's agreements or understandings reached behind the scenes. In fact, these were as important or more important than the formal election laws. These understandings consisted of promises by the non-party, opposition candidates not to advocate either communism or support of the Taiwanese Independence Movement. Non-party candidates also agreed not to state that they were representing any of those prosecuted (and in jail) as a result of the Kaohsiung Incident. The government in turn promised that the opposition candidates could otherwise have complete freedom of expression. In fact, non-party candidates were guaranteed that the government would control, or, if need be, suppress, veterans and other groups that might interfere with their activities. Taiwan's police organizations were ordered to protect and furthermore not to harass in any way independent candidates. [11]

In short, before December 1980, the groundwork was laid for the most open, competitive, and meaningful election in the nation's history. The election was made even more significant by the unprecedented number of seats in the elective bodies of government allocated to the territory under the control of the Republic of China. A total of 205 seats in the National Assembly, the Legislative Yuan, and the Control Yuan were to be filled by open competitive elections: 76,97, and 32 positions respectively. The number of delegates to be elected to the National Assembly was five times the number elected in 1969. The number to be picked by the electorate to the Legislative Yuan was slightly less than double the number elected in 1973 and 1975. The number of seats to be contested for the Control Yuan was sixteen times that elected in 1969 and more than double the number elected in 1973.

In assessing the significance of the number of seats put up for election, one must again consider the fact that many of the members then serving in these bodies were too old to participate actively in debate and their attendance rate was low. Furthermore, with the high rate of attrition due to death or serious illness, the elected candidates, though still in a minority, had time on their side. This was, of course, offset to some extent by the fact that the overseas Chinese (28 percent of the Legislative Yuan and 17 percent of the Control Yuan) rather than the local population, "elected" some additional seats. The Kuomintang in reality picked "elected" representatives of the overseas Chinese. Also, members of the Control Yuan were still elected indirectly, and the National Assembly remained in most respects a less than dynamic decision making body in terms of debate or wielding political power.

The Campaign

The campaign took place in an exhilarating atmosphere. The KMT claimed to represent policies of successful economic growth; material benefits; and a safe, secure, and peaceful society. The KMT also took credit, generally justifiably, for social welfare programs for the poor, better housing, and health insurance and unemployment benefits—issues with which independents and *tang wai* candidates also identified. [12]

Although the opposition was not unified, either formally (since that was illegal) or in spirit (due to factionalism), the candidates generally agreed on enough issues to write a *tang wai* platform. This platform included the following demands or suggestions: (1) more seats should be placed up for election in the National Assembly, Legislative Yuan, and Control Yuan; (2) popular elections should be held for the governor of Taiwan province and the mayorships of Taipei and Kaohsiung; (3) more Taiwanese should be appointed to government positions; (4) new political parties should be allowed to form; (5) the scope of freedom of press, speech, assembly, and the like should be broadened; (6) campaigning for elections should be less restricted; (7) the Temporary Provisions of the Constitution, particularly the articles that established martial law should be abolished; (8) earlier political trials should be reviewed and most or all political prisoners released; and (9) the KMT should relinquish many of the powers and prerogatives that in other political systems belong to the government and not to a political party.[13]

During the campaign some *tang wai* candidates vociferously assailed the government and the KMT on issues such as bribery, graft, corruption, and special privileges. Many chided the establishment for allowing overpaid, senile delegates to hold positions in important elected bodies of the government. Some even compared the KMT to the Chinese Communist Party and complained of the Republic of China's human rights record as well as the human rights records of nations with which Taipei still had diplomatic ties.[14] Many assailed the government for an ineffective foreign policy, mentioning specifically the loss of diplomatic ties and the new unofficial relationship with the United States.

Local citizens were literally flabbergasted at the candidates' actions and vitriolic statements made during the campaign. In fact, during the several weeks before the election there were numerous citizen complaints, both from opponents and supporters of the independent candidates, asking why the police were not arresting the most provocative candidates for threatening public order. Some observers predicted that unrestrained campaign activities would lead to anarchy. Others expressed delight at what they described as a free-for-all campaign and the sudden democratization of the political process.

Observers noticed citizens attending political rallies sponsored by the most extreme candidates often looking behind them and to the side expecting the police to close in at any moment to stop the speeches. But this didn't happen. Many wondered why veterans or other right wing groups did not try to break up public gatherings or speeches given by the most outspoken, anti-government candidates.[15] The answer, or course, was that understandings had been reached about this in advance and the police were instructed to protect opposition candidates.

Some *tang wai* candidates complained that police were harassing them, but in almost every case it was apparent that if the police had been intent upon obstructing their campaign or preventing them from saying what they were saying, the candidates in question would have been silenced or dragged off to jail before the campaign activities reached the tense pitch that they did. Hence, few believed charges of police interference or harassment; most often they were seen as a calculated effort by *tang wai* candidates to win sympathy from the masses and find an excuse to condemn the government.

A number of independent and *tang wai* candidates made issue of the unfairness of the nation's capitalist system. They immediately discovered, however, that this was not a "hot button" issue. Clearly there was no public sentiment for changing the economic system. Moreover, a number of noted scholars offered quantitative, empirical evidence in rebuttal, showing that Taiwan's economic growth had provided a more equitable distribution of incomes and material goods than was present in most Western countries.

Opposition candidates also tried to make political capital of Taiwan's serious environmental problems. The electorate generally regarded environmental destruction as a problem, but it was not one that generated much excitement. The large majority of the population felt that economic growth was more important, at least for the moment, than environmental concerns. Many also perceived that the government was doing all it could to deal with the most serious problems—air and water pollution. Some *tang wai* candidates also condemned the use of nuclear energy, but they found few listeners. The same was true for the critics of high defense expenditures. Most of the population perceived that a strong defense was necessary to protect Taiwan from external threat. The People's Republic of China had in recent months provided grist for this argument in the form of threats to use force to "bring Taiwan back into the fold."

The KMT officially nominated only 42 candidates for the National Assembly and 38 for the Legislative Yuan competition. Since a total of 402 candidates ran (5 were disqualified), independents and *tang wai* candidates were given a nice opportunity in terms of numbers. On the other hand, the large group of candidate, though it reflected a greater interest in the election and a genuine feeling of competition, meant that the average number of candidates per seat was larger: 2.76 as opposed to 1.48 for the by-election held in 1972 and an average of 1.77 for seven elections for the Taiwan Provincial Assembly held between 1954 and 1977. Thus, victory depended more on good organization than in previous elections and the KMT knew this.

The election took place with no serious irregularities or even credible accusations of anyone stuffing ballot boxes or intimidating candidates or voters or in any other way rigging the election. Election officials made greater efforts than usual to be certain that no one voted twice and that no ballots had to be invalidated unless the voter wanted to cast a blank or protest vote. Ballot boxes were translucent and vote counting was done in the eyes of the public. Final tallying was done on television, with local totals telephoned in by each precinct.

Voter turnout was somewhat lower than in previous elections because of bad weather on voting day: 66.43 percent cast ballots for delegates to the National Assembly; 66.36 voted for Legislative Yuan representatives. Turnout was lowest in Taipei and below average in other large cities; it was higher on the offshore islands. In terms of voting groups or blocs, professional and women's associations recorded the highest turnout at over 77 percent.[16]

The Election Results

Deciding the victor after the election was somewhat complicated. The KMT won 63 of 76 seats in the National Assembly contest for a score of 82 percent of the seats up for election. The ruling party's success, of course, was facilitated by overseas Chinese and professional organization voting overwhelmingly for the KMT. In the Legislative Yuan competition, the KMT won 56 of 70 seats for an 80 per-cent victory margin. In terms of numbers alone it was clearly a KMT win.

Although *tang wai* candidates did not make a good showing in terms of the seats gained and the percentage of wins, they could still boast of victory for several reasons. First, several *tang wai* candidates were among the biggest victors in terms of the number of votes won by a single candidate. Moreover, some of these winners were the most controversial and the most critical of the government.[17] Also, *tang wai* candidates did better than in previous elections, thereby demonstrating a favorable trend. Another reason to argue for an opposition victory (or at least a good performance) was the fact that a number of KMT candidates bolted the party and joined the ranks of the independents. This made the KMT appear less united and evoked questions about its future election victories. Finally, the public generally seemed sympathetic toward *tang wai* candidates and their platform and did not negatively associate them with the violence of the Kaohsiung Incident to the degree of just a few months before.

KMT officials were generally delighted with the election results in spite of the *tang wai* candidates' claim of victory and what, from an objective point of view, seems to have been an election where there was no overall winner. The KMT did well in Taipei and other large cities, proving that the rural-urban shift, which some sociologists had argued was hurting the party's base of support, was not a factor working against the ruling party. Social alienation resulting from urbanization and a rising material culture was similarly not a serious problem. Nor did the KMT suffer from lack of unity in the context of new planks in the party platform. Most important, the party fared well in spite of the unusual freedom allowed during the campaigning and what amounted to permitting party-style organization on the part of *tang wai* candidates.

Another factor of great significance was that some of the most anti-KMT opposition candidates were repudiated by the electorate. So were some of the *tang wai's* most important campaign issues. Lastly, the KMT ran with a majority of Taiwanese candidates; this gave an impression that the KMT had successfully bridged the gap between Taiwanese and Mainlander and that it was no longer a Mainland Chinese-dominated party—a view challenged, however, by the *tang wai*, which was almost exclusively Taiwanese.[18]

Generally the election was a credit to the nation's political development and to an informed and enlightened electorate. Most of the victorious candidates, whether KMT or *tang wai*, were Taiwanese—thereby further rectifying the Taiwanese-Mainlander imbalance in the elected organs of government. The level of education of the candidates was high: Of candidates winning seats in the National Assembly, 4 held Ph.D. degrees, 6 had M.A. degrees, and 45 possessed B.A. degrees; in the case of the Legislative Yuan the figures for academic degrees were 8, 9, and 42 respectively. This upgraded the level of education of these two bodies considerably. In addition, the age of victorious candidates was also low: an average of 45 for the National Assembly and 44 for the Legislative Yuan.[19] This made both bodies much younger.

Most winning candidates were businessmen who, according to some observers, would guarantee continued close ties between the government and the business community and ensure continuity in domestic policies. They may also facilitate stability in politics in general since businessmen were generally winners in local elections during the 1970s and appear to be the group most interested in politics and most capable of providing the type of leadership needed by the nation. A less pro-business viewpoint is apparent among victorious *tang wai* candidates, however, signifying to some extent a new, and perhaps growing, concern with social welfare, workers' rights, and environmental problems.

Ideologues fared poorly in the election. During the campaign many candidates de-emphasized their ideological views—especially if strong, or if identified with a specific ideological stand. Most who campaigned on a platform of ideology lost. A number of candidates employed sensationalist techniques in their campaigns, several hiring movie stars and other celebrities. These candidates were not very successful. A sizable portion of candidates followed public opinion polls in building their platforms or simply took a stand on many issues that seemed to be favored by the electorate. Others took an extremist or critical stand on some issues, in many cases even when it was obvious that if victorious they would not be able to rectify the problems discussed—or at least do so quickly or alone. The electorate was generally skeptical of both of these categories of candidates, thereby proving these tactics to be less than effective.[20]

In terms of less positive trends, those with money, and particularly those willing to spend large sums in the campaign, were generally winners. The average candidate spent around U.S. $500,000 during the campaign.[21] Personal fortunes in many cases were used, but many candidates made promises of favors to contributors if elected. The problem of "money politics" will be discussed again later. Needless to say, it was a rapidly emerging problem.

Those with personality and charisma fared better in the election, though this had to be combined with local support and influence for it to be meaningful. Oratory ability and good looks helped candidates, but obviously less so than in most Western nations' elections; in fact, some candidates made no public speeches, having others speaking on their behalf, and still won. Education was a qualification to boast about—in fact, very much so. It was considerably more important than in either past elections or in elections in Western democracies as reflected in opinion surveys and in winning candidates. Experience was also valuable, helping candidates about as much as in elections in Western countries. A high level of loyalty toward the constituency was considered important by voters, as was an ability to maneuver effectively in politics so as to influence law making and other decisions to the benefit of one's constituency.

When the election was over, government officials moved quickly to remove campaign posters, close candidates' headquarters, and end the "political holiday." On the other hand, the end of the campaign did not mean that no new precedents had been set or that the degree of freedom to criticize the government witnessed during the election was nothing more than a temporary phenomenon. Nor did it mean that in future elections the same openness and competitiveness would not prevail. In fact, although things seemed to return to normal in terms of excitement and intense public debate, there were certainly no warnings or repression carried out to make sure that progressive politicians and the public understood that the "holiday" had ended. On the contrary, the public was to some extent enervated by the election "ordeal" and wished to return to pre-election quiet and calm.

Clearly, in terms of competitive elections, a foundation was built. In short, the 1980 precedent-setting election appeared to mark a transition from what theorists would call an authoritarian/technocrat system to a democratic-development one. Thus, it is important to put this election into perspective and examine its impact on Taiwan's democratization and political development. First, however, it is necessary to look at the political issues in Taiwan that survived this momentous election and the immediate implications of the 1980 election.

It is clear that although *tang wai* candidates generally stressed the issues mentioned in their "platform," there was a great deal of difference in terms of the emphasis given to each tenet or issue. Many candidates never once mentioned some of them. Others emphasized only one or two planks. Obviously not all the tenets of the platform were as popular with the public as most *tang wai* candidates or objective observers might have assumed. It is also apparent that beneath the superficialities, the *tang wai* proposals in many ways differed very little from the KMT platform, at least as the latter planks were emphasized by most KMT candidates.

Generally, there was little public support for abandoning the Temporary Provisions and getting rid of martial law. Although this appears to be clearer after subsequent elections, candidates who stressed opposition to either in their speeches received acclaim from only a small portion of the electorate and in only a few cases did it help their campaigns. The same is true of the proposals to review the cases of political prisoners and give greater attention to human rights concerns. The reasons these issues were not as popular as *tang wai* candidates anticipated is that they contradicted the public's strong concern about maintaining public security and social and political stability. It also seems that in the minds of the voters these issues were associated with excessive westernization, an increase in crime and other social problems, and too much attentiveness to the advice of foreigners.[22] In short, a feeling of nationalism conflicted with these issues.

Although there was deep concern among voters for reforming the political system, they generally limited their support to democratic reforms promised by the government within the rubric of the Constitution and Sun Yat-sen's Three Principles of the People (although ideology itself was not a popular issue) rather than extending it to any Western model or solution. In other words, the public seemed to support rather sweeping improvements in the political system yet also saw rapid change as conflicting with stability; indeed public opinion regarding political reform was contradictory.

Also, notwithstanding the loss of diplomatic ties with the United States, which followed a long series of diplomatic defeats from 1969 to 1978 and seemed to precipitate opposition demands for change, foreign policy issues were not important during the election. In fact, it was quite apparent that foreign policy played only a small role in influencing either candidates or voters. Relations with other nations were mentioned only infrequently by candidates and was not to be an issue that got much voter attention during the campaign. However, one exception may be cited: If the issue of "Taiwanizing" can be seen as a foreign policy issue, then foreign policy was important. Obviously the electorate wanted a government that concerned itself with Taiwan's problems and opposed perpetuating the myth of ruling all of China. If one translates this into a two-

China policy or a one-Taiwan, one-China policy, or separatism, then that was one foreign policy issue that was of considerable concern.

In the domestic arena the public displayed strong support for a free-market economy and capitalism. Some *tang wai* candidates advocated socialism or socialist-like programs; this position attracted little sympathy. In fact, they alienated many voters. This situation might have been different if the government had not expended considerable effort for several years in the realms of health insurance, low-cost loans for workers to buy houses and apartments, unemployment benefits, and job safety. The electorate seemed to perceive that sufficient progress had been in these areas or was in the works.

The same was also true of the environmental problems, even though to the objective viewer environmental destruction was quickly becoming critical. *Tang wai* candidates were simply unable to make much of ecological concerns, probably because they did not try hard enough or because economic growth was considered a higher priority by most voters. Thus, both the KMT and the *tang wai* can be faulted for not taking up an issue that should have been of considerable concern. Likewise with sanitation, flooding (including sewers), and traffic problems. All of these things were of concern to the voter but apparently not enough. And because of the newness of this kind of election, the focus of attention was on other issues of immediate concern.

Conclusions

As a result of this election *tang wai* candidates began to assume a new role in Taiwan's politics. They could take credit for the fact they had helped make the system competitive in terms of party versus non-party electioneering. On the other hand, because a cohesive platform did not emerge from the *tang wai* candidates campaigning, there were no special bread and butter issues (as opposed to issues relating to the political system, civil and political rights and so forth) that could be identified that strongly with one side or the other and, as a result, the nature of future party competition remained uncertain. This may be attributed to the fact that it was the first real experience in a competitive, open national election for the *tang wai* candidates and because they emphasized too many issues that were not as important as they thought. Also, *tang wai* candidates, because of the election rules, had only local influence and reputation. Even after the 1980 election, it was clearly too early to predict how these questions would be dealt with.

It appeared that the KMT also faced some fundamental problems that it showed no signs of dealing with effectively. One basic question related to the role of the KMT as a mass party. Should it continue to be a large party? The disadvantage, namely that party discipline is difficult to impose, was very apparent in this election especially because there were a large number of KMT members who ran for office without party approval. The number of candidates doing this—and winning—was large enough to warrant concern. At the time, in fact, the problem portended to be a serious problem in the future.[23]

Another problem for the Kuomintang was that it was associated in the minds of the voters with the government to the extent that most errors made by the government, including unpopular decisions and problems associated with red tape and bureaucracy are blamed on the KMT. In contrast, the party does not always get credit by association for government policies that are successful or beneficial to the public. This seems to be a factor of political behavior in the Republic of China that is not unlike most Western democracies; the political culture discriminates against the party in power. What, if anything, can be done to change this tendency is uncertain. In any case, KMT leaders faced this dilemma in 1980 as it began to anticipate future elections.

Sociologists and political analysts have predicted for some time that the ruling party would lose support in the cities and voting trends in earlier elections seemed to support this point. However, the KMT dealt effectively with this problem through good organization. It may be that the urban cynicism expressed toward KMT policies in the past, as well as the large number of younger and more restless voters, will be equally a problem for *tang wai* candidates as they evolve into an unofficial or pseudo-party. Frequently during the campaign, Taipei voters openly expressed disbelief that *tang wai* candidates would pretend that they could solve problems when in office when, in fact, they would have no authority or power over such issues. They also criticized many who exaggerated their ability to change the system. In fact, some candidates made promises and statements that Taipei voters and the press immediately labeled ridiculous.

One final observation: The two other legal parties fared very poorly in the 1980 election. Their performance was disappointing to those who hoped that they would gain strength and win significant voter support, thereby giving rise to a competitive party system without changing or circumventing the Temporary Provisions. Therefore, the 1980 election suggested that if independent or *tang wai* candidates were to consider joining one of the two smaller parties, they should abandon this hope. Likewise, if one thought that *tang wai* candidates as a group might consider joining en masse one of the two small, but legal, parties, the prospects seemed very dim.

Endnotes

1. See J. Bruce Jacobs, "Taiwan in 1979: 'Normalcy' After 'Normalization,'" *Asian Survey*, January 1980, p. 85.

2. See Theodore Hsi-en Chen, "Taiwan's Future,"*Current History*, 77, No. 449 (September 1979), pp. 71–73, 83–84, for further details regarding the difficulties caused by the U.S. decision to break diplomatic relations.

3. See Hung-mao Tien, "Uncertain Future: Politics in Taiwan," in Robert B. Oxnam and Richard C. Bush, eds., *China Briefing 1980* (Boulder, CO: Westview Press, 1980), pp. 87–94.

4. For further details, see John F. Copper, "Taiwan in 1980: Entering a New Decade," *Asian Survey*, January 1981.

5. See John F. Copper, "Taiwan's Recent Election: Progress Toward a Democratic System," *Asian Survey*, October 1981, pp. 1032–1033.

6. See Copper, "Taiwan in 1980," for further details. This was the account that was given in the foreign media at the time.

7. This was true in part because several of the defendants were rather formidable intellectuals and were able to present a cogent case in defense of their actions. At the same time, the government did not seem to be prepared or did not care to engage in debate on the moral and philosophical significance of the event. See Hung-mao Tien, "Uncertain Future," p. 89, for further details.

8. See Harry Hsin-i Hsiao, "Political Development in Taiwan Since the Normalization of the Sino-U.S. Relationship," in Hung-mao Tien, ed., *Mainland China: Taiwan and U.S. Policy* (Cambridge, MA: Oelgeschlager, Gunn and Hain Publishers, Inc., 1983), p. 163.

9. See *The Public Officials Election and Recall Law, Republic of China* (Taipei: Hwang Hwa Publishing Company, 1980).

10. Efforts were made to deal with these complaints at this time. Much more, however, was done later.

11. For details, see Copper, "Taiwan's Recent Election," p. 1035.

12. *Tang wai* candidates generally advocated more social programs, welfare, and higher taxes, especially on high incomes. This platform had less voter appeal than anticipated for two reasons: one, it contradicted *tang wai* candidates' view that the government already interfered in individual activities too much, and two, the government had already instituted a host of welfare programs, and a shortage of labor had already had a strong income-leveling impact.

13. See various issues of *Ba-shih Nien-tai* (The Eighties), published by *tang wai* leader Kang Ning-hsiang. C.f. Jurgen Domes, "Political Differentiation in Taiwan: Group Formation Within the Ruling Party and the Opposition Circles, 1979–1980," *Asian Survey*, 21, No. 10 (October 1981), p. 1017.

14. These charges were made in public speeches and on posters at various campaign headquarters. The most noticeable were at the campaign headquarters of *tang wai* candidate Huang Tien-fu on a main street in Taipei, an area frequented by foreign tourists.

15. This observation is based upon interviews in Taipei and several other cities in Taiwan at the time. Most people obviously did not know about the compromises and the gentleman's agreement made between the government and the *tang wai*.

16. See Annual *Review of Government Administration, Republic of China 1981–82* (Taipei: Research, Development, and Evaluation Commission, Executive Yuan, 1983), p. 24.

17. In fact, a number of those connected with the "Kaohsiung Incident" in 1979 were elected, including relatives.

18. Over 90 percent of the KMT candidates in this election were Taiwanese.

19. "KMT Wins Elections," *China Post* (Taipei), December 8, 1980, p. 1.

20. For further details, see Copper, "Taiwan's Recent Elections," *Asian Survey,* October 1982, p. 1037.

21. Ibid.

22. There was a fairly widespread perception that the election was being held in large part for the benefit of the United States. This author was in Taiwan at the time and felt that a fairly sizeable number of people resented this, although they did agree with the other reasons for the election.

23. This view was expressed by a number of KMT leaders at this time, sometimes in public.

Chapter Two
The 1983 National Election

On December 3, 1983, Taiwan held its fifth national supplementary election. More important, this was the Republic of China's second competitive national election, and therefore confirmed the institutionalization of such elections. At least it proved that the 1980 competitive election was not just an isolated, one-time event. The KMT again performed well against a real opposition—though it still had many advantages and independent politicians were still in some important ways handicapped.

In this election, 71 candidates were chosen to the Legislative Yuan, including 16 picked to represent trade, professional organizations and other groups. In addition, 27 were chosen to represent the overseas Chinese. However, since this was an "off-year" contest, there was no election of delegates to the National Assembly or Control Yuan. Nevertheless, this was an important election; it was the first national election since the competitive 1980 election and, like that election, it witnessed a campaign and struggle pitting the Nationalist Party against the *tang wai*, or a group of non-party candidates thereby proving the genuineness of party competition in national elections. It also tested still another set of election laws.

Pre-Election Politics

Prior to the election, on July 8, 1983, President Chiang Ching-kuo signed and promulgated a new Election and Recall Law. The 1980 national election, as well as local elections in 1981 and 1982, had shown that the earlier set of election laws were defective in a number of respects and it was clear that revisions and changes had to be undertaken. Suggestions for revision of the Election and Recall Law had been made even before the 1980 election just after it had been promulgated. More serious post-election proposals after three other elections led to formal discussions that subsequently resulted in a new set of laws.

205

The Election and Recall Law of July 1983 was in effect a major revision of the earlier set of laws. Forty-nine of the 113 articles were altered. The three general areas of change were: preventing acts of violence during the election, eliminating vote buying and bribery, and prohibiting illegal campaign activities. All were serious problems during the 1980 election and in subsequent local elections. Moreover, throughout 1983 the increased level of emotionalism about the pending election, which promised to be more competitive, caused many to fear that violence might occur, disrupting the election and reversing the progress made toward democratization so far. Also, very serious actions had to be taken to control vote buying and illegal campaign activities.

Specifically, the new Election and Recall Law made a number of important procedural changes that to some degree altered the electoral system and the democratic processes related to it. The Control Yuan, previously chosen through indirect election, or ballots cast by the Taiwan Provincial Assembly and the Taipei and Kaohsiung city councils on a local constituency basis, had suffered from a scandal involving vote buying. In fact, it was rumored that in the 1980 elections, one candidate had purchased six votes from Taiwan Provincial Assembly members for around U.S. $3 million.[1] Provisions in the new Election and Recall Law made this more difficult and at the same time made the Control Yuan more representative of the population, inasmuch as delegates elected to the Provincial Assembly would now choose delegates representing a larger geographical area and a broader spectrum in terms of views and experience. The change favored the Nationalist Party, however, since it worked to split the *tang wai* and independent vote. It is not surprising that the non-KMT opposition strongly opposed the change.

To reduce the incidence of various illegal campaign activities, penalties were increased for campaigning before the official election period opened. More detailed restrictions forbidding the posting of signs and other forms of political advertising in places other than those approved by the Election Commission were written into law. The new Election and Recall Law also standardized the size of campaign pamphlets and limited the number of campaign vehicles. Firecrackers were banned (because of injuries caused by them in the last elections), and collective campaigning was made unlawful at privately-sponsored meetings during the first week of the campaign.

The new law prohibited candidates from using the mass media for political campaigning and made illegal parades and demonstrations a more serious offense. Television and other forms of mass media were not allowed under earlier 1980 election laws and a number of candidates had complained of these restrictions. Yet, the new law went even further in restricting the use of the mass media by political candidates. In this regard, those who drew up the new set of laws cited public opinion in formulating these regulations. The majority of the electorate had expressed opposition to candidates buying television time—which, being especially expensive in the Republic of China, would favor wealthy candidates. The Central Election Commission also sought to avoid the sticky problem of equal time that has become so controversial in Western countries. Clearly more laws (which would have been extremely controversial) would have been needed if television campaign advertising had been allowed. In contrast to the changes made in electing the Control Yuan, other provisions in the new law generally found favor with independent candidates.[2]

The new Election and Recall Law also delineated more specific penalties for violations of the law and defined illegal acts more clearly than the old law. Penalties for vote buying and bribery, for example, were explicitly set and the punishment increased in severity. This provision even extended to the voter who might show his vote before putting it in the ballot box. Ceilings were also imposed on campaign spending according to the size of the electoral district, the number of elected offices to be filled, and the consumer price index. This limit ranged from NT$3.5 million (U.S.$87,500) in the smallest district to NT $5.4 million (U.S. $135,000) in the largest for the 1983 supplementary election.[3] Candidates were also prohibited from receiving contributions from foreign governments, groups, foundations, or individuals and could not make contributions to other candidates in the same election.

The public generally agreed that a new set of election laws had to be written and supported of the results. In fact, polls taken after the new Election and Recall Law was completed and debated in the media reflected a high level of public level. Clearly, firmer election regulations were needed and more specific definitions of illegal acts and punishments were required to make elections fairer. The feeling about the excessive use of money in elections was particularly intense.

Tang wai candidates agreed with most of the provisions of the new law, though they felt that some of the provisions discriminated against them. Not having sufficient voting strength to prevent the inclusion of these parts of the law, *tang wai* members of the Legislative Yuan boycotted the session that approved it. However, this protest was not a very serious matter and can be interpreted as going on record in registering a complaint. There was little controversy afterwards, especially regarding provisions other than those that were seen to unduly weaken or restrict opposition candidates.[4]

As soon as the new Election and Recall Law went into force, potential candidates started preparations for the December election accordingly. During the period from October 29 to November 2, 177 candidates registered with various election commissions. Candidates for professional or other groups drew lots to decide their election numbers on November 14. December 3 was the date set for the election of legislators to replace those whose terms would expire January 13, 1984, in accordance with both constitutional provisions and the new Election and Recall Law. Candidates registered in six regular voting districts or for balloting in Taipei or Kaohsiung City. Eight days were allocated, according to the election law, to self-sponsored forums and seven days to government or election committee-run campaigning.

The Campaign

During the period of self-sponsored forums, which began on November 17 and ended November 25, 2,971 such meetings were held, 542 in Taipei. An average of 1,000 people attended for a total of more than 2 million people during this period.[5] Chen Ming-tang, a *tang wai* candidate, topped all other candidates by holding 46 meetings. Some candidates, however, decided to forego self-sponsored forums. Two candidates from Taipei and eleven candidates island-wide refused to appear in public at all. The so-called silent candidates were generally unknown to the public and had little confidence in their ability to attract an audience.[6] A much larger number of self-sponsored meetings were on the eighth day, just before the government-sponsored meetings started. Campaigning during the period was in general orderly and problems were few despite the heated nature of the issues being debated and the intensity of the competition among candidates was intense. The Election Committee issued only seven warnings for minor offenses committed by candidates and their workers during this period.[7]

Government-sponsored forums were held from November 26 to December 2. Thirty-seven forums were allocated for Taipei, including 5 for professional and other groups; 16 were arranged in Kaohsiung, including 3 for professional and other groups; and 263 were held elsewhere, including 45 for professional and other groups.[8] According to the new Election and Recall Law, each candidate could speak for only fifteen minutes at a time and in a sequence set by the Election Committee. The government-sponsored forum, unlike the self-sponsored forum, required candidates to speak in person. Most of the candidates gave "packaged" speeches, but the grouping of many candidates together created in essence a debate atmosphere. Candidates were banned from giving speeches at other occasions during this period; they were even prohibited from talking in public about non-election issues. Several candidates violated this provision in the election law by participating in weddings, birthday and tea parties, and other events—as they had before the campaign started. One candidate, Huang Tien-fu, allowed (or perhaps instructed) his campaign workers to call a news conference to discuss the "unfair treatment of prisoners." Some described this as flaunting the election law; others interpreted his actions as legal. On this issue, the new Election and Recall Law was clearly not explicit enough.[9] In any event, the government took no action.

Another candidate, Fang Su-min, distributed a campaign pamphlet that included a picture of Teng Hsiao-ping (Deng Xiaoping in Pinyin—leader of the People's Republic of China). The government immediately seized these pamphlets, but not before it was reported in newspapers throughout the island. Fang wanted to be provocative and test the Election Commission and the new Election and Recall Law. However, her gesture was not construed as necessarily advocating communism inasmuch as the picture made reference specifically to United States-People's Republic of China relations.[10] In any case, the government took no action against Fang, probably because it did not want to be charged with obstructing democratic practices. Subsequently, since the government was pleased with the election and did not want to sully its image abroad, it did not pursue the case.

In addition to making numerous public speeches, candidates made announcements via trucks with loud-speakers. They also had their campaign workers put up campaign posters and do other forms of advertising. Both of these types of campaign activities were, however, much more restricted than during the 1980 election. Candidates were limited to five trucks each and allocated specific places to put up posters. A number of candidates complained that this restriction limited their freedom of speech. The public, however, generally felt that it made the campaign more orderly, eliminated noise pollution, and reduced the problem of cleanup afterwards—all of which were serious annoyances during the 1980 campaign. Surprisingly there was no major split between Kuomintang and *tang wai* candidates on these issues. However, on the use of students as campaign workers, *tang wai* candidates were almost unanimous in protesting new restrictions in the Election and Recall Law. The candidates and the public alike generally accepted the ban on firecrackers.

The new law demanded the standardization of handbills in terms of size and style. Some handbills, however, were made to look like news releases in order to attract more attention.[11] An inordinately large amount of handbills had been used during the government-sponsored forums because of the restriction on the amount of time the candidates were allowed to speak. The law also prohibited candidates from hiring entertainers or performers who were not officially approved campaign workers. Views expressed by both candidates and the public were more mixed on these and other restrict-ions.

Many *tang wai* candidates started their campaigning with advertisements in magazines that they owned or campaigned informally for a long period before the election period began. Many used the news or political magazines during the campaign. The government took action against a number of such publi-cations—banning four issues of one, confiscating ten issues of another, and suspending the publication of five magazines for a year.[12] Nevertheless, the number of *tang wai* magazines proliferated during the months preceding the election, with the most important claiming circulation of 15,000 or more.[13] Moreover, there was general agreement that the magazines were able to say many things they were prohibited from saying in the past, even in 1980. *Tang wai* candidates admitted that freedom of the press had increased, compared to any time in the past, notwithstanding the bans.[14]

Tang wai candidates generally campaigned on such issues as democracy, greater political participation for Taiwanese, human rights and civil liberties (in particular, freedom of speech), the lifting of martial law, and the Republic of China's status in the world community.[15] There was a "gentleman's agreement" between the government and *tang wai* candidates early on to the effect that the latter could campaign on any issue and say anything except that they could not advocate Communism or Taiwanese independence or claim to represent those jailed after the "Kaohsiung Incident." The former two provisions were also later written into the Election and Recall Law. Still, a number of *tang wai* candidates spoke of "self-determination" for Taiwan, which most voters recognized as a word that had been cited by a witness during a recent hearing of the U.S. Senate Foreign Relations Committee in November 1983 to advance Taiwanese indepen-dence (since the matter had been talked about a lot in the media). The Election Commission subsequently asked candidates not to use the term since it was "confusing and misleading" and sounded like those using it were advocating Taiwanese independence.[16] A number of *tang wai* candidates continued to use it anyway.

Many *tang wai* candidates harshly criticized the government for keeping special privileges; allowing pollution to get worse; not doing anything about traffic problems, flooding and other social problems; and not controlling eco-nomic crimes.[17] Most of the electorate considered these valid criticisms. Never-theless, most *tang wai* candidates were unable to offer cogent or realistic solu-tions other than those already being implemented by the government to deal with the problems.

Kuomintang candidates stressed the following themes in their campaign: Taiwan under KMT leadership had attained remarkable economic progress; political change must be evolutionary, not revolutionary—lest everything that had been gained economically be lost because of political mistakes (making reference at times to Vietnam); the nation faces an external threat—the People's Republic of China—and this threat can be dealt with only if the people remain united and keep the faith; the government and the people must transcend ethnic and other differences (referring to Taiwanese-Mainlander differences), especially in view of the fact that an overwhelming proportion of the population has a common Chinese ancestry. In short, the KMT was standing on its record while advocating peaceful and moderate solutions to Taiwan's problems.

KMT leaders played well-known popular songs at their rallies or made reference to themes in them in their campaign literature. These themes usually underscored planks in their platform and were already familiar to most voters. This proved to be a clever and effective way of putting across their campaign positions while winning sympathy and support for their platform.[18] It also reflected sophisticated advertising techniques and professionalism in electioneering.

The KMT also devised clever responses to *tang wai* campaign issues. KMT candidates specifically criticized the slogan of self-determination, arguing that this concept applies only to people under colonial rule. They also criticized *tang wai* candidates for campaigning on non-election issues and constantly mentioning the 1979 Kaohsiung Incident. Some KMT candidates in their speeches satirically noted that they had no relatives in jail—making reference to seven *tang wai* candidates that were wives, brothers, other relatives, or even attorneys of those jailed following violence in Kaohsiung in December 1979.[19] KMT candidates also underscored the logic of their platform while chiding the emotionalism, inexperience, and lack of realism of *tang wai* candidates.

KMT candidates even criticized the government for having special privileges (joining the *tang wai* on this theme) and called for more government action to deal with pollution, traffic, and other problems. Like the *tang wai,* they also called for more democracy and individual freedoms. At times, the KMT seemed to avoid identification with the government. Generally, however, KMT candidates spent more time applauding the progress made in economic development, but also in the realms of human rights and social freedoms (which they argued could only follow economic development or were inevitable outcomes of the economic growth the government had engineered). Nearly all KMT candidates supported the continuation of martial law, and during the campaign they were able to cite a timely poll indicating great public support for keeping it.[20]

The KMT's campaign reflected a new identity for the party separate from the government and the bureaucracy. This is important since it suggested that the KMT in the future no longer wanted to be regarded as an official or government party. Such a change, of course, is necessary if the KMT is to win election victories based on its professionalism and its public support instead its special status. It also means that the KMT can no longer claim "official party" status and will probably have to end many of its ties to organs of the government.

A number of both KMT and *tang wai* candidates criticized each other on both substantive and personal issues. A popular issue was overspending during the campaign. One KMT candidate was named the "golden cow" by other candidates for his lavish spending. Several candidates were "single issue" candidates; one named his campaign headquarters the "human rights gas station" and used it to campaign almost solely on that issue. Another candidate accused the government of nepotism, making this the main theme of his campaign.[21] Many used emotional appeals. This was especially true of *tang wai* candidates, some of whom frequently made references to relatives or friends in jail. Some implied in public that if they lost the election they would not be able to do anything in public again due to the loss of face suffered. One candidate had his wife, a locally famous opera star, do much of his campaigning. She stated repeatedly that she could not appear in operas again if her husband lost, trying to intimidate the voters to vote for her husband.

The KMT had two internationally famous athletes—Chi Cheng (formerly an internationally famous Olympic runner) and Yang Chuang-kuang (former "Iron Man of Asia") among its candidates. Thus the party frequently made reference to the health of the nation and its informal diplomacy abroad when promoting these candidates. Both added sparkle to the KMT's campaign, and both contributed to the pluralistic image of the party, since the former was Hakka Taiwanese and the latter an aborigine.

Generally, the KMT platform as well as party campaigning were based upon logical arguments concerning the party's qualifications and ability, the government's and the nation's achievements to date under its leadership, and its candidates's experience. This approach was clearly conservative compared to the *tang wai's* campaign. *Tang wai* candidates argued that insufficient progress had been made to date in realizing the Constitution, implementing democracy, and in the fulfillment of human and civil rights guarantees. They also scored the government's "return to the mainland" policy and the idea of one China as silly, though these issues were not overly stressed since they smacked of advocating communism or Taiwanese independence. Although most voters may not consider such policies realistic ones, they nevertheless opposed radical changes in them so as not to provoke Beijing (which has made it clear that Taiwan independence will provoke military action) or foster political instability.

On the whole, the KMT was united during the campaign. Some party members did not get the KMT to nominate them or officially sanction their candidacy and thus bolted from the Party. One or two bitterly criticized the KMT leadership and supported the *tang wai* in election issues. Generally, however, the KMT maintained party unity and discipline.

The *tang wai* formed a kind of election or nominating committee *(hou-hsuan hui)* and thus had "official candidates" and a platform. Thus, as in 1980, the *tang wai* was for all intents and purposes a political party, even though forming new political parties were still forbidden under the Temporary Provisions. In fact, the nation seemed no closer to formally dealing with this contradiction than three years earlier. Essentially the *tang wai* was allowed to do everything a political party does, but was not allowed to be a legal party. This seemed at the time to be an issue that would be resolved in a Chinese way—by time and inaction.

During the campaign, the *tang wai* split into what some described as two factions: a moderate, or "reform within the system" group, and an extreme, or "reform the system itself," group.[22] This, description, however, may be an over-simplification since the *tang wai* was in reality even more factionalized than these categories suggest. The publications put out by moderate and extremist candidates were not coordinated and many simply attacked all other candidates. Thus, both during and after the campaign, it was difficult to predict in what direction the *tang wai* was going in terms of its role as a new political force. Some were speculating that it would split into several "parties." Others thought it was simply suffering from lack of unity as a result of its "adolescent" status and that it remained a weak, unorganized pseudo-political party.

The Election Results

The results of the election were unequivocally a victory for the Kuomintang. KMT candidates won 62 of the 71 seats being contested; the *tang wai* won only 6; others won 4. Prior to the election, the KMT held 57 of the contested seats; thus, it gained 5. The tang *wai* had 9, suffering a loss of 3.[23] (Independents had 4 before, and 1 was added because of population increases.)

Of the 58 candidates officially nominated by the KMT, 56 won—or 96.55 percent. (Calculating on the basis of candidates approved by the KMT but not officially nominated, the figure is 87.32 percent.) Of the "officially" recommended *tang wai* candidates, 6 of 25 won, or 24 percent. Thirty-seven of the

KMT victors were incumbents, or 63.78 percent; 21, or 36.21 percent, were newly elected. In contrast, the *tang wai* returned only 2 incumbents.[24]

On the other hand, the KMT won 73.1 percent of the popular vote, down slightly from 1980. Official *tang wai* candidates won 19 percent of the popular vote, nearly the same as in 1980. Counting independent and *tang wai* candidates together, their vote was 26 percent—up slightly from 1980.[25] Whichever way the opposition is defined, non-KMT candidates received only about half of the seats they should have received judging from their popular vote count—reflecting poor organization, bad campaign strategy and a lack of unity.

Of the victorious candidates, 66 were Taiwanese and 5 were Mainlanders.[26] Both *tang wai* candidates and winners were overwhelmingly Taiwanese; in fact, there was only one exception. This was natural since it is regarded as a Taiwanese "party." But a large majority of both KMT candidates and victors were also Taiwanese, reflecting the decade-long "Taiwanization" of the ruling party—which was carried a step further in this election, with the KMT supporting an even larger percentage of Taiwanese candidates than in the 1980 election. Hence, Taiwanese became much better represented in the Legislative Yuan as a result of this election, even though this was not a breakthrough inasmuch as it was also true of the 1980 election and elections previous to that.

Eight women were elected, or slightly over 10 percent. All won by a large percentage. Three were *tang wai*; 5 were KMT.[27] According to rules in the Temporary Provisions, one woman must be elected for every five to ten legislators. Since women won a sufficient number of seats to fulfill this requirement, no special action was required. The *tang wai* candidates who were women tended to be more progressive or radical than their male counterparts, whereas female KMT candidates were even more traditional or conservative than their male counterparts. The average age of the women elected was forty-five—slightly older than male winners.

The ages off the winning candidates is also worth mentioning. Thirteen were in their thirties, 40 in their forties, 17 in their fifties, and only 1 was over sixty. The youngest candidate was 38. The average age of elected candidates was 44.85.[28] In short, it was a young group of new representative that was elected to the Legislative Yuan. *Tang wai* candidates and winners were slightly younger than their KMT counterparts, as was true in 1980; the gap, however, narrowed in 1983.

The level of education of winning candidates also rose compared to 1980 and previous elections; there were 10 high school graduates, 40 with college, university, or technical degrees; 21 with graduate education. Eleven victorious candidates had M.A. or Ph.D degrees.[29] The candidates were very well educated compared to their counterparts in other countries. KMT candidates and winners had higher educational qualifications than *tang wai* candidates and winners.

The election brought 6,741,937 people to the polls, 63.17 percent of the eligible voters.[30] The turnout was slightly lower than in the 1980 election and below average for elections in Taiwan. This was true notwithstanding the good weather almost island-wide. There were various explanations for the low voter turnout. Too many candidates turned off many of the voters by resorting to emotional appeals. Many candidates promised things they could not deliver, turning the campaign into a contest of "promising and lying." Money played too large a role, discouraging many potential voters. Some of the electorate decided that increased political freedoms included the right not to vote.[31] It is uncertain how big a role any of these reasons played, but all were mentioned by those who did not vote.

As usual, the voter turnout in Taipei was less than the national average: 62.92 percent. Kaohsiung registered 64.14 percent—somewhat above the national average. Voters went to the polls more in the rural areas and less in the cities. The highest voter turnout was on the islands of Quemoy and Matsu.[32]

The majority of KMT winners, as well as the party's biggest vote-getters, generally stuck to the party platform and can be described as moderates who based their campaigning on issues. Few can be defined as ideologues. Most victorious KMT candidates conducted a clean campaign. A large majority stressed their experience and education. Most praised the government yet also maintained some distance to avoid being identified as insiders.

Most of the *tang wai* winners would be categorized as "progressives" or "radicals." Four of the seven relatives or attorneys of those jailed after the Kaohsiung Incident won. In counting the victors, moderate *tang wai* candidates did not fare well. Even the leader of the moderate *tang wai*, Kang Ning-hsiang, lost. This prompted a number of foreign reporters to conclude that the *tang wai* would be more radical in the future since the voters had repudiated the moderates and supported more radical candidates.[33] Since elections are always complex events, this explanation is no doubt an oversimplification. Furthermore, there is considerable evidence to support quite a different conclusion regarding the *tang wai's* performance in this election. Further analysis is needed to explain why moderate *tang wai* candidates fared so poorly.

The biggest vote-getter among the *tang wai*, Fang Su-min, probably received more votes out of sympathy than out of support for her radical views.[34] Shortly after the trial of the Kaohsiung defendants (including her husband), her two daughters and her mother-in-law were murdered. The crime was uncharacteristically for Taiwan not solved. Fang took her only remaining child to the United States and returned to Taiwan shortly before the election.

During the campaign she carried pictures of her mother-in-law and children and told the story of their murder in her speeches and campaign literature. She campaigned actively and energetically. On a number of occasions she provoked the audience to become emotional and even to throw money at her.

In contrast, moderate Kang Ning-hsiang, standing on his laurels, generally refused to campaign. He expected an easy victory. The polls predicted his win, which until the day of the election seemed certain. Kang's attitude, his meager campaign effort, his split with the *tang wai* radicals, and the fact that running against him was a disenchanted KMT candidate that did not have party approval and appealed to poorer and less educated voters in Kang's district, probably explains Kang's defeat more than a shift of *tang wai* voter support from moderate to radical candidates.[35]

Huang Tien-fu, a *tang wai* incumbent from the same district as Kang but defined as a radical, lost for many of the same reasons Kang lost: the split in the *tang wai* and competition from a KMT rebel candidate. Furthermore, most *tang wai* candidates who emphasized the Kaohsiung Incident, martial law, and human rights in their campaigns lost their audiences and ultimately were not voted into office. Ideological *tang wai* candidates, as in the 1980 election, generally lost. Except for the fact that there was a larger number of victors among more "radical" *tang wai* candidates than among moderates, there is little evidence for a shift in support to the radical wing.

It can also be argued that the *tang wai* "moderates" are really misnamed; they are simply more experienced or have had more contacts with the government. Since the *tang wai* vote in large part represents a protest vote, as witnessed by the fact that few *tang wai* incumbents won, it naturally did not favor those defined as "moderates." In contrast, the so-called "radical" vote may better be defined as a protest vote.

In terms of big individual winners in the election, Lin Keng-shen, a male Taiwanese, age forty-eight and a member of the KMT, was the biggest winner, receiving 141,941 votes.[36] Lin was an excellent campaigner and could boast of experience in politics, a clean record, a good education, and the support of other leading politicians. His support came primarily from voters who viewed him as highly qualified and who expected a good performance from him. The second largest vote-getter was Yu Chen Yueh-ying, a female Taiwanese, age fifty-seven, who was recommended and supported by the *tang wai*. Yu was well-known because her father-in-law was one of the important *tang wai* politicians in the 1970s and was arrested following the 1979 anti-government protest that followed the U.S. breaking of diplomatic relations with the ROC. Yu may be described as somewhat moderate among the radical *tang wai* politicians.

Fang Su-min, already mentioned, was the third largest winner in terms of number of votes. She benefited from a huge sympathy vote and from the help of other *tang wai* candidates—including "moderate" Kang Ning-hsiang. She also had a strong base of support in her hometown, and because of this some competing candidates dropped out of the election early, leaving more votes for her.

Victorious *tang wai* candidates generally were bigger vote-getters than their KMT counterparts, which reflects good individual efforts but poor collective planning. KMT candidates were more consistent in their campaigning and showed more cooperation with other party members in terms of helping others to victory. They also had help from KMT officials in other branches of the government. In contrast, some *tang wai* candidates got help from *tang wai* representatives in the National Assembly, the Legislative Yuan, the Control Yuan, and sympathetic local government officials. But in relative terms, this strategy was not very profitable.[37]

Conclusions

A number of implications can be drawn from the results of this second national election with party (or party versus *tang wai*) competition. It was an important election simply because it was held. Some had described the 1980 election as unique or as an "election holiday," suggesting that it was staged for foreign observers and did not set a precedent in terms of genuine political change or democratization. Obviously this charge is no longer credible. The 1983 election was even more open and competitive. At the same time, however, it was less exciting because it was the second one and because understandings between and among the competitors had become customary. In addition, the new Election and Recall Law improved upon the previous set of laws and made smoother and fairer elections possible.

The election mirrored three processes going on politically in the Republic of China: democratization, Taiwanization, and rejuvenation.[38] Democracy was visibly in action even more than in previous elections because the candidates were less inhibited about exercising free speech. Candidates were, however, more aware of what they should not say in terms of what the public did not want to hear. Thus, there was more genuine free speech and fewer wild promises, statements, or criticism.

The political system was Taiwanized inasmuch as the overwhelming majority of winning candidates were Taiwanese. The KMT, often thought of as a party of Mainlanders, successfully promoted mostly Taiwanese candidates. Thus it can truly be said to be a party of all citizens.

The political system was rejuvenated inasmuch as a legislative body that had an average age of seventy-eight was made younger. The newly elected are more energetic and will tend to dominate debate in the Legislative Yuan even though they are still in a minority in terms of numbers. Considering the fact that many of the older members do not attend Legislative Yuan sessions, and when they do they lack the ability or the energy to engage in debate, the yuan is already functioning as a democratically elected body.

Some critics have argued that the results indicate this election was less competitive—because the *tang wai* lost. In fact, looking beyond the number of winners and losers, one finds that the election results were mixed. For example, the KMT won a slightly smaller percentage of the popular vote than in 1980. Moreover, the reason for the KMT victory in this election can be attributed largely to two factors: better planning and superior strategy. Also, the KMT had more candidates. The KMT nominated 58 candidates for 41 seats in contrast to 1980 when it nominated 38 for 70 seats. Fewer KMT members ran without the party's nomination: 6 with approval and 28 without permission (42 fewer than in 1980). Party discipline was maintained much better and members who resisted were effectively punished. This produced a more unified campaign effort and helped foster cooperation and consistency in KMT electioneering. This, plus careful and studious planning, won the election for the KMT.

If one wants to add something, it might be the opposition's lack of experience and unity. Not even the staunchest opponents of the KMT accused it of rigging the election. Some criticized certain provisions of the new Election and Recall Law that discriminated against the *tang wai*. But few had any illusions that this is why the *tang wai* did not do better. Its lack of organization, party infighting, inferior qualifications in terms of education and experience among its candidates, and its use of emotionalism and frequent reference to non-issues, for the most part, explain its performance.

It seems likely that the *tang wai* will learn from this election and will do better in the next one. Better planning and a well-thought-out election strategy should improve its showing in 1986. More pragmatism will also help. Some *tang wai* candidates who won because of sympathy votes will most likely not perform well in debates in the Legislative Yuan or will learn some lessons in political realism very quickly. Some already appear to have adopted more moderate views. The losers will probably teach a lesson to others who will run in future elections: that the voting public is concerned with issues and that professionalism in politics is a sine qua non for victory. The KMT demonstrated a high degree of professionalism in this election. This in considerable part explains its victory. It also explains why the party was able to make concessions to the *tang wai* allowing it to compete quite freely and to organize and behave as a political party. One can expect that this policy will set a precedent for future party competition. It also confirms some of the conclusions made about the 1980 election and comments made in previous chapters: that democracy is evolving through competitive elections and party politics. However, it does not necessarily mean that a two-party system is developing. If the *tang wai* remains factionalized, the Republic of China will likely evolve into a one-party-dominant system as exists in Japan. In this connection, it is worth noting that there are no working two-party systems anywhere in East Asia.

If this election is a guide to the future, there will be less voting along ethnic lines; the military will not influence as many votes as in the past; the electorate, becoming younger, will reflect "younger" issues; and interest groups will probably weaken, as will almost all traditional groupings to which politicians appeal. Replacing interest groups will be professional groups and newly forming blocs based upon new interests. The business community and the press will be even more influential in future elections.

Seats representing professional and other groups will probably become more competitive in the future. In past elections, candidates representing these groups were almost assured election if they won the support of the group or got the KMT nomination. Usually, they had both and were only "elected" in a pro forma manner. During this election, these seats became subject to KMT–*tang wai*, as well as Young China Party and Democratic Socialist Party to some degree, competition. In fact, there was some heated campaigning for professional groups' nominations compared to the past.[39] It is likely that the race for these seats will become even more competitive in the next election.

Opinion polling was more important in this election than in previous ones. More candidates paid attention to polls in determining what issues to stress in campaigning. The polls did not prove worthy, however, in predicting winners.[40] But this sophistication is likely to come. People in Taiwan are becoming less suspicious of polls.

The role of the press has also been changing. It is playing a bigger role in campaigns and elections. Before and during this election, there was much more editorializing than in the past. The press obviously influenced more votes than before. Candidates made special efforts to cultivate the press and did things to attract press attention. Some candidates, especially *tang wai* candidates, focused their attention on their own publications. But this was a diminishing trend. More channeled their energies and attention to the established newspapers, both local and national.

Money politics was a less serious problem than in the 1980 election, in large part because of the more vigorous controls established via the new Election and Recall Law and the more severe penalties for violations. There was less vote buying, bribery, and vote showing (to prove to the buyer that he actually bought a vote) in this election than in the past. The use of money, however, still plagues Taiwan's elections. It seems to be a problem, judging from the 1983 election, that cannot be resolved easily, if at all. Taiwan has simply become too affluent too quickly. Maintaining the status quo or making marginal progress may be the best that can be expected.

Violence, violations of the election laws, and other behavior detrimental to the institutionalization of democratic procedures were not serious problems. Incidents of violence, intimidation, and other irregular behavior were, in fact, minimal. In this election, the control of violence was facilitated by a high level of public concern about crime, which was increased at the time because of several incidents of crime during the campaign period that did not relate to the election but required stern police action. In any case, there seems to be sufficient public concern and support for police organizations that future elections will not see lawlessness, notwithstanding the changed atmosphere of Taiwan's elections and continued apprehension by many that this will occur.

In short, the 1983 election in the Republic of China signifies continued campaign competitiveness, democratization, and political development. It marks another step in a long process of democratization that over the past ten to twelve years has rapidly accelerated. Taiwan should now be regarded as a model or prototype for other nations to follow. It has democratized quickly without a bloody revolution. The 1983 election is further proof that credit is due for these accomplishments.[41]

Endnotes

1. This "rumor" was reported by several *tang wai* magazines.

2. For further details, see "Revised Election Law Paves Way for Orderly Vote," *Free China Weekly,* July 3, 1983, p. 1.

3. For further details, see "Goals Set for Election in December," *Free China Weekly,* October 2, 1983, pp. 1–2.

4. For example, *tang wai* magazines at this time said very little in opposition to the new election law other than criticizing certain provisions. No effort was made to start a movement against the new election law.

5. *China Post,* November 2, 1983, p. 1.

6. Ibid.

7. Ibid.

8. *China Post,* December 2, 1983, p. 1.

9. Ibid.

10. *China Post,* December 3, 1983, p. 1.

11. *China Post,* November 29, 1983, p. 1.

12. Maria Shao, "Taiwan Opposition Gears Up for Elections," *Asian Wall Street Journal Weekly,* October 17, 1983, p. 15.

13. Maria Shao, "As Taiwan Elections Near, Opposition Seeks Unity," Asian Wall Street Journal, October 17, 1983, p. 15.

14. Ibid.

15. See Maria Shao, "Opposition Courting Sympathy Vote in Campaign for Taiwanese Elections, " *Asian Wall Street Journal,* November 28, 1983, p. 16.

16. *China Post,* November 22, 1983, p. 1.

17. For a synopsis of *tang wai* views, see *Min Chu Jen* (Democratic Person), December 1, 1983.

18. See "The Way They Were Won," *Free China Review,* 34, No. 1 (January 1984), pp. 57–62.

19. See *Hsuan Chan* (Election Battle), November 26, 1983.

20. According to a poll taken by the Republic of China Public Opinion Polling Association in November, more than 80 percent of respondents said that martial law in no way inconvenienced them in their daily lives. Another 9.83 percent said martial law caused them some inconvenience, and 1.35 percent replied that martial law caused them considerable inconvenience. See *China Post,* December 2, 1983.

21. In fact, one *tang wai* candidate accused a number of high officials of being related by blood or marriage to other officials. Several of the accusations, however, were mistaken. See *China Post,* November 30, 1983.

22. See "A Triumph for the Kuomintang," *Asiaweek,* December 16, 1983, p. 23.

23. For details on the winners and losers and further figures on the election, see *China Post,* December 3 and 4, 1983, and *Free China Weekly,* December 4, 1983.

24. Ibid.

25. This figure would vary somewhat depending on how *tang wai* and especially independents are defined. Several observers put the *tang wai* popular vote a bit higher, around 29 percent, but argue it was essentially the same as in 1980. See, for example, Maria Shao, "Taiwan's KMT Scores Big in Election," *Asian Wall Street Journal,* December 5, 1983, pp. 1, 10.

26. The term Mainlander here is defined to include sons and daughters of Chinese born on the mainland who came to Taiwan in 1949. Some argue that they should be regarded as Taiwanese since they have never been to China.

27. One of the female winners among *tang wai* candidates was not regarded as *tang wai.*

28. "6.7 Million Voters Select 71 Legislators: Democracy Moves Forward in the ROC: KMT Wins Huge Vote of Confidence," *Free China Weekly,* December 4, 1983, p. 1.

29. Ibid.

30. See China *Post*, December 4, 1983.

31. Ibid.

32. Ibid.

33. See, for example, Maria Shao, "Taiwan's KMT Scores Big in Election."

34. See ibid. Also see "A Triumph for the Kuomintang," *Asiaweek,* December 16, 1983, p. 23.

35. See Andrew Tanzar, "Strategy Wins Out: The Ruling Kuomintang Outmaneuvers a Disorganized Opposition," *Far Eastern Economic Review,* 122, No. 50 (December 15, 1983), p. 17.

36. See *Free China Weekly,* December 4, 1983.

37. See Tanzar, "Strategy Wins Out," p. 15 for further details.

38. See Steve Lohr, "Voting in Taiwan is a Sign of Gains," *New York Times,* December 5, 1983, p. A7.

39. See *China Post,* November 25, 1983, for a description of some of the competition for professional and other group seats.

40. This was not only true of the polls that predicted Kang Ning-hsiang would be an easy winner. Many other polls published during the campaign were also incorrect regarding voting for specific candidates as well as voter turnout and trends. See, for example, "Voting Results Predicted in Local Papers," *China Post,* December 1, 1983, and "Two of Ten Non-Partisan Legislators Expected to Retain their Seats," *China Post,* December 3, 1983, and compare the predictions with the actual results.

41. For a short analysis of the election in terms of its importance to the United States, see A. James Gregor, "Election Proves Democracy is Alive and Well in ROC," *New York Tribune,* January 26, 1984, p. 1B.

Chapter Three
Taiwan's 1986 National Election:
Transition to Democracy

On December 6, 1986, voters went to the polls throughout Taiwan in what many have since called a watershed election. Some said it pushed forward the political modernization process in this island republic by perhaps a decade or more. Other observers declared the election was proof that the Republic of China had made the transition from an authoritarian political system to a democracy. Clearly politics, especially electoral politics, changed as a result of this election and its campaign.

This was the sixty-eighth major election held in Taiwan over the past three decades. It was the first, however, in which the competition was organized in the form of a legally constituted party—even though the government had not yet fully recognized it as such. The newly formed Democratic Progressive Party (DPP) nominated candidates who ran as "party" members, whereas their predecessors had run as a group of non-party or independent opposition candidates. DPP candidates carried green and white "party" flags. The media and the electorate referred to the DPP as a political party. Hence, this election was dubbed—and, in fact, was—the first two-party election in Chinese history.

The 1986 election must also be seen in relation to events during 1986, particularly announcements by President Chiang Ching-kuo that the government in the not-too-distant future would end martial law and allow the formation of new political parties. The year 1986 was clearly a time of significant political change in Taiwan.[1] This election was its capstone.

The Political Context of the Election

During the first half to two-thirds of 1985, the government and the ruling Nationalist Party or Kuomintang (KMT) passed through what might be called a period of malaise. A number of trends were less than positive—including economic growth (compared to the past) and unemployment (increasing, though still low compared to other countries). The country also faced some rather serious problems and crises. Early in the year the Henry Liu case (the murder of a San Francisco businessman) broke, implicating top military intelligence officials in Taipei. The foreign media took the line that the KMT had killed a U.S. citizen because he had written something uncomplimentary about the government, and in particular about President Chiang Ching-kuo. A number of U.S. newspapers harshly criticized the government and implicated other officials by association. The subcommittee on Asia of the House Foreign Affairs Committee held hearings during which several noted Congressmen sought to use the event as a reason to end arms sales to Taiwan.[2]

The collapse of the Tenth Credit Union, the second largest financial conglomerate in Taiwan, weeks later further undermined the credibility of the government and the ruling KMT. It was monumental in terms of its size and the number of businesses and investors affected—involving more than one hundred companies collectively worth more than U.S.$3.5 billion. The collapse gave the impression that the government was not properly managing the economy and that corruption and malfeasance were widespread.

On top of these problems the country witnessed a number of highly publicized accidents that many blamed on the government. There were two coal mine disasters; also tainted wine (from the government's Wine and Tobacco Monopoly) got onto the market, poisoning several people. Then there was unfavorable press over the arrest of a Taiwan-born (but with U.S. citizenship), Los Angeles newspaper owner in Taiwan. There were also rumors about President Chiang Ching-kuo's health and increased speculation about the problem of his successor. Some, especially opposition politicians, charged that he did not have one.

By mid-year the KMT seemed to be heading for an election defeat in November. However, the ruling party deftly handled the challenges, which in the end were not as dire as they had appeared. Thus, an election loss was averted. By the time of the campaign the Henry Liu case was seen by most voters as an instance of one or two officials acting on their own against a double or triple agent (who had done intelligence work for Washington, Taipei, and Beijing). The Tenth Credit scandal was in part put to rest when several officials, including two cabinet members, stepped down. Moreover, insufficient government regulation, rather than corruption, was eventually seen as the problem. The public was unsure it if wanted more regulation in view of the fact that a free and open market (although maybe too free) had given Taiwan its miracle economic development. The other problems as well seemed to pass so that, by November, they were no longer seen as terribly important. The nation's most serious "problem" was its growing foreign exchange position, the result of a huge trade surplus. Some observers commenting about the problem said that it was one that most developing nations wish they had.[3]

The Nationalist Party also appeared to be taking the coming elections in stride showing its willingness to adjust to new political realities in order to help its candidates to electoral victory. In March the KMT held its third plenary session of the party's twelfth Central Committee. At that meeting several new members were appointed to the important and powerful Central Standing Committee. The new appointments mirrored progressive changes in the direction of Taiwanization, democratization, and a younger leadership of the party. Some even speculated that the older, less flexible and more authoritarian-minded leaders of the party no longer held the balance of power in top party decision-making bodies.[4]

A few months later, President Chiang Ching-kuo (also chairman of the KMT) ordered the formation of a twelve-member committee to study the status of martial law and the ban on the formation of new parties; the committee was also to examine the problem of an aging National Assembly and means of improving local government. The first two "tasks" were by far the most important. What was meant by "studying" martial law and the ban on new parties was, in essence, finding a way to get rid of both and figure out how the system could best be pushed ahead on the road to further democratization without evoking political chaos or instability.

On the subject of legalizing new parties, *tang wai* leaders proposed that they be allowed to have permanent offices countrywide in the form of the Tang Wai Research Association for Public Policy (TRAPP). TRAPP would serve as a permanent national "party" organization that could coordinate "party" activities during periods when elections were not pending. This would help give the *tang wai* the status of a real political party, though it had been so labeled during previous election campaigns. It indeed had a platform, "party" funds, and a unified campaign. In May, the government, upon the recommendation and support of President Chiang, approved TRAPP.

Additional meetings (which included *tang wai* officials as well as scholars and others) were held to discuss the proposals to abolish martial law and formally allow new political parties to form. The issue was not whether to carry out these decisions, but how. Nor were there any really intractable issues between the two sides relative to implementing the proposals.

The substance of national security legislation that would replace martial law was an issue, but not a divisive one. The public did not consider martial law offensive or bothersome (according to public opinion polls), but it did see the abolishment of martial law as necessary to fulfilling the goal of democratizing the system. Notwithstanding the public's support of martial law, on May 19 (the thirty-eighth anniversary of its enactment) demonstrators organized to protest what they considered "unfair and undemocratic impediments to freedoms guaranteed in the Constitution."[5]

The formation of new parties was not as hot an issue as some had anticipated because the *tang wai* was already in most respects a political party. Older KMT officials opposed giving it legal status for various reasons, including the notion that allowing it to operate as a party, informally and without official sanction, seemed to be the most cautious means of allowing party competition to develop. Moreover, a significant number of opposition politicians were not enthusiastic about the offer of legal status since the *tang wai* was in large part a protest party, and winning legal status, some perceived, could be a liability rather than an asset in the coming election campaign. The *tang wai* lacked a base of support in the sense that parties in Western countries can identify potential voters by region, social class, and the like; thus, the protest vote was viewed as crucial.

Underscoring the "protest party" nature of *tang wai*, four of its members were jailed for libel in early June. Opposition leaders viewed the court action as an attempt to prevent their candidates from running in the December election, charging that it was instigated by the KMT. On June 9, 5,000 demonstrators protested the eight-month sentence meted out to a *tang wai* politician (for libeling a university professor in an article in *Neo-Formosa* magazine). It was described as the largest demonstration since the 1979 Kaohsiung Incident.[6]

In August TRAPP organized a rally at an elementary school in Taipei, attracting 50,000 participants and onlookers. The gathering was attended by the executive director of the U.S. National Democratic Institute for International Affairs, giving the impression that the United States supported TRAPP and an end to the ban on political parties. In fact, some perceived his presence as a sign of U.S. pressure on the government to "open up" the coming election.[7]

Taipei City Councilman Lin Cheng-chieh (also publisher of the opposition magazine *Progress Monthly*) was sentenced in early September to eighteen months in jail on the same charge as the others: libel. Lin somehow evaded the police for a while. He then appeared at the steps of the Presidential Office Building, and in front of a large crowd, smashed a clock (the word for "clock" being a homonym of "end" or "final")—signifying his "had it" attitude with the government. This provoked several days of protest demonstrations in Taipei and other large cities in Taiwan attracting large numbers (thousands at times) of people.[8]

On September 9, protestors in Taipei formed a large street march—the first led by the opposition since the Kaohsiung Incident in 1979. The march attracted even more participants and spectators than the earlier event and seemed to inject both unity and enthusiasm into the opposition movement. It also appeared to enhance public support for *tang wai* politicians. Meanwhile, the government's contention that the court decisions against *tang wai* notables were not influenced by any other branch of the government or the ruling Nationalist Party, though true, was not very convincing.[9] This problem fueled "demonstration fever." On September 28—without further consultations with the KMT, the government, or Chiang Ching-kuo's committee—135 *tang wai* politicians, after a meeting at the Grand Hotel in Taipei, announced that they had decided to form the Democratic Progressive Party (DPP). The announcement was provocative because it was still illegal to form a new political party. Yet it seemed apparent to almost everyone that the ban on new parties would be lifted and that the DPP's "crime" was one of simply acting prematurely—which was not very serious. It was also obvious that the *tang wai* made this move (rather than continuing discussions with the committee) in order to avoid the perception that it was a creation of the KMT or born out of *tang wai*–KMT cooperation.

A few days later President Chiang, in a meeting with Katherine Graham, owner of the *Washington Post*, affirmed that martial law would be lifted and that new political parties would be allowed to form. Judging from the tone of the president's statement and considering the person to whom the announcement was made (the news was reported with some fanfare in the *Post*), it was a promise to be taken seriously.[10] This statement was subsequently underscored when the president blocked action by the Ministry of Interior to file charges against the DPP for violating the prohibition against new political parties.

The KMT approved a proposal in mid-October whereby martial law would be replaced by national security legislation patterned after laws in the United States and other Western democracies. Although it was assumed that this action would take some time to be formalized by the Legislative Yuan, most thought that the legislation would pass because the KMT controlled the majority vote in that body. In the meantime, martial law enforcement for all intents and purposes was held in abeyance. Hence, the DPP assumed that the elections would not be held under the constraints of martial law and that the ban on forming new political parties would not be enforced.

On November 8, You Ching, one of the most visible leaders of the DPP, told Japanese reporters that the DPP had a membership of 2,500 and expected to grow to 100,000 in less than a year.[11] He declared the DPP's objective was to "break KMT one-party monopoly rule and build a welfare society after the Western European model." He also said that the DPP stood for "self-determination" and wanted Taiwan to be readmitted to the United Nations (though he did not say how this might be accomplished or if he meant that the Republic of China's name should be changed).

The DPP announced its "party" organization and leadership on November 10. Oddly, the DPP was structured after Leninist organizational principles. Opposition politicians had long cited KMT "hypocrisy" because of structuring the ruling party after these "Communist" tenets of party organization. Apparently they were not impressed with the organizational structures of the Western political parties. They had studied various party structures (including those in the United States) but ostensibly considered unity and party discipline too important to adopt the organizational structure of any of them.

Chiang P'eng-chien, a relatively little-known member of the Legislative Yuan, was elected chairman of the DPP in what appeared to be a close and divisive vote. You Ching and several others were in contention. Inside observers said the decision was a compromise and that the DPP's most well-known and most charismatic leader (meaning You Ching) was not picked to head the DPP because of factional infighting. Many called Chiang's appointment a mistake. Subsequently P'an Li-fu, a DPP Standing Committee member representing activists from the south of Taiwan, threatened to resign and take representatives of Ping Tung County with him. A serious party split seemed in the offing.[12]

Because those involved realized that party unity was a sine qua non to compete successfully in the December election, a formal split was avoided and party unity, at least on the surface, was restored. Obviously something had been learned from the *tang wai*'s disappointing performances in past elections. Moreover, the DPP had to maintain party unity if there was to be a two-party election—which the polls showed the public wanted. Individually, DPP leaders had to consider public opinion not only for the sake of the party but also, in most cases, for the sake of furthering their own candidacies—since most of them were running for office in December.

President Chiang meanwhile announced that, to become a legal party, three conditions must be met. New parties must: (1) abide by the Constitution (meaning, among other things, foreswearing violence), (2) renounce communism, and (3) deny supporting independence. These conditions did not seem onerous. The opposition had long supported the Constitution; it had even criticized the KMT for not upholding it, especially in its original form. Few *tang wai* politicians had even hinted at supporting communism as it had no appeal among the electorate. And, the DPP had been critical of Taiwanese

Independence Movement activities in the United States and Japan and eschewed direct contacts with the movement in either place.[13]

The DPP, however, refused to accept the president's three conditions, ostensibly because the new party did not want to give the impression it was colluding, or even cooperating, with the KMT. DPP leaders, in fact, sought to accentuate differences between their party and the KMT. The DPP openly challenged the KMT's policy of reconquering the mainland and instead called for separation from the People's Republic of China. The DPP's charter even contained a "plank" that stated that the future of Taiwan should be "decided by the residents of Taiwan." Many interpreted this to mean the DPP was advocating self-determination and/or ties with the Taiwanese Independence Movement. DPP officials, however, pointed out that the two were not the same.

Meanwhile, a nationwide opinion poll was conducted (and published in one of Taiwan's largest newspapers), that reflected public support for the president's decision to lift martial law and to allow new parties to form. However, more detailed public opinion queries suggested that the public had not changed its view about martial law but rather remained supportive of it. The poll also indicated public disapproval of the formation of the DPP.[14] In light of this poll, the president's actions apparently represented a commitment to create a wholly democratic system—therefore the public supported him. Martial law, even if supported by the public, had to go in order to realize the bigger objective: democracy. The DPP's suddenness in forming and its violation of the law in doing so apparently alienated a sizable portion of the public. Alternatively, the DPP's stated tenets on a number of issues had that effect.

In any event, the lines were being drawn between the KMT and the DPP on several important issues. Polarization was not so serious, however, as to make the election process unworkable. Most wanted the system to work. Moreover, it was clear the DPP was going to participate in the election as a party, even though legal status was yet to be granted. Blocking its participation would have hurt Taiwan's political development and sent the wrong signals domestically and internationally.

The Election Campaign

On November 14, a week before the campaign began, seven U.S.-based dissidents returned to Taiwan to support the DPP and "democratize the elections." The leader of the group, Lin Shui-chuan (who had been in the United States since 1982 after finishing a prison term in Taiwan), was refused entry because he presented no travel documents. Some of the other members of the group also failed to show passports; the rest declined entry when Lin was detained. The group started a scuffle with police before they left, causing a scene that soon became a campaign issue for the DPP.[15] DPP candidates, looking for an election issue to rally their supporters, charged the government and the ruling KMT with supporting police brutality and with subverting democracy.

With this backdrop, the campaign began on November 21 with candidate-sponsored forums and speeches. This phase lasted for eight days. Prior to the onset of the campaign period, a number of candidates held "teas" and other "parties" as a way of starting their campaigning early—in violation of the Election and Recall Law.[16] KMT candidates generally observed the election rules in this regard. During the period of candidate-sponsored forums, more than 500 meetings were held. Moderate DPP candidate Kang Ning-hsiang held the most: forty-three. Opposition DPP candidates Hsiao Yu-chen and Chou Ching-yu held thirty-seven and thirty-six respectively.[17] Candidates generally attracted good crowds, but according to several observers (including myself) these crowds were not as large as in the past two elections. There also seemed to be a larger discrepancy in the size of the audiences attracted to different candidates.

Following the period of private campaigning, public forums sponsored and arranged by the Election Commission were held for seven days. There were 721 such meetings throughout the country. Because the place, order of speakers, and time of presentation were assigned, the public forums in some ways resembled debates between political candidates in the United States and in other Western democracies. Certainly they enabled the electorate to compare candidates' views and various other qualities.

According to opinion polls conducted both before and during the campaign, the issues the electorate perceived as important differed markedly from those the candidates thought were central. Voters surveyed in Taipei indicated that traffic, air pollution, and public safety were their biggest concerns. They ranked the formation of new political parties below a dozen other issues in importance. In Kaohsiung, voters rated public safety as their first concern, followed by traffic and air pollution. The formation of new parties was not even among their top twenty concerns. In contrast, candidates in Taipei replied that social welfare, foreign relations, national security, and human rights were their foremost concerns. They put the top three issues as ranked by the voters below fourteen other issues. Candidates in Kaohsiung stated that social welfare, economic freedom, foreign relations, and national security were the most important campaign issues.[18]

The discrepancies (which also existed in previous elections) may be explained by the fact that none of the issues the voters regarded as the most important, with the possible exception of the crime issue (part of the public safety problem), could be sensationalized or used to attract attention. Certainly they were not issues that could be used to excite listeners at rallies. Candidates thought that they had to attract a devoted and committed group of supporters (to enlist as campaign workers and activists) first. They also perceived that they needed to attract public attention to get their campaigns off to a good start; without this they would be viewed as boring and could not build momentum.

Many candidates seemed to believe they could ignore the issues the voters considered important early in the campaign and address these issues only when asked or when other candidates did so. Some said they could bring up these issues during the "less interesting" government-sponsored forums. Many candidates, furthermore, pointed out that nearly all candidates took an identical position on these issues, that is favoring more orderly traffic, less air pollution, and less crime. Even specific means of handling these problems did not differ among candidates very much, at least not enough to build candidate identification or image.

During the campaign, KMT candidates in general espoused more conservative positions and DPP candidates took more liberal views. However, few candidates presented themselves as ideologues, inasmuch as this was not a mark of success in previous elections. Hence, liberal and conservative views on many issues were not very clear much of the time. Finally, a considerable disparity of views within each party blurred differences between them.

Still, the two parties were different enough that party identification was not difficult. DPP candidates consistently called for more press freedom and freedom of speech and advocated expanding civil and political freedoms. They were in agreement that campaign regulations were too restrictive, that the campaign period needed to be lengthened, and that limits on campaign spending needed to be broadened or lifted (notwithstanding public concern about "money politics" and a serious problem of vote buying in previous elections). KMT candidates were usually stronger advocates of law and order and reducing crime. As a rule, they favored keeping the present election rules or changing them only slightly (even though the election laws were not working very well). KMT candidates as a group expressed satisfaction with the nation's progress in broadening civil and political liberties.

DPP candidates supported increased social welfare and made this a major issue in the campaign, just as the *tang wai* had in previous campaigns. KMT candidates took credit for the nation's economic prosperity, and they boasted of successful social welfare legislation and work done by the KMT in this area. KMT candidates also claimed credit for low unemployment and the nation's low disparity of income, which, they said, made social security less necessary than in other countries.

DPP candidates advocated a more aggressive foreign policy, in particular, arguing for policies that would get the country back into the United Nations and other international organizations. They did not, however, cite any specific means for doing this and appeared to lack any feasible plan. They did, in contrast, have concrete proposals regarding the Asian Development Bank: Remain in! KMT candidates, when they talked about foreign policy issues, stressed the government's successful economic and cultural diplomacy and defined past "diplomatic failures" as inevitable, not as mistakes.

DPP candidates criticized the government's "three nos" policy and in its place suggested "contacts while maintaining separation" with the People's Republic of China. As was the case with most foreign policy planks, they did not elaborate on how this should be done. They criticized the nation's large defense budget and suggested that more money should be spent on social programs, unemployment insurance, and the like. KMT candidates generally espoused the position that Beijing could not be trusted and therefore "opposed negotiating with the Communists." They were critical of "unrealistic" DPP foreign policy proposals, though they generally avoided talking about retaking the mainland, which the DPP labeled as grossly unrealistic. For the most part, KMT candidates supported current defense spending.

Foreign trade issues were rarely discussed. Likewise, Taiwan's large trade surplus with the United States and currency revaluation were not important election issues. This was so in spite of growing tensions with the United States over trade and rapidly growing foreign currency reserves that threatened to touch off inflation.

The DPP talked about democracy and the need for greater freedoms for candidates to say and do as they desired in order for the political system to become truly democratic. Its members charged that the KMT monopoly of the media and the country's one party-system precluded real democracy. The main opposition party continued to indict the KMT for not allowing genuinely free elections and for lack of fairness in the election system, especially the system's bias toward the ruling party. KMT candidates spoke of the need for political and social stability as a precondition for democracy and accused DPP candidates of naivete in this regard. They also accused the opposition of "reckless" and unrealistic talk about democracy, which KMT officials labeled foolish and dangerous since it would "play into the hands of the Communists."

The most sensitive issues were self-determination and DPP street politics, labeled by the KMT as lawless and anarchic. Views on both issues became polarized during the campaign. Some KMT candidates construed DPP candidates' statements as advocating independence, which, they said, was treason. Others said the DPP played into the hands of the Taiwanese Independence Movement and the Communists. Many argued that the DPP's advocacy of self-determination was either already realized, since Taiwan had a legally constituted government, or was an unnecessary provocation. The People's Republic of China underscored the latter point when a press spokesman for the Ministry of Foreign Affairs publicly assailed the DPP's advocacy of self-determination during the middle of the campaigning.[19]

KMT and DPP differences on the touchy issues were amplified when dissident Hsu Hsin-liang tried to return to Taiwan from the United States. Hsu had left Taiwan under indictment for treason before the Kaohsiung Incident in 1979. He subsequently applied for and was granted political asylum in the United States. Not having been an important official or opposition spokesman at the time (a county magistrate), he was unable to win much of a following in the United States or much support back home—though his name was remembered through his brother, who was running for office at this time in his home district. However, Hsu became better known immediately before the campaign. Claiming to represent the DPP in the United States, he became intensely critical of the Taiwan government and vowed to return to Taiwan as an "Aquino."[20]

Some DPP leaders repudiated Hsu's claim to represent the party in the United States. They amplified this rejection when his advocacy of terrorism and terrorist tactics were documented in Taiwan's newspapers at the time, some in rather lurid detail.[21] This association embarrassed the DPP and caused many in the opposition to distance themselves from Hsu and the Taiwanese Independence Movement. Still, DPP leaders perceived Hsu's return as an opportunity to rally their forces and win public sympathy and support for their cause. Demonstrations and rallies during the spring and summer had that effect;so, they asked themselves, why not now? Thus the DPP prepared for Hsu's rumored arrival on November 20.

DPP leaders were also plainly aware of the fact that the government had ordered the police and other authorities to behave with the utmost restraint and leniency in order to prevent anything from happening during the campaign that would be construed by the foreign press as sullying an otherwise fair election or oppressing democracy. Thus, the DPP assumed they could organize demonstrations at the airport without fear of retaliation. So they joined in mass to meet Hsu.

Many KMT candidates, meanwhile, opposed the government's "excessively lenient policy" toward protest demonstrations. They saw it as creating a situation in which the DPP was given carte blanche to advocate radical policies, undermine government authority, and create a situation verging on a breakdown of law and order. Others, however, opined that the public's fear of anarchy would work to the KMT's advantage. They saw a repeat of the Kaohsiung Incident of 1979, when the opposition alienated the population by creating political instability that threatened to escalate into chaos.

In any event, 20,000 demonstrators gathered at the airport when Hsu was rumored to arrive. They turned over and burned police cars, threw rocks, and hit, kicked, and insulted police officers—including women officers. One reporter videotaped a scene of a demonstrator in a shoving fracas with police, after which he doused his head with animal blood or paint taken from a sack in his pocket, then claimed that he had been beaten by police. This incident was reported by several large newspapers and the television networks. It clearly damaged the image and reputation of the DPP. So did the fact that the opposition was seen to have started the violence and the widespread belief that police acted with restraint. One public opinion poll recorded an immediate 3 percent drop in voter support for the DPP.[22]

The DPP officially repudiated the violence, perceiving that it was creating a serious backlash. DPP leaders also cried fowl. Then, in order to effect damage control, the DPP showed its own tapes at its campaign offices and elsewhere in public. These tapes showed only the police throwing rocks and using water cannons and tear gas. One tape, which the DPP played repeatedly, showed the demonstrators being pushed away by police; this "movie" they dubbed "The Ugly Cop." DPP leaders also decried media reports on the incident that they said unfairly favored the KMT. On one occasion, DPP supporters held a rally to burn copies of the *United Daily News*—one of Taiwan's largest papers—which had reported that the violence was started by DPP supporters and was organized by the opposition party.[23]

Hsu later managed to get to Taipei from the Philippines. But he was discovered before disembarking at Taipei International Airport, and the plane carrying him was forced to leave before it was widely known that he had arrived. Subsequent repeated efforts by Hsu to get to Taiwan failed. His campaign to play the spoiler role or become "Taiwan's Aquino" thus ultimately failed.

Besides the "Hsu incident," the campaign was full of antics and tricks. Even before the campaigning started, a number of candidates publicly accused their opponents of sexual and financial misconduct. Several filed suits against opposing candidates prior to and during the campaign. Organized rumor-mongering was common. Candidates frequently hired audiences to support their speeches and forums and to disrupt their opponents' speeches by using firecrackers, car horns, and other noise makers. A number of DPP candidates had their workers cut the electricity during their speeches; they could then blame the disruption on KMT "operatives."

Some campaign workers printed counterfeit ballots and placed them in their opponents' offices, after which they telephoned election officials. Campaign workers also called voters during the night, using opposing candidates' names. Phony handbills were printed by some candidates to misrepresent opposing candidates. In short, campaign dirty tricks were widespread; many of them were reportedly learned from studying election campaigns in Western democracies.

Candidates and their workers and supporters regularly violated election laws by using too many handbills or larger posters than prescribed by law and by campaigning in places that were restricted. "Illegal" marches were commonplace. Political advertisements were put in the newspapers in violation of the Election and Recall Law. Some candidates did television commercials to get more exposure, in violation of the spirit of the election law. In short, election rules were blatantly and frequently flaunted.[24]

Yet there was little violence. Nor was there frequent breaking of important election rules or laws. DPP politicians burned KMT flags but did not burn any national flags. They used unflattering terms (such as "pig" on some occasions) to describe the president, but when this seemed likely to create a backlash they refrained from any mention of the president or other high officials. KMT candidates accused the DPP of disregard for social stability and of lawlessness; they did not accuse them (or at least not very often) of treason or sedition.

Some DPP candidates talked about "revolution." Several claimed to be "Corazons"—making reference to President Aquino of the Philippines. Yet few opposition candidates' statements could be construed as advocating revolution. Many DPP candidates referred obliquely to self-determination; few mentioned the Taiwanese Independence Movement. Fewer still made any mention of Beijing or communism. When the People's Republic of China condemned the advocacy of self-determination by DPP candidates, the latter usually did not reply.

In short, the election was full of technically illegal actions on the part of numerous candidates. But most knew that the law would not be rigidly enforced. Some wanted to break the law to draw attention to their campaign. Others sought to test the law. Still others didn't know what the law meant. This situation made many of the campaign regulations almost meaningless. Some even opined that the Election and Recall Law was not, in fact, working and that it should be regarded as defunct. Still, the system did work. In fact, some said the system was strengthened because it was able to work "under stress."

The Election Results

There were 306 candidates registered to compete for 73 seats in the Legislative Yuan and 84 seats in the National Assembly—a total of 157 seats. There were 169 candidates for National Assembly seats and 137 for Legislative Yuan seats. Of the 306 candidates, 179 represented the Nationalist Party or Kuomintang, and 44 represented the newly formed Democratic Progressive Party. The rest were independents or representatives of the two minor parties.

The KMT won 59 seats in the Legislative Yuan and 68 in the National Assembly. Translated into a margin of victory, the ruling party captured 80.8 percent and 80.95 percent, respectively, of the seats contested in these two elected bodies of government. In popular vote the KMT won 66.3 percent and 60.2 percent, respectively, in the two contests. On the basis of these figures, the ruling party could easily claim a victory.[25]

The KMT also performed well on the basis of electing a high proportion of the candidates it nominated. In fact, no KMT candidate who did not have the party's official endorsement won in the election. Party discipline, in short, was maintained, which had not been the case in previous elections. Finally, many KMT candidates claimed to be at a disadvantage because DPP candidates were more free to engage in tricks and antics. The KMT restrained its candidates and acted to prevent or minimize violations of the Election and Recall Law. Thus, KMT candidates asserted that their performance must be judged in view of a serious handicap during the campaign.

The KMT may be proclaimed the victor in another sense. It was due for a defeat in the sense that electorates tend to be fickle and change their minds about political participants whether they are performing well or not. The KMT had won the two previous national elections (in 1980 and 1983) and (according to most observers) the nationwide local election in 1985. In popular vote as well as in seats, the KMT did better in these elections than in major elections during the 1970s. Additionally, the fact that the public wanted two-party competition seemed to indicate that the KMT was destined to lose.

Another factor was the KMT's election strategy, which in this election (unlike in previous elections) was not clearly superior to that of the opposition. In other words, the ruling party lost this advantage. Some observers even contended that the KMT had become complacent. In at least one case the KMT did not calculate the electorate correctly. The party's military candidate, retired Air Force Chief of Staff Chen Hung-chuan, lost because of a dilution of the vote in his district. This loss reflected bad planning. The KMT also showed signs of some disagreement among its candidates concerning how to counter the DPP's platform, meaning whether to take a tough line against the opposition party or not.

Finally, the KMT did well in spite of the fact that the DPP had the momentum. Rallies and demonstrations in the months preceding the election gave the opposition both unity and a spirit of cooperation, not to mention a feeling that it was making democracy work. Many, if not most, opposition politicians perceived their cause to have historical significance. Events during the campaign focused attention on the new opposition party and its candidates. Just before the election DPP leaders boasted they would win 30 percent of the popular vote. They did not win that much.

The DPP also claimed victory. In several respects its claims were more credible than the KMT's. The DPP won 12 and 11 seats respectively—double the figure the *tang wai* had won in the previous election for the Legislative Yuan, and an increase of 4 over the previous National Assembly contest. It won 16.4 and 13.1 percent of the seats contested in the elective bodies, which was impressive when compared to the opposition's past record. Over half of the DPP candidates were elected—23 of 44. The DPP's popular vote was also several percent-age points above that attained by the *tang wai* in previous elections: 22.2 percent in the Legislative Yuan election and 18.9 percent in the National Assembly con-test.

The DPP, moreover, did not suffer from the factionalism that plagued the *tang wai*. No DPP candidate won who was not officially endorsed by the DPP leadership. There were no "unofficial" DPP candidates and none left the party or refused to follow the party platform at least nominally. In fact, DPP party unity reduced the number of independent candidates drastically. Seven joined the DPP before the election. Only two seats in the Legislative Yuan and four in the National Assembly were won by candidates not officially nominated by the KMT or the DPP. One Democratic Socialist Party candidate won (in the National Assembly race). The China Youth Party, with two and three candidates in the Legislative Yuan and the National Assembly races respectively, failed to elect a candidate. In short, the election seemed to be much more a contest between the KMT and the opposition, which in this case coalesced to become the DPP, than previous elections.

The DPP also had the big vote-getters; the top four winners in the Legislative Yuan contest—Hsu Chung-shu, Hong Chi-chang, You Ching, and

Hsu Kuo-ta—got the largest number of popular votes among all winning candidates. DPP candidates were also the top vote-getters in five of the eight electoral districts.

The DPP fared especially well in the capital city and in Taiwan's second largest city, Kaohsiung, capturing over 30 percent of the popular vote in both. Since some consider the big cities, especially Taipei, bellwethers, the DPP could look ahead to an even better performance in future elections.[26] It also had another plus from a strong showing in the capital city—a psychological advantage in terms of its impact on the legislation process.

The DPP also performed well in spite of the fact that economic growth projections published just before the election made the government and the KMT look good. The electorate going to the polls was looking at an economic growth of 10.7 percent for the year. Clearly the public was pleased with the KMT's performance in economic growth terms. The announcements that martial law and the ban on new political parties would be rescinded likewise helped the KMT. That the KMT had nominated a slate of candidates that was generally young, reform-oriented, and Western-educated also made the KMT attractive to the voter.[27]

The bottom line was that most observers felt the election results suggested more a victory for the DPP than for the KMT. Clearly the DPP's performance as measured against its past record was astoundingly better. The KMT's was not; it gained seats in the National Assembly but lost in the Legislative Yuan. The DPP had the biggest winners. In terms of the popular vote, perhaps the best indicator of success, the DPP did better and the KMT did worse.

Conclusions

An assessment of the results of the election suggests still other conclusions. It is no doubt accurate to say that the nation, particularly in terms of good press abroad, and political modernization were bigger winners than either party or any candidate. The government may also be given credit for delivering on promises to make the country democratic: The voters wanted a more competitive party system to advance democracy, and they got it.

Reflecting the electorate's feeling toward the electoral process in this election, the voter turnout was higher; 65.4 percent—compared to 63.17 percent in the previous comparable election. There had been a gradual decline in voter turnout in elections in Taiwan until the 1985 nationwide local election. However, because it was a local election, some considered the better turnout a fluke, not a signal of a reversal of the downward trend. The higher turnout in this election could thus be seen as a positive sign and perhaps as sufficient proof that voter alienation or cynicism about the political process had not grown.

Female candidates did well in the election, winning 6 seats in the Legislative Yuan and nine in the National Assembly. In other words, women captured just under 10 percent of the seats in the Legislative Yuan and over 10 percent in the National Assembly race. The largest vote-getter in the Legislative Yuan race was a woman. Again, like past elections, the performance of female candidates in this election compares very favorably to most Western democracies, even better than most in this regard.[28]

The education level of winning candidates was also high. Only 4 winners in Legislative Yuan contests and twelve for seats in the National Assembly did not have an education beyond high school. Twenty-three and 15 candidates, respectively, in the two races had graduate education. Over 31 percent of winning candidates for Legislative Yuan seats had graduate education—a very good mark compared to counterpart lawmaking bodies in Western democracies. Nearly 95 percent were college educated or had an equivalent degree. There were 23 candidates with Ph.D. degrees; 20 (or 86.95 percent) won.[29]

The age of victorious candidates is also instructive; the mean age was 46. The average age of winning candidates in the Legislative Yuan was 45.9; in the National Assembly contest it was 47.2. The majority of winning candidates in both elections were in their forties. In neither race did a candidate over 69 win.[30] This suggests that the voters wanted representatives with both experience and sufficient energy to serve in the jobs for which they were chosen.

A number of less quantifiable indicators also reflect positive signals. As in past elections, candidates emphasizing ideology did not fare well. Radical candidates also did poorly, compared to previous elections, especially non-KMT candidates. Several that talked about revolution during the campaign did not win. Kang Ning-hsiang, a well-known opposition candidate who had lost in the previous Legislative Yuan election (many say because of his moderate position) won big in this election. The KMT's biggest winners were moderates or progressives: Chao Shao-kang in Taipei and Hung Chao-nan in Taichung. Chao said throughout the campaign that "a vote for me is a vote for reform."[31]

Money also seemed to be less a factor in this election than in previous elections. Most observers (including myself) perceived that vote buying (both with money and gifts) and expensive campaigning were less prevalent. Clearly, most victorious candidates were not known as much for their large or lavish campaign spending as had been the case in previous elections. Certainly "money politics" did not seem as great a problem—notwithstanding the country's continuing economic growth and prosperity. It may be that accusations and publicity about vote buying and excessive campaign spending in recent elections and during the campaign for this election had some impact.

A poll taken after the election showed that the populace perceived that the election reflected progress—by nearly seven-fold over those who perceived that it did not. Over 60 percent replied that the election was fair—nearly five times as many as those who thought it was unfair. Vote buying was also judged to be a less serious problem (confirming what observers perceived), with nearly 70 percent saying that they did not think it was a serious problem in their district or did not personally know about any such incidents. Those polled, however, seemed to perceive the problem was more serious elsewhere.[32]

Most considered the election to have gone smoothly in view of the existence of a new party and the fact that it was the first true party competition in a national election in Taiwan. Because it was generally understood that the government was not going to enforce most of the campaign rules, many felt the election, especially the campaigning, would not be orderly. But there were very few serious incidents during the campaign and none during the voting.

Clearly there was no overwhelming issue that divided the nation; the candidates for the most part debated "bread and butter" issues. Sensitive or controversial issues were used primarily as attention getters, and this worked because the system was "on trial," as were the democratic process and political modernization. This was as it should have been, considering the country was in a transition phase evolving into a democratic system at a very high rate of speed.

Most observers concluded that it was a landmark election and that Taiwan deserved credit for taking another big step toward a democratic political system. Certainly progress was the big winner.

Endnotes

1. For further details, see John F. Copper, "Political Developments in Taiwan in 1986," *China News Analysis*, January 15, 1987, pp. 1–9.

2. For details, see John F. Copper, "Taiwan: New Challenges to Development," *Current History*, April 1986, pp. 168–171.

3. See John F. Copper, "Taiwan in 1986: Back on Top Again," *Asian Survey*, January 1987, pp. 89–90.

4. See "ROC Sets a Model for All Chinese, Chiang Says," *Free China Journal*, March 31, 1986, p. 1. For a comparison with the previous Central Standing Committee, see Edwin A. Winckler, "After the Chiangs: The Coming Political Succession on Taiwan" in Richard C. Bush, ed., *China Briefing, 1982* (Boulder CO: Westview Press, 1983), pp. 103–121.

5. *Facts on File*, October 24, 1986, p. 799.

6. Ibid.

7. Agency France Press, August 15, 1986 in Foreign Broadcasting Information Service—China (FBIS), August 18, 1986, p. 2.

8. Paul Mooney, "Opposition in the Streets," *Far Eastern Economic Review*, September 25, 1986, p. 18.

9. Ibid.

10. See Daniel Southerland, "Taiwan President to Propose End to Island's Martial Law," *Washington Post*, October 8, 1986, p. 3.

11. See Carl Goldstein, "The Opposition Party," *Far Eastern Economic Review*, November 20, 1986, p. 36.

12. See Ramon H. Myers, "Political Change and Democratization in the Republic of China 1986," *Free China Journal*, December 1, 1986, p. 2.

13. DPP leaders made such statements at the time the party was formed. For further details, see John F. Copper, "Political Developments in Taiwan 1986."

14. See "Gearing up for Elections," *Asia Bulletin*, November 1986, p. 35.

15. Copper, "Political Developments in Taiwan in 1986."

16. This had been a problem in previous elections. Candidates could circumvent the Election and Recall Law by holding private birthday parties and teas, which were in reality political meetings. No solutions to this problem had been found.

The Taiwan Political Miracle

17. "By-Election Campaigning to Enter 2nd Stage Today," *China Post*, November 29, 1986, p. 3.

18. "Poll: Citizens, Candidates Differ on Election Issues," *China Post*, November 12, 1986, p. 3.

19. For further details on Beijing's attitude, remarks, and threats, see "The Peking Factor," *Asiaweek*, December 21–28, 1986, p. 29.

20. Carl Goldstein, "Barricaded Tarmac," *Far Eastern Economic Review*, December 11, 1986, p. 16.

21. See "Dissident Enters Illegally Flying Under False Colors," *Free China Journal*, December 8, 1986, p. 2. Several of Taiwan's major newspapers carried stories citing Hsu's advocacy of violence and reprinted some of his writings about the use of terrorist tactics during the campaign.

22. "The People Spoke Their Minds," *Asiaweek*, December 21–28, 1986, p. 25.

23. Ibid.

24. See, for example, "Videotaping Questioned"; "Nonpartisans Insulting Head of State, Newspapers Say"; "Nonpartisans Get Warnings for Street Demonstrations," *China Post*, November 27, 1986, p. 12.

25. See "Voting Heavy, Smooth-Running in Apparent Landslide for KMT," *China Post*, December 7, 1986, p. 3.

26. "The People Spoke Their Minds," p. 25.

27. Ibid.

28. This compares to 4.6 percent in the U.S. Congress—2 percent in the Senate and 5.28 in the House of Representatives.

29. See *North American Daily* (in Chinese), December 9, 1986, p. 2.

30. Ibid. Also see "People's Voice Loud, Clear," *Free China Journal*, December 15, 1986, p. 2.

31. See "The People Spoke Their Minds,"*Asiaweek*, December 21–28, 1986, pp. 24–29.

32. See *China Times* (in Chinese), December 7, 1986, p. 1.

Chapter Four
Taiwan's 1989
National and Local Elections

On December 2, 1989, the electorate in Taiwan went to the polls to pick 101 members of the Legislative Yuan, 77 members (or a plenum) of the Provincial Assembly, 94 members of the Taipei and Kaohsiung city councils, and 21 county magistrates and city mayors. This was one of four very important elections in Taiwan's recent history—in fact, in the 1980s—and it played a vital role in pushing the democratization process ahead.[1]

Observers noted that this election was in many ways the culmination of rapid progressive change in the electoral processes in Taiwan. It was also another watershed election in several respects because the opposition Democratic Progressive Party (DPP) attained what most consider a resounding victory, giving it the status of a serious opposition party and perhaps auguring in the beginning of a two-party system in Taiwan. There was also widespread discussion of Taiwan independence, which caused relations with the People's Republic of China to become a campaign issue as it had never been before.

The election was preceded by several important "legal changes" in the system (since the last national election in 1986) that affected the election process. First was the enactment of the Civic Organization Law, which made it legal to form new political parties.[2] Thus, for the first time the Nationalist Party or Kuomintang (KMT), faced a genuine legal opposition. However, it was unclear in the months prior to the election whether the opposition would take the form of one main opposition party or many. Nearly forty parties formed; eighteen parties entered candidates in the race.

Second, the government had just revised the Public Officials Election and Recall Law.[3] Control over election campaigns and other enforcement of election laws was thus transferred from the military to civilian organizations. The new law also expanded political participation and made elections more competitive in form. The Democratic Progressive Party (DPP) characterized the revisions as democratic, but it complained that there were too many restrictions on electioneering and that the law discriminated against opposition parties in a number of critical ways. DPP leaders particularly complained about the short campaign period and the ban on television advertising, which they charged did not hurt the KMT since it owned or controlled all of the TV networks.[4] KMT candidates complained that the "equal access" to media coverage in the revised law treated the ruling party unfairly since it was much larger. The smaller parties disagreed. The KMT and the DPP chided the unrealistic restrictions on campaign spending. Both lauded provisions that were aimed at discouraging "whimsical candidates" and hurt smaller parties and independents; the two major parties felt these provisions made the process more rational.

Third, early in the year the Legislative Yuan passed the Law on Voluntary Retirement of Senior Parliamentarians.[5] In enacting this bill, the Legislative Yuan sought to reduce the number of delegates to the elected bodies of government who were voted into office before the government moved to Taiwan in 1949 (and subsequently frozen or replaced with appointed members). This was a sensitive issue because the opposition regarded these delegates to the National Assembly, the Legislative Yuan, and the Control Yuan as illegitimate. DPP candidates mocked them in public and asked them to "step down or hurry up and die," charging that they were an obstacle to democracy. The KMT argued that they were duly elected and should be allowed to retire with respect. The issue reflected the fact that Taiwan's political system assumes one China, a position the KMT supports and the DPP labels ludicrous. The KMT's one-China policy, however, had the support of both Washington and Beijing.

Another systemic change affecting the campaign and the election was the inauguration of a primary election system by the KMT, with the DPP immediately following suit. This had several consequences. The primaries weakened the KMT leadership's control over the nomination process. As a consequence, some ruling party incumbents were not nominated, creating serious intra-party problems for the KMT. Also, the military and veterans gained a larger voice in the nominating process, since their turnout was high and they voted as a bloc in the primaries. The KMT because of this nominated more Mainland Chinese than usual. Primaries caused problems for the DPP as well, but in the context of the DPP's already serious differences on central issues and leadership, the process was not as disruptive for the DPP as it was for the KMT.[6]

This was the first election in Taiwan since the termination of martial law in July 1987 and the January 1988 end of a ban on new newspapers. It was also the first since the death of Chiang Ching-kuo in January 1988 and the succession of a Taiwan-born president. Plus, it followed the opening of significant contacts with the People's Republic of China. Finally, it came in the wake of the Tiananmen Massacre—which some linked to an urgent need to keep Taiwan separate from China and which led some to talk about and even advocate independence. The election results were generally unexpected. Only the KMT and the DPP emerged with meaningful representation in the elective bodies of government. Other parties and independents did poorly. More important, the DPP victory exceeded the predictions of most experts. This gave rise again to speculation about the evolution of a two-party system, the impact of opposition politicians on the decision-making process in the future, and much more. The KMT, though still in control and even at times claiming victory in a fair and even contest, generally perceived the election as a setback.

The Campaign

The campaign began officially on November 17 for the Legislative Yuan race and on November 22 for the other contests. The period was formally divided into two parts: the privately conducted campaigns followed by officially sponsored public sessions. In fact, however, the campaign had begun much earlier, technically in violation of the election law. As in previous election campaigns, candidates, in order to circumvent the restrictions, held teas and birthday parties and gave "educational speeches." Observers viewed these events as "early campaign" efforts.

The DPP's "early campaign" was highlighted by the return of a number of dissidents, mostly anti-KMT figures, from abroad, mainly from the United States. Many came carrying U.S. passports with different spellings of their names and in this way escaped detection. Hsu Hsin-liang was the most famous. Hsu, who was under indictment for treason, had tried to return for the 1986 election, only to be detained at the airport and sent back. This time he returned on a fishing boat and was arrested, which made it difficult for the government to ignore him. In fact, he said that he had come back to stand trial, something he had previously been denied. Former U.S. Attorney General Ramsey Clark attempted to travel to Taiwan to represent him but was not granted an entry visa. In jail, Hsu was allowed to talk to news reporters; thus, he could draw attention to his case while rallying his supporters. On October 10, supporters besieged the detention center where he was held, sparking a riot that resulted in injury to a number of onlookers and police officers.[7]

Another was Lin Yi-hsiang, whose mother and daughter had been mysteriously murdered following the Kaohsiung Incident in 1979. Lin returned to Taiwan at this time and shortly after published what he called the "basic law" of the "Republic of Taiwan." The text was printed in two of Taiwan's large newspapers. The Justice Ministry initiated proceedings against him as well as the newspapers, but the ministry did not act quickly enough. Lin's "basic law" became well known and was widely discussed throughout Taiwan during the campaign.[8]

A third famous dissident who returned was Kuo Pei-hung. Kuo, chairman of the U.S.-based World United Formosans for Independence, was on the wanted list in Taiwan for sedition. He came back without notice before the campaign and organized his followers for a "grandstand play." On November 22, during an evening political rally, he stepped out of the crowd and onto a platform and then to a podium. He proceeded to give a highly emotional and inflammatory speech attacking the government and the KMT. This excited the crowd, most of whom knew him or knew of him and expected the police to close in at any moment and arrest Kuo. The police attempted to do exactly that, but when they moved in someone turned out the lights. Kuo and hundreds of his supporters donned identical black masks, and in the confusion Kuo escaped. The police, and the government, were thoroughly embarrassed by the incident. Subsequently DPP candidates exhibited or wore similar black masks at their rallies—black symbolizing their blacklisted colleagues who could not return to Taiwan or could not run in the election. After some deliberation, the Election Commission banned the use of masks by candidates.[9]

Just before the campaign period started, thirty-two DPP candidates belonging to the New Tide faction, which advocated Taiwan independence, announced the formation of the "New Country Alliance" and called for a new constitution and the election of all members of Taiwan's elected bodies of government. This move pushed the independence issue further to the forefront of the campaign, presenting a challenge to the government and the KMT—and to Beijing.[10]

The KMT responded, though not in kind. KMT legislators pushed a tough anti-crime bill through the Legislative Yuan, timing its announcement just before the election. Government officials also initiated several special crime control efforts, including dragnets that brought in large numbers of wanted criminals, some of whom were associated with the DPP. Beijing assailed the advocates of Taiwan independence, referring to the "evil consequences of the policy of two Chinas," and promised to make a "strong response."[11] Nationalist Party leaders widely quoted Beijing's threats.

The government, with KMT prompting, also announced a number of bills and actions that party leaders hoped would help KMT candidates. Though many had been on the agenda for some time, they were given special emphasis or a different spin. In mid-November the KMT published a campaign advertisement saying that a vote for the KMT would be a vote for a bullish stock market, implying that voting for the DPP would cause the market to fall, thereby hurting nearly 4 million owners of shares of stock (one fifth of the population and perhaps half of the voters).[12] The government, apparently at the instigation of KMT leaders, also backed down from investigating investment houses that had been criticized for creating an atmosphere of wild financial speculation in Taiwan. Officials also suddenly decided against imposing a higher stock transaction tax to dampen stock speculation.

When the campaign period started, the government ordered 10,000 extra police on duty to keep order. Riot police in full gear patrolled areas where they thought violence might occur. Government spokesmen said this precaution was justified by the rise of crime in Taiwan in recent years. Moreover, crime usually escalated at election time because criminals took advantage of the fact that campaigners and their assistants often carried large amounts of cash and many other people were preoccupied with the campaign. There were other reasons for concern about violence during the campaign. Chen Yung-yuan, an independent candidate for a Legislative Yuan seat, had been shot on the street in Changhua, apparently by gangsters who had tried to extort money from him. The death of Yu Deng-fa, the founder of the opposition movement in southern Taiwan and father of Yu Chen Yueh-ying, who was running for Kaohsiung county magistrate, also attracted attention. Yu probably died of natural causes (as the coroner had reported); however, DPP leaders claimed he had been murdered. DPP candidate Hsu Jung-shu's office was torched, and TV host Hu Kua, a KMT supporter, reported numerous death threats.[13]

The DPP complained about the police, but many of its candidates requested the same police protection that was offered to other candidates. Many also hired their own bodyguards. A police dragnet launched during the campaign resulted in 5,000 arrests and the seizure of hundreds of handguns smuggled from China.

DPP candidates and their aides accused the KMT of vote-buying at nearly every rally. In private, however, DPP leaders admitted that its candidates were also engaging in the practice. The prosecutor's office of the Supreme Court offered a reward of $NT 200,000 for evidence of vote buying, but with few results. Certainly this effort did not hinder the practice much. However, one expert said that vote buying was only a 20 percent guarantee of a vote for a specific candidate.[14]

Spending in excess of legal limits was also commonplace. DPP candidates accused the KMT of using funds from party-owned companies in illegal ways. Wu Li-yi, a KMT candidate, shocked an American election observer team when he stated publicly that he would spend NT $30 million (over U.S$ 1 million) on the election and his DPP opponent would spend double that. Like their KMT counterparts, DPP candidates clearly had money to spend, as reflected by their well-heeled campaigns, gift giving, and lavish parties. Observers noted that vote buying and illegal campaign spending were the result of Taiwan's economic boom combined with the now greater importance of elected officials in influencing economic decisions. Most regarded the growth of "money politics" as unfortunate but also inevitable.

Almost daily the DPP charged that the KMT possessed a monopoly over television coverage and T.V. political advertising since all three of Taiwan's stations are owned by either the KMT or the government. Late in the campaign, the DPP decided to do something about this. Announcing it in advance, the DPP began broadcasting from a "guerrilla station." DPP leaders subsequently claimed to be in the process of establishing a permanent station in the Philippines to broadcast opposition views to Taiwan. DPP candidates meanwhile sold videotapes of their speeches, of anti-KMT demonstrations, and of the rally where Kuo Pei-hung had appeared and then disappeared.[15]

Both parties took a number of opinion surveys during the campaign. Many distorted the results; some were completely fake. One opposition candidate even sued a polling organization over an inaccurate survey. The KMT published several surveys indicating that most of the population did not support Taiwan independence. The DPP responded with polls indicating that virtually no one wanted to unify with China and be ruled by the Chinese Communist Party, implying that the majority favored separation and thus independence. Completely different results were obtained by asking the question differently. Both sides also published inaccurate poll data predicting the election outcome.[16]

So-called "snails without shells" (people with sufficient incomes, but unable to afford decent housing) staged mass "sleep-ins" in expensive residential areas and in conspicuous places in several of Taiwan's large cities during the campaign.[17] Some observers said the DPP was behind these demonstrations. "Water buffaloes without skin" (people who could not cheat on their income tax because of withholding) also complained in organized public appearances.

A large number of candidates slandered opponents. Many filed lawsuits against their rivals. A retired military man slapped Kaohsiung county commissioner Yu Chen Yueh–ying in the face while she was campaigning. It was not uncommon to see organized group heckling candidates or honking car horns to disrupt their speeches. Meanwhile, candidates beheaded chickens while swearing to be honest politicians, took vows in temples, and engaged in a multitude of other campaign antics.[18]

Some opposition candidates compared the Presidential Square in Taipei with Tiananmen Square in Beijing. Others said that if the KMT stole the election its leaders would have to leave as Ferdinand and Imelda Marcos left the Philippines and that they would probably take all their treasures and money with them. Some accused the old-guard KMT of "refusing to die." Many spoke in Taiwanese only, saying that it was the "language of the people," in contrast to Mandarin Chinese, the ruling class language. And many accused top leaders of having multiple wives or of other moral indiscretions.

Ju Gau-jeng, the "KMT's Rambo," accused opposition candidates of stupidity with regard to the independence issue and said they were ignorant and uneducated. He even declared that some of his critics "should be exterminated." He bragged of his large following and claimed credit for changing the KMT's foreign and domestic policies single-handedly.[19]

Attracting more attention than other candidates, New Country Alliance members responded to authorities in Beijing who criticized their advocacy of independence by staging public burnings of People's Republic of China flags and challenging Deng Xiaoping and other Communist leaders to use military force against Taiwan. Many cursed Deng and other Chinese leaders. One DPP candidate sent an invitation to Premier Li Peng to come observe the election.

The single candidate drawing the biggest crowds, however, was Hsu Hsiao-tan of the Labor Party. Hsu, who had been a stripper, ran on a platform of "supporting the arts" and "openness in government." Depicting both, she distributed a campaign poster with a picture of herself, nude, breaking through a KMT emblem. At one point she challenged her opponent, also female, to a debate in English and a comparison of nipples.

Toward the end of the campaign uncertainty prevailed in the stock market, causing the Tai Index to register its biggest drop ever in a single day. The next day it rose a record amount.[20] The government, on behalf of the KMT, according to opposition critics, issued a statement on the stock transaction tax a couple of days later hoping to cause the market to rise. The stock market stabilized but slid downward during the last few days before the election.

The day before the election, when KMT General Secretary James Soong announced that thirty-four of the elder parliamentarians would be retired, DPP leaders cried foul. They responded similarly when a statement by Deng Xiaoping, to the effect that he would solve the "Taiwan problem" in five years probably from "inside of Taiwan," was published the day of the election. DPP leaders said this news was calculated to frighten the electorate from voting for opposition candidates.[21]

The newly organized Campaign for Clean Elections sought to oversee the election. It published several tracts on human rights problems in Taiwan and a list of those candidates engaging in vote buying. Because it was an arm of the DPP (according to the KMT), most of the accused were naturally ruling party candidates. Two to three hundred foreign reporters covered the election along with several U.S. election observer teams, including one composed of five members of Congress.[22]

Campaign Platforms

The kind of campaign just described generally overshadowed the two parties' platforms and strategies prior to the election. Still, however, both need to be assessed in-depth in order to understand the results of the election (since many voters did not decide their vote on issues) and how the campaign affected future elections and the political development process.

The KMT's platform remained much the same as in previous elections. It claimed credit for the Taiwan economic "miracle" and the high standards of living and prosperity it produced. It also claimed to have engineered political development. The KMT similarly portrayed itself as the party of experience, which could keep the nation "on track" in terms of prosperity and stability. More specifically, its agenda consisted of capitalism mixed with the right amount of social security and welfare, a trade-led growth economy, and a shift to a capital- and knowledge-intensive economy. The KMT claimed also to be a party of progress and a "party on the go" that would lead the nation ahead.[23] It took a tough stand against crime and advocated social stability. Finally, it promised actions to deal with bread-and-butter issues such as air pollution, traffic, and water problems.

The only ideological issue of importance in the KMT's platform was anti-independence. Party leaders promised to maintain their one-China policy and to keep Chinese territory and culture intact. Candidates who sought to give this issue a positive spin cited the "Taiwan model" for reform on the mainland. Some KMT candidates, however, ignored or played down the one-China idea, choosing to concentrate on domestic issues.

The KMT appealed to farmers and the business community more than to other groups, but it claimed to represent the whole nation rather than specific groups or narrow interests. Its program was basically conservative, which it said fit with the traditionalism and conservatism of Chinese culture. It lauded education, hard work, honesty, and merit. It also spoke of morality in government.

KMT strategists sought to portray the DPP and most of the other new opposition parties as composed of radicals and hotheads who associated with criminal and lower-class elements. The KMT pictured the opposition as having little experience, espousing unrealistic programs, and pursuing an agenda that might bring the country to ruin economically and to war with the mainland.

The DPP's campaign platform listed "political order based on democracy and freedom" as its first item. Party briefings and campaign literature focused on "real democracy" and more political and civil liberties. DPP leaders pointed out that to have democracy the KMT must cut its ties with the government and end its control of the media and its "illegitimate" relationship with numerous industries and businesses. They stressed that constitutional guidelines such as checks and balances must be respected and charged the KMT with being in power too long.[24]

The DPP's main tactic was to make the electorate believe that, in order for Taiwan to become democratic, the public must support the DPP. In short, a DPP victory—or even a better performance in the election—would signify that the elections had been competitive and therefore that political modernization was taking Taiwan in the direction of democracy. In this connection, party leaders insisted that Taiwan must become democratic in order to parry efforts by Beijing to incorporate Taiwan.

The DPP platform called for balanced economic and financial administration, which in more specific terms meant full employment, a fairer tax system, improvements in transportation, and environmental protection. It proposed an improved welfare and social security system. The DPP also advocated a "peaceful" foreign policy and mentioned specifically cutting the size of the military, ending hostilities with the mainland, and participating in international organizations.

Most frequently mentioned in DPP candidates' speeches were the unfair advantages possessed by the KMT, the KMT's hold on the government, the long reign of the senior parliamentarians, and KMT vote buying. They charged that under the KMT, political change had not kept pace with economic development. Although the party itself did not take a specific position on the issue of Taiwan's independence, it did cite self-determination in its platform. Moreover, nearly all of its candidates argued that unification with China was a stupid idea that had no public support and that something must be done (meaning to keep Taiwan separate) in response to Beijing's terrible human rights record and its threats toward Taiwan. DPP leaders chided the KMT's wait-and-see policy and the idea that time was on Taiwan's side.

The DPP made a clear and strong appeal to only one interest group: labor. The party made reference to farmers' problems, but not strongly. In other words, DPP candidates did not expect to win many votes in rural Taiwan. Although they did not try to appeal to specific socio-economic or occupational groups or focus on geographic regions in Taiwan, DPP leaders aimed to attract anti-government, anti-KMT protest votes. The DPP also appealed to the democratic-minded and to those with a socialist inclination. Its program was clearly more liberal than conservative when measured against the KMT's platform or by definitions used for political parties in Western countries.

The DPP stated that its strategy for election victory was to seek power at the local level and "surround the center." This statement, especially the terminology, sounded like Mao's 1940s strategy used to defeat the Nationalists. The Communists' guerrilla war strategy aimed to defeat the Nationalists by prevailing in the countryside first and later surrounding and strangling the cities. Many, in fact, understood the allusion. On the other hand, DPP leaders also vowed that in this way they could get the KMT accustomed to sharing power. In any event, the DPP had some other reasons to adopt such a game plan: because the DPP was more capable of winning local elections than national elections, and local elected positions are powerful and are springboards for national elective office in Taiwan.[25] Thus the plan constituted what some called a positive approach.

As in previous elections, the platforms of both parties failed to reflect very well what the voters thought were the most important issues. The biggest election issue as reflected in most polls was crime. Following were pollution and traffic. Taxes, water control, and other tangible issues were also important. Economic growth was an issue, but only in the sense that the electorate wanted sustained growth; few wanted higher growth rates. Trade was also an issue, but this was a matter of keeping trade on track. Social security, health insurance, and welfare were important, but what the public wanted in these areas was unclear.[26]

Not only did the two parties not focus on these basic issues, but their positions on them did not differ very much. Both parties called for a crackdown on crime. The KMT claimed to be the party of law and order, and most citizens perceived it as such. However, because big increases in crime in Taiwan had occurred on the "KMT's shift," its position on law and order was somewhat less than credible. Some even said that the KMT had become too soft and was making too many concessions to democracy. Others said the KMT did not mind the increasing crime rate since this was an issue that favored a KMT vote. On the issues of pollution and traffic and on a number of other substantial issues, the KMT was seen by the electorate as more competent to handle the problems, but also as the party that allowed the problems to become as serious as they were. The KMT advocated lower taxes, yet it had increased taxes considerably over the years. Most voters expected even higher taxes to pay for more social welfare if the DPP were to rule the country, but they did not think seriously in terms of that happening and thus did not show much worry over higher taxes.

The choice between parties, in the last analysis, was more a matter of supporting either the status quo or more democracy. The KMT had a better agenda; the DPP had in its favor the democratization issue. To some extent ethnicity was important: Mainlanders favored the KMT; Taiwanese identified with both parties, though the DPP was seen as a "Taiwanese party." On the issue of Taiwan independence the choice between the two parties was clear, though the meaning of that term was not. Meanwhile, nearly every candidate's campaign was to a great extent personal, emphasizing differences between himself or herself and the opponent.

The Election Results

The Election Commission was not able to announce all of the results of the election by midnight on polling day as it had promised. Despite the more refined and sophisticated vote tallying system, accusations of vote fraud and demands for recounts slowed down the process. The DPP had organized protest demonstrations in advance, either thinking that its candidates would be cheated or assuming they would lose (and wanted to embarrass the KMT if possible). In most cases, however, the DPP candidate either was victorious or the KMT candidate won so clearly that alleged irregularities were not taken seriously. Yet a couple of exceptions caused protest demonstrations to go on for two or three days.

In the Legislative Yuan contest the KMT won 72 seats, the DPP 21, and others (meaning independents) 8; these numbers represented 71.3 percent, 20.8 percent, and 7.9 percent of the seats, respectively. In the Provincial Assembly race, the KMT won 54 seats, the DPP won 16, and others 7; this was 70.1 percent, 20.8 percent, and 9.1 percent of the seats. In the country magistrate and city mayor races, the KMT won 14, the DPP 6, and others 1, or 66.7 percent, 28.6 percent, and 4.8 percent. For the city council races, the respective tallies were: KMT 36, the DPP 14, and others 1, in Taipei, and the KMT 29, DPP 8, and others 5, for Kaohsiung.[27]

In comparison to the number of seats each held before the election (as a result of the 1986 election in the case of the Legislative Yuan and the 1985 election for the other races), the KMT lost ground in every category: by 6 seats in the Legislative Yuan, 5 in the Provincial Assembly, 3 in the county magistrate and city mayor offices, 2 in the Taipei City Council, and 3 in the Kaohsiung City Council. In the legislative race the DPP gained 9 seats. Since the DPP had come into existence in 1986, after the previous local election, DPP gains other than in the Legislative Yuan election were all new. However, if one assumes the DPP is the successor to the *tang wai,* the DPP made significant gains in those races.

Besides reflecting a broad and significant DPP victory, which will be discussed further below, the election results indicate that third parties were unprepared. The new opposition parties, in short, failed to prove they had, or could build, a base of support. Only the Labor Party won a seat—a single place on the Kaohsiung City Council. The two older parties, which were aligned with the KMT failed to demonstrate any viability: The Young China Party lost the two seats it held in the Legislative Yuan and its one seat in the Provincial Assembly, and the China Democratic Socialist Party lost its only seat in the Provincial Assembly. Similarly, independents did less well than in previous elections, losing ground in all of the races except the Legislative Yuan race. Although it may be too early to draw conclusions, this is strong evidence that a two-party system, not a multiparty system, is evolving in Taiwan. In any event, December 1989 witnessed a two-party election victory.

Because there was a larger number of candidates than in previous elections, a significantly smaller percentage of contestants won: 33.2 percent for Legislative Yuan seats as compared to 73 percent in the 1986 election. In this sense the election was much more competitive than other recent elections. In addition, few incumbents won office, but this happened in large part because few ran. Only 48 of the 304 candidates for Legislative Yuan seats were incumbents. Of those, 7 lost. This translates into 70 percent newcomer winners.[28] In many cases incumbent legislators decided to run in other elections, many of them viewing some of the other offices, especially county magistrate, as more important. KMT-DPP competition was also more intense for magistrate offices, thereby causing both parties to try to put their best candidates up for these races, in a number of cases pulling them from other contests.

Family members or relatives of known political figures generally did well. Relatives of the presidents of the Legislative Yuan, the Judicial Yuan, and the Control Yuan all won seats. Two sons of the former mayor of Kaohsiung won posts running on the KMT ticket. Yu Chen Yueh-ying, who was reelected Kaohsiung county magistrate, saw her son elected to the Legislative Yuan and her daughter elected to the Taiwan Provincial Assembly. Chang Po-ya was elected to the Legislative Yuan and her sister Chai-yi was elected mayor; their mother was a noted local politician. Meanwhile, several candidates ran in place of their husbands or wives. However, some kin of known political figures lost, such as You Ching's brother, who ran for the Legislative Yuan.[29]

A number of candidates appear to have won considerable sympathy vote. Chen Shui-bian, who campaigned in a wheelchair because of a recent accident, won. Yeh Chu-lau, whose husband burned himself to death in April while under investigation for sedition after his opposition magazine was closed, won a seat in the Legislative Yuan. A number of candidates who had served jail terms were elected. Several won who campaigned on the independence issue, and some won after declaring they could avoid jail if elected.

Mainlander and female candidates did well, especially in the Legislative Yuan. Mainlanders won 19.2 percent of the seats; female candidates won 14.1 percent. Over 25 percent of KMT winners of Legislative Yuan seats were Mainlanders—the result of the military vote in the primary. Almost 20 percent of KMT winners were female, in part because the KMT had entered more female candidates than ever. Less than 6 percent of DPP victors were Mainlanders or women.[30] The increase in the number of Mainlanders (all second generation) was five-fold. (Only three had won seats in the 1986 election.)

Some observers said this marked an end to the KMT's "affirmative action" policy designed to run more Taiwanese candidates. It needed to be reversed, many said, since the percentage of KMT Taiwanese candidates in recent elections had exceeded the percentage of the Taiwanese in the population. Moreover, many applauded the young Mainlander candidates as a force for reason and democracy, since most advocated phasing out senior parliamentarians and reforming the KMT yet were more moderate on other issues. Some said the ethnic backgrounds of candidates had faded in importance. In any event, Jaw Shau-kong, a second-generation Mainlander, won the third largest number of votes nationwide. Another Mainlander, Yu Mu-ming, was the top vote-getter from the southern Taipei area.[31]

The educational level of winning candidates was high but did not show an increase from the last election. In fact, it dropped. This change was due in part to the larger number of DPP winners and the fact the DPP did not give the same emphasis to educational qualifications as the KMT. The level of experience of winners was also less for the same reason. Putting a positive twist on these facts, many observers said educational qualifications had been overemphasized in past campaigns and interpreted lack of experience in politics to mean "new blood" with broader experience.[32] The average age of winning candidates was somewhat higher, though for victorious candidates for Legislative Yuan seats it was almost the same.

Voter turnout was 75.4 percent of an estimated 12 million eligible voters. This was up markedly from the past two elections. In fact, voter turnout was the highest in ten years. Inasmuch as campaign rallies were not attended as well as in the last three elections, voter interest seemed to have been hidden. Alternatively, perhaps voters were interested but based their decisions on information from other sources.[33]

In light of the election results, the KMT could, and in some cases did, claim victory. The ruling party won 60 percent of the popular vote and more. The ruling party won more than two-thirds of the seats in every category: in the Legislative Yuan, 71.3 percent (69.6 percent not counting the thirteen of eighteen vocational seats); in the Provincial Assembly, 70 percent; in the Taipei City Council, 67 percent; in the Kaohsiung City Council, 67 percent; in the races for county magistrates and city mayors (taken as one category), 67 percent. The KMT accomplished this while making the playing field level or almost level and in spite of the fact that many voters favored the opposition, not because of its platform or its candidates, but in order to make the system democratic. Finally, by comparison with elections in Western democracies, the vote was a resounding victory for the KMT.

Still, few observers viewed the election as a KMT victory; rather, most saw it as a major setback. All of Taiwan's major newspapers carried headlines that proclaimed a KMT defeat. The KMT held an emergency meeting the Sunday morning after the election to discuss the results, and most at the meeting considered it an effort to discover what went wrong. Party Secretary General James Soong stated solemnly: "We calmly accept the upset."[34]

DPP leaders unequivocally viewed the election as a defeat for the KMT and a victory for their party. The DPP won 31 percent of the popular vote. An additional 9 percent of the popular vote went to independents, most of whom favored the DPP. DPP leaders declared after the election that they had accomplished this in spite of tremendous disadvantages: The playing field was not level owing to extraordinary KMT influence over the media; the membership of the party was small (20,000 compared to 2.5 million KMT members); and the DPP was only three years old. DPP leaders also noted that the purported split over the issue of independence had not proven real. In addition, they pointed out that all other competing parties had failed.[35]

In terms of popular vote, the DPP registered an increase of nearly 10 percent from the previous election in 1986. In total number of seats, the gain was even more impressive—25 percent. The DPP made advances at every level of government. In the Legislative Yuan election the DPP won 9 more seats for a total of 21. Since 20 are needed to introduce legislation, this was a breakthrough. In the city council elections, the DPP doubled its representation in Kaohsiung and gained 40 percent in Taipei over what the *tang wai* had won in 1985. In the Taiwan Provincial Assembly, the DPP made a smaller, but still impressive, gain.

The biggest DPP victory came in the county magistrate races. Many consider the county magistrate the most powerful popularly elected official in Taiwan, and the DPP campaigned hard for these slots. In these races the DPP won 38 percent of the popular vote, compared to the KMT's 53 percent. It won six magistrates (Taipei, Ilan, Hsinchu, Changhua, Pingtung, Kaohsiung). As a result, the DPP gained control of the executive offices of the county governments wherein 40 percent of the population lives, including the capital city. The KMT had never before lost more than four magistrate races.

Anti-KMT independent county magistrates have in recent years destroyed police and intelligence agency records on county employees and have tried to withhold tax revenues from the national government. In so acting they caused major problems for the national government and the KMT. Now DPP magistrates can do this, and much more, if they choose. They may try to disestablish KMT organizations, especially KMT branches, within or close to county or city governments. They may seek to restructure local police systems. They may institute local health insurance programs and unemployment and welfare systems. The DPP will certainly exercise considerable political influence in the counties for the next four years and probably beyond.

The DPP also can claim victory inasmuch as most of the candidates that the KMT tried hardest to defeat won. You Ching, winner of the county magistrate seat in Taipei County, site of the capital city and the home of President Lee Teng-hui and other top government leaders, is the best example. In addition, many of the most radical and controversial DPP candidates won. The majority of DPP winners were of the New Tide faction, the most vociferous advocates of Taiwan independence.

Implications for Taiwan's Polity

Most observers would say of the December 1989 election that the DPP did better than most expected and that it should be credited with a victory, perhaps a big victory. Furthermore, the DPP will be a force to be reckoned with politically in Taiwan for the foreseeable future. The success of the DPP also means that Taiwan has a meaningful, organized opposition and that competitive elections and competitive politics are now well established. This translates into the following: Taiwan has made another big stride toward a democratic system.

Some observers, in fact, say that Taiwan is no longer just becoming a democracy; it already is one. Some opposition candidates stated during the campaign that Taiwan has democratized faster than any other nation in the world over the past few years. Others admitted that they consider Taiwan the most democratic country in East Asia, save Japan. These statements may be premature; yet clearly Taiwan has in a number of significant ways made the transition from an authoritarian to a democratic system.

Not all of the important hurdles in the political modernization process have been crossed, however. Nor are political stability and tranquility necessarily guaranteed. Democracy is not without costs. The DPP victory will probably mean greater, not less, tension between the KMT and the opposition. No doubt there will be difficult relations between the national government and the county and city governments for some time. Decision making may, in fact, be paralyzed on some issues. Discord between the two parties could spread into other realms.

The nation will no doubt be polarized further on the issue of Taiwan independence as a result of this election. The most vociferous pro-independence candidates won, but so did their loudest opponents and the advocates of the future unification of Taiwan with China. This situation injects an ideological issue into Taiwan politics that may not be auspicious. Ethnic politics may also gain prominence because ethnic issues were amplified by candidates who made issue of differences in political viewpoint and advocacy based on provincial or group identification. Similarly, special interest groups played a greater role in this election than in previous electoral contests. In fact, there were many complaints that candidates were toadying to interest groups while ignoring the silent majority. There is also evidence that special interests and money politics reinforced and strengthened each other. Efforts to check money politics in Taiwan clearly have not succeeded, though vote buying or its equivalent seems to be the result more of economic prosperity than of increasing corruption.

Party politics, for better or worse, are apparently a fact of political life in Taiwan. Party competition normally facilitates the democratic process, but it also creates partisanship and other undesirable effects. Partisanship indeed seems to have taken root in Taiwan.

The election results indicate that some events and campaign tactics had a different impact on the voters than originally anticipated. There was clearly some misinterpretation of how advocacy of certain issues would influence the electorate. Both parties made some fairly serious errors during the campaign, though the KMT made more.

Many observers felt that the events in China in June—the Tiananmen Massacre—would help the KMT at the polls. Initially, the PRC's actions did have a salutary affect on the KMT's campaign efforts: They made the government and the ruling party in Taiwan look good by comparison; students were not being killed with tanks and machine guns in Taipei. The Tiananmen Massacre also solved the KMT's problem of formulating a "mainland policy"—which in 1988 and early 1989 was an especially knotty issue. After Tiananmen, the KMT did not need to worry about this very much. But these issues came back. DPP candidates to some extent successfully portrayed themselves as similar to the Beijing students and in this way won some sympathy from the electorate. More important, the DPP found a poignant argument for self-determination, Taiwan independence, or whatever version of separation it advocated; Tiananmen and the repression that followed justified Taiwan eschewing contacts with China and rejecting unification in the near future. As one DPP candidate put it: "Beijing's brutality justifies calls for separation." Certainly separation at the time of this election—less than six months away from Tiananmen—did not look like a radical notion; rather, it seemed the only sensible policy.

Events in Eastern Europe and the Soviet Union also helped the DPP. Democracy seemed to be "breaking out around the world." This being the case, pushing for even more democracy in Taiwan did not seem out of place. The KMT had taken the position that it had introduced democracy to Taiwan at a very rapid pace, but the DPP said it was not fast enough. The DPP in this context seemed to be right.

The DPP's disadvantage in not having access to television was no doubt exaggerated; otherwise the DPP could not have done as well as it did. In fact, survey polls indicate the electorate did not base its decisions much on TV, clearly not as much as in many Western countries. Moreover, the DPP was able to both make this an issue of fairness (and thus democracy) and offset the handicap of not being able to use television very much with effective advertising in newspapers, magazines, and other places.

The KMT, and many outside observers, overestimated the importance of what they saw as a split within the DPP. KMT leaders did this intentionally to some extent to support their position that the DPP was a group of ruffians—the rationale being that because they were ruffians, naturally they could not get along with each other. Differences over whether to advocate independence have been around for some time, and they continued during this election for the DPP, but they did not cause a serious split. In any event, the DPP was not very dependent on party discipline; instead it relied on activist candidates and personalities to win.

In contrast, although the KMT was not seen as factionalized there were serious differences within its ranks over the pace od democratization and the possibility of making certain concessions to level the playing field for the DPP. Some KMT candidates seemed to desire fair competition with the DPP and thus did not try as hard as they could have in the campaign. The issues of patriotism and separation also confused KMT candidates. A major split in the KMT was never imminent, but differences in viewpoint did clearly affect the ruling party's performance.

The KMT also made some rather serious errors in strategy. KMT notables in the government appeared to try to control the stock market in order to influence the election outcome. They also tried to use statements made by Deng Xiaoping and pronouncements from Beijing to counteract the DPP's call for independence. To a sizable portion of the electorate this tactic appeared to be a cynical effort at manipulation. Moreover, KMT leaders seemed to give too much emphasis to educational standards so as to portray the DPP as low-class hoodlums. Thus, in picking candidates they relied too much on educational qualifications and not enough on charisma. This made the KMT look elitist and helped give the DPP an image of a common man's party.

The KMT underestimated the sympathy vote and unwisely tried to use logical arguments against it. It put too much reliance on opinion surveys, while trying to use them to influence voting. Both had bad results. The KMT may also have been overconfident. At times it seemed to be. It also appeared less professional and less on the ball than in the past. A number of the members of foreign election observer teams noted this problem. Changes in personnel may have been the cause. A decline in morale as a result of Chiang Ching-Kuo's death may also explain it. Similarly, a number of KMT leaders seemed to be locked in a power struggle with others in the party. President Lee Teng-hui was still new in office, and though his public image was very good, he had yet to resolve some internal party disputes and convince many party stalwarts of his leadership abilities.

DPP candidates made much of the fact that they were underdogs, and this ploy worked. They won the protest vote and the sympathy vote. DPP candidates also benefited from the widely held view that a vote for them was a vote for democracy. To some, a vote for the DPP would encourage the KMT to do better. Thus, there was a large bloc of votes that did not necessarily support the DPP but nevertheless helped it in the election. Most voters, in fact, did not consider the possibility that the DPP might win sufficiently to rule the country and did not worry about the party's shortcomings. Finally, some, assuming the KMT could not lose at the national level, reasoned that the DPP would view winning local office a priority, thereby making part of the system more competitive and perhaps more efficient.

In sum, the DPP's strategy and performance in the campaign were considerably better than most observers had anticipated, and the KMT's were worse. This fact, plus the DPP's attraction of the protest vote and the vote for competitive elections and democracy, help explain the DPP's gains. But so do world events, such as Tiananmen, the democracy movements in Europe, and the pending collapse of communism. Deng's threats in this context amplified the help these events gave the DPP. Events in Japan, too, had an effect: The ruling conservative Liberal Democratic Party, which had been in power for nearly thirty-five years. Many in Taiwan modeled their politics after Japan; this being the case, the KMT could look forward to a long period of rule in an essentially one-party-dominant system. However, the Japanese electorate's rejection of the Liberal Democratic Party in the summer and the LDP's subsequent difficulties sent another signal to Taiwan's voters.

All of these factors could be reversed in the next election. Thus 1989 seems to suggest a rise of the opposition and competitive democracy in Taiwan; it does not mean a demise of the KMT.

How DPP politicians perform in office will surely influence the next election. By 1992 the DPP will no doubt be seen to some degree as a ruling or government party—certainly at the local level. The DPP will have to campaign on its record next time. That may be an advantage; in Chinese politics, it helps to be an incumbent. Yet being an outsider, at odds with the KMT, proved a boon in this election. In the next three years the DPP will have to come to terms with the KMT and compromise, or paralyze the system—either of which may hurt their image with the protest voter.

The DPP will also have to reconcile many of its election promises and statements with reality. DPP candidates spoke of a "peaceful foreign policy" and of reentering international organizations, including the United Nations. Fulfilling these promises will be very difficult. The DPP will have to defend many of its "socialist" policies in the context of the failure of both communism and socialism around the world. They will have to cope with the female vote, which is growing in influence in Taiwan. The KMT has a better record with both women candidates and women's issues. The DPP will also have to deal with the image that it is dominated by narrow objectives and appeals to special-interest groups rather than the national interest. Finally, it will have to deal with the crime issue, which certainly will not be easy.

Meanwhile, the KMT will no doubt learn something from this election setback. How the KMT will respond to this "defeat" is difficult to predict. It has been a party that has dealt with all kinds of adversity in the past. It may be able to improve its image based on Taiwan's democratization, its enhanced role in global economic affairs, and what some call Taiwan's new identity. It may be able to adjust to breaking its ties with the government and its control of television and a large number of corporations and enterprises. It can probably also change from an election strategy that emphasizes morality in government to a strategy built on tough political campaigning in a pluralist country.

In any event, it is clear that the election process and democracy have been advanced by the 1989 national election. Probably future analysts will say it was furthered by a big notch.

Endnotes

1. The other three were in 1980, 1983, and 1986. For details on past elections, see John F. Copper with George P. Chen, *Taiwan's Elections: Political Development and Democratization in the Republic of China* (Baltimore: University of Maryland School of Law, 1984); John F. Copper, "Taiwan's 1985 Elections," *Asian Affairs*, Spring 1986, pp. 27–45; John F. Copper, "Taiwan's 1986 National Election: Pushing Democracy Ahead," *Asian Thought and Society*, July 1987, pp. 115–136.

2. Excerpts of this law were published only in typewritten form by the Government Information Office in Taipei at this time.

3. *The Public Officials Election and Recall Law of the Republic of China* (Taipei: Shine Chin Enterprises Co., Ltd., 1989).

4. These complaints were made by Shih-yuan Tsai, deputy secretary general of the Democratic Progressive Party, during a briefing to an election observer team in Taipei during the campaign. They are also contained in a typed booklet entitled "Taiwan According to the DPP" given to members of the observer team.

5. This statute has been printed in English and is available in typed form from the Government Information Office in Taipei.

6. See Wu Wen-cheng and Chen I-hsin, *Elections and Political Development in Taiwan* (Taipei: Government Information Office, 1989), pp. 16–18.

7. Lincoln Kaye, "On the Defensive," *Far Eastern Economic Review*, October 19, 1989, p. 26. For details on Hsu's earlier attempts to return, see Copper, "Taiwan's 1986 Election."

8. For details, see *China Post*, November 11, 1989, p. 12.

9. "No more marks allowed, Election Commission Says," *China News*, November 30, 1989, p. 12. See "Kuo Pei-hung's parents ask police to stop hunt," *China Post*, November 27, 1989, p. 12, for further details on the impact of the case during the campaign.

10. See James McGregor, "Taiwan Poll Renews Independence Issue," *Asian Wall Street Journal*, November 30, 1989, p. 1.

11. See "Guarding Against the Ideological Trends of Taiwan Independence," *Liao-wang*, November 27, 1989, pp. 21–22, translated in FBIS (China), November 29, 1989, p. 52.

12. See "KMT ad misled investors into purchasing shares," *China Post*, November 26, 1989, p. 8.

13. See "Shadow of Violence," *Asiaweek*, December 1, 1989, p. 35.

14. See *China Post*, November 28, 1989, p. 12.

15. See Lincoln Kaye, "Television Tangle," *Far Eastern Economic Review*, November 30, 1989, pp. 23–24.

16. "Opposition Candidate Sues Group over Inaccurate Survey," *China Post*, November 30, 1989, p. 11. Also see "KMT Projects Winning 70 Percent of Votes" and "DPP Comes Out on Top in NTU Simulated Poll," *China Post*, November 30, 1989, p. 11.

17. "'Snails without Shells' Endorse 18 Candidates," *China Post*, November 30, 1989, p. 12.

18. See Ho Ying, "Tactics and Strategies Within the Combat Zone," *China News*, November 30, 1989, p. 12.

19. Ibid., p. 23.

20. See James McGregor, "Taipei Stocks Bounce Back by Record 6.5%," *Asian Wall Street Journal,* November 30, 1989, p. 1.

21. "Candidates Engage in Last-minute Campaigning on Eve of Election," *China Post,* December 2, 1989, p. 12.

22. "300 Newsmen, Observers Here for Election," *China Post,* December 2, 1989, p. 12.

23. For a summary of the KMT's platform and strategy, see "Campaign Strategist," (Interview of Wang Shu-ching, chief commissioner of the KMT City Committee, by Chen Yi-ming), *Free China Review,* December 1989, pp. 32–37.

24. See "Taiwan According to the DPP" (mimeographed brochure given to foreign observers by the DPP during the election).

25. For further details, see James McGregor, "Taiwan's DPP Pins Hopes on Local Posts," *Asian Wall Street Journal,* December 1–2, 1989, p. 1.

26. The issues the voters were most concerned about were little different from those of other recent elections. The interests of voters in urban areas were different from those of voters in rural areas. In some cases the polls reflected contradictory interests; for example, voters favored increased social security and health insurance, but not higher taxes.

27. Final election results were published in *China Post* and *China News,* December 4, 1989.

28. "7 Legislators Not Reelected; 70% of Parliament Newcomers," *China Post,* December 4, 1989, p. 12.

29. "Political Dynasties Flourish as Family Members Are Elected," *China Post,* December 4, 1989, p. 12.

30. These calculations are my own, but are based on a number of local newspaper reports on winning candidates.

31. "2nd Generation Mainlanders Do Well in Poll," *China Post*, December 4, 1989, p. 12.

32. "Newly Elected Officials by Age and Educational Background," *China News*, December 4, 1989, p. 12.

33. For details, see "Voter Turnout," *China News*, December 4, 1989, p. 12.

34. See "Worst Poll Setbacks for KMT in 40 Years," *China Post*, December 4, 1989, p. 1.

35. For DPP victory statements, see various articles in *Independence Evening News* (in Chinese) December 3 and 4, 1989.

Chapter 5
Taiwan's 1991 Second National Assembly Election

On December 21, 1991, the electorate in Taiwan went to the polls to select delegates to the National Assembly—one of the nation's three parliamentary bodies and the organ of government empowered to elect the president and vice president, amend the Constitution, and perform various other duties. This was Taiwan's fifth competitive election at the national level.[1]

This election was considered by many a watershed event because it was Taiwan's first national election that was not a supplemental election. The "elder" National Assembly delegates (along with their counterparts in the Legislative Yuan and the Control Yuan, the other two elective bodies in Taiwan's tri-parliamentary system), who were elected when the government ruled all of China, or the mainland in addition to Taiwan, either resigned shortly before the election or signed a document promising to step down. Thus the new National Assembly will no longer be made up primarily of delegates elected before the government moved to Taiwan or purport to represent districts in China. Instead it will have merely token representation of "Chinese living abroad." Since the new delegates will, with a few exceptions, represent Taiwan, this election constitutes a big step forward in the democratization process, though it may also mark the further separation of Taiwan from China politically.

This election is also important because the new or Second National Assembly will have the task of revising Taiwan's Constitution—an important matter that has been pending for some time. This will involve deciding fundamental issues such as how the president and vice president are elected and whether Taiwan is a presidential or cabinet system of government, among other things. It could, in fact, mean much more if, under the rubric of streamlining the government and changing the relationship between the central government and local governments, the delegates make more far-reaching changes in the nation's basic law.

Some observers, however, viewed the election as having little importance. The National Assembly, after all, is not a law-making body. There was even serious debate, in the context of devising a system for directly electing the president and vice-president, of reducing its powers, making it little more than an electoral college. There also was voter apathy. The issue of constitutional change did not excite the electorate. The parties and candidates likewise did not do a good job of communicating the gravity of the job of constitutional revision. Meanwhile a number of candidates discussed "bread-and-butter" issues that were not relevant to the decision-making powers of the National Assembly. This dampened the political debate over constitutional change and gave the appearance that the process was not working correctly. Finally, it seemed that many voters were perhaps bored by national elections that have become frequent and routine in Taiwan.

This lack of enthusiasm prevailed despite an unprecedented focus on a very controversial issue—Taiwan independence—by candidates of the opposition Democratic Progressive Party (DPP). The DPP platform called for establishing a "Republic of Taiwan" following a national plebiscite to decide the country's future. The Nationalist Party, or Kuomintang (KMT), along with a number of government officials, labeled this proposal treasonous. The government, under KMT leadership, was then forced to decide whether to disqualify the main opposition party or take legal action against some of its leaders and candidates and then suffer public criticism for ruining a democratic election, or let the matter go. It opted for the latter.

A number of minor parties entered the race. However, only two, the Chinese Social Democratic Party and the National Democratic Independent Political Alliance, nominated a sufficient number of candidates (the minimum being ten) to qualify for television time. In any event, all third parties failed to field enough well-known candidates and patently lacked good organization, and consequently the minor or smaller parties did not perform well during the campaign. Also, they found some election rules discriminated against small parties. When the votes were counted, all of the third parties were disappointed. Not even the main opposition Democratic Progressive Party did well. It was unanimous that the KMT won the election hands down.

The election was conducted with fewer irregularities than the national elections of the 1980s in Taiwan. Democracy had apparently taken root. After the election, many observers said Taiwan had made another major stride forward on the road to a democratic system. Few nations, perhaps none have performed so well in democratizing, without bloodshed, so quickly.

Pre-election Politics in Taiwan

Following President Chiang Ching-kuo's death in January 1988, the ruling Nationalist Party experienced internal disunity. Vice President Lee Teng-hui became president without opposition and in a constitutional manner, but he was not the choice of many in the ruling party to be president, and even more, party chairman. Lee, however, overcame an early challenge, one that sought to make him a temporary chairman or make the chairmanship a rotating position. At the 13th Party Congress held in mid-year he successfully promoted party reform that democratized party rules and at the same time strengthened his own position in the party.[2] But these efforts did not put the matter of the KMT's leadership to rest.

His opponents assailed his dictatorial manner plus his flirting with the opposition. Some even accused Lee of supporting Taiwan independence—heresy to many KMT stalwarts. Most felt that he could not fill the shoes of previous president and party head Chiang Ching-kuo. All of this perpetuated serious dissension in the ruling party, causing some to describe the party as seriously split. Exacerbating the centrifugal tendencies, well-known party organizer John Kuan, who many considered the genius behind the Nationalist Party's past election victories, was seriously at odds with Secretary General James Soong. Soong, who supported President Lee to head the party and gained in stature because of that, was described by Kuan's associates and others as Lee's "hatchet man."[3]

These difficulties led, though to what extent is controvertible, to an important election defeat for the KMT in December 1989. This setback at the polls caused KMT officials to ponder the party's leadership and the problem of factionalism in the party. The KMT's stance on further political reform and its relationship with the opposition party were also hotly debated.

In the spring of 1990, President Lee faced another dilemma. He had to be elected (or reelected, if one considers he had been elected vice president and had the presidential mandate at the time) president by the National Assembly to a new six-year term. But he wanted quick political reform, including retiring the "senior" members of the National Assembly who had not stood for reelection since the government moved to Taiwan in 1949 or had been appointed as replacements. In short, Lee needed the support of those he wanted to force into retirement. Lee caused a controversy at this juncture by naming Li Yuan-zu as his vice-presidential running mate. Li was considered an unknown and too old, too tied to the Chiang family, and at worst a "political hack." A popular Taiwanese politician, Lin Yang-kang, joined forces with Wego Chiang, Chiang Kai-shek's second son and former President Chiang Ching-kuo's half-brother, to challenge President Lee. This incident further divided the ruling party.[4]

Notwithstanding serious opposition and a hostile, or at least unfriendly, National Assembly, President Lee and his choice for vice president were elected in March. Meanwhile, 10,000 students gathered at Chiang Kai-shek Memorial in downtown Taipei to protest the method of electing a president (though not President Lee's election) and the Temporary Provisions of the Constitution, which undermined the guarantees of political and civil rights in the Constitution. President Lee met with the students and vowed to act to bring about these and other reforms. He specifically promised a "National Affairs Conference" to debate major issues of political reform—including constitutional change—which, as an expert on constitutions, Vice President Li would lead.

In May, in his inauguration speech, President Lee again pledged his support for constitutional reform. Needless to say, it was the major agenda item at the National Affairs Conference when it convened the next month. Scholars, overseas Chinese, officials, and opposition politicians were invited to join the meeting, which was intended to be a kind of constitutional convention. President Lee's major objectives were to build consensus on political reform and to lay the groundwork for constitutional changes that were needed to mold the democratization process as it proceeded several steps further.[5]

He also sought the retirement of the elder parliamentarians. The Nationalist Party had earlier, in 1989, pushed a law through the Legislative Yuan asking for their retirement; many resisted, however, and questioned the law's constitutionality. Just before the National Affairs Conference began, the Grand Council of Justices, the legal body responsible for interpreting the Constitution, ruled that those members of Taiwan's parliament (meaning the National Assembly, the Legislative Yuan, and the Control Yuan) elected by mainland constituencies had to retire by December 31, 1991. But this ruling was also challenged. Thus, one of the main topics of discussion at the National Affairs Conference was persuading or forcing the retirement of the "elder" National Assembly members. In fact, this issue was seen as a sine qua non if the Constitution was to be amended democratically.

In April 1991, President Lee called an extraordinary session of the National Assembly (only the second ever held) and proposed a draft of ten additional articles to be added to the Constitution. These articles provided the basis for the election of a second, or new, National Assembly later in the year. More specifically, it was decided that an election would be held before December 31 and that an extraordinary session of the Second National Assembly would be convened within three months after the election to discuss the issue of the Constitution.

The terms of the delegates to the Second National Assembly was set at four years and two months, meaning their tenure in office would expire before they could elect a president under the present system. Hence, their mandate was almost solely to amend, or possibly rewrite, the Constitution.[6]

In May, President Lee announced an end to the "Period of National Mobilization for Suppression of Communist Rebellion," or the state of war that existed between the Nationalist and Communist Chinese governments, or between Taiwan and China, which provided the legal basis for the Temporary Provisions. This was a necessary first step to terminating the provisions. The Temporary Provisions were subsequently abolished, and "Additional Articles" guaranteeing political and civil rights went into full force. This step constituted what many called the "first phase" of constitutional revision; the second phase was to follow the election of a new Second National Assembly.

Subsequently, the government took steps to make some important revisions in the Public Officials Election and Recall Law of 1980 (though revisions had been made in 1983 and 1989). In fact, changes were made that affected the upcoming election. The campaign period was shortened to ten days in response to public complaints that the campaign activities were too disruptive. Regulations were tightened on campaign spending. Also, candidates were for the first time allowed to use television, although TV time was allocated to political parties rather than to individual candidates.

Article 1 of the Additional Articles and the Election Law provided for an election of 219 seats (of which 19 are reserved for female candidates, if that many females are not elected) from special municipalities, cities and counties in the election districts (of which there are 58) in addition to 6 Aborigine delegates, 3 to be chosen from lowland areas and 3 from highland areas. Another 100 national constituency delegates were to be chosen and given proportionally to the political parties receiving at least 5 percent of the vote, 20 of whom will represent "Chinese living abroad." In all, 325 delegates were to be chosen by the electorate in the December 1991 election.

The Party Platforms and Strategies

The Nationalist Party's platform was very much like its platform in previous elections. The ruling party took credit for the nation's economic growth, social change, political modernization and all of the other progress Taiwan has made in the past four-plus decades. Party officials and candidates preached stability and attacked the "violence-prone candidates" of the Democratic Progressive Party. They characterized DPP leaders as uneducated, low-class hoodlums and rebels. They frequently asked the electorate rhetorically: "Do you want to live in a country ruled by the DPP?" They also hit the DPP's economic plans as unrealistic, socialist, and likely to harm the country's economy. KMT candidates similarly assailed the DPP's independence plank as divisive, treasonous, and dangerous (because it might provoke an armed attack on Taiwan by the People's Republic of China).

The KMT's main slogan used during the campaign was: "reform, stability and prosperity." These words, according to the head of the party's Cultural Affairs Division, James Chu, came from a computer analysis of ideas and suggestions contained in letters to party leaders during several months leading up to the election. He said the campaign slogan also fit the party's general views. The KMT, he declared, wanted political reform and rightfully took credit for the political modernization the nation had experienced so far, including getting the elder parliamentarians to retire, and holding this, the nation's first non-supplementary election. He said the country needed stability in the context of rapid economic, social, and political change. Finally, he said everyone wanted continued economic growth and prosperity.[7]

Chu and other KMT officials, however, said the party had not reached a decision on the matter of how the president and vice president should be elected. They reported that opinion polls revealed a divided electorate and said that they wanted to hear more from the voters on the question before deciding what the party's position would be. It seemed, however, that the KMT favored an indirect system for choosing the president or that it was split on the issue. In contrast, the KMT, unequivocally supported the direct election of the governor of Taiwan and the mayors of Taipei and Kaohsiung. On the matter of whether to revise the Constitution or rewrite it, the KMT clearly favored the former. Its slogan was: "Maximize the benefit of constitutional reform, minimize the social cost." Yet party leaders privately admitted they may choose to make numerous and important changes. More specifically, they said they would seek to streamline the Office of the President, the Legislative Yuan, and the Control Yuan and to improve the relationship between the central and local governments. Several spoke of shifting tax money to local governments where it would be used more efficiently. Some even spoke of altering Taiwan's political system in the direction of federalism by transferring powers from the central government to the local governments and of changing the ill-defined relationship between the president and the premier caused by ambiguity in the Constitution as to whether Taiwan has a presidential or a cabinet system of government.[8]

Another campaign slogan used by the KMT was: "To support President Lee, please vote for the KMT." The party perceived that President Lee Teng-hui had a highly favorable image and that the electorate felt he was doing a good job. They also calculated that using his name would attract many Taiwanese votes, since he is Taiwanese. At the same time, it would help counter some of the tenets of the Democratic Progressive Party's platform that appealed specifically to the Taiwanese "ethnic" voter.

KMT leaders likewise made issue of the "weak performance" of DPP county magistrates elected in 1989. Others made reference to the DPP as a party already in power, trying to counter the DPP slogan that a vote for the DPP is a vote for a two-party system and democracy.

In this vein, KMT candidates and party leaders alike made frequent note of the "fact" that a higher voter turnout would favor the KMT because the "silent majority" favors the ruling party. This was quite unlike the situation in 1989 when many voters were upset with KMT over factional fighting and favored the DPP in order to advance democracy. This time it was different, they said, because of the DPP's performance, the fact that people were fed up with DPP antics and its advocacy of protest and violence, plus the KMT's recent good performance in promoting economic growth and rational political change.

The Democratic Progressive Party put in its platform, and its candidates advocated, many of the often-heard tenets of the main opposition party: full employment, a fairer tax system, environmental protection, welfare for the poor, social security, national health insurance, a peaceful foreign policy, and reduced military spending.[9] The main parts of its platform remained generally unchanged from the 1989 campaign.

DPP candidates made an issue of fairness in the election or a "level playing field" and accused the KMT of monopolizing political power and of unfair campaign tactics. They specifically mentioned the KMT's ownership of large enterprises (which provide large amounts of campaign money) and its control over the media. DPP leaders also assailed election rules that favored the KMT and the latter's efforts in buying votes. The DPP publicized its weak financial position in comparison to the "rich" KMT—a comparison given credibility by the fact that the DPP mortgaged its headquarters building just before the campaign started to pay election expenses.[10]

The DPP departed from its past campaign strategy by advocating Taiwan's independence in a new and more direct way: by putting it into the party platform. This made it a much more controversial issue than it had been in the past when the DPP made only indirect reference to it in party literature and candidates spoke of it but usually stopped short of stating clear definitions or policies.

Also, there had been considerable variance among DPP candidates who supported independence. Reaction in the party was mixed for making independence a central elect-ion issue and putting it in the platform, thereby challenging the government to charge the party, or its candidates, with treason. Hsu Hsin-liang, DPP secretary-general, in fact, noted that most DPP leaders did not favor making this a plank in the platform, but the majority of the Central Standing Committee did, and thus it was passed at a party conference on October 13. According to DPP leaders whom I queried on this subject, those who favored calling specifically for an independent Taiwan perceived that the DPP's other campaign issues would not attract voter interest because of their lack of relevance to this election.[11] They felt that this issue was what the party stood for and perceived emphasizing it was a good strategy. They reasoned that the DPP had profited during the last election campaign from making point of the fact that, in view of the Tiananmen Massacre (in Beijing in June 1989), Taiwan should obviously not be ruled by the People's Republic of China and should instead seek formal separation. Developments in Eastern Europe also had an impact.[12] Some also linked independence to the issue of constitutional revision—since the present Constitution embraced a one-China position.

During the campaign it became evident that advocating independence was not productive. Hence, the DPP—or at least most candidates—switched gears and instead emphasized their stand against the KMT's unification policy. They called this policy unrealistic and stupid, and, if sensible at all, so far in the distant future that it was meaningless to talk about it now. Changing their approach in midstream, however, created a problem for some candidates in that many voters thought they had dropped their advocacy of independence or at least were confused by what they said.

The DPP's second important campaign issue was the direct election of the president. Its leaders said (and this went into the party platform) that a directly elected president would be more responsive to the people and that the political system would thereby be more democratic. They also said that this was what the people wanted and contended that the KMT did not want direct presidential elections "because it would put political power in the hands of the people." DPP leaders said this issue was connected to the independence issue inasmuch as a directly elected president would be seen to be more a "Taiwan president" than a "Republic of China president."

A third and much less important DPP campaign tenet was a call for a more positive foreign policy. This included, DPP leaders argued, returning to the United Nations. When confronted with the argument that joining the UN was not possible because, among other things, Beijing would use its veto, they responded that the rapid changes in the world (especially in the communist bloc) indicated that it was not so unrealistic and that UN membership should be seen as a long-term objective that should receive immediate attention. The DPP also advocated an international or global foreign policy and better relations with China, though its opposition to both investment in China and political contacts with Beijing seemed to indicate otherwise. Also, the DPP refused to acknowledge the fact that the one-China policy espoused by the United States and most other countries of the world would probably not change.[13]

The platform of the Chinese Social Democratic Party (CSDP) called for a "social state" that "emancipates productivity and fairly distributes economic wealth." It also stated: "We are personalistic liberals." Elaborating on these slogans, one of its spokesmen said in a private interview that the platform drew philosophically from Confucius, Mencius, and Kant. He declared that liberalism and socialism provided the historical context in which democracy grew. Further, the CSDP said the party stands for "world peace, a revival of nature, human dignity, and social justice" plus the "liberation of women, the right to work, and the humanization of labor."[14]

In its campaign the CSDP criticized both the KMT and the DPP, saying that the voters "do not favor either extreme." Its candidates described the KMT as too old and out-of-date, and the DPP as having "betrayed the people" because it espoused radical policies and engaged in "ethnic politics." They also argued that it was healthy to have a third party. Relative to the purpose of the election—to elect delegates to the National Assembly who would revise or replace the Constitution—the Chinese Social Democratic Party advocated a cabinet system of government with a weak ceremonial president.

The National Democratic Independent Political Alliance (NDIPA) did not write a party platform in the same sense as the other parties. Being simply a rubric or umbrella organization for non-party candidates designed to help them offset some of the disadvantages of not having a party, particularly to get television time, the NDIPA announced that it would allow its candidates to express their own views, thereby placing them under no constraints. The Alliance did, however, express some commonly held anti-KMT and anti-DPP views and advocated the position that democracy would be better served if there were more independent candidates.

The Campaign

In late November, 637 men and women filed candidacy for the December 21 election: 471 for the directly elected seats and 166 for the party-chosen or national constituency seats. Sixty–seven parties officially registered, though only 17 submitted candidates. In addition to the candidates officially registered with party affiliation, parties "supported" a number of other candidates. When the campaign began, there were 468 candidates for the 225 regional seats. Five parties sponsored 136 candidates for 80 national seats. Three parties named 24 candidates for 20 "overseas" Chinese seats.[15]

The campaign officially began December 10, giving candidates only ten days in which to win over the electorate. Many, however, had actually started campaigning much earlier by holding political meetings, giving interviews to news reporters, and the like. In addition, teas, parties, and banquets provided venues for candidates to communicate with the voters. Most serious candidates also had a number of spokespersons working for them before the campaign period began. The parties similarly publicized their platforms in advance of the campaign period.

A number of new rules or guidelines made this election a unique and unprecedented one. The most noticeable of the changes was the use of television in the campaign. Although the Election Commission permitted candidates to use the television medium to advertise during the campaign, it stipulated that a political party must have at minimum ten candidates in order to qualify. Only four parties met this requirement: the Kuomintang, the Democratic Progressive Party, the Chinese Social Democratic Party and the National Democratic Independent Political Alliance. They were allotted 215 minutes, 94 minutes, 45 minutes and 35 minutes, respectively, based on the number of their candidates. As it turned out, however, television advertising was not as effective as it was thought it would be, and certainly did not have the effect on voter choice as it does in most Western countries. Clearly it did not afford an advantage to the four main parties that some pundits assumed it would. Meanwhile, other candidates and even candidates from the major parties advertised on illegal cable systems that have been in use throughout the island for some years and used videotapes in lieu of actual television broadcasts to present themselves and their ideas.

The major systemic changes were the type of ballot and the voting districts. Taiwan, for this election, adopted a single-entry ballot for fifty-eight multi-member districts. The multi-member district system favored the smaller parties. With three to ten winners allowed in each electoral district, KMT candidates would naturally run against each other. The smaller parties could support a single candidate, putting all of its strength and resources into an effort to win one seat. The DPP could use this strategy as well, although not in all districts. The single-entry ballot, however, favored the KMT. For that reason, it was opposed by the DPP and some of the other parties, though the DPP was most vocal in complaining. DPP resistance, in fact, led to some bitter confrontations in the Legislative Yuan in the spring and prompted DPP legislators to boycott sessions for five weeks.

The DPP also accused the KMT of gerrymandering, but since the electoral districts did not cross any county boundaries and were generally considered "logical," this charge did not stick. The two parties also disagreed on some other issues. For example, the KMT wanted academic qualifications for candidates—at least a high school diploma. The DPP opposed this. The KMT wanted to calculate the number of proportional representation seats allocated to the parties based on the average number of votes in the districts; the DPP wanted to count the total vote. On these issues the KMT won.

Another change in the electoral system affected special-interest groups: They were no longer given the special preferences for representation they had in past elections. Professional, labor, and other groups lost the allocation of seats they were guaranteed in previous elections. The Aborigines, in contrast, were given two special districts, as noted above. In addition, women were still granted a minimum number of seats (though this had not been necessary in most recent elections because a more than sufficient number of women were elected) and were thus entitled to be proclaimed winners even if they had a lower number of votes than one or more male candidates.

Voters were allowed to vote either for a political party or an individual but not both, a system opposed by many. Some, however, regarded this system as temporary and opined that the German formula (which allows one vote for an individual candidate and another vote for a political party) which the DPP advocates, will probably be adopted in the future. The single member vote in a multi-member district is unique; it is used only in Japan and Spain, in addition to Taiwan.

The most frequent complaints heard by the Election Commission were that the campaign period was too short, that candidates did not obey campaign rules, and that the independence plank advanced by the DPP in October was too provocative. Midway through the campaign, however, the commission noted that both complaints and irregularities were fewer than in previous elections. Clearly the government had made a major effort to make the polling process easy and smooth. Still, there were more than 80,000 election officials to supervise the campaign and the voting.

Polls taken during the campaign indicated that more voters were interested in party affiliation and fewer in personal charm, political views, and social connections compared to previous elections. Many said they had not decided for whom to vote. Seventy percent said they were going to decide who to vote for during the campaign. Most said that the mass media, including television, were not very effective in influencing their vote. According to a China Television poll, nearly three-fourths of voters said they were clearer on issues than during most elections.[16] A Gallup poll taken during the election reflected KMT voting strength increasing considerably during the campaign, suggesting the ruling party was peaking at the right time. This same poll also registered considerable dissatisfaction with the DPP—mostly over "bad behavior," and one-quarter of those surveyed did not like the DPP's platform. Nine percent said they initially favored the DPP but changed to support the KMT.[17]

The campaign was not without antics, charges and countercharges in public and even lawsuits. Chen Shui–bian, a DPP member of the Legislative Yuan, published what he said was a KMT document that revealed the KMT had devised a plan to mobilize the military to vote for its candidates, which he charged violated the "neutrality" of the military in politics. He also said he had proof that the KMT planned to abolish the National Assembly and the Control Yuan at some time in the future. Another DPP candidate filed multiple lawsuits against Taiwan Governor Lien Chan and Minister of Interior Wu Poh-hsiung during the campaign.[18]

The day of the election DPP leaders accused the Tainan County Election Commission of having 86,000 extra ballots and thus of trying to rig a KMT victory. Election Commission officials replied that they had destroyed the extra ballots in front of commission members and had videotapes of this event. This response, however, did not prevent a DPP-inspired protest resulting in injuries to several people.[19] The DPP also voiced loud complaints when a student candidate was disqualified, even though students have long been banned from running for election in Taiwan.

During one campaign rally a KMT candidate said that, if elected, the DPP would "turn Taiwan's money into toilet paper." A DPP candidate retorted that the KMT is "the only party in the world still playing the China card." Alliance candidates on several occasions bowed before audiences begging them not to allow "golden cows" (meaning wealthy candidates from the KMT) and the DPP to "pollute politics" in Taiwan. Candidates of all parties asked the voters not to vote for candidates who sought to buy votes. The KMT allocated 1,700 party officials to investigate illegal election practices, particularly by DPP candidates.

The DPP offered a reward of NT$ 1 million for information on candidates practicing bribery.[20]

The KMT took advantage of its control of the government to make announcements and even pass laws that would help KMT candidates. The ruling party, however, was circumspect in doing this because of the fact that its last-minute passage of a law on stock market transaction taxes during the 1989 campaign had backfired, with the media and the electorate seeing it as a blatant and unfair attempt to manipulate the voters. The DPP again asked the voters to vote for its candidates if they favored a competitive party system and democracy; but this plea was not heard as often as in 1989 since many people now viewed the DPP, as, to some degree at least, an "insider" party. The smaller parties engaged in publicity stunts but did not want to be labeled as radical groups or advocates of violence since the elect-orate seemed unsympathetic to such antics.

The Election Results

The evening of the election and the next day virtually all of the major newspapers, radio stations, and television station commentators proclaimed that the Nationalist Party won the election. Academics and other political observers agreed. In counterpoint, the Democratic Progressive Party lost, they said. So did the other two parties thought to be serious contenders and the other minor parties.

The Nationalist Party won 6.05 million of the 8.5 million votes cast, or 71.2 percent of the popular vote. The DPP won 2.04 million, or 23.9 percent. The Chinese Social Democratic Party and the National Democratic Independent Political Alliance attracted fewer than 200,000 votes each, for 2.2 and 2.3 percent, respectively, of the popular vote. In terms of seats, where the scorecard is more important, the KMT won 179 of the 225 district seats contested, or 79.6 percent. The DPP won 41 seats, or 18.2 percent. The Chinese Social Democratic Party failed to win even 1 seat. The alliance won 3; independents won 2. Based on the 5 percent rule—the percent of popular votes needed to qualify for national seats—the KMT received 60 (of 80) regular national seats and 15 (of 20) overseas Chinese seats. The DPP received 20 and 5 respectively. The other parties received none. Thus the KMT obtained a total of 254 of the 325 seats contested in this election, or 78.2 percent. The DPP garnered 66 seats for 20.3 percent. KMT wins, together with the 64 seats that were party holdovers (elected in the 1986 election), gave the KMT 318 seats of the 403 in the new National Assembly. The DPP came out with 75.[21]

Given that the KMT overall won 60 percent of the popular vote in the 1989 national election and the DPP 31 percent, the results of this election showed a more than 10 percent increase in the popular vote for the KMT. It was also a KMT victory in the sense that its leaders and election strategists said they hoped for 70 percent of the popular vote and received slightly more than that. KMT officials also declared that their aim was to attain 75 percent of the seats in the National Assembly so that they could amend the Constitution unimpeded by the DPP. The ruling party exceeded that goal by more than 3 percent and with the holdovers, more than that. The DPP's performance was way below what its leaders predicted, though it was clear that some of its predictions were inflated or unrealistic.[22] Furthermore, the DPP missed the 25 percent needed to block or influence amending the constitution and missed the 20 percent needed to propose motions on the floor of the National Assembly.

Most observers said the KMT victory was a personal victory for President Lee Teng-hui and Secretary General James Soong. President Lee had promised a new National Assembly without delegates elected decades ago on the mainland. He succeeded in getting the elder parliamentarians to resign. He also succeeded in getting a majority of his own supporters elected to the National Assembly. This will be crucial in case the present system of electing a president remains in force and President Lee decides to run for another term (although he has said he will not). Even if he does not run for president again, it was a triumph for President Lee insofar as he had for some time made constitutional revision a major political issue and had personally called for important changes during the campaign—in contrast to some in the KMT who opposed anything but minor changes.

It was a victory for Secretary General James Soong; he was the party's election organizer and strategist. Soong ran an election campaign using professionals. They understood voting behavior and the ruling party's strengths and weaknesses. The KMT thus ran a well-coordinated, efficient campaign and avoided ideological issues as much as possible. This strategy worked. It was also a Soong conquest in that many in the party would have blamed Soong had the KMT not performed well in the election.

The election proved a major setback for the New Tide faction of the DPP. The New Tide put the independence issue in the DPP's platform, which, according to post-election analysts, was the main reason for the DPP's defeat. Former DPP Secretary General Huang Hsin-chieh said after the election that the independence issue "cost the DPP dearly." Only two independence activists won seats in the National Assembly. Even Lin Cho-shui, the originator of the independence plank, was defeated.[23]

The minor parties and independents lost even worse. The KMT and the DPP together got 95 percent of the votes, leaving only 5 percent for other parties and independents. (Independents and third-party candidates had gotten around 10 percent of the popular vote in previous elections.) The bad performance of third parties and independents was more serious than just a loss in the popular vote column. They garnered less than 2 percent of the seats contested.

The difficulties of smaller parties and non-party candidates did not end there. Because none of the third parties got 5 percent of the popular vote, they had to sacrifice NT$2.4 million (nearly US$100,000 U.S.) in non-refundable deposits. The CSDP and the NDIPA, in addition, lost deposits for television time for failing to get one-tenth of their candidates elected. Finally, campaign contributions to these parties could not be taken as tax deductions because the five percent rule affects this. In short, the smaller parties and independents suffered in this election from a system that in a number of ways was stacked against them.[24] In fact, observers suggested at the time that the Chinese Social Democratic Party and the National Democratic Independent Political Alliance, plus a lot of other smaller parties, would soon disappear from Taiwan's political scene.

Still, the Alliance received more than 10 percent of the popular vote in three countries and more than 7 percent in five. In one, Taitung, it garnered 22.5 percent. This success suggested that, in certain parts of the country at least, there was still support for independent candidates or third parties. The Chinese Social Democratic Party topped 3 percent of the popular vote in only two countries, Hsinchu and Taichiang, and there only by a small margin: 3.06 and 3.60 percent, respectively.[25] Yet its hopes remained alive to some extent because it is a personalistic party to a considerable degree and its leader is still popular. A broader base of support or an increase in its leader's following may make it possible for the party to compete in future elections.

The KMT performed best in rural Taiwan, but not in the south and not in the east (except for Hualien). This makes sense because it is a conservative party, though it is noteworthy that the DPP is often seen as a native Taiwanese party and Taiwanese live more in the rural areas than in the cities, where Mainland Chinese are concentrated. The KMT's success in rural areas suggests that ethnic politics is on the decline or the appeal to ethnic identification for votes simply did not work very well. The south, and perhaps eastern Taiwan would clearly be an exception.

The KMT received less than 50 percent of the popular vote in only one county: Taitung (in the south). It received less than 60 percent of the vote in only three counties: Taitung, Ilan in the east, and Chiayi in the south-central part of the island. The KMT's biggest gains were also in rural areas. It scored

The Taiwan Political Miracle

an increase of more than 20 percent of the popular vote in six counties or cities. One, interestingly, was Kaohsiung (Taiwan's second largest city), which had been a DPP stronghold: The KMT gained 64 percent of the popular vote, up from 41 percent in 1989 (one of its worst performances). The Kaohsiung performance suggests that the KMT may have learned to campaign in an urban, mostly Taiwanese city, though local circumstances also help explain its gains.[26]

The DPP recorded its best performance in Kaohsiung City and in Tainan County, with more than 30 percent of the popular vote in each (32.8 and 32.0 percent, respectively). Its good performance in Kaohsiung City, though a decrease of 5.8 percent of the popular vote from the 1989 election, can be explained by the poor performance of independent candidates there compared to 1989. The DPP did the worst in Hualien County, incidently Taiwan's poorest county (though prospering in recent years), and in Taipei County (the suburbs of Taipei to a large extent), where it got only 6.24 and 6.9 percent, respectively, of the popular vote. In Taipei, which some pundits say is the bellwether area in Taiwan politics, the KMT did better than in 1989, gaining 6.1 percent more of the popular vote. The DPP declined in terms of popular vote support by 10 percent.[27]

In terms of putting younger, more educated representatives into office, the election tally is quite phenomenal. Including those chosen by the parties to form the national constituency, only 31, or 9.5 percent are over 60 years of age. Twelve new delegates are less than 30; 75, or 23.1 percent of those elected, are less than 40, and 199, or 61.3 percent, are under fifty. Forty-three of those elected, or a whopping 13.2 percent, have a Ph.D. degree. (The number of Ph.D.s may well be the highest in the world for such a parliamentary body.) There are 104 victors with graduate degrees, or 32 percent. A large majority, 85.5 percent, have a college or technical education.[28] This is in stark contrast to the old National Assembly that was aged and not well educated. The old National Assembly had few with higher education and averaged in age in the eighties. In short, the new National Assembly will be younger, more highly educated and more dynamic than the one it replaces. This change will certainly affect Taiwan's political future.

Female candidates fared well, though they did not perform up to the standards of earlier elections, with 21 winning sufficient votes to be elected. Three were pushed ahead of male candidates who had a larger number of votes. Thus, the total of victorious female delegates was 24—still well above the number guaranteed in the election law and higher than in most other countries. Chu Li-ling, a KMT candidate from Taichung, at age 24 was the youngest winning candidate.[29]

Conclusions

The 1991 Second National Assembly election was in several respects Taiwan's most important election contest to date. Taiwan has become more a democracy as a result of this, the nation's first non-supplementary election. One of its parliamentary bodies now represents the people of Taiwan as such bodies do in Western democracies. No longer does the claim of one-China, and representation of areas not under government control, impede the democratization process. The other two parliamentary bodies will soon follow suit.

Notwithstanding antics and irregularities, this election was also the smoothest national election in Taiwan since elections became competitive in 1980. It reflected a maturing on the part of the voters as well as less patience with candidates who engage in show tactics, exaggerate their qualifications, make wild promises, or use or cause violence in the campaign. The number of undecided voters—twice the number usually found during election campaigns in Western democracies—may also suggest that voters are learning to be swayed less by sensationalism and show tactics. On a positive note, voter turnout, at 68 percent, was considerably lower than in the last elect-ion.

The KMT's resounding victory means that the ruling party has a better mandate to rule than at any time in the past four-plus decades. One observer even asserted: "The KMT had never had legitimacy since it came to Taiwan; now it does." The KMT also has public approval to amend the Constitution (rather than rewrite it) and to come up with a revised system to elect the president. It can also claim broad public support to decide some other fundamental issues of government and will no doubt because of its election victory make decisions about the kind of political system for Taiwan that will last for years to come. This mandate does not necessarily mean, however, that the KMT will reject DPP suggestions. Certainly the latter's calls for a more direct and democratic system to choose a president will be heard, since the KMT was split on this issue during the campaign and may remain divided.

Many conditions favored the KMT win. The economy was doing well and there was a strong public feeling that the KMT would be better able to ensure continued economic prosperity. The stock market crash in 1990 (following the DPP's victory in 1989) made this an especially salient factor. The KMT's call for social and political stability after a decade of street politics, including large numbers of demonstrations and protests, attracted voters who had become tired of protest, or cynical. The KMT's platform was practical, which seemed to fit the times. Its slogans, though perhaps simplistic, appeared to be appropriate at a time when the public could not get excited about voting for a candidate to revise the Constitution (which few have read). The KMT's professionalism also worked to its considerable advantage in the context of a new electoral situation that was complicated to say the least. Engineering a campaign strategy that would prevent candidates from competing with others in their own party and encourage them to use resources effectively proved important. The DPP was not so good at this. Moreover, it suffered from factional fighting and lack of unity. It also had financial problems, partly resulting from its internal feuding. Another factor was that the DPP leaders had not performed especially well in office. The party had to run on its less than good record to some extent.

The KMT's victory, however, should not be exaggerated. Much of its success was due to the fact that its candidates were able to learn from past mistakes (particularly during the 1989 campaign), avoid party factionalism, and benefit from the DPP's errors in this campaign. These factors aside, the KMT did not perform that much better than in earlier elections. What the KMT can boast of, however, is that it performed well at a critical time even though the system had become fairer and the playing field more level. Perhaps this means that the KMT's past popularity was indeed real popularity and that the public truly understands its accomplishments.

The DPP made a serious mistake with the independence issue. It is obvious from the election results that it should not have put the independence plank in the platform—which required the party to then define its terms and policies. In the past DPP candidates used the independence issue much more effectively: by mentioning it to attract attention, which it did very well, and then avoiding saying much more. Defining independence meant drawing inclusive and exclusive lines. It required defining "Taiwanese." Are the children of mainland Chinese born on Taiwan Taiwanese? What about the Hakka? In short, what the independence issue did was make it difficult for the DPP to attract new voters while turning off some old supporters. It excited some of the party's committed voters but did not enhance its appeal to the electorate.

The DPP was much more effective attacking the KMT's unification (of China) platform. They put KMT candidates on the defensive by asking when this would happen and suggesting that, if now, it would mean Taiwan would be ruled by a communist government. But the DPP did too little too late with this tack. Moreover, KMT candidates cleverly played down the unification issue during the campaign or simply defined it as a long-term goal.

The DPP was also hurt, by comparison with its election victory in 1989, by the fact that voting for the DPP was no longer seen to such a degree as in the past a vote for a two-party system and thus for democracy. In the past, a significant number of voters thought the DPP presented a needed alternative and that a competing party facilitated democratization. This feeling was less evident in 1991. World events also helped the DPP in 1989: Rapid political change in Eastern Europe and the massacre of students in Beijing made the party more popular. The DPP's demands for democratization and its calls for independence were not so radical in that context. Things were different in 1991. In fact, in 1991, the KMT was seen by most people as more the force behind democratizing the country—by getting the elder parliamentarians to retire.

The DPP charged the KMT with gerrymandering, controlling the media, engaging in machine politics, and buying votes. All of these charges were true, but making any of them a campaign issue was difficult. Unfairness in drawing the lines of electoral districts was not very credible in view of the fact that the minor parties and independents charged the DPP with complicity, even proposing rules that hurt them. The KMT had the advantage of being able to influence or control a good part of the media. But it was patently less able to do so than in past elections. The DPP got a lot of media coverage. It had television time. But it did not use either very effectively. Machine politics, a more legitimate DPP complaint, was not something that the voters understood very well. Vote-buying was a problem, but it has been in all recent elections in Taiwan and there seemed to be diminishing evidence that it worked or that it could prove much of an advantage since so many candidates did it. Moreover, the first major case of vote-buying that be-came public during the campaign involved a DPP candidate. Thus, DPP charges of vote-buying did not stick.

Other DPP campaign errors were also in evidence. It nominated too many candidates causing it to spread its resources too thin. It also put some less qualified candidates in public view, giving the KMT's complaints about the DPP in this regard credence.

The fact that the DPP performed as well as it did, and the other parties and independents didn't gave rise to more sanguine forecasts about the evolution of a two-party system in Taiwan. There were 67 political parties registered at the time of the election and 17 entered candidates. But only 5 nominated candidates for national seats. Only 4 obtained television time. And only 2 did well in the vote count. Thus a two-party system. At least that conclusion seemed to be a valid one based on this election. Alternatively, one can argue that, in view of the fact that the KMT won almost four times as many seats as the DPP, Taiwan's party system should be seen as a one-party system or a one-party-dominant system. And several facts—that forming a party in Taiwan is easy, that new ones find getting some support a rather simple matter, and that the voting system in some ways favors a multiparty system—all seem to suggest that third parties and independents will be around for a while. The large number of electoral districts, and agreements between the KMT and the DPP in the Legislative Yuan, which in effect weaken or punish smaller parties, will have the opposite effect. Thus, where Taiwan is going in terms of a party system is still unclear.

In any case, Taiwan appears to have made another big step forward in its democratization process, and, as has been the case since 1980, elections have made a major contribution. Clearly election politics in Taiwan reflect its fast-moving political modernization process.

Endnotes

1. For an analysis of previous elections in Taiwan, see John F. Copper with George P. Chen, *Taiwan's Elections: Political Development and Democratization in the Republic of China* (Baltimore: University of Maryland Law School, 1984), and John F. Copper, *Taiwan's Recent Elections: Fulfilling the Democratic Promise* (Baltimore: University of Maryland Law School, 1990).

2. See John F. Copper, "The Kuomingtang's 13th Party Congress: Reform, Renovation, New Blood, New Politics," in Cynthia L. Chennault, ed. *Modernizing East Asia: Economic and Cultural Dimensions of Political Change* (New York: St. John's University Press, 1989), pp. 53–55.

3. For further details, see June Teufel Dreyer, "Taiwan in 1989: Democratization and Economic Growth," *Asian Survey*, XXX, No. 1, January 1990, pp. 53–55.

4. See June Teufel Dreyer, "Taiwan in 1990: Finetuning the System," *Asian Survey*, XXXI, No. 1, January 1991, pp. 59–61.

5. James Robinson, "The ROC's National Affairs Conference," *Issues and Studies*, 26, No. 12, December 1990, pp. 23–35.

6. See Hung-mao Tien, *Brothers in Arms: Political Struggle and Party Competition in Taiwan's Evolving Democracy* (New York: The Asia Society, 1991).

7. I was in Taiwan during the campaign and the election. The above comments are based on my interview with the director of the Nationalist Party's Cultural Affairs Division.

8. The above came from my interviews with a number of KMT officials. Also see China News Agency report of November 14, 1991, in *Foreign Broadcasting Information Service—China* (hereafter *FBIS*), November 15, 1991, p. 83.

9. These items come from the DPP's platform provided to me in written form during the campaign.

10. On the other hand, the DPP had a sizable number of rich candidates, and the party had considerable financial help from the business community.

11. See Julian Baum, "Opposition Cues," *Far Eastern Economic Review*, December 19, 1991, p. 11.

12. See Neil S. Robbins, "Enter the Dragon," *Washington Post*, December 15, 1991, p. E5. It is also worth noting that Yang Shangkun, president of the People's Republic of China and the leader behind the Tiananmen Massacre, had just warned Taiwan independence advocates that "those who play with fire will be burned to ashes."

13. These observations came from my interview with a DPP spokesperson on December 17, 1991, during the campaign.

14. The above is taken from the Chinese Social Democratic Party's platform and my interview with a party spokesperson on December 18, 1991.

15. See China News Agency Report of December 11, 1991, cited in *FBIS—China*, December 11, 1991, p. 66.

16. See "70% Voter Turnout Hoped," *China Post* (International Edition), December 19, 1991, p. 16.

17. "45% of Voters Undecided," *China Post*, December 20, 1991, p. 16.

18. "DPP Stages Election Stunt," *China News*, December 17, 1991, p. 3.

19. "County Vote Challenged," *China Post*, December 21, 1991, p. 16.

20. See "Campaign Snags Bared," *China Post* (International Edition), December 18, 1991, p. 1.

21. See Jeremy Mark, "Taiwan's KMT Set to Dominate Assembly," *Asian Wall Street Journal*, December 23, 1991, p. 1, for a good compilation of election statistics.

22. In what was generally considered a realistic prediction, DPP leaders at the onset of the campaign said they hoped for 30% of the seats. See China News Agency report entitled "National Assembly Election Campaign Underway," December 11, 1991, in *FBIS—China*, December 11, 1991, p. 66.

23. See Y. C. Chen, "DPP's Independence Platform Bombs; 'Wrong' Move Admitted," *Free China Journal*, December 24, 1991, p. 7.

24. Ibid.

25. Based on a data chart in *Hsin Hsin Wen* (The Journalist), December 23–29, 1991, p. 15.

26. Ibid.

27. Ibid.

28. See table in *Shih-chieh Jih-pao* (World Journal), December 22, 1991, p. 10.

29. "24-Year-Old Elected to Assembly Seat," *China Post*, December 24, 1991, p. 3.

Chapter Six
Taiwan's 1992 Legislative Yuan
Election

On December 19, 1992, voters in Taiwan went to the polls to choose delegates to the Republic of China's national lawmaking body, the Legislative Yuan.[1] This was the sixth competitive national election in Taiwan beginning with the 1980 election.[2] It was the nation's fourth two-party election contest and the second non-supplemental election.

Observers called the election the nation's most important political contest ever. It was Taiwan's first ever non-supplemental or plenary election of the Legislative Yuan. With a more level playing field because of changes in the law allowing free discussion of an independent Taiwan, a new election law that made campaign contests fairer and a political system favoring two political parties, the opposition Democratic Progressive Party (DPP) had an opportunity to win enough seats to win big, even become the ruling party. In fact, the DPP hoped to gain a sufficient number of seats that in a future boycott of a legislative session it could have a major impact.

Several months prior to the election, the two major parties were suffering from internal feuds to the degree that they seemed to be heading toward serious factionalism. Members of both parties registered as candidates without party approval. Some terminated their party membership and ran as independents. Some were expelled from their party. Two top government officials resigned just before the deadline for registration in order to run, thus flaunting the primaries and the regular nomination process. However, as the election date approached it became evident that internal factionalism was much more a problem for the ruling Nationalist Party, or Kuomintang (KMT), than for the opposition DPP.

Whereas it seemed after the last election that third or minor parties and independents would have little influence in future Taiwan elections and that a two-party system had fully evolved, this time it looked like minor parties were poised to challenge the two main parties during the campaign. Over 100 candidates ran as independents or with party affiliation rather than as party nominees, nearly one-fourth of the total. Two parties, besides the KMT and the DPP, nominated more than five candidates, giving them a share of the time allocated for TV advertising. One, the Truth Party, was new and was hardly known to Taiwan's electorate. The other, the Chinese Socialist Democratic Party, seemed to be making a comeback after a poor performance in the 1991 election.

A much larger number of candidates than usual entered the race. This was no doubt the product of Taiwan's increasingly more pluralistic society and the greater importance of politics to Taiwan's manifold interest groups. Democratization and the growing visibility and importance of the Legislative Yuan were also factors. In any case, the increased competition promised to make the campaign and the election more contentious. In all voting districts the KMT endorsed more than one flagbearer, and in most endorsed several. In many districts the DPP also had multiple candidates. Candidates thus ran against not only representatives of the other party, but also against candidates of their own party.

Pre-election polls indicated that voters were not making up their minds early and many would vote for preferred candidates rather than by political party. Opinion surveys also reflected decreased voter enthusiasm about the two main parties, but more so about the KMT.

There were multitudinous charges of vote buying by both sides, but particularly by the DPP against KMT candidates. Since so much was at stake and the competition so intense, and because the practice was so ingrained and Taiwan so prosperous, it was virtually impossible to prevent this as well as various other forms of illegal campaign activities. The Central Election Commission went to extraordinary means to deter election cheating, including offering large rewards for information about vote buying. Several religious organizations got involved, trying to ensure that the election was fair. Poll watch groups also were formed.

The campaign was marred by more violence than usual. Before the campaign started more than forty candidates requested police protection. Many borrowed bulletproof vests. There was a reported assassination attempt just before the election, but it was uncertain at the time whether it was real or bogus. Many candidates resorted to grandstanding and sensationalism.

A number of noted personalities returned from abroad before the election. Some came back to be chosen as national or Overseas Chinese delegates. Others, including several famous dissidents, returned to campaign or to send a political message.

Ideological and partisan political issues in some unprecedented ways pervaded the campaign. Foreign policy issues were more important than in previous elections. Specific or tangible issues were given less attention.

This campaign was clearly the most exciting in Taiwan since the first competitive national election in 1980. Notwithstanding emotions, vote buying, violence, and campaign antics, the election was seen by most observers as fair and was judged as contributing to the further democratization of the nation.

Pre-election Politics in Taiwan

The Kuomintang entered 1992 riding high after an election victory in the December 1991 National Assembly election. The opposing Democratic Progressive Party was chastised by the electorate for pressing the independence issue and putting it into the party's platform and the campaign. Other political parties and independents likewise had performed poorly. The KMT, in short, came away from that election with a stunning victory and a mandate the ruling party had never had before.[3]

With a new sense of confidence on its forth-fifth anniversary, the KMT dared to publish a report on the "February 28 Incident" (of 1947) when thousands of Taiwanese were killed by the Nationalist Chinese Army. It then proceeded to make further amendments to the Constitution, giving the National Assembly increased duties and its members four-year terms. The provincial governor and county magistrates were made elected offices. The Control Yuan was restructured to become a semi-judicial organ of government.

However, the report on the February 28 Incident divided the party over the issues of whether to pay compensation to victims' families and how to respond to the opposition call to make the date a national holiday.[4] In addition, when making constitutional changes, the issue of whether the president and vice-president should be elected directly or indirectly by the voters created an impasse for the KMT's leadership. Ruling party leaders could not agree and postponed a decision. Paralysis over both issues also drew attention to what appeared to be serious personal differences between President Lee Teng-hui and Premier Hau Pei-tsun, and to growing factionalism in the party.[5]

Still, in May, Taiwan's sedition law was revised, making it no longer a crime to discuss Taiwan's independence or communism. And in July the minister of interior announced that the infamous Black List (of individuals who could neither leave nor enter the country) had been reduced from 282 to 5 names. At almost the same time the Taiwan Garrison Command, which had been responsible for keeping social order and which used censorship and military courts to accomplish this, was abolished.[6]

Political liberalization, however, was accompanied by concern on the part of the public that change was proceeding too fast and the perception that crime was becoming a serious problem—exemplified by McDonalds closing fifty-seven fast-food restaurants in April after bombs exploded in three, killing a policeman and injuring four people.[7] The question of independence also persisted, even though it had been a losing issue in the 1991 election: Economic ties with China were increasing and this trend seemed to favor those who advocated a one-China policy or unification. The president and the premier represented different views on this issue and each had followers, thus further feeding party factionalism.

Primary elections in August accentuated centrifugal forces in the KMT. Even before the primaries were held controversy arose. In late July, the Central Standing Committee of the KMT canceled sixteen of the twenty-nine primaries, noting that primaries were optional and that in many cases regional offices could decide the nominations without them. Premier Hau argued that the primaries caused confrontations between candidates, were a financial burden, and allowed factions to mislead voters. But he decided to honor the results of the primaries already held, which patently advantaged his wing of the party. Critics pointed out that only one-third of party members voted in the primaries; also the formula weighing the votes of cadres and officials equal to the votes of all other party members favored conservative candidates with military and government support.

The Democratic Progressive Party suffered from bad publicity during its primaries over vote buying by party members who wanted to be selected for national constituency seats during primaries held on August 30.[8] This, however, did not get much attention compared with the KMT's problems.

For the KMT, difficulties caused by the nominating process persisted. The next month a Legislative Yuan caucus of KMT members blasted the party leadership for unfair procedures in the nominating process and proposed that all incumbents be eligible to run in the December election. The caucus then sent a resolution to the KMT's nominating committee asking for t a revised list of candidates, in order to get reversed the party's decision on twenty–seven of the seventy–three incumbents who were rejected. Caucus members assailed the KMT leadership for seeking to punish disobedient legislators as a way to root out factionalism in the party. They also opined that Legislative Yuan members should have been represented on the nominating committee. Subsequently, leaders of two KMT factions, the Wisdom Coalition and the New KMT Alliance, were barred from campaigning. Lee Sen-fong, leader of the latter faction, said he planned to set up a political body to operate outside of the Legislative Yuan. Jaw Shao-kong, the popular Environmental Protection

Agency head and former member of the New KMT Alliance, supported Lee's proposal while hinting that he would resign from his position and campaign for a Legislative Yuan seat.

On the heels of this crisis, elder members of the Legislative Yuan, who were slated to resign at the end of the current session, announced that they would not simply step down. Nine signed up for national constituency seats and thirty-two signed a letter sent to Premier Hau demanding that national seats be equally distributed between Taiwanese and Mainland Chinese—reflecting concern that the Legislative Yuan would be dominated by Taiwanese and that this would adversely affect the KMT's one-China policy. This constituted another instance of "ethnic" differences in the KMT.[9]

In late October, in the context of eroding party solidarity, the KMT decided to use its "severest punishment" against four Legislative Yuan members who had voted in defiance of the party's orders to uphold a proposal regarding the stock transaction tax. The party memberships of the four were terminated. Observers said this was done to salvage party discipline and to fend off public criticism of the KMT for engaging in "money politics"—since the four were known for close ties with several large enterprises, including Hualon Business Group, which was headed by Oung Ta-ming, a KMT candidate under indictment for fraud.[10]

At this juncture the party was presented with still another crisis: the resignation of Finance Minister Wang Chien-shien. Wang had created a serious row over a proposal to alter the method of taxing land, suggesting it be based on the actual sale price rather than government-assessed prices. A public opinion poll taken at this time reflected 62 percent of the public approved of his proposal. Scholars, 780 of whom signed a petition to back Wang's view, also supported Wang. However, the Taiwan Provincial Assembly and the Kaohsiung City Council did not like Wang's position and passed resolutions calling for his resignation.[11] After Wang resigned, he entered the Legislative Yuan election race, causing an imbroglio in the KMT, since candidates had already been chosen and were already planning their campaign strategies based on the current lineup of contestants.

At nearly the same time, a number of KMT Legislative Yuan members called on the Cabinet to adopt a two-China policy, or what they called a "Taiwan first policy." This request further polarized the party into Taiwanese and Mainland Chinese groups, or what were already known as "Mainstream" and "Non-Mainstream" factions. In the midst of this controversy, Jaw Shao-kong resigned as head of the Environmental Protection Administration and declared his candidacy for a Legislative Yuan seat.

These announcements put KMT leaders in a real quandary. If the party allowed Wang and Jaw to run as KMT candidates, party discipline would be undermined and election strategy made more complicated. In addition, other candidates would be angered and demoralized. If not given the party nod, Wang and Jaw would run as independents and compete with KMT candidates. The votes they garnered would not count as KMT votes in allotting seats to the national and overseas constituencies.[12] The KMT allowed the two to run, but without party endorsement.

These difficulties, on top of a number of other serious problems, prompted James Soong, secretary general of the KMT, to threaten to resign. Soong, who was nicknamed "chief of the fire brigade" for his successful role in quelling intraparty disputes, was said to be exhausted from dealing with intractable problems and with the endless feuding between both the factions and individual party members.[13]

All of this controversy hurt the KMT's image with the electorate. On November 24, an opinion survey was conducted showing only 25.9 percent of respondents would vote for the KMT. More respondents agreed than disagreed that the "one-China, two-China" controversy was the result of factional politics. The poll did not reflect strong support for the DPP but rather indicated that voters were undecided (27 percent) or would cast their votes for individual candidates without regard to party affiliation (35 percent). Although opinion polls are not as reliable or heeded as much in Taiwan as they are in Western democracies, the KMT was concerned.[14]

On November 27, the KMT's discipline committee voted to expel another party member: Chen Je-nan. Chen had publicly advocated a one-China, one-Taiwan policy in contraposition to the KMT's one-China stance. President Lee Teng-hui tried to intervene and ordered the committee to reconsider. But Chen increased his attacks, calling Premier Hau and three other KMT senior officials "traitors to Taiwan." It was too late for the KMT to cancel Chen's party nomination, so party leaders instructed voters to choose other KMT candidates and not vote for Chen.[15] The Wisdom Coalition faction, which Chen belonged to, subsequently blamed the discipline committee for "working for conservative rightists" in the party and cited some members of the KMT for advocating air flights to China in violation of the party line.[16]

The DPP experienced similar problems at the time. In mid-November founding member and former Finance Committee chairman Hsu Ming-teh quit the party, saying that it had fallen under the control of "a few eloquent lawyers-turned-politicians adept at power struggles."[17] But the DPP's troubles seemed nothing compared to the KMT's.

Throughout the year Taiwan's U.S. $300 billion-plus Six-Year National Development Plan was also the subject of controversy. The KMT drew criticism over various projects because of their high costs, corruption involved in the bidding process, economic disruption, and logistical problems. Premier Hau, who had launched the plan in 1990, was singled out for much of the blame. Minister of Transportation Eugene Chien was frequently accused of corruption.

External events also influenced the electorate's perception of the KMT in the months leading up to the election. Most important, and certainly the biggest in terms of news, was the loss of diplomatic ties with South Korea. In August, Seoul announced that it was forthwith establishing formal diplomatic links with Beijing. This was a tough blow for Taipei inasmuch as South Korea was one of two "important" nations (the other being South Africa) recognizing Taipei and was the only large or medium-sized Asian country with ambassadorial ties with the Republic of China.[18] The loss was to some degree offset by establishing relations with Niger at the time and with the increasing hope for membership in the General Agreement on Tariffs and Trade. The subsequent U.S. decision to sell F-16 fighter planes to Taiwan was also a win for Taipei. But these victories did not compensate in full for the loss of ties with Seoul, and both had a price tag.

The dollar cost of Taiwan's diplomatic successes, which critics of the government talked about frequently, would not have mattered much had it not been for the fact that the economic news at the time was bad. In September, Council of Economic Planning and Development head Shirley Kuo warned that the people were spending too much and that capital investment was markedly declining. She declared that state enterprise investment had dropped from 37.12 percent in 1990, to 9.59 percent in 1991, and to 1.98 percent so far in 1992. Public-sector investment as a whole was also lagging and increases in private investment did not offset these declines. Meanwhile, consumer spending was up, to over one-half of the nation's gross national product GNP), thereby accounting for more than three-fourths of the nation's growth.[19] A month later, the government published figures that indicating that Taiwan's GNP increase for the year was projected to be 6.4 percent rather than the 7 percent predicted earlier, because exports had fallen—down 6.7 percent in September compared to a year earlier. The revaluation of the N.T. dollar was said to be the reason, in addition to the shrinking manufacturing sector. At the same time inflation hit 7.4 percent—the highest in a decade.[20] All of this, plus the fact that the economy of the People's Republic of China was growing at a rate almost double Taiwan's, was unsettling.

The Campaign

The campaign began officially (unofficially with teas, parties, policy discussions, and other activities months earlier) on December 9 and lasted for ten days. A total of 403 candidates from various political parties, plus independents, ran for 161 Legislative Yuan seats—a number based on Taiwan's population six months prior to the election. Taiwan had seventy-one political parties at the time, but only fourteen fielded candidates and just four—the KMT, the DPP, the Chinese Social Democratic Party (CSDP), and the Truth Party—had more than five contenders, the figure required for television advertising.[21]

The KMT slated 124 candidates for the 29 electoral district seats or the regional constituency; the DPP supported 59. The CSDP nominated 22, the Truth Party 5, the Chinese Union Party 4, the Chinese People's Action Party 2, and the Labor Party 2. Seven other parties nominated 1 candidate each. For the national or at-large constituency, made up of party-selected candidates, the KMT nominated 27, the DPP 16 and the CSDP 3. For the Overseas Chinese constituency, which represented Chinese elsewhere and helped maintain Taiwan's one-China policy, the KMT listed 6 and the DPP 3.[22]

The line-up of candidates was unprecedented in several respects. First, a total of 348 candidates stood for 125 regional seats. This was a ratio of about 2.8 to 1—the highest in any national election in recent years. Some called this a "candidate explosion." It meant that there would be more losers than winners and signaled much more intense competition during the campaign. Furthermore, some large and important districts were much more crowded with candidates than others: 206 candidates were vying for 64 seats in the 13 most competitive districts. The number of candidates was especially high in the cities of Taipei, Kaohsiung, and Taichung and in Taipei County. Second, of the 348 candidates for regional seats, 123, or more than one-third, were independents or not affiliated officially with any political party. This was largely the product of party factionalism in the KMT and the DPP and a weakening of party discipline, both prompting a large number of party members to run without endorsement. More than forty KMT and DPP members had left their parties to run as independents—most from the KMT. Third, two very popular KMT candidates, Wang Chien-shien and Jaw Shao-kong, ran without party affiliation, and thus were competitors with other KMT candidates.[23] All of these factors made the election more complex and charting strategies more difficult for both the candidates and the parties.

The campaign was noticeably more lively than those before other recent elections for a number of reasons. The Legislative Yuan was more important than the other elective branches of government, and this was not a supplementary election. A number of wealthy individuals sought political fame. Influential local families wanted national status. Ambitious young politicians wanted to further their political careers. Interest groups sought representation. All of this reflected social pluralism in Taiwan; but it also mirrored the fact that many perceived that they had more to win or lose in the political process. Also, political decision making was becoming more decentralized.

Because of the election defeat in 1991, which DPP leaders saw as resulting from too much emphasis on the independence issue, the DPP sought to challenge the KMT on issues of substance. The opposition party fielded a number of candidates that were strong on issues, many of whom had not run in 1991 in order to prepare for this election. Also, the DPP entered candidates in every district and acted as if it might win big enough to gain control of the Legislative Yuan—if not in 1992, then sometime in the future. For the first time ever, simply according to the numbers, the KMT could lose control of an elective organ of government.

The platform of the ruling KMT did not differ markedly from its 1991 platform. Party leaders used the slogan "prosperity, security, progress." Most saw no reason to change what had worked in 1991. The party issued a twenty-point platform that set forth specific KMT policies to be presented to the electorate during the campaign. The most important planks were: promoting a one-China policy and the unification of China, advancing political reform, pushing the Six-Year National Development Plan, speeding up local autonomy, enhancing the social welfare system (by introducing a national health plan and by providing more public housing, among other things), punishing corruption, and improving the tax system. Other items included advancing the nation's pragmatic diplomacy, bolstering the national defense (through an "elite troop" policy and more military R & D), eliminating sex discrimination, upgrading industrial productivity through more investment in research and technology, and supporting cultural development.[24]

The KMT's platform clearly did not contain much that was new or sensational. Party leaders reckoned that a new agenda was not necessary in view of the party's success in 1991. In addition, there seemed to be some difficulty with putting new ideas into the platform in view of intra-party feuding. Some of the planks in the platform were already the cause for divisions in the KMT. The one-China policy was not supported, at least with enthusiasm, by many members of the party. The Six-Year National Development Plan had run into problems, as noted earlier. The national health plan was not new. Tax changes were controversial and divisive. The other planks were hardly attention grabbers.

KMT leaders supplemented the platform with talk about the party's success in promoting economic development and democracy. But, while its economic accomplishments were certainly credible—Taiwan being an emulated model of economic success—problems were more on the minds of voters during the campaign than usual. KMT leaders boasted of constitutional reform, especially eight amendments that were passed peacefully in May. Yet some of the amendments were neither important nor controversial, and the KMT could garner only partial credit for the democratization process, since many voters perceived that the two-party system, made possible by the DPP's successes, contributed to the political modernization process by forcing the KMT to take the actions that it did.

In contrast to the KMT's little changed platform, the DPP's was quite new and different in a number of respects. Two months before the election the party released a policy white paper that set forth a seventeen-point common platform for its candidates. The six most important points became the basis for the DPP's "three antis and three pros" slogan: opposition to military rule, privilege, and money politics and support for tax cuts, direct presidential elections and self-determination. Although the DPP could not make a case that Taiwan was ruled by the military (which did not seem to be its real purpose anyway), it was able to rally supporters, and to a lesser extent voters, against Premier Hau. Hau was a four-star general before becoming premier. He was Mainland Chinese. His views about one-China seemed inflexible, particularly as he was seen more and more as a minority in his own party. He also appeared to deliberately overstate Taiwan's economic ties with China so as to support his one-China policy (based on economic linkages). In short, the DPP found in Hau a convenient enemy. The DPP's attack on privilege made pointed reference to the KMT's special status as a ruling party that had "infiltrated" the government and owned a large number of profitable, government-connected enterprises. The DPP's strategy, which appeared to be an effort to exploit class politics, was abetted by the fact that the gap between rich and poor in Taiwan had been growing and had gotten considerable attention in recent years. The DPP's assault on money politics was not new, but it took on a special salience because of the KMT's problems and the growing concern about corruption and recent financial scandals in Taiwan. Similarly, the DPP's advocacy of tax cuts had been enunciated before, but gained some credibility now owing to controversies over tax issues prior to the campaign. The DPP's apparent contradiction in advocating tax cuts while advancing more welfare didn't appear so serious in view of financial scandals that exposed serious government corruption and waste. DPP candidates were quick to point out, when asked about increasing social welfare costs, that the sale of KMT-owned enterprises would easily pay for their program and that these funds, together with cuts in military spending, made tax cuts also feasible. Likewise the call for direct presidential elections was not new, but it took on new meaning after the KMT failed to act on the matter, having promised to do so. The DPP's increased popularity also weakened the KMT's claim to be the party that has promoted democracy. Finally, the DPP cleverly advocated "self-determination" instead of "independence." Though mostly a difference in semantics, the change made the DPP's platform seem much less provocative and more in consonance with the electorate's view.[25]

In more specific terms the DPP called for the following: writing a new Constitution with provisions for a directly elected president (limited to two four-year terms); establishing a unicameral parliament (after abolishing the National Assembly, the Examination Yuan, and the Control Yuan); pursuing economic policies that distinguish clearly between the public and private sector, and privatizing state enterprises; joining the North American Free Trade Association instead of thinking of a "greater China economic bloc"; reassessing the Six-Year National Development Plan (though no concrete steps or goals were cited); altering the nation's foreign policy by abandoning the one-China position and applying for admission to the United Nations and other international bodies under the name "Taiwan"; and instituting a new comprehensive social welfare system that protects the people's right to work, distributes wealth more equally, and helps the poor and underprivileged.

On the opening day of the campaign, KMT leaders met with government officials and candidates and used this event as a tactic to draw attention to the party's policies and candidates. President Lee Teng-hui met with the speaker of the Kaohsiung City Assembly. KMT General Secretary James Soong presented party flags to candidates at Sun Yat-sen Memorial in Taipei.[26] In contrast, DPP Chairman Hsu Hsin-liang, as if he were campaigning himself, declared at the opening of the campaign period that the DPP stood for cutting income taxes, changing land transaction taxes, and strengthening social welfare—which he said "was opposite the KMT." DPP Secretary General David Chiang said the DPP would try hard to attract women, students, and young workers.[27]

For a number of candidates, however, the start of the campaign was less peaceful. Fistfights broke out in Kaohsiung and Taichung. In Kaohsiung, candidate Su Chiu-chen and his supporters pelted a statue of Chiang Kai-shek with eggs. Six policemen were injured when his supporters tried to climb on top of the statue. Tsai Kuan-lun, an independent candidate and leader of the Four Seasons Gang, known for his critical attitude toward the DPP's independence stance, held a provocative national flag-raising ceremony outside DPP headquarters.[28] Chen Je–nan, who had been expelled from the KMT only days earlier, threw eggs at the Kaohsiung City Election Commission office.[29] Labor Party candidate Hsu Hsiao-tan, a former stripper, gave a speech in front of the Kaohsiung police headquarters, asking the police to protect her from gangsters, while demanding a retraction from her rival candidate who said that she had starred in a pornographic movie.[30] Several candidates sued their rival candidates. Lion dances, parades, and firecrackers started many campaigns, many of them in violation of election laws. Loudspeakers were used to interrupt others' campaigns. One candidate's campaign truck was set on fire. It was even reported that several candidates had tried to poison the food at their rivals' headquarters to disable their campaign.[31]

The second day of the campaign, Chang Chun–hong, a well-known DPP candidate, set up a makeshift radio station to broadcast his campaign platform. Chang claimed that the DPP's loss in the 1991 election was the result of the KMT's control of the media. Supporting his complaint, a major Chinese-language newspaper at this time ran a story saying that the KMT had ordered Taiwan's three television stations to give more attention to KMT candidates in their reporting.[32] The next day Chang protested to the Government Information Office while applying for a permit for his station. Chang was not given a permit, nor was legal action taken to stop him from broadcasting.[33] At this same time a well-known radio personality was barred from running in the election because he did not have a high school diploma. He campaigned anyway, saying he felt he should be able to run notwithstanding his low educational attainments, and that he wanted to serve as a check on the KMT.[34]

Meanwhile, the KMT and the DPP attacked each other in television advertisements. The KMT depicted the DPP as violence-prone and a party that could lead street demonstrations but not govern the nation. The DPP mocked Premier Hau Pei-tsun and labeled the KMT "a party of corruption and political persecution of opposition politicians." The Chinese Social Democratic Party, in contrast, used low-keyed presentations and urged voters to vote for incorruptible candidates, regardless of their affiliation. The Truth Party called for more morality in the campaign. Although most viewers said they thought the advertisements were well done and well presented, most said they did not influence their vote.[35]

There were numerous reports of vote buying and other forms of election fraud. The DPP, on the fourth day of the campaign, publicized the cost of votes in various districts. The secretary general of the DPP said that votes were going for N.T.$1,000 to $3,500 in the southern district of Taipei, with one "Golden Ox" offering N.T.$5,000 (about U.S.$200) for one vote. Halfway through the campaign thirty-three cases of vote buying had been reported and one community leader had been arrested for buying votes for a KMT candidate.[36] This and other problems prompted Interior Minister Wu Poh-hsiung to warn the public about vote buying and the presence of counterfeit ballots, while mentioning that some candidates might proclaim themselves winners before the votes were tallied in order to accuse their opponents of cheating when the final results were published.[37]

After the DPP published specific information about vote buying, which included some names of candidates, several community leaders sued the DPP for libel.[38] Meanwhile, a private think tank with opposition sympathies published a report linking a number of candidates with business groups. The report, published by Cheng She, identified twelve "notorious" candidates, plus another fifty-six, as having used government privilege to transact land deals; forty-two were KMT candidates and four were DPP.[39] Another election watch group, the Parliamentary Observers Association (POA), published a list of legislators it rated as the best and worst. Ten of the best twenty were KMT members, nine were DPP candidates, and one was from the Social Democratic Party. All ten of the worst were KMT members. Two incumbent legislators immediately filed suit against the POA.[40] KMT Secretary General James Soong criticized both groups for unfair analysis, overrating the importance of speechmaking, and not considering some other kinds of leadership work.[41]

Opinion surveys published at this time indicated that more voters than not believed that vote buying was no more serious than in past elections. Polls also reflected that few people's votes were influenced by vote buying. Other surveys, however, showed that a large number of people had been approached by vote buyers and that more voters felt that vote buying should be stopped.[42]

A number of outsiders got involved in the campaign. A group of Hong Kong and Macao Chinese criticized President Lee's one-China policy as "not convincing." A foreign election observer team was quoted by the press saying things indicating they were making efforts to help the DPP's campaign. Jiang Zemin, general secretary of the Communist Party in the People's Republic of China, said that China would "take resolute actions if Taiwan appeared to be going independent."[43] This report prompted the government to criticize "foreign interference" in the election. Some well known Chinese, both in Taiwan and elsewhere, made statements intended to influence the campaign. Peng Ming-min, known as the "father of Taiwan independence" and who returned to Taiwan from the United States just before the campaign, publicly denounced vote buying and the prohibitions on many campaign activities.[44]

As the campaign drew to a close, more antics, some seemingly in desperation, plagued electioneering. Chen Je-nan, who had been expelled from the KMT, led supporters to destroy a newspaper office in Kaohsiung.[45] One candidate claimed that he had been shot in an assassination attempt the last day of the campaign, but because of lack of physical evidence (the candidate was wearing a bulletproof vest at the time), the police doubted his story.[46]

Election Results

Despite the plethora of antics, sensationalism, and illegal activities during the campaign, voting was generally carried out without incidence. Part of the reason for the smooth voting process was the 50,000 police who were stationed at the polling places, plus other precautions taken to prevent the violent protests that occurred during the 1989 Legislative Yuan election. There were also fewer complaints than in previous elections, probably because the campaign was regulated more effectively. But, votes were counted quickly and the results posted earlier than in previous elections. Problems arose regarding the vote counting in two districts, yet these did not interfere with the central vote counting.

The voter turnout was 72.02 percent. This was an increase of almost four percent over the 1991 election. The turnout was 67.60 percent in Taipei and 75.06 percent in Kaohsiung—Taiwan's two largest cities. In Taiwan's twenty-one largest cities the turnout averaged 72.48 percent. On the offshore islands it was 80.72 percent.[47]

The KMT won 61.67 percent of the popular vote—73 of the 125 regional seats, 19 of the national constituency seats, and 6 of the Overseas Chinese seats for a total of 96 seats or 59.6 percent of the total delegates to the new or second Legislative Yuan. This margin of "victory" will clearly make it possible for the ruling party to continue to dominate the Legislative Yuan.[48] Moreover, by the standards of elections in Western democratic countries, the KMT won in quite an impressive way.

But the KMT did not consider the election results a victory. Secretary General James Soong said that night: "Our party is very dissatisfied with the outcome." He subsequently tendered his resignation, although there was no indication at the time that it would be accepted or that he deserved blame for the loss.[49]

The vote tally indicated a KMT defeat in the sense that the ruling party won much less than the 71 percent of the popular vote it got in the 1991 election. Furthermore, the popular vote won by the KMT was by almost any standard below what its leaders had wanted or hoped to win. Other KMT officials besides Soong also regarded the results as bad news for the party. The media almost unanimously spoke of a KMT setback the next day.[50]

In contrast, the DPP won 37 of the contested seats, plus 13 appointed seats. This gives the main opposition party 50 seats in the new Legislative Yuan or 31.1 percent of the total. The DPP's 50 seats in the new Legislative Yuan compares to 19 it held before the election. DPP candidates were frontrunners in 14 of the 29 electoral districts, or 4 more than the KMT—though the KMT fielded twice as many candidates. Add to this the fact that 6 of 11 members of the DPP's executive committee won. And 62.7 percent of DPP candidates competing in the contests won, compared to 58.4 percent of KMT candidates. In the popular vote column, the DPP won 36.09 percent of the popular vote—a figure much above the DPP's previous performances. Finally, in both popular vote and seats won, the DPP did much better than either its leaders or KMT leaders had anticipated. It also bettered what most pundits had predicted.[51]

After the vote counting was over, DPP Chairman Hsu Hsin-liang broke open champagne bottles. He proclaimed the election a resounding DPP victory. He also called it a defeat for the KMT. Other DPP leaders, the media, and observers agreed. Clearly the DPP was happy with the election outcome and could, by most criteria, call it a win.

The Chinese Social Democratic Party won one seat, its leader Ju Gao-jeng gaining victory. Having endorsed 22 candidates its percent of winners was 4.5 percent with 1.54 percent of the popular vote. The Truth Party fared even worse; it failed to elect even one candidate. Independents and other third party candidates likewise fared poorly. As a single category they won less than 1 percent of the popular vote—0.8 percent. They fielded 142 candidates, but only 14 won—again less than 1 percent.

Assessing the balloting another way—by not counting the votes of candidates who ran without the party's formal approval as party winners—the picture is a bit different. The assessment of the winners and losers remains the same, but is amplified somewhat or considerably in some cases. Counting this way, the KMT received only 53 percent of the popular vote. This figure represents a nearly 20 point drop in the popular vote from the 1991 election. It is also the lowest popular vote for the KMT in any election in Taiwan. Using this way of calculating the popular vote, the DPP's percentage drops to 31 percent instead of just over 36 percent.[52] But this is still good when compared to its 23.9 percent in 1991 or its 28.2 percent in 1989, the latter representing its best performance prior to this election. Hence, picking winners and losers using this method of calculating the results, the KMT suffered a much bigger loss, while the DPP still made a significant gain. Whether this is a fair way of measuring the performances of the two major parties is a matter of debate. Most of the independent candidates were KMT members. Two were the top vote-getters. They will probably remain KMT members and will vote with the ruling party in the Legislative Yuan. Yet they also divided the party and may continue to do so in the future.

Noting individual winners and losers is also helpful in assessing the meaning of the election results. In terms of total votes, Jaw Shao-kong and Wang Chien-shien—two KMT government officials who resigned just before the campaign to run without party endorsement—were the biggest vote-getters. Jaw, with more than 230,000 votes, bested all other candidates by more than 100,000 votes. Wang was second with more than 120,000 votes. Both represent the Non-Mainstream faction of the KMT. Thus they helped the Non-Mainstream "defeat" the Mainstream faction. Their victories also underscore the problems caused for the KMT by the nominating process and the difficulties the ruling party has with factionalism. The third largest vote-getter was Lu Hsiu-yi, a DPP candidate in the Taipei northern district. Lu, an incumbent legislator, has been known as one of the DPP's most radical personalities, notably on the independence issue. The fourth largest winner, and the female candidate winning the largest number of votes, Chu Feng-yi, is a KMT Non-Mainstream faction member who was supported by the military. The fifth vote winner, Su Huan-chi, is a DPP member known for his support of independence. Thus, the five biggest winners represent more extreme views, at least on the independence issue, and their popularity seems to reflect a polarization of the electorate.[53]

A number of controversial candidates won: Oung Ta-ming, who was convicted earlier in the year for breach of trust for his role in Taiwan's largest stock scandal ever; Chen Je-nan, who was dismissed from the KMT for his opposition to the party's one-China policy and who called several top leaders of the party, including Premier Hau, traitors; Ju Gao-jeng, head of the Chinese Social Democratic Party and known for his grandstanding and confrontational style; Chen Sui-bian, one of the most activist of DPP legislators; and Stella Chen, who faced a prison sentence of up to twelve years for sedition. Oung and Chen, however, won by narrow margins.

Some notables also lost: Hsu Hsiao-tan, the so-called "porn queen," lost by a very small margin. Kao Tsu-ming, who reported an "assassin" attempted to kill him, was defeated. Huang Hsin-chieh, former head of the DPP, failed, although the balloting was contested after the election.

Notwithstanding Oung Ta-ming's win, together with Wu Tung-sheng's victory in Hsinchu County, most wealthy candidates, or "Golden Ox" politicians, lost. Furthermore, many winning candidates, including many frontrunners, had spoken out strongly against money politics. The electorate seemed to be disgusted with money politics and candidates who perceived they would win by spending more than their competitors during the campaign or by buying votes.

Female candidates did well at the polls, though this is not particularly unusual for Taiwan. There were 36 female candidates in the district contests; 12 were elected. Just under 10 percent of the victors were women. As noted above, Chu Feng-yi was the fourth largest vote-getter overall. She was also the top vote recipient in her district—as were two other female candidates in other districts. Journalist-turned-lawmaker Chou Chuan, a KMT member, won without her party's support.[54] In Taipei, Kaohsiung and eight other districts where women are guaranteed seats, female candidates won in the regular competition. This impressive performance caused some to speculate that the constitutional provision giving female candidates seats if not enough women are elected—a kind of affirmative action rule—is no longer needed and may be ended.[55]

The winning candidates, as usual, were well–educated. Fifteen, or 12 percent, held a Ph.D. degree; 32, or 25.6 percent, held an M.A. degree; 48, or 38.4 percent, were college graduates; 13, or 10.4 percent, were graduates of a "specialty" or vocational school (after high school); and 17, or 13.6 percent, were only high school graduates.[56] The election also produced younger candidates. Only 3 candidates above sixty years of age won, or 2.4 percent; 33, or 26.4 percent, were below forty; 55, or 44 percent were in their forties; and 34, or 27.2 percent, were in their fifties.[57]

Most of the candidates of both parties, as well as independents, were Taiwanese, or Chinese whose parents were born in Taiwan, as opposed to Mainland Chinese, those who came after World War II or their descendants. The KMT, which is regarded as a Mainland Chinese party by many Taiwanese (even though its membership is around three-fourths Taiwanese), fielded more than 83 percent Taiwanese candidates. Similarly, most of the KMT winners were Taiwanese. The exception was in Taipei. In Taipei 20 of 29, or 60 percent, of KMT candidates were Mainlanders. And most won. In fact, Mainlanders did well in Taipei generally, winning 33 of 68 seats contested.[58] This reflected a much higher voter turnout of Mainland Chinese than Taiwanese voters. It was also a product of the rise of activist second-generation Mainlanders. In all, 35 Mainlanders will have seats in the new parliament, nearly all from Taipei.

In contrast, the DPP ran all Taiwanese candidates, with one exception, and that candidate was not elected. In short, the DPP gave the appearance of being an ethnic party. In fact, critics said it had become a party of "Taiwanese only." The

DPP, however, broadened its base of support in terms of appealing to women and farmers—two DPP weaknesses in terms of voter support in the past. The election results clearly indicate a victory for the Non-Mainstream KMT faction, which is composed primarily of Mainland Chinese who advocate a one-China policy and generally support Premier Hau. In contrast, the Mainstream faction, which is more moderate and supports President Lee, did poorly. The DPP's New Tide faction, which strongly advocates independence, did well; the Formosa faction, which is more moderate, did not do as well. This comparison suggests a radicalization of both parties and a weakening of President Lee's power. Such a conclusion however, is contradicted by the DPP's victory being a de facto defeat for Premier Hau and his faction, since DPP strategists targeted both. Moreover, the DPP, as a party, took a much less radical stance on independence and, probably because of that, performed much better at the polls.

Conclusions

The 1992 Legislative Yuan election, notwithstanding the problems of illegal campaign activities, money politics, vote buying, violence, antics, and sensationalism, contributed significantly to the further democratization of Taiwan's political system. By most accounts the election was competitive and fair and was carried out smoothly. Observers, including some government spokesmen who declared that Taiwan had arrived at an advanced stage of democracy, were probably not too far off the mark.

On the other hand, the results of this election clearly strengthen the argument that Taiwan has a two-party system. For most this seemed to be a good sign. This argument was heard after the 1989 election, when the Democratic Progressive Party performed well. At that time the DPP was unified and spoke for a much strengthened opposition in Taiwan. After the 1991 election, when the DPP did not perform as well, there was more talk of Taiwan's party system being a one-party-dominant system. Although this election does not offer final proof to settle this argument, it does bolster the two-party system argument. Similarly, the performance of the minor parties offered strong evidence that a multiparty system is not in Taiwan's future.

On the other hand, there was some mention during the campaign and in its wake that Taiwan may be heading toward a three-party system. Those who said this made reference to the split in the KMT between the Mainstream and Non-Mainstream factions and noted that this may continue to plague the majority party for some time. They suggested that in the future the Mainstream may align with the DPP on the one-China issue and perhaps some other issues. President Lee's faction of the KMT was obviously weakened because of its poor performance in this election. Thus, while worthy of only speculation at this juncture, cooperation between the Mainstream KMT and the DPP may become a possibility in Taiwan's evolving party politics. Yet, such a scenario makes several assumptions: (1) the inability of the leadership of the ruling party to resolve its internal differences, (2) an escalation of factional differences, and (3) a division of control over the party's vast financial resources.

Clearly, factionalism was a problem for the KMT during the run up to the campaign as well as during the campaign. It is certainly an important factor explaining the KMT's poor performance. The relationship between the president and the premier was a particularly divisive one. The one-China or two-Chinas issue similarly proved destructive for the KMT. It clearly split the ruling party and made it a less able performer during the campaign—much as it did the DPP in 1991. The KMT also seems to have miscalculated the public's perception of this issue. Rejecting independence in 1991 did not mean that the electorate favored unification or a one-China policy. Assuming so was a mistake. Perhaps the KMT should declare without equivocation that debate on the issue is not productive and should be avoided. It might advocate maintaining the status quo or resolving the problem in the future, but not now—which indeed seem to be its policy. It might even admit that the issue cannot be resolved in Taipei or Beijing and that Washington holds the key. Clearly Beijing's use of force to resolve the "Taiwan issue" would fail if the United States intervened and would succeed if it did not.

Another variable to consider in assessing the election results is that the KMT's advantage in talent, professionalism, and financial resources proved to be less critical in this election—in the context of factionalism in the party and a complicated election. Moreover, the two factors seemed to accentuate each other. Thus, the ruling party lost its focus on important issues. Clearly, the KMT needed to stress issues more than it did. It also needed to inject some fresh ideas into the campaign. It didn't. Perhaps the KMT has learned a good lesson: that it cannot win an election as it did last year or the year before (meaning with-out new issues or strategies). The political milieu in Taiwan changes too fast for that.

That the KMT (or at least the conservative, Non-Mainstream faction) appeared to abandon, or indeed did abandon, its anti-Communist ideology by advocating friendly ties with China while giving much importance to the implications of economic ties with the mainland was unique for this election. This may have been a big factor in causing disarray in the party and may have rendered impossible a platform with an understandable ideological underpinning. Though changing its ideology to adjust to reality (if the reformists in China are indeed in control) may have been a good decision, it was, in the short run, disruptive. In the long run, getting rid of its anti-Communist philosophy may be very good for the KMT.

The DPP also gave some appearance of being factionalized. But being a smaller party that is adept at confrontational politics, the DPP can look divided, and perhaps even be at conflict within, without adversely affecting its performance. This is to some extent the nature of the DPP. It may be its strength. Yet the DPP also showed more professionalism in this election than in past elections. Its election strategy was much more cogent and clever. It seemed to learn a lot from its 1991 defeat. Most important, it avoided making independence the main issue in its platform. It did not abandon it, but it did not box itself in by defining it too clearly. One might say the DPP let the KMT fight over the problem.

The DPP also fielded generally more well-known and, in many senses, better candidates than the KMT. It was able to do this because it did not run its best people in the 1991 National Assembly election, seeing the Legislative Yuan election as more important. It also had a number of candidates who were committed to democracy and good government and opposed to money politics. It thus won the image of "the party of change" when it came to the issues of vote buying, money politics, and corruption. This reputation no doubt explains why the DPP won the support of a number of organizations devoted to better government and more students and young people than in previous elections.

The DPP campaigned more on issues the voters were concerned with than in previous elections, and it was on the winning side of most of them. The DPP also presented its stand on issues to the voters much more clearly than in the past and without radical overtones. Also, due to circumstances, it made many of its attacks on the KMT stick. Because of the bad publicity surrounding recent scandals, the DPP was able to label the KMT a party of the rich, of corruption, and most of all, of vote buying. Never mind that vote buying was not much more serious, if at all, than in previous elections or that doing it helped the poor and was thus income and wealth equalizing; the DPP found it an effective issue to damage the KMT's image. Meanwhile, the KMT was not very effective in portraying the DPP as a party of extremists who are not interested in or capable of governing the nation.

The DPP also managed to use the ethnic factor effectively against the KMT. It took aim at Premier Hau throughout the campaign in large measure because he represented Mainland Chinese rule that most Taiwanese wanted to bring to an end. Large numbers of Taiwanese wanted to vote for Taiwanese candidates, and the DPP represented the Taiwanese. President Lee is, of course, Taiwanese; however, the DPP, by drawing attention to his feud with Premier Hau, whom he appointed, cast doubt on the KMT's ability to bridge the "ethnic gap." Though the antipathy between Taiwanese and Mainlanders has diminished markedly in recent years, it is still something to exploit in an election campaign, or at least it was in this one.

The DPP also benefited from events, both domestic and international, during 1992. The political scandals that plagued the nation during the months prior to the campaign clearly helped the DPP. As the party was out of power, it was not identified with the problems. The KMT was—even though in many cases it was not culpable. The unexpected slower economic growth also hurt the KMT. KMT leaders were able to use economic issues to their advantage in previous elections; that was not the case this time. Likewise for foreign policy issues. The KMT lost credibility because of the diplomatic break with Korea. Its one-China policy seemed to be responsible. At minimum, it made the DPP's position—that the nation should appeal to the international community as Taiwan and not China—appear more reasonable. Beijing's capacity to block any new initiative by Taipei to establish global contacts seemed still limited by its isolationism and pariah image; thus, Taipei's foreign policy seemed to be in need of new initiatives as the DPP advocated.

Much of this analysis suggests that the DPP's victory cannot be taken for granted in the sense that it will necessarily perform as well or better in the next election and that only more time is needed, perhaps five or ten years, as some DPP leaders have suggested, before the DPP is the ruling party. In the past four elections, the KMT and the DPP have, almost taking turns, performed better and worse. This trend seems to suggest a cyclical pattern. The next election may be the KMT's turn again. This possibility will certainly be more likely if the KMT learns a lesson from its defeat and acts to overcome its internal frictions and fact-ionalism. Alternatively, if the DPP experiences internal division or conflict, or if it does not prove itself as capable in office as out of office (there being a contradiction between wanting to oppose and wanting to rule), the KMT will do better at the polls.

Clearly, the DPP will have more influence over policy making, especially lawmaking, as a result of this election. Though still in a minority, it will be able to make its positions heard in the Legislative Yuan. The KMT will not be able to ignore the DPP in lawmaking as it has in the past. A DPP boycott, if it chooses this means of influence, will be much more effective—both in the sense of the work of the Legislative Yuan and in terms of public opinion. The DPP's program will also benefit. Even if the DPP cannot pass legislation, the KMT may try to preempt some of the tenets of its program. This has happened in the past, and seems even more likely now.

There may also be some downsides to the DPP "victory." Taiwan-China relations are likely to suffer as a result of the DPP victory. Beijing favored the KMT in the election. The DPP generally opposes more extensive ties and better relations with China. Its victory may also increase political instability in Taiwan, at least in the short run. After the election there was an increase in the number of people leaving for the United States. Nevertheless, Taiwan has adjusted to competitive elections very well since 1980. Both its leaders and the electorate seem to understand there is a price to be paid for democracy and that a democratic system has many defects.

Endnotes

1. The Legislative Yuan is one of three parliamentary bodies in the national government of the Republic of China. The other two are the National Assembly and the Control Yuan. The National Assembly elects the president and vice president, and may recall them, and amends the constitution. Some consider it little more than an electoral college, though it has recently played an important function in amending the nation's basic law. The Control Yuan is an oversight branch of government chosen by provincial and special city councils, but effective February 1, 1993, it will no longer exercise the power of approving presidential nominations and will in essence become a semi-judicial body of government.

2. For an analysis of previous elections, see John F. Copper with George P. Chen, *Taiwan's Elections: Political Development and Democratization in the Republic of China* (Baltimore: University of Maryland School of Law, 1984); John F. Copper, *Taiwan's Recent Elections: Fulfilling the Democratic Promise* (Baltimore: University of Maryland School of Law, 1990); and John F. Copper, "Taiwan's 1991 Second National Assembly Election," *Journal of Northeast Asian Studies*, Spring 1992.

3. See Copper, "Taiwan's 1991 National Assembly Election," *Journal of Northeast Asian Studies*, Spring 1991, for further details.

4. Julian Baum, "Unfinished Business," *Far Eastern Economic Review*, March 19, 1992, pp. 30–31.

5. See John F. Copper, "Taiwan," in *Colliers Encyclopedia Yearbook,* for further details.

6. Julian Baum, "Changing the Watch," *Far Eastern Economic Review*, August 13, 1992, p. 24.

7. Julian Baum, "Extortion in Taiwan," *Far Eastern Economic Review*, May 14, 1992, p. 61.

8. See Tammy C. Peng, "DPP ready with white paper for year–end election," *Free China Journal*, September 4, 1992, p. 2.

9. "Retired legislators staging a comeback," *China Post*, October 1, 1992, p. 1.

10. "KMT to crack whip," *China Post,* October 30, 1992, p. 1.

11. "Mediocre KMT polls showing seen," *China Post*, October 12, 1992, p. 16.

12. "Temporary gains seen from KMT's approval of poll bids," *China Post,* November 11, 1992, p. 1.

13. *China News*, November 16, 1992, p. 2.

14. "Polls shows KMT landslide not sure," *China Post*, November 25, 1992, p. 1.

15. "KMT expels Chen Je-nan," *China News*, November 28, 1992, p. 1.

16. "KMT expulsion stirs deep anger and hurt," *China Post*, November 30, 1992, p. 1.

17. "DPP leader to go it alone," *China News*, November 11, 1992, p. 2.

18. Julian Baum, "Teasing the dragon," *Far Eastern Economic Review*, October 16, 1992, p. 34.

19. Allen Pun, "Imbalance in public, state spending," *Free China Journal,* September 4, 1992, p. 3.

20. Julian Baum, "Export Worries," *Far Eastern Economic Review*, October 22, 1992, p. 46.

21. These figures, as well as information on the reason for the number of seats, etc., were provided by the head of the Central Election Commission in an interview on December 15, 1992.

22. See data chart in Tammy C. Peng, "ROC heads to the polls; first full legislative election in 44 years," *Free China Journal,* December 4, 1992, p. 7.

23. See R. L. Chen, "Election will be most complex in 40 years," *China Post,* November 20, 1992, p. 1, and "Too many candidates chasing too few seats," *China Post* (editorial), November 25, 1992, p. 2.

24. Part of this analysis is based on a meeting with KMT leaders, particularly the head of Cultural Affairs, on December 14, 1992. The KMT platform is cited in Susan Yu, "KMT goes to the polls confident of victory, but ready for a fight," *Free China Journal*, December 11, 1992, p. 7.

25. This assessment is based on a meeting with DPP spokespersons on December 15, 1992 and a synopsis of the DPP's platform provided to me at that time. Also see, Tammy C. Peng, "DPP is ready for uphill battle; exploits divisions within KMT," *Free China Journal*, December 15, 1992, p. 7.

26. "KMT heads meet with officials," *China News,* December 10, 1992, p. 2.

27. "DPP putting more than ever into election," *China News*, December 10, 1992, p. 2.

28. "Fistfights and firecrackers mark first day of campaign," *China News*, December 10, 1992, p. 1, and "Carnival start to election," *China Post*, December 10, 1992, p. 16.

29. "200 Chen fans pelt election committee building with eggs," *China News*, December 10, 1992, p. 2.

30. "'Porn queen' asks police for support," *China News*, December 10, 1992, p. 2.

31. "Election rivals seek to taint food supplies," *China Post*, December 10, 1992, p. 16.

32. "DPP hopeful sets up radio station in defiance of law," *China Post*, December 11, 1992, p. 16.

33. "Candidate leads protest against media monopoly," *China Post*, December 12, 1992, p. 16.

34. "Radio personality to continue campaign," *China News*, December 12, 1992, p. 2.

35. "KMT, DPP trade barbs in TV commercials," *China Post*, December 12, 1992, p. 16.

36. "Votes can cost NT$5,000," *China Post*, December 13, 1992, p. 12.

37. "Election commissioner warns of vote rigging."

38. "DPP faces libel suits filed by Keelung leaders," *China Post*, December 14, 1992, p. 12.

39. "Candidates linked with business groups," *China Post*, December 14, 1992, p. 16.

40. "The best and the worst government lawmakers," *China News*, December 14, 1992, p. 3. The ratings were based on attendance, proposal legislation, and participation in debates.

41. "KMT blasts 2 think tanks over unflattering reports," *China News*, December 15, 1992, p. 16.

42. There were numerous polls published during the campaign and many stories and reports on vote buying. See, for example, "Candidates can't shake

vote–buying," *China News*, December 15, 1992, p. 1, and editorial in *Chung Kuo Shih Pao* (China Times), December 20, 1992, p. 9.

43. "Jiang warns against calls for Taiwan independence," *China News*, December 17, 1992, p. 1. Beijing, however, was relatively silent during the campaign, at least compared to 1989 when a large number of threats were made against DPP candidates for their statements about Taiwan independence. See "Peking mum on Taiwan election: MAC," *Express News* (Taipei), December 19–20, 1992, p. 2.

44. "Pong speaks his mind about government and elections," *China Post*, December 15, 1992, p. 16.

45. "Expelled ruling party member leads violence," *China Post*, December 19, 1992, p. 16.

46. "Police suspicious of candidate's claims to being shot," *China News*, December 19, 1992, p. 1.

47. "KMT wins easily, but opposition makes big gains," *China News*, December 19, 1992, p. 1.

48. See "KMT loses ground to opposition party," *China Post*, December 20, 1992, p. 1.

49. Sophia Wu, "Soong offers to quit post," *China News*, December 21, 1992, p. 1.

50. The latter observations are based on news items in a dozen Taiwan newspapers as well as opinion pieces. They are also based on conversations with reporters, party leaders, and scholars after the election.

51. Data mostly drawn from articles in the *China Post* and the *China News* of December 20 and 21, 1992. See also Julian Baum, "The hollow centre," *Far Eastern Economic Review*, January 7, 1993, pp. 14–15.

52. See Jeremy Mark, "Taiwan Opposition Gets Big Lift in Poll," *Asian Wall Street Journal*, December 21, 1992, p. 1, for an assessment of the election using this way of counting the popular vote.

53. See Rodney Chan, "Jaw wins most votes, Wang takes second," *China Post*, December 20, 1992, p. 12.

54. See Allen Pun, "Fat cats deflated in election bids; voters reward enemies of graft," *Free China Journal*, December 22, 1992, p. 7.

55. *Chung Kuo Shih Pao* (China Times), December 20, 1994, p. 10.

56. *Ching Chi Jih Pao* (Economic Times), December 20, 1992, p. 1.

57. Ibid.

58. *Chung Kuo Shih Pao* (China Times), December 20, 1992, p. 7.

Chapter Seven
Taiwan's 1994 Gubernatorial
and Mayoral Elections

On December 3, 1994 voters in the Republic of China, or Taiwan, went to the polls to elect the governor of Taiwan province, the mayors of the two metropolitan cities (Taipei and Kaohsiung), plus delegates to the Taiwan Provincial Assembly and the two metropolitan city councils. This election may be categorized as the seventh "important" election in this island republic—beginning with the country's first competitive national election in 1980, another in 1983, the nation's first two-party election in 1986, a "victory" (meaning a much better than expected performance in popular votes and the seats won plus a big gain over the previous election) for the opposition Democratic Progressive Party (DPP) in 1989, the first plenary or non-supplemental election in 1991 (for the National Assembly), and another non-supplemental election (this time for the more important Legislative Yuan) in 1992.[1]

Though not technically a national contest, this election was "larger" in some respects than past national elections. It was also a significant election for several reasons. First, the governor had never been elected before. Second, the mayors of Taipei and Kaohsiung had not been elected since 1964 and 1977, respectively, these jobs having been subsequently made appointed positions.[2] Third, it was Taiwan's first important "three-party" election. Finally, the election was thought to be a barometer for two elections to come: the second non-supplemental election of the Legislative Yuan in December 1995 and the first direct election of the president in March 1996.

Laying the groundwork for this election, the Republic of China had amended its Constitution in 1992 and the Legislative Yuan had enacted legislation in mid-1994 making the governor and two metropolitan mayors elective officials.[3] Many felt these actions constituted another major step in the direction of making Taiwan's polity a fully democratic one. They also satisfied an important demand made by the opposition Democratic Progressive Party: that these jobs be made elective offices.

The months prior to the election were filled with events that made the campaign atmosphere tense. Members and supporters of the three main parties and a number of candidates hurled accusations of corruption and misconduct (including, of course, financial and sexual) at each other. All three parties made demands for the resignations of opponents and filed lawsuits as campaign tactics. Several top party officials and even candidates were arrested for various crimes. A number were expelled from their parties, some promising revenge. And a recall petition against four standing Nationalist Party or Kuomintang (KMT) legislators was filed but then nullified by specific legislation. New Party (NP) and DPP supporters met head-on on several occasions, leading to bloody clashes.

The most attention-getting of events was the serious debate, emanating from several quarters about an invasion of Taiwan by the military of the People's Republic of China (PRC). Topping this off, in November, less than a month before the election, gunners on one of Taiwan's Offshore Islands accidently shelled a village on the coast of the PRC—after which an opposition politician said it was a deliberate political act.

The campaign began in the context of recent modest successes for the ruling Nationalist Party or Kuomintang (KMT). In December 1993 there were year-end elections for city mayors and county magistrates. Though the DPP increased its popular vote from 38.3 percent to 41 percent, it lost one seat and failed to attain what it had promised. Chairman Hsu Hsin-liang subsequently resigned. In January 1994, the ruling Nationalist Party won an even more impressive victory in local elections for city and county councils and mayors and executive chiefs of small cities, townships, and villages. In the councils, the KMT won 67.4 percent of the seats; in mayor and executive chiefs races, it won 82.2 percent of the seats contested.[4] There were also smaller elections in June and July.

Still, all was not happiness by any means for the ruling party. The KMT's election victories were followed by widespread charges of vote-buying and other irregularities. Public and opposition pressure prompted the Ministry of Justice to take strong punitive actions, indicting or removing from office a number of KMT officials. Then, because of the emergence of the New Party in August 1993, the KMT had to deal with competition on both its left and right. The KMT leadership soon found campaigning was more complicated than in the past against only one opponent.

The campaign was enlivened by ethnic politics and the issue of Taiwan independence versus unification (*t'ung-tu wen-t'i*). Accusations, threats, and tricks abounded, including bomb threats. The election was also a more competitive election than previous ones in terms of the number of candidates and the money spent—not to mention the fact that it was a three-party race. Where Taiwan was headed in terms of its political party system and future elections was also brought to question.

There were a variety of opinions about who won the election. In fact, one could easily make an argument for each of the three parties being victorious. Obviously the cause of democracy won notwithstanding the plethora of irregularities and violence during the campaign. It was likewise clear that the electorate was interested in the electoral process and the evolution of democracy in Taiwan as reflected by the high voter turnout and the public attention given to the candidates during the campaign.

Pre-election Politics

The year 1994 was an eventful or "hot" period in Taiwan politically, particularly in the months preceding the election. Clearly what transpired in the months before the campaign influenced the election's outcome. The legal issues relating to the election, however, had an earlier history, as did the formation of the New Party.[5]

The opposition had long complained about the fact that the governor and the mayors of Taipei and Kaohsiung were appointed. Soon after the DPP was formed in the fall of 1986, its leaders made issue—in fact, strongly—of these positions not being elective offices.[6] The KMT could not disagree, and its leaders, in turn, promised to change the situation soon; in fact, they mentioned 1989 as a deadline for making the mayors elected officials.[7] The matter was discussed at the National Affairs Conference in the summer of 1990.[8] It was subsequently resolved when additional amendments were added to the Constitution in 1992.

However, the Ministry of Interior's work drafting new self-government laws (required by the Constitutional amendments) continued into mid-1994 without tangible results. As a consequence, Premier Lien Chan noted at one point that the election might have to be delayed past December. DPP leaders replied that the KMT wanted to hold the election at a later date to give the people time to forget the recent vote-buying scandal. Meanwhile, two well-known DPP lawmakers advocated not participating in the governor's race since the party had long advocated abolishing the provincial government.[9]

The formation of the New Party also has a relevant background. After Lee Teng-hui became president in January 1988 following President Chiang Ching-kuo's death, opposition grew in the KMT to turning over national executive power to a Taiwanese (as opposed to Mainland Chinese). This marked the beginning of a fissure in the party along ethnic lines. In addition, a number of KMT leaders perceived that President Lee was not committed to the goal of one China but rather favored an independent Taiwan—though Lee consistently spoke in support of one China. By the time of the 1992 Legislative Yuan election, factions had formed in support of and in opposition to Lee (called the Mainstream and Non–Mainstream factions respectively). This split had a very visible impact on the KMT's performance at the polls in 1992.[10] The Non-Mainstream faction did well, but the DPP's outstanding performance was attributed to the fact that the Non-Main-stream had divided the KMT, benefiting the opposition.[11]

In August 1993, when the KMT held its Fourteenth Party Congress, the gulf between the two factions became even wider, prompting some Non-Mainstream KMT members to form the Chinese New Party, later renamed the New Party.[12] The NP advocated a one-China policy. It also charged the KMT with corruption. It labeled the DPP as a party of advocates of violence and separation.

The months leading up to the campaign period witnessed events that also affected the voting. In addition, there were disputes within and among the parties, accusations, threats, lawsuits, acts of sensationalism, and violence. Think tanks, lobbying groups, and academics also made their voices heard.

In January, former Premier Hau Pei-tsun published his memoirs, *With a Clear Conscience*, wherein Hau assailed President Lee for arrogating too much political power. The charge had resonance because the KMT had just pushed a bill through the Legislative Yuan formalizing the National Security Council and the National Security Bureau, evoking opposition accompanied by violence in a legislative session and also debate about whether Taiwan had, or should have, a presidential or cabinet system of government.[13] Friction between the KMT and the NP and between the two factions in the KMT worsened as a result.

Just weeks later President Lee visited three countries in Southeast Asia—the Philippines, Indonesia, and Thailand—and met the head-of-state of each. This was only Lee's second visit abroad as president and was considered by most observers a break-through in the nation's diplomacy.[14] Clearly the ruling party benefited from Lee's trip, particularly given the DPP's criticism of Taiwan's isolation in the world community. Lee's successful diplomacy to a small degree diverted attention away from domestic political problems.

In late March, twenty-four members of a tour group from Taiwan visiting China were murdered. The PRC attempted to deflect attention from the incident with quick trials and executions and refused to cooperate with Taiwan authorities in investigating the matter. Officials in Taiwan, responding to public outcries, condemned Beijing's actions using uncomplimentary language reminiscent of the

Cold War days.[15] Polls at this time indicated a big drop in favorable public opinion toward the PRC and reunification.[16] Subsequently, Taipei suspended various cultural and educational exchange programs with China. As a result of this tough stance the KMT appeared to benefit, this time at the expense of the NP.

Meanwhile, the murder of a naval officer revealed the likelihood of deep corruption in Taiwan's arms procurement.[17] Weapons purchases had to be temporarily stopped for the first time ever. Following on the heels of this scandal the media disclosed that there was an on-going investigation into vote buying in all but one of Taiwan's cities and counties as a follow up of earlier elections, in particular of candidates for speakers and deputy speakers.[18] The gravity of the situation prompted a group of KMT members to form the Alliance for Democratic Reform to clean up the party.[19] Justice Minister Mao Ying-jeou, however, handled the matter promptly, gaining credit for a job well done for himself, the government, and the KMT; still, the KMT was tainted. The DPP's troubles were less by comparison, but the main opposition party still got considerable unwanted publicity about a lawsuit filed by eleven members who had been pressured, they said, unjustly, to withdraw from the party. This incident was said to weaken the DPP's influence in Kaohsiung.[20]

In April, President Lee gave an interview to a Japanese reporter, in Japanese (which Lee speaks very well), relating the bitter experience of Taiwanese after the Nationalist Chinese arrived at the end of World War II and assumed political control over the island. He referred to KMT rule in the interview as like that of a "foreign power." His remarks, some of which were taken out of context, angered the NP, not to mention the People's Republic of China.

On a trip to Latin America in May, President Lee stopped in Honolulu where he was denied the right to disembark and stay overnight. Many Americans, and particularly members of Congress, viewed this slight as petty and mean-spirited. Congress, as a consequence, began to push the Clinton administration to upgrade relations with Taipei. Lee also seemed to win sympathy at home. As it turned out this incident had a strong delayed impact.

In early summer, author Chen Lang-ping published *August 1995: China's Violent Invasion of Taiwan*—which instantly created public controversy. Though not an academic argument, but rather sensationalism, the book strongly incited citizen concern about relations with Beijing and Washington as well as about Taiwan's future. *August 1995* also amplified the pro-independence and anti-independence positions taken by the two opposition parties.

In July, Minister of Interior Wu Poh-hsiung resigned from office. Wu, considered one of the most popular Taiwanese politicians, and a KMT contender for the nomination for governor, also announced that he would not be a candidate in the governor's race. This left the nomination to James Soong. Wu's decision prevented a dispute within the ruling party over its nominee.

The Council on Economic Planning and Development issued a "green light" (a very positive economic evaluation) on the economy in August. It also raised the projected growth for the year to 6.2 percent.[21] This good news was followed by the first substantive political talks between Taipei and Beijing. Several issues, such as hijacking, illegal immigration, and fishing rights, were discussed. Both the better economic outlook and seemingly improved relations with the PRC benefited the KMT.

Meanwhile, 1,000 protestors, angry about the government shutting down illegal radio stations, staged a mass demonstration. Twenty-six people were injured; eleven were jailed. Also attracting public attention, a member of the City Council in Kaohsiung was attacked and killed near his home.[22] And a DPP member of the Legislative Yuan faced disciplinary action for threatening Premier Lien on September 6.[23] The fallout of these events in terms of helping or hurting the three major parties was mixed.

In mid-September, the KMT held a mobilization meeting that was described as its biggest ever. Instead of cooperating against the KMT, the two opposition parties engaged in violent clashes in Kaohsiung on September 24. Four hundred people were involved, and more than eighty people were hurt, including the NP's candidate for mayor. A number of vehicles were turned over or burned.[24]

President Lee's invitation to attend the Asian Games was subsequently withdrawn under PRC pressure and Taiwan's membership application to the United Nations was rejected by the Steering Committee of the General Assembly. At the same time, however, Washington announced that the Clinton administration would "re-adjust" U.S. Taiwan policy to allow for higher level meetings and a change of name of Taiwan's representative offices in the United States. This followed criticism of the Clinton administration by members of the Congress over offending President Lee in May.

The Republic of China held its first public military games, timed to respond specifically to exercises held by the People's Liberation Army on the mainland in late September. The display featured the Taiwan-built Ching Kuo fighters and helicopters fitted to attack submarines or troops landing on the beaches.[25]

On October 2, the first television debates by candidates were held, even though the campaign had not officially started. The debates featured the candidates for the Taipei mayor position and were very popular—getting 40 percent of viewers. Incumbent Mayor Huang Ta-chou performed poorly according to analysts, after which local bookies gave him only a thirty to one chance of winning. Jaw Shao-kong, of the NP, scored the best, though he did not seem to gain much on DPP candidate Chen Sui-bian. Both of the latter candidates criticized Mayor Huang in harsh terms, with Jaw referring to him as the "nincompoop mayor."[26]

The NP at this juncture suffered from an internal rift when a KMT member and friend of Jaw's was threatened by Yok Mu-ming, head of the NP. Seeking to take advantage of the situation, the KMT asked Jaw to return to the KMT, but he refused.[27]

In the meantime, a number of high ranking politicians of all three political parties were found deeply embroiled in a stock scandal after the stock market dropped more than 1,000 points, or 15 percent of its value. Police raided the home of Oung Ta-ming, a KMT legislator elected in 1992. Even though he had been convicted of securities fraud, a number of politicians went to his house—apparently to prevent police from taking records that might implicate them. DPP legislator Hou Hai-hsiung was subsequently expelled from his party. NP members were on Oung's board or were his advisers. KMT politicians were implicated in larger numbers, though the opposition parties were not able to exploit the situation.[28]

Following on the heels of this incident, KMT legislators revised a provision in the nation's election law invalidating a recall effort against party legislators who had supported Taiwan's fourth nuclear plant. Otherwise this would have been the first ever recall petition placed on the ballot during an election.[29] Not long after this controversy the KMT ousted three candidates running without the party's endorsement. At the same time, party officials tried to keep Kuo Yen-sheng in the party even though the Taichung City Council speaker had been convicted of a crime.[30] These events reflected poorly on the KMT.

By this time campaign fever had already become intense. Campaign posters, political advertisements and flags were visible almost everywhere in the cities. Even taxi drivers became partisan; they not only pasted party insignia and advertisements for candidates on their taxis, but also asked customers before getting in their taxis about their voting preferences and refused those who did not support the same candidate or party as themselves. In several cases this led to fistfights and other violence.[31]

In early November, just before the official campaign began, the DPP issued a position-paper saying that troops should be withdrawn from the Republic of China-held islands of Quemoy and Matsu near the mainland. The DPP's position created such a negative reaction that DPP Taipei mayoral candidate Chen Sui-bian promptly announced that he was opposed enunciating such a policy "before the Chinese Communists...pledge that they will give up the idea of invading

Taiwan." In a damage-control effort, Chen made a quick trip to Quemoy where he said that the DPP's position had been misunderstood. He asserted that he had "absolutely no intention of abandoning the islands."[32]

As the formal campaign period approached the campaign strategies of the three parties became clearer. The KMT planned to stress its record for creating economic development and maintaining political stability while taking advantage of President Lee's good popularity ratings. Their campaign would be professionally run and well financed. The DPP and NP were going to stress change—since they were running mainly against KMT incumbents. Both parties had to engage in fund- raising at the same time. The NP said it hoped to raise nearly all its campaign money from small donations. DPP leaders spoke of pressing social and welfare issues. They also planned to appeal to the ethnic Taiwanese vote. They said they would use cable television to get their message across. NP planners tried to make issue of corruption and aimed at the young and women voters while promoting Chinese nationalism.[33]

The Campaign

Though campaigning began in force before the formal campaign period, months before, in fact, officially the race for governor started on November 8 for a period of twenty-five days. The races for mayors got underway on November 18. And the contests for Provincial Assembly and city council seats were launched on November 23. Generally the election period was short, but there was less disagreement about this as there had been in the past.[34]

Huang Shih-cheng, chairman of the Central Election Commission (CEC), admonished candidates that they must demonstrate sportsmanship and compete fairly. He also warned against violations of the election laws and conduct that might disturb the campaign.[35] Meanwhile, the CEC prepared the largest election-monitoring group ever assembled in Taiwan as well as an unprecedented number of police and security personnel to protect candidates and keep order.

Four hundred and fifty candidates registered for 175 Provincial Assembly and city council seats. Fourteen entered the respective races for governor and mayor. This made for an unusually high ratio of candidates per seat. The KMT had a much larger number of candidates than the other two parties—fielding nearly 80 percent of all candidates—calculating it could win more seats this way.[36] Five candidates competed for the governorship: incumbent Governor Soong Chu-yu (more often known as James Soong) from the KMT; Chen Ting-nan, representing the DPP; Ju Gau–jeng, the NP's candidate; Wu Tzu, of the Taiwan

People's United Party; and Tsai Cheng-chih, running as an indepen-dent.[37] The group mirrored an array of different backgrounds and experience. As a whole, however, the candidates were well educated, well qualified, young, ener-getic, and dynamic. According to the election law, a contestant needed 4 million votes of just over 10 million eligible voters to win.

James Soong began his campaign by taking leave from office and lighting a "fire of victory" at his headquarters in Taichung. His supporters launched a parade. Chen Ting-nan began his campaign also in Taichung with a drum beat to mark the beginning of the twenty-five-day campaign period and by "declaring war on the incumbent governor." In a public ceremony, he ate some locally grown potatoes, symbolizing the local or native Taiwanese and asked Taiwanese to vote for Taiwanese. Ju Gau-jeng began his campaign in Taipei by reading a passage from a Chinese classic that demonstrated his determination to win. Wu Tzu began by describing his party and asking voters who were not satisfied with the other parties to vote for him. Tsai Cheng-chih issued a statement together with thirty-five other independent candidates calling on voters to support independents to avoid "big-party monopolization."[38]

The CEC scheduled twenty-eight public political forums in addition to two television forums for the gubernatorial candidates. The first regular forum was held on November 9 in Taichung. Approximately 10,000 people (plus 3,000 police) attended this event, the first of its kind for a gubernatorial election contest. Ju spoke first. He attacked incumbent Governor Soong and DPP candi-date Chen and called for converting the Taichung military airport into an inter-national one and for building a rapid transit system. Soong cited the need for stability and blasted DPP efforts to "overthrow the current political system." DPP hecklers in the front row yelled during his talk, saying he should speak in Taiwanese. Chen assailed Soong for neglecting local cultural and for bragging too much about his own record. Wu called for support of his party as an alter-native. Tsai criticized the "election culture" of Taiwan and money politics and said 3,000 police at such an event was abnormal.[39]

The campaign strategies of the three major candidates, Soong, Chen, and Ju, became apparent from the outset. Soong boasted of his record and his experience. He also made note of the fact that President Lee had appointed him governor in March 1993 and supported his candidacy, as did Premier Lien Chan. He promised to "serve in office rather than dominate," alluding to his caring attitude reflected by his visits to all of his constituent offices in the past year.[40] He also talked about good government, moderation, and stability, and criticized the DPP's plank of "changing the sky" (meaning promoting major change), which he char-acterized as radical, de-stabilizing, and dangerous. He specifically criticized the

DPP for advocating withdrawing from Quemoy and Matsu and giving the islands to the PRC, saying that if the DPP's desires were put into effect "clear blue skies would turn red." Soong spoke in Taiwanese at many rallies, stressing the fact that Taiwan was his home (even though he came from the Mainland when he was young). He also tried to play down ethnic differences between Taiwanese and Mainlanders.[41]

Chen Ting-nan began with a more negative campaign strategy, attacking Soong as "alienating himself from Taiwan culture" and for alleged links with construction companies that provided him with offices and provincial banks that paid for his advertisements. He hit the KMT for "official corruption, improper links with big business and tolerance of organized criminal gangs." He said that one year of KMT rule of the provincial government cost NT $60 billion (U.S. $2.4 billion) in corruption yet government officials said there was no money for the senior citizens' pensions that Chen supported. Chen said he would launch a "new government movement" to transform the provincial government into a clean, effective, and high-quality administration.[42] Chen ignored the other candidates in his diatribes.

Ju Gau-jeng, on the other hand, focused his attention on attacking all of the other candidates. He said President Lee was "acting like an emperor," criticized Soong for refusing to allow Taiwanese television programs when he was director general of the Government Information Office, and accused Chen of exaggerating the success of the "so-called Ilan experience"—referring to his tenure as magistrate of Ilan County from 1981 to 1989. Ju also spoke of wiping out the shame felt by Chinese since the Opium War.[43]

On November 13, the people of Taiwan saw their first ever government-sponsored television campaign event. Each candidate was given fifteen minutes to state what he would do as governor. Analysts later said all of the candidates performed well and made their points clearly.[44] Meanwhile, several candidates rented computers to send taped political messages to constituents by telephone. This was also a first.[45]

Four candidates competed for the Taipei mayor position: incumbent mayor Huang Ta-chou of the KMT; Chen Sui-bian, carrying the DPP banner; Jaw Shao-kong, representing the NP; and Jih Rong-ze, running as an independent. Five competed for the mayorship of Kaohsiung: incumbent mayor Wu Den-yih of the KMT; Chang Chun-hsiung for the DPP; Tang A-ken, representing the NP; Shih Chung-hsiung, an independent; and Cheng Te-yiao, also an independent.

On November 18, the day of the official launching of the mayoral campaigns, Jaw Shao-kong visited city government offices, and talked to workers and met people at the entrance of National Taiwan University, his alma mater. Chen Sui-bian met with elderly citizens at Youth Park and repeated his promise that those over the age of sixty-five would receive pensions of NT $5,000 per month and that children under three would get free medical care if he were elected. Later in the day he met with a local women's group. Huang Ta-chou visited a public market in the suburbs and a local temple.[46]

Jaw dropped a bombshell as the campaign formally got started. He accused President Lee Teng-hui of a "conspiracy" with the opposition DPP to accomplish Taiwan's independence before Hong Kong was returned to the People's Republic of China in July 1997. He said: "These crazy methods will bring us our doom." Also Jaw spoke of KMT corruption. Chen's strategy was aimed at incumbent Mayor Huang. He spoke of "classified" documents that proved Huang's malfeasance in office, citing in particular problems with the rapid transit system. He also referred to Huang as a "dishonest mayor who is not capable of telling residents the real problems."[47] Huang adopted an "in between" or moderate strategy, saying that hasty unification and Taiwan independence were both wrong, while calling Jaw's charges against President Lee absurd. He spoke of his record, noting successful projects such as changing the course of the Keelung River and building Ta-an Forest Park and the Chunghua Commercial Center. He portrayed himself as a "practical and patient person as opposed to those with talents for showmanship and sweet talk."[48]

The gubernatorial race and the Taipei mayoral race overshadowed the Kaohsiung mayoral race, both city council races, and the Provincial Assembly race. Relatively little press attention was given to the latter contests. Incumbent mayor of Kaohsiung, Wu Den-yih, campaigned on his record, a strong one, and talked of stability and moderation. The other mayoral candidates adopted less middle-of-the road positions. KMT candidates for other offices generally spoke of the need for stability, while boasting of the party's record, especially on economic development. They warned of chaos and a business downturn if another party prevailed. DPP candidates emphasized the need for change and advocated an independent Taiwan. NP candidates spoke of KMT corruption and DPP violence and about a unified China. Campaign issues and party struggles were generally more visible in the races for governor and Taipei mayor; local issues were more salient in other campaigns.

On November 18, just as the race for mayors officially opened, an unlicensed television station founded by the DPP began broadcasting. A party spokesperson said that there was bias in the three government-run channels favoring the KMT and thus a ruling party monopolization of the channels of communication. The Government Information Office declared that it would take action against the station because it violated the Telecommunications Law and Radio and Television Law and because the pirate station had affected the people's rights and interests.[49]

Meanwhile, the KMT announced that, if its candidates for governor and mayors won, there would be a decrease in the individual payments made to the National Health Insurance Plan to 20 percent of the total fee. The other parties cried fowl.[50] Jaw Shao-kong subsequently declared that he would build more public housing to help the "snails without shells" (people that cannot afford to buy a house).[51] Other candidates made similar promises.

A few days later, an NP candidate threatened to sue President Lee for the closing of three alleys near his residence. Another threatened to blow up the Presidential Office because of President Lee's "disrespect for Sun Yat-sen and the late President Chiang Kai-shek." He panicked police when he showed up with what appeared to be a remote control device. Another candidate asked fellow candidates to sign written pledges recording their campaign promises in writing. Still another called a "press conference in the air" by meeting with news reporters in a helicopter.[52]

The NP mobilized supporters for a march in Taipei near the headquarters of mayoral candidate Chen Sui-bian on November 20. An estimated 50,000 participated—40,000 more than the parade permit asked for. NP leaders sought to give the appearance of mass public support for their candidate for mayor. In a subsequent appearance on television, Jaw Shao-kong proclaimed his version of the "three-nos" policy (after a government foreign policy position using that name): no second term for President Lee; no plebiscite on Taiwan's future; and no declaration of independence.[53]

At almost the same time, James Soong offered a reward of NT $100,000 for information about vote buying in response to accusations by Chen Ting-nan that his campaign workers were engaging in the practice.[54] The next day, a DPP legislator accused Soong of having thirteen workers on his staff who had been convicted of electoral fraud.

Some days later, a candidate for Taipei City Council brought a group of people to the Tamsui line of the Taipei Mass Rapid Transit System for a test ride, even though the line was not yet open. In an unrelated incident, a fake bomb was found at NP headquarters.[55] The next day, an anonymous letter about Jaw Shao-kong having a mentally retarded son was printed in the newspaper. Soon after that, Rebar Group filed suit against the DPP for slander regarding alleged money the company had given to Mayor Huang.[56]

President Lee Teng-hui joined the fray in replying to Jaw Shao-kong's charges. In addition, he described the promises by the DPP to senior citizens as "cheating." Lee, at the same time, noted that people in Taiwan "are all Taiwanese as they drink the same water" (in response to DPP statements that Taiwanese should vote only for Taiwanese candidates).[57] President Lee meanwhile campaigned for various KMT candidates.

A number of other events and incidents sparked controversy and created excitement. Some were coincidental; others were planned by the candidates, their workers, or the parties. Several seemed to benefit one party or another or certain candidates.

The Congressional election in the United States, a landslide for the Republican Party, was seen as auspicious for Taipei. Tu Chou-seng, director of the Department of North American Affairs in the Ministry of Foreign Affairs, noted that Republicans had been more friendly to the Republic of China than Democrats and said he anticipated more U.S. support.[58] This seemed to be good news for the ruling KMT. Subsequently, the murder of a policeman in Taipei by gangsters and the kidnapping of a Taiwan businessman in the People's Republic of China got headlines.[59] These stories may also have helped the KMT since they underscored concern about crime, which was a KMT plank. However, Japan's refusal to invite President Lee to an Asia-Pacific Economic Cooperation forum had the opposite effect. The same might be said of the suicide of a Marine major general who had been charged with improperly using defense funds—since the KMT has advocated larger defense spending and is the ruling party.[60]

On November 14, Xinhua News Agency (of the People's Republic of China) reported that army forces stationed on Little Quemoy (meaning forces from Taiwan) had fired on the village of Tatou on the outskirts of Amoy injuring four people, two seriously. Taipei initially denied that its military had fired on the mainland, but it was soon disclosed that indeed this had happened. Though an accident that was quickly resolved, the matter did create tension between Taipei and Beijing for a few days. It also brought the security issue front and center during the campaign.[61]

Election Results

The election results, in terms of defining winning and losing parties, were mixed. All of the political parties had cause for both satisfaction and disappointment. All claimed victory in some ways; all expressed some disappointment.

If one assumes that the KMT's performance should not necessarily be measured against the percentage of votes it received in past elections, that it is now competing with two parties rather than one (and, therefore, does not have to win 50 percent of the vote to rule), and that virtually all ruling parties in democratic countries throughout the world have been voted out of office in recent years, one can easily say that the voters gave the KMT a victory. Most observers, in fact, came to this conclusion.

There were other reasons for speaking of a KMT win. The KMT got the most votes. The vote tallying for the gubernatorial and two mayoral races saw the KMT win 52.05 percent, the DPP 39.4 percent, and the NP 7.7 percent.[62] The KMT also reversed a decline in popular vote it had experienced in elections since 1991, while the DPP witnessed its first drop in popular vote since 1989.

The governorship, the most important race, the KMT won handily. Some called it a "landslide victory" for the ruling party.[63] James Soong won 4.7 million votes, almost 1.5 million more votes (of 8.5 million total) than his closest rival, or 56.2 percent of the popular vote, compared to Chen Ting-nan's 38.7 percent. He also took all but one of the 21 cities and districts in the country; Chen won only in his own home area. In addition, Soong won in a number of counties controlled by the DPP. In the Provincial Assembly contest, the KMT also won a comfortable majority of 48 seats in this 79-member body. The *United Daily News*, one of Taiwan's largest newspapers, reported that this meant that there would be "no radical change in the political landscape."[64]

The KMT also won the Kaohsiung mayoral race. Incumbent Mayor Wu Den-yih received 54.46 percent of the popular vote, easily defeating the DPP's Chang Chun-hsiung, who got only 39.29 percent. The NP got 3.45 percent and others won 2.8 percent. This victory was a special one for the KMT since Kaohsiung's population is overwhelmingly Taiwanese and has in the past strongly supported independence and the DPP. It was even labeled the DPP's "holy ground." Following the vote tallying, DPP Chairman Shih Ming-teh described the results as "too shocking."[65] In the Kaohsiung City Council race, the KMT emerged a winner with a majority of 23 seats in this 44-member body. This means Mayor Wu can probably function without serious opposition. On the other hand, the KMT also lost 6 seats in this body, while the other parties and independents all gained.

The ruling party lost 7 seats in the Provincial Assembly, or 10.7 percent of its strength. This hardly suggests a victory. Commensurately, the DPP gained 7 seats for a 8.3 percent gain (from 16 to 23). In addition, the NP gained 2 seats, its first ever seats in the Provincial Assembly. Independents kept 8 seats.

If these were not important setbacks, the Taipei mayoral race was. The KMT's candidate, Huang Ta-chou, won only 25.9 percent of the popular vote, less than the vote received by either the DPP's candidate or the NP's candidate.

The ruling party's performance here was called an embarrassing defeat by the media and most observers.

The KMT simultaneously lost its majority on the Taipei City Council, finishing with only 18 seats in this 52-member body—17 seats fewer than before the election. This represents a loss of over 38 percent of its representation and was viewed as a major setback for the ruling party. Clearly, the KMT will no longer dominate the political agenda in the nation's capital.

The DPP had some difficulty saying this election was a win. In the popular vote column in this election, the DPP overall declined. After the vote tallying, some DPP officials admitted the election was a defeat. On the other hand, the DPP gained in seats and won the coveted and important Taipei mayorship. To many DPP members as well as independent observers, this was important enough to conclude that the DPP was not defeated and maybe even came out of the election a winner.

The DPP's win in the first popular election for the mayor of Taipei in thirty years was significant by all accounts. Chen Sui-bian got 43.7 percent of the popular vote to defeat Jaw Shao-kong, the NP's candidate, who had in 1991 won the largest number of votes cast for any candidate in the Legislative Yuan election that year, as well as the KMT's incumbent Mayor Huang. Many called this a crucial and big victory for the opposition party. In fact, it would be difficult to make any other interpretation.

In the Taipei City Council the DPP also made gains: from 14 to 18 seats. And in the Taiwan Provincial Assembly and the Kaohsiung City Council the main opposition party won more seats: in the Provincial Assembly up from 16 to 23 (for a 8.3 percent gain), as mentioned above, and in the Kaohsiung City Council going from 8 to 11 (for a 5.6 percent increase). These were quite important gains.

It is more difficult to assess the NP's performance in terms of labeling it a winner or loser since the party was just over a year old at the time of this election and had never participated in a major election campaign before. However, some analysis can be made based on expectations as well as some other factors.

Many observers thought the NP had a good chance of winning the Taipei mayorship. Jaw Shao-kong had a fine political track record and was an energetic and effective campaigner as he had demonstrated during the 1992 Legislative Yuan campaign. His strategy seemed sound and he attracted large crowds at his rallies during the campaign—probably bigger than Chen's and certainly bigger than Huang's.[66] Thus his defeat was a big disappointment to his party.

Because of this, there was speculation that Jaw may have won the race had the KMT not recommended (if indeed the KMT did do this), that its members and supporters should vote for DPP candidate Chen Sui-bian when it became evident that Huang had little chance of prevailing. The KMT certainly appeared to have cause. Some well known members of the KMT in the Non-Mainstream (anti-Lee) faction had openly supported Jaw during the campaign, angering the KMT's Mainstream and Lee's supporters. Included were Chiang Wei-kuo, Chiang Kai-shek's son, and, some say former Premier Hau Pei-tsun.[67] The KMT leadership also tried without success to get the NP to end its campaign and rejoin the KMT. In any event, an official of the ruling party made an announcement to the effect that KMT supporters should vote for Chen, though it is unclear whether or to what degree top KMT leaders were involved.[68] This tactic surely made a difference, but whether Jaw might have won had this not happened is much more difficult to say. Chen won by a margin of more than 10 percent of the popular vote.

The NP elsewhere performed poorly, no doubt below expectations. In the governor's race and in the Kaohsiung mayor's race, NP candidates won only 4.3 percent and 3.5 percent, respectively, of the popular vote. The NP made gains in the Provincial Assembly and the Kaohsiung City Council races—from 0 to 2 seats in each—but these can hardly be considered of much consequence.

All was not bad news for the New Party, however. The NP did very well in the Taipei City Council race—winning 11 seats there. Moreover, it fielded only 14 candidates, giving it the highest percentage of winners among the three seriously competing parties. Perhaps even more important, the NP, as a result of this election, now holds the balance of power in the Taipei City Council. Neither the KMT nor the DPP has a majority, and for either to pass bills or take other actions, they will require votes of the NP's council members. Hence, the NP can claim at least one victory and will certainly accrue some political influence from that victory.

The voter turnout in this election was very high, 76.76 percent, signifying a strong interest in the election on the part of the electorate. In fact, the percent of eligible voters casting votes was the highest for some years. It was a very impressive 80.58 percent in Kaohsiung. The security and ethnic issues may have heightened voter participation. So, too, events leading up to the campaign period and during the campaign. Also, this was the first election of the Taiwan governor and the first election for a long time for the two metropolitan mayors. Finally, the weather may have helped. The high turnout, notwithstanding the reasons, probably indicates that elections have not become tiresome or that the voter has become apathetic.

The education level of the candidates was high. Two of the three most important KMT candidates hold a Ph.D. degree. James Soong received his degree from Georgetown University in the United States. All three DPP candidates hold a law degree. Chen Sui-bian graduated number one in his class at National Taiwan University, the country's best academic institution. The level of education of the winners overall was very impressive: 5.1 percent hold a Ph.d. degree, 16.6 percent hold an M.A., 53.7 percent have a B.A. or B.S. degree and 22.7 percent have a high school diploma. Only 0.6 percent have only a middle school education, and only 1.1 percent just primary education.[69] Nevertheless, the level of education of victor-ious candidates was much below that of the winners in the 1991 National Assembly election and the 1992 Legislative Yuan election.[70] However, the difference between the organs of government before and after the election was not so pronounced in terms of educational qualifications as had been the case in the National Assembly and Legislative Yuan after the 1991 and 1992 elections.

The age of candidates and winners was low. There was no candidate for governor or mayor over 58; 97.1 percent of the winning candidates in the Provincial Assembly race and the city council races were under age 60; and 77.1 percent were under 50.[71] This election, in fact, produced the youngest group of winners ever in a major election.[72]

There were 178 female candidates, including 1 each for the governor and two mayor races, 79 for the Taiwan Provincial Assembly, 52 for the Taipei City Council and 44 for the Kaohsiung City Council.[73] Although no female candidate won a major position, women won a sufficiently large number of seats in the Provincial Assembly (where they are guaranteed constitutionally eight seats) and in the city council races such that they obtained more than 10 percent of the seats without using the Constitution's "affirmative action" provisions for women.

Conclusions

This election was clearly one of Taiwan's most important. But, was it *the* most important to date? Was it *the* major step toward democratization of the political system of the Republic of China? Was it *the* most exciting election ever in Taiwan?

In 1980, Taiwan had its first competitive national election. Competitive democratic nation-wide elections started then. The nation held its first two-party election six years later in 1986—the first ever in a Chinese nation. The 1989 election prompted many observers to say that Taiwan had become a democracy, since the opposition party seemed to have some hope of acquiring power. The

1991 election was Taiwan's first non-supplemental election—meaning the "elder parliamentarians" who represented districts on the mainland had departed and the National Assembly now virtually represented only Taiwan (though there were seats for overseas Chinese). It was an election also that gave the ruling party its first democratic mandate and allowed the KMT to change the nation's Constitution. The next year, 1992, saw an even more important non-supplemental election for the Legislative Yuan, a victory for the DPP, and more speculation that it would be the ruling party within a short period of time. Which of these elections was the most important in terms of advancing democracy is difficult to say. Or was the election just held the most important? They all made major contributions.

The 1980 election, being the first competitive national election, was probably the most exciting. The 1986 election, the first two-party election, was also historically significant, as was the 1991 election when the DPP made independence a central issue during the campaign. But the 1994 election was close. Elections, more frequent in Taiwan than in most nations, have become routine, some say. Although this is certainly not so in the sense they have lost their air of excitement. This campaign was full of antics. There was also an unusual amount of violence. One observer said that the number of security people made it appear Taiwan had become a "police state" again. Yet few, if any, thought this was so. Few if any thought the election had not contributed to democracy in Taiwan or that Taiwan was not a democracy.

What about cheating, corruption, and especially, vote buying? Certainly all of these things were part of the campaign and no doubt affected the results in some ways. The amount of money spent during the campaign was astounding. Most candidates spent more than their counterparts in elections in the United States or Japan. Yet vote buying seemed to be less a factor than in previous elections. It had been given considerable negative publicity, and clearly candidates and their workers were intimidated by so many arrests. Voters in Taipei especially were probably not influenced very much by it. They made their decisions based on other factors. Island-wide issues and ideological positions, not to mention party affiliation, were more important than personalities, especially compared to past elections, thereby making vote buying a less effective tactic. The impact of television was greater.

More was spent on advertising. It was estimated that candidates spent up to one-fourth of their campaign budgets on media advertising, with newspaper advertisements taking the most money.[74] In fact, this election may have set a precedent in that respect. Future candidates may well allocate more energy and money to various forms of publicity.

Was the KMT hurt by vote-buying accusations? The ruling party has this image and it was obviously tainted by arrests and convictions following the last election, as some of these cases were still news. But the DPP was also implicated and the timing was particularly bad for the main opposition party. The party expelled several of its members just before the campaign. The NP used the corruption and vote-buying issues. But this was not an issue of enough importance to give the NP a meaningful edge. Many people shrugged off vote buying as a consequence of affluence. Some cited it as simply related to lobbying, which is something present in all democracies. Some even said vote buying was good since it put money in the pockets of poor people. All in all, it did not seem as much a factor in the voting results as it appeared it would. Meanwhile, the KMT was advantaged by its favorable financial position (the richest party in the world) and better organizational skills in this more complicated election and, in the case of the gubernatorial election, one covering a larger amount of territory and more voters. But the KMT's record was also good and its leader, President Lee, was very popular.

Did this election destroy the argument that a two-party system is evolving in Taiwan? Clearly this election was a three-party race in most respects. Yet it seems premature to say that Taiwan is evolving toward a three-party system. Voting districts, regulations on forming political parties, and a number of other laws help small parties and favor a multi-party system.[75] Yet other electoral laws and regulations, such as qualifying for television time and tax deductions, do not. They favor a two-party system. Moreover, the NP is still much smaller than the DPP. In fact, it is said to be a party that does not have supporters or influence south of the Tamsui River which runs through Taipei. Its political role, as a matter of fact, will be limited pretty much to the Taipei city government until the NP can build an island-wide support system and win some local elections. Yet it is literally a new party. It grew fairly impressively during its first year, which other minor parties have generally failed to do. It has a good record in electing a high percentage of its candidates. In this election, its "batting record" in that respect was better than the KMT's or the DPP's. Thus, one might say that its future is uncertain and Taiwan's political party system is still evolving.

As was true in the 1989 election and elections after that, external issues have had much more salience than in the past. In this election, foreign policy matters were much more important. The issue of stability and the nation's security were connected to relations across the Taiwan Strait and threats made against Taiwan by the People's Republic of China (of course, exacerbated by the publication of a book about an invasion, which nearly every voter heard about, and by Taiwan's troops firing on a village on the mainland during the campaign). The prospect of better relations with the United States was also on the minds of voters. The foreign policy issue helped the KMT, since it got credit for some successes and benefited from some sympathy at other times.

What about major domestic issues that influenced voters? The economy is always an issue in Taiwan's elections. But there was little new in the economic realm and certainly nothing to cause fear among the voters. The fact that the economy was doing well no doubt helped the KMT since it is the ruling party and is the party of the status quo. Meanwhile, the DPP probably did not do as well as anticipated with the pension and other welfare issues because of the growing realization that government spending has become a problem. In 1994, for the first time in many years, the government's budget was cut. High taxes and economic competitiveness, particularly for Taiwan's exports, seemed to overshadow the need for more government spending.

During the campaign, the KMT was frequently identified as the moderate party—with the DPP on its left and the NP on its right. Some called the DPP a socialist party, the KMT a capitalist party, and the NP a nationalist party. This, perception, of course, was a gross oversimplification. In fact, it might erroneously suggest that the KMT can solicit cooperation from either end of the political spectrum and thus in the future form a coalition with either if necessary, and counterpointwise that the DPP and NP will never cooperate with each other. This is far from the case, as has already been seen. Though it seems unlikely that the DPP and NP can cooperate in a major election, especially the coming presidential election, they will no doubt work together on issues of mutual advantage. It is hard to say what party alignments there will be in the Taipei City Council. DPP-NP cooperation is likely at times, perhaps often.

The ethnic issue proved to be more complicated than it appeared before and during the campaign. Clearly there was ethnic voting. But for a Taiwanese to vote for a Taiwanese was not that simple. Issues mattered. The DPP, which pushed this theme, is identified as a leftist party inclined toward socialism; yet most Taiwanese are conservative and live in rural areas. Most are in business or farming, professions that favor a conservative or rightist government. Most favor a secure political environment. Other issues of concern to voters were, moreover, juxtaposed beside the ethnicity of the candidate. Hakka voters no doubt identified with President Lee more than with the idea of voting for Taiwanese of Fukien origin. When the ethnic issue was used against James Soong, voters must have pondered: Soong has a Taiwanese wife; the two Taiwanese running against him have Mainland Chinese wives. Then, voters must have asked whether Taiwan now isn't ruled by Taiwanese: President Lee, a majority of the KMT's Central Standing Committee, Premier Lien, a majority of the cabinet, and the overwhelming majority of local officials are Taiwanese. The fact that the parties seemed to divide on ethnic lines with the DPP a Taiwanese party, the NP a Mainland Chinese party (though this is so only in Taipei), and the KMT a multi-ethnic party probably made the ethnic issue seem more important than it really was.

Related to the ethnic problem, the issue of Taiwan independence versus unification was clearly a campaign issue that benefited certain parties and candidates. It did not play as well for the DPP as anticipated; KMT candidates countered it quite well by pushing the security and stability issues. They also said it might unnecessarily provoke the PRC. Chen Sui-bian avoided talking about of the issue on many occasions even when provoked by his opponents. He even picked Retrocession Day (when Taiwan was turned over to the Republic of China by Japan) to state his views on the subject. He sounded like he repudiated it in the case of the Quemoy and Matsu controversy. With Taiwan heading closer and closer to the People's Republic of China economically while moving further away politically, it was difficult to say what the future might be or should be for Taiwan in this regard. Thus, when the KMT supported the status quo and called for unification sometime in the future, though this appeared to be a poor answer to such an emotion-laden question, it seemed to be the right position to most voters.

The DPP and the NP both sought to compete with the KMT. But in terms of geography they did not do very well. Most of the rural vote stayed with the KMT. This left the DPP and the NP to compete for votes in the cities. The KMT has an advantage in rural areas because of its superior organization and some say finances (to buy votes). Being an incumbent party with a good record also helps.

Vote splitting was more common in this election than in the past. On the one hand, that may simply have been a factor of three parties rather than two appealing successfully to the electorate. Yet, vote splitting may well become common in the future, making it more difficult to design campaign strategies and do voting analysis.

The polls were more accurate than usual. They accurately predicted the winning candidates well before the campaign period started. The pollsters may have been helped by the fact that broad issues played a bigger role in this election, as did ideology. Personalities were less important. Voters seemed to have decided earlier, not waiting to the last minute to make up their minds as they have done in some recent national elections.

What does this election say about the Legislative Yuan election that is coming at the end of 1995 and the nation's first direct presidential election in the spring of 1996? Many saw it is as a practice run. Others said it would be a bellwether and would enable observers to predict the outcome of these elections. This may be so inasmuch as the election showed what a three-party contest would be like in Taiwan. Likewise, it allowed the parties to practice planning for a large election. Also, broad issues and ideology will probably not change that much before the next election. But what can be said of a more specific nature? Certainly President Lee's ability to campaign and his popularity were apparent. Some have noted that he has never been elected by the voters to any high office and for that reason his ability to campaign and appeal to the voter may be doubted. Given how he helped candidates in this election, the fact that he was elected by the National Assembly rather than by popular vote would hardly seem to matter. The KMT's professionalism and its record on both domestic and foreign policy were important in this election and no doubt will be in 1995 and 1996. Yet predicting it a winner in the next election is problematic. Victors (meaning the winning party) in past elections have tended to become complacent after a win. There is also a history of cyclic patterns in Taiwan's elections. Similarly, Taiwan's political system is still undergoing change that makes forecasting hard. Voters are splitting the ticket. Campaign spending changed in this election, favoring political advertising; this may become a permanent feature in campaigning.

It does appear that James Soong's strong showing helped President Lee and will make it easier for him to win the presidential election, assuming he runs. Yet few have doubted he will win. It appears that optimistic predictions about the DPP winning either of the coming elections have been dampened somewhat. Yet much depends upon what the parties and candidates do on the job. Some KMT officials have voiced the opinion that they hoped the DPP would win the mayorship of Taipei as it would disadvantage any party to try to rule a city that is so unmanageable. Yet that stance may be more rationalization than good sense. Chen Sui-bian has a real opportunity to prove that he and the DPP can govern the nation's capital effectively and may win the confidence and support of the electorate in so doing.

Will one or more of the candidates, particularly winners, be propelled into the presidential campaign in 1996? Probably not. The winners have important jobs and promises to fulfill in these jobs. Moreover, campaigning will start too soon. Furthermore, James Soong probably could only be a strong candidate with President Lee's support. If Lee runs, as most think he will, this becomes an academic question. If he does not, it is uncertain whom he will support.

Whatever else may be said about the election, a proposition that can hardly be challenged is that it was a step forward for democracy. It also gave a new twist to the concept of national election (since it was bigger and more complicated in many ways than most national elections). That Taiwan may have to think about a three-party system, that elections are not simple, that Taiwan's polity is still evolving and external issues (which are difficult to anticipate or use) will continue to be important are also reasonable conclusions.

Endnotes

1. For details on Taiwan's earlier elections, see John F. Copper with George P. Chen,*Taiwan's Elections: Political Development and Democratization in the Republic of China* (Baltimore: University of Maryland School of Law, 1984); John F. Copper, *Taiwan's Recent Elections: Fulfilling the Democratic Promise* (Baltimore: University of Maryland School of Law, 1990); John F. Copper, *Taiwan's 1991 and 1992 Non–Supplemental Elections: Reaching a Higher State of Democracy* (Lanham, MD: University Press of America, 1994).

2. Taipei was named a special municipality in 1967 and the elected and standing mayor, Henry Kao, was appointed mayor. Taipei's status as the capital city and its large population—in excess of 1 million—were given as reasons for the change. In 1979, elected and standing mayor Wang Yu-yun was appointed mayor when Kaohsiung reached a population of one million and was designated a special municipality. Taipei has had eight appointed mayors. Kaohsiung has had five.

3. The constitution was amended in 1991 by ten Additional Articles and again in 1992 by eight more Additional Articles. The National Assembly subsequently distilled these articles into ten Additional Articles. Article 8 restates and clarifies provisions for the election of the Taiwan governor and the Provincial Assembly. Elected mayorships are not mentioned, since the regulations concerning this issue were changed by law originally and changed again by legislation.

4. See, for details, James A. Robinson, "Local Elections in Taiwan, 1993–94," *The Political Chronicle*, Winter/Spring 1994–95; also see Yu-shan Wu, "Taiwan in 1994: Managing a Critical Relationship," *Asian Survey*, January 1995, pp. 67–68, for information on the political context of these elections.

5. According to the constitution of the Republic of China (Article 113), a provincial governor is to be elected by the people of the province. In April 1948, however, a constitutional amendment was passed called the "Temporary Provisions Effective During the Period of National Mobilization for Suppression of Communist Rebellion." Subsequently the governor became an appointed official. In 1991, the National Assembly abolished the Temporary Provisions.

The position of mayor of Taipei was made an appointed office in 1967. According to the government and the KMT, this change was necessary because the nation's capital was more than just a city. According to the opposition, because a non-KMT politician had won the position and KMT feared he would use it to challenge the government or build a following and eventually run for higher office, it was made an appointed office.

The position of mayor of Kaohsiung was made an appointed office later—officially because the city reached a population of over one million and there-fore was a metropolitan city.

6. See Alexander Ya-li Lu, "Political Opposition in Taiwan: The Development of the Democratic Progressive Party," in Tun-jen Cheng and Stephan Haggard, eds., *Political Change in Taiwan* (Boulder, CO: Lynne Rienner Publishers, 1992).

7. See Ping-lung Jiang and Wen-cheng Wu, "The Changing Role of the KMT in Taiwan's Political System," in Cheng and Haggard, eds., *Political Change in Taiwan* , p. 104.

8. See Constance Squires Meaney, "Liberalization, Democratization, and the Role of the KMT," in Cheng and Haggard, *Political Change in Taiwan.*, p. 105.

9. See Susan Yu, "Law changes may delay governor, mayor races," *Free China Journal*, June 17, 1994, p. 1.

10. See Copper, *Taiwan's 1991 and 1992 Non-Supplemental Elections*, chapter 3.

11. Ibid.

12. For details on the KMT Congress and the formation of the New Party, see John F. Copper, "The KMT's 14th Party Congress: Toward Unity or Disunity," *Journal of Chinese Studies*, October 1994. The New Party was formed by seven

KMT members, six of them legislators. By the summer of 1994, the New Party claimed a membership of 40,000, though many belonged to other parties also since the NP allowed dual membership. For further information, see Susan Yu, "New Party showing gains, but leaders hope for more," *Free China Journal,* August 12, 1994, p. 3.

13. See Julian Baum, "Breaking the Rules," *Far Eastern Economic Review,* January 20, 1994, p. 14.

14. See *Keesing's Record of World Events,* January 1994, p. 39862.

15. See "Murder of Taiwan Tourists Sours Relations; Support for Taiwan Independence Reaches Record High," *Asian Bulletin,* June 1994, p. 31.

16. See ibid., p. 32. The number of people expressing pro-independence sentiment was the highest ever recorded in a poll taken in Taiwan—27 percent.

17. See Julian Baum, "Arms and Greased Palms," *Far Eastern Economic Review,* March 3, 1994, p. 14.

18. Julian Baum, "One Dollar, One Vote," *Far Eastern Economic Review,* March 24, 1994, pp. 27–28.

19. "Government Launches Anti-Corruption Campaign," *Asian Bulletin,* May 1994, p. 30. The alliance, on the other hand, denied it was a faction or that it wanted to change any basic KMT policies.

20. Ibid.

21. "CEPD, July equals eight months of green light," *Free China Journal,* September 2, 1994, p. 3.

22. China News Agency, September 3, 1994, cited in Foreign Broadcast Information Service—China (hereafter FBIS), September 8, 1994, p. 93.

23. China News Agency, September 6, 1994, cited in FBIS, September 8, 1994, p. 93.

24. See Susan Yu, "Pace of Election Quickens," *Free China Journal*, September 30, 1994, p. 2.

25. Julian Baum, "Show of Might," *Far Eastern Economic Review*, October 13, 1994, p. 24.

26. Julian Baum, "Face to Face," *Far Eastern Economic Review*, October 20, 1994, p. 29.

27. "Jaw refuses to go back to the KMT," *China Post*, October 12, 1994, p. 1.

28. Julian Baum, "Fast Friends," *Far Eastern Economic Review*, October 27, 1994, p. 30, and "38 may be charged in stock probe," *China Post*, October 27, 1994, p. 1.

29. "KMT lawmakers crush recall," *China Post*, October 21, 1995, p. 1.

30. "KMT to oust 3 candidates," *China Post*, October 27, 1995, p. 1.

31. Julian Baum, "Down and Dirty," *Far Eastern Economic Review*, November 14, 1994, p. 24.

32. Dennis Engbarth, "Taipei Mayoral Candidate Defuses Controversy," *South China Morning Post*, November 3, 1994, p. 3, cited in FBIS, November 3, 1994, pp. 60–61.

33. Susan Yu, "Opposing parties gear up for governor, mayor votes," *Free China Journal*, August 18, 1994, p. 2.

34. DPP leaders and candidates had often complained in the past about the short campaign period. But the public generally favored a short campaign because of the disruption it caused and the fact that Taiwan has so many elections. See sources cited in footnote 1 for further details on this issue in the past.

35. China Broadcasting Corporation, November 7, 1994, cited in FBIS, November 7, 1994, p. 80.

36. "Candidates nominated for poll," *Asian Bulletin*, November 1994, p. 25.

37. The Taiwan United Political Party was not an official party at this time. It announced that it had written a charter and planned to apply for party status soon. It was comprised of both KMT and DPP members. Its leaders hoped to appeal to people who were dissatisfied with the two main parties. For additional details, see "Campaigning for Mayoral Elections Reaches Climax," *Asian Bulletin*, January 1995, p. 28. The independent candidate was actually a KMT member who ran without the ruling party's nomination. However, he was categorized as an independent.

38. Susan Yu, "Race for Taiwan provincial governor gets under way," *Free China Journal*, November 11, 1994, p. 1.

39. "Governor hopefuls hold Taichung rally," *China Post*, November 11, 1994, p. 1.

40. Soong had visited 309 villages and towns in the province over the previous eighteen months. See "Strengths and weaknesses of the governor candidates," *China Post*, October 14, 1994, p. 2.

41. For further details, see Dennis Engbarth, "Governor Candidates Given 15-Minute T.V. Slot," *South China Morning Post*, November 14, 1994, p. 8, cited in FBIS, November 14, 1994, p. 93. Also see ibid.

42. Ibid.

43. Ibid.

44. R. L. Chen, "First gov't backed TV campaign takes place," *China Post*, November 14, 1994, p. 1.

45. Yeh Ching, "Candidates now calling voters," *China Post*, November 14, 1994, p. 1.

46. "Taipei mayor race in high gear," *China Post*, November 19, 1994, p. 1.

47. Ibid.

48. Ibid.

348 The Taiwan Political Miracle

49. "DPP TV station to go on the air today," *China Post*, November 18, 1994, p. 1.

50. "Lower insurance premiums promised," *China Post*, November 18, 1994, p. 1.

51. "Jaw hopes to build affordable housing," *China Post*, November 18, 1994, p. 1.

52. Stephanie Low, "Candidates campaign for attention," *China Post*, November 23, 1994, p. 1.

53. R. L. Chen, "50, 000 march for NP," *China Post*, November 21, 1994, p. 1.

54. "Reward for vote buying evidence," *China Post*, November 21, 1994, p. 4.

55. See "Election Tidbits," *China Post*, November 24, 1994, p. 4.

56. "Election Tidbits," *China Post*, November 25, 1994, p. 1.

57. "DDP cheats senior citizens: Lee," *China Post*, November 26, 1994, p. 1.

58. Yeh Ching, "U.S. poll result seen as benefit for ROC," *China Post*, November 11, 1994, p. 1.

59. For further details, see major stories in the *China Post* on November 10 and 17, 1994.

60. See reports in the *China Post* on November 14 and 22, 1994.

61. For further details on the incident, see *Wen Hui Po*, November 16, 1994, p. A2, cited in FBIS, November 16, 1994, p. 54.

62. China News Agency, December 3, 1994, cited in FBIS, December 5, 1994, p. 94

63. Ibid.

64. Cited in *Far Eastern Economic Review*, December 15, 1994, pp. 14–15.

65. Julian Baum, "Split Ticket," *Far Eastern Economic Review*, December 15, 1994, p. 16.

66. The media reported that his rallies were bigger. Many of those attending, however, may have been bused in from Taipei county, where Jaw had strong support, and were not eligible to vote in the Taipei election.

67. Chiang Wei-kuo openly endorsed Jaw. Hau Pei-tsun, when asked about a report that endorsed Huang, contradicted what Huang said.

68. This incident subsequently resulted in a legal suit that is still in progress. Thus, details about the incident are not available or are not clear.

69. Wen-hui Tsai, *Toward Greater Democracy: An Analysis of the Republic of China on TAiwan's Major Elections in the 1990s* (Baltimore: University of Maryland School of Law, 1994), p. 29.

70. See Copper, *Taiwan's 1991 and 1992 Non–Supplemental Elections*, p. 37 and 77. In the National Assembly elected in 1991, for example, 13.2 percent have Ph.d. degrees and 32 percent have graduate degrees.

71. Tsai, *Toward Greater Democracy*, p. 30.

72. See figures cited in sources listed in footnote 1 for comparisons.

73. "Candidates finish registration," *China Post*, October 15, 1994, p. 1.

74. See Stephanie Low, "Candidates spend billions on ads," *China Post*, November 15, 1994, p. 4.

75. For details, see John F. Copper, "The Role of Minor Parties in Taiwan," *World Affairs*, Fall 1992.

Chapter Eight
The Evolution of Political Parties
in Taiwan

Over the past two decades, a salient argument about the course of political modernization in developing countries has concerned whether political parties and party competition have played a vanguard role. The answer is generally no. In fact, some observers have concluded that the evolution of political parties is perhaps not as important as originally assumed.[1]

However, Taiwan is an exception. Political parties have evolved there. So has party competition in elections. In fact, the 1986 election in Taiwan is one of the few instances of a two-party election being held in a developing country that was not led to it by a colonial experience and/or by a mother country. It was, moreover, the first two-party election among Chinese people anywhere in any Chinese nation.

Inasmuch as Taiwan is widely acclaimed as a model of economic development, and more recently a model of political modernization, its experience with political parties and party competition in elections is likely to be seen among Third World leaders, and perhaps even Western scholars, as precedent-setting.[2] The evolution of political parties in Taiwan has certainly attracted considerable media attention, and to many appears to be the driving force behind the democratization process in this nation.

Prima facie evidence about the Taiwan experience indicates that a number of conditions facilitated the development of political parties and made parties important to political modernization. In general, political parties should develop rather late in the political modernization process; their growth should be evolutionary or slow; the government (and the official or ruling party) must welcome party competition (which means the ruling party must reform earlier than other political parties or at the same time); the citizens, and to some extent political leaders, must favor party competition and see it as a sine qua non for democracy; and the political system must be able to withstand and/or absorb competition and its accompanying disruptions.

351

All of these conditions seem to have been met in Taiwan in recent years. That being the case, one can say with some degree of certainty that political parties have become a permanent feature of the political system. All indications are that they will continue to play a central role in the democratization process. One may even say that, considering the present role of political parties in Taiwan, democracy has made a "breakthrough" or has already proceeded to a fairly high stage of development.[3]

In this chapter, I examine the "early" stages of party development (meaning before the 1980 national election), the development of party competition in the 1980 election, the "legalization" of political parties in 1986, the subsequent formation of the Democratic Progressive Party (DPP) from a group of independents and *tang wai* (meaning "outside the party," that is the Nationalist Party) politicians, and the appearance of additional political parties. I will conclude by assessing the progress made and the possible future courses of party development and the party system in Taiwan.

Early Political Party Development

Historically, opposition politics in Taiwan took the form of family or local competition in a feudal political system. Under Japanese rule (1895 to 1945), Taiwan was a colony and Tokyo discouraged the development of any kind of political opposition, save a late and half-hearted effort to prepare Taiwan for independence when it was evident that Japan would lose the war. Hence, before the end of World War II, political parties had not evolved in Taiwan and there was no organized political opposition that could easily or quickly evolve into a political party or parties.[4]

When the Nationalist government assumed jurisdiction over Taiwan in 1945 following the Japanese defeat, it brought with it the political party system then in operation in China. There was a dominant ruling party—the Nationalist Party, or Kuomintang (KMT). Party politics thus did not play a insignificant role in democratizing Taiwan's policy at this time; in fact, the Nationalists ruled Taiwan in an authoritarian manner much as the Japanese had done. Since new political parties were not allowed to form in Taiwan after 1949 following the Nationalists' defeat on the mainland and the KMT's move to Taiwan, Taiwan remained a one-party system. The KMT controlled the government as it felt was its role. It did not encourage and generally did not allow party competition (though there were two nominal opposition parties). A challenge to the KMT was usually viewed as subversive or Communist-inspired.

The KMT's dominance of the political system, however, was not without opponents and critics. Both grew out of widespread dissatisfaction with Nationalist rule after 1945, and particularly after February 1947 when the Nationalists suppressed a Taiwanese rebellion and killed a significant number of Taiwanese, including many local leaders. This opposition became broadly known as the Taiwanese Independence Movement, or TIM. Because it was seen as subversive, the government adopted various measures to suppress it. Hence, the TIM (including any part or faction of it) could not evolve into a legitimate political opposition organization or party. It, in fact, remained underground. This inhibited it's ability to become an effectively organized movement, politically or otherwise, in Taiwan.

Instead it organized abroad, particularly in Japan and the United States. From its foreign bases it supported opposition politicians in Taiwan. But this effort was not very effective. The TIM's overseas organizations did not coordinate their activities very well.[5] A further difficulty was that the TIM became faction-ridden. Some of its factions espoused radical views and sanctioned terrorist methods, including the overthrow of the Nationalist government by violence or guerrilla warfare. Others favored an evolutionary democratization of the political system that would eventually result in Taiwanese local rule but they did not have an action program.

The Presbyterian Church in Taiwan also became a locus of opposition politics, though for the most part it espoused the same anti-government themes as the TIM. Rather than acting as an opposition group itself (which might have developed into a de facto opposition party), the church for the most part helped the TIM. The Presbyterians provided the TIM with communications links and reputedly with foreign support. At times during the 1950s and 1960s, it was rumored that the Presbyterian Church and its missionaries had U.S. Central Intelligence Agency support and that it was for this reason that they advocated a two-China policy. This perception had two rather different consequences: First, it helped give the TIM some credibility which it needed. Second, however, it conveyed the impression to many in Taiwan that the TIM had foreign rather than local support.[6] Since the TIM's operations in Taiwan were largely a matter speculated about, neither view really evolved.

Because the KMT felt threatened by the TIM (and perhaps any opposition), it used its political influence to pass legislation (specifically laws based on the Temporary Provisions to the Constitution) that prohibited the formation of new political parties and restricted the activities of various other "civic organizations." Martial law enforced the Temporary Provisions; more than that, it intimidated opposition politicians. In this context the KMT monopolized political party functions.

Within a decade or two, the KMT began to reform and became a locus of competitive politics itself. By expanding its membership to include Taiwanese, the KMT enlisted, and then absorbed, many potential opposition politicians. Taiwanese did not necessarily abandon their opposition points of view when they joined the KMT and consequently infused the KMT with some internal "party" competition. This occurred gradually, but it increased in importance with time.

Hence, as the nation experienced economic growth and social change, and when it needed avenues of channeling varying political views into policies, the KMT was able to provide these avenues while not allowing other parties to represent or channel dissent. Conflict over policies was resolved internally within the ruling party. This arrangement did not fully meet the need for competition in politics; but it did go a considerable way, especially at first.

The origins of party competition (in this case meaning between or among parties) began with the appearance of independent politicians, who, discreetly or sometimes openly, iterated anti-KMT views. The most prominent was Henry Kao, who as mayor of Taipei became known as an opposition politician. In 1964, he campaigned for, and was elected to, a second term, whereby he gained even greater recognition as an alternative to the KMT. At that time, independents held the mayorships of three of Taiwan's largest cities (Taipei plus Tainan and Keelung). Independents also ran for and won a number of positions in local government and in the Taiwan Provincial Assembly.

In 1967, however, the government transformed Taipei (and later Kaohsiung) into special "municipalities" and asserted the right to appoint the executive officers thereof. This move temporarily halted what appeared to be a budding opposition movement. Nevertheless, independent politicians continued to provide the nation with a kind of cautious platform for opposition politics. In ensuing years, independents opposed the KMT in both national and local elections, though they did not constitute a threat to KMT rule.[7]

In the 1970s, social change occurred much more rapidly than ever before in Taiwan's history as a product of its miracle economic growth. Consequently Taiwan became socially pluralistic. This and other changes reinforced the need for a genuine political opposition. In short, social and economic issues increasingly had political ramifications, and political solutions were more frequently called for. Social and economic progress, as well as advances in mass education based on free-market capitalism, demanded democracy.

In 1968, national educational reforms included provision for nine years of compulsory schooling. This had considerable social impact. According to surveys conducted at this time reflecting peoples' own perceptions of their class status, 50 percent of the population considered itself middle class. Meanwhile, more than 40 percent of Taiwan's population became urban dwellers. These changes had the effect of breaking down traditional social ties and evoking new ones. A popular culture developed.[8]

With 1.5 million tourists arriving yearly and more and more citizens going abroad, especially to Japan and the United States, Taiwan was also more and more being influenced by Western culture and ideas. Better employment opportunities caused many former students to return from the United States, where employment opportunities had begun to decline. Their return reinforced the need for political change.

By 1975, independent opposition politicians began to organize. Huang Hsin-chieh and Kang Ning-hsiang founded the *Taiwan Political Review*—a journal that advocated democracy, opposition, and competitive politics. Other developments occurred, some sanctioned by the government and the KMT, some not. Independent politicians, who for all intents and purposes constituted an opposition, gradually evolved into the political "group" known as *tang wai*, meaning literally "outside the party (the party being the KMT) but implying a kind of club of independent politicians. *Tang wai* politicians began to develop a program, mutual objectives, and even a platform. They also campaigned for each other, even though election laws made this difficult.[9] By 1978, the *tang wai* was poised to evolve into a preliminary or proto-political party. It might have become a true opposition party had it not been for certain events that transpired at that time.

Clearly *tang wai* was attracting more of a following and support than the TIM had. There were very obvious reasons for this. The main one was that the TIM relied on violence and terrorism. In 1970, TIM activists made an attempt on then Deputy Premier Chiang Ching-kuo's life when he was visiting New York City. In 1976, TIM supporters caused a sensation when they exploded several bombs in public places in Taiwan. Several people were killed. The vice president's hand had to be amputated as a result of a letter bomb explosion. In 1978 a TIM-related movement known as the People's Liberation Front sent threatening letters to foreign businessmen, demanding that they leave Taiwan.

These events led to a crackdown on TIM groups in Taiwan. Whereas in previous years it had become easier for TIM supporters to communicate with their leaders in the United States and Japan, the government now made it extremely difficult. The TIM's activities, meanwhile, gave the impression to people in Taiwan that it was a terrorist organization (though this was only partly true). This reputation caused public support for the group to wane. Thus, the

TIM seemed to lose what hope it had of becoming a legitimate opposition in Taiwan.[10] The violent image also hurt the *tang wai*. While TIM was not linked with *tang wai*, and was eschewed by a majority of *tang wai* politicians, its actions had a negative impact on the *tang wai* movement because they led the government to take a less accommodating attitude toward political competition than it might have otherwise. Also, because of the violence image a large segment of the population formed a negative attitude toward political opposition.

In the meantime, however, in 1975 Chiang Kai-shek died and his eldest son, Chiang Ching-kuo, became premier. In 1978, Chiang Ching-kuo became President. CCK, as he was known, was a reformer and a populist. He visited the countryside every weekend and spent much of his spare time with peasants and workers. He gave amnesty to political prisoners. He launched anti-corruption campaigns and adopted measures to bring more Taiwanese into the KMT and the government; in fact, he recruited Taiwanese at a rate considerably higher than their percentage of the population to make up for past under-representation. In 1979, when he was elected President, he nominated Shieh Tung-min, a Taiwanese, to be his vice president. This turn of events weakened ethnic Taiwanese support for the *tang wai*.

Not only was there reform in the KMT "from above"; KMT activists also began to push for reform from below. One was Hsu Hsin-liang, who had garnered a reputation as an activist reformer within the KMT in the early 1970s. In 1977, after the KMT refused to nominate him as a candidate for the 1977 election, since many of the party's elders saw him as too radical, he ran on his own. Meanwhile, he published a critical memoir of his years in the Provincial Assembly and rallied a number of college students to his cause. Hsu won in an election marred by voting irregularities, evoking an anti-government backlash, later known as the Chungli Incident. But his victory was allowed to stand.[11]

Hsu subsequently brought together an intellectual movement that demanded that the government grant much broader political liberties and more democracy, and, in particular, allow opposition politics. Indeed, anti-government, anti-KMT magazines and other forms of expression flourished at this time. Publications were often banned or removed from the newsstands, but they usually reappeared or were copied and sold. Often, they had a bigger impact than they would have if they had not been banned. In the context of increasing demands for political freedoms, CCK's "reform from above," and in a country on the move economically and socially, political reform seemed unstoppable.

Considering the number of older KMT members who were resistant to change, however, Hsu went too far in his efforts to reform the KMT. Even some non-KMT politicians considered him too radical. However, his extreme views enhanced the position of more moderate reformers or progressives in the KMT. A progressive movement grew within the KMT and supported CCK's reforms; but it also created an independent agenda that would survive him and continue reform in the party after CCK's death.

The *tang wai* reached at a critical juncture in 1978. It may or may not have been accepted by the KMT and the population as a whole. One cannot be sure. In any event, in December President Jimmy Carter unexpectedly announced that the U.S. would establish formal diplomatic relations with the People's Republic of China, and that the U.S. embassy in Taipei would be closed. As a consequence, the national election, just days away, was canceled. The *tang wai*'s hope of becoming an opposition party was put on hold.

The loss of diplomatic ties with the United States (and the defense treaty after one year) undermined the credibility of the government and the KMT. Events favored more radical elements among the opposition who argued that the situation was desperate and required drastic solutions. As a result, during 1979 the *tang wai* split into a moderate faction headed by Kang Ning-hsiang (publisher of the magazine *The Eighties*) and a radical group headed by ex-political prisoner Shih Ming-teh and various of his supporters, including a core group associated with the magazine *Formosa*. The latter, in the context of what many perceived as a critical time, grew to dominate the opposition movement.[12]

During the summer and fall of 1979, the radical opposition, particularly the *Formosa* magazine group, expanded its following. In mid-December, the *Formosa* magazine group organized a demonstration in the southern city of Kaohsiung that turned violent. A number of police were injured, some seriously, trying to contain a street demonstration. Whether the "Formosa group" intended to initiate violence is uncertain. It had been joined by local gangs and that the police publicized this and (though no doubt exaggerated) their injuries and the scope of the violence and this influenced public opinion. The government cracked down and ordered the arrests of those responsible, including the *Formosa* magazine group and its leader Shih Ming-teh.

Initially, public opinion had favored the Formosa group, but its extreme views and the December incident frightened many people. The government took advantage of this situation. Those arrested were given public trials. In fact, they were given an opportunity to hit the government with a number of charges in court, especially for its authoritarianism, unfulfilled promises of democracy, and the country's diplomatic isolation. Yet the public sided with the government, giving it and the KMT an opportunity to eliminate some of the radical opposition and compromise with the more moderate opposition. This compromise paved the way for rewriting the election laws and holding Taiwan's first national competitive election in 1980, and thus helped Taiwan make the transition to having a real opposition and "party" competition.[13]

"Party" Competition

Taiwan had held "supplemental elections" for the National Assembly, Legislative Yuan, and Control Yuan in 1969, 1973, and 1975, respectively. These elections, however, were not competitive to any degree, not even considering the fact that a sizable number of independent candidates ran. Moreover, they were not significant politically, except that they caused Taiwan to be over-represented in the elected bodies of government that were assumed to represent all of China. However, they set in motion an important trend toward making these bodies represent only Taiwan, thereby becoming truly representative bodies of government. The 1977 local elections were characterized by "party" competition between the KMT and the *tang wai* candidates, but they did not have national significance. Moreover, few regarded these elections as setting any kind of precedent in terms of the electoral or party system.[14] Nevertheless, Taiwan had taken a step forward.

During 1978, President Chiang Ching-kuo initiated major steps toward creating more competitive and more meaningful elections. He forced the KMT to accept competition by the *tang wai*. However, as noted above, the 1978 election, which might have seen the beginnings of "party" competition at the national level was canceled. The confrontational politics that follow-ed might have escalated and had a de-stabilizing effect in Taiwan had it not been for the U.S. Congress passing the Taiwan Relations Act (TRA) in April. That piece of legislation restored the government's credibility and gave Taiwan an increased sense of security from foreign enemies—that is, the People's Republic of China. But, it also made calls for further democratization more urgent. The United States had for some time encouraged, or, more bluntly, applied pressure for, democracy in Taiwan; it was now continuing to do so more formally, de-recognition notwithstanding. This pressure served to strengthen the cause of the moderate reformers, especially after December 1979.

In May 1980, after the "Kaohsiung Incident" trials, but in the middle of serious public debate about the nation's future, the government wrote a new Public Officials Election and Recall Law. Government officials, particularly the Election Commission, consulted scholars, other experts, and the opposition. A number of contentious issues were resolved, many to the satisfaction of the opposition. Some issues were not resolved formally but proved amenable to "gentlemen's agreements." The new law did not legalize the *tang wai* as a political party. However, this was not a real issue since the *tang wai* could not really compete with the KMT anyway. Its organization was inferior, or at least incomplete, and its members knew relatively little about campaigning. The *tang wai* also lacked financing and suffered from internal factionalism and was engaged in severe disputes about the tenets of the party "platform."[15]

Nevertheless, an atmosphere of competition between the KMT and the *tang wai* developed in the course of the campaign. Each side had a platform, issues, and candidates. KMT candidates took credit for the nation's prosperity, high employment, equality of incomes, consumerism, and social welfare programs, and advocated a continuation of the policies that had created the present situation. The *tang wai* called for more democracy; more seats up for election in the National Assembly, Legislative Yuan, and Control Yuan; popular elections for the governor of Taiwan and mayors of Taipei and Kaohsiung; the legalization of new political parties; more government appointments for native-born Taiwanese; increasing scope for freedom of speech, press, and assembly; fewer campaign restrictions; the end of the "temporary provisions" and the emergency decree (or martial law); a break between the KMT and the government; and divestiture of public enterprises.[16]

Tang wai candidates went on the offensive. The populace of Taiwan was literally astounded by the animated, sometimes unrestrained campaign atmosphere. Observers were, in fact, flabbergasted by the unprecedented criticism leveled at the KMT and the government by *tang wai* candidates. KMT candidates were more restrained. They tried to appear dignified, calling for a peaceful election and stability, noting that these were essential to a functioning democracy. Most KMT candidates took *tang wai* criticism as constructive, or, when it was not, argued that the electorate would repudiate those candidates "who did not behave as gentlemen." Both sides became aware of limits to their approaches to the campaign. The KMT learned that it had to accept democracy. The country needed it and the electorate demanded it. The opposition learned that it had to be more moderate and realistic to win over the voter. Both found out how to deal with the other under the scrutiny of the public.[17]

The KMT won 63 of the 76 National Assembly seats up for grabs, for a score of 82 percent. Ruling party candidates won 56 of 70, or 80 percent, of the Legislative Yuan seats. After the election, KMT leaders claimed a landslide victory in an election that was for the first time open and competitive. KMT spokesmen asserted that they had won in spite of handicaps, such as the easing of restraints on the opposition. They, however, also perceived that the KMT was associated to much with the government in the minds of the public and therefore was blamed for mistaken government policies, even when the KMT was not involved. Clearly the election gave the KMT confidence that it could win in competitive elections. It likewise gave the Party's leaders a feeling that the public appreciated what the KMT had accomplished over the past two decades in terms of economic growth and political stability.[18] But they also sensed a need to separate party and government functions.

The *tang wai* also claimed victory, noting that its candidates as a group had done better than in previous elections. This accomplishment, their spokesman pointed out, suggested a trend toward even greater success in the future. The *tang wai* did not split, and it appeared that the public had not associated most of its candidates with the violence of the Kaohsiung Incident. Finally, several *tang wai* candidates, including some who espoused radical positions or were associated with the Formosa group, were among the biggest winners.[19]

Most radical candidates, and nearly all of those who based their campaigns on ideology, lost. The electorate sent them a message. Most of the successful candidates had a good educational background and experience in government and/or business. As a whole, the victorious candidates made the democratic process look good. Most of the candidates, particularly most of the winning candidates, were Taiwanese, thereby helping to rectify the imbalance between Mainland Chinese and Taiwanese in politics at the national level. The majority of the KMT's slate of candidates was Taiwanese, and most won. These victories furthered the image of the KMT as a broad-based party instead of a party of the Mainland Chinese.[20]

More important still, the election proved that competitive elections could work. In traditional Chinese culture, opponents are generally regarded as enemies, rebels, or traitors rather than contestants in the "game" of politics. This election, however, affirmed the possibility of a loyal opposition. Acceptance of this concept constituted perhaps the most vital step in Taiwan's transition to democracy. Also significant was the perception that the election laws had worked properly, although it became evident that further refinements were necessary.

Some observers viewed the election as evidence that the political system was, or had become, democratic "from the bottom up." They noted that long-standing party competition between the KMT and a unified or organized opposition at the local level had now reached the level of national politics. Many Taiwanese had claimed that previously there had been a bifurcated political system, with a Mainlander-dominated, authoritarian system at the national level, yet a relatively democratic system on the local level. Now, democracy might be said to have "seeped up." Many KMT and government officials of mainland origin felt that they, rather than the Taiwanese, deserved credit for this development. First, they noted they had prevented factionalism from destroying democratic processes locally and had laid the foundation for democracy at the national level by first affording a safe and secure environment where democracy could work. Second, they claimed they had engineered economic growth, which was a necessary precondition for democracy. In making these arguments, they cited the numerous failures of democratic "experiments" in other countries as evidence.[21]

The discrepancy in viewpoints did not really matter and was certainly not an impediment to further democratization. In fact, it may have been a blessing, since both sides could take credit for what had happened and focus on making further progress.

After the election, some claimed that it was not really precedent-setting. Because it was an "election holiday," meaning it was staged, it would not be repeated. But most observers thought it was more than a single incidence of democracy for the benefit of outsiders, particularly in the United States. Local elections in 1981 and 1982, another national election in 1983 (though not including election of the National Assembly), and a nationwide local election in 1985 all demonstrated that the latter view was correct. The 1980 election had indeed initiated a new, competitive party system in Taiwan.[22]

Clearly the *tang wai* had become the basis for an opposition political party in Taiwan. Yet it needed to evolve and grow before it could become real competition for the KMT. The government (read KMT) had yet to give the *tang wai* legal status. The events of the early 1980s and the mood of the population at this time suggested that the *tang wai* should be made legal. But that was another hurdle to cross; both the KMT and the public were still apprehensive.

The 1986 Election: The KMT Versus the DPP

The KMT's impressive performance in the 1980 and 1983 competitive national elections and the intervening local elections helped calm its conservatives' fears that the party could not win elections against a real opposition. Some even concluded that the KMT would be a better party by facing competition. Others believed that the *tang wai* could not rule the country, or in fact even improve its position greatly, without becoming more moderate on a number of important issues. This view, in fact, in turn helped convince KMT progressives to allow genuine and formal party competition. Meanwhile, pressure from various fronts increased for continued democratization.[23]

In early 1986, the government again up-dated and revised the Election and Recall Law, consulting opposition politicians and commissioning public opinion polls in the process. Officials also examined the election laws of a number of Western democracies. The KMT at this juncture not only started to dissociate itself from the government but began to play a more assertive role in political change, notably electoral reform.[24]

Meanwhile, Chiang Ching-kuo continued to send signals that democracy would evolve quickly in Taiwan. In early 1985, he publicly "pledged" that the "Chiang Dynasty" would end with his death and that a relative would not succeed him. This assurance implied that Vice President Lee Teng-hui would be the next president and would run the country, (though perhaps with the benefit of collective rule). Since Lee is Taiwanese, the announcement signified a possible transfer of political power to native-born Taiwanese. CCK took determined actions to ensure that his promises were fulfilled. He sent the only one of his sons who was rumored to be a contender for political power to Singapore. He also declared that the military would not play a role in politics in the future and took measures to see that this, in fact, could not happen. His actions included the transferral of several top military leaders, some to ambassadorships and others to different jobs out of the country.[25]

In early 1986, President Chiang ordered the formation of a twelve–member committee to study, among other things, the ban on the formation of new political parties. The implication was that the ban would soon be ended. Meetings were subsequently held between the KMT and *tang wai* leaders for the expressed purpose of working out plans for the legalization of the *tang wai*. Some, especially older KMT politicians, did not want the *tang wai* legalized. They reasoned that a more cautious and prudent policy would be to keep new political parties illegal during a "transition phase." Ironically, many *tang wai* leaders agreed, since they believed that their illegal status strengthened their image as an anti-KMT, anti-government organization and therefore helped them recruit new members. They could thus be certain of winning the 15 percent of the vote that is found in almost all countries that typically oppose the regime in power. They were concerned as well that if the *tang wai* became legal too easily, another opposition group, such as the TIM, might be able to win that 15 percent protest or opposition vote. But the majority of both sides wanted the *tang wai* legal.[26]

On September 26 (a special day being Confucius' Birthday), 185 *tang wai* leaders met in the Grand Hotel in Taipei and subsequently announced that they had formed the Democratic Progressive Party (DPP). Their action was technically illegal since the law banning the formation of new parties had not been rescinded or changed. However, CCK instructed the government not to take action. A few days later, in an interview with Katherine Graham, publisher of the Washington *Post*, President Chiang promised to end martial law and the ban on forming new parties.[27] Nearly everyone believed that the DPP would become a real party and compete openly with the KMT in the December election.

It did, in fact, just that. In November, the DPP announced a "party" organization and leadership. One of its top leaders declared that the DPP had a membership of 2,500 and that this number would grow to 10,000 within a year. DPP leaders then announced that they would break the KMT's "one party monopoly rule." They also declared that they stood for a welfare society built on the Western European model, wanted Taiwan back in the United Nations, and supported "self-determination" (meaning Taiwan's permanent separation from China).[28]

Chiang P'eng-chien was elected chairman of the DPP by a close and divisive vote that seemed to portend a split in the party. However, because of the pending election, strenuous efforts were made to keep the DPP united. DPP leaders and candidates were acutely aware that the public wanted a democratic election and perceived that party competition was a necessary ingredient. Interestingly, public opinion polls did not show support specifically for the DPP; in fact, they reflected public disapproval of the formation of the DPP. But the same polls mirrored public support for party competition.[29] Thus the DPP reckoned it had an asset that should not be squandered.

During the campaigning, DPP candidates were viewed by the public as representing an (or *the*) opposition party. The name "Democratic Progressive Party" did not actually appear on ballots, since the DPP was not yet technically a legal party, but the name appeared regularly in the press. The DPP also had its own flag and platform and, in essence, everything that legal political parties have. KMT candidates even referred to DPP candidates by that appellation.[30]

On major issues the KMT and the DPP clearly espoused different views. The DPP called for more rapid democratization; the KMT's calls for political stability tacitly endorsed only gradual changes in the status quo. KMT candidates advocated continued economic prosperity; DPP candidates wanted more economic equality and welfare. The DPP advocated a more aggressive foreign policy, but it did not offer alternative policies or even tangible ideas about what the country should do. DPP spokesmen assailed the KMT's "three nos" policy toward the People's Republic of China, but without advocating closer ties.

DPP leaders refused to reach an agreement with the KMT and the government not to advocate communism or Taiwan's independence. They knew that being associated with communism—to which they were in any case ideologically opposed—would only hurt their public image. They were also aware that "independence" was a highly sensitive and divisive issue even among their most loyal supporters, so they made reference to "self-determination"—advocating that the people of Taiwan should decide their own future. Learning from the 1980 election, the DPP eschewed ideological candidates. Thus, while maintaining an opposition image, they avoided extreme positions and practiced what might be called restrained sensationalism. They were likewise careful to avoid making too many promises.[31]

The KMT won 59 of 78 seats up for the Legislative Yuan and 68 of 84 seats for the National Assembly. The ruling party's margin of victory was just over 60 percent in both races, with over 66 and 60 percent, respectively, of the popular vote. A high proportion of KMT candidates were elected. None won without party endorsement, as had occurred in previous elections, including the 1985 nationwide election. In view of all these circumstances, the KMT felt it could legitimately claim victory.[32]

The DPP won 12 and 11 seats, respectively, in the two elections. This was double the number it had won in the previous Legislative Yuan election and 4 more than in the previous National Assembly election. DPP candidates were also among the biggest vote-getters. Finally, the DPP did not split.[33] Clearly the DPP had cause for celebration. It could, and did, claim victory. And its claims were in some ways more credible than the KMT's.

Observers considered it a two-party election—Taiwan's first. Pundits subsequently spoke of the evolution of a two-party democratic system. Most felt that democracy and two party elections were related. Almost everyone considered it an important, watershed event. No two-party election had ever been held in any China—not in the People's Republic of China, Hong Kong, or Singapore.

Still, it remained uncertain where the country was heading in terms of party competition and electoral politics. Whether the DPP was a loyal opposition or not was questionable. Whether it was a viable political party also was in doubt. There would be an opposition in future elections, but was that to be the DPP? Would the DPP split? Would other parties form and succeed? These remained serious questions.

DPP Factionalism and other Political Parties

Although the DPP remained united throughout the campaign and the election, as soon as the election was over internal strife became evident and the new party seemed in danger of splitting into two or more parties. There were, in fact, a host of serious problems that fostered centrifugal tendencies within the DPP.

One was leadership. The vote for a party chairman had been close, and it was divisive. In many respects, the outcome was a compromise. The DPP's most charismatic leader, Yu Ching, was still waiting in the wings. Clearly the issue of who should lead the party had not been resolved. Not only that, regional leaders appeared to present other challenges, and even appeared to be asking for local autonomy.

A second cause of tension within the DPP involved issues. The independence issue was both the most controversial and the most difficult to resolve. Some DPP members wanted to advocate independence for Taiwan; others did not, or only wanted to have the right to advocate independence. Still others used the term self-determination or advocated that the people of Taiwan should decide the future of the country. Neither party leaders nor the rank and file could decide. Yet neither could they drop the issue; it was too important.[34]

The DPP's relationship to the KMT was also a problem. Some felt the DPP's success depended upon winning the hearts and the votes of the anti-government, anti-KMT segment of the population. They feared that if the DPP did not keep its anti-government/KMT stance, the party would lose an important base of voter support. Yet DPP leaders, especially those who had been elected to the Legislative Yuan, had to cooperate with the KMT to accomplish reforms or even basic legislation. If they did not, they would be viewed as negative and obstructionist; the KMT would implement the reforms anyway and take full credit.[35]

Reforms themselves were a problem. Some DPP members enthusiastically supported them, even when proposed by the ruling Nationalist Party. Others automatically opposed anything the KMT put forth—reforms included. This dilemma was particularly apparent in the spring of 1987 during discussions on the termination of martial law. Some DPP leaders took the position that the new National Security Law was only a substitute for martial law: "old wine in new bottles." Others contended that martial law had indeed been terminated and that this created an advantageous, or even, some said, a "revolutionary," situation advantageous for the DPP.[36]

DPP leaders were also undecided about the party's role. Should they or should they not grandstand in the Legislative Yuan, and was it wise to promote or lead street protests and demonstrations? Some DPP legislators sought to cause problems, even chaos, in legislative sessions. As a matter of practice, some started fights. This activity attracted press attention and gave the DPP publicity. But in general it did not give the DPP a good image; in fact, it seemed generally to have the opposite effect. Opinion surveys at the time indicated that the public was becoming less rather than more sympathetic to most DPP methods. In particular, the public began to see many of the demonstrations as supported by DPP-hired hoodlums and opportunists.[37]

The DPP also experienced difficulties stemming from its relationship to the Taiwanese Independence Movement and groups and individuals connected to TIM in the United States. When activist Hsu Hsin-liang, who had TIM backing, tried to return to Taiwan from the United States just before the 1986 election, DPP members went to the airport in mass to meet him. They insisted that he be allowed to return and formed a protest demonstration at the airport, provoking a confrontation with the police. However, most DPP members did not want him back; he threatened to compete against the top leaders of the DPP for influence within the party. The DPP wanted financial support from anti-KMT groups in Japan and the United States, even the TIM; but DPP leaders did not want advice or competition from these groups. The question soon arose whether Taiwanese with U.S. citizenship should be allowed membership in the DPP. The DPP could not have it both ways and this became another cause of DPP faction-alism.[38]

Lack of DPP unity made recruitment more difficult. When it was formed, the DPP predicted it would attract a large membership within a year. In early 1987 it predicted a membership of 50,000 soon. It did not realize this goal. In fact, the DPP patently failed in recruitment efforts. Antics, which often struck observers as childish, violence and DPP unwillingness to cooperate with the KMT alienated many KMT progressives who had favored allowing the DPP more opportunity to compete. The media also began to criticize the DPP more harshly. Its leaders were ill-prepared to adjust to this situation.[39]

The emergence of other political parties was also a factor that hurt the DPP. Or, one might argue that other parties formed mainly because of the DPP's failure to become recognized as *the* opposition party. In any event, a spate of other new parties formed during 1987 and 1988.

In July 1987, when the Chinese Freedom Party organized to oppose the DPP, eight hundred people attended the inauguration ceremony. Though not competitive with the DPP for voter support, the Freedom Party engaged in pro-government, patriotic demonstrations (which the KMT was unwilling to do), thereby drawing some media attention away from the DPP. This offset the DPP's singular role as the party of protest that leads all activist demon-strations.[40] The Freedom Party also took up some of the same issues as the DPP—for example, corruption in the government. Finally, the formation of the

Chinese Freedom Party had the effect of making the DPP appear an extremist group while making the KMT appear moderate.

In September and October, the Democratic Liberty and the China Democratic Justice parties formed. Neither party attracted a large following, but the announcements by these two new parties suggested a continuing trend toward more parties as opposed to the evolution of a single opposition party.[41]

In November, Wang Yi-hsiung, a DPP leader elected to the Legislative Yuan in December 1986, left the DPP and formed the Labor Party. It started with 500 members. And, unlike the other new parties, it appeared to have considerable potential to grow. The Labor Party immediately gained the support of several unions. It subsequently won acclaim from a large number of workers by fighting for reinstatement of a worker who had been fired by the Chungshin Textile Company, and for opposing the revision of the Labor Union Law sponsored by the government Labor Commission. Inasmuch as the Labor Party's intellectual leaders opposed Taiwan independence and the party openly said the DPP's record on labor was poor, there seemed little hope for cooperation with the DPP. In fact, formation of the Labor Party threatened to take support away from the DPP and dash any hope the DPP had of building a base of support among workers.[42]

Following the formation of the Labor Party, another spate of new parties organized: the China Democratic Justice Party in October 1987; the China People's Party in November 1987; the New-Socialist Party (actually the reestablishment of a party formed in November 1947 in China); the United Democratic Party in March 1988; the Chinese Republican Party in March 1989; and the China Reunification Party in March 1988.[43]

These parties espoused a variety of political views and published a host of political objectives. The New-Socialist Party, for example, advocated unifying China peacefully, though it did not say how this could be done. It also came out for cooperation between management and labor and for abolishing the state-run Liberty Lottery. The Neo-Socialist platform propounded the political philosophy of Confucius and Mencius and claimed the support of an unspecified "two hundred top leaders" in Taiwan. The Chinese Republican Party, when it was launched, called for the "salvation of China and the promotion of world peace." It claimed a beginning membership of 1,748.[44]

As of mid-1988 there were several other parties in the process of organizing. These included the China Patriotic Party, the China Reunification Party, the Women's Party, and the China Farmers' Party. In July, the Buddhist Association of the Republic of China voted to form an election committee and back their own political candidates.[45]

All of the above-cited parties formed in violation of the ban on new parties just as the DPP had in September 1986. Most of them competed with the DPP more than the KMT. Some formed from factions of the DPP. All organized in large measure because of the new political system not only allowing de facto new parties but encouraging them to form. In addition, the DPP had failed to become recognized as *the* opposition.

Conclusions

A political party system has evolved in Taiwan in recent years that both embodies and promotes party competition. This competition first took the form of independent politicians running for office either uncontested or against KMT candidates. They were handicapped by not having a party organization and the help or support of other opposition candidates. So, in the 1970s, they began to organize. The resulting "outside the party" group, or *tang wai*, became the basis for party competition. Although the political system was built for and assumed only one party, it began to change or accommodate as progressive elements in the KMT saw the need for new parties to represent opposition views and to help the system adjust to the rapid economic and political development the nation had experienced. The success of the *tang wai* and the failure of the TIM reflected this process.

This progress culminated in a KMT versus *tang wai* competitive party election in 1980. Competition, however, was still informal since forming new parties remained illegal. Some observers noted that the gradual development of political party competition made the process work; others noted that party competition had fortunately occurred rather late in the political development process. Movements against corruption and efforts to support government efficiency, "affirmative action," democracy in local politics, and other changes preceded real or meaningful party competition. Many activists in this latter group argued that the preconditions for party politics were a secure environment, economic development and an educated electorate, all of which took time to realize.

Inasmuch as the nation was quite polarized on some important issues up to 1980, in retrospect it seems to have been wise to allow party competition only after the political system had undergone considerable maturation. Others point out that the nation was very divided on a number of important political issues in 1980 and that the election dampened strong feelings about these issues and undermined some radical views as the public repudiated out-of-the-mainstream candidates. In any event, the development of political party competition should, according to the "Taiwan model," come late rather than early in the process of political development.

A genuine two-party election impressed observers of Taiwan politics in 1986. In fact, it seemed at that time that a two-party system had evolved. But this was probably wishful thinking. The U.S. political system had been to a large degree the model of political development for Taiwan. Also, many scholars in Taiwan had assumed that a two-party system was better; it had a history of greater political stability than multiparty systems. Also, the opposition had to be unified to do well in an election, since the KMT had not suffered any kind of open split.

This was not to happen, or at least that seems to have been the situation. The newly formed Democratic Progressive Party was plagued with factionalism from the start. It lacked a strong and widely accepted leader. Disagreements on some issues caused the party to split. Meanwhile, KMT progressives began to represent some of the same ideas as the DPP—in many respects more cogently and certainly more rationally. Thus some of the impetus for an opposition party was lost.

It is also important to note that the public demanded party competition because it associated it with democracy. Political development, it was assumed, could not continue without party competition. Yet that did not necessarily mean a two-party system. Japan, viewed as a model by many in Taiwan, had a one-party-dominant multiparty system. Nor did public support for democracy translate into support for the DPP. To the extent that it did, the DPP frittered that advantage away. More accurately, the DPP was not ready to govern; nor was the public ready for it to lead. The KMT had a superb reputation for engineering economic development, social change, and political stability. Ironically, its success, not its failure, created public demand for democracy and party competition.

Another factor was the appearance of many new parties following the *tang wai's* precedent-setting announcement that it had formed the DPP in September 1986. The other new parties represented a wide variety of views and objectives. They seemed to mirror the fact that the public was uncertain where the nation was going in terms of a party system. Who should represent political change and who should stand as the opposition was yet to be decided. It also reflected the reality that when the ban on new parties was lifted, it was done so by presidential proclamation. It was not done by legislation that might have created the framework for a two-party system. In a sense then, the DPP's haste to become a formal opposition party may have been self-defeating.

Now the parties are testing the waters. Events thus far seem to indicate that the KMT will continue to rule and that the opposition will be divided and weak. In other words, the opposition will compete with itself for some time, or perhaps into the foreseeable future. Again, this is the Japanese model.

Thus, a one-party-dominant system seems to be Taiwan's future, at least for some time. A weak opposition seems preferable to most other alternatives in a number of respects. Chinese political culture has traditionally demanded a strong leadership, and the KMT has provided this. CCK's accomplishments and his memory now reinforce this aspect of Chinese political culture. Things may be changing, but this change will most likely be evolutionary, not revolutionary. Meanwhile, the KMT has become a large—perhaps a mass—party that represents virtually all large sectors of the population of Taiwan, including Taiwanese who in the past were alienated from the KMT.

Although party competition has been institutionalized, a loyal opposition that is ready to rule when issues and public support change has yet to develop. When that happens, perhaps a two-party or, more likely, a multiparty system will result. But that may be a decade away.

Endnotes

1. Jorge I. Dominques, "Political Change: Asia, Africa and the Middle East," in Myron Weiner and Samuel P. Huntington, eds., *Understanding Political Development* (Boston: Little Brown and Company, 1987), p. 44.

2. For a general discussion of political development in Taiwan, see John F. Copper, *A Quiet Revolution: Political Development in the Republic of China* (Lanham, MD: University Press of America, 1988).

3. Ibid.

4. See George H. Kerr, *Formosa: Licensed Revolution and the Home Rule Movement, 1895–1945* (Honolulu: University of Hawaii Press, 1974). Tokyo even discouraged the study of politics and other social sciences in colleges and universities in Taiwan. Japanese rule of Taiwan, in short, was efficient and the people experienced improved living conditions and political stability, but not democracy.

5. See Joseph Martin, *Terrorism and the Taiwan Independence Movement* (Taipei: Institute of Contemporary China, 1985), regarding the radical goals of some TIM factions. KMT efforts also split the TIM and caused disputes between its supporters in Japan and the United States.

6. According to many observers, a two-Chinas or a one-China, one-Taiwan policy was evolving in the United States by the 1960s.

7. See Thomas B. Gold, *State and Society in the Taiwan Miracle* (Armonk, NY: M. E. Sharpe, Inc., 1986), p. 91.

8. Ibid, p. 113.

9. See John F. Copper with George P. Chen, *Taiwan's Elections: Political Development and Democratization in the Republic of China* (Baltimore: University of Maryland Law School, 1985).

10. See footnote 5.

11. See Gold, *State and Society in the Taiwan Miracle,* p. 115.

12. Ibid, p. 117.

13. See Copper and Chen, *Taiwan's Elections,* Chapter 4.

14. Ibid.

15. Ibid.

16. Ibid, Chapter 5.

17. Ibid.

18. Ibid.

19. Ibid.

20. Ibid.

21. Ibid.

22. See John F. Copper, "Taiwan's 1985 Elections," *Asian Affairs*, Spring 1986.

23. There appeared to be various factors influencing the democratization process. A financial scandal in 1985 caused both the government and the population to reexamine the political processes. U.S. pressure on Taiwan to reduce repressive activities increased after the killing of Henry Liu in San Francisco (though he had spied for Peking) by a gang that implicated government officials in Taipei. Taiwan's per capita income reached $5,000—a figure that many political development theorists say produces pressure for political development.

24. See John F. Copper, "Political Developments in Taiwan in 1986," *China News Analysis*, January 1987.

25. For details, see John F. Copper, "Taiwan in 1986: Back on Top Again," *Asian Survey*, January 1987.

26. See "Politics in Taiwan, 1985–86: Political Development and Elections," in Hungdah Chiu, ed., *Survey of Recent Developments in China (Mainland and Taiwan), 1985–86* (Baltimore: University of Maryland School of Law, 1987).

27. Donald Southerland, "Chiang Envisions Change for Taiwan," *Washington Post*, October 18, 1986, p. A18.

28. See John F. Copper, "Taiwan's 1986 National Election: Pushing Democracy Ahead," *Asian Thought and Society*, July 1987.

29. Cited in ibid.

30. Ibid.

31. Ibid.

32. Ibid.

33. Ibid.

34. The DPP had consistently refused the government's request that it drop any mention of Taiwan independence from its platform or campaign. Some interpreted self-determination to be the same as Taiwan independence; some did not. Some used another phrase, that the "population of Taiwan should decide its future."

35. This issue split the leadership as well as the rank-and-file. Those who supported KMT reforms were labeled "traitors" by some DPP members. They responded that many DPP members were only capable of "grandstanding" and could not do anything constructive.

36. See John F. Copper, "Taiwan's State Security Law: Old Wine in New Bottles?" *Journal of Defense and Diplomacy*, October 1987.

37. Numerous newspaper articles in 1986 and 1987 made reference to the fact that many political demonstrations were composed of a large percentage of demonstrators "shipped in" from other parts of the country who were paid for their time. It was also widely reported that gang members, troublemakers and hoodlums were hired to demonstrate.

38. The DPP eventually adopted a policy of allowing only Republic of China citizens to hold membership in the DPP.

39. Some said that the DPP had been given a "grace period" from press criticism. DPP leaders cried foul when the media began to report widely on their failures to recruit, their internal difficulties and their contradictory policies. One particularly pointed criticism was that the DPP, which had long chided the KMT for its Leninist organization, used the same organization system for the DPP.

40. See *Keesings Contemporary Archives*, September 1987, p. 25378.

41. Ibid, February 1988, p. 35716.

42. *China Post*, February 13, 1987, cited in *Foreign Broadcasting Information Service—China* (hereafter *FBIS*) February 18, 1987, p. VI.

43. The formation of these new parties was reported in various issues of FBIS at the time the said party announced it.

44. See FBIS, March 1988, p. 66, and *FBIS*, March 10, 1988, p. 55.

45. *Free China Journal,* August 3, 1988, p. 3.

Chapter Nine
Opposition Politics in Taiwan

Opposition politics, or the presence of a meaningful and generally strong opposition, has been viewed by many writers as evidence of the growth of democracy in the Republic of China, or Taiwan, over the past four-plus decades. Opposition politics is seen as related to competition in the realms of interest articulation and interest aggregation and to a free press. An opposition party, or parties, is also seen as essential to meaningful elections and to reform in election politics. An opposition guarantees openness in government and helps ensure that corruption will not degrade the system and that important political issues are dealt with fairly and discussed within the public purview.

Inasmuch as most scholars in Taiwan agree that the country has made rapid progress in the direction of democracy—some saying faster than any nation in the world in the past decade—one may presume that opposition politics in Taiwan have played an important role in that process. It is also true that the political opposition and its organizations, especially political parties, have undergone considerable progress in the past forty-five to fifty years. Clearly, opposition groups in politics in Taiwan have assumed an increasingly important role over the years. One must certainly consider the fact that, inasmuch as Taiwan may be a model based on its achievements in political development, its opposition politicians, movements, and parties are worthy of study.

In addition to the importance and special roles of the opposition, a study of opposition politics reveals that, although the style of political opposition has changed and there are many new aspects of that opposition and many new entrants into the field as well, many of the old forms of opposition politics remain. In fact, some of the old opposition tactics and people compete with the new.[1]

Finally, the future of Taiwan's party system and the polity itself will be profoundly affected by the nature, thrust, and organization of political opposition groups in the nation. At this juncture, it may be predicted that the political opposition may fragment, resulting in a multiparty system. Others say it will coalesce, resulting in a two-party system. There are also options in between. Moreover, ruling party relations with the opposition will affect the nature of the system. In short, one may say that the future success or failure of opposition politics in Taiwan will determine its party system and will affect many of its policies, both domestic and foreign.

In the following pages I will assess the growth or evolution of opposition politics, the beginning of an organized and meaningful opposition in 1980, the subsequent proliferation of opposition groups, the strengthening of the opposition after 1986–1987, and finally, the future of opposition politics and their impact on Taiwan politics in the 1990s.

Opposition Politics to 1980

Before 1949 Taiwan had a tradition of political opposition to such a degree that Chinese historical records often cited Taiwan as a land of rebellion and a place of political unrest and instability. In fact, it was for those reasons that Taiwan was considered a place "beyond the pale of Chinese civilization." In other words, Taiwan was considered unruly.[2]

The foreign colonial powers—the Dutch and the Spanish—similarly found Taiwan difficult to bring under control. Their experience was that the local population was tough and resisted being placed under any kind of political or legal jurisdiction.

During the period of Chinese rule from 1683 to 1895, there were three major rebellions against Chinese authority, as well as frequent uprisings. Chinese officials did not consider Taiwan a favorable place to serve and often noted that Taiwan was difficult to rule because of political opposition. Some historians have observed that Taiwan had acquired a tradition of opposition from the Malay civilization brought to Taiwan by the aborigines, in addition to a tradition of resistance to authority found in Hakka culture. They also mentioned the fact that Taiwan has been quite cosmopolitan during most of its history, with ideas coming in that were incompatible with arbitrary government and that engendered political opposition movements.[3]

The Japanese also found Taiwan hard to control, notwithstanding the fact that the local population had been disenchanted with Chinese rule. However, there was severe factionalism in the local population at this time, in fact, to the degree that many citizens perceived that Japanese rule was preferable to local "warlordism." In any event, Tokyo used Draconian methods to pacify the population and quell any opposition to Japanese rule. The Japanese army battled guerrilla warfare for the first three years of their colonial rule and encountered frequent subsequent protests, even though Taiwan prospered and became the most modern and advanced place in Asia outside of Japan proper.[4]

It is also worthy of note that the local population of Taiwan twice tried to establish a republican form of government wherein a political opposition was formalized and legitimized. A home-rule movement also influenced Taiwan's politics for some time. Toward the end of the Japanese colonial period when Tokyo realized that it would lose World War II the people of Taiwan were allowed to form representative bodies and were given at least a degree of self-rule.[5]

After the war, the people of Taiwan chose to become part of Nationalist China—in large part because of the population's awareness of the constitutional movement in China and the vital (and legal) role an opposition played in that political system. The Nationalist Constitution, which Taiwan's local leaders had read, guaranteed various civil and political rights, including the rights to form political movements and conduct protest.[6] Though the rebellion in Taiwan in 1947 is usually interpreted as a reaction against an economic downturn and the oppression of the local population by Nationalist Chinese carpetbaggers, it should also be considered a backlash in response to unfulfilled promises of opposition rights and democracy. It was not possible for the Nationalists to deliver upon these promises because of the war against the Communists at the time and the fear that communism had made or might make inroads in Taiwan—problems that were not well understood in Taiwan.

After 1949, the Nationalists encountered few situations that could be categorized as revolt or even opposition to the government. Many have argued that this was true because the Taiwanese leadership was decimated during the military suppression of the 1947 rebellion and cowed after that. It is also a fact, however, that as a result of their defeat by the Communists on the mainland, the ruling Nationalist government adopted policies that were much more democratic and tolerant of a political opposition. The Nationalists allowed a formal and meaningful political opposition in local jurisdictions. It is clearly worthy of note that Taiwan had its first island-wide election in 1950, just one year after the Nationalist defeat and retreat to Taiwan.[7]

In the 1950s, opposition politicians were very active in local politics in Taiwan. The Nationalist Party and the government in many respects encouraged this for two reasons. First, Nationalist officials could play the role of intermediary in preventing local factions from engaging in destructive internecine struggles that would render local government unworkable. Second, the Nationalists were obligated to fulfill at least in part the Constitution they had brought with them. (In contrast, they rejected opposition at the national level because of the continued threat of communism.) Almost no Nationalist Party members or government officials advocated changes to the Constitution that would not allow democracy or even legitimize opposition politics; they simply said that the process had to develop in an orderly (meaning slow) process.[8]

Because of the nature of the political system in Taiwan—wherein local politicians can quickly move up to positions in the central government—opposition politics soon seeped upward. Another reason this happened was because the Nationalist Party sought to become a mass party and made strenuous efforts to recruit locally-born Chinese or Taiwanese; in doing so they recruited many new members with a political opposition style and mentality. Meanwhile, many of the Chinese from the mainland, especially younger ones, learned some ideas about opposition politics from the local population. They likewise began to emulate some of the ideals put forth in foreign political philosophy, particularly Western notions of democracies. They also observed the requirements for political change resulting from Taiwan's economic growth and the need to accommodate U.S. demands for democracy realizing the importance of Taiwan's military and political ties with the United States.

By the early 1960s, opposition politics in Taiwan had already risen into national politics. The most important manifestation of opposition politics was the participation of independent politicians in important elections and their rise in notoriety. Henry Kao, who ran for mayor of Taipei, built a career as a local opposition politician. Though he and a number like him were preempted or destroyed by Nationalist Party leaders who feared political opposition, they set a precedent that others could, and did, follow.[9] Political opposition also influenced Nationalist leaders to undertake reforms in the party and in the government to foster a fairer, more responsible, and more honest government. An attempt was also made to establish an opposition political party, but that was crushed. It was too early for the government and the ruling party to tolerate direct and challenging opposition parties; anyway, they were illegal under the Temporary Provisions.

In the 1970s, Taiwan's political system was influenced by rapid economic development and social change—among the fastest of any nation in the world. Foreign ideas also influenced Taiwan politically. Increasing commercial contacts, returning students (especially from the United States and other Western democracies) and Taiwan's need to compete with the People's Republic of China (PRC) for diplomatic status were all factors. Many also perceived that genuine competition in national politics in Taiwan was necessary, meaning democracy had to be realized and only in this way could Taiwan convince Western countries and the international community that Taiwan should determine its own future rather than being forced to unify with the People's Republic of China.[10]

Additionally, in the 1970s independent, essentially now opposition, candidates began to organize. They called themselves *tang wai* (or "outside the party"—meaning the Nationalist Party) politicians. Notwithstanding the law against forming new political parties, they established a platform, helped each other in elections, and acted like a political party. They evolved into what many observers said was for all intents and purposes an "opposition party."

Political Opposition, 1980–1986

By the late 1970s, *tang wai* politicians had become more numerous and better organized. They looked forward to the day when they could openly participate in politics, especially in elections in the form of a legal opposition party. Inasmuch as political modernization was proceeding at a rapid pace in Taiwan, many thought this time was not too far in the future. Not only were competitive politics thought to be close at hand, but many opposition politicians and activists perceived that they needed to push aggressively the case and even challenge the ruling party and the government.

President Jimmy Carter's decision in December 1978 to de-recognize the Republic of China and establish formal ties with the People's Republic of China, in the minds of many opposition politicians added urgency to the task. Others felt that, at this time of crisis the opposition should support the government and redefine the national interest in coordination with the ruling party rather than making an open challenge.

In early 1979 and throughout that summer and fall, the opposition movement split on this issue. More radical or aggressive elements, affiliated with the *Formosa* magazine, became very critical of the government's policies and the lack of democracy in the country. They felt that quick democratization was the only thing that could save the country since it would prove that Taiwan was different from the People's Republic of China and should be given a choice about its future. In other words, they perceived that otherwise Taiwan could not resist Beijing's overtures to discuss reunification and Taiwan would be absorbed by the PRC and Taiwan would suffer grave consequences. The situation, they thought, was urgent. The voices of moderate opposition politics were drowned out in the debate as the government came to view the opposition as opportunists and as dangerous. The KMT and the government perceived opposition politicians as fomenters of chaos, which would provide an opportunity for enemies of the government (meaning China) to take advantage of the situation.[11] They did not agree that immediate democracy would save the country.

This polarization of views got worse and in late 1979 during a planned protest march led by the *Formosa* magazine group in Kaohsiung led to a confrontational situation. Up to this time, public opinion seemed to favor the advocates of quick democratization. After violence broke out, however, the majority of the population—fearing chaos and anarchy—sided with the government. The opposition, seeing its mass support collapse, and the ruling party, perceiving that the situation had become serious enough to require compromise (meaning promoting democracy more aggressively), changed their views regarding accommodation with the opposition—which was not led by somewhat more moderate leaders (the radical leaders having been jailed or having gone into hiding). Though the government subsequently put several of the opposition leaders on trial for the Kaohsiung Incident, ruling authorities decided to negotiate with the opposition (especially more moderate opposition leaders) and proceed with an open and competitive election. They rewrote the election law and laid the groundwork for a different kind of election in December 1980.[12]

The 1980 election was thus a competitive one. It was the first such national election in Taiwan's history. *Tang wai* candidates criticized the government and ruling party in language never before heard in public. Issues were broached that were provocative. The campaign was truly an exciting, exhilarating political contest. Voters were utterly flabbergasted by many of the charges. Some were frightened.[13]

After the election, some opposition politicians charged that it was staged to impress foreigners and to make them think that Taiwan now had democracy. Others said it was an "election holiday" that would not impact post-election politics and would not be repeated. Yet the 1980 election had a lasting impact in terms of the opposition becoming, at least to a degree, legitimate and viewed by many as a loyal opposition.[14]

Kang Ning-hsiang, a member of the moderate opposition, was elected to the Legislative Yuan, and from "inside" continued to call for an end to martial law. His magazine, *The Eighties,* began publishing again. In mid-1981 the *tang wai* (now with some of the trappings of a political party) organized for the November local elections. The election was fair and went smoothly, particularly as judged by those who remembered the last local election in 1977, when violence broke out in Chungli, causing a major incident. This was not a national election, but it did indicate which direction the nation was going (and that was toward democracy). Other subsequent less important elections indicated the same thing.

In 1983, another national election was held. As in 1980, this election was competitive. Many observers spoke of the *tang wai* as *the* opposition. Others referred to the *tang wai* as a political party. This was Taiwan's second competitive and open (and to many, democratic) national election. It proved that the 1980 election had not been just a show or an anomaly, that competitive politics had truly arrived and that Taiwan had a real opposition.

The opposition fared poorly at the polls, however. It was factionalized between moderate and more radical opposition policies. Furthermore its leadership split on the same issue. Lack of realism and the absence of a good election strategy also hurt the *tang wai* at the polls. Many observers said the opposition had to regroup and adopt more sensible policies. Radicals were again in control. Kang Ning-hsiang lost his election bid and the radicals seemed to be in control of the opposition.

The *tang wai* had been beaten in what most called a fair election. Its candidates, however, said the election was not fair and that the "playing field was not level" because they were not a legal party and election rules discriminated against opposition politicians. *Tang wai's* desire for legal status and the election setback, which many blamed on the radicals, moderated its policies.

In coming months the *tang wai* found it difficult to respond to Nationalist Party reform initiatives or to take advantage of the ruling party's difficulties when they arose. The opposition began to realize more and more that the public wanted democracy and this meant an opposition party. But, how to translate that desire to the advantage of its own candidates was yet to be understood clearly.

In 1986, at the initiative of President Chiang Ching-kuo, three major reforms were promised: ending martial law, canceling the ban on new parties, and democratizing the elective bodies of government (meaning ridding these bodies of members elected when the government ruled the mainland or those appointed later to fill vacancies). Other reforms were also discussed, but the three cited above influenced the future of opposition politics most.

Tang wai politicians took Chiang Ching-kuo's promises seriously. Yet they decided that, in order not to appear as a party created by the Nationalist Party and the government, and thus under their control or beholden to them, they had to act even before the formalization of the law allowing the establishment of new parties. They also wanted to be seen as *the* opposition party and were cognizant that other opposition groups may try to form a political party. Hence they met in September 1986 and announced that they had formed the Democratic Progressive Party (DPP). They put forth a platform that was clearly different from the ruling party's and vividly an opposition one. Their leadership was of the same character and was even hostile toward the ruling party and government.

The Democratic Progressive Party entered the December 1986 election contest as a recognized political party and an alternative to the KMT. The press and the population considered the DPP a political party. Some, even most, viewed it as *the* opposition party. The ruling Nationalist Party tried to play down the DPP's importance, but they, too, regarded it as a political party, even though it was not yet legal.

As a result, the 1986 election was in practice a two-party election. This was the first ever two-party election in a Chinese nation. Singapore had never had one, even though it was considered a democratic nation. Hong Kong likewise had not had such an election. Certainly the People's Republic of China had not. Taiwan thus had, between 1980 and 1986, held not only competitive national elections but a national two-party election. Many even speculated that Taiwan now had an established two-party system and that the opposition had become fully legitimate and a permanent part of the political landscape. Many also said real democracy had resulted from this.[15]

Post-1986 Opposition Politics

Although the DPP doubled its representation in the Legislative Yuan in the 1986 election, most viewed the contest as a Nationalist Party victory and a poor showing for the opposition. Ironically, the Nationalist Party victory may have been fortuitous for competitive politics in Taiwan, as the ruling party gained confidence that it could win in fair election contests with a legitimate opposition party. Similarly, DPP leaders learned that they had to improve their campaign strategies and tactics and take more seriously their opposition role. More important, they had to decide if the DPP was going to be a "loud voice" (a term not at all complimentary in Chinese) opposition or a genuinely contending political party.

During 1987, younger, more radical members of the DPP gained even more control over the party's leadership. They sought to continue street politics and demand more radical reform. They also complained about the unfair advantages of the Nationalist Party and protested the ruling party's policies and its links with the government. Meanwhile, the Nationalist Party dampened DPP calls for reform by promoting its own reform package, which included a policy change allowing Taiwan's citizens to visit the mainland. This news caught the DPP off-guard. In fact, many of the KMT reforms created a dilemma for the DPP concerning whether to support or oppose them.[16]

In the fall of 1987, the DPP claimed 7,000 new members. But DPP leaders had called for the recruitment to win 50,000 new members.[17] The size of the party thus remained much smaller than hoped. In addition, factionalism continued to plague the DPP.

Meanwhile, in July 1987 the ruling party oversaw the termination of martial law. For years, martial law had been, according to virtually all opposition politicians and activists in Taiwan, the major obstacle to a genuine opposition, free elections, and democracy. It was also labeled a trait of autocracy and fascism and more. The DPP sought to label the move a meaningless gesture, calling the new National Security Law "old wine in new bottles"—meaning that martial law had not really ended (though there were other voices in the DPP about this). Legal experts, political observers, and the Western media, however, thought differently. Things had changed; this was a turning point. A number of DPP leaders also wanted to take a different tack: that the end of martial law presented a new opportunity.[18]

Although the law did not legalize new parties or labor unions strikes, it did remove what many called psychological barriers to open competitive politics and thus gave opposition groups a greater opportunity to organize and compete for support and votes in an election. It made for a much more free press and paved the way for important changes in the legal system.

In the context of a factionalized DPP and a political system that made it easy for small parties to form and a range of opposition voices, the end of martial law evoked the formation of a number of formal opposition political parties. In fact, within twenty months Taiwan had twenty-one new political parties.[19]

Several of these parties drew strength away from the DPP. The Chinese Freedom Party, which formed just as martial law ended, used the same media politics tactics used by the DPP. The Labor Party, which announced its formation in November, was organized by a disenchanted DPP leader. It threatened to attract Taiwan's labor vote, to which the DPP appealed, but with limited success. Other new parties tended to split the opposition, even though a significant number of them were right-wing parties that were disaffected by the Nationalist Party's "move to the left" politically. These parties hurt the DPP because they, like the DPP, engaged in street politics that the KMT eschewed and thus drew media attention away from the DPP. They also made the DPP appear more radical and the KMT middle-of-the-road.

Factionalism and the independence issue continued to plague the DPP. During 1988, in meetings in April and October (the annual party congress), the independence issue seriously divided the DPP leadership and the rank and file.

So did a leadership struggle. All of this aided Nationalist Party efforts to portray the DPP as a party of thugs and low-class rabble-rousers.

In May 1988, Taiwan experienced its worst outbreak of protest and public disturbances in forty years. It started when farmers began a peaceful protest to get the government to buy rice at higher subsidized prices and extend medical insurance to farmers. DPP activists and supporters joined by a number of hoodlums enlarged the demonstration while turning it into an anti-government rampage that resulted in injuries to 500 people. The incident alienated many middle-class citizens and polarized the opposition. It also created some question as to whether the DPP was in control of anti-government protest opposition or not. Some blamed the DPP; others said that the DPP played only a belated and secondary role.[20] In either case, the DPP had not benefited as it had hoped it would.

In mid-summer, the Nationalist Party convened its Thirteenth Party Congress. The ruling party at this meeting democratized its rules and procedures and for the first time elected a majority of Taiwanese to the powerful Central Standing Committee. In some ways the Nationalist Party adopted more democratic rule than many parties in Western democracies employ. And with a chairman and most of the top decision-making body Taiwanese, it could no longer be seen as a Mainland Chinese party. These progressive changes presented a challenge to the DPP.[21]

In ensuring months, other inauspicious events for the main opposition party included the emergence of more new political parties and the continuing feuding between factions within the DPP. Clearly 1988 was not a good year for the DPP. To most observers it appeared that the political opposition in Taiwan was seriously fragmented and would remain in that condition for the foreseeable future. This situation translated into Taiwan remaining a one-party-dominant system with a number of weak opposition parties. Understandably the DPP's prospects in the coming December 1989 election seemed dim.

This situation, however, changed in 1989. The ruling Nationalist Party and the government failed to handle the issue of unelected (meaning those elected when the government ruled all of China or their appointed replacements) members of the three elected bodies of government. In the context of democratization they were an embarrassment and the KMT wanted to get them to retire quietly. But most refused. The controversy grew and played into the hands of radical DPP politicians. The DPP seemed in this context to be the true advocate of democracy.

The situation in Europe also worked auspiciously for the DPP. Communism (a one–party system) was falling and democracy (a multiparty system) was replacing it. The new democratic forces were aggressive and radical. In comparison to Eastern Europe, the DPP did not appear to be making extreme demands. In fact, it seemed to be simply asking for reasonable progress toward democracy in Taiwan. It could even argue that Taiwan's democratization was too slow; the rest of the world was going faster. The DPP shunned the image of being too radical and a party of extremists who disregarded peace and stability in Taiwan, and world events helped in this regard.

Still another world event also facilitated the DPP's unity and its competitiveness in the December 1989 election. In June 1989, the People's Liberation Army (the PRC's military), acting on orders of the Chinese Communist Party, massacred students with tanks and machine guns in Tiananmen Square. The Nationalist Party looked very good by comparison and said so. More important, however, the DPP could argue that its call for independence or self-determination (however it was phrased), heretofore considered radical, was eminently logical in view of the PRC's treatment its "best and brightest." During the election campaign DPP candidates made a point of this. They cursed Chinese leaders in Beijing and burned PRC flags in public—almost always receiving cheers from observers. Thus, the DPP was able to turn the issue for which they had been long criticize—calling for independence—into one that worked to their advantage.[22]

Meanwhile, the Nationalist Party suffered an internal hemorrhage. In the spring, President Lee Teng-hui had to stand for reelection (by the National Assembly). This event underscored the undemocratic nature of the system since the National Assembly is the least representative of the elected bodies of government in the Republic of China of Taiwan's population. President Lee was challenged, and in the course of events bitter rivalries surfaced in the party, not to mention public criticism of President Lee by members of his own party. President Lee was forced to appeal to the unpopular National Assembly delegates in order to get the needed votes for a victory, which he did finally receive. The whole chain of events gave the public the impression that the Nationalist Party had problems and that many of the criticisms that it had leveled against the DPP were also true of itself.

All of these factors, as well as the DPP not suffering more internal problems, led to the feeling among the electorate that to have a democracy (which was perceived now as very important) there had to be party competition. Many, in fact, supported the DPP for this reason. Meanwhile, the other opposition parties failed to cash in or convince the voters that a vote for them would also further the cause of democracy.

The result: The December 1989 election was a big victory for the DPP. Although the Nationalist Party continued to rule, it had lost strength. The DPP gained. Other opposition parties meanwhile failed to perform. Across the board, they lost what strength they had in the elective bodies of government. After the election many commentators spoke of a two-party system again (meaning the Nationalist Party versus the Democratic Progressive Party). Some were projecting how many years it would be before the DPP would rule the country, given a continuation of the present trends, or discussing how the DPP could chart a path to win a majority in the elected bodies of government.[23]

Conclusions

Opposition to political authority in Taiwan has been a characteristic of its population throughout its history up to the present. This comes from its geography; its history; a tough, striving people; contacts with other parts of the world; and, more recently, the desire of the population for self-rule and democracy. It clearly cannot be said that the population of Taiwan is docile and lacks revolutionary ideas or energy.

Opposition politics in the modern sense was created by the Japanese. But it did not grow to become meaningful or to affect the policy. Albeit many scholars would argue to the contrary, political opposition was tolerated to a degree comparable to most developing countries under early Nationalist rule. This, in fact, made local politics in Taiwan quite democratic in the 1950s and 1960s. Democracy in local politics began to seep up in the 1970s, just at the time that the nation's economic development and social change (both faster probably than any nation on earth) created the need for democratic institutions. Thus were laid the foundation stones for the democratization of the national polity.

The transition from local to national politics, or a turning point, came in 1980 with the first competitive national election. At the time neither Taiwan's own leaders nor its population knew where this was going. Within three years competitive elections were viewed by most as a permanent part of the system. Taiwan had democracy in its national politics as well as in its local politics. Opposition forces had made this possible.

The opposition had evolved by this time from scattered local independent politicians who once in a while criticized the KMT, to better-known opposition politicians running in meaningful national elections (but usually not going anywhere or being preempted), to the creation of the *tang wai*—a loosely organized opposition party (though it was by definition not a party). The *tang wai* through the 1970s behaved more and more like a party; in the 1980s most voters in Taiwan assumed it was a true opposition party.

If it wasn't a real opposition party in 1980, it was in 1986, when it became the Democratic Progressive Party. The election that year was seen by both sides and the electorate as a two-party affair. This was doubtless a premature conclusion; but viewing the system as having evolved into a competitive party system was not.

The failure of the DPP to become *the* opposition because of factionalism and the ease with which new parties could organize after the termination of martial law in mid-1987, made it appear that a multiparty system was developing. However, if the ruling Nationalist Party continued to do well in spite of a real opposition, the system would change instead from a one-party system to a one-party dominant system with a weak and presumably divided opposition, as in Japan.

At the time of this writing, the structure of the political system is still changing and the strength and structure of opposition parties is subject to speculation. There is clearly, however, opposition politics in Taiwan. And that has changed the system to a democratic or near-democratic one.

Endnotes

1. See John F Copper, *A Silent Revolution: Political Development in the Republic of China* (Lanham, MD: University Press of America, 1988), for further details on this point.

2. See George H. Kerr, *Formosa: Licensed Revolution and the Home Rule Movement,1895–1945* (Honolulu: University of Hawaii Press, 1974), Chapter 1.

3. Ibid.

4. Ibid, Chapter 2.

5. Ibid.

6. This came from emulating the U.S. Constitution. See John F. Copper, "Taiwan: The U.S. Factor," in Ray S. Cline and Hungdah Chiu, ed., *The United*

States Constitution and Constitutionalism in China (Washington, DC: U.S. Global Strategy Council, 1988).

7. The importance of this is discussed in John F. Copper with George P. Chen, *Taiwan's Elections: Political Development and Democratization in the Republic of China* (Baltimore: University of Maryland School of Law, 1984), Chapter 1.

8. Ibid.

9. See Hung–mao Tien, *The Great Transition: Political and Social Change in the Republic of China* (Stanford: Hoover Institution Press, 1989), Chapter 4.

10. See John F. Copper, *Taiwan: Nation–State or Province?* (Boulder: West-view Press, 1990), Chapter 5.

11. See Copper and Chen, *Taiwan's Elections*, Chapter 5.

12. Ibid.

13. Ibid.

14. Ibid, Chapter 6.

15. See John F. Copper, "Taiwan's 1986 National Election: Pushing Democracy Ahead," *Asian Thought and Society,* July 1987.

16. See Tien, *The Great Transition*, chapter 4.

17. *Asia 1988 Yearbook* (Hong Kong: Far Eastern Economic Review, Ltd., 1988).

18. See John F. Copper, "Ending Martial Law in Taiwan: Prospects and Implications," *Journal of Northeast Asian Studies,* Summer 1988.

19. For further details, see John F. Copper, "The Evolution of Political Parties in Taiwan," *Asian Affairs,* Spring 1989.

20. *Asia 1989 Yearbook* (Hong Kong: Far Eastern Economic Review, Ltd., 1988), p. 231.

21. See John F. Copper, "The KMT's 13th Party Congress: Reform, Democratization, New Blood," in Cynthia Chenault, ed., *Modernizing East Asia: Economic and Cultural Dimensions of Political Change* (New York: St. John's University Press, 1989).

22. See John F. Copper, "Taiwan's 1989 Election," *Journal of Northeast Asian Studies*, Spring 1990.

23. Ibid.

Chapter Ten
Minor Parties in Taiwan

As of the end of July 1990, Taiwan had fifty-two minor parties.[1] In fact, all of the Republic of China's political parties may be classified as minor parties with the exception of the Nationalist Party or Kuomintang (KMT), and the Democratic Progressive Party (DPP), based on the size of their membership and their performance in the last national election.[2]

Taiwan has traditionally had minor parties; however, none ever seriously challenged the Nationalist Party in what was a one-party system before the 1980s. Minor parties likewise never constituted a real opposition; nor did any seem to have much hope of growing into a meaningful contending party. The impetus for new political parties to form occurred when President Chiang Ching-kuo indicated, in 1986, that martial law would be terminated and the ban on the formation of new political parties lifted. They emerged in mass following the end of martial law in July 1987.

Forming a political party in Taiwan is now easy, and as a result many new parties have been announced in the past few years. This trend will probably continue unless some legal restraints are applied. There is considerable doubt, however, whether one or more of the new parties will ever exert any meaningful influence in an election or in Taiwan politics generally because of the nature of the electoral system and what appears to be cooperation or collusion between the two major parties to prevent this.

The presence of a large number of political parties, however, in the meantime has prompted some observers to call Taiwan's political party system a multi-party one. Others argue—based on the miserable performance of all parties except the KMT and the DPP in the national election in October 1989—that Taiwan has a two-party system.

In this chapter I assess the presence of minor parties before and after martial law, their proliferation after martial law was terminated, the system in which they organized and now operate, the performance of the minor parties in the last election, and some other aspects of minor party politics. Lastly, some scenarios regarding the future of minor parties will be presented.

Minor Parties Before and After Martial Law

Taiwan had two minor "opposition" parties in the 1940s that originated on the mainland: the Young China Party (YCP) and the China Democratic Socialist Party (CDSP). At various times, observers thought these parties might gain in strength and become true opposition parties; this, however, has not happened.

The Young China Party is the oldest, founded in 1923. In April 1947, the YCP joined in a coalition with the KMT, winning 237 seats in the National Assembly and 14 in the Legislative Yuan. In addition, four party members were made commissioners in the National Political Council. After the government moved to Taiwan in 1949, the YCP left the government (or, more accurately, its close association with the KMT) and tried to become a true opposition party. It recruited locally-born Taiwanese and tried to win some local elections.[3] In 1960 two of its members joined in a failed effort to found the China Democratic Party, which was strongly anti-KMT.[4]

Since 1960, however, the YCP has been allied with the KMT to the extent that it is often called a satellite party. The YCP has received financial help from the KMT and generally adheres to the KMT line on domestic and foreign affairs—taking a somewhat stronger line on environmental issues, privatization, veterans benefits, and the reunification of China, however. The YCP has been recently represented in the National Assembly, the Legislative Yuan and the Control Yuan.[5]

The YCP's membership is estimated at 20,000—making it by far the largest minor party. However, it has failed to grow or attract increasing support from the electorate or from those active in politics in Taiwan. Since 1949, it has not received more than 1 percent of the total popular vote in a national election.[6] In the wake of ending martial law and the growth of opposition politics and a two-party or multiparty system in the 1989 national election, the YCP lost the two seats it held in the Legislative Yuan and its single seat in the Provincial Assembly.[7]

The China Democratic Socialist Party was formed in 1946 in Shanghai and fled with the KMT and the Nationalist government to Taiwan in 1949. At that time it was a coalition partner with the KMT. The CDSP failed, however, to gain even a semblance of opposition status after that. It suffered from lack of an independent platform, lack of voter support, and factionalism. It has had a small representation in all three elective bodies of government—the National Assembly, the Legislative Yuan, and the Control Yuan—and in local bodies of government.[8] But after the 1989 election the CDSP had virtually no such representation—losing the only seat it had in the Provincial Assembly. Its membership is estimated at 6,000 and is not increasing.[9]

In April 1986, after President Chiang Ching-kuo instructed members of the KMT's Central Standing Committee to examine the prospect of lifting martial law and legalizing the formation of new political parties, the die was cast to get rid of what was essentially a one-party system in Taiwan. As a consequence the YCP and the CDSP no longer served as a token opposition. Even before President Chiang's order evolved into legislation ending the ban on forming new political parties, a group of politicians known as the *tang wai* (or "outside the party"), which had functioned as a meaningful opposition in national elections beginning in 1980, had established, in September 1986, the Democratic Progressive Party (DPP). The DPP participated in the December 1986 national election as a "fully accredited party" in the minds of most voters and observers.[10] In the 1989 election the DPP "won" a startling victory with gains in every election contest and has since come to be regarded as *the* opposition by many political observers. In fact, it is viewed as the second of two major parties in a two-party system.[11]

Meanwhile, after the Legislative Yuan officially ended martial law in July 1987, a spate of new political parties appeared on the scene. By March 1989, Taiwan had twenty-one more political parties—for a total of twenty-five–parties. Twenty-three of these, however, must be classified as minor parties.[12]

There were several reasons for the formation of so many new parties. First, at this juncture, whether the Democratic Progressive Party would succeed in becoming a sufficiently strong opposition party to challenge the KMT was questionable. The DPP was plagued by factionalism and recruitment was not going very well, certainly not up to the announced expectations of DPP leaders. Moreover, it was having difficulties soliciting funds. Finally, the DPP did not perform as well in the 1986 national election as party leaders had predicted.[13]

A second reason was that the independence issue, which was a central tenet of the DPP's platform, stirred considerable controversy and opposition. In fact, a number of the minor parties that formed at this time did so in reaction to the independence issue; in other words, they opposed the separation or fragmentation of China and thought that Taiwan should be considered a part of China.[14]

Third, many political activists perceived that the KMT had moved to the left in response to foreign pressure and DPP prodding and in an effort to win what it perceived to be the vote of the silent majority in the center. Some also said that the KMT sought to take options away from the DPP by itself advocating or becoming socialist. Thus, most of the new parties that appeared at this time were right-of-center parties in terms of issues and ideology (though most of the parties were not ideological as such).[15]

Fourth, those interested in forming political parties often felt that neither the KMT nor the DPP represented voting groups or blocs that needed to be represented. This was true of the ruling party because the KMT took many voting blocs for granted. It was also the case for the DPP because of its dependence on the protest vote, which represented extreme views and interests but left behind numerous large interest groups that constituted genuine blocs of voters.

Finally, election laws in Taiwan were such that forming a political party was very easy. There were no real restraints on party formation; one could form a party almost simply by filing. Demonstrated voter support in an election, a meaningful membership, a budget, even party activities were not required. The Civic Organizations Law, passed in early 1989, further clarified the status of political parties, preserving the minimal qualifications for political party status. The law required that a party founder be twenty years of age and that the party have thirty members—hardly qualifications that would impede the formation of more parties or force already-existing minor parties out of business.[16]

The Chinese Freedom Party (CFP), which formed in July 1987, was an activist party like the DPP—except that it generally promoted views diametrically opposed to the DPP. Some said the CFP's central policy or purpose was to attract media attention away from the DPP and to engage in pro-government demonstrations that the KMT was unwilling to stage.[17]

A few months later, in November 1987, the Labor Party registered with the Ministry of Interior. A former DPP leader formed the Labor Party, stating that neither the KMT nor the DPP represented labor. With a large labor force in Taiwan that was not well organized by a union or unions and not linked strongly to any political party, there seemed to exist a good opportunity to represent labor and win labor votes. There were several intense labor disputes at the time that further aided the Labor Party's cause.[18]

Other parties of various stripes formed during this time. A socialist advocacy party formed. One supported Confucius and Mencius. Another called for world salvation. A Buddhist party was also founded. And there were many more.[19]

However, all of these minor parties—even the Labor Party—failed to perform in the December 1989 national election. The DPP did well, as did the KMT. The ruling KMT was hurt by serious internal problems and suffered from a poor campaign strategy. Its leaders later admitted "defeat," even though the ruling party won a large majority of the popular votes and most of the seats contended in the election. It thus appeared that Taiwan was heading toward a two-party system, one in which minor parties would play little if any role.[20] Some observers speculated that the KMT and the DPP wanted a two-party system and had conspired in some meaningful ways before and during the election against the other parties. The new election law, written in 1989 prior to the election, clearly discriminated against "frivolous parties" in some significant ways.[21]

But the law did not deter new parties from forming. In fact, the new election law seemed to encourage more parties to announce, as more new ones appeared immediately before and after the election. The reasons for these parties forming seemed much the same as earlier, although most of the new parties forming after 1989 were right-of-center parties and thus were reacting to the DPP election "victory," the DPP's advocacy of independence, its media-attracting antics, and its general promotion of controversy. Some perceived that the developing two-party monopoly offered new parties a special opportunity to represent interests ignored by the KMT and the DPP.

Party Approaches and Strategies

The minor parties that have formed in Taiwan since the lifting of martial law—both before and after the 1989 national election—have tended to be more ideological than their Western counterparts, notwithstanding the fact that ideological candidates had not fared well in election contests since 1980. The explanation is that it was not their major objective to campaign in an election and win seats in an elective body of government; rather, a cause or historical mission was the goal of most of the minor parties.[22]

Why? Because most of Taiwan's new minor parties were formed by intellectuals or unsuccessful politicians (or both) and leaders who have not served in office or were out of office. Most were in some way disgruntled. Also, many minor party leaders were not serious about politics in the normal sense of the word; rather, they sought to oppose the DPP, express patriotism, oppose the KMT, make headlines, solicit money, or use the party rubric to start a business or consolidate an existing commercial enterprise.[23]

Most of the new minor parties have been national as opposed to local parties and reflect causes and issues that affect much of the nation's population. They are generally not parties that advocate decentralization of political power or "states' rights" in the American sense. Similarly, the minor parties are generally not supported by religious groups or faiths, nor are they dependent on a region or a local political issue or issues. Hence, new parties cannot be said to cause national disintegration; rather the opposite, since most oppose Taiwan independence or localism of any sort.[24]

Because of the nature of Taiwan's electoral system—especially the multiple member electoral district system in Legislative Yuan elections and something less than that in county magistrate and other county office elections—minor party candidates, when they have entered election competition seriously, have had to be very selective. They have to seek to win offices where they can maintain their less than middle of the road status yet do not need to appeal to the electorate in general or a broad segment of it.[25]

The Labor Party and the Workers Party, two of Taiwan's most successful minor parties, however, are exceptions to the rule of not appealing to a special class and many of the other generalities made above. The Labor Party, as noted earlier, was established in late 1987, a few months after the end of martial law. Its founders were socialist intellectuals and labor activists. The head of the Labor Party, Wang Yi-hsiung, was a DPP Legislative Yuan member and a labor lawyer. The party's manifesto declared the hope that the party could become the vehicle and spokesman for Taiwan's 7 million-plus labor force. It supported trade unionism and sought to become a major political force like labor parties in a number of European countries. It was clearly the perception of Labor Party leaders that both the KMT and the DPP had failed to represent workers and were trying to appeal to business interests too much, and that it was therefore possible to attract worker organizations into their party.[26]

The Workers Party formed in March 1989, after breaking from the Labor Party. Its leadership was also made up of left-wing socialists, intellectuals, and labor activists. It broke with the Labor Party over both personalities and issues (considering the Labor Party too pragmatic).

Both the Labor Party and the Workers Party failed to perform up to even low expectations in the 1989 National election. The Labor Party ran a female candidate who had been a stripper. She undressed publicly during the campaign, promised an "open" campaign and challenged her opponent (also female) to a debate in English and a comparison of nipples. She was not elected. Many observers felt this discredited the Labor Party in the minds of both workers and the public.[27] In the same election, the Labor Party chairman lost in his election bid, as did the party's other candidates. Ditto for candidates of the Workers Party.

There are a host of reasons for their election failures. Most important, the DPP came to be perceived as *the* opposition party that alone could challenge the ruling party. It thus got nearly all of the anti-KMT, anti-government, and protest vote. Few voters cast votes for minor party candidates to promote democracy or protest current policies or conditions.[28] Both parties also suffered from last-minute KMT and DPP efforts to win labor votes. In fact, the two leading parties noticeably began to be more effective in attracting worker support shortly before the election. The Labor Party and the Workers Party also lacked grass-roots organization and financial strength.

Both parties, however, survived the 1989 election defeat. Both had sufficient membership to make them more serious contenders than the other minor parties. The Labor Party had an estimated 5,000 members; the Workers Party had more than 3,000. This compares to 1,000 or less for the other minor parties, excluding, of course, the Young China Party and the China Democratic Socialist Party, the two older minor parties.[29]

The remaining minor parties also failed in win many votes in the 1989 election. But the "two-party" election and the ill fate of minor parties in that election contest did not discourage most minor parties from hanging on or even new ones from forming. The primary reason was that most did not seek to do well in this election or any future election. Rather, they had other goals.

In the spring of 1990, ten to twelve of the minor parties came out in support of Lin Yang-kang and Chiang Wei-kuo for president and vice president, respectively, in opposition to President Lee Teng-hui. Most or all of these parties were right-of-center parties made up more of Mainland Chinese (those moving to Taiwan after World War II) than locally-born Taiwanese. Some also ran candidates for the presidency at this time, though their efforts were not considered at all serious.

In ensuing months there was little activity among the minor parties. They remain exactly that—minor, or perhaps even insignificant, parties. As of mid-1990 the fate of the minor parties appeared quite uncertain. It depended to a large extent upon changes in the rules regulating parties, election laws, and future elections.

Problems and Prospects for the Minor Parties

Taiwan's older minor parties, meaning the China Youth Party and the China Democratic Socialist Party, despite having a larger membership and better organization than most of the other minor parties, seem to have little hope of substantial growth or the ability to attract voter support and thus succeed at the polls. They seem destined to be viewed as adjuncts to the KMT and thus can offer little in terms of "another voice." Consequently it is likely that they will decline further in importance in coming years and will have little effect on Taiwan's political future.[30]

It could be different if the KMT experiences serious factionalism or splits in an irreparable fashion. One might imagine a situation in which one faction may see sufficient advantage in offering an alliance or partnership with one or both of these parties. Clearly such an alliance would not present serious difficulties for either side. Such a coalition might also include some of the other right-of-center parties.

One (or both) of the labor parties, however, appears to have better prospects of gaining membership and winning seats in an election.[31] Their success depends on a number of factors. One is the success, or failure, of the KMT and the DPP to represent labor in Taiwan. If the KMT and the DPP fail to attract labor, or damage each other seriously with the labor vote, the Labor Party or the Workers Party, or both, will benefit. These two parties will likewise gain by building better ties with Taiwan's labor unions if they can do this in coming months. Their future to a large extent will also be determined by the course of labor organization and unionization. This is clearly yet to be decided.

Both of the minor parties representing or trying to represent labor did poorly in the 1989 election; yet, these losses may not be particularly meaningful. Taiwan's political system in terms of electoral politics is changing rapidly, and one election does not seal the fate of a political party movement or candidate. The DPP has been counted out at times. Some were quite pessimistic about the DPP not many months after its 1989 election victory.[32]

The two minor parties representing labor may choose to join or cooperate in the future. Merging would give them added strength. Abandoning their socialist ideology would doubtless help in recruiting the labor vote. Socialism does not have much appeal in Taiwan owing to the fact that most citizens feel it promotes laziness and poor-quality production and thus would be contrary to the national interest. Taiwan must maintain quality control and efficiency to compete internationally, its economic growth being highly dependent on exports. Yet, Taiwan's workers seem destined to organize to a greater extent, and doing so probably means establishing ties with a political party or parties or even forming (or having) their own party.

One cannot be sanguine about the future of any of the other minor parties. They are too small, are not seen as serious, and have not performed credibly in any election. Moreover, they have in no way proven themselves to be contenders for political power and cannot offer their supporters anything in terms of spoils or rewards.

Still, the nature of Taiwan's political system—at least in the sense of allowing new parties to form easily and survive—determines that Taiwan in the immediate future will have a multitude of political parties. If legislation is passed requiring political parties to win a certain percentage of the vote in an election or gain a certain membership within a set period of time, then the minor parties will die. Or at least most of them will. KMT-DPP collaboration to kill the minor parties might certainly be successful especially through legislation that discriminates against them. A change in the voter district system could also have this effect; a single member district system would be disastrous to the minor parties, especially if they were required to win a certain portion of the vote to participate in future elections.

Yet, there are many reasons for thinking this will not happen. The DPP benefitted from the fact that forming a political party was easy. It is still having difficulties recruiting. There is a possibility it will split and thus become vulnerable to minimum voter support laws. Therefore, the DPP seems unlikely to support such legislation in the near future. The public opposes laws aimed at destroying the small political parties, labeling these laws undemocratic. For now at least, there is public support for allowing political parties to form easily and keep their present status.[33]

The minor parties would improve their election chances and their ability to influence political decisions in Taiwan if they were able to form a coalition or coalitions. And, while it seems unlikely (perhaps virtually impossible) for a large number to join together, for two to ten or fifteen to join forces may be feasible. In fact, several parties have already joined together in one or two cases.[34] Coalition politics among the minor parties hence seems to have some potential.

A weakening of the KMT's strength and a decline in its prestige would also help the minor parties, especially assuming that the DPP does not commensurately benefit from the KMT's problems. Inasmuch as the KMT occupies a big space on the political spectrum, the ruling party is vulnerable from both right and left, though the KMT is somewhat more vulnerable from the right since the DPP is seen as a left of center party. Consequently, most minor parties are rightist parties. If the KMT alienates conservatives, as has been evidenced in the past several years in efforts to preempt the DPP's platforms by taking up some of its campaign planks, a number of the minor parties may benefit. Clearly, the KMT has been moving to the center or left politically.[35]

If the KMT splits, one, or some, of the minor parties could immediately become competitive, especially if one or more could take over some of the KMT's support base and/or sources of financial power. However, the more likely possibility is that they will form a coalition with one of the KMT factions if and when the KMT loses a great deal of strength or suffers from a more serious factional split.

A DPP split would also be beneficial to the minor parties, particularly those on the left of the political spectrum. Several leftist minor parties might attempt to build a meaningful opposition to the KMT in the wake of a DPP "failure." Alternatively, leftist parties could align with a DPP faction or form a coalition. Or, if the DPP fails to gain in strength, they could grow to attain the status of an opposition party among a group of opposition parties—similar to Japan's opposition parties.

The evolution of some important election issues in Taiwan could also benefit the minor parties, or at least some of them. If the Taiwan independence issue becomes heated and divides the KMT and/or the DPP, or the two major parties are not effective in dealing with independence and try to be too moderate, conditions may allow some minor parties an opportunity to rise in popularity. Such a scenario seems more likely if the KMT shifts its view on this issue. Many of the minor parties, it should be noted, are "unification" parties.[36]

The environment is another issue that may benefit minor parties. Both the KMT and the DPP to some degree lack credibility on this issue. The KMT has allowed the problem to get worse "on its shift." The DPP has offered few serious ideas, and its leaders, many now in office in the counties, do not seem to be acting in very functional ways to support ecological improvement. The DPP has some links with the Greenpeace movement, though these ties may not last. In the future, a minor party may establish such links or an environmental party may form.[37] Another possibility would be for the movement to become unpopular, thereby hurting the DPP and causing it to disassociate from environmental issues. This development might pave the way for a single-issue environmental party to form at some future date.

There also are some interest groups in Taiwan that may want party representation and find the KMT or the DPP less than receptive. One example is the farmers.[38] Some businesses may see a need for more direct representation and thus decide to form a party or support a presently existing minor party. Representing business generally may be difficult in the future for the KMT. Both farmers and businessmen are represented by the KMT, but to many now well enough. Some professions may also want a party.

The possibilities for the minor parties, though not good, are not bad either. Minor parties thus seem likely to be around for a while. Conditions must change, however, before they can play a significant role politically in Taiwan.

Endnotes

1. This figure was provided by a member of the Election Commission in Taipei in August 1990.

2. Membership data alone may provide a different picture, as will be noted below.

3. See *Republic of China Yearbook 1989* (Taipei: Kwang Hwa Publishing Company, 1989), pp. 194-5.

4. See Hung-mao Tien, *The Great Transition: Political and Social Change in the Republic of China* (Stanford: Hoover Institution Press, 1989), p. 92.

5. Ibid.

6. Ibid.

7. See John F. Copper, *Taiwan's Recent Elections: Fulfilling the Democratic Promise* (Baltimore: University of Maryland School of Law, 1990), p. 78.

8. See *Republic of China Yearbook, 1989,* p. 195.

9. See Copper, *Taiwan's Recent Elections*, p. 78.

10. See ibid, pp. 45-59.

11. See John F. Copper, "The Evolution of Political Parties in Taiwan," *Asian Affairs,* 16, No. 1 (Spring 1989), pp. 3-21, for further details.

12. See *Republic of China Yearbook, 1989,* p. 197.

13. See Copper, *Taiwan's Recent Elections,* p. 61-62.

14. One can see this simply by looking at the names of the minor parties.

15. Probably 80 percent of Taiwan's minor parties are right-of-center in terms of their ideological tenets.

16. See *Tung Yuan Chan Luan Shih Chi Jen Min Tuan Ti Fa* (Law on the Civic Organizations During the Period of Mobilization) (Taipei: Ministry of Domestic Affairs, 1989).

17. See Copper, "The Evolution of Political Parties in Taiwan," pp. 16-17, for further details.

18. Ibid.

19. Ibid.

20. See Copper, *Taiwan's Recent Elections*, p. 78, for further details on this point. See pp. 93-95 and 97-98 for a more general discussion.

21. See ibid.

22. See Ya-li Lu, "Party Politics in the Republic of China on Taiwan," in King-yu Chang, ed., *Political and Social Change in Taiwan and Mainland China* (Taipei: Institute of International Relations, 1989), for further details.

23. Ibid.

24. Ibid.

25. This was especially evident in the 1989 national election.

26. See Tien, *The Great Transition*, pp. 102-3.

27. There was some speculation at the time that the KMT helped finance this candidate surreptitiously in order to embarrass the Labor Party.

28. Tien, *The Great Transition*, pp. 102–3.

29. Estimates of party strength are based on conversations with a number of observers of party politics in Taiwan during July and August 1990. I assume most figures published on party membership are not accurate.

30. This opinion is shared by most political observers in Taiwan. In fact, I have not heard a serious voice to the contrary.

31. Again, this opinion is shared by many experts in Taiwan.

32. This was noticeably true in Taiwan in July and August 1990. DPP leaders expressed concerns over financial problems and recruiting at this time.

33. I asked a number of experts, including both scholars and officials, about this. There was no consensus about where Taiwan was heading in this respect. However, most did not expect any change immediately.

34. Six minor parties allied to sponsor a candidate in the 1989 election, though this effort did not get very far. See *Tzu-li Wan-pao* (Independence Evening News), May 3, 1989, p. 3.

35. Some observers opine that this is the reason why most of the minor parties are right-of-center parties.

36. This is apparent from the names of many of the minor parties.

37. Several observers in Taiwan said this me in July 1990.

38. The farmers are represented by a minor party at the present time.

Section III
Foreign Policy and Diplomacy

Introduction

This section examines the foreign policy and diplomacy as well as the national security policy of the Republic of China from 1949, when the Nationalist Chinese government and the Nationalist Party, or Kuomintang (KMT), moved to Taiwan, up to 1996. The central theme is that, as is usual for developing countries, a more democratically formulated foreign policy with increased domestic inputs has coincided with Taiwan's political development. Diplomacy has also become more important while becoming increasingly more like public relations.

And yet, Taiwan's foreign policy was, from the beginning of the relocation of the Republic of China to Taiwan in 1949, unique. Taipei found its relations with Washington the key to its very survival. The United States became its protector. Coinciding with close U.S.–Republic of China relations and Taiwan's center-stage role in the struggle against communism, Taipei sought to represent all of China plus Chinese living outside of China—the Overseas Chinese—in the world community and in international organizations, including the United Nations—and, for some time, succeeded. Hence, Taiwan's diplomacy required public support and democratization. After all, the Republic of China was "Free China."

The Republic of China was likewise a front-line state in the East-West struggle during the Cold War. This status made it a focus of attention for the Western media—which expected more from Taiwan in terms of democratic political change and an open style of diplomacy than they did from other developing nations. The Western press criticized and often condemned Taiwan when expectations were not met. Taipei thus formulated its foreign policy and conducted its diplomacy under considerable scrutiny.

This being the case, the Republic of China's foreign relations were very important, even critical to the nation's image, not to mention domestic politics. Moreover, Taipei did not have the option of isolationism or even avoiding regional much less international problems. It became a member of the capitalist, democratic bloc and assumed many of the obligations of this choice.

Two other variables were, of course, critical: The People's Republic of China (PRC) was Taipei's enemy. The United States was its close friend and provider of aid and security. Taiwan's foreign policy makers recognized these two nations as more important than others. In fact, other nations were unimportant by comparison. This situation has remained true, although much has changed in "relations across the Taiwan Strait." Taipei's policies vis-à-vis Beijing can hardly be characterized as dealing with an arch-enemy anymore. Still, Taiwan is under Beijing's threat, potentially even an more formidable threat now due to the PRC's increased military capabilities. As a result, Washington's protector role remains critical.

As the formulation of Taiwan's foreign policy made the transition from an autocratic to a democratic style with the evolution of political development, leaders in Taipei found it convenient to boast of democracy in Taiwan and use its new image to cope with, or parry, Beijing's claim that Taiwan is its property and its pressure to negotiate reunification. Almost whenever this question was broached leaders in Taipei would respond that they represented a democratic nation and the people should decide. Obviously the populace was undecided; so were the nation's leaders. Thus, resolving the matter of being a "divided nation"—that is, the question of whether there are two Chinas or one, or whether Taiwan should be an independent nation or unified with China—had to be postponed.

Taiwan's economic development was also a determining factor in its foreign policy making. It made Taiwan a success story, especially in comparison to the People's Republic of China. It gave Taipei economic clout. It also reinforced the continued pursuit of democracy and a democratic foreign policy. Part of the reason economic development engendered a democratic foreign policy was that Taiwan had become dependent upon the Western nations' markets and penetrated by Western ideas. At first this was troublesome; later it proved very advantageous. Taipei was apprehensive about it when it wanted to restrain the process of democratization or felt threatened by it. Otherwise it liked it. With the coming of the new world order, Taiwan's economic power and influence became even more important and Taipei talked about this. How can it be denied a meaningful global role and/or be isolated by Beijing when it is such an important economic player? The answer, thought Taiwan's policy makers, was axiomatic.

Likewise, Taipei could ask the world community to respect its right to decide. Democratization in Taiwan began to accelerate at nearly the same time the Republic of China was "expelled" from the United Nations and became seriously isolated on the world stage. Taiwan thus used its new status as a democratizing nation, or a fledgling democracy, to seek sympathy from members of the world community, and, especially, for its right to choose its future status (whether a sovereign nation or part of China, or something in between). To a large extent it was successful in this effort. More recently, it has managed to embarrass the world community by making a bid to participate in the United Nations and other international organizations: the new world order supposedly being non-ideological, and universal.

Unlike other aspects of its foreign policy making, Taiwan's security policies remain basically unchanged in terms of enemies. Clearly the new world order, which is supposed to be peaceful, has not provided Taiwan with a less threatening external environment. In fact, since the People's Republic of China has lost its main enemy (the Soviet Union), it can, and it has, repositioned its military forces to focus on the Taiwan Strait and intimidate or coerce Taiwan even more.

This being the case, Taipei has had to maintain an even higher level of military readiness and buy more and better weapons and/or build its own, while giving security considerations an even more central role in foreign policy formulation. This requirement in turn affects the domestic debate about democracy. In the context of Beijing's threats, is it wise to declare independence? Probably not. Is it wise to consider reunification? Similarly, probably not. Certainly Taiwan cannot get a good bargain under duress. Since Taiwan's political system hinges on its status as a sovereign nation, or not, its policies toward Beijing impact its domestic politics at the core.

The importance of the United States economically to Taiwan has declined; yet in terms of Taiwan's security Washington is still critical. It is a fact that if the People's Republic of China were to launch an invasion of Taiwan, without the interference of U.S. forces, it would succeed. If the United States intervened, it would not succeed. Washington thus holds the key to Taiwan's future, which Taipei duly recognizes.

The first chapter in this section deals with Taipei's policy strategy vis-à-vis the two nations that are most important to it: the United States and the People's Republic of China. This piece focuses on the 1970s, when Taiwan had to adjust to the loss of the China seat in the United Nations, the subsequent decrease in the number of nations maintaining diplomatic relations with Taipei, and finally, the end of formal ties with the United States, its only superpower ally and best friend. This article should serve as a useful background reference for the next chapters.

Chapter 2 is about the Fishing Islands, or the Senkaku Islands (in Japanese), or the Tiaoyutai Islands (in Chinese). In 1971, these uninhabited islands 100 miles north of Taiwan became the focus of controversy because they were soon going to be returned by the United States to Japan along with the "rest of" the Ryukyu Chain. Moreover, it was reported that there were large undersea deposits of oil near them. The islands, which were not geologically part of the Ryukyu Islands, were claimed by Taiwan based on use and because they were part of the mainland continental shelf and Taiwan claimed China. Beijing also staked a claim. The dispute marked the first time public opinion in Taiwan influenced foreign policy, though in this case the public's reaction was not that spontaneous. The issue is also of interest because it has not been resolved, though Taiwan no longer makes serious claim to the island.

The third chapter concerns Taiwan's strategic or global alternatives in coping with the problem of the United States "abandoning" Taiwan in 1979. On the heels of Taipei being "expelled" from the United Nations, Taipei lost ground fast in the war with Beijing for diplomatic relations. This was traumatizing. Taipei's options, as many saw its situation, were: (1) to establish ties with the Soviet Union; (2) to go nuclear (i.e., build an atomic bomb); and (3) to declare independence. Though all of these options involved serious downsides, and Taiwan's policy makers never seriously considered any of them, an examination of these possible policies is nevertheless instructive. Interestingly, these choices are still around, though Taipei is no more serious about them and is pursuing other policies instead.

Chapter 4 focuses on Taiwan's legal status. In the context of its inability to make a credible claim to represent China in the global community beginning in the 1960s and much more seriously in the 1970s, and with Beijing aggressively pursuing claim to Taiwan, the question arose: Does Taiwan belong to China? Or can it claim national sovereignty? Based upon both the traditional definition of nation-state and the modern definition (altered by recent practice and United Nations actions), the Republic of China, or Taiwan (if it wishes to change its name, which is not really relevant to its legal status), can easily claim nation-state status. In short, Beijing's claim to Taiwan is weak.

Chapter 5 discusses the Taiwan Relations Act (TRA). In the wake of the U.S. decision to break diplomatic ties with the Republic of China, actions taken by the U.S. Congress repaired or reestablished relations through legislation setting forth specific policy toward Taiwan. (Incidentally, the United States had never before severed formal relations with a nation with which it was on friendly term. Nor had the Congress ever written a law setting the parameters for U.S. foreign relations with a specific country.) The TRA spoke of Taiwan as a legally constituted nation-state, although it avoided using the term Republic of China. By so acting, Congress created a second China policy (in contrast to the China policy of the White House) or two U.S. China policies, and, according to some, reestablished needed ambiguity in America's China policy. Though Taipei liked the TRA and felt it restored its sovereignty in U.S. eyes and offered America's protection after the defense treaty was allowed to lapse, its leaders did not often praise the TRA because of its wording—using the terms "Taiwan" or the "people of Taiwan," rather than Republic of China.

Chapter 6 assesses the August Communiqué negotiated between the United States and the People's Republic of China in 1982. In this agreement the U.S. pledged to decrease and eventually end arms sales to Taiwan. This contradicted provisions in the Taiwan Relations Act and was seen by some as a "sellout" of Taiwan. Since leaders on both sides said things immediately that repudiated it, or at minimum presented very different interpretations of it and talked about assumptions or conditions, others questioned the significance of the agreement and whether it was in any way ominous for Taiwan. Some said it was merely an effort by the Reagan administration to succor Deng Xiaoping who was America's friend and was under attack by opponents at home who wanted to make issue of Taiwan and weaken his leadership. Still others said it constituted a needed adjustment in U.S-China relations which had become too close given the realities of national interests on both sides and the nature of international politics.

Chapter 7 analyzes Taiwan's diminishing diplomatic ties at this time and its diplomatic isolation in the wake of its loss of the U.N. seat and U.S. ties. The 1970s and early 1980s were a low point in terms of Taiwan's diplomatic setbacks. Subsequently, Taiwan began to recover. It did this by substituting informal relations for formal diplomatic ties and through flexibility in its foreign policy. It also had economic clout and began to be regarded a democracy. Both were clearly to its advantage. By the early 1990s, it was clear that Taiwan was not isolated and was not going to be.

The subject of Chapter 8 is Taiwan's security. Taiwan is a nation under threat by a nearby (100 miles away) major power, the People's Republic of China, that says Taiwan's government is illegitimate and claims its territory. Moreover, Beijing frequently reiterates a much earlier-stated vow to "liberate" Taiwan by military force and sends agents to Taiwan to engage in spying and espionage. Hence it is natural that security concerns impact Taipei's foreign policy making process. This must be understood to comprehend Taiwan's foreign policy and diplomacy.

Chapter 9 considers whether the Taiwan Relations Act has stood the test of time and how it has been regarded in Beijing, Taipei and Washington. When it was passed into law in the United States some said that it would soon be forgotten and that the Department of State, which generally did not like Congress interfering in the making of foreign policy and specifically disliked the TRA, working with the People's Republic of China would destroy or undermine it. This did not happen. In fact, the record of the TRA was, after a decade, a good one. This continues to be the case and probably will be in the future.

Chapter 10 deals with Taiwan's response to the new world order, focusing on changes in its domestic, economic, foreign, and security policies designed to adjust to a different global system. Taipei did not count the People's Republic of China out after the Tiananmen Massacre and continued to deal with Beijing in 1989, perceiving that three global economic blocs would characterize the new world, and Taipei and Beijing were going to be bloc partners. Taiwan also continued to democratize, seeing democracy as the "wave of the future." And it began to use its economic clout more, seeing the key of influence in the world now as more economic and less military. The new world order had eliminated or weakened Beijing's external threats, however, and Beijing could focus more of its military forces on the Taiwan Strait area. Thus, Taiwan did not benefit in security terms from a new era of peace, and purchasing arms and maintaining and even augmenting its military forces became more important.

Chapter One
Taiwan's Strategy
and America's China Policy

In 1971, the United States made a volte-face in its China policy. The causes of this reversal were myriad. One was the Vietnam War and Peking's influence over its protégé, North Vietnam. Another was the fear in Washington that an escalation of Sino-Soviet hostilities might lead to nuclear war and involve the United States. A third was that America's stance toward China was the subject of criticism in many Third World countries; thus it seemed clear that Washington could not continue to isolate Peking and in particular keep it out of the United Nations much longer. Finally, many scholars and statesmen in the United States argued that the international system was evolving away from bipolarity; hence, improving relations with China would help dispel one of the rigidities that characterized the old style of international relations. In any event, the reasons for a rapprochement with China were manifold and compelling.

Because Taiwan was considered a major obstacle to closer relations with Peking, President Nixon signed a joint communiqué after negotiations with the government of the People's Republic of China (PRC) in early 1972 that mentioned the "Taiwan issue." In the Shanghai Communiqué, the U.S. concurred (though obliquely) with Peking's position that Taiwan is a part of China. Nixon also committed the United States to withdraw its 8,500 troops from Taiwan. Subsequently, an across-the-board cut was made that left just 3,000 U.S. troops on the island. U.S. warplanes also were relocated and Washington cut military aid to Taipei. Finally, Congress invalidated the resolution under which President Eisenhower promised U.S. help in the defense of the Nationalist-held offshore islands of Quemoy and Matsu.

In spite of subsequent leadership changes in both the United States and the PRC, détente remained a major foreign policy tenet on both sides. In 1975 President Ford reaffirmed the support for the Shanghai Communiqué during his visit to China. In route back to the United States after the trip, in a public speech in Hawaii, he asserted that U.S. friendship with the People's Republic of

China "is becoming a permanent feature of the international landscape." Shortly after, in early 1976, he sent a letter to China's new premier, Hua Kuo-feng, reiterating his commitment to pursuing better relations. Soon Thomas Gates was appointed head of the liaison office in Peking—with ambassadorial status. Meanwhile, Henry Kissinger visited Peking and conferred with Chinese officials on the topic of formal diplomatic ties. Both sides seemed to agree that diplomatic relations should be established without delay. However, because of Mao's illness and eventual death in 1976 and a U.S. election, a final decision was held in abeyance.

During the presidential campaign, candidate Jimmy Carter promised improved relations with the People's Republic of China. So did the Democratic Party's platform. Since taking office, President Carter has pledged publicly on more than one occasion to seek closer relations with China—meaning, to most observers, establishing formal diplomatic relations. In an apparent effort to fulfill this promise, Carter has sent a number emissaries to Peking to discuss issues that may be seen as related to forging diplomatic relations, including many who are influential in foreign policy making. Most analysts thus predict that an exchange of embassies is not far off.

In Taipei, U.S. officials have hinted that they will start phasing out or closing down operations soon. The U.S. ambassador to the Republic of China, Leonard Unger, a man who some have speculated was sent to Taipei for that purpose, said recently that ultimately the "nature of U.S.-Republic of China relations will change."

When the United States closes its embassy, Taipei will be recognized by no important nation. Following the closing of the U.S. embassy, probably within a very short time, most of the fewer than twenty-five countries that retain ambassadorial ties with Taipei will end them. Other corollary difficulties will no doubt arise. American investment in Taiwan will decline because such investment is now guaranteed by the U.S. government, and that guarantee is tied to diplomatic relations. Other sources of foreign investment may be difficult to find. Trade with the United States will no doubt be affected. This is very important because America took 37 percent of Taiwan's exports last year. Either the U.S.-Republic of China defense pact will be automatically nullified, or Washington will give a year's notice to cancel it. U.S. military aid will certainly be reduced if not cut.

Many observers feel that when this happens Taipei will be forced to seek some sort of accommodation with Peking that will lead to an eventual reversion of the island to Peking's jurisdiction. They argue that the situation has been all downhill in the past six years for Taiwan and that Taipei has few, if any, options —none of them promising. Without the United States, they say, Peking can use economic and military pressures to compel the Nationalist Chinese government to bargain and eventually capitulate.

Others, however, contend that the United States will not abandon Taiwan, which has been its historical ally, friend and a showcase of American aid. They also note that Taiwan has considerable support if it makes a bid for independence, including the support of public in the United States. In addition, Taipei has some other options. Finally, Peking has more critical matters to worry about, the most important being worsening of Sino-Soviet relations.

In any event, Taiwan is at a crossroads. Reflecting that fact, its leaders have to chart a future course for Taiwan. Past policies will not suffice. An examination of Taiwan's recent actions and its newly formulated policies indicate that Nationalist Chinese leaders have, in fact, designed a strategy to deal with the shock of America's move to Peking, which they now perceive as inevitable. In formulating a policy they must taken into consideration a number of variables. First, Nationalist leaders have to worry about Taiwanese demands for an independent Taiwan. This issue has serious domestic ramifications. Second, Peking can veto Taiwan's admission to the United Nations, and it will no doubt win on a vote concerning whether or not the Taiwan Question is a domestic matter. Thus, Taipei cannot hope for much international support. Third, leaders in Taiwan state that they can survive the impact of the loss of U.S. recognition and time will eventually be on their side in terms of maintaining the nation's sovereignty and autonomy.

An assessment of Taipei's strategy is made in the following pages. The political, military, and economic dimensions of the plan are analyzed separately in the next three sections. The last section contains conclusions concerning the possibility for the success of Taipei's policies and the importance of the issue to the world.

Taipei's Political Calculations

In the political realm, Taipei's strategy is to delay Washington's move to Peking for as long as possible. In the meantime, it must quietly abandon its claim to represent China in the global community while seeking support in the United States on the "Taiwan Question" (meaning Taiwan's right to chose its own future, or not). Leaders in Taiwan know that Washington will eventually establish formal diplomatic ties with Peking and that they cannot prevent this. They also know, however, that the United States is Taiwan's only important friend and ally at present and think that America will not abandon Taiwan completely when it makes the move to Peking. They likewise calculate, as their new policies indicate, that they can influence Washington's Taiwan policy.

In order to impact America's decision on Taiwan's future, Taipei has made special efforts to present its side of the problem to relevant people of influence in the United States. In the past two or three years, Taipei has invited numerous members of Congress, congressional staff personnel, journalists, and scholars to visit Taiwan. All have been treated royally in the hope that they might return to the United States with a favorable impression of Taiwan. The list of invitees is both bigger and different from former ones: It includes both liberals and conservatives. In Taiwan they are allowed to see what they want and talk to whomever they want. But, Nationalist Chinese leaders, whenever they have an opportunity, talk about friendship and good relations, and point out that the Shanghai Communiqué is intentionally vague on the question of Taiwan and that Washington has made no final decision on the question (which many Americans, even those in the know, do not realize).

Taipei has also pulled out all stops to encourage tourism. In contrast to past policies, which discouraged travel to Taiwan and therefore too many foreign contacts with local citizens (for fear that they may learn about democracy and make increasing demands for it), the government is now doing all it can to increase the number of foreign guests. This more liberal policy toward foreign visitors also applies to students and retired or vacationing U.S. military personnel. Taipei espouses the doctrine of "see what you want to see, good or bad"—while noting that the People's Republic of China does not allow freedom of travel on the mainland and that very few foreign tourists are given entry visas to the PRC. Taiwan's leaders also flaunt progress in individual liberties, democracy, and social and economic development in Taiwan, again making contrasts to the mainland. Observers contend that Taipei wants to attract more foreigners, especially Americans, because their "advertising" for Taiwan might eventually influence foreign public opinion. It also allays criticism of Taiwan as a less-than-free country.

Taiwan has also expended considerable energy and money in the United States to increase cultural and other less official contacts. Three new consulates have been opened in the United States since the Shanghai Communiqué was concluded, and various athletic, entertainment, and cultural groups have been sent to tour U.S. cities. Special efforts have likewise been made to preserve contacts with and win the support of Chinese living in the United States. Taipei would hardly make these efforts if it did not think that it could influence the American people and that this in turn might affect decision makers in Washington.

In marked contrast to its past policy, Taipei now talks about deciding its own future instead of liberating the mainland and even cites the principle of self-determination when discussing Taiwan's status. Its representatives in the United States have purchased advertising space in several large newspapers to present its case—meaning its right to decide—to the public. In addition, friends of Nationalist China have written numerous letters to editors of American newspapers and magazines, specifically suggesting that a "will-of-the-people" criterion be used when discussing the "Taiwan Question." They present the argument that ignoring the wishes of the people of Taiwan would be undemocratic and contrary to the principles on which the United Nations and other global institutions are based.

Taipei's position in various international organizations is also telling. With the exception of the United Nations, Taipei has not withdrawn from world organizations when Peking has been admitted unless it has been forced to do so. Instead, Taiwan maintains an active membership. This is new. Likewise, Taipei endeavors to play a part in international forums, economic summits, athletic meets, and so on. Since it cannot represent China, it must have in mind representing an autonomous Taiwan, at least temporarily. This suggests, along with evidence already presented, that Nationalist Chinese leaders have, for all intents and purposes (though, of course, they don't say this) adopted a "two Chinas" policy or a "one China, one Taiwan" policy.

Despite this new and probably far-sighted policy toward the United States and the world community, at home Taipei still espouses a doctrine of retaking the mainland. At first glance this strategy appears to be inconsistent and unrealistic. However, considering all of the variables, it may not be at all unwise. The anti-Communist posture justifies the continuance of the minority government of Chinese that went to Taiwan when Chiang Kai-shek left the mainland in 1949, as well as the postponement of constitutionally-guaranteed civil rights. The calls for deciding its own future or as the opposition would say, for self-determination, which has been made in the United States and elsewhere, increases the danger of demands for proportional representation and "full democracy" by Taiwan's newly active opposition that are mostly native-born Taiwanese. These demands threaten political stability in Taiwan at a critical juncture. Clearly, increasing political freedom and boasting of its human rights progress as Taipei has been doing carries with it the peril of encouraging dissent. The return-to-the-mainland policy and a nominal one-China policy help keep demands for greater freedoms and more democracy within bounds and justifies (in the name of national security) periodic harsh crackdowns against protesters.

Taipei's refusal to negotiate with the Communists is a policy line taken for similar reasons. There is fear on the part of the "ethnic" Taiwanese that the Mainlanders who hold political power will sell them out by making a deal with Peking before surrendering political power to the majority Taiwanese. Though some say the government in Peking has intentionally planted such rumors, and that is very possible, it is clearly a natural apprehension. This might explain why Taipei refused Peking's offer in 1976 to repatriate Nationalist prisoners, which ended in a propaganda victory for Mao. It elucidates other actions by the government, especially an unyielding attitude toward Peking at various times that has created bad publicity for Taipei.

Meanwhile, more Taiwanese are encouraged to participate in the government by joining the Nationalist Party or seeking government employment. At the Nationalist Party Congress held in November 1976, for the first time the majority of representatives were Taiwan-born. Also, the proportion of Taiwanese applying for government jobs in the past two or three years has been greater than the proportion of Taiwanese in the population. Efforts have even been made toward reconciliation with Taiwanese Independence Movement leaders in Japan and in the United States. Nationalist Chinese leaders underscore the realities: The Shanghai Communiqué undermined the cause of Taiwanese independence, and now Taiwan-ese and Mainlanders are in the same predicament regarding Peking's threat of incorporating Taiwan.

Nationalist Chinese leaders do not want to declare that Taiwan is independent or officially abdicate claims to the mainland, however. This would have dangerous implications. And, it might also unnecessarily provoke Peking. Why do that if time is on Taipei's side? Chinese officials in Taipei doubtless hope that Taiwan can maintain an ambiguous status in the near future and that someday Taiwan will become simply another representative of the Chinese people, like Singapore. But that will take time.

In short, Taiwan's political policy for coping with the problem of U.S. recognition of Peking may be regarded as a goodwill campaign. It acknowledges that public opinion in the United States favors recognition of China but not abandoning Taiwan. It also realizes that Taiwan's traditional support in the United States (in the form of the China Lobby) is inadequate. Nationalist Chinese leaders, however, perceive that Washington may defer the Taiwan Question to the United Nations or that world opinion may in some other way have a bearing on their future. They know that the people on Taiwan, Taiwanese and Mainlanders alike, do not want to be incorporated by China. If they are allowed to choose their destiny, there is no question that their choice will be for remaining separate from the PRC. Nationalist Chinese leaders know their cause is furthered by at least paying lip service to democratic principles; so Chiang Ching-kuo and other leaders make trips to rural areas in Taiwan and speak to the farmers, the poor, and the young. Concern for human rights is publicized, but almost always in comparison to mainland China. More leniency has been shown toward political prisoners, but most notably in those cases that have gained attention abroad. Taiwanese are invited to participate in politics and are given some positions of real importance. Though some of this may be facade, it does represent a definite change from the past, and it has resulted in good press for Taiwan in the United States and elsewhere.

Taipei's Military Calculations

Taipei's military policies relate to and complement its political strategy in regard to the matter of U.S. relations with the PRC. Nationalist Chinese leaders seek to delay U.S. recognition of the PRC and the withdrawal of American troops, knowing that Peking will not use military force against Taiwan as long as they are there. And they see the two issues as connected. More realistically Taipei hopes to keep U.S. troops in Taiwan at least until Washington recognizes Peking and, if possible, for at least a year thereafter—during what will be a critical period for Taiwan. In the meantime, Taiwan is making a concerted effort to attract American weapons builders to Taiwan and is purchasing U.S. military technology and sophisticated weapons to build up its own defenses.

In terms of specific policies, Taiwan has issued a number of warnings to U.S. military leaders, and to the American public as well, that Taiwan should be maintained as a U.S. fortress in the wake of the loss of Indochina. They also present the case that the Sino-Soviet dispute is spurious and may be a trick to get the United States to relax its guard (even though the evidence suggests that Taipei knows that the dispute is real). The Nationalist Chinese military, however, has made no effort to activate hostilities with Peking to force Washington's hand, knowing that it would be counterproductive to preserving even temporarily defense ties with the United States.

Meanwhile, Taipei continues to grant U.S. military advisers in Taiwan a high protocol status and invites other American military decision-makers to Taiwan for inspection tours and visits. Nationalist Chinese leaders clearly want to preserve their good relations with the U.S. military, knowing that the Pentagon has a considerable influence on U.S. policy making and that it favors a sovereign Taiwan. In fact, it is said that no U.S. general or admiral favors a total U.S. troop evacuation from Taiwan. Moreover, the Joint Chiefs of Staff have gone on record recommending a residual U.S. presence on Taiwan as a means of guaranteeing its security once the United States breaks diplomatic relations with Taipei.

Regarding the U.S.-Republic of China mutual defense treaty, Nationalist Chinese leaders consider the treaty will be in force for at least twelve months after de-recognition (since a year's advance notice is legally required by either side to abrogate the pact). Though some argue that the treaty would be automatically invalidated if the United States switched its embassy to Peking, Taipei does not agree with this interpretation. Moreover, Taiwan seems prepared to make an issue of the validity of the treaty when Washington makes the move to Peking. Taipei might win in such an effort; in fact, it may have already succeeded inasmuch as neither the White House nor the Department of State has said that the treaty would be nullified by de-recognition.

An important related facet of Taipei's military strategy is to attract U.S. arms manufacturers to Taiwan to set up subsidiary companies or to aid Taiwan's growing arms industry. Taiwan is investing heavily in its own weapons building and it needs foreign technology and aid. The United States is the best source. To date, Taipei has been successful in attracting several American companies to Taiwan. Northrop Corporation, for example, is building F-5E fighter planes in Taiwan, which are now being purveyed to the Nationalist Chinese air force. Huey helicopters, U.S.-designed tanks and artillery, and M-14 rifles are also locally-made. Among Taiwan's purchases from U.S. companies is a U.S. $34 million air defense system from Hughes Aircraft. This was one of the largest single contracts for military equipment a U.S. company has signed with a foreign country.

The purpose of all this is, of course, to defend Taiwan against an attack from the mainland. But the publicity given to increased military preparedness is also aimed at the populace of Taiwan—to give them assurance that their government can and will defend the island. It is also directed at the international community, which wonders whether Peking can invade Taiwan without destabilizing international politics. Last but not least, American arms manufacturers, which have political influence in Washington, DC, will be more committed to Taiwan's survival.

Concurrent with its efforts to build a local arms industry, Taipei has implemented a policy that clearly reflects that defense rather than offense (retaking the mainland) is now paramount. The size of its air force and navy, as well as its reserves, have been increased, while the strength of the army has declined. This policy gives military planners a single objective, making their tactics simpler and more credible. Just as important, it is a move that makes Taiwan's overall foreign policy appear to be that of a nonbelligerent nation seeking to develop on its own and wanting merely to control its own destiny.

Meanwhile, Taipei appears to be trying to tie its security to Japan's, thereby indirectly keeping Taiwan under the protective wing of the United States. Nationalist Chinese leaders know that the United States regards Japan as the cornerstone of its Asian defense policy and will continue to defend Japan. Furthermore, the U.S.-Japanese defense treaty contains provisions for evoking cooperation in the event of overt hostile acts against Taiwan. Thus, Taipei did not object in 1969 when Japanese Prime Minister Sato said that Taiwan was "within Japan's defense zone"—even though this statement may have been construed as a violation of the Republic of China's sovereignty. Since then it has tried to encourage the continuation and restatement of this policy. Over the past few years, moreover, Nationalist Chinese leaders have held frequent meetings with conservative Japanese leaders, particularly those with close ties to the Japanese military, to discuss the future of East Asia. Taipei has used these talks to point out the problems Japan will experience if Taiwan is incorporated by China: Japan's oil lifeline would be vulnerable; its trade might be disrupted; and its influence in South and Southeast Asia would be reduced.

Nationalist China also maintains contacts with the Soviet Union to use as leverage against Peking. Soviet representatives have gone to Taiwan periodically in recent years, and Taipei has sent both official and unofficial spokesmen to Moscow. "Unofficial" spokesmen in Taipei have stated publicly on several occasions that Taiwan might grant the Soviet Union base facilities on Taiwan or the Pescadores Islands, particularly if the United States withdraws its military forces after it diplomatically recognizes Peking.

Several points of mutual interest stand out if one wishes to speculate about cooperation between Taipei and Moscow. Nationalist Chinese forces tie down a large number of troops in adjacent provinces on the mainland that might otherwise be sent north to areas near the Sino-Soviet border. Moscow's growing naval presence in the Pacific and its interests in South and Southeast Asia mean that it desires to keep the Taiwan Strait open and limit China's naval expansion. Finally, neither Taipei nor Moscow want Peking to be able to pressure Japan militarily.

Taipei wants the Soviet Union as a friend and ally in reserve, and it seeks to convey the message to Peking that if the United States evacuates its forces, Taipei still has alternatives. Although switching defense ties from Washington to Moscow would be very problematic for Taipei, and would involve political and economic bonds that would doubtless be less advantageous, its "Russian connection" serves as a big bargaining card vis-à-vis Peking. Some even suggest that Taipei's return-to-the-mainland policy is maintained partly at the Kremlin's request (in order to keep more PRC forces in southern China) and that, as a quid pro quo, Moscow will initiate hostilities on the Sino-Soviet border should Peking prepare to launch an invasion against Taiwan. It is also possible that Taipei hopes to bargain with Peking to the effect that there will be no Soviet bases on Taiwan in return for no Chinese military buildup in Fukien Province across the Taiwan Strait.

Another "card" that Taipei holds is its nuclear program and the possibility of building atomic bombs. Nationalist Chinese decision makers have given a high priority to the development of nuclear energy—even though other forms of energy are more economical. This may be seen as a purposeful effort to create speculation concerning Taiwan's potential as a nuclear power. Its efforts to train nuclear scientists in the United States in areas that go beyond the use of nuclear energy for peaceful purposes is further confirmation. Taipei ostensibly sees its progress in this area as a means to counter a military threat from the mainland. Furthermore, it makes any conflict between the Nationalist and Communist Chinese, explicitly, an invasion of Taiwan, a matter of international concern.

Taipei's Economic Calculations

Several facets of Taiwan's economic policies also reflect that it anticipates problems connected with the likely U.S. diplomatic departure. Most apparent is the emphasis given to short-range growth without concern for future downtrends and inflation. Taipei is deliberately planning an economic boom in anticipation of less readily available capital and probably a decline in trade when the United States recognizes and establishes formal diplomatic ties with Peking. Nationalist Chinese leaders also foresee the possibility of Peking employing economic warfare tactics to force Taiwan to negotiate incorporation. Rapid growth will help prevent this as well as pessimism and defeatism which would be injurious to the morale of the government and the resistance of the people to Communist overtures. Likewise, economic expansion is good for Taiwan's image abroad and bolsters economic contacts with other countries, helping to supplant the loss of political ties.

Most obvious in Taiwan's accelerated economic growth plans are the "ten projects." These are massive public-sector projects that require huge investment and government supervision and support. They include two seaports, an international airport, a shipyard, a steel mill, a petrochemical complex, a superhighway, a new rail line, and the electrification of several existing rail lines. Nuclear power plants are also included. The projects will be completed by the end of the decade at a cost of $5 billion, or one-half of Taiwan's current annual gross national product. Half of the investment will come from abroad.

Notwithstanding the fact that economic growth will be influenced in a positive way, various liabilities involved with these projects are apparent. First, it has become necessary to import construction materials and machines at a high cost and to the detriment of Taiwan's balance of payments. Second, the projects are taxing present port facilities as well as internal transportation facilities. Third, a labor shortage is being created in many areas, putting a strain on the private sector of the economy and on social stability.

Clearly, the simultaneous construction of so many large public works is questionable economics: Not only will they compete with each other for skilled labor and technicians, but they are highly inflationary. These projects were originally designed to stimulate economic growth in order to compensate for political defeats resulting from the flight of embassies from Taiwan (after President Nixon announced his trip to China and Peking was voted into the United Nations). The projects, however, are still accorded a high priority and have early completion dates. The continuation of rapid growth economic policies and now accelerating growth further clearly involves risks to domestic economic and political stability.

Taiwan's economic policies take several other factors into consideration, particularly the state of the economy during the recent few years. First, expansionary growth was needed to bring the country out of a serious recession caused by the oil crisis of 1973. In 1974, Taiwan's gross national product increased by less than 1 percent, while per capita income dropped slightly. In 1975, economic growth returned to a reasonable 5 to 6 percent. In 1976, it was over 12 percent. The return to rapid growth at this time probably deterred the development of a recession mentality, which would have fostered pessimism and weakened the nation's resistance to Peking's enticements and intimidation. A continuation of a high rate of growth do this again; in short, it will be salutary in terms of coping with the ordeal of a U.S. evacuation.

Rapid economic growth similarly ensures rising per capita income and reduces the likelihood of rebellion or opposition to the government. Since the government will face a legitimacy problem when the United States withdraws, this "ounce of prevention" may prove to be crucial. Nationalist Chinese leaders are no doubt aware of the fact that political unrest is not usually prevalent in an environment of high economic growth. They are also aware that this is particularly relevant to Taiwan, since the Taiwanese are a majority in the business sector and are also among the poor and dissatisfied.

Fast growth is likewise good for Taiwan's global image and contributes to increasing commercial contacts with foreign countries. These ties are valuable in that they supplant political relationships and establish an interdependency, which may sway the decisions of nations that otherwise might not care whether or not Taiwan remains self-governing. Taiwan's future may well become an international question, and vested interests will support Taipei's cause. The same is true of attracting foreign investment. A high growth rate makes possible larger investment input and foreign borrowing, which evokes a greater concern abroad for Taiwan's future independence.

Finally, while Taiwan's rapid economic growth has the disadvantage of forcing infrastructure changes and creating a financial crises for businessmen in sectors of the economy that rely on low labor costs, it prompts innovation and new industries. It also induces greater specialization and technology use. This is an advantage in that it reduces the worry about economic competition from Peking which can dump similar products on the market at low or below-cost prices (and has been recently doing so). China does not produce in sufficient quantity many of the products now being developed in Taiwan and probably will not be able to do so in the future. Rapid economic growth could preserve this situation. It would also make incorporation less beneficial for Peking, because China would have to maintain Taiwan's ties with the world economy, meaning accepting of capitalism, or oversee the deterioration of Taiwan's economy and no doubt relocate a sizable portion of the population. Rapid economic growth, particularly in high-technology and specialized industry, promotes cultural changes that will too make the integration of Taiwan with the mainland difficult.

In its endeavors to generate business ties and foreign investment, Taiwan has pointedly aimed at nations that will play paramount roles in determining Taiwan's future: namely the United States and then at Japan. Last year, foreign investment in Taiwan totaled over $1.3 billion; nearly half of this came from the United States. Japan followed a close second. In the case of U.S. investment, Taipei has sought to attract large U.S. companies, especially those that are known to have political influence in Washington. With Japan, in contrast, Taiwan has invited small investors so as to avoid competition between U.S. and Japanese companies and to involve Japanese businessmen in Taiwan in such a way that they cannot recover their investments should Taiwan lose its autonomy. Considering Taiwan's size and economic situation, its debt is clearly bigger than it need be. Its arrears to the United States and Japan are noticeably very large.

Taiwan's efforts to maintain a high level of trade, investment and other economic ties with the United States and Japan involve some risk. One could argue that Taiwan is dangerously dependent on the United States, where protectionist sentiment is strong, and on Japan. Taiwan's planners, however, opt to increase commercial ties with the two countries that will have the greatest influence on Taiwan's future. Taipei has thus adjusted the balance of payments to maintain influence with these two important friends. Specifically, Taipei has made moves to correct its overly favorable balance of trade with the United States over the past three to four years, and it has publicized this in the United States. It is now buying American products even though in many cases they are more expensive than goods of comparable quality elsewhere. Taipei allows a huge balance of trade deficit with Japan. Besides allowing an unfavorable balance of trade with Japan, Taiwan is permitting Japanese companies on the island to make very large profits.

This strategy makes sense for two reasons. First, China is now giving high priority to economic development, based in large part on increased trade with the West. Japan and the United States are China's most important trading partners, and Peking cannot afford to alienate business leaders in these two countries. Meanwhile, Taipei is seeking to alter many of the U.S. regulations and laws governing America's trade and investment abroad, particularly rules that would discriminate against Taiwan once it loses diplomatic recognition.

Conclusions

Taiwan's strategy to deal with U.S. diplomatic recognition of Peking is replete with contradictions. Nationalist Chinese leaders must maintain a return-to-the-main-land policy both to placate the old hands in the Kuomintang and to alleviate Taiwanese fears that they will make a deal with Peking. They have to oppose negotiations for the same reason. They do not want to bargain with Peking on Taiwan's future; they want to remain free of ties to China. Yet they have to convince Washington that they are reasonable. They want U.S. military support, but they cannot force a crisis situation to keep it, as this would be counterproductive. They must persuade America that they are concerned for democracy and human rights, yet in the eyes of the local population, America has overdone both. They must preserve political stability and must worry about an escalation of demands for political rights; since the Nationalists constitute a minority government, political rights are dangerous.

Because of these dilemmas, Taipei is following a low-key policy. This gives the impression that Taiwan has no policy and is perhaps fatalistic about the future. Likewise, it gives the impression that Peking will win on the issue of the Taiwan Question. The alternative would be for Taipei to openly declare its independence as the Republic of Taiwan—which for reasons already mentioned has serious disadvantages. Anyway, Taipei can make this move later if it perceives a need. At present, Taipei appears to have a number of assets it can exploit, and it has some options. Thus its policy, though plagued with seeming contradictions, appears to be quite appropriate given the circumstances. And, with what little evidence there is to offer, it appears to be working.

Taiwan has considerable support in U.S. government circles on the issue of its right to chose its future. There is less support, however, on U.S. nonrecognition of Peking and almost none for Taipei's return-to-the-mainland policy. Taiwan's retreat from the latter two issues will probably augment U.S. support on the former. Public opinion in the United States clearly favors Taiwan's sovereignty by a large margin. In fact, Taipei was the originator of at least one recent public opinion poll on the subject and has done all it can to publicize the results. Public opinion may indeed play a significant role, since U.S. decision makers seem equivocal on the issue of Taiwan. Washington's stance at present seems to be that Taiwan's status is a "Chinese question." Clearly, this is not true. Taiwan's future is in the hands of the United States. There is little hope that Taipei and Peking can negotiate a peaceful solution.

It would not be in Japan's interest for Taiwan to be incorporated by China—another point that Taipei privately mentions to Japanese leaders. Unification would allow China to close the Taiwan Strait and possibly prevent Japanese passage (which China could easily do if it opted to employ naval force in the Taiwan Strait). It would also give China a stronger bargaining position with Tokyo regarding the settlement of territorial issues in the vicinity of Okinawa and, more important, the ownership of vast undersea oil reserves in that area. The same applies to the Soviet Union. The Kremlin is locked into a serious conflict with China, and presumably, after Peking resolves the Taiwan issue, it will make a stronger claim to "lost territories" in the Soviet Union. Both Tokyo and Moscow would prefer to see Taiwan self-governing and independent. Taipei has thus maintained good relations with both countries— obviously better than other circumstances would justify.

The Taiwan Independence Movement is now weak and factionalized. Thus, Chinese Nationalist leaders have conveyed to the Taiwanese the message that they will continue to rule Taiwan but that their exclusive hold on political power will be relinquished in the near future and assimilation will eventually resolve all differences. That the two groups have almost identical interests in avoiding incorporation is a picture presented by the government—and it is being understood. The differences separating Taiwanese and mainland Chinese are being buried by time and official policies. Nationalist Chinese leaders must still worry, however, about diehards in their party who oppose Taiwanese participation in the government and also about radical Taiwanese who want independence on the basis of expelling Mainland Chinese or reducing their status to that of a persecuted minority group. At the present time, no perceivable polarization has occurred even though the Taiwanese Independence Movement has perhaps been helped by the granting of more political freedoms in Taiwan.

Optimistically, Taipei hopes that Washington will recognize two Chinas, following the Soviet precedent of recognizing two Germanys. Considering China's need for American support (to cope with the Soviet military threat) and the fact that China's economic development plans are now founded on increased trade with the West, as well as the acquisition of technology and investment funds, this scenario may not be out of the question. Another potentially auspicious solution for Taiwan would be for the United States to follow the "Japan formula"—to recognize Peking and retain a "liaison office" in Taipei but keep a U.S. military presence in Taiwan and extract a nonaggression pledge from Peking. These solutions are certainly preferable to relying on Japan, which is militarily weak compared to China, or using the Soviet option, which would certainly imperil Taiwan's commercial relations with the West and hurt its economic development.

Taipei can also make a good case for independence. Taiwan has been de facto a separate nation for twenty-eight years. It has had ties with the mainland for only four years in this century. Historical connections are likewise weak. Taiwan is clearly a viable nation. Its size, population, and economy are all larger than at least a third of the member states in the United Nations. Nevertheless, Taipei does not want to anger Peking. It is not advantageous to do so. Nationalist Chinese leaders perceive that the case for independence, if it needs to be made, can best be made gradually.

Taipei can present the Taiwan Question as an international issue. If China were to invade Taiwan it would probably result in casualties upward of 1 million, and it might take months before Peking could succeed in pacifying the island's population. Taiwan's military forces are equipped with modern weapons and in terms of strategy are totally programmed to defend the island. Peking might choose the nuclear option, but Taiwan might have its own to use in return. In any case, this conflict could not go unnoticed by the rest of the world. Meanwhile, Taiwan is gradually garnering friends and commitments from the international community. Certainly Peking's claim that Taiwan is a domestic issue will have less and less support as time passes.

Taiwan's foreign policy today manifests a great deal of realism and flexibility. One of Taipei's principal tactics is to keep the world guessing; moralism is being played down. Taipei's actions reflect the realization that Taiwan's best future does not lie in becoming part of the People's Republic of China. Hence, Nationalist Chinese leaders seek to maintain Taiwan's autonomy as a sine qua non. Lastly, Taipei's stance reveals an understanding of Taiwan's place in the world and a comprehension of the influence of world politics on Taiwan's future; also, it shows an ability to adapt to the world situation. Thus, its policy vis-à-vis the pending U.S. establishment of diplomatic ties with Peking may well succeed.

Chapter Two
The Fishing Islands Controversy

During 1971, several small islands located between Taiwan and Okinawa became a locus of contention in the Far East involving Japan, the Republic of China, the United States—and to a lesser extent the People's Republic of China, the Republic of Korea, and the Republic of the Philippines. The territorial dispute that ensued attracted considerable attention, especially in the Republic of China or Taiwan. Demonstrations over this issue occurred in a number of major cities of the world—in some cases resulting in violence. This, of course, amplified the dispute and increased the attention given to it in the press.

The controversy over the islands was complicated by the complex and sensitive relations among the nations involved and larger issue at stake: petroleum. Thus, for a short time at least, the contention over these islands, which are almost worthless except for the undersea oil in the area, became a barometer reflecting more crucial issues.

Historical Background to the Dispute

The Fishing Islands (called the Senkaku Islands in Japanese and the Tiaoyutai Islands in Chinese) are situated just over 100 miles northwest of Keelung, the northern port city of Taiwan. There are eight islands in the group, ranging from .02 to .07 of a square kilometer in area. The largest island of the group is called Wu Jen in Chinese (meaning "without people"); it is also called Tiaoyutai ("fishing stage"). This island is the largest island in the chain; but, like the other islands of the group, it has no source of food or water and is characterized by steep, rough slopes. None of the islands has ever been inhabited.

The East China Sea Monsoons and the Japanese Current both influence the Fishing Islands. Since the Japanese Current flows from the south northward, it is difficult for small boats from the Ryukyu Islands to get there against the current. This explains why for centuries the islands have been relatively isolated

429

from the rest of the Ryukyu chain. U.S. jurisdiction over the Ryukyus since World War II also accounts for the fact that Japanese fishermen have not used the islands in recent years as much as Chinese fishermen, even though the islands are much closer to the Ryukyus than to Taiwan.

During the Ming Dynasty (1368 to 1644), the Ryukyu Islands were politically organized as a kingdom that was a vassal state of China. This relationship continued through part of the Ch'ing Dynasty (1644 to 1911). Both Ming and Ch'ing records, however, note that the Fishing Islands were not a part of the Ryukyu Kingdom. When Ming and Ch'ing ambassadors were sent to the Ryukyu Kingdom, they followed the Japanese Current and recorded in their ledgers seeing several small islands "before reaching the boundary of the Ryukyu Kingdom."[1] Nevertheless, no Chinese historical record ever included the islands as a part of China.

During the 1700s, the Ryukyu Kingdom began paying tribute to Japan as well as China. In 1789, Japan sent occupation forces to the Ryukyus and subsequently laid claim to them. Later Japan proposed to the Chinese government an exchange of "four small islands in the southern Ryukyus" for revision of Japan's commercial treaty with China. Officials of the Ch'ing Dynasty court refused this overture on the basis that the Ryukyu Kingdom was still a vassal state of China.[2]

In 1872, the King of the Ryukyu Kingdom was taken to Japan to pay homage to the emperor. He was reduced in rank, thus bringing the Ryukyu Kingdom under the implicit jurisdiction of Japan. China was too weak and preoccupied with other problems at the time to make any meaningful protest.

Following the Sino-Japanese War of 1894–1895, Japan received sovereignty over Taiwan and the Pescadores Islands from China. This consolidated Japan's control of the island territory from Japan southward to the Philippines. The Fishing Islands, if not Japanese territory before, were now clearly under Japan's rule. In fact, almost nothing was heard about the islands for some time after this.

During World War II it was proclaimed at the Cairo Conference that Japan would be "stripped of all the islands in the Pacific" that it had "seized or occupied" since the beginning of World War I, and that all the territories Japan had "stolen" from China, such as Manchuria, Formosa, and the Pescadores, would be "restored to the Republic of China." Japan was also to be expelled from other territories which it had taken by "violence and greed."[3] The status of the Ryukyu Islands (and the Fishing Islands) was not mentioned, however, and could not be assumed by the wording of the proclamation.

According to several authors, the United States expected to occupy Taiwan and the Pescadores after World War II.[4] Such a U.S. action would have postponed the issue of Japanese territory to a later date when a peace treaty could have been concluded. In the final assault on Japan, however, United States forces bypassed Taiwan and attacked Okinawa in order to gain a base close enough to the main Japanese islands to carry out heavy bombing missions. Taiwan and the Pescadores did not become battlegrounds and were not occupied by Allied troops. Therefore, they were turned over to the Republic of China at the end of the war in accordance with the Cairo Declaration. The United States occupied the Ryukyu Islands, including the Fishing Islands.

The Current Dispute over the Fishing Islands

In September 1951, Japan signed a treaty of peace with forty-eight Allied nations in San Francisco. According to the treaty, Japan renounced all right, title, and claim to Formosa and the Pescadores. The Ryukyu Islands were made U.N. trust territories under U.S. control. Although the agreements made at Cairo were referred to, they were not formalized or legalized by the San Francisco Treaty. Moreover, because of the large number of nations signing the San Francisco Treaty, this treaty took on the status of an international agreement, and it may be seen to have superseded the Cairo agreements. Owing to the Chinese Civil War and the Nationalist Chinese defeat, the government of the Republic of China (which moved to Taiwan in 1949) signed a separate treaty of peace with Japan; its provisions were almost entirely copied from the San Francisco Treaty.

In ensuing years, the status of the Ryukyu Islands, which were controlled by the United States, was questioned by neither Japan nor the Republic of China. Similarly the People's Republic of China said nothing. During the Kennedy administration reference was made by officials in Washington, including the President himself, to Japan's "residual sovereignty" over the Ryukyu Islands. Thus it was assumed that the United States planned to return the Ryukyus to Japan at some date in the future. However, subsequent to Kennedy's statements, but before President Nixon's official declaration of reversion on November 21, 1969, a number of important events transpired.

Paramount among the interim events was the discovery of possible deposits of oil north of the Taiwan Strait and in the vicinity of the Fishing Islands. Speculation about large oil deposits was made by the Economic Commission for Asia and the Far East in late 1968 following an investigation by the commission (which was not made public immediately). Taipei, when it heard of this, decided to drill for the oil and called upon foreign oil companies to cooperate with the China Petroleum Company in the effort.

Japan responded by conducting its own investigation to ascertain if oil was present and determine the size of the deposits. By mid-1969 preliminary explorations had been completed that supported earlier reports of undersea oil deposits; in fact, it was stated at the time that the area could have one of the world's ten largest reserves.[5] Forthwith, the Japanese government announced that it was appropriating $280,000 to carry on "continued research."[6]

In 1970 the dispute over the Fishing Islands became open and hostile. Taipei made a legal claim to the islands, this time on the basis of the 1958 Continental Shelf Convention, which said that any country was entitled to exploit offshore resources lying within a depth of 200 meters or beyond "where the depth of the waters admits of the exploitation of natural resources."[7] Although the depth of the ocean between Taiwan and the Fishing Islands exceeds 200 meters, the continental shelf (from mainland China) may be seen to extend to the Fishing Islands. The latter provision in the Continental Shelf Convention seemed to apply in Taipei's favor.[8] On this basis the Republic of China granted concessions to the Pacific Gulf Petroleum Company to exploit the oil resources in the vicinity of the Fishing Islands.[9]

The Continental Shelf Convention, however, was not ratified by the Legislative Yuan of the government of the Republic of China until August 1970; and it appears that it was signed specifically for the purpose of making the claim on the Fishing Islands. It also appears that Taipei's claim to the oil resources on the continental shelf of China could be seen (in addition, of course, to reflecting a need for oil) an attempt to show its mettle against improving relations by both the United States and Japan with the People's Republic of China. A month after the convention was signed by Taipei, Foreign Minister Wei Tao-ming notified the Japanese government that the Republic of China would exercise its sovereign rights over the Fishing Islands.[10]

Meanwhile, the Japanese government took additional steps to claim the islands. Tokyo asserted that the "Senkaku Islands" had been inhabited by Japanese until the end of World War II, and that the islands had been a part of Ishigaki City in the southwestern Ryukyus.[11] Further, Tokyo claimed that an Okinawan citizen held a deed to the islands; this citizen, whom the Japanese government named, allegedly received the islands from his father who had discovered them. The father's claim to the islands was said to have been legalized in 1896 and again in 1931. Also, Tokyo pointed out that the owner of the islands paid $400 yearly in taxes on the islands and, in addition, that one of the islands was rented from him by the United States government (meaning the U.S. Navy) for $11,000 per year.[12]

In December 1970, a meeting was called between representatives of the governments of the Republic of China, Japan, and the Republic of Korea (because oil deposits were also thought to exist on the continental shelf of South Korea and beyond) in Tokyo. The gathering was apparently held to resolve the issue of the oil in the area—in particular, to decide how it should be divided between the three countries—before the controversy over the Fishing Islands could give rise to more serious problems.[13] A joint committee was formed for ocean development research and the exploitation of undersea oil resources; otherwise, no notable decisions were forthcoming, or at least none were made known.

Apparently no agreement could be reached on either the oil or territory issue. The following March the Japanese press reported that the Republic of China had contacted Japan for technical assistance to make further efforts to exploit offshore oil in the Taiwan Strait.[14] Immediately, the government of the Republic of China denied the authenticity of this statement.[15]

Meanwhile, beginning in January, Tiaoyutai demonstrations were held by Chinese students in a number of large cities in the United States, including New York, Washington, DC, Chicago, Seattle, San Francisco, and Los Angeles. In New York, demonstrations were staged in front of the United Nations building and in Washington, DC, at the Japanese embassy.[16] A "Tiaoyutai Movement" was also launched in Hong Kong. In all cases, demonstrators claimed Chinese sovereignty over the Fishing Islands. The timing of these demonstrations was clearly coordinated with Taipei's negotiations with Japan on the undersea oil. A number of sources averred that the demonstrations had been planned and carried out by the government in Taipei.[17]

In April 1971, ignoring the demonstrations, the United States government announced that the Fishing Islands would be returned to Japan. This was the immediate cause for renewed demonstrations and protest.

In Hong Kong, parades were held and violent disturbances occurred, resulting in some injuries and the arrest of a number of young people.[18] In and near Taipei, demonstrations were held on university and college campuses, after which demonstrators went to the United States and Japanese embassies to present their grievances. Emotional slogans, such as "Don't wait until a second Yalta Treaty is signed" and "Tiaoyutai is ours," were heard. Nevertheless, the demonstrations were orderly and peaceful, apparently reflecting the fact that they were supervised by government authorities. Some students at the schools where the demonstrations took place intimated that government representatives at the schools called on certain students to participate and instructed them as to the purpose and limits of the demonstrations.

Following the demonstrations in Taipei, the U.S. ambassador to the Republic of China stated in a special press conference that the United States had not made a final decision on returning of the Fishing Islands to Japan.[19] At nearly the same time, however, the U.S. State Department warned American oil companies that they should not enter into any agreement to exploit undersea oil in the Taiwan Strait without prior State Department advice. Pacific Gulf heeded this advice by not continuing with its planned explorations.[20]

This move suggested that Washington probably wanted to hold the status of the Fishing Islands in abeyance. In June, when the reversion of Okinawa was made official in the form of a ceremony between the United States and Japan, there were no special provisions for the Fishing Islands, presumably meaning that they were to be returned to Japan along with the Ryukyu Islands. The treaty ceremony was followed by further demonstrations in front of the Japanese and U.S. embassies in Taipei. In addition, Nationalist Chinese warships held maneuvers around the Fishing Islands for several hours on June 29.[21]

Conclusions

The United States was apparently motivated to return the Fishing Islands to Japan in the belief that the islands are a part of the Ryukyu Islands and rightfully belonged to Japan. The hastiness of the decision and the absence of any efforts to placate feelings in Taipei suggest a coolness toward the Republic of China, perhaps because of Nationalist Chinese pressure to discourage Washington from continuing friendly gestures to Peking and the use of demonstrations about the Fishing Islands' status to make this pressure known.

The U.S. government, in approaching better relations with the People's Republic of China, may also have wanted to avoid a dispute with Peking on the issue of the islands. On two occasions, Peking announced that the Fishing Islands belonged to the People's Republic of China.[22] However, these claims were not made very strenuously, and greater stress was placed on the issue of misusing natural resources as opposed to a territorial claim. It may be seriously doubted that Peking planned to make a real bid for the islands. Moreover, Washington's cooperation with Taipei, by allowing U.S. oil companies to drill oil in the Taiwan Strait, would doubtless have been just as offensive to Peking as returning the islands unceremoniously to Japan (if this is what the United States indeed did).

Washington's decision also seems to have been prompted more by efforts to disengage militarily in Asia in accordance with the Nixon Doctrine. Such plans meant that American allies had to be persuaded or forced into accepting greater responsibility for the defense of Asia. The Fishing Islands problem may, in fact, help push Japan in coming years into a new role in Asia. The director general of the Japanese Defense Agency has already announced that the Fishing Islands would be included in Japan's defense network in 1972.[23]

There is little doubt that Taipei sparked the dispute over the Fishing Islands because of strained relations with both the United States and Japan over the issue of their relations with Peking. It might be speculated that Taipei wished to publicly renew its claim to represent all of China by claiming these islands, since they are part of the mainland continental shelf. It is also possible that the Nationalist Chinese government wanted to sound out or apply pressure in Washington and Tokyo in the context of the impending issue of Chinese representation in the United Nations.

Other issues may also have been germane in fostering Taipei's actions. For example, Nationalist officials had charged that the Taiwan Independence Movement was getting official support in the United States and Japan, and it seems that this was not just fabrication.[24] Finally, the controversy over the Fishing Islands was no doubt caused in part by unproductive negotiations on the oil to be taken from beneath the sea in the area. It is quite possible that Japanese officials stalled the negotiations believing that time was in Japan's favor. Or Tokyo may have wished to be extra cautious in view of its delicate relations with Peking, while Taipei wanted an immediate solution to the problem.

It is clear that the tiny islands have little intrinsic value. Once the problem of the oil and the political problems between the governments involved are resolved, the problem of sovereignty can probably be decided with little or no difficulty. In fact, if the issue is allowed to pass without further ado in Taipei, the islands will no doubt revert quietly to Japan in 1972 along with the rest of the Ryukyu Islands. Japan, however, does not want to lose sovereignty over the islands; that is an important matter to Japan. It would weaken its territorial claims in the north and hurt its claim to the undersea oil in the area around the Fishing Islands. Japan—the world's largest importer of oil—needs this oil. For this reason, Japan cannot make any significant concession on the territorial issue.

The Republic of China's claim to Fishing Islands is weak. It is based upon historical records of dubious validity and the fact that the islands are a part of China's continental shelf. Even maps in Taipei show the islands to be a part of the Ryukyu chain. Moreover, the Nationalist Chinese claim on the islands was made only after oil was discovered beneath the sea in the area.

Taipei's legal claim to the islands, which was already shaky, was further undermined by Peking's admission to the United Nations in early 1971. In the opinion of most nations, if the Fishing Islands are part of the continental shelf, they should belong to the People's Republic of China. Finally, the China Petroleum Company in Taiwan does not have the machinery and technical skills to exploit off-shore oil at this depth, and it is doubtful that Taipei can enlist the help of a foreign oil company with the problem of sovereignty undecided.

Demonstrations and protest over the Fishing Islands, obviously directed by the Nationalist Chinese government, seem patently related to issues other than sovereignty over the small islands. Because of the likelihood that Peking will capitalize on the issue (pro-Communist students were thought to have participated in the demonstrations in both the United States and Hong Kong), it is unlikely that more demonstrations will be held. In August it was so rumored in Taipei and indeed no new demonstrations have taken place since.

The problem of the Fishing Islands in large part represented disagreements between Washington and Taipei and a period of instability in the relations between the two countries, as did the bombing of U.S. agencies and businesses in Taiwan and hostilities shown toward Americans living in Taiwan at that time. Most likely, the Nationalist Chinese government has now accepted the fact that the United States cannot continue to ignore Peking, and at the same time that the United States does not plan to repudiate its commitments to Taipei. If this is true, there will probably be little heard about the Fishing Islands, except for the drilling of oil in coming months.

Endnotes

1. *Shih Liu-ch'ou Lu San-chung* (Three Historical Records on the Ryukyu Islands) (Taipei: Taiwan Provincial Government Printing Office, 1970), p. 11.

2. *Tiao-yu-t'ai Lieh-yu Wen-t'i* (The Tiaoyutai Islands Question) (Taipei: Overseas Publishing Company, 1971), p. 26. Also see ibid.

3. For the text of the Cairo Declaration, see *United States Relations with China* (Washington, DC: U.S. Government Printing Office, 1949), p. 249.

4. See, for example, Franz H. Michael and George E. Taylor, *The Far East in the Modern World* (New York: Holt, Rinehart and Winston, Inc., 1964), p. 448.

5. *New York Times,* August 28, 1969.

6. *New York Times,* September 1, 1969.

7. For the complete text of this treaty, see Gerald J. Mangone, *The Elements of International Law* (Homewood: Dorsey Press, 1967), p. 188. This treaty went into effect on June 10, 1964. An analysis of the application of this treaty to the Republic of China's claim to the Fishing Islands is found in Ch'ou Hung-ta, "Tsung Kuo-chi Fan-kuan-tien Lun Tiao-yu-t'ai Lieh-hsing Wen-t'i," ("The Tiaoyutai Islands Problem from the Standpoint of International Law") *Ta-hsueh* (University), January 1971.

8. John Gittings, "Scramble for Oil in the Far East," *Guardian,* December 18, 1970.

9. The exact nature of the agreement between the Republic of China, the China Petroleum Company and Pacific Gulf Oil Company was not clear at this time. For later comments on the agreement, see *New York Times,* January 30, 1971.

10. *China Post,* August 22, 1970 and September 5, 1970.

11. *Japan Times,* September 1, 1970.

12. For a summary of the basis of Japan's claim to the Fishing Islands, see Robert Liu, "Japanese Daydream,"*Okinawa Morning Star,* June 19, 1971.

13. It is noteworthy that the representatives sent to this meeting were financial representatives of the governments concerned.

14. *Yomiuri,* March 12, 1971.

15. *Central Daily News,* March 16, 1971.

16. See *New York Times,* January 30, 1971, for details on these demonstrations.

17. A number of Chinese students in the United States at this time told me that the demonstrations were organized by Nationalist Party members among the Chinese students in the United States. In the case of one of the demonstrations

in the United States, I was personally acquainted with the leader of the demonstration and know this to be true. A number of students from Hong Kong told me the same thing concerning the demonstrations and protest movements in Hong Kong.

18. *Okinawa Morning Star*, July 9, 1971. Demonstrations were also held in London and other cities at this time.

19. *China Post*, May 19, 1971.

20. Two weeks earlier, Pacific Gulf's exploration ship left Taiwan. An appeal was made by Taipei to Pacific Gulf to go on with the work; the appeal did not attain results, however. For more details on this matter, see *New York Times*, April 14, 1971.

21. *Okinawa Morning Star*, July 4, 1971.

22. *People's Daily*, December 29, 1970 and May 1, 1971. The December article assailed the Republic of China for trying to make a deal with Japan and the Republic of Korea on the undersea oil. On May 1, a claim was made to the Fishing Islands.

23. *Japan Times*, May 20, 1971.

24. *Far Eastern Economic Review*, May 20, 1971. The press in Taiwan criticized the United States on a number of occasions for its handling of the assassination attempt on Chiang Ching-kuo's life when he was in New York by members of the Taiwanese Independence Movement and for not allowing extradition of the criminals.

Chapter Three
Taiwan's Options

On December 15, 1978, President Jimmy Carter announced that the United States would grant formal diplomatic recognition to the People's Republic of China PRC) and withdraw recognition from the Republic of China (ROC). He also stated that the U.S. defense treaty with the Republic of China would be terminated after one year, and acknowledged that Taiwan was a part of China. The administration subsequently suggested the term "corporate state" of China when discussing Taiwan's status—apparently assuming that it would be incorporated by the PRC some time in the future.

Although Washington's decision to establish formal diplomatic ties with Peking was expected by Taipei, the way it was done and the other agreements were not. The ROC government, in fact, had anticipated that the United States would use either the German formula (recognizing two Chinas) or the Japanese formula (formal recognition of Peking with some arrangement for informal ties with Taipei). The former was an optimistic view but was nevertheless regarded as possible since the Soviet Union had been able to recognize two Germanys and because the United States seemed as important to China as the Soviet Union was to West Germany. Although the Japanese formula was less advantageous, it was regarded as more likely inasmuch as the Chinese Communist leadership had indicated publicly to U.S. officials that it was willing to accept this approach to negotiations. In fact, Premier Teng Hsiao-p'ing had suggested that the United States might simply reverse the locations of the embassy and the liaison office. Since the American liaison officer in Peking had ambassadorial status, this move would not have been a serious setback for Taipei.

Hence, the announcement that the United States would recognize Peking and de-recognize Taipei in conformity with the three conditions that Peking had set earlier—that is, Washington would close its embassy in Taipei, withdraw U.S. troops from Taiwan, and terminate the defense treaty—undoubtedly came as a surprise and, in fact, was a shock to the Chinese Nationalist leadership. President Carter also acknowledged in the joint communiqué that Taiwan was a part of

China, and in subsequent statements indicated that he genuinely accepted this view.

Although President Nixon had referred to only one China in the Shanghai Communique, he resorted to ambiguous language in doing so, stating, "Chinese on either side of the Taiwan Strait agree that there is only one China." He also promised the ultimate withdrawal of U.S. troops from Taiwan, but made this contingent upon "peace and stability in the area." In addition, the term "self-determination" was used in the US side (the English version) of the Shanghai Communiqué. Finally, President Nixon at the time repeated long-held positions on U.S. relations with South Korea and Japan that were opposed to those of the PRC leadership and subsequently stated on a number of occasions that Taiwan's security and U.S. ties with Taiwan would be maintained. (Henry Kissinger had originally suggested that the United States concede to Peking the point that Taiwan was Chinese territory, but Nixon rejected this advice.)

Furthermore, during three administrations, from the signing of the Shanghai Communiqué on February 28, 1972, to Carter's announcement on December 15, 1978, U.S. officials had on more than fifty occasions declared or promised that Taiwan's security would be maintained. According to the ROC deputy foreign minister, the White House had promised more than twenty times that the U.S.-ROC defense pact would not be abrogated.

Taipei had other reasons for feeling confident about the defense treaty. The United States Senate in the summer of 1978 passed a resolution by the unanimous vote of 94 to 0 declaring that the president should consult with the Congress before ending any treaty then in force, making special reference to the U.S.-ROC defense pact. Subsequently, the House of Representatives gave its support to the resolution. Public opinion in the United States was also favorable to Taiwan: Americans opposed termination of the defense agreement by a ratio of three to one and opposed de-recognition by a slightly wider margin.

There was cause for desperation in Taiwan. Taipei was stunned and angered by Carter's moves. And, not only the way it was done but also the context in which it happened made it worse. Taiwan's diplomatic position had eroded seriously since the United Nations vote, on October 25, 1971, to seat Peking and eject Taipei. Only twenty-three countries still maintained formal diplomatic relations with the ROC in December 1978. Taipei had no security agreement with any other nation and relied completely on the United States for its strategic defense and for arms. Moreover, Peking had on a number of occasions vowed to liberate Taiwan by force if necessary, and shortly before Carter's announcement the PRC held military exercises that involved the use of amphibious and landing forces of the kind that would be used in an invasion of Taiwan.

Although the situation as perceived by ROC decision makers was not an immediate crisis inasmuch as the defense treaty with the United States remained in effect until the end of 1979, Taipei no doubt felt betrayed. More important, it anticipated domestic political instability. It also expected an emergency situation immediately after the termination of the treaty or at minimum some time in the near future.

Despite these developments, the ROC leaders repeated their determination never to enter into negotiations with Peking on Taiwan's status, or anything else for that matter. And clearly the population rallied to the government's cause. There can be no question that the people of Taiwan, in spite of strong differences of opinion on other issues, unequivocally opposed Carter's acknowledgment that Taiwan "is a part of Communist China," and the implication that Taipei should negotiate with Peking concerning reversion. Although there were no opinion polls to support a judgment on this question, most observers who are knowledgeable about the situation in Taiwan agreed that an overwhelming majority of the population opposed incorporation into the PRC. It was also clear that most of them would be willing to fight to prevent this.

In this context, it is instructive to examine Taiwan's options in the period ahead. In the following sections, the three most obvious choices will be discussed: (1) declaring independence; (2) aligning with the Soviet Union; (3) developing nuclear weapons. Although the disadvantages for Taipei in exercising any of these options may seem so great as to rule them out as real possibilities, the untenable position in which Taiwan now finds itself suggests that it may be forced to take them seriously. Furthermore, there is evidence that Taipei is now in the process of implementing all three options, at least tentatively. These options, it should be pointed out, can be carried out slowly, with subtlety, in part in secret, and possibly with little worry over the ramifications.

The Independence Option

The most obvious option for Taipei is to declare publicly that it is giving up its claim to be the legitimate government of all of China and likewise to any territory governed by the People's Republic of China. This announcement would present to the world, including the U.S. Congress and the American people, the impression that Taipei is responding to its present dilemmas with realism, while underscoring the fact that President Carter's statement acknowledging Taiwan is a part of China was not in consonance with the desires of the population of Taiwan or with other political realities. In this context, ROC leaders might even argue that Taiwan really was never part of China. Taiwan has been administratively (organized as a province) of China for fewer than fifteen years (though China ruled it for two centuries) in the entire 5,000 years of recorded Chinese history. Moreover, on numerous occasions in the past, Peking renounced its claims to Taiwan. In 1895, Peking ceded Taiwan "in perpetuity" to Japan. Mao and other PRC leaders in the 1930s stated that Taiwan was not a part of China. In 1951, Japan formally gave up its claim to Taiwan in a treaty with the Republic of China, and no mention was made of any claim or right to the island that might be vested in the People's Republic of China.

Taipei could then propose a plebiscite—a device frequently employed to settle territorial disputes—to determine Taiwan's future. This method was used to determine the future of other territory formerly part of the Japanese empire, including Okinawa, and is generally supported by the United Nations and the world community as the best way of resolving territorial claims and making claim to nation-state status.

Taipei would have the choice of whether to change its name or not. If it remained the "Republic of China," it could simply redefine its borders and continue normal diplomatic relations with the twenty or more countries that still maintain ties with Taipei. This would be an advantage in that this title is used in the literally thousands of treaties and other agreements that Taipei has with other countries. It also represents less of a break with the past. Alternatively, Taipei could change its name to the "Taiwan Republic," and thereby accentuate its independent status and the breaking of its links with China. This decision might induce a number of countries to extend recognition that might otherwise not do so. (Some countries that have broken relations with Taipei have reportedly promised to restore diplomatic ties if Taipei declares its independence and changes its name.) Taipei would also be able to pressure a number of foreign companies operating in Taiwan or that have large investments there to change the name of the host country in various contracts and agreements, thereby underscoring Taiwan's independent status. The same thing could be done with airlines and shipping companies that wish to traverse its air space or territorial waters. Similarly, Taiwan could apply for membership in a number of international organizations in which Peking could not exercise a veto or where representation is given to nation-states without regard to political qualifications, or where individual citizens can hold representation. Taipei's application for United Nations membership, even though it would no doubt be vetoed by Peking, would probably win considerable support and even sympathy from members nations, since Taiwan would be the only nation (with the exceptions of North and South Korea) to have sought membership and been refused.

In the process of declaring its independence, Taipei would probably be well advised to withdraw from the offshore islands of Quemoy and Matsu. This action would sever the last remaining link between Taiwan and China, both geographically and historically, and would better position Taiwan to defend its territory against an attack by Communist China— by avoiding a situation whereby a large number of its forces might be killed or taken captive while clearly placing it in a defensive posture.

Although the repercussions of such a move would in many ways be undesirable, the decision could be timed and implemented in such a way as to minimize the liabilities. If the move were made soon, it would take advantage of the transfer of Chinese Communist troop away from the Taiwan Strait area and the resulting lower force levels on the mainland coast opposite Taiwan. Currently, Peking would need time to prepare an invasion, and its threats of intimidation against Taiwan are less than credible. Both the continuation of the U.S.-ROC defense pact until the end of 1979 and confrontations with the Soviet Union and Vietnam argue against Peking taking any military action against Taiwan in the immediate future. Thus, Taipei's rupture of the last vestiges of its ties with mainland China probably would not provoke any immediate reaction from Peking, and the world and the United States would have time to accept Taiwan's move as a new reality.

Taipei could alternatively delay announcing its independence until such time as Peking becomes more dependent, both politically and economically, upon the United States and Japan, assuming Peking could not thereafter afford to alienate Washington or Tokyo. Clearly Peking is becoming increasingly dependent on both Japan and the United States for the success of its economic modernization program and is trying to ally politically with both against the Soviet Union. This strategy will inevitably limit its future freedom of movement with respect to Taiwan. The same thing can be said more generally with respect to its efforts to improve its overall image in the international community and within various international organizations. Or, Taipei might choose to assert its formal independence more gradually and indirectly. In fact, it can be argued that it has already moved in this direction by refusing negotiations with Peking. This refusal and the claim to be the legal government of Taiwan, which it says is backed by the overwhelming support of its people, is tantamount in some respects to a declaration of independence.

Taipei has certain policy choices available to support its claim to independence, in the event that Peking seeks to bring pressure against it. Taipei could, for example, negotiate with Vietnam, the Philippines, or Malaysia concerning the future of certain territories it claims or holds in the South China Sea, and which Peking also claims. Such a move would be certain to complicate relations between those countries and the PRC. Taipei could do almost the same thing by abandoning its claim to the Senkaku Islands north of Taiwan, which were returned to Japan by the United States along with Okinawa. Taipei might apply for immigration visas for several million of its citizens to go to Japan and other nearby countries, and to the United States, because of fear of persecution under PRC rule. This action could force these nations to face up to the realities of the problem and to regard it as something other than simply a domestic Chinese issue. Conceivably, Taipei might also resort to terrorist tactics similar to those used by the Palestine Liberation Organization to win attention for its claim to self-determination, although it is certainly aware that few people in the nations it hopes to influence in other ways would support such methods.

Indeed, an independence policy of some kind should be expected in reaction to President Carter's dramatic initiative. The implementation of such a policy, if gradual, probably does not involve undue risks from Taipei's point of view. This is not only because Taipei is already in a very difficult situation, and would weigh such a course against the risks already present; it also knows that the White House decision was taken against the sentiment of the Congress, the American people, and even world opinion. A declaration of independence would put the Carter administration in a difficult position. It would accentuate the differences between the White House and the Congress, as well as underscore the lack of public support for at least one aspect of American foreign policy. It would inevitably cause some strain in U.S. relations with Communist China as Washington groped for the appropriate response to what would be an increasingly awkward new political reality.

The Soviet Option

A second option for Taipei is to seek closer relations with the Soviet Union leading to an agreement that would afford Taiwan some of the security it will lose when the U.S.-ROC defense treaty lapses at the end of 1979. Many observers have argued that such a development is not likely because of Taiwan's vital commercial relations with the West. It is also argued that Taipei could not trust the Kremlin. But there are also counter-arguments. First, a secret agreement would not endanger Taiwan's commercial or other ties with the West and Japan. Second, it is uncertain in any event that Soviet ties with Taiwan would in any case interfere with Taiwan's present foreign economic relationships. Soviet political and military ties with a number of other countries have not hurt their capitalist-oriented economy or trade. Third, Taipei has undoubtedly come to distrust the United States, especially in view of the timing and modalities of Washington's recognition of Peking and abrogation of the defense treaty after numerous assurances to the contrary. For the moment, at least, Taipei could hardly perceive the Soviet Union as being less reliable than the United States.

There is some reason to believe that there may already be a number of agreements or informal understandings in effect between Taipei and Moscow. Ever since 1960, when the Sino-Soviet break became formal, and especially after the onset of the Cultural Revolution in China in 1965, there has been growing evidence that the Soviet Union no longer perceived the incorporation of Taiwan by China to be in its best interests. In 1965, pictures of the flag of the Republic of China were published in the Soviet Union, constituting (in Peking's view, at least) Moscow's recognition of the ROC being a sovereign nation. The following year, a Soviet magazine called Taiwan a "state," and in 1967, this same term appeared in an official Tass release. In 1970, coinciding with Vice President Agnew's trip to Asia, the Soviet press called Taiwan a "country." In 1968, Victor Louis, a well-known unofficial representative of the Soviet government, visited Taiwan and conferred with Chiang Ching-kuo, who was then defense minister. In 1971, the Soviet Union's United Nation's representative made reference to a "two-Chinas solution" to the Chinese representation question then before the world body.

Other facts suggest that the Soviet Union has a military interest in Taiwan and that this view is reciprocated in Taipei. The ROC's armed forces tie down large numbers of Chinese troops across the Taiwan Strait in Fukien Province that might otherwise be shifted to the north to reinforce Chinese divisions on the Sino-Soviet border. In 1969, after the flare-up on the border, and coinciding with Moscow's demands that Peking negotiate forthwith, paramilitary forces from Taiwan raided a military installation in Fukien Province. China's defense planners announced the next year that in the event of escalating hostilities with the Soviet Union, China would also have to prepare for an invasion from the east. Since the Soviet Union does not possess adequate capabilities for landing forces on the Chinese coast, this had to refer to Taiwan. At almost the same time, Peking accused Taipei of holding talks with Soviet military representatives in Tokyo on problems of mutual interest. In 1973, just two days before Ambassador David Bruce went to Peking to head the U.S. "liaison office," two Soviet warships passed through the Taiwan Strait and circumnavigated the island. This was the first time that Soviet naval vessels passed through the Taiwan Strait since World War II. After President Carter's announcement on December 15, 1978, that the United States would grant recognition to the People's Republic of

China, it was rumored that Soviet ships were again in the Taiwan Strait and had signaled to military installations on the coast of Taiwan.

Evidence on the Taiwan side also indicates a change in both attitude and policy toward the Soviet Union over a period of years. In the early 1960s, the government-controlled press in Taiwan stopped criticizing the Soviet Union as harshly as it had formerly; contrary to past practice, it also began to discriminate between Soviet and Chinese communism. In 1969, the year after Victor Louis's trip to Taipei, the ROC minister of education traveled to the Soviet Union on a semi-official visit, accompanied by newspaper reporters. Chiang Ching-kuo's wife, who is Russian and whom he married in the Soviet Union, was subsequently seen in public more frequently, and the press was allowed to photograph her—again contrary to past practices. On a number of occasions, officials in Taipei have said (though always unofficially or off the record) that Taiwan plans to provide the Soviet Union with bases if the United States moves its embassy to Peking. In all cases, the reports were subsequently denied; but in view of the number of them, and the fact that the officials reportedly making them were not punished, it must be that they had official sanction, at least as trial balloons. The most recent reports were made by a Greek newspaper editor who spent several weeks in Taiwan in 1975 and by South Korean sources in August 1978. It is also noteworthy that a member of the National Assembly in Taipei made a similar statement at a meeting of that body after Carter's announcement on granting diplomatic recognition to Peking in December 1978.

Peking's statements of reaction which go beyond those already mentioned provide further evidence of the possibility of a Soviet connection. In April 1978, for example, Peking charged that secret conversations were going on between Moscow and Taipei in Vienna; and in July, Peking charged "collusion" between the Soviet Union and Taiwan. There is no question that Peking is concerned about the prospect of military and other ties between Moscow and Taipei. Communist leaders in Peking have frequently commented on the possibility of talks between the two.

Clearly Taipei and Moscow have parallel interests, which have been brought into focus by the U.S. decision to recognize Peking diplomatically, especially in the fashion it did. Moscow perceives that the United States is allying (having already an alliance with Japan in place) with China to form an alliance against the Soviet Union, and that the Kremlin's strategic interests in Northeast Asia are threatened. Ties with Taiwan would counter this and at the same time might enhance Soviet efforts to establish what it calls an "Asian security system" (better perceived of as a Soviet-Asia security system), which interestingly Taipei does not oppose.

Although Taiwan's defenses are strong, ultimately the island would need outside help to repel an invasion. A Soviet promise to keep Sino-Soviet border tension high enough to prevent Chinese troops from massing in Fukien Province, to deliberately heighten tensions if such a reinforcement effort began, or to interdict an invasion across the strait by the use of Soviet naval forces would all help Taipei deal with this threat. The presence of Soviet military bases in Taiwan, would even more serve to increase Taiwan's security in the event of an invasion.

The Nuclear Option

A third option for Taiwan is to go nuclear. Again, many observers argue that Taipei cannot and will not exercise this option for a host of reasons. There is, however, considerable evidence that Taiwan has already gone some distance in this direction. Clearly, like the other options cited above, it is not an all-or-nothing decision. Taipei could go up to the last step prior to an actual test or build weapons in secret without testing them; in either case, it would retain a measure of ambiguity as to its nuclear status.

The argument that Taiwan has nuclear weapons capabilities is widely accepted. Scientists in Taiwan have been doing research on nuclear energy since the early 1950s. To date, more than a thousand scientists from Taiwan have received advanced nuclear training at institutions in the United States. Since 1961, they have had use of a nuclear reactor and thus an opportunity to carry their research to more advanced levels. Taipei has also purchased equipment abroad to build three nuclear power plants with two nuclear generators in each. One generator is now in use and a second will go on stream in August this year. In the 1980s, nuclear power will—according to recent estimates—produce more than 40 percent of Taiwan's electricity. The by-products of these power plants could provide the raw materials for a number of nuclear bombs if diverted to that purpose.

One of Taiwan's nuclear research reactors was purchased from Canada shortly before Ottawa granted diplomatic recognition to Peking. As a result of cutting diplomatic ties, the reactor is no longer subject to inspection. Furthermore, the reactor was almost identical to the one that Canada sold to India, which was instrumental in India's engineering a "nuclear explosion" in 1974. Taiwan also has a facility for reprocessing spent fuel, which is probably the most important step in moving from the peaceful use of nuclear energy to the production of bombs. In fact, in 1976, it was reported that the Republic of

China had secretly reprocessed some of the nuclear fuel it was using for experimental purposes.

Westinghouse, the company that has contracted with Taiwan to build two of its nuclear power plants, and also the U.S. Energy Research and Development Administration, the Joint Committee on Atomic Energy of the Congress, and the CIA, have all judged Taiwan to be a potential nuclear power. In 1975, Premier Chiang Ching-kuo was reported to have stated that Taiwan has both the facilities and the capabilities to make nuclear weapons and has considered building a nuclear arsenal. In other statements, Taipei has denied that it has any intention of building nuclear weapons; presumably, however, the long-term validity of such assertions would depend on the ROC's perceptions of its security situation.

Together with the capability to build nuclear weapons, Taiwan also has a credible delivery system. Taiwan's F-4 and F-5 jet fighter planes can be fitted to carry nuclear weapons. Since these planes were used by U.S. military forces in Taiwan and were so equipped at the time, presumably the ROC Air Force already has the know-how for this. Republic of China military forces may also be able to deliver an atomic warhead by missile. Its engineers have ostensibly acquired the sophisticated technology necessary to build the inertial navigational systems used in missiles. In the past year, Taiwan has displayed locally built missiles. If it does not yet have a missile system capable of delivering nuclear weapons, it surely will have before long. In any event, in view of Taiwan's demonstrated capabilities to infiltrate men and material into China, it may not need such a sophisticated delivery system. It might deliver them "by hand."

The question then is: Will Taipei see the need to go nuclear? The Republic of China signed the 1968 Nuclear Non-Proliferation Treaty, and in 1970 ratified it. Both, however, were done when the Republic of China was a member of the United Nations. In 1971, it was expelled from the world body. Thus, it could be argued that it now has no responsibilities under the treaty. As a consequence, Taipei's decision may rest on how it perceives its guarantees under the non-proliferation treaty. The United States and the Soviet Union have both guaranteed non-nuclear signatories protection from threat or attack by other nuclear countries. If Taipei sees this as effectively applying to Peking, then it will probably forgo the decision to go nuclear. In view of President Carter's statement that Taiwan is a part of China, however, Taipei cannot reasonably assume that this will be the case.

Looking at Taipei's situation another way, in the event that Peking is able to convince the United States and other important countries that the Taiwan question is purely an internal or domestic matter, Taipei may be compelled to exercise the nuclear option to prove that this is not the case. Certainly Taiwan could gain world attention by announcing the attainment of nuclear status or by testing a nuclear device. This course of action would undoubtedly strengthen Taipei's claim to be recognized as a sovereign nation. Similarly, Taipei may see an advantage in going nuclear if Peking threatens Taiwan in order to force it to negotiate incorporation, or if the PRC starts making long-term preparations, such as increasing force levels in the part of China near Taiwan or acquiring landing craft, for military action against Taiwan. Finally, the burdensome costs of conventional weapons needed to guarantee its security may persuade Taipei to exercise the nuclear option.

It bears repeating at this point that Taipei can complete all of the initial steps in the process, or even build weapons, both in secret and thereby avoid the unfavorable public repercussions of going nuclear. Indeed, it may already have nuclear weapons. Alternatively, Taipei can continue to keep the world guessing about its nuclear capabilities even if it doesn't have any and doesn't plan to, while encouraging the belief that it may be close to having, or already has, nuclear weapons. This course would have almost the same effect as going nuclear without the accompanying problems.

Conclusions

Taipei may adopt any of the three options just discussed. It might exercise two or all of them simultaneously. The decision to implement any or all of the options could be made immediately or in the more distant future. The options may also be put into force gradually. Though all of them entail risks and undesirable repercussions, disadvantages or liabilities may be minimized by moving slowly or secretly.

This situation creates potentially serious problems for the United States in Asia. What is the United States to do if Taiwan exercises one or more of its options? What will be the impact on U.S.-China relations? How will Japan react and how will this affect Sino-Japanese relations? More important, how will U.S.-Soviet relations be affected? These are questions that need to be given considerable thought. The implications for all of them are serious.

All of the options pose dangers to the stability of East Asia but no doubt would inevitably involve the United States. One should recall in this context that the United States fought its last three wars in Asia. Such action by Taiwan could lead to a deterioration of relations between China and the Soviet Union or between the United States and either or both of the two Communist superpowers. The triangular relationship is in many ways a fragile one. Likewise, Japan's role in Asia and its relations with China, Taiwan, and Southeast Asia, not to mention the Soviet Union, would also be seriously affected.

One alternative for the United States, mindful of the gravity of the possible results of a decision by Taiwan to exercise any or all of its options, is to explicitly and unilaterally, or in concert with the Soviet Union, promise Taipei nuclear protection under the 1968 Nuclear Non-Proliferation treaty, including protection against an attack by Communist China. Similarly, the United States could go beyond what the Congress did in April to broaden the scope of US support for Taiwan's security, or make these "guarantees" more explicit and more formal. Another choice would be for the United States to redeploy the Seventh Fleet back to the Taiwan Strait in order to forestall its use by Peking as an invasion route. Washington could rationalize this decision in terms of the rapid Soviet naval buildup in the region. Since Peking has suggested that the United States bolster its naval strength in the Pacific area, it could hardly oppose the decision. Another choice for the United States would be to provide Taiwan with more sophisticated weapons. The decision to withhold weapons sales to Taiwan is of grave concern in Taipei and does not bode well for Taipei in the context of the coming termination of the U.S.-ROC defense pact.

Finally, the United States should deal with Taiwan as a nation-state and help bolster its image in this respect. The people of Taiwan do not want to be incorporated or ruled by China, and it is not in the U.S. interest to allow this to happen. The credibility of the United States, upon which rests its strategic posture in Asia, would be undermined if it were to abandon a loyal ally. U.S. support for a world legal order and a pluralist state system would similarly be questioned by the global community if Taiwan were taken over against its will by the PRC. The same would be true of U.S. human rights policy. It is one thing for the United States to acknowledge Peking's claim to Taiwan. It is quite another to go beyond mere acknowledgment and leave Taiwan with no alternatives but to take options that are dangerous for itself, the United States, and the world.

Chapter Four
Taiwan's Legal Status:
A Multilevel Perspective

In October 1981, President Ye Jianying, China's "head of state," made a public announcement (directed to Taipei) that the People's Republic of China was offering Taiwan very "liberal and reasonable conditions" by which Taiwan could "return to the motherland." Ye declared that Taipei had to give up the name "Republic of China" and its flag and that after reversion it would not have an independent foreign policy. Everything else, he said, was negotiable. Taiwan's political system could remain intact and so could its economic system. In the United States and other Western countries Ye's offer was portrayed by the media as reflecting China's reasonableness not to mention its desire to settle the problem of Taiwan's status, legal and otherwise, amicably.

Little attention was given by either the U.S. government or the Western media to the fact that, to accept Ye's offer Taipei would have to surrender its status as a sovereign nation-state—something it has possessed for more than thirty years. What Ye categorized as "not negotiable" is indeed vital to the sovereignty of any nation, including the Republic of China or any future regime on Taiwan. Thus Taipei's reaction was understandably negative. Only if one takes China's view that Taiwan is not a sovereign nation-state, but rather is simply "part of China," can the offer be considered generous.

Why did this become an issue at this time? The answer: The U.S. decision made in December 1978 (to be effective January 1, 1979) to de-recognize the Republic of China and establish relations with the People's Republic of China precipitated Ye's announcement. The United States had been Taiwan's protector and more for three decades; thus, after the break in relations, Taiwan's status in the eyes of some observers became tenuous. Furthermore, in addition to granting diplomatic recognition to the People's Republic of China, the United States declared that it supported a one-China policy.

Washington's policy regarding Taiwan's legal status, however, in several important respects was unclear, and remains so. In the 1960s, the two-Chinas policy or one-China and one-Taiwan policy evolving in the United States was seen by most as simply a recognition of reality. In 1972 the Shanghai Communiqué reversed this trend, seemingly establishing a one-China policy.[1] The decision to grant diplomatic relations to the People's Republic of China seven years later, and the Carter administration's formal acknowledgement that there was "only one China and Taiwan was a part of China," seemed to reaffirm this latter policy.

Nevertheless, the Carter administration allowed a defense treaty with the Republic of China to remain in force for a year. Even more important, the U.S. Congress subsequently wrote the Taiwan Relations Act (TRA), which gave Taipei access to U.S. courts and various other privileges generally given only to sovereign nation-states. It also guaranteed Taiwan U.S. weapons "sufficient to meet its needs." In so acting, Congress, for all intents and purposes, returned to Taipei its sovereignty and nation-state status even though the TRA referred to the "people of Taiwan," rather than the "Republic of China."

Meanwhile, all Western European countries that did not already have formal relations with Beijing (with the exception of the Vatican) plus Japan established diplomatic ties with the People's Republic of China during the 1970s and in doing so broke relations with the Republic of China. Nevertheless, in almost all cases they maintained pseudo-diplomatic ties with Taipei and increased trade and other kinds of contacts. They, furthermore, generally said very little about Taiwan's status as a nation-state, regarding the issue as a Chinese or U.S. problem.

The Soviet Union during the 1950s and 1960s consistently took Beijing's side on the issue of Taiwan, though during the two Offshore Islands crises the Kremlin patently did not give Chinese leaders any meaningful support in their efforts to get "their" territory back by force. In recent years Moscow has on occasion referred to Taiwan by its official name, the "Republic of China" (also calling it a "nation") and has published pictures of the Republic of China's flag in official magazines, thereby suggesting support for its nation-state status. The Soviet Union has also sent representatives to Taipei and, according to Beijing, has held defense-related talks with the Taiwan government.[2]

Third World countries have not taken and do not now generally take a serious interest in Taiwan's status, as a nation or not, unless they have received or are receiving aid from Beijing or Taipei or have important trade or ties with one or the other. Most Third World nations recognize the People's Republic of China, but a significant number retain ties with Taipei. As a result of its increased ties with the Third World, in 1981, for the first time in a number of years, the Republic of China gained in terms of the number of nations giving it official recognition.[3]

Some observers feel that Taiwan's status as a sovereign nation should be of concern to other nations and to the world community inasmuch as its fate has serious implications for international law. Furthermore, Taiwan's position might affect the status of separatist or self-determination movements in other areas of the world, which most nations either support or oppose (though many change their view depending on the situation). More important still is the fact that Taipei, if it perceives that its survival is threatened, may decide to seek an alliance with or assistance from the Soviet Union; this decision could seriously affect Sino-Soviet relations and ultimately stability in the region. Or Taipei may decide to go nuclear. It does have this potential capability. Finally, it could declare itself a new and separate nation with no ties with China.

All of these possibilities evoke the question of Taiwan's legal status. To whom does Taiwan belong? Is it a part of China? Should it legally remain independent? In seeking answers to these questions, one must consider at least four factors: historical evidence, declarations and treaties made in the modern period, the Republic of China's qualifications for nation-state status, and the United Nations definition of nationhood and its guidelines or practices regarding the disposition of disputed territory.

Historical Evidence

The original inhabitants of Taiwan were people of Malay ancestry who probably arrived by boat from the south. Taiwan is mentioned in early Chinese records, but clearly not as a part of China. Rather, it was referred to as "Liu Chiu"—the name for the Ryukyu Islands that are now part of Japan. Chinese started migrating to Taiwan from Fukien Province across the Taiwan Strait about a thousand years ago, but they severed their contacts with China when they did so. The Chinese government did not regard this migration as a colonizing effort: In fact, it was unlawful for Chinese subjects to leave China.[4] During the period of Western colonization, Taiwan, or Formosa, as the island has been called by Westerners, came under European control with no protest made by Beijing.

During the seventeenth century Taiwan experienced Chinese political control for the first time. However, this rule was by what most historians call a government-in-exile. Moreover, only a fraction of Taiwan was under central authority, and this government lasted only a short time. Subsequently, jurisdiction by China was established, but this was Manchu rule, not Chinese (as China was under Manchu control). And it was over narrow areas on the coast. The interior of the island (most of the island's land area) remained controlled by aboriginal groups, who signed treaties with Western powers.[5] This situation continued into the nineteenth century.

It was not until late in the nineteenth century that the Chinese immigrants or "Taiwanese" came to constitute a majority of the population. Even then they occupied or controlled considerably less than half of Taiwan's land area. Peking continued to regard Taiwan as a land inhabited by barbarians (by definition not Chinese), and it remained illegal for Chinese to go to Taiwan. And, though there was some migration from China, most of the island's population growth came from natural increase.

In the 1850s the United States was interested in a coaling station on Taiwan and also needed ports there for its entrepôt trade. Contact was made with the Chinese government concerning the status of Taiwan, and American officials were told that China did not claim title to or jurisdiction over Taiwan. Subsequently a recommendation was made to the U.S. president that the United States make Taiwan a colony. This proposal was rejected, though not because U.S. authorities considered Taiwan to be a part of China. Subsequently, in 1874, Japan complained to Peking about the killing of shipwrecked Japanese on Taiwan, at which time China again disclaimed jurisdiction and refused any responsibility. This response confirmed to Tokyo the view that Japan also took of Taiwan: that this was not part of China.

Despite these official rejections of claim to Taiwan, some Chinese officials sought to incorporate Taiwan into the Chinese empire, and the government of Fukien Province at times maintained some form of political ties to Taiwan, not to mention ties of kinship. Finally, as a result of repeated prompting by provincial authorities, Taiwan, in 1887, was made a province of China. Nevertheless, only eight years later, at the end of the Sino-Japanese War, China gave Taiwan to Japan. According to the Treaty of Shimonoseki, Taiwan was transferred to Japan "in perpetuity." Inasmuch as Taiwan had been a province of China for such a short time, plus Peking's earlier disclaimers of ownership, China's action generally went unopposed in the West. Moreover, gaining territory as a result of war or conquest was clearly established in international law. Japan's move to incorporate Taiwan into the Japanese empire was therefore considered legitimate. Finally, in ensuing years Peking made no effort to repudiate the Treaty of Shimonoseki.

When Japan took control of Taiwan, Chinese residents were given an opportunity to retain their Chinese citizenship and return to China. Less than two tenths of 1 percent so decided. Some Taiwanese opted for independence, and a "Republic of Taiwan" was formed and supported by a segment of the Taiwanese community. This turned out to be only a short-lived effort, however, and Japanese rule was soon firmly established and local opposition or protest evaporated.[6]

During the next fifty years, Taiwan was a part of Japan. Japanese was used by government officials and in the education system in Taiwan, though Taiwanese—a language derivative of the Fukien dialect of Chinese—remained in use by most of Taiwan's Chinese inhabitants. The population adopted Japanese customs and ways of thinking, yet retained local (Chinese) customs as well. "Taiwanese," as the Chinese on Taiwan called themselves, respected Japanese rule and Taiwan's economic progress that was engineered by Tokyo, though they did not think of themselves as Japanese.

Modern Declarations and Treaties

During the first part of the twentieth century, no challenge was made to Japan's rule of Taiwan or its incorporation into the Japanese empire. Peking said nothing. Nor did any foreign power contest Japan's legal right to Taiwan. In the 1930s, Mao, Lin Piao, and others later to rule China averred that Taiwan was not part of China and on several occasions put it in the same category as Korea and other nations on China's periphery.[7]

This situation changed, however, with the beginning of the war between China and Japan in 1937. Having no reason to be concerned about amicable relations with Tokyo, China announced that it disputed Japan's incorporation of Taiwan into the Japanese Empire. Though initially this claim had no support among other nations to give it any measure of legality, in the Cairo Declaration in 1943 the United States and the United Kingdom proclaimed that Taiwan was territory "stolen by Japan" and should be returned. However, like China's statement, this was a wartime declaration and even U.S. allies did not regard it as legal. In fact, since it was a joint declaration made with the government of the Republic of China, it was seen by most Western nations, including many in the United States, as little more than an effort by President Roosevelt to keep China in the war against Japan.[8] Certainly it did not have the legal standing to negate the Treaty of Shimonoseki. Observers also pointed out that it contradicted the Atlantic Charter, which proclaimed that future territorial transfers should be based on the wishes of the people residing therein.

As the war's end drew closer, the provisions of the Cairo Declaration were repeated at Potsdam. However, the Potsdam Proclamation was still only a wartime declaration and had little or no legal status. Furthermore, a surrender and a peace treaty were yet to be negotiated with Japan. Thus Taiwan's legal status was a question not dealt with directly and at the end of the war was an issue that was basically ignored by the United States and its allies.

The surrender agreement did not mention Taiwan's status either; it was left to a formal peace treaty. Japan, in the meantime, withdrew its colonial officials from Taiwan, and the government of the Republic of China established jurisdiction over Taiwan—generally with the support of the local population. Soon, however, problems arose. In 1947, when Taiwanese rebelled against Nationalist Chinese authority, it was clear that a large segment of the population was unhappy with the island's political situation. Despite the population's dissatisfaction with the Nationalist Chinese government, however, there was no appeal to Communist leaders, who by then controlled a sizable portion of China. Moreover, although many Taiwanese viewed independence as desirable, they also saw it as unrealistic.

In 1951, Japan signed a peace treaty with the allies. Meanwhile, the People's Republic of China was established on the mainland as the Nationalist Chinese army and government fled to Taiwan to regroup. Neither China signed the peace treaty, which in any case said only that Japan renounced claim to Taiwan and the Pescadore Islands. The next year Japan signed a separate peace treaty with the Republic of China in which it again renounced claim to Taiwan. This treaty, however, was vaguely written. Some articles refer to the Republic of China, others just to China. Some of the articles in the treaty imply that the territory of the Republic of China includes only Taiwan and the Pescadores; others do not say. Whether Japan legally surrendered sovereignty over Taiwan to the Republic of China is thus uncertain. At that time, however, the territory in question was almost coterminous with the Republic of China (except the offshore islands), and though the People's Republic of China was the de facto if not the de jure government of China, or at least the mainland part of China, Japan never mentioned the transfer of Taiwan to the People's Republic of China.

Subsequently, the Republic of China entered into a number of treaties and international agreement limiting its territory to that which it currently administered, namely Taiwan and the Pescadores, or, depending on the treaty, the offshore islands of Quemoy and Matsu as well. The United States-Republic of China Defense Pact signed in 1954 limited the Republic of China's territorial jurisdiction to Taiwan and the Pescadores. The Republic of China's membership in most international organizations did not specify its territorial jurisdiction, and most nations that granted recognition to the Republic of China did not mention this point. After the early 1950s, most nations that recognized the People's Republic of China only took note of or concurred with Beijing's claim to

Taiwan and did not themselves declare or offer the opinion that Taiwan and the Pescadores were territories of the People's Republic of China. Hence, if any legal status was established, it was that Taiwan was not part of the People's Republic of China but rather belonged to the Republic of China. Meanwhile, the Republic of China became thought of as synonymous with Taiwan and the Pescadores and these were assumed to be its legal territory.

The United States, in the 1972 Shanghai Communiqué, expressed the view that there was only one China but stated this in a rather oblique way, saying that this was a position held by the governments on both sides of the Taiwan Strait. The document made no mention of the wishes of the people of Taiwan, though it did speak of and support self-determination in other contexts. Thus, in spite of the fact that the Shanghai Communiqué is generally understood to have ended the evolution of a two-China policy in the United States, it may have hinted that the wishes of the population of Taiwan should be considered and even supported. At least it left open the possibility of an independent Taiwan. Washington asserted that it did "not challenge" Beijing's claim to Taiwan, but this phrasing may be taken to mean that it did not necessarily support it or consider it a legal claim either. In any event, that document, being only a communiqué, was not legally binding.

In December 1978, President Carter, while conferring diplomatic recognition on the People's Republic of China, acknowledged that Taiwan was a part of China. However, he made no commitment to see that this union was accomplished; nor did he make any effort to put forth a legal argument to support his statement that Taiwan was part of China. Carter might have consulted with the World Court, sought the opinion of other national leaders, or offered a U.S. position. He did not do so. After December 1978, the United States referred to the "people of Taiwan" when referring to Taiwan, but continued to deal with the government of the Republic of China as though it were synonymous with the people of Taiwan. Americans continued to travel to Taiwan under visas entitled "the Republic of China." Taipei, through the Taiwan Relations Act passed by Congress several months later, retained the right to use U.S. courts and other privileges belonging to legally constituted and recognized nation-states.[9] In late 1980 President Carter granted Taiwan's representative in the United States diplomatic immunity.

The Republic of China's Qualifications

The Republic of China's, or Taiwan's, legal status may also be judged by four traditional or standard qualifications. Both traditionally and in modern usage, nation-states are defined by territory, population, government, and the capacity to enter into relations with other nations.

The Republic of China's territorial size (including only Taiwan and the Pescadore Islands), though not large, is bigger than one-third of the members of the United Nations. It is often mentioned that the Republic of China makes claim to all territory under the jurisdiction of the People's Republic of China, plus Outer Mongolia; thus the Republic of China is a government-in-exile or its legitimacy will be resolved when the Chinese Civil War is finished. Few, even in Taipei, however, consider this claim as legitimate or meaningful, and the means commonly discussed to realize it seem unrealistic.

In any case, a more important point is that the Republic of China's territory has not changed in more than thirty years and should, therefore, be considered stable. It has tenuous jurisdiction over the offshore islands of Quemoy and Matsu, which are very close to the mainland, plus some other small islets there. But abandoning claim to this territory would not affect the size or territorial integrity of the nation in a significant way. In short, the Republic of China can be thought of as made up of Taiwan and the Pescadores, plus the territorial seas around them that the Republic of China can defend and that are seen by foreign nations as belonging to that government.

The population of the Republic of China is larger than that of most of the members of the United Nations. It is also stable; there has been no meaningful migration or other movement of people into or out of Taiwan in the past thirty-plus years. The People's Republic of China claims jurisdiction over all Chinese, including those born in Taiwan, and counts Taiwan's population in its census; but most other nations (and international law) do not consider this fact relevant to a legal claim. Moreover, this claim has been sullied to some extent by Beijing's unwillingness to welcome or even allow the unrestricted immigration of ethnic Chinese born in Vietnam (who are also included in their census).

The populace of the Republic of China is loyal to their government as reflected in the paying of taxes, serving in the military, and the like. They regards themselves as Chinese but are also aware of a gulf between Taiwan and the mainland in terms of ideology, culture, and economic development. Citizens of the Republic of China generally see their future in terms other than linking up with or being ruled by a government on the mainland.

The government of the Republic of China is stable by almost any global standard or criterion. There have been no irregular transfers of executive authority. The crime rate, incidents of riots and demonstrations, and the level of opposition to the government are all low compared to the majority of nations in the world. The voter turnout in elections is much higher than in most nations, even Western nations, as is popular representation in political parties. There is an independence movement abroad, most active in the United States and Japan, that demands that Taiwan be ruled by the native-born; but it does not present a threat to the government. It does not even maintain effective communications with its supporters in Taiwan, who are few in number. Moreover, this movement does not advocate that Taiwan be ruled by the People's Republic of China; in fact, it strongly opposes Taiwan becoming part of People's China or being ruled by Beijing. Thus, by any objective standard, especially a legal one, the government of the Republic of China is a legally constituted and viable one. It is sometimes pointed out that it is a minority government—of Chinese who came from the mainland in 1949. This, however, would not make it an illegal government since nearly all countries in the past have been ruled by some kind of minority (and many are today).

The Republic of China has full diplomatic ties with more than twenty nations. This figure is not large, but it compares with the number of embassies in most small Third World countries. It may decline in future years, yet according to most scholars of international law, this would not be evidence of the nation-state's extinction. Taipei maintains representation in a number of international organizations and has extensive trade and other contacts with more than 140 other countries. Its representation in the more important international organizations will no doubt decline in the future. Still, it will be able to maintain a presence in some international organizations, such as those that do not discriminate against divided nations or competing regimes and those that allow representation by citizens or organizations rather than by national representatives.

Meanwhile, the Republic of China has established informal contacts with foreign nations to substitute for the loss of diplomatic ties, and these ties will no doubt increase.[10] Clearly, the Republic of China is not diplomatically isolated. In fact, if commercial, cultural, economic, and other ties, plus tourism, are seen to represent diplomatic status, Taipei must be ranked among the most active capitals in the world.

In conclusion, using the first three traditional criteria of nationhood, the Republic of China easily meets nation-state requirements; in fact, it may be said that its qualifications are outstanding, and events short of war seem unlikely to change them. Using the last standard, Taipei does not measure up quite so well.

If both formal and informal diplomatic contacts are taken into consideration, however, the Republic of China stands at least among, and probably above, most Third World countries.

United Nations Guidelines

United Nations practice is also helpful in ascertaining Taiwan's qualifications as a nation-state and, therefore, its legal status. U.N. usage generally discounts the historical argument in making territorial claims. It also regards wartime proclamations as propaganda and hence not legally binding. Its definition of "nation-state" includes the aforementioned territory, population, government, and relations with other countries, but it interprets these liberally, thus making nation-state status open to almost all self-governing territories or prospective self-governing territories, except mini-states. Nation-state status is also based on membership in international organizations, but it is not necessarily tied to membership in the United Nations, as Switzerland's lack of membership demonstrates. Finally, self-determination is crucial to determining territorial jurisdiction or claims.[11] Thus, United Nations practice favors the Republic of China's sovereignty, though a local self-determination movement might change this.

Could this change? Because the People's Republic of China has no control over the territory or population of the Republic of China, and gaining such control would require military force, the former is legally constrained and the latter's independent status protected by the United Nations doctrine of nonacquisition of territory by force. The U.N. Charter clearly applies this principle to cases where nonmembers are involved, and according to most legal scholars, this would be extended to "competing" regimes as well. Thus the Republic of China should not legally be able to lose it sovereignty or nation-state status by force of arms.

What about Taipei's lose of representation in the United Nations? Since the Republic of China was a member of the United Nations from its founding until 1971—in fact, was a permanent member of the Security Council—it was by U.N. usage clearly a legally constituted nation-state during that period. Inasmuch as the United Nations did not repudiate the Republic of China's legal status by admitting the People's Republic of China and unseating the Republic of China, it can be assumed that the ROC still meets the U.N. definition of a legal nation-state even after the loss of U.N. membership. (It should be noted that Taipei did not apply for membership under a different name, and by holding to the claim to represent all of China, made the decision to "expel" it unavoidable.) This assumption is further substantiated by the fact that the Republic of China retains membership in a number of U.N.-affiliated organizations and by the fact that the U.N. did not transfer the Republic of China's debt to the People's Republic of China and did not cancel it.[12]

An even more important tenet of U.N. usage that alters or creates international law that bears on the disposition of contested territory is that of self--determination. U.N. practice upholds the view taken from the Atlantic Charter that territorial transfers should be made only in accordance with the wishes of the population of the said territory. Although this concept is most often applied to former colonial territory, it can have much wider application. In any case, it should have direct application to Taiwan's legal status since Taiwan was a colony of Japan for fifty years prior to 1945.

Even if one argues that Taiwan's former colonial status became irrelevant as a result of its reversion to Nationalist Chinese control after World War II, the concept of self-determination as it is used by the United Nations still has application to Taiwan inasmuch as it has been used on several occasions to determine the legally constituted governments of nation-states. It has also been used in cases of irredentist claims. Hence, self-determination may be taken as the basis for Taiwan's future legal status whether Taiwan is seen as once part of China and now independent, or as an area where there are two contending regimes disputing control over a territory and a population.

Tied to the concept of self-determination is the use of the plebiscite to decide the future of disputed territory and populations. Plebiscites have been conducted under the aegis of the U.N. in several places in recent years. A U.N.-sponsored plebiscite might be suggested as a legal, and certainly a reasonable, way to resolve the issue of Taiwan's status. Reinforcing this argument is the fact that a plebiscite was used to determine the future of Okinawa, territory also taken from Japan as a result of World War II.

If a plebiscite were held in Taiwan, the result would clearly reflect a desire by the population not to be a part of the People's Republic of China. The expected expression of the people's wishes would probably be something like 99 percent or more against being ruled by Beijing.[13] Whether a plebiscite would sup-port the present government or the name Republic of China is less certain. It probably would. Recent public opinion polls indicate a high level of public satisfaction with the government's performance.[14] Even if they did not, this would mean only that the Republic of China would be constrained to change its national title, the structure and composition of the government, or its leadership. It would mean little else.

The Prevailing Argument and Future Possibilities

Using two means of ascertaining Taiwan's legal status, historical evidence and the treaties and proclamations made relating to Taiwan during and after World War II, Taiwan's legal status is somewhat ambiguous. The Republic of China's legal authority over Taiwan is supported, but not definitively so. Neither argument supports the position that Taiwan should be considered a part of the territory of the People's Republic of China, however. Clearly neither gives any support to the view that Taiwan belongs to the regime called the People's Republic of China.

The definition of "nation-state" in both international law and U.N. usage supports the Republic of China's continued existence and its rule of Taiwan. This judgment, however, assumes to some extent that the population of Taiwan supports the ruling regime. Since the government of the Republic of China is constituted at the top by Chinese who came to Taiwan in 1949 and who are in a minority in Taiwan, there is some question about this support. Yet there is no evidence of a desire on the part of the majority to exterminate or do violence to the ruling minority. Rather, there is a perceived need for the "modernization" or democratization of the leadership, though to a considerable extent this has been accomplished through elections in recent years, especially since 1980.

Thus, although a more complete implementation of democracy would no doubt engender changes in the ethnic composition of organs of the government, it would not likely lead to the creation of a new government or make illegitimate the government of the Republic of China. Moreover, democracy would be expected to evoke greater demands for formal independence by the population of Taiwan, which would, of course, underscore the Republic of China's status as an independent and sovereign nation-state and contradict Beijing's claim.

The People's Republic of China's claim to Taiwan is based primarily upon a historical claim and the argument that it is the legal successor to the Republic of China.[15] As we have already seen, the historical argument is weak inasmuch as Taiwan was not populated by a majority of Chinese until the mid-nineteenth century; moreover, according to Chinese law, Chinese were there illegally. The claim to jurisdiction over people of Chinese blood, which often accompanies this view, is not considered an argument of any merit in international law.

The argument that the People's Republic of China is the successor to the Republic of China is similarly not a cogent one inasmuch as the latter still exists. Certainly, if that government were disestablished and a "Republic of Taiwan" established, the People's Republic of China would hardly be persuaded of the invalidity of its claim.

Chinese leaders have also mentioned the occupative and proximity arguments in their claim to Taiwan. The former suggests that China was a colonizer of Taiwan in the past and therefore has title, since a Chinese government ruling the mainland assumed governing authority from Japan. This argument, however, would legalize Japan's past rule of Taiwan, a position Beijing has consistently argued against. Furthermore, it might—if we are to accept Chinese leaders' protests during the more than two and a half decades after the 1950s that Taiwan was under the "occupation of American imperialism"—support the view that the United States has a legal claim. The proximity argument could not be entertained seriously since Taiwan is too far away, and such an argument could similarly make the Ryukyu Islands and the Philippines a part of China.

Several apparent trends in international law are also relevant. The historical argument and the argument made from past treaties are becoming less important while the qualifications for nationhood are becoming less rigid or demanding. Commensurately, the current U.N. definition of nation-state, compared even to the recent past, gives much weight to the principle of self-determination. Thus the use of the plebiscite to determine the desire or demand for self-determination, and therefore legal status, is stronger now than ever before.

The prevailing argument, then, is that Taiwan is legally ruled by the Republic of China, at least until the population of the island expresses a desire to change this status. The fact that this regime once ruled China and since 1949 has claimed jurisdiction over all of China is not germane to the title question. The Republic of China could have changed its name in 1949 and can in the future. It is important to recall in this connection that the leaders of the People's Republic of China made an assertive claim to Taiwan only after the Nationalist regime fled there in 1949, not when Taiwan was a part of the Republic of China from 1945 to 1949.

Considering practical realities along with the legal arguments, there seem to be three possibilities concerning Taiwan's future. One, Taiwan can become part of China, assuming the two governments, the People's Republic of China and the Republic of China, agree to make Taiwan a part of China and the people of Taiwan concur. At this juncture this scenario seems extremely unlikely. Two, one of several independence movements may promote or force marked changes in the composition and policies of the government of the Republic of China and in the process establish what would amount to a new regime with a new name. Similarly, a U.N. plebiscite taken in the context of a conflagration between the Republic of China and the People's Republic of China or a foiled attempt by the latter to "liberate" Taiwan might produce the same result. Three, the Republic of China might officially repudiate its claim to represent all of China and proclaim itself another China, or simply Taiwan (a Chinese nation but one that does not claim to represent Chinese elsewhere). This is a policy that is already evolving naturally, though perhaps slowly.

Of the alternatives, the third seems clearly to be the closest to a legal answer and is also the most practical solution. Thus the prevailing legal argument and reality seem to coincide and should be mutually reinforcing. It is also the only solution that can be realized democratically and that is in consonance with the views of most nations of the world, U.N. practice, and trends in international law about this kind of problem.

Endnotes

1. This view has been contested. Evidence cited that the United States had not fully accepted a one-China policy in 1972 is the fact that the Shanghai Communiqué simply states that both sides (meaning Beijing and Taipei) agree that there is one China. The United States did not officially say that it accepted this view. Furthermore, the Shanghai Communiqué is very vague, perhaps reflecting differences on the issue of Taiwan, or uncertainties on the part of Washington. Finally, President Nixon is said to have refused at the time to agree that Taiwan was a part of China and apparently rejected China's four conditions for further normalization.

2. See *Washington Post,* December 2, 1968, and March 23, 1969, and *New York Times,* January 12, 1970.

3. The newly independent Republic of Nauru granted recognition to the Republic of China that year.

4. For further details on these points, see James W. Davidson, *The Island of Formosa, Past and Present* (New York: AMS Press, 1977).

5. See Sophi Su-fei Yen, *Taiwan in China's Foreign Relations, 1836-1875* (Camden, CT: Shoestring Press, 1965), pp. 136-39.

6. George H. Kerr, *Formosa: Licensed Revolution and the Home Rule Movement, 1895-1945* (Honolulu: University of Hawaii Press, 1974), Chapter 2. Kerr, however, argues that the desire for independence on the part of the Formosans remained.

7. See Edgar Snow, *Red Star over China* (New York: Random House, 1938), pp. 88-89.

8. Winston S. Churchill, *Memoirs of the Second World War* (Boston: Houghton Mifflin, 1959), p. 753.

9. The Taiwan Relations Act states that "whenever any law, regulation, or order of the United States refers or relates to a foreign country, nation, state, government, or similar entity, such terms shall include, and such law, regulation, or order shall apply with respect to the people of Taiwan." By this provision, some argue, the U.S. Congress accorded Taiwan de facto diplomatic recognition.

10. U.S. de-recognition, in fact, prompted some nations to upgrade their ties with Taipei. It may also be relevant that some nations have apparently pledged to reestablish an embassy in Taipei if the Republic of China declares its independence and changes its official name.

11. For details on the U.N. view of nation-state status, see Rosalyn Higgins, *The Development of International Law Through the Political Organs of the United Nations* (London: Oxford University Press, 1963), pp. 54–55.

12. This conclusion may be drawn from the similarity in U.N. action on Indonesia's membership after it withdrew from the organization in 1965.

13. No such poll has ever been taken, so this statement must be based upon observation. However, I have, during several years of residence in Taiwan over the past two decades, met very few who would advocate or see any benefit in Taiwan becoming part of the People's Republic of China. Moreover, even those scholars who advocate that Taiwan should be incorporated by the People's Republic do not argue that there is any meaningful support among the population in Taiwan for this.

14. Several polls are cited in John F. Copper, "Taiwan in 1981: In a Holding Pattern," *Asian Survey*, January 1982.

15. For further details on the People's Republic of China's legal claim to Taiwan, see Hungdah Chiu, "Certain Legal Aspects of Recognizing the People's

Republic of China," *Occasional Papers/Reprints in Contemporary Asian Studies*, University of Maryland School of Law, Number 5, 1979.

Chapter Five
The Taiwan Relations Act as Viewed from Beijing and Taipei

On December 15, 1978, President Jimmy Carter announced that the United States would establish formal diplomatic relations with the People's Republic of China and at the same time would break official ties with Taiwan. Two weeks later, on January 1, 1979, Washington and Beijing issued a joint communiqué on their "normalization of relations." The "Normalization Agreement," as it became known, said that the United States "acknowledges the Chinese position that there is but one China and Taiwan is part of China." But it also declared that the United States would "maintain cultural, commercial, and other unofficial relations with the people of Taiwan." These statements would obviously evoke conflicts. Furthermore, the communiqué was very brief and, in fact, engendered controversy because many important questions were left unanswered. Most important among them was the status of Taiwan as viewed by the United States.

Congress, as the Carter administration anticipated, took action to resolve this situation as well as the problems caused by the fact that the White House had "abandoned" an old friend and ally not to mention an important "political entity" that could hardly be viewed by the United States as something other than a legally constituted nation-state. The result was an unprecedented law: the Taiwan Relations Act (TRA). Enacted in March and signed by President Carter in April, it became the first ever legislation to delineate U.S. relations with a foreign "country." Furthermore, the TRA created a dichotomy in American China policy. Some said that it created two China policies—one advanced by the executive branch of government, and one by the legislative branch, or Congress. The former viewed Taiwan as part of China legally and assumed the reunification of China in the not-too-distant future. The latter considered Taiwan a legally constituted nation-state, meaning that it could become a part of China if it wished, whenever it desired (or not).

This duality in U.S.-China policy, though confusing, was in many respects convenient. It created needed ambiguity. Washington and Beijing, notwithstanding common interests, especially in dealing with the growing Soviet military threat, still disagreed on many important matters. They had also in very recent times been archenemies and many on both sides perceived the other as dangerous or hostile. The TRA made it possible for American diplomats to blame the Congress for U.S. relations with Taiwan, particularly when dealing with Chinese officials from Beijing who felt the United States should abandon Taiwan. It fittingly obfuscated the matter of Taiwan's future. Whether Taiwan should be governed by Beijing or instead should remain an independent nation was something that could not be resolved at this time, and perhaps not even in the distant future. It encouraged Beijing and Taipei to approach unification peacefully and (in Beijing's case) to avoid trying to resolve the problem by force.

U.S.-China policy since 1979, in fact, may be viewed as having been founded on these two documents. Two other documents—the Shanghai Communiqué, signed when President Nixon visited Beijing in 1972, and the "August 17 Communiqué" of 1982, in which the United States promised to end arms sales to Taiwan (which was, for all intents and purposes, repudiated immediately after it was concluded by leaders on both sides, while the Department of State later said that it lacked legal standing, though it was not formally nullified or canceled)—are said to compete with or help interpret the Normalization Agreement and the Taiwan Relations Act. The Shanghai Communiqué and the August Communiqué, in fact, do very little to define U.S. China policy. The former is largely a statement of views by both sides, mentioning also some areas of agreement, while generally avoiding some thorny issues (namely Taiwan). It marked the end of a period of hostility between the United States and China and the beginning of a new relationship—but no one was clear about what that would be at the time. The latter represented an effort to smooth over a specific trouble spot (for Deng Xiaoping) in U.S.-China relations: namely continued U.S. arms sales to Taiwan.

In this chapter I will assess the conditions leading up to the Taiwan Relations Act and Beijing's and Taipei's perception of this ground-breaking legislation. How the two view the Act is clearly a reflection—perhaps a barometer—of how they view Washington's China policy. Their response to the TRA also mirrors how they see each other and the prospects for friendly, or unfriendly, relations and ultimately reunification or continued separation.

U.S. China Policy and the Taiwan Relations Act

In order to understand Beijing's and Taipei's response to the Taiwan Relations Act and how the two have viewed it during the thirteen years since its passage, it is necessary to look at the context in which the act became a central part of America's China policy. Clearly, the TRA was not an impulsive move on the part of an uniformed Congress. Leading members of Congress took cognizance of U.S.-China relations up to that time, particularly points of disagreement. They understood America's global commitments and the views of other members of Congress and the U.S. public as well as moral imperatives and legal constraints on foreign policy making. Thus, the reactions of the two Chinas to the TRA can be considered responses to U.S. foreign policy broadly defined as well as the changes made in China policy in 1979.

To comprehend Congress's perspective, it need be noted that the legislative branch of government was intimately involved with and supported United States' relations with Nationalist China prior to World War II.[1] During the war, Washington rendered crucial military and economic assistance to Chiang Kai-shek and counted on his armies to tie down a million or more Japanese troops that would otherwise have been freed to fight U.S. forces in the Pacific. There was some disappointment in Chiang on the part of U.S. military leaders, particularly General Joseph Stilwell; nevertheless, the United States continued to aid the Nationalists after World War II in their fight with Mao and the Chinese Communists. This lasted until Chiang was defeated in 1949.

The United States officially "washed its hands" of involvement in China's civil war in 1949 and for a brief time hoped to establish amicable relations with Mao. This was not to be, however; Mao joined the Soviet bloc—an action that turned the U.S. government as well as the American public against him. As a natural consequence, when the Korean War began President Truman reversed America's neutral, hands-off stance and ordered the Seventh Fleet into the Taiwan Strait to block an invasion of Taiwan by Mao's military forces that were at the time poised to take the island.

Following the defeat of Japan, the United States had hoped that a democratic China would play a stabilizing role in East Asia and that good relations with China would help promote democracy and preserve American interests in the region. The feeling was also widespread that Japan was not capable of becoming a democracy and in any event would not recover from its defeat to become a major power again. Hence the Communist victory in China and the inability (or unwillingness given the circumstances) to establish relations with the new government in Beijing were shocks for American policy makers and the

American people. In reaction to this "loss of China," the Department of State was purged of so-called Communists and Communist sympathizers (including virtually all of its China experts) and blame was case on Chiang Kai-shek. Both were irrational reactions.

East Asia subsequently became a part of the bipolar struggle. In response to Mao's victory, the United States supported the Nationalist government on Taiwan and treated it as the legitimate government of the Chinese people. Washington agreed with Chiang's claim that Mao's regime was illegitimate and that Chiang would liberate China from the "Communist bandits." The United States demonstrated its resolve in 1954 when Mao tried to wrest the Offshore Islands (Quemoy and Matsu—small islands close to China that were not conquered when Mao defeated the Nationalists) from Chiang. The U.S. navy helped the Nationalist Chinese military supply and reinforce the islands, and Mao backed down. President Eisenhower then proposed, and Congress approved, the United States-Republic of China Defense Pact. Subsequently, via the Formosa Resolution, passed by Congress in 1955, the treaty's provisions were extended to the Offshore Islands. In 1958, following another crisis over the Offshore Islands, the U.S. navy placed nuclear artillery on the island of Quemoy and intimidated Mao to bring an end to his assault on the islands.[2]

U.S. policy makers, however, realized that Washington might have overcommitted: The Nationalists could start a conflict that might draw the United States into a broader war with Beijing.[3] This, plus the realization that Mao's regime was not going to collapse and the Nationalists would not likely liberate China from communism without U.S. help, prompted a policy shift in Washington toward a two-China (or a one-China, one-Taiwan) policy. Had it not been for the Vietnam conflict, which escalated after the Gulf of Tonkin incident in 1964 and the Great Proletarian Cultural Revolution, launched by Mao in late 1965, which radicalized and isolated China, a formal United States two-China policy might have evolved.

When he assumed the presidency, Richard Nixon had a mandate to disengage from Vietnam. In the spring of 1969, he thus announced new tenets of U.S. foreign policy, which became known as the Nixon Doctrine. According to this doctrine, the United States would end the Vietnam War and never again fight an Asian land war. This policy, however, assumed a drastically different relationship with the People's Republic of China. Meanwhile, Sino-Soviet relations had deteriorated to the point that the two engaged in a "war" on their border at almost exactly the time Nixon announced the shifts in U.S. foreign policy. Hence both Washington and Beijing were prepared for a rapprochement that would end their twenty-year-long state of mutual hostility. In fact, because of a perception of a growing Soviet threat espoused by both, they were willing to change the relationship dramatically—from archenemy to friend and perhaps even ally. President Nixon's visit to China in early 1972 was a natural consequence of a new U.S.-China relationship. There, he signed, with Chinese leaders, a document that became known as the Shanghai Communiqué. Because of their past unfriendly relationship and still many outstanding differences, each side inserted into the communiqué a unilateral statement of policy. The document thus reflected considerable lack of agreement. But the two also included positions of mutual agreement, including their concern over Soviet hegemonism. Regarding the matter of Taiwan, about which they obviously disagreed, they spoke in ambiguous terms. The United States said that it "did not challenge" Beijing's view that Taiwan was part of China. This phrase could be (and was) interpreted to mean either that the United States agreed with Beijing's view or that it did not agree. Incorrect English, inaccuracies (that the people of Taiwan favored unification), and unclear statements further clouded the document. Ambiguity was necessary at this juncture.[4] Mao had already broken a promise not to deal with the United States until the Taiwan "issue" was resolved. Nixon seemed to betray Taipei and his anti-Communist principles by making the trip.

In the following months, U.S.-China relations improved. Washington and Beijing sought to counter Soviet expansionism. The United States avoided an arms race with the Soviet Union that was unpopular and lacked support at home in the wake of the defeat in the Vietnam War by building friendly relations with China. In short, Washington used its relationship with Beijing as leverage against the Kremlin. Beijing diverted resources that would otherwise have gone to the military to counter America's "threat" to China. China, with U.S. help and support, became a legitimate player in world politics and used this to parry Soviet intimidation. The U.S. and China began to trade in fairly significant amounts. Cultural and other exchanges were broadened. A "China fad" hit America; an "America fad" hit China. Both sides viewed the world as a changed one: one that had evolved from a bipolar world of two superpowers to a more flexible multipolar world.[5]

U.S.-China relations might have become even closer and formal diplomatic ties established had it not been for the Watergate scandal, which prompted President Nixon's resignation in 1974; America's "defeat" in the Vietnam War in 1975 (China was supposed to help the United States disengage from Vietnam with honor.); and Mao's death in 1976. Alternatively, relations may not have improved. U.S.-China relations were, in fact, quite "normal" given their past hostility and the fact that many points of disagreement remained. One can only speculate about this. Clearly, the Taiwan "issue" could not be resolved amicably.

When Jimmy Carter became president, he showed little interest in China. Unlike Nixon and Ford, he did not view the world in multipolar, realpolitik terms. Rather, he saw the gap between north and south (or rich and poor nations) as the paramount world problem. He thought that peace could be pursued by friendly, unilateral overtures toward Moscow. China did not play a crucial role in U.S. foreign policy making in this context.

But in less than two years Carter changed his view about China. He increasingly needed a foreign policy victory after a number of setbacks, including the SALT treaty (which was withdrawn by the White House after submission to the Senate) and the Panama Canal treaty (which cost Carter considerable support in the Congress and with the American public). This was even more true as Carter began to realize that his popularity was falling, and his hopes for reelection had diminished. Bureaucratic politics also played a role. The Department of State sought relations with Beijing in order to have more representation abroad. State also wanted to play a bigger role in China-policy formulation. The Defense Department and Carter's national security adviser, Zbigniew Brzezinski, advocated formal ties with the People's Republic of China to use as leverage against the Kremlin. President Carter's personal and party advisers wanted him to establish formal diplomatic ties with China for still another reason: The China "breakthrough," they noted, had bolstered President Nixon's popularity and was viewed in retrospect as a high point (and perhaps even as a redeeming one) in his presidency. They saw formal China ties as affecting in a positive way Carter's image and reelection prospects.[6]

Given the disparate (and certainly difficult to coordinate) sources of support for establishing formal relations with Beijing, together with contrary views in Congress, among the public, and elsewhere, not to mention Taipei's potential for organizing opposition, President Carter decided to pursue formal relations in secret. He chose to announce the decision in mid-December, just before Christmas and when Congress was in recess.

Viewing President Carter's action as unnecessarily and wrongly secret and as having "abandoned Taiwan"—a friend and ally (the United States never before having broken a treaty with an ally without cause)—Congress decided, in January 1979, to rectify the situation. It did this in a nonpartisan manner. Democrats provided the impetus and leadership for writing the legislation that became the Taiwan Relations Act. Republicans supported the effort. President Carter threatened to use the veto if what Congress did ran counter to his China policy. Congress intended for the TRA to change Carter's China policy and it did. Yet President Carter signed it into law without ado.

Because of its importance and particularly because it laid a permanent foundation for U.S. China policy (particularly U.S. Taiwan policy), both Beijing and
Taipei watched with great interest and concern. Both had strong yet complex
views about the act. Both continued to react to the TRA months later. These
responses are quite instructive.

Beijing's Response to the TRA

Beijing's early response—to Congress debating and then passing legislation
called the Taiwan Relations Act—was almost like no response at all. This may
appear odd in view of the fact that the act virtually recognized Taipei's sovereignty, extended a guarantee of arms sales, and made Taiwan's security a "U.S.
interest" in a way equal to or better (for Taipei) than the defense treaty. In
addition, there were economic guarantees and calls for continued democratization
and an improved human rights record (which were certain to increase the separation between China and Taiwan). There are two reasons for this near absence of
criticism or comment: one, Beijing had already adopted a policy of friendly
pursuit of Taipei, and two, China was about to go to war with Vietnam.
    In mid-December 1978, when President Carter announced the United States
would establish formal diplomatic relations with Beijing and break its ties with
Taipei, Deng Xiaoping offered trade, aid, and other ties to Taiwan. He also
extended an offer of landing rights in Beijing and Shanghai. At the same time he
promised that China would "not pursue an aggressive policy toward Taiwan."
Deng apparently calculated that the U.S. decision had put Taipei in a difficult
predicament and that Taiwan's government could not refuse to negotiate. Or,
perhaps he wanted to give the impression that Taipei would submit to talks in
order to justify the new relationship with the United States. In other words, he
wanted to convey the message at home in order to head off his critics, that
Taiwan could be recovered through peaceful means and that this was a distinct
asset of his pro-U.S. diplomacy.
    This policy of friendly overtures toward Taiwan was even more evident in
January after Washington and Beijing established formal ties.[7] China's National
People's Congress issued a "Message to Taiwan Compatriots" stating that China
hoped Taiwan would "return to the motherland" and "work together for the great
cause of national development." The message pledged that Beijing would consider "present realities" in Taiwan and respect the status quo there. The National
People's Congress also called on its own government to establish the appropriate administrative organs to manage mutual visits, postal and transportation

links, and trade—the so-called "three exchanges." At the same time, Beijing announced that it would end its alternate-day shelling of the Nationalist-held island of Quemoy.

In January, Deng met with eighty-five U.S. Senators visiting China. He did not mention the Taiwan Relations Act, even though this was a major item on Congress's agenda. He might have asked them not to pass such a law. [8] Alternatively, he could have made suggestions about which provisions should or should not be in the act. Deng was preoccupied with increasing tensions with Vietnam that led to a Chinese invasion of the northern part of Vietnam in mid-February. Yet he undoubtedly knew that he would face political trouble over the "Taiwan issue" in the future and that on the matter of unification he was vulnerable vis-à-vis his critics on his political left.

Officials in the Chinese embassy in Washington attended the hearings and debates that led to the passage of the Taiwan Relations Act. But there was noticeably little reaction. When the TRA was signed into law by President Carter in April, the Chinese government delivered a note of formal protest to U.S. Ambassador Leonard Woodcock in Beijing. The language was not strong, however: The TRA was "unacceptable."[9] No stronger statement followed.

This was quite unlike the response from the press in China. In fact, the very different reaction from the media reflected differences over Taiwan policy between the Left, which controlled the media, and the Right, or Deng's reformist supporters, in the Chinese Communist Party and the government. The Left did not agree with Deng's pro-U.S. policy and consequently did not concur with his assumption that good relations with Washington would "bring Taiwan back into the fold." Xinhua, the official Chinese news agency, said the TRA would "do great harm to U.S.-China relations if passed as now worded." Xinhua went on to make an issue of the fact that the TRA "recognized a separate government in Taiwan" and blocked Beijing from seizing Taiwan's official property in the United States (as would be allowed if Beijing were the successor government). Ostensibly under pressure, Deng publicly, but belatedly, assailed the TRA as violating the Normalization Agreement while stating that it could "threaten" U.S.-China relations.

In the coming months, Deng, on various occasions, was chided by the Left. His friendly overtures to Taipei were met with ridicule and rejection and his "conciliatory" policy toward the United States was seen as "surrendering on the Taiwan issue." This situation evoked an interesting shift in Beijing's Taiwan policy. In December 1979, when an anti-government demonstration supported by the Taiwan independence forces broke out in the southern city of Kaohsiung, Deng sided with the Kuomintang (KMT) against the demonstrators—a marked change in Beijing's policy, which had for years condemned the KMT's domestic policies and encouraged the native-born Taiwanese to overthrow the government. Deng had to side with the KMT, which, even though critical of communism, espoused, at least nominally, a one-China policy and condemned the separatists.

After the debate in Beijing over Taiwan subsided, Deng generally avoided the issue. Deng's main concern was economic development and this depended on U.S. help. Deng knew the United States would not change its Taiwan policy; Congress had already seen to that. Thus, he tried to placate his opponents and prevent them from undermining relations with the United States, upon which the success of his economic reforms depended. However, he remained sensitive to any criticism that his overtures toward Taipei had not worked. In January 1980, he referred ambiguously (to observers in the United States at least) to the reunification of Taiwan as a "great issue." Later, he linked it to peace in Asia but without being specific, while pointedly not criticizing the United States.[10]

In the summer and in late 1980, the political Left was provided with ammunition to use against Deng on the Taiwan question. In mid-year, President Carter announced a resumption of arms sales to Taiwan (frozen at the time that diplomatic recognition was granted to Beijing). Deng's opponents were highly critical. Then, in October when the United States granted diplomatic privileges to Taiwan's "representatives" in Washington, the Left went on the attack again. The *People's Daily* said this move represented a "two-China policy" and opined that it would "reverse the good trends in U.S.-China relations." The Chinese media also attacked Ronald Reagan, who was campaigning for the presidency at this time, for his pro-Taiwan declarations. When he asserted that the TRA did not prohibit a liaison office in Taipei, Xinhua labeled his statement "pure fabrication." The *People's Daily* subsequently charged that Reagan had "insulted one billion Chinese people."

After Reagan became president, the Chinese media (still representing the party Left) continued to make an issue of Taiwan. It focused on the matter of arms sales. In the spring, when Secretary of State Alexander Haig visited Beijing, various Chinese newspapers declared that U.S. arms sales constituted a de facto policy of reestablishing the defense treaty. In July, on the occasion of the sixtieth anniversary of the founding of the Chinese Communist Party, General Secretary Hu Yaobang scored the United States "for not seeing a contradiction between the TRA and the Normalization Agreement."[11]

By the middle of 1981 or, if not then, certainly by late in the year, Beijing's view (including Deng's) of Sino-American relations started to shift. Chinese leaders began to perceive that, because of a shift in the "global balance of forces," (meaning the restoration of a Washington-Moscow balance because of the Reagan military build-up) and the Kremlin's more friendly posture toward Beijing, China was in a "swing" position vis-à-vis both the United States and the Soviet Union and could exploit this advantage—a view that had some vague factual basis. The belief that there was a split in the U.S. leadership on China policy, especially regarding U.S. relations with Taiwan, was also a factor. Both views were promoted actively by the Left. Deng thus found himself under increasing pressure to do something about U.S. arms aid to Taiwan. Arms sales, Deng's opponents argued, undermined Beijing's efforts to either cajole or force Taipei to negotiate reunification, and China, given the new situation, should pressure the United States to change its policy.

Beijing downgraded its relations with Holland over the issue of its submarine sales to Taiwan in early 1981. Some saw this as a signal to the United States regarding arms sales to Taipei. In any event, Chinese leaders began to perceive that there was less of a need for closer relations with Washington as a result of a changing world balance of power. At the same time, Deng's economic program (which was seen by the Left as restoring capitalism in China) came under fire. Deng hence became even more vulnerable to criticism. He needed to do something about the "Taiwan issue," which had become in a sense his "Achilles' heel."[12]

In June 1982, former Senate leader Howard Baker visited China. Deng told him of the difficulties he faced because of his "capitalist" reforms. He also talked about U.S.-China relations and the Taiwan issue. He suggested that Congress amend the TRA, though he added that he did not think this would happen. Deng may have been trying to sidestep his opponents by giving them the impression that he was trying to persuade Washington to alter its China policy, particularly its policy on Taiwan. Alternatively, he may have sought to influence the State Department and the president by exaggerating his predicament and the strength of his opposition on the political Left.

In any event, the United States responded. The State Department sought to succor Deng by agreeing to limit arms sales to Taiwan. Secretary of State Haig, who led the effort, reasoned that Deng was pro-U.S., that he was reforming China in a way that was to the advantage of the United States and world peace, and that Deng's opponents would turn China to the left (and backward) politically and evoke a return to a hostile, isolationist China if the United States did not help him.

The result was the "August 17 Communiqué" of 1982, in which the United States declared that it did "not seek to carry out a long-term policy of arms sales to Taiwan" and that such arms sales will decline and eventually end. Washington also reiterated a policy of not "infringing on China's sovereignty" or "pursuing a two-China policy." President Reagan, who was only tentatively convinced the communiqué was necessary and was anxious not to appear to be selling out Taiwan, the next day said the agreement was linked to a peaceful solution only of the Taiwan problem. Deng, because his opponents were "watching and waiting," had to repudiate Reagan's statement, which he did. Thus, the agreement seemed to be meaningless. Still, it may have helped Deng.[13]

Another interpretation is possible. Deng may have realized he was unable to alter U.S.-China policy in any significant way. The communiqué was thus only a diversionary tactic. Anyway, the next month, at its 13th Party Congress, China adopted what it called an "independent foreign policy" line (canceling the "united front" policy of aligning with the United States against the Soviet Union). Western scholars labeled it an "equidistance (between Washington and Moscow) policy" designed to exploit China's "swing role" in a triangular power game involving Washington, Beijing, and Moscow. With the United States no longer an "ally," Beijing could not expect (at least Deng could say so) Washington to force Taipei to negotiate reunification (which it clearly was not doing). Deng could also promote other "important" foreign policy issues over which he had better control.

In the ensuing years, Chinese leaders periodically complained that the United States was not abiding by the August 17 Communiqué (which Washington interpreted as requiring arms sales reductions over a very extended period of time and oddly not necessarily decreasing in dollar amounts because of the inflation factor). Beijing also complained that the United States was circumventing the agreement by transferring weapons technology to Taipei, enabling it to build its own advanced jet fighter plane, while helping Taiwan to develop sophisticated anti-submarine warfare capabilities. However, little else was said about the Taiwan Relations Act. Chinese leaders did not like it, but apparently they understood that Congress would not change or rescind it. So they ignored it. It likewise became less an issue of disagreement between the Left and Right because it had become less controversial over time and other issues in the meantime had become more critical. Also, there grew a realization that as China's role in world affairs expanded, it needed to give the appearance at least of reasonableness in its foreign policy. The global community did not deny Taiwan's sovereignty and certainly did not approve of Beijing using military force against Taiwan. Even Third World countries did not support Beijing's Taiwan policy because that would have dealt a blow to the cause of self-determination.

In any event, Deng would argue that Taiwan was not in danger of falling into the hands of another power (namely, the Soviet Union or Japan) as Beijing had earlier feared and that economic relations were blossoming across the Taiwan Strait (to China's economic advantage, while making unification more likely). Taipei at this time changed its policies on trade and investment with China. Trade between the two expanded at a rate of nearly 50 percent annually during the mid and late 1980s—reaching the tidy sum of $1.5 billion in 1987, nearly doubling to $2.7 billion in 1988, and growing by more than a billion to $3.8 billion in 1989. Investment grew at a similar pace. And tourism from Taiwan at this time brought in $1 billion to $2 billion in foreign exchange.

In early 1989, on the tenth anniversary of the Normalization Agreement, Beijing celebrated the event. Foreign Minister Qian Qichen reiterated the often-heard line that the Taiwan issue was a major obstacle affecting the "steady development" of relations between the United States and China. He said that he hoped that the United States would uphold its one-China policy. He did not, however, mention the Taiwan Relations Act. [14] Three months later, the anniversary of the enactment of the Taiwan Relations Act passed without comment from high officials. At this time Beijing's policy may best be described as a dual strategy of cajoling Taiwan on the one hand, and searching for friends in the United States (including such people as former President Nixon and former Secretary of State Kissinger) to build a kind of new China "lobby" to promote China's interests, with the eventual goal of undermining or destroying the TRA, on the other. But the latter goal was a long-term one.

As of mid-1989, when China's relations with the United States, not to mention with the rest of the world, suffered severe damage by the Tiananmen Massacre, this strategy had produced few if any results. In the wake of Tiananmen, Beijing realized it was completely futile to try to get the U.S. Congress to alter or annul the TRA. Congress was not in a friendly mood toward China. In fact, it sought to punish China by criticizing China on human rights, limiting high-tech sales, and possibly canceling China's Most Favored Nation status. Because of Tiananmen, Beijing also had less influence with the State Department and the White House and its friends in the United States. Meanwhile, U.S. relations improved with the Soviet Union. With the decline and fall of communism and the breakup of the Soviet "empire," America's view of China changed still further. Because the Soviet Union was no longer a threat to the United States, China's stock (meaning the usefulness of the "China card" as leverage against the Soviet Union's military power) fell.

Chinese leaders, both left and right, realized that criticizing the TRA in view of a Congress that was very angry at the People's Republic of China would not be wise. Thus Beijing remained almost mute on the subject. Even members of Congress visiting Beijing in the month following the Tiananmen Massacre did not hear mention of the TRA. Beijing, nevertheless continued to respond to events in Taiwan, with the Chinese media strongly supporting reunification and a one-China policy while condemning any separatist proposals. In late 1991, the Chinese press assailed Democratic Progressive Party leaders for putting Taiwan independence in the party's platform, former U.S. Attorney General Ramsey Clark for supporting them, and the KMT for its "three no's" policy, but no connection was made between any of these and the TRA (even though the advocates of Taiwan independence often cited it). Moreover, Beijing threatened no specific actions. Premier Li Peng at the time seemed to mirror Chinese policy. Referring to Taiwan independence in a major policy speech, he declared blandly that "peaceful reunification ... is the trend of the times."[15] He did not criticize the United States.

However, in the wake of the collapse of the Soviet Union, Beijing criticized the United States for becoming a "hegemonist power" Chinese leaders also vented their hostility toward several other countries about their relations with Taipei, such as the Philippines which had debated a Taiwan Relations Act of its own. And China responded with anger to suggestions that the TRA "model" could be used by various nations of the world in establishing relations with the Baltic nations and other breakaway republics of the former USSR. It similarly condemned the "Hong Kong Policy Act" proposed in the U.S. Congress at this time (in part because it resembled the TRA), which sought to draw attention to promises made by Beijing in 1984 when Hong Kong's reversion was negotiated with the United Kingdom.

In summary, Beijing has been and remains adamantly opposed to the Taiwan Relations Act and ultimately hopes to persuade or pressure the United States to annul it. But at the moment, Chinese leaders see little hope of success in getting it either amended or overturned. Finally, the TRA is less an issue of contention between the Left and Right in China as it has to some degree become an old and less useful issue politically. If these conditions change, Beijing will likely go on the offensive against the TRA once again. Otherwise China will probably continue to ignore the TRA as much as possible.

Taipei's Response to the TRA

On December 15, when President Carter announced that the United States would establish formal diplomatic relations with the People's Republic of China and break relations with the Republic of China, Taipei reacted with anger and surprise. Taipei's immediate response was to put the military on alert, close the stock market, and cancel a national election. Even though there had been talk of the United States establishing ties with Beijing for a number of years—in fact, seriously, since President Nixon visited Beijing in 1972—the decision was still unexpected. Taipei was not forewarned. The nation, in short, was stunned.[16]

After a few days, Taipei issued a formal policy statement. It called the decision "regrettable" and said that Washington should "change its mind." It said further that the Republic of China would "under no circumstances" enter into talks with Beijing. In fact, officials in Taipei repeated emphatically the three no's policy: no contacts, no negotiations, no compromise. Taipei announced the establishment of a "defense fund" to compensate in part for the pending cancellation of the U.S.-ROC defense treaty (even though this was not to happen for one year). The government asked for public contributions. Later, when Deputy Secretary of State Warren Christopher visited Taipei to work out the details of unofficial relations between Washington and Taipei, angry crowds threw eggs and stones at his car in an unusual demonstration of public outrage. Some observers said the government had staged the event, or at minimum had encouraged it. Clearly President Carter's decision had hurt the credibility of the government in Taiwan and many officials, not to mention citizens, were angry.[17]

On December 28, President Chiang Ching-kuo announced five principles (continuity, reality, security, equality and governmentality) upon which future relations with the United States should be based. These principles were vague but represented a much calmer and more rational response on Taipei's part. They, incidentally, can be seen as components of the Taiwan Relations Act written in the next few months.

During January, February, and March, while Congress was working on the Taiwan Relations Act, Taipei made few specific comments. Regarding relations with the United States, Taipei's position remained that the United States had "made a mistake" and that formal diplomatic relations should be restored. Officials in Taipei said Washington had "played into the hands of the communists." This quite unrealistic response can be explained by the fact that the government was still experiencing damage control problems and it feared that the political opposition would try to exploit the situation. Officials wanted to engender feelings of anger and disappointment in the population to prevent a shocked citizenry from blaming the government for the loss of ties with Washington. There were also genuine feelings of emotion in the leadership because Taiwan, a long-time trusted and loyal ally of the United States, had been, they felt, jilted.

When the Taiwan Relations Act was written into law and signed by President Carter, it was evident that Congress had in essence restored Taiwan's sovereignty and guaranteed Taiwan's security and economic health. Still, Taipei did not react in a positive way. Officials took note of the fact that the TRA throughout referred to "Taiwan" and did not use the country's formal name, "Republic of China." They called this insulting. Some said there was no reason for the United States to have such legislation. Some said it constituted interference in the Republic of China's domestic affairs.

Meanwhile, Taipei's representatives in Washington kept abreast of the debate in Congress on the TRA. They carefully analyzed the legislation from various perspectives, including its impact on U.S.-China policy. They provided some input behind the scenes. When the legislation was passed by Congress, they supported it—though without fanfare.

In Taipei, most top government officials, including President Chiang and Premier Sun Yuan-suan, were pleased with what the U.S. Congress had done, though they continued to talk tough in reply to overtures from Beijing. Taipei, in fact, sent mixed signals. Taiwan's anti-Communist propaganda was toned down. Officials in Taiwan and the press stopped referring to the government in Beijing as a "bandit regime." More important, Taipei, in the context of a situation wherein Taiwan might have been expected to feel some desperation, repudiated its so-called "options": ties with the Soviet Union, going nuclear, and declaring independence.[18] Clearly, Taiwan felt some comfort from the TRA. Apparently its leaders felt its provisions provided sufficient guarantees that Taiwan did not need to change its foreign policy in any meaningful way.

In a few months, government officials began to take note of the fact that the foreign press had been quite "understanding" of Taiwan. It had not taken the position that Taiwan had lost its sovereignty or that the U.S. decision to break diplomatic relations with Taipei could be interpreted as supporting the opposition in Taiwan. The Western media generally spoke favorably of Taiwan (which it was not very accustomed to doing) and supported Taiwan's nation-state status and its right to self-determination (which meant that Taipei should have the right to decide if it wanted to become part of China). The foreign press continued to sympathize with the opposition in Taiwan, but this was noticeably more because of its call for democracy rather than independence.

As a result, Taipei began to make policy statements based on U.S. China policy as set forth in the TRA. In reply to Beijing's overtures, Taipei made some of the following points: If, as Beijing suggested, Taiwan could have its own military after a reunification agreement, then why should Beijing oppose the weapons sales provision in the TRA? If China wanted Taiwan to prosper (another provision in the TRA), why should it try to isolate Taiwan and endeavor to have Taipei expelled from international organizations, many of them financial? And why did Beijing continue to threaten Taiwan with military force and thereby challenge the TRA?

Some Taipei leaders even suggested open support for the TRA and foreign and domestic policies that could be built or predicated on it. Their argument was that the TRA needed support: that Beijing would undermine it, the American public would forget it, and the communiqués (the Shanghai Communiqué of 1972, the Normalization Agreement, and in 1982, the August 17 Communiqué) would adumbrate it. Their suggestions were heard but not adopted as policy. Instead, a policy of quiet support evolved, the rationale being that Taipei should not give the impression that it was dependent for its survival on the U.S. Congress.[19] After all Congress was a legislative body and did not normally make, and certainly did not conduct, U.S. foreign policy. U.S. China policy would continue, they reckoned, to be made primarily by the executive branch of government, with the TRA serving as a constraint. Taiwan's policy makers also continued to deem it insulting. Finally, Taiwan's leaders did not want to give the impression that the TRA alone guaranteed the nation's security. They instead sought to build Taiwan's deterrence capabilities, which they calculated would supplement or complement the TRA.

Another factor also helps to explain why most political leaders in Taipei did not want to openly or directly support the Taiwan Relations Act: An increasingly strong and vocal opposition in Taiwan was calling for a policy of independence and permanent separation from China, and drew attention to the fact the government's popularity had been damaged by the loss of formal ties with the United States. Nationalist leaders feared that this combination spelled trouble. And that was to prove true. During 1979, the opposition became more aggressive and openly critical of the government. Opposition leaders frequently cited the TRA and the support of the U.S. Congress for democracy in Taiwan and linked this to an independent Taiwan. Some even sensed that the government, because of the loss of credibility resulting from breaking relations with the United States, could be overthrown. This unrest culminated in a crisis in December 1979 in the southern city of Kaohsiung, when the opposition organized an anti-government protest that turned violent.

In 1980, after the period of crisis had passed, some government officials began to argue that Taiwan's stance vis-à-vis the independence advocates should be more flexible. They argued that the TRA did not support a two-China policy. Furthermore, they said, the TRA had to be seen in relation to or in combination with the Normalization Agreement. The latter enunciated a one-China policy. They likewise argued that Beijing would not allow Taiwan to declare independence and that the United States would not help independence advocates because of Washington's view of the importance of its ties with China. (U.S. officials made statements at this time to support this view.) Others contended that reform was under way in China, beginning with Deng Xiaoping's ascendancy in 1978, and that Taipei had to take cognizance of that. At this time, Taipei's leaders were under pressure from the business community to pursue more meaningful economic ties with China in view of the fact that China provided economic opportunities and many of Taiwan's businesses were beginning to feel the pinch of rising labor costs, a closing U.S. market, and other problems.

There was also a widespread feeling in Taiwan that—whether, in order to satisfy the TRA, win support from the global community, or placate the opposition—Taiwan had to democratize. In December 1980, Taiwan held its first competitive national election. It was successful. As a result, Taipei's leaders began to boast of democracy in Taiwan. In September 1981, when president Ye Jianying of the People's Republic of China issued a "nine-point" statement regarding the reunification of Taiwan, Premier Sun responded that this could be possible "on the basis of Sun Yat-sen's Three People's Principles." This concession constituted a major departure from the three no's policy. Moreover, it represented a degree of confidence not seen before on the part of the leadership of Taipei.

In 1982, as noted above, the Reagan administration signed a communiqué with Beijing promising to limit arms sales to Taiwan and ultimately terminate those sales. Arms sales had been promised in the Taiwan Relations Act, so the communiqué seemed to both contradict and undermine the act. Taipei noted on a number of occasions that the TRA had guaranteed arms sales. But Taipei's protests were neither strong nor strident. High officials in Taipei ostensibly calculated that Taiwan needed to build its own arms and that the communiqué did not state that the United States would halt the transfer of military technology to Taiwan. Furthermore, since it was waging a popularity "war" with Beijing for global support, Taipei did not want to appear too aggressive; instead it wanted to give the impression of it being a small, "underdog" nation that simply wanted the right to choose its future democratically.

Taiwan held its second competitive national election the next year in 1983. Some observers said democracy was taking hold. The 1980 election no longer appeared to be a one-time show for foreign consumption as some critics had suggested. In 1986, President Chiang Ching-kuo promised that the ban on forming new political parties would be lifted. (Taiwan, in fact, already had a strong opposition group that was organized almost like a political party.) Immediately, the Democratic Progressive Party announced its formation and challenged the Kuomintang in the December election. The result was the first ever two-party national election in Taiwan; in fact, it was the first two-party election in a Chinese nation. In 1987, Taiwan ended martial law. In 1988, Chiang Ching-kuo died and Taiwan had its first Taiwan born president. Critics of Taiwan's authoritarian political system had said many times that this would never happen. In mid-1988, the Kuomintang held its 13th Party Congress and instituted reforms that democratized the ruling party, in many ways beyond that of Western parties. At that same meeting the KMT adopted a "mainland policy" that envisioned more contacts with Beijing perhaps (one might speculate at least) leading to better relations and eventual reunification. In 1989, the Democratic Progressive Party "won" an election victory, increasing its popular vote and capturing a large number of local executive offices.

Changes in both domestic policy and foreign policy—democratization and a policy of opening up relations with China—seemed to be to some degree a response to the Taiwan Relations Act. The act had called for democracy in Taiwan. It anticipated better relations between Taipei and Beijing (at least less hostility on Taiwan's part toward China) but left open the matter of reunification. The government in Taipei clearly wanted to deserve the support of the U.S. Congress, not only because of its impact on U.S. China policy but also because it influenced Beijing and global opinion. Taipei wanted to keep the matter of reunification an open question—one to be decided according to its schedule and on its terms.

Officials in Taipei meanwhile made serious efforts to comply with the TRA's call for improvements in the human rights situation in Taiwan. Not long after the passage of the TRA, Taipei established a human rights organization and made genuine efforts to improve its human rights condition, though the TRA was not mentioned as the reason for these efforts.[20] Subsequently, when the issue of reunification was mentioned by Beijing or others, Taipei's usual response was to cite human rights abuses in China. Taiwan's human rights record had indeed improved and was much better than China's. The human rights issue was thus a good arguing point for Taipei. Tibet was specifically mentioned, because of the horrendous human rights abuses there and the fact it was an "autonomous region" in the People's Republic of China, just as Taiwan would be after reunification, according to Deng Xiaoping. Taipei found many sympathetic ears, especially after the June 1989 massacre of Democracy Movement students in Tiananmen Square in Beijing.

Taipei even responded to critics of its trade surplus by noting that the TRA had given Taiwan a special economic status in the United States and that the trade deficit was partly a result. American policy makers found it difficult to reject this explanation. Officials in Taipei who sought to avoid an isolationist foreign policy, which had some attraction because of Taiwan's diplomatic defeats, sometimes credited the TRA with its policy of staying in the Asian Development Bank and other global institutions and its open trade policy, which began to include trade with Communist nations.

In the late 1980s, Taipei began officially to give credit and even praise to the TRA for "helping Taiwan overcome a diplomatic crisis in 1979" and establishing what it called a "statutory basis for continuing the U.S. commitment." Government publications also mentioned that the Republic of China had become one of the top ten exporting nations in the world, that foreign exchange controls were being lifted, that there were meaningful elections, and that visits to the People's Republic of China would be approved. The TRA was cited, in this context, as "welcoming a new era."[21]

In the past few years it has been even clearer that Taipei supports the TRA and does not want it altered or weakened. In 1991, when Taipei officially ended the state of war with China, observers noted that the TRA had provided the stability Taiwan needed to do this. Others remarked that the TRA was a contributing factor to democratic reform in Taiwan and in particular that it enabled Chiang Ching-kuo to end the "Temporary Provisions" (which had circumvented constitutional guarantees of civil and political rights).[22]

Conclusions and Forecasts

Since the passage of the Taiwan Relations Act, both Beijing and Taipei have come to accept this notable piece of legislation as setting the parameters of U.S. China policy. Both have formulated policies of accommodation. In both Beijing and Taipei, the act caused domestic political controversy, resulting in disputes within the top leadership over the act's provisions versus its national policy. Opposition to the act revealed factionalism in both leaderships and different perspectives regarding relations with the United States. The policies of Beijing and Taipei have differed and continue to diverge—with Beijing opposing the act and Taipei supporting it. And this is likely to continue to be the case.

Beijing both fundamentally and strongly opposed the Taiwan Relations Act when it was formulated. Its leaders did not say so immediately because of a more pressing issue at the time: the conflict with Vietnam. Washington's economic support, essential to China's economic reforms, was also a factor. Opposition to the TRA came from the opponents of economic and political reform on the left of the political spectrum in China. It was seen as the "Achilles' heel" of the rightist reformers—Deng and his supporters. They had abandoned Communist ideology and had substituted for it Chinese nationalism. Hence, they could justifiably be assailed for "abandoning" China's "sacred territory." When Deng's economic reforms did not produce as much as expected or evoked problems (such as corruption, crime, and the like), his opponents argued that ties with the United States were not so desirable or beneficial as the reformists said or that Deng was slavishly cultivating better U.S. relations for personal reasons. In so doing, they said, he was forsaking the longstanding policy that Taiwan is a part of China and should be returned. It was primarily through the media that they made this case.

Deng was compelled to answer his critics. Often he had to assail the TRA. He refused to repudiate the use of armed force to recover Taiwan. He pressured the United States in 1982 to sign an agreement limiting arms sales to Taiwan, an agreement that would negate the most controversial provision in the TRA and the one that was most often used against him by his opponents. Deng's opponents had argued strenuously that if the United States were to continue to sell arms to Taiwan, Taipei would never need to negotiate reunification.

Gradually, other issues became more central in the ongoing struggle between the political Left and Right in China. Moreover, while the Left could complain about Deng's failure to do anything about the "Taiwan issue," it was unable to offer a reasonable alternative solution. Moreover, it did not possess the will (or perhaps the stupidity) to launch a military attack on Taiwan. Thus the issue waned. Deng was deft in handling the problem by adopting, when necessary, the left's line and advocating a tougher policy vis-à-vis Taiwan. (The United States apparently understood this, as Washington generally ignored his threats and warnings.) Finally, the media, which was for the most part controlled by the political Left in China, could complain about the "Taiwan issue" and the reformists' inaction, but in the long run Taiwan was not a good issue. There was also a basic contradiction in Deng's opponents' position about Taiwan: the political Left in China was isolationist or at least focused more on domestic than global issues. Why then should it expend its energies talking about Taiwan? Its leaders could say it was a domestic issue, but considering political realities in or outside of China, it was not. Finally, the Left in China found that mentioning Taipei was a problem: Taiwan's successes in economic and political development were an embarrassment for the hard-liners, since they proved the wisdom of the policies advocated by the right reformists.

In Taiwan, the opposition to the TRA came from the other end of the political spectrum—the political Right. The TRA was seen as insulting because it used the term "Taiwan" and not "Republic of China." Opposition politicians liked it and quoted it. It called for improvements in the human rights situation in

Taiwan, which was interpreted as interference in the nation's domestic affairs. It was seen as supporting radical democratic change. It embodied a U.S. two-China policy.

But rational minds prevailed. The TRA was soon seen to provide damage control for the government. It returned to Taiwan its sovereignty. It, in essence, restored the U.S. defense commitment to Taiwan. It provided a needed undergirding for Taiwan's continued economic stability and growth. It afforded the legal basis for Taiwan to maintain relations with the most important country in the world and its largest trading partner. In general, it was seen as supporting Taiwan and favoring Taipei over Beijing.

Early on in Taiwan, there was strong support for the TRA in the Ministry of Foreign Affairs (MOFA). But MOFA did not have much clout. Opposition politicians on the political Left supported the act, but many were not enthusiastic about it. It did not lay the groundwork for an independent Taiwan, but simply gave Taiwan a choice about its future. Reformists in the KMT and the government supported it, but they had to do so cautiously because control of the party remained in the hands of the old guard. Finally, the groups just mentioned that supported the TRA were not able to coordinate their efforts and were ideologically far apart.

As time passed and as the emotional response of America's "abandoning" Taiwan subsided and the realization that the Carter administration had acted in a way not in consonance with American public opinion became more evident, support for the TRA increased. Factional politics, with one side supporting the act and the other opposing it, never really became serious. The political opposition in Taiwan was unusually ambivalent about the TRA. Its members cited provisions in the act that favored better human rights in Taiwan and democracy; but these were strong visible trends before the TRA became law in the United States. Thus, the government in Taiwan was given credit for democracy and a better human rights condition—not the TRA. The opposition could not make a case that the KMT or the government opposed the act; consequently it was not a good campaign issue. Nor could they say that it supported an independent Taiwan. The act, as most interpreted it, gave Taiwan a choice. Which choice Taiwan wanted to make was uncertain. Finally, most of the opposition to the TRA was vented in KMT meetings and became muted. Gradually, hard-liners were persuaded that supporting the TRA was in the national interest. Meanwhile, moderates in the party pointed out that the Communists in Beijing opposed it, thereby embarrassing some hard-liners.

What predictions can be made regarding Beijing's and Taipei's future stances toward the TRA? It appears likely that Beijing will generally keep silent about the TRA in the foreseeable future—that is, until there is a chance to pressure the U.S. government to have it rescinded. When that happens, Chinese leaders can be expected to jump at the opportunity. But such a situation seems unlikely. Beijing will no doubt continue to try to rally support in the United States among its friends to have the act changed or scrapped, but to make strong efforts in this direction it would have to see some hope of success. In short, Beijing will likely remain waiting in the wings for an opportunity to successfully oppose the TRA. A more vicious factional struggle in the Chinese Communist Party or government could change this; that kind of struggle is less than likely, however, since there has been a reconciliation of views between Left and Right on certain issues, particularly foreign policy matters.

Taipei will certainly continue to support the TRA. It is not too likely, however, that Taipei will openly or enthusiastically support the TRA. Taipei, after all, has to deal with the White House and the Department of State, both of which advocate a one-China policy (that says that Taiwan is a part of China) and are hostile toward the TRA. Taipei, moreover, does not expect them to make an overt policy shift. Taipei also understands that Congress is usually only temporarily or tangentially concerned with foreign policy issues. If it is asked to interpret the TRA it is difficult to predict the result. Taipei knows this as well.

Taiwan's leaders have taken note of the fact that the Western media supports the TRA as well as Taipei's sovereignty, as does U.S. public opinion and the international community. Taipei will no doubt make some note of this in the future, especially when it feels pressure from Beijing to discuss reunification on China's terms. On the other hand, Taipei has opened up meaningful contacts with Beijing and will probably continue to improve relations with the mainland in the future. Inasmuch as unification is probably a long way off (or will never happen, in the view of the opposition), the TRA provides Taipei with a framework for dealing with China in the interim.

The U.S. perspective on the TRA and any changes in that view naturally will affect both Beijing and Taipei. Though there appeared some cause, in the first few years after the TRA became law, to believe that it may erode over time as a foundation stone of U.S.-China policy, this has not happened. There is still some possibility that Congress may change its stance toward Taiwan, or toward China, and thus choose to revise or rescind the TRA, or that it will become preoccupied with other problems and ignore it. But for now this seems unlikely. The Department of State and the White House (during the Carter administration) took exception to the TRA. The former regarded it as an encroachment on its turf. It still holds this view; but it has also gotten accustomed to the act and has found it, at times at least, convenient. The act has made U.S. China policy confusing, which in many respects it needed to be, and that will probably remain the case given what some consider a regression in U.S.-China relations in recent years.

All concerned parties, the United States, China and Taiwan as well as members of the international community—have to give the TRA some credit for maintaining a working relationship between the two Chinas and the United States at a critical time. It was a factor contributing to stability during a period of rapid change. The post-Cold War era does not seem to offer a different situation in this regard even though the world is different in so many other respects.

Endnotes

1. See John F. Copper, *China Diplomacy: The Washington-Taipei-Beijing Triangle* (Boulder, CO: Westview Press, 1982), pp. 1-6, for additional details on early U.S.-China relations.

2. See A. Doak Barnett, *Communist China and Asia: A Challenge to American Policy* (New York: Vintage Books, 1960), pp. 47-52.

3. For details, see Thomas E. Stolper, *China, Taiwan and the Offshore Islands* (Armonk, NY: M. E. Sharpe, Inc., 1985), Chapter 5.

4. See Copper, *China Diplomacy,* pp. 31-35.

5. Ibid, pp. 5-6.

6. See ibid, pp. 6-12, for details.

7. Ibid, pp. 75-78.

8. Ibid, p. 68.

9. Ibid.

10. See Robert G. Sutter, *Chinese Foreign Policy Development After Mao* (New York: Praeger, 1986), p. 99.

11. See Copper, *China Diplomacy*, pp. 70-71, for further details.

12. Ibid, p. 72.

13. Ibid, pp. 46-56.

14. Shang Rongguang, "Anniversary of Normalization of Sino-U.S. Relations Marked," *Beijing Review*, December 26, 1988-January 1, 1989, pp. 11-12.

15. "Meddling in Taiwan Will Get Nowhere," *Beijing Review*, September 23–29, 1991, p. 9.

16. See Copper, *China Diplomacy*, pp. 88-95, for details.

17. Ibid, p. 88.

18. Ibid, p. 89.

19. Ibid, p. 90.

20. Actually, two human rights organizations were established at this time. One was concerned with human rights both in China and Taiwan. The other, launched by opposition politicians, focused mainly on Taiwan.

21. See annual editions of *The Republic of China: A Reference Book*, published by the Government Information Office in Taipei.

22. The statements were made to me by officials in Taiwan.

Chapter Six
The Second Shanghai Communiqué

On August 17, 1982, the governments of the United States of America and the People's Republic of China (PRC) concluded an agreement that subsequently became known as the "second Shanghai Communiqué" or the "August Communiqué." It was the fourth formal agreement on U.S.-China relations reached between Washington and Beijing—the others being the Shanghai Communiqué of 1972, the Normalization Agreement of 1978 and the Taiwan Relations Act of 1979.

This August Communiqué was seen by some observers as needed in order to deal with or resolve the growing tension in U.S.-China relations over the "Taiwan problem," though it was described by both sides at the time as a further step in improving relations between the two countries. The central theme or issue cited in the communiqué was U.S. arms sales to Taiwan. And, in this document the United States promised to reduce and eventually end such sales.

Immediately after the communiqué was made public both sides presented their own interpretations, which even to the uninitiated observer were radically different. Both the content of the communiqué and the interpretations given afterwards were likewise full of ambiguities and contradictions.[1] For example, the United States declared its intention to reduce arms sales to Taiwan "leading over a period of time to a final solution." Several words or phrases in this statement seemed deliberately unclear. In fact, "intention," "over a period of time" and "final solution" were all ambiguous. Indeed using such words made the document suspect. The PRC reportedly pledged a "peaceful solution only" to the Taiwan issue; yet it was uncertain if this was really the case.

U.S. officials argued that the communiqué was consistent with the Taiwan Relations Act (TRA). However, since the TRA specifically guaranteed the sale of weapons to Taiwan sufficient to meet its defense needs consistency hardly seemed to be the case. In fact, just the opposite. In addition, though clearly Beijing's interpretation, President Reagan declared that the communiqué should not be taken to mean that Washington would put pressure on Taipei to negotiate

491

with Beijing. Chinese officials in Beijing said that the communiqué declared and meant that the United States would terminate completely its arms sales to Taiwan without any conditions, though this was not Washington's view.

The communiqué mentioned a "peaceful settlement" of the Taiwan problem, which Washington took (and President Reagan said so unequivocally) as being linked to the U.S. pledge to reduce arms sales. In other words, from the U.S. point of view this was a pre-condition. U.S. officials even described the "peaceful solution only" (of the Taiwan issue) provision as a policy statement made by the People's Republic of China for the first time.

People's Daily, China's most official newspaper, subsequently denied there was any tie between the two.[2] As for the "precedence" of the Chinese alleged agreement not to use force to resolve the Taiwan issue, this was something that the United States government had on numerous occasions argued was their understanding of Beijing's policy; therefore, it was hardly unprecedented in terms of what the U.S. sought. China had talked about it before, but had not made any promise (and didn't on this occasion, according to Deng Xiaoping).

After provisions in the communiqué were discussed by pundits, two questions immediately arose: Did the communiqué state anything new in terms of U.S.-China relations? And, if not, what was the need for the negotiations and for such a formal official document. Clearly the communiqué did not set forth any new policies in terms of overall Washington-Beijing relations as it focused exclusively on U.S.-Taiwan relations. Nor did it reflect any true understanding or agreement between the United States and the People's Republic of China if one looks at the statements made about the communiqué by both sides. Finally, it did not clarify earlier agreements (thought it did mention them) or say anything about either nation's relations with other countries.

On the other hand, the communiqué did serve several purposes. Most important it smoothed relations between the two countries at what seemed to be a critical juncture, especially for China. In short, it helped China's strongman Deng Xiaoping (who was a good friend and perhaps ally of the United States and who was reforming China in the direction of free market capitalism, free trade, and openness—as opposed to Mao's self-reliance and isolationism). Deng faced a domestic political crisis at the time. It may, looking in retrospect, have saved Deng from being overthrown or his power drastically curtailed or weakened.

In terms of its long-term significance, the agreement put some needed vagueness back in U.S. China policy which had been lost during the Carter administration due to explicit promises and statements made during and following the establishment of formal diplomatic relations. (The Normalization Agreement was very specific unlike the Shanghai Communiqué negotiated by

President Nixon in 1972.) While the Taiwan Relations Act contradicted the Normalization Agreement and thus created a "dual" U.S. China policy (one from the executive branch of government and another different one from Congress) and thus created a more ambiguous China policy, it, on the other hand, created what seemed to be at least a firm policy regarding U.S. arms sales to Taiwan and consequently caused difficulties for Deng.

This situation worsened during the first part of the Reagan administration when Alexander Haig was Secretary of State. Haig favored a friendly and positive U.S. policy toward China, which he thought was useful since it afforded Washington leverage against the Soviet Union and felt was needed to keep the Department of State in command of relations with the PRC. He also believed Deng was in trouble and wanted to help him. Chinese leaders, in particular Deng Xiaoping, took literally U.S. pronouncements about the importance of U.S.-China relations since they supported China's modernization efforts and could also be used against the Kremlin or at least were thought helpful to counter Soviet threats and pressure. The problem of arms sales thus presented a special vexing problem for Deng.

President Reagan realized that close ties between the countries had spawned special interests that wanted to see closer relations while others and the populations of the respective nations were beginning to see disadvantages in the relationship. This gap translated into certain policy making organs of government working in tandem with certain outside interests (the Department of State and certain businesses in the United States and Deng's supporters and those benefitting from economic reform in China) favoring building a more intimate partnership or alliance between the two countries. Others opposed this. The product was conflict over relations with the other in both countries.

In terms of what appeared to be a deterioration in U.S.-China relations, the communiqué may have been very much needed. For several months prior to the signing of the document Washington and Beijing had been taking swipes at each other on a host of issues and for a variety of reasons, mainly relating to disappointments in the relationship and efforts to placate opponents of official policy in both countries. Disappointments had resulted from too many expectations and false hopes. Reagan's critics carped that he was constantly endangering U.S-China relations. Deng's foes said he was making China dependent on the United States and had abandoned Taiwan. Clearly something was needed, if only something cosmetic, to end this friction or bring it under control.

The nature of the international system and other foreign policy concerns and problems were related. U.S.-China relations were founded on the view that the global system was no longer characterized by bipolarity and that the system had evolved into a multipolar structure.[3] By 1981, the evidence seemed to be mounting that this view had been premature or exaggerated, or was even untrue. Moreover, even if true, both sides needed to maintain considerable flexibility in their relations to make that kind of system work.

In addition, there was cognizance in many quarters (both in the United States and China) that U.S.-Soviet relations were more important than U.S. relations with China. Washington had to negotiate nuclear arms control and other problems and such talks were not in consonance with better U.S.-China relations. Similarly, Beijing had abandoned its support for the Third World and had seemingly given up being the leader of the Third World—all for better relations with the United States. This exacted a toll on the Chinese leadership.

Notwithstanding the reports of a number of analysts at this time, it seemed clear that neither the Taiwan issue nor Reagan's anti-communist rhetoric, which the media warned threatened U.S.-China relations, was really a problem for leaders in Beijing. Both Mao and Zhou Enlai had expressed the view that the Taiwan matter could be resolved in a hundred or even a thousand years. Deng Xiaoping at this time gave no reason to believe that it could not still be this way. Then one had to ask: What benefit would Beijing get from incorporating Taiwan? The PRC would have to allow the island virtual autonomy (which would be difficult for it to do given its domestic political situation) or risk a grave loss of face for mismanaging it. Clearly Taiwan had to keep its free market economy and extensive trade ties to prosper. Then, could the U.S. abandon Taiwan given the over-whelming majority of its population saying that it does not want to be ruled by Beijing? The causes of human rights and democracy would, in so acting, be seriously undermined.

During the presidential campaign in 1980, Beijing did not react in a very negative way to candidate Reagan's campaign statements about Taiwan. Deng and other Chinese leaders considered President Carter a good friend, but also saw him as a weak and indecisive leader. In fact, they preferred Reagan's policies vis-à-vis the Soviet Union. When he took office, Reagan maintained Washington's pro-Beijing (especially relative to Moscow) policies and in a number of ways went further than President Carter in pleasing China. On no important issue of substance did he give Chinese leaders cause for disappointment other than regarding issues that were already causing problems.[4]

Thus, it appears that the difficulties in U.S-China relations were not over matters that related to Reagan's intimate feelings toward Taiwan. They seemed much more to reflect disillusion on both sides and opposition politics in both countries, but especially in China. Below an effort will be made to explain the August Communiqué in its recent historical context as well as the situation at the time it was negotiated. Some observations will be made concerning the impact it has had on smoothing out U.S.-China relations.

Finally, it should be noted that the issuance of the communiqué was deliberately timed, in the Chinese case (meaning Deng), to offer proof of progress in U.S.-China relations at a critical crossroads. Deng had scheduled the 12th Party Congress for early September. For the Reagan administration, the November election was approaching. Neither, but especially Deng, wanted to be in a situation where foreign policy could be viewed as problematic.

U.S. Disappointments with China

For the United States, relations with the People's Republic of China began to improve after Richard Nixon became president in 1969. Nixon hoped that he could get Beijing to help the U.S. extricate itself from the Vietnam quagmire. The Nixon Doctrine, which in 1969 became a pillar in United States foreign policy in East Asia, in fact, made the assumption that better relations with China would make it possible for American to get out of the Vietnam War with honor and avoid such wars in the future.[5]

America's prestige globally was also at a low point because of the Vietnam War. Washington was no longer seen as the protector of world peace as was its reputation for some years after World War II. Sour relations with China had also been unproductive in terms of the U.S. image abroad. Mending relations with Beijing and bringing China into the international community could improve America's image problems and likely enhance its influence in world affairs. Similarly, U.S. productivity, technology, management and its political system were no longer admired abroad as they once were, though they all had a good reputation in China. China's praise of the United States was appreciated and played well at home.

Another expectation was that China could resolve the problem of the Soviet Union outpacing the United States in weapons building and possibly forcing the U.S. to backdown in a future showdown (the reverse of what Washington did to the Kremlin during the Cuba crisis because of its lead in strategic weapons). Some even suggested that close ties with China would make it unnecessary for the United States to match Soviet defense spending ever. In short, the China connection, it was thought, would serve to offset the problem of the Soviet Union's growing military superiority over the United States.[6]

Subsequently, American businessmen began to perceive—a view encouraged by Washington—that the opening of China would create a vast market for

U.S. products. This, it was thought, would do wonders for American business. Some even opined that it would guarantee a bullish stock market into the forseeable future. Many U.S. businessmen, in fact, dreamed of fat contracts and lucrative deals with China.

Expectations tended to be self-perpetuating and hopes in one area reinforced those in another. The public was conditioned to think of China as a friend if not an ally and to anticipate much from U.S. ties with China. Reflecting how far this went, a public opinion poll taken in 1980 reflected that 34 percent of Americans did not think China had a communist political system and 54 percent believed that China was America's leading trading partner.[7] (China was not one of America's top ten trading partners. China trade, in fact, constituted less than one-tenth of U.S. trade with either Canada or Japan and had never exceeded U.S. trade with Taiwan.)

By 1978, much of the euphoria had evaporated. China had not been successful in helping the United Sates get out of Vietnam with honor. Instead the U.S., in the eyes of both Americans and the rest of the world, lost its first war ever. Whether China had tried to help the U.S. avoid this or not was of little consequence. (Beijing, in fact had made some effort, but Soviet influence over Hanoi prevailed.) Beijing was therefore blamed.

For various reasons, including the still perpetuated belief (perhaps wishful thinking in view of the lack of alternatives) that China could offset the growing military might of the Soviet Union, together with the fact the Carter administration needed to do something exciting and decisive at a time when opportunities for either were scarce and the White House was being seen more and more as incompetent, President Carter, in 1978, made the move to establish full diplomatic relations with Beijing. This restored and perpetuated many of the chimerical hopes and expectations about China relations. It created another China "fad."[8]

However, in the next few years China again proved to be a disappointment. The Chinese leadership overextended itself in terms of its ability to engineer development, at least in the sense that it would engender business opportunities for American companies. Moreover, Beijing gave U.S. businessmen little preferential treatment and many of the post lucrative contracts instead went to Japanese companies. Also, many contracts were canceled or changed causing many American businessmen to report that China was not a good market and that Chinese were often confused about their own economic plans or could not implement them. Others got the impression they were cheated or that China thought that American companies were in the economic aid business.

Deng's candor and his new policies that included publishing grim figures on China's economic conditions (to justify his reformist policies) further discouraged American businessmen, especially those who had not yet investigated the Chinese market. Deng disillusioned the American public as well. Those who had idealized Maoist ideology and egalitarianism were repulsed by his modernization program and the extent to which Deng was restoring capitalism and a class system in China. As a result the average American developed a lot of negative impressions of China—not what he or she had been led to believe before this.

In 1979, China began publishing economic statistics after a long hiatus. These figures ware particular revealing. According to Beijing's official records (which no doubt underestimated the strength of the Chinese economy in order to qualify for lower interest loans from international lending institutions), the per capita income in Taiwan was thirteen to fourteen times higher than China. Yet Taiwan "suffered" from a population density several times higher and lacked both natural resources and energy which were plentiful in China. Rural per capita income in China was officially put at U.S.$48 per year—on par with Bangladesh, which Henry Kissinger had referred to as an "international basket case."[9] Clearly something must be wrong in China; or at least the United States had been given the wrong impression regarding China's desire for trade rather than economic assistance.

In 1979, China's thought-to-be impressive military capabilities were debunked when it performed badly in a short war with Vietnam. Later in the year, U.S. defense officials published an estimate that China needed U.S.$50 to $60 billion to improve its military in order to have a meaningful defense against the Soviet Union.[10] This was a sum the United States could clearly not afford. Therefore, it was seen as doubtful whether the U.S. could help China become a counterweight to the Soviet Union even if it were willing to. Meanwhile the Soviet Union began to give the impression that U.S.-China strategic ties were not of any real consequence. In fact, in some cases, it made pointed and successful efforts to embarrass the U.S. for using China as leverage against the Kremlin.

Coinciding with these disappointments the China fad began to wear out and interest in China in the United States started to wane. Visiting China was no longer so exciting. China's respect for the United States meant less and less; it also had a bad side in that many Americans, wittingly or unwittingly, took advantage of special privileges in China (reminding some of the days of Western imperialism), while others sympathized with Chinese students who were demanding democracy in China.

China's Disappointments With the United States

A similar situation obtained on the Chinese side. Beijing perceived a need for improved relations with the United States as relations with the Soviet Union deteriorated in 1968 following the Soviet invasion of Czechoslovakia and the Kremlin's announcement of the Brezhnev Doctrine (which the PRC interpreted to mean that Moscow challenged Chinese sovereignty, and believed the use of force to be justified to preserve bloc unity, even, and especially against, China). The following year, in the Spring of 1969, when tensions between the two escalated, resulting in fighting on their border, the United States tilt toward China may have prevented Moscow from taking military action against Beijing.[11] Soviet military leaders at the time of the border fighting, which incidently involved artillery and other heavy weapons, advocated strong action against China includ-ing an invasion of Beijing to install a new leadership or, at minimum, the elimi-nation of China's nuclear capabilities.

Chinese leaders had cause to believe, or at least hope, that the United States would align with China broadly and more permanently and thereby nullify or offset the Soviet threat against China. Instead, the United States allowed its military spending to continue to decline, giving the Kremlin the opportunity to fill the power vacuum in Asia caused by the U.S. withdrawal after the Vietnam War. While Chinese leaders realized Washington's problem (most important being the unpopularity of the military and defense spending in the wake of the Vietnam War), they generally believed that U.S. leaders were not acting willfully enough in trammeling Soviet expansionism. They felt the U.S. could do much more in the realm of organizing U.S., European and Japanese cooperation to counter Moscow. Beijing also expected the U.S. to use technology transfers, commercial ties and grain sales as a means to punish Soviet "hegemonism"— which Washington did not do, or at least consistently or effectively.[12]

After 1978, there were several important specific instances of Chinese dis-enchantment with the United States. The first occurred immediately after the two countries established formal diplomatic relations. Deng Xiaoping made a trip to the United States where he was given royal treatment and broad (and favorable) press coverage. While in the United States, he publicly condemned Vietnam's occupation of Kampuchea and spoke of "teaching the Vietnamese a lesson." Inasmuch as there were no apparent differences between the U.S. and China on the Vietnam issue and because China was in effect implementing U.S. policy (Washington being unable to act because of public opposition to getting involved in Southeast Asia again yet apparently wanting to), Deng no doubt expected American support when he invaded the northern part of Vietnam soon after he returned to Beijing from his America trip.[13] Instead the Carter administration's reaction was one of surprise and an expression of hope for peace.

Beijing was likewise sorely dismayed with Washington's initial response to the Soviet invasion of Afghanistan. Washington imposed a grain embargo on the Soviet Union and scolded the Kremlin, but did little else. The Carter administration subsequently announced that the U.S. was sending weapons to the Afghan guerrillas, but did not do much to follow up on this (at least in China's eyes). Carter also let it be known that China and other countries would send arms and other aid. This caused some embarrassment (though perhaps mainly due to lack of official consultations and the fact there was a lack of consensus in the Chinese leadership about the wisdom of U.S.-China military cooperation) to Beijing.[14] There was still another problem: With Soviet troops having secured the narrow border with China, Beijing could only send arms through Pakistan. Furthermore, it risked a confrontation with the Soviet Union and gave the Kremlin an excuse for taking action against the PRC elsewhere and even justified to some its presence in Afghanistan because of Chinese "interference" and involvement (which Moscow made a point of). Washington also attempted to "punish" the Soviet Union by expanding military cooperation with China, but this produced no immediate reaction and was seen by many as an unsuccessful bluff. In short, Chinese leaders perceived that the United States did not handle the situation well.

The crisis in Poland was another case. Beijing sided with the United States early on by criticizing Soviet policy in Poland. However, when Washington indicated that it expected China to support Solidarity (and thereby condemn the Polish Communist Party and its ideology as well as the political system in Poland), Chinese leaders were miffed. This, in the eyes of Chinese leaders, would have been tantamount to repudiating their own party and political system while inviting labor problems in China.

The arms sales issue (U.S. sales to the PRC), which paralleled all of the above-mentioned crises and problems, deserves special mention. The U.S. had cited the possibility of weapons sales to China in the late 1960s and the topic was frequently broached through the 1970s. Some military or dual-use equipment was, in fact, sold to China during the mid-1970s. After the Soviet invasion of Afghanistan, the topic was discussed much more seriously in Washington and in the U.S. press. To the Chinese government, however, the willingness of the U.S. to sell arms to the PRC was not a coveted prize; instead, for a number of reasons, it presented problems. First, weapons sales seemed to be tied to accepting U.S. arms sales to Taiwan. Some officials in the Carter administration said this and the media picked up on it. Second, it was not clear how China would pay for U.S. weapons. In the context of Deng's modernization program China could ill-afford to spend much more on defense. Third, what controls would the United States have over the weapons once they were delivered became a sensitive matter. Would U.S. military advisors be sent to China? What leverage would this give the U.S. over the Chinese military? Cognizant of the fact that China had a very bad experience with the Soviet Union in this realm in the 1950s, Beijing's leaders were naturally very apprehensive.

Chinese leaders were also aware of the debate among U.S. defense officials regarding arms deliveries to the PRC. Generally the debate was humiliating to China. U.S. officials often cited the fact that China was recently an enemy in two wars—in Korea and in Vietnam—and averred that this should not be forgotten. Many also expressed fear of a Sino-Soviet rapprochement, insinuating that China could not be trusted. Others argued that the United States alone had to face the responsibility of coping with Moscow's growing military strength and that in terms of the global military balance China was almost irrelevant: China could not project military power and could not even do much in terms of countering Soviet military power in Asia except in a case where Soviet troops might invade China, which seemed at this time unlikely.[15]

China likewise experienced disenchantment with its economic ties with the United States. During the 1970s, the United States expressed great enthusiasm about Deng's modernization program. In fact, almost nothing was said in the U.S. in official circles at least, that was negative about Deng's "four modernizations"—not even that they were over-ambitious or unrealistic. Thus Chinese leaders concluded that they might expect a lot of help from the United States in making the economic reforms work.

The U.S. did help. American provided a lot of free or cheap technology. It granted most favored nation treatment, giving China access to the vast American market (which incidently was not granted to the Soviet Union and most other communist countries). The U.S. provided loans and credits on concessionary terms while the American government guaranteed private business investment in China. All of this amounted to economic aid. Still Beijing was not satisfied. Why?

The United States moved too slowly on all fronts. Or there were strings attached. In addition, serious problems developed that Chinese leaders apparently did not anticipate. Free or cheap technology was provided by the United States; but it was in many ways restricted. Also much of it was not useful to China given the state of the development of its economy. The American market was open to China; yet the sale of textiles was affected by quotas. The result: China suffered from a serious balance of trade deficit with the United States. While it was able to cover this with loans and credits, many Chinese leaders forecast getting into serious debt to the United States (known only recently to most Chinese as the leader of the neo-colonialist, imperialist bloc).

Then, when loans were extended to China, they were not generous by the standards of U.S. aid and loans to poor counties in the past. Washington was now less able to give economic assistance in considerable measure because the public was not supportive of it. Furthermore, many U.S. officials were not willing to allow other recipients of U.S. aid to suffer in order to be more generous to China. Chinese leaders did not understand this very well.

Further adding to the problem of the Chinese perception of the U.S. "connection," after a brief period following the launching of the modernization program, China experienced quite rapid economic growth; but that growth rate subsequently declined. In 1981, the increase in the gross national product was quite small.[16] Measured in U.S. dollars, since there was a devaluation of China's currency, growth was negative. As a result, Beijing had to cancel around 1,500 development projects to save hard currency. The development budget was slashed from U.S.$8 billion to $1.6 billion—reflecting the fact that something was seriously wrong. Why was this happening if the United States were such a good friend?

In short, by 1980–81, Deng witnessed what some said was a failing of the modernization program. Although it may have been over-ambitious and poorly planned from the start, to Chinese leaders the United States deserved some of the blame.

All of this caused Deng's critics to become more vocal and stronger. They brought into question the value of U.S.-China relations and cited the pitfalls. More important, they could, and did, broach the Taiwan matter and United States arms sales to Taiwan as evidence that the U.S. link was bad and should be broken or at least reduced in importance.

The Impact of Disappointments on Policy Making

The bursting of the bubble of high expectations in Sino-American relations had two noticeable effects on policy making on both sides. Members of the decision making process involved in formulating and carrying on U.S.-China relations in both Washington and Beijing experienced some isolation from the rest of the decision making machine and became the frequent brunt of criticism from other policy making organs as well as the media and the public. Each side also began to engage in some rather strident at times criticism of the other side in order to stave off opposition to its policies of maintaining overly good relations or improving relations.

In the case of the United States, the Department of State was the subject of some strong criticism of its China policy. This took the form of critics attacking State for repudiating U.S. commitments to Taiwan, a former ally and trusted and loyal friend and a showcase of American aid, while even revealing a willingness to abandon Taiwan. The latter, it was charged, would have serious implications for U.S. security policy in Asia and would undermine U.S. support of human rights and international law (since the population of Taiwan did not want to be governed by Beijing) and democracy (since Taiwan has made measurably more progress in democratizing its political system than China). Critics also argued that the State Department was not competent in negotiating with China—making many concessions and getting little or nothing in return. U.S. China policy, and to some extent U.S. foreign policy, to the more extreme critics, was "made in Beijing." Furthermore, U.S.-Soviet relations suffered as a result of improved U.S.-China relations. This, it was said, would exacerbate world tensions and increase the likelihood of an East-West conflict. Specifically mentioned was the fact that close U.S.-China relations undermined efforts to reduce the level of nuclear weapons—because China opposed any arms limitations talks between the U.S. and the Soviet Union to which Beijing was not invited (and inviting China was unrealistic).[17]

In response the Department of State argued that U.S.-China relations must not be allowed to deteriorate. Officials at State argued that years of progress in building the relationship and converting Beijing from an arch-enemy to a friend would be lost and relations would return to the "ugly" status of the 1950s. The "China card" was often mentioned, but most of the time indirectly or by implying the argument that the U.S. must maintain some leverage against the Kremlin to ensure that the Soviet Union would act with restraint. Both positions, however, suffered from some rather serious defects. In view of the large volume of trade between China and the West (which the U.S. to a large extent controlled by its leadership in this realm), it seemed highly improbably that U.S.-China relations would deteriorate markedly, particularly regress to the situation of the 1950s. China had built its economic development plans on trade and could hardly change this. Similarly there was little evidence that China provided much useful leverage in dealing with the Kremlin. In fact, several instances could be cited to support a quite different view. Worthy of note, the onset of better U.S.-China relations was followed almost immediately by increasing Soviet involvement in Southeast Asia, to the detriment of the United States interests there. Some even cited thee U.S. defeat in the Vietnam War as happening because of the rapprochement with China. The U.S. and China formally establishing diplomatic ties was followed by the Soviet invasion of Afghanistan. There were other pieces of evidence.[18]

On the Chinese side, the Deng leadership was assailed for allowing the American connection to ruin Chinese efforts to establish itself as a leader of the Third World countries and to even abandon Third World causes. Deng's opponents even suggested that China's Third World policy had been sacrificed to better Washington-Beijing ties or was "made in Washington." Having even more salience, they also pointed out that the U.S. had reneged on its one-China policy and had allowed Taiwan policy, or at least the Taiwan Relations Act, to dictate U.S.-China relations. Thus, Taiwan, they charged, continued to behave as a sovereign nation, refusing overtures by Beijing to negotiate its future as part of China. Deng's critics also contended that his modernization program, which was seen as inextricably tied to good relations with the U.S., engendered inflation, unemployment, smuggling, black marketing, bribery, racketeering and special privileges for foreigners similar to the days of Western imperialism. Similarly, they mentioned Deng's failures to maintain respect for the Chinese Communist Party, youth problems, materialism, mammonism and prostitution.[19]

While there did not seem to be much support in China for returning to Maoist policies, Deng's reforms were nevertheless hurt by his alienating the military (by cutting their budget and undermining their prestige), reducing the size of the bureaucracy (which threw many government workers out of a job) and by the dimming prospects for rapid economic development. In fact, a sizeable number of Communist Party members questioned Deng's leadership, giving rise to speculation in the Western media that the reforms, and even Deng himself, may not survive.[20]

Deng responded by underscoring the Soviet threat and the Kremlin's "hegemonist" and "aggressive" foreign policy and the grave danger the Soviet Union imposed to China. This was to some degree credible though there had been no serious Soviet military actions against China since 1969 and the border situation remained generally the same as it was more than a decade earlier. Deng also pointed out that the American connection was crucial to China's economic development (which was certainly true) and that pro-China forces in the Department of State and elsewhere in the U.S. government must not be alienated or their influence undermined by China being too critical of the United States.

The above-described situation prompted sniping and criticism by officials in the United States and China who were supportive of good relations in order to offset or preempt the critics. In the case of the United States this came primarily from the White House. In the case of China, Deng himself made charges against the U.S.

On the U.S. side, the Reagan administration began to respond in a positive manner to Soviet proposals to hold arms talks especially those aimed at reducing the level of strategic weapons. Beijing was not mentioned or invited to the meetings. Since China was a nuclear power, it would appear that it should have some voice in such negotiations. Also ignoring China seemed to contradict the notion of a "China card" to play against the Kremlin. The same applied to proposed talks with the Soviet Union on other issues and some hints by the United States about trying to restore detente. Clearly U.S. Soviet policy was being made without giving much deference to China. Similarly, Beijing admonitions against selling grain to Moscow, taking a tougher stance against Soviet aggression in Europe, and other advice generally went unheeded.

United States policy toward Vietnam also showed signs of departing from full agreement with China. In early 1982, Washington pushed for a coalition government in Kampuchea and suggested that better U.S. relations with Vietnam may be to the benefit of both countries. Beijing was not happy to hear this. There were also increasingly visible signs that Washington and Beijing were disagreeing over Afghanistan.

In mid-year, Reagan personally took two jabs at the leadership in Beijing when speaking of communism "belonging on the ash heap of history" while not discriminating between Soviet and Chinese brands of communism, and in another statement in which he assailed China as an exporter of illegal drugs to the Western market.[21] The latter problem, according to some observers, if indeed serious might have been discussed in private. A slowdown in helping build nuclear power plants in China, restrictions on Chinese students in the United States having access to classified studies, and efforts to crackdown on China obtaining technology from American companies may fit also into the same category of matters that did not need to be made public. In short, there was some official unfriendliness toward China at this time which seemed intentionally provocative.

The same kind of things transpired on the other side. In order to deal with his critics on the political Left, Deng in several public statements, expressed an aloof attitude toward the possible deteriorating of U.S.-China relations. In one specific statement concerning the decline in Sino-American ties because of Taiwan, Deng is reported to have said: If that is to happen, let it be." Later, in response to American supporters of Taiwan who referred to Taiwan as an "unsinkable aircraft carrier" (suggesting its strategic importance to the United States), a Chinese official responded that this was an expression of "imperialist logic." In January, Beijing unofficially charged that leaks about American intelligence gathering installations in China near the Soviet border were aimed at hurting China diplomatically and militarily.[22]

Ostensibly following Deng's orders and probably attributable to troublesome U.S.-China relations, during 1981 and 1982, Beijing made some moves to improve relations with Moscow. Anti-Soviet propaganda was carefully toned down seemingly to set the stage for possible Sino-Soviet negotiations. Then, contrary to the practice of the recent several years, the term "hegemonist" was used to describe both the Soviet Union and the United States—instead of just the former.

In some other realms, Beijing took actions to back up its angry words toward the United States. During the first half of 1982 China did the following: It increased trade with Poland after the U.S. applied sanctions against that government, thereby undermining this element of U.S. policy. It criticized United States policy in Central America and Washington's siding with Britain during the Falkland Islands crisis. It opposed U.S. Middle East policy more strongly than at any time for a number of years. And it renewed its demand that the United States pull its military forces out of South Korea (after being silent on this issue for some time).[23]

In short, both sides seemed to need concessions from the other in order to justify continuing efforts to improve relations, much less sustain moderate to good relations. The public and political opposition on both sides seemed increasingly hostile (while venting that hostility in the form of open criticism and suggesting alternative policies became more and more common). Both sides, at least in public, were less enthusiastic about better relations than in the recent past and perceived there was little or no advantage in pursuing closer ties and considerable cause to see certain disadvantages in the relationship.

The Future of U.S.-China Relations

Based on the above assessment it is clear that U.S.-China relations before the two nations negotiated and signed the second Shanghai Communiqué or the August Communiqué were at a low point and relations portended to deteriorate even further. At minimum the relationship had become sensitive and was under fire from domestic critics on both sides.

Inasmuch as the communiqué seemed to resolve the most sensitive issue (especially for China) plaguing U.S.-China relations, it may indeed have prevented relations between the two countries from imploding. In short, in may have saved the good will and important and useful ties built between Washington and Beijing since 1969.

The agreement helped China's strongman Deng Xiaoping deal with his adversaries at a critical juncture. At least this seems a reasonable conclusion in view of the Party Congress convened the next month during which time Deng pushed through a series of reforms which altered both the organizational structure and the top leadership of the party that favored his capitalist reforms and in the long-term helped ties with the United States.[24] One may therefore reasonably interpret the communiqué as an effort by the United States to help Deng cope with his hard-line critics on the political left who wanted to preserve Maoism, isolationism and hard-line communism and whose power and influence had increased in recent years and especially in recent months. And it worked.

Though not so vital to President Reagan, his administration also benefitted by the communiqué given the acceleration of media and Democratic criticism of his foreign policy and in particular his ability in particular to keep relations with China on track. Some predicted that he would ruin close relations between the two countries which three previous administrations had so carefully and success- fully cultivated. Clearly Reagan did not like this criticism.

The communiqué, on the other hand, may have been concluded with other purposes or thoughts in mind. As has been already noted it added needed flex- ibility to U.S.-China relations. Put in perspective, some thought that relations between the two countries would inevitably experience problems as they had become closer than they should have given the degree of mutuality of national interests. Improving U.S.-China relations has patently happened at the expense of good U.S.-Soviet relations. Better relations between Washington and Beijing to a large degree assumed continued bad U.S. relations with the Soviet Union. Since cordial U.S.-Soviet relations were more important than good U.S.-China relations, one might say that U.S.-China ties needed some adjustment. After all the Soviet Union was able to destroy the United States with its nuclear arsenal; China was not.

The U.S.-Soviet relationship was also the cornerstone of the global system. Thus some were saying that for Washington to pursue better relations with Beijing constituted a bad ordering of priorities and did not reflect realism about international politics. Hence, while the "China card" was useful in dealing with the Kremlin, it could not be taken too far (and it had been). From the beginning (which was only now being realized clearly) it was a dangerous game.

A similar argument can be made regarding Sino-Soviet relations. Washing- ton may indeed have prevented an escalation of hostilities between the two communist giants in 1969 when it sided with Beijing during the border fighting.

There did seem a real danger of the Kremlin, under the pressure of military leaders, escalating the conflict and engaging in a broader or more serious war with China. But this passed. By 1982, the border was no longer a flashpoint. Hence a U.S. tilt no longer seemed functional (if it was at the time or for any length of time after the border conflict) in terms of maintaining global stability.

Continued strained relations between China and the Soviet Union were clearly not in the U.S. interest insofar as the two became permanently aligned against the other and their conflict spread from the border and party and other matters to efforts to undermine each other's interests throughout the world. This clearly was not an auspicious trend.

While it was definitely not in the U.S. interest for Moscow and Beijing to rebuild the alliance that opposed the American presence in Asia in the 1950s, the danger of this has also passed. Both distrusted the other and a meaningful alliance between them seems out of the question; if it were to be considered seriously it would be a long-time possibility, not a short-term one. In any event, working alliances usually depend upon economic and political ties rather than expediency alone and neither seem likely for Beijing and Moscow soon, with both having built trade and other commercial relations with the West.

Those who argued for better U.S.-China relations in the past also seemed to ignore some of the constraints of international politics. The Nixon administration assumed the international system to be more multipolar than it really was. It had not evolved away from bipolarity yet; and subsequently it did not. Soviet military power ultimately had to be matched by the United States alone. Or at least this was the assumption of the Reagan administration and Reagan did that. Thus multipolarity faded.

In any event, if the global system did evolve into a multipolar one U.S.-China relations probably became too close as that system assumes a great deal of flexibility in making friends and allies. The U.S. and China had become too close and too reliant on each other; or at least many thought so. Furthermore, looking deeper into the evolving international system, a sober judgement of China revealed that China was a regional actor, not much of a global one. This meant that U.S.-China relations had relevance mainly to East Asia.[25] Thus, there was a read danger in the United States relying on China too much.

China also sacrificed due to close relations with the United States. It lost ground in its bid to lead the Third World. This was important to China for psychological reasons at least and prompted opposition to Deng's excessively pro-American policies.[26] Intimate Sino-American relations exacted other costs for Deng, including charges of allowing China to become the victim of imperialism once again, economic inequity, crime, social instability and more.

And, of course, one must add to this the accusation that was most difficult to refute or cope with, that Deng had abandoned any hope of recovering an important part of China's "lost and sacred territory"—Taiwan.

The best future course for U.S.-China relations may, in fact, be one that seeks a shift of emphasis by both from their "alliance" and fewer expectations about the other in terms of help. Political and strategic relations certainly need to be de-emphasized. Realism needs to become more a part of the relationship.

If the August Communiqué allowed Washington and Beijing to defuse the Taiwan issue which threatened to blow up U.S.-China relations while injecting more moderation and less grand expectations into the relationship then it was a good thing. It may, in fact, have helped U.S.-China relations get passed a major impasse or crisis and become more "normal."

Endnotes

1. See, for example, Richard Nations, "Framework for the Future," *Far Eastern Economic Review*, August 20–26, 1982, pp. 12–13.

2. Cited in ibid.

3. For a discussion of China's changing global perspective at this time, see John F. Copper,"China's Global Strategy," *Current History*, September 1981.

4. Even on issues of style Reagan in some ways pleased Beijing. The PRC ambassador was the first to see Reagan after he became president. Also during Reagan's first year in office, Taiwan's representatives had trouble seeing or communicating with the president.

5. The Nixon Doctrine said this. Also, see Henry Kissinger, *White House Years* (Boston: Little, Brown and Co., 1979), p. 224.

6. For further details, see Richard H. Solomon, "The China Factor in America's Foreign Relations," in Richard H. Solomon, ed., *The China Factor: Sino-American Relations and the Global Scene* (Englewood Cliffs, NJ: Prentice-Hall, 1981), pp. 22–26.

7. Jeremiah Novak, "Worldly Jeremiads: The Paper Tiger," *Worldview*, February 1982.

8. For a discussion of U.S. China policy and the Carter administration's decision to grant diplomatic recognition to the People's Republic of China, see William R. Kintner and John F. Copper, *A Matter of Two Chinas* (Philadelphia: Foreign Policy Research Institute, 1979)

9. Novak, "Worldly Jeremiads."

10. *New York Times*, January 4, 1980. This figure came from a Department of Defense study.

11. See A. Doak Barnett, *China and the Major Powers in East Asia* (Washington, DC: Brookings Institution, 1977), p. 194. It is worthy of note that the Soviet Union announced its "Asian Security Plan"—which most observers saw as directed against China—that same year.

12. See Michael Oxenberg, "The Dynamics of the Sino-Soviet Relationship," in Solomon, ed., *The China Factor, pp. 67–68.*

13. See Lucian W. Pye, "The China Factor in Southeast Asia," in Solomon, ed., *The China Factor*, p. 241.

14. See several stories in the *New York Times*, February 10, 1979, for further details.

15. Ibid., February 16, 1981 and July 10, 1981.

16. See *U.S.-China Business Review*, March-April 1982, for further details.

17. For further details, see John F. Copper, "Sino-American Relations: Reaching a Plateau," *Current History*, September 1982.

18. See Robert L. Downen, "Reagan Policy of Strategic Cooperation with China: Implication for Asian-Pacific Stability," *Journal of East Asian Affairs*, Spring-Summer 1982.

19. See, for example, *Asiaweek*, June 11, 1982.

20. This was noticeable during 1981 when Deng's reforms didn't seem to be making much progress. Also opposition to Deng seemed to be growing in China.

21. See *Facts of File*, June 11, 1982.

22. See "Quarterly Chronicle and Documentation," *China Quarterly*, June 1982.

23. Ibid.

24. See David Bonavia, "Stalemate in Peking," *Far Eastern Economic Review*, September 17–23, 1982.

25. See John F. Copper, *China's Global Role: An Analysis of China's National Power Capabilities in the Context of an Evolving International System* (Stanford: Hoover Institution Press, 1980).

26. It should be noted that sacrificing China's leadership of t he Third World bloc, after the "Taiwan issue" was the most frequently heard criticism of Deng's foreign policy at home. See Milinda Liu and Larry Rohter, "China Shuffles the Cards," *Newsweek*, October 4, 1982.

Chapter Seven
Taiwan's Diplomatic Isolation: How Serious a Problem?

In recent years, scholars, especially China specialists, have frequently asserted that Taiwan, or the Republic of China (ROC), is diplomatically isolated. Assuming it is, they have questioned whether it can survive as an independent, sovereign nation-state. The answer to this question clearly has implications for the future of China—whether it will continue to be a divided nation —and the situation in East Asia in general. How it is resolved may also affect the future of small nations, certainly those nations with territory claimed by larger powers.

Those who argue that Taiwan (meaning the ROC for the purposes of diplomatic legitimacy, assuming that the terms are in essence synonymous) is diplomatically isolated say that Taipei is not represented in any important governmental international organization, that it has no official diplomatic ties with any large or influential nation, and that Beijing has effectively sequestered Taipei on the diplomatic front. They observe that Taiwan's diplomatic status is incongruent with its trade and economic power, but the former, they say, is more important. Thus the ROC will lose its nation-state status notwithstanding the fact that it is a model of economic success and an economic power.

Some of these "pessimists" assert that it might have been otherwise. In other words, Taipei might have avoided being in the diplomatic predicament it is in had it opted for a two-China, or one-China, one-Taiwan, policy at some time in the past. Most say that it should have done this in the mid-1960s, before its important friends decided to establish formal diplomatic relations with Beijing, or at least before 1971, when Taipei was expelled from the United Nations (or, more accurately, lost the China seat). Many who hold this view contend that the ROC might have made a foreign policy volte-face during the Cultural Revolution (especially during its violent phase from 1966 to 1969) and won global support for a two-China policy, and this is the only way Taipei might have survived diplomatically. More recently some (granted, a minority) have argued that Taipei had another opportunity in 1989 in the wake of the Tiananmen Massacre and again failed to take advantage of the situation.

Others—those we may call "optimists"—argue that because of Taiwan's increase in diplomatic ties in recent years, albeit with small, less important nations, Taipei has reversed the trend. Numbers are crucial, they assert. They also note that diplomatic ties are now less vital to nation-state status as the United Nations has defined that term and that Taiwan's sovereignty has not been challenged seriously by any nation that has moved its embassy to Beijing or diplomatically recognized the People's Republic of China (PRC) in recent years. Most of these nations have said little or nothing on this matter; many have refused to. Taipei meanwhile has about the same number of embassies abroad as many small, Third World countries—countries which are not considered diplomatically isolated. Finally, Taipei has markedly increased its informal ties with other countries, especially those of an economic kind, and these are now becoming very important in a world increasingly structured on economic blocs as the military blocs break up in the wake of the end of the Cold War.

Historical considerations as well as current trends shed some light on the question of whether Taiwan is diplomatically isolated or. After the defeat of the Nationalists on the mainland of China and the establishment of the People's Republic of China (PRC) in 1949, Taipei, for several reasons, did not suffer from diplomatic isolation as might have been expected. First, the issue of a "Communist" and a "free" China became a part of the bipolar struggle and most Western bloc nations refused to establish relations with the government of the People's Republic of China even though it de facto controlled and ruled China. Beijing caused many countries to be more adamant about this by its abuse of foreign diplomats, including U.S. diplomats, in 1949 and 1950, and by taking a hostile attitude toward the West and the international community, not to mention flouting diplomatic rules and protocol. Similarly, because the PRC espoused the position that it could use the establishment of formal diplomatic ties as a bargaining chip to gain political advantage, many countries rejected ties at least temporarily. (For example, several nations that offered Beijing recognition did not immediately receive a favorable reply: Pakistan, Ceylon, Afghanistan, Norway, Finland, the U.K., the Netherlands, and Israel. The PRC to this day, in an effort to win favor among Arab nations, has not responded to Israel's offer.) Thus, it seemed that PRC leaders were not engaged in a diplomatic contest with Taipei. As a consequence, in 1950 Taipei had twice as many foreign embassies as Beijing.

In the mid-1950s, Beijing changed its position and began trying to win diplomatic ties with certain Third World countries. Chinese leaders sought to break out of the isolation imposed on China by the United States and the United Nations. Beijing also sought to discredit Taipei, apparently feeling that this was now possible. PRC foreign aid was hence linked to establishing formal ambassadorial ties. Its diplomacy generally focused on Southeast Asia and the Middle East and was directed toward building meaningful ties with important or "leadership" nations in the two regions that would encourage other countries there to recognize Beijing. China was moderately successful in this effort.

In the early 1960s, Beijing renewed its efforts to gain diplomatic legitimacy. It had all but abandoned hope of conquering Taiwan, having failed in two attempts to wrest the Offshore Islands (Quemoy and Matsu) from Taipei. Chinese leaders were also motivated by what they considered Soviet attempts, as well as American efforts, to isolate China—the Sino-Soviet dispute having become a more serious and a public issue in 1960. Beijing's diplomatic efforts, however, still were aimed at selected (generally defined as revolutionary or anti-imperialist) Third World countries; the PRC did not yet decide to make an effort to be a legitimate member of the international community. Thus, in 1963 Taipei still led in the diplomatic contest by a significant margin: fifty-eight to forty-two.

In 1964, a major Western country, France, gave the diplomatic nod to the PRC (though the U.K. had done so earlier because of the need to deal with Beijing on Hong Kong). This might have set a precedent causing Beijing to win the contest for diplomatic legitimacy and Taipei to become isolated, but it did not. Indonesia, Beijing's important ally in Southeast Asia and a country that Chinese leaders believed might help the PRC gain hegemony over the region, broke with Beijing after an attempted Communist coup there failed and the army assumed power. Shortly after this, the chaos of the Great Proletarian Cultural Revolution enveloped China and Beijing recalled all of its diplomats except its ambassador in Egypt. Beijing also alienated a number of nations by aggressively promoting its revolutionary ideology where it had embassies or other representative offices. The PRC made few, if any, serious efforts to win diplomatic support from nations around the world for the next five years.

In the 1960s, however, there were both vague signals and direct evidence that the United States was moving toward a two-China policy and would eventually seek to establish some form of ties with Beijing. In Taipei, some leaders initiated debate on whether to allow dual recognition and try to maintain ties with countries determined to have an embassy in Beijing. The forces against a two-China policy won out, strengthened by the problem of the legitimacy of the Taipei government, which was founded on the claim to represent all of China. The government, composed largely of Mainland Chinese who went to Taiwan in 1949, as opposed to "Taiwanese" Chinese who were born there, would appear to be a carpetbagger government if Taipei did not claim to be part of "greater China." Those arguing against dual recognition, in addition, could point out that Beijing was not making any headway in winning the "war" anyway owing to chaotic conditions in the PRC, which at this time showed no signs of change. In retrospect, some say that Taipei made a very serious error. However, given the fact that it subsequently made rapid progress in resolving the ethnic problem between Mainlander and Taiwanese Chinese while democratizing the political system, thus making it possible to claim sovereignty based on democracy and the people's will, a second opinion is warranted.

In 1970, however, Canada and Italy, two important Western countries, opted for Beijing and granted diplomatic status to the PRC. This was a bad omen for Taipei and threatened to set a precedent. Taipei remained ahead in the recognition contest: sixty to fifty-three, with two nations saying they recognized both and fourteen having formal ties with neither. But this was soon to change.

Though the decisions by Canada and Italy might have set in motion a bandwagon effect, it was the United Nations decision in 1971 to seat Beijing and "expel" Taipei (or rather change the occupant of the China seat) that prompted a host of nations to open talks with the PRC with the intent of establishing diplomatic relations. Another relevant factor was that Henry Kissinger had just made a trip to Beijing, laying the groundwork for President Nixon to go the next year, dramatically altering what other nations perceived was the U.S. position on Beijing's legitimacy and its right to represent the Chinese people in international politics.

By 1973 the tide had clearly shifted; the PRC had formal diplomatic ties with eighty-five nations; Taiwan had only thirty-nine. By 1973, 45 percent of those nations that had formal diplomatic relations with Taipei in 1971 had abandoned the Republic of China for the People's Republic of China. The situation continued to worsen for Taiwan until Taipei had official ties with only twenty-one countries in 1975. Taiwan made a slight rebound, and in 1977, Beijing had 111 and Taipei had twenty-three. Nevertheless, the number of embassies in Beijing continued to increase.

Taipei's diplomatic losses can be accounted for in large part by Beijing's efforts to isolate Taiwan and destroy its legitimacy as a nation-state together with its international standing. Nevertheless, in many instances, most of the nations that granted the PRC the diplomatic nod (all but eight) did not accede to Beijing's claim that Taiwan was its territory. They simply "took note of" Beijing's claim.

Meanwhile, as early as 1970 Taipei began successfully to substitute commercial and cultural diplomacy for formal diplomatic relations. In fact, one can argue that part of the reason for its spate of diplomatic defeats was its own decision to try to play a different game, one at which it could succeed. In short, Taipei caused some of its losses. In any event, Taipei made what many people said was a realistic change and succeeded to a large degree in preventing its isolation. This policy incidentally coincided with efforts in Taiwan to democratize the political system—in what looks in retrospect to be a studied decision to redefine the legitimacy question in terms of "people's choice" or democracy. In other words, decision makers in Taipei understood that the question of its sovereignty and its survival as a nation would ultimately be influenced by its image (whether Taiwan was a democracy or an authoritarian dictatorship), and that democratization meant survival. It was thought in Taipei's decision-making circles that the perception of the international community, especially the United States, would be an important variable regarding whether or not Taiwan would be isolated by Beijing and whether or not it would survive as a nation-state.

Taiwan suffered another blow to its legitimacy in 1978 when the Carter administration decided to switch formal diplomatic recognition from Taipei to Beijing. In this move, Taipei lost its only superpower contact; moreover, it no longer had formal diplomatic relations with the most important nation in the world and by a large margin the most important country to Taiwan—militarily, politically, and economically. At the time it appeared to many that Taiwan had suffered such a serious shock and such a blow to its diplomacy, even its informal diplomacy, that it would not survive.

However, such was not to be the case. The U.S. Congress wrote the Taiwan Relations Act (TRA) a few months later, redefining U.S. policy toward Taipei. Some said that the administration had repudiated Taiwan's sovereignty and the Congress gave it back. Moreover, Congress, in the TRA, offered a new security commitment to Taiwan (by, in essence, replacing the defense pact with a provision in a U.S. law, which in some ways was broader and hence better) and guaranteed Taiwan's continued economic growth with appropriate legal provisions. At the same time, Congress (again in the TRA) expressed its desire (actually appearing like a demand if seen in context) for better human rights and democracy in Taiwan. In other words, Congress linked Taipei's legitimacy and U.S.-Taiwan relations to democracy in Taiwan. All of this reduced the shock of the diplomatic break and compelled Taipei to continue the commercial and cultural foreign policy it had already embarked upon and to enter a global popularity contest based on its progress toward attaining a democratic system.

Taipei, at this juncture, decided to continue its membership in the Asian Development Bank—notwithstanding the fact that the PRC was to be admitted and that Taiwan had to accept an embarrassing change of title (to "Taipei,

China"). Meanwhile, Taipei began to take a more innovative stance toward Communist bloc nations. Decision-makers in Taipei reasoned that if the weakening of the bipolar system were to hurt its diplomatic status it could take advantage of the new international climate to pursue informal ties with nations it had eschewed in the past. Some Communist countries were quite willing to deal with Taiwan, for the same reason (that the bipolar system was waning), and found trade and other economic relations with Taiwan profitable.

Taipei, probably in considerable measure in response to its diplomatic situation, began to pursue democratization in a more aggressive fashion. In 1980, the year after the TRA was passed and signed into law by President Carter, Taiwan had its first national competitive election. Although democracy and diplomacy were not publicly or formally linked, to many top decision-makers in Taiwan this was axiomatic.

In 1983, Taiwan had another competitive national election. In 1986, it had the first two-party election in Chinese history. Press laws were subsequently changed. In 1987, Taipei terminated martial law. In 1988, the Nationalist Party, or Kuomintang, democratized party rules and brought reform into the party, saying that the majority party should operate democratically in order for the country to be a democracy. Clearly the die was set to advance the democratization process faster and in ways that would change Taiwan's political system and, more important, its image in the world. The purpose, as far as foreign policy makers were concerned, was to maintain the nation's legitimacy and its sovereignty.

As a result of the June 1989 Tiananmen massacre, of students asking for better government, human rights, and democracy, the People's Republic of China was no longer in a good position to continue to isolate Taiwan diplomatically. In fact, it had, by its own actions, diplomatically isolated itself and caused the People's Republic of China to be regarded as a pariah nation by many members of the international community. A host of nations cut their embassy staffs. Many important nations severed or reduced economic and trade ties. Some spoke of breaking diplomatic relations. International financial organizations stopped or put a hold on loans to China, and people throughout the world reacted negatively and stopped traveling to the PRC.

This seemed like an ideal opportunity for Taipei to exploit the situation by asking some countries to recognize or re-recognize it diplomatically and/or allow Taipei into some important international organizations. Alternatively, it was an opportunity for Taipei to formally and publicly announce a two-China policy of some kind, probably a one-China and one-Taiwan policy. Clearly, world community sympathy would have been on Taipei's side were a statement of separation or independence to provoke hostile actions by Beijing.

Taipei chose not to exploit the situation, at least very much, for several reasons. First, Taiwan had a similar opportunity (a comparable situation in some important respects) during the Cultural Revolution. But, as Taipei's decision makers pointed out, the Cultural Revolution ended and Taipei was in a worse situation afterward than it would have been otherwise. Taiwan suffered a major loss of diplomatic support at the close of the turmoil in China and in the wake of its several years of isolation. Nations were quick to forgive and forget. Taipei did not want this to happen again.

Second, Taipei viewed the world as one where barriers were breaking down, not being erected. Communism was in collapse. Hence, while taking advantage of Beijing's predicament, Taipei would be "rowing against the stream" in terms of the changes that were going on in the world. Many leaders in Taipei thus perceived that rather than try to isolate China, Taiwan should act to promote the demise of communism there. That could not be done by adopting a policy of trying to accelerate Beijing's isolationism.

Third, the government and ruling Nationalist Party in Taiwan had been carrying on a balancing act in terms of democracy and pursuing contacts (or breaking down barriers) with Beijing. Democracy in Taiwan promoted independence and therefore an end to ties with China. In other words, an independent Taiwan would be the product of further democratization. Yet, many in the leadership thought the calls for independence would provoke internal instability, anger the United States and the international community, and thereby hurt Taiwan diplomatically. Hence, to maintain the balance, Taipei had to maintain contacts with China and not exploit Beijing's predicament.

Fourth, many in the decision-making ranks in Taipei thought that Taiwan's foreign policy was on the right track and did not need a major overhaul: Its one-nation, two-governments (or areas) policy and its flexible diplomacy were working. By this time Taipei had several more countries on its side diplomatically—up to twenty-seven from a low of twenty-one. Trade and cultural offices had increased markedly in number. Many nations that had been hostile toward Taiwan in the past—such as Canada and Australia—were now sending missions and establishing commercial offices in Taipei. These ties seemed unlikely to be lost again even if China's image improved.

In the summer of 1990, Taipei's decision makers seemed to be vindicated inasmuch as Beijing still sought to hurt Taiwan diplomatically but was less capable of doing so. Because of Beijing's efforts at isolating Taiwan, Taipei lost one of the last two important countries with which it had formal diplomatic ties—Saudi Arabia. (South Korea was the other.) Also, Singapore and Indonesia were poised to go to Beijing with diplomatic offers, and subsequently they did; though Taipei had formal ties with neither, their decisions to recognize Beijing and establish formal diplomatic ties were still a defeat of sorts. Yet Taiwan was not isolated; in fact, these losses caused little alarm in Taiwan or pessimism among those observing Taiwan.

These events were nothing like the loss of U.S. diplomatic ties, perhaps because the population of Taiwan had become accustomed to Taipei conducting foreign relations without formal diplomatic ties. Alternatively, the public now had a different attitude toward Taipei's foreign policy—that it was succeeding, not failing (as appeared to be the case in 1978). Taiwan's Ministry of Foreign Affairs certainly could cite various diplomatic victories to offset its losses. Most important, Taiwan was successfully beating back Beijing's efforts to isolate Taiwan, and in so doing avoided the necessity of going to the negotiating table to bargain away its sovereignty to the PRC.

Thus, while suffering the loss of ties with one important country, Taipei increased its formal ties with smaller countries, thereby improving (in numbers at least) its performance in the diplomatic contest. It did this in large part with a foreign aid program inaugurated in 1988 to help poor countries. Its purpose was to establish formal diplomatic ties with some small countries that had no need for diplomatic ties with Beijing or, just as important, those willing to adopt a two-China policy. Critics pointed out that Taiwan was buying diplomatic ties (some said renting) and that the countries willing to deal with Taiwan in terms of formal relations were all small, unimportant ones. But numbers were important. Taipei's foreign policy decision makers perceived that the nation needed official ties with twenty to thirty countries in order to preclude being seen as lacking one of the essential qualifications for nationhood.

In late 1990, Taipei reestablished formal ties with Nicaragua. This was hardly insignificant inasmuch as it gave Taipei diplomatic relations with every Central American country. A nation could not be considered diplomatically isolated if it maintained relations with a whole bloc of nations. It also was interpreted by some as suggesting that the end of communism might help Taipei. Alternatively, Taipei had economic clout in a world where economic power had replaced military power.

Meanwhile, Taipei received unprecedented visits by Soviet economic and political leaders. The new authority of "local governments" in the Soviet Union gave them the prerogative to carry on some form of diplomacy, and Taiwan benefited. There was considerable speculation as to what this might mean. Almost simultaneously, Saudi Arabia decided to allow Taipei to continue to keep its embassy there—an unusual precedent. And Bolivia permitted Taipei to set up a consulate and use its official name (the Republic of China) and flag, while it maintained formal ties with Beijing. Finally, Canada (which had been quite hostile toward Taipei for some time) and Australia publicly upgraded their informal missions in Taiwan.

Some in Taiwan at this time asserted that Taiwan's informal cultural and economic diplomacy was working. They said it did not need to accomplish a breakthrough because the Tiananmen Massacre had changed Beijing's status in the global community; what it needed instead of formal diplomatic exchanges was a favorable trend toward more contracts of various kinds and to avoid being "contained" and isolated. And in this respect things were going well.

Given the situation described above, it seems fair to say that Taiwan is not now diplomatically isolated and is not going to be. This conclusion, however, does not answer the question asked at the beginning of this chapter: Can Taiwan survive as an independent nation-state? Answering this question depends upon defining the terms. Taipei has clearly not been in a position of finding nations of the world rallied against it, nor has it had difficulty in sustaining or even building trade and cultural relations or sending its citizens to other parts of the world as one would think would be the case if it were losing its sovereignty. But can it improve on the situation?

It can be argued that Taipei missed an opportunity in the 1960s to put forward a two-China policy. Had it done so, it is presumed, it would not be in the situation it is in now. That is, it would have legitimacy apart from China, would still be in the United Nations and other international bodies, and would not have to "stoop" to adopting informal diplomacy. However, there is a major "but" to contend with in making this argument. Such a policy probably would have created an independent Taiwan but would no doubt have "disturbed" (perhaps impeded) the democratization that followed. It may have created such inner tensions and undermined the credibility of the government, which was an ethnic minority government, to such an extent that what happened in terms of Taiwan's miracle political modernization would not have followed. Those who argue that Taipei did not miss an opportunity say that democratization had to come first and that Taiwan's foreign policy had to be built on it. They also argue that time was on Taiwan's side. These are a persuasive arguments.

It is still possible to argue, from an even different angle, that domestic politics is the determinant of foreign policy. Democracy is proceeding at such a rate in Taiwan that it is impossible to slow it, much less stop it. It is clearly pushing Taiwan along a different path than the one the PRC is following. It has also built support (at least sympathy) globally for Taiwan's plea that it should decide its own future democratically—which means resisting Beijing's efforts (for the immediate future at least) to incorporate Taiwan.

And yet, Taipei and Beijing are both members of the Pacific Rim bloc. Furthermore, economic ties are bringing them closer together. A more aggressive foreign policy, that is, one that includes dealing with Beijing, also offsets the separation tendency while it supports Taipei's freedom of choice. Democracy alone, or democracy too fast, would, in the minds of some at least, create a kind of ethnic nationalism that would build barriers between Taiwan and China and between Taiwan and the rest of the world as well, and this would not be good.

It is also a contention of those who ask for a cautious policy that if time is on Taiwan's side then there must be a balance between establishing links with the mainland and independence and that an impetuous decision to officially declare separation is wrongheaded (notwithstanding the fact that given the Tiananmen Massacre it is justified). Taipei can maintain its sovereignty; why make an issue of it? This is a more potent argument if one gives any credibility to Deng Xiaoping's threats to use military force against Taiwan if it declares independence. Even if one does not believe Deng, he or she must give some consideration to the fact that Deng has opponents who are willing to exploit his weaknesses (and Taiwan is one of those). And they may promote an aggressive policy toward Taiwan. Finally, one must recall that China invaded Vietnam and used the military against unarmed students; that is testimony to the fact it may do something rash.

One may also argue that it is better for Taiwan to be n ow searching for its identity and making efforts to keep its sovereignty in the context of a changing international system than it would have been for it to have declared a two-China policy in the 1960s. Clearly the world, and the international system, are changing. People and nations are finding new identities. Taiwan is a nation in such a position. It needs its sovereignty; yet it also needs to be global in its outlook, and associating with China is essential to that. (It doesn't want to isolate itself by refusing contacts with the PRC.) What that may lead to, if anything, is a question that must be left to the future. Hence, Taiwan, in the interim, must not only avoid being isolated but must also pursue a foreign policy that gives it an enhanced status in the world; it does not have to decide its formal relationship to China at the moment.

Chapter Eight
Taiwan's Security:
Problems and Prospects

The important security problems facing the government of the Republic of China (ROC), or Taiwan, can be traced to the takeover of the China mainland by Mao and his Communist followers in 1949 and the establishment of the People's Republic of China (PRC) that year. The PRC planned an invasion of Taiwan a few months later to destroy the Nationalist Chinese military and government. That effort was interrupted by the Korean War. In fact, Taiwan was saved by that war and a consequent change of policy on the part of the U.S. government, which had just months before foresworn any more involvement in the Chinese civil war, seeing the Nationalist Chinese cause as a lost one.

During their takeover of the mainland of China, the Communists also failed to "liberate" several islands on the coast of south-central China—the most important being Quemoy and Matsu. These islands remained in Nationalist hands. They were subsequently heavily fortified. Chiang Kai-shek, in fact, hoped to use them as the springboard for a counterattack on the mainland and the recovery of China from the Communists.

During the Korean War, Nationalist Chinese leaders espoused some hope that the United States and its allies would help Taipei with its mainland recovery effort. After the intense part of the war turned to stalemate in 1951, however, this hope began to dim. Subsequently, the United States and other Western governments signed a peace treaty with Japan aimed at preserving the status quo in East Asia. Taiwan, as a result, seemed safe from a PRC invasion but unable to "liberate" China from communism.[1]

In 1954, a crisis ensued when PRC forces laid siege to Quemoy. The United States rendered assistance to Taipei and subsequently signed a defense pact with the ROC government again formalizing the status quo in the region. The PRC attack-ed the Offshore Islands again in 1958, but for a second time managed only to create a crisis. Though it may not have been Beijing's intention to wrest these islands from Taipei, and instead its objective may have been to test its alliance with Moscow, the event demonstrated the resolve of both Washington and Taipei to keep the islands in Nationalist hands.[2] Taipei at the same time demonstrated its ability to control the airspace over the Taiwan Strait and its capacity to defend Taiwan.

However, because of a high-level defection in one of its intelligence organizations in the early 1960s, the ROC lost much of its active underground operation on the mainland, which, in any event, had been deteriorating with age.[3] This setback, plus the fact that Taipei did not make any significant initiatives to "liberate" the mainland during the Cultural Revolution, when the PRC was in chaos, seemed to signify that the ROC had little or no hope of bringing down the PRC government. As a consequence, Taipei's military posture vis-à-vis the PRC (its only enemy) became almost exclusively a defensive one.

Both the Cultural Revolution and the Vietnam War provided Taipei with a period of respite from pressures resulting from the waning struggle between East and West, which had up to that time provided Taipei with allies and political support for its claim to represent China in the United Nations and elsewhere. During the Vietnam conflict Taiwan served as a rear base of some significance for the United States, and Taipei hoped to continue playing this role in return for U.S. security guarantees as well as political support for the ROC government.

However, by the onset of the 1970s (underscored by the Nixon Doctrine in 1969), it appeared that this strategy was no longer viable. Beijing was eventually going to defeat Taipei diplomatically, which it did in the battle for United Nations representation in 1971. A host of countries, including Japan in 1972, subsequently switched their diplomatic recognition to Beijing. In response Taipei looked for—and probably considered—other options. These included defense ties with the Soviet Union, nuclear weapons, and a declaration of "independence" (meaning abandoning any claim to China or ties to the mainland in hope of winning either diplomatic or defense support from some important countries of the world).[4] None of these "options," however, turned out to be either desirable or feasible.

Taipei lost formal diplomatic ties with its only superpower friend and ally (and the only country with whom it had a defense treaty) when the United States withdrew its recognition and moved its embassy to Beijing in January 1979. The U.S.-ROC defense pact was terminated after the expiration of the year's grace period. Taiwan had to fend for itself. Congress, however, subsequent to de-recognition, wrote the Taiwan Relations Act, thus providing a "substitute" for the defense treaty—depending on one's views, a better or worse substitute.

In any case, Taipei decided that it would pursue a policy of maintaining a "substantial level" of deterrence against the PRC while at the same time trying to survive politically by demonstrating its worthiness for global support (most important of which was the United States' support) through promoting political development, notably the democratization of the political system.[5] Recently some of its leaders have asserted that Taipei cannot win the struggle against Beijing militarily or economically but that it can win politically. Following that line of thinking, Taipei is stressing its so-called "defensive position" militarily and its "right" to refuse to negotiate with Beijing and chose its future politically.

On the military side, a purely defensive posture is easier and cheaper. Nevertheless, a credible level of deterrence against Beijing requires purchases of weapons from the United States. And this has become a fractious issue between Washington and Beijing. In fact, under pressure from the PRC, in August 1982 the Reagan administration promised to reduce arms sales to Taiwan and eventually end them. Taipei has endeavored to "take up the slack" by buying more military technology, by producing its own weapons, and by making arms purchases elsewhere. It has been somewhat successful in all three efforts.

Taiwan's Threat Perception

The threat to Taiwan's security, in the minds of its strategic planners as well as the population, emanates exclusively from one nation: the People's Republic of China. Unlike other Asian countries, especially to the south, Taiwan does not perceive the revival of Japanese militarism to be a serious threat, probably because Taiwan's leaders are aware of Japan's military weaknesses and perceive that this situation will not change in the near future. Neither does it perceive a threat from the Soviet Union, even considering its rapid military buildup in the area.

The view from Taiwan is that the PRC constitutes an overriding military threat—one that is so proximate and so large that others pale by comparison. In fact, Taipei sees both Japan's military strength, and to a lesser extent the Soviet presence, as offsetting the PRC threat. For that reason, Taiwan has expressed no serious opposition to increased Japanese military spending or its assumption of a greater defense role in Asia. Nor has it said much about the Soviet presence in the area. (Taiwan's defense relationship with both will be discussed in further detail below.)[6]

One of Taipei's considerations is a nuclear attack on Taiwan by Beijing. After all, the PRC is a nuclear power. This, however, is not a paramount worry for Taipei for a number of reasons. If the PRC were to carry out a nuclear attack, it (and its leaders) would be regarded as a monster by the international community for years to come. This fact serves to deter a nuclear threat or even the use of nuclear weapons for intimidation purposes. In fact, Chinese leaders have gone on record as denying any intention of using nuclear weapons to "liberate" Taiwan, and they have not threatened their use even in the context of intimidating Taiwan with military force. Moreover, it would be illogical for Beijing to render nuclear destruction to Taiwan since it wants it intact. Still, there is some fear in Taiwan of irrationality on the part of Beijing.

A seemingly major consideration among Taiwan's defense strategists and its military is the fact that the PRC has the largest standing army in the world, manifestly larger than Taiwan's. It would certainly be able to defeat Taiwan's army even though the latter is better equipped and trained. Underscoring what it perceives as a central part of the PRC's strategy, Beijing used its military numerical superiority in the Korean War and in Vietnam. The PRC has not stationed a large number of its People's Liberation Army forces adjacent to Taiwan, however. It would need an estimated forty divisions if it were to launch an invasion of Taiwan, and Taipei would easily be able to anticipate an invasion if it were preceded by a troop buildup across the Taiwan Strait.[7]

The threat of a PRC invasion, or the perception of it in Taiwan, is also reduced by the fact that a long, drawn-out war and large numbers of casualties would be likely to draw in other powers who would at least put pressure on Beijing to end an invasion. Since Taipei would become aware of any plans in advance and could make preparations both militarily and politically, it would be able to draw attention to the crisis and likely get one or more major powers to tilt toward Taiwan, or at least intimidate Beijing to reverse course. Hence, the use of its manpower advantage is not a threat of the magnitude one might think, though it still is a major consideration in Taipei.

In contrast, ROC leaders are very concerned about a PRC naval threat to Taiwan. The PRC's navy is superior to the ROC's in frigates, patrol ships, missile craft, and coastal craft. Only in destroyers does Taiwan have an advantage. Naval forces could be used by Beijing for a surprise attack—one Taipei could not prepare for easily either militarily or politically. The biggest threat comes from the PRC's submarines, which number more than forty in its East Sea Fleet. If undetected, PRC submarines could easily destroy the ROC's navy as well as its commercial fleet. They could also effectively enforce a blockade of Taiwan and keep the naval craft as well as shipping vessels from other nations away from Taiwan.

Taipei is likewise gravely concerned about the PRC's air force and its superiority in number of aircraft. Based on the number of aircraft it possesses, a sustained, determined effort by Beijing would certainly result in the destruction of the ROC's air force (even though Taiwan could be expected to have an advantage in kill ratio). This would then make it possible for PRC bombers to destroy targets on Taiwan at will. Meanwhile, Taipei would be less able to cope with PRC submarines if the latter maintained air superiority around Taiwan.

A PRC air attack on Taiwan, in fact, is generally considered Taipei's biggest "first concern," because it would facilitate bombing and submarine attacks and it might come with less warning than either a People's Liberation Army invasion or a naval attack. Certainly PRC jet fighters can be repositioned more easily and quickly than its navy or army. An air attack would certainly give Taipei less time to get prepared or to try to get other nations concerned or involved.[8]

It is for this reason that recently Taipei has expressed serious apprehension about and opposition to the United States for helping the PRC to upgrade its jet fighters with better radar and avionics. PRC advances in this realm have to some extent been off-set by improvements in the ROC's air-to-air missiles, but probably not sufficiently so. It also explains Taipei's concern to upgrade its jet fighters or buy more advanced fighters.

Taipei's defense planners generally perceive that they cannot and do not need to be able to counter all of the PRC's aircraft, since some would be needed to defend its northern and southern borders. Thus, the Soviet threat and the Vietnamese threat tie down a certain portion of the PRC's air force. Also, in the minds of Taiwan's leaders, Beijing cannot be expected to sacrifice proportionally as many planes (or ships) as it would men. Hence, being able to destroy a significant number of aircraft and ships is sufficient to maintain a high degree of deterrence against Beijing.

Finally, Taipei is obviously concerned about a coordinated air-sea-ground invasion. In fact, planners view this as the major threat scenario to Taiwan. In dealing with a coordinated attack, Taiwan must prepare for all three components and consider each in relationship to the other while trying to build its own coordinated defense.[9]

Though a coordinated air-sea-ground invasion is the biggest military threat, Taipei regards the most likely scenario to be the announcement of a blockade, or a "paper blockade," which would result in a cutoff or reduction of Taiwan's foreign trade. Second would be the use of an actual blockade against the island to attain military objectives without an actual war. In fact, Taipei's planners see either scenario as likely, either alone or as a precursor to a coordinated air-sea-ground invasion.

Inasmuch as Taiwan is economically highly dependent on trade, even a partially effective blockade would exact immediate and serious costs. The commercial ships of other nations would probably be scared off rather easily. Insurance rates would jump immediately. A paper blockade could be put into effect at any time and might be used over and over. It may even be used as a tool of harassment or in an effort to discredit the ROC government in the eyes of its business community and foreign trading partners.[10]

Foreign defense specialists also cite an attack on the Offshore Islands as a high probability threat, though Taipei's planners generally play down this possibility. The PRC could, according to foreign defense experts, surround and force the surrender of ROC forces on Quemoy and Matsu with ease. Given the large number of Taiwan's forces on these two islands—close to one third of the ROC army—such an event would be a disastrous blow to Taiwan both strategically and psychologically.

Taipei's position is that the islands are not as vulnerable as they appear and that they could serve as a base of operations for offensive assaults on the mainland in the event of a conflict. In reality their value seems to be more political, keeping alive the government's hope to some day rule China (which to most observers is not likely). Having the Offshore Islands also provides reason to restrain the advocates of self-determination (who, in the context of the rapid democratization of Taiwan's political system, have become more active) since they provide a link between Taiwan and the mainland. Holding the islands may also discourage a PRC attack on Taiwan, since their being in Taipei's possession is seemingly proof (since independence advocates suggest they be abandoned) that Taiwan is not seeking independence—an action Beijing claims is justification for an armed attack. Thus, Taipei's policy is more logical than it appears at first glance.

Taiwan's Military Capabilities

For its size and population, Taiwan has quite formidable military capabilities. It is one of the top thirty nations in the world in defense spending. With 25.1 persons per 1,000 population in the military, it leads other nations in Northeast Asia with the exception of North Korea in the percent of its population under arms. It is also a major purchaser of arms.

Taiwan's armed forces in regular service number 444,000.[11] Its reserve forces are 1,470,000 (most of those in the army). The army is 290,000 strong; the air force 77,000; and the navy, 380,000 (plus 37,000 marines). Taiwan's defense budget in 1985-1986 was U.S. $3.9 billion. This expenditure exceeds or compares with other nations in Asia except the People's Republic of China and Japan. Taiwan's standing military as well as its reserves are larger than Japan's. And both its military manpower and its military budget are only slightly smaller than those of either North or South Korea.

In terms of the composition of its military forces, Taiwan has a mix that reflects an overwhelming defensive posture and thus its perception of a need to maintain deterrence in the defensive rather than the offensive sense. This carries obvious advantages. Because of the concentration of its forces on a single object- ive and a single enemy, it is more capable of realizing a high level of deterrence than if it espoused a broader military policy.

Taiwan, however, has no strategic nuclear forces, such as Intercontinental Ballistic Missiles (ICBMs), Intermediate-Range Ballistic Missiles (IRBMs), or Submarine Launched Ballistic Missiles (SLBMs). It presumably has no nuclear warheads, though Taiwan is regarded by military experts as a "nuclear capable" country. It has the money, materials, and scientists to build a nuclear weapon, probably within six months or less, if it opted to do so. In fact, it was rumored several years ago that Taiwan was close to building a nuclear weapon but decided not to, because of pressure or guarantees from the United States. Taipei at the time denied this, probably reflecting a policy of not going nuclear, though it gave the impression at that time (and subsequently) that it could or that it might have nuclear weapons. In early 1988, such rumors spread again when the United States openly expressed some concern about Taipei's intentions. Taipei's coy policy, if that is an accurate description of its policy, avoids the problems associated with going nuclear while retaining some deterrence, because, in the minds of a potential aggressor, Taiwan might have nuclear bombs. In Taiwan's case this has the distinct plus of not allowing the world community to ignore Taiwan or assume that there would be no repercussions in allowing Taiwan to be taken forcibly by the People's Republic of China. It also lends support to the argument in the United States that arms aid to Taipei is more likely to prevent a conflict in the region than ignite one.

Taiwan's army is composed of two armored divisions and twenty-two infantry divisions. In the event of a war or national emergency, Taipei could, by calling up the reserves, put nearly 2 million soldiers on duty. The ROC can move troops to and from the Offshore Islands easily, though this may not be possible in the event of a war or serious confrontation with the People's

Republic of China. Taipei does not intend to use its troops in other regions of the world; thus, its limited ability to carry on combat missions elsewhere is not relevant to its defense posture.

The most important mission of the ROC army would be to defend the island of Taiwan from an invasion by the PRC close to shore or when it reaches land. Taipei possesses special weapons for use against landing craft and to counter an invasion of soldiers swimming in from thousands of small boats a mile or so offshore (which is a possibility). Artillery and air-exploding devices similar to mines would cause large numbers of casualties for invasion forces trying to swim in or land in small crafts. Taiwan's shoreline, which to a large extent is controlled by the military, could also be mined and covered with artillery barrages in the event of an invasion.

The ROC army could also defend against paratrooper landings. And it could, for a time at least, prevent landing forces from moving toward populated areas or to other areas on the island to join with other enemy forces or launch an attack on its military bases.

This it is capable of doing, though in a long, drawn-out war, the PRC, with its army of nearly 3 million and reserves and militia numbering more than 100 million, would be able to conquer the island. Taipei, however, believes that it has a good measure of deterrence because an invasion of Taiwan could cost the PRC up to a million lives. Clearly Beijing would have to activate the reserves and use militia forces or divert a large portion of its regular army to undertake such an invasion, and it probably has some reservations about doing that. Taipei also calculates that an invasion, which might result in loss of life on the two sides numbering 2 million or more, would attract the attention of the major powers and the world community, which would act to stop such a war.[12] This reality makes Taipei's deterrence even more credible.

The ROC navy is also primarily a defensive one. It has no bombers or fighter bombers. It is strong in destroyers (twenty-seven) and weak in most other categories. Taiwan has two submarines of an older vintage and two on order that are considered attack submarines that would be used against PRC submarines in the event that it sought to quarantine or blockade the island.[13] However, against more than one hundred submarines the PRC might deploy, or even a much smaller number, ROC defense efforts could not ultimately succeed. What the ROC navy could do, however, is challenge a paper blockade or a partial blockade. Recently added to Taiwan's navy are ship-to-ship missiles. These would be used against PRC ships in the event of either a blockade or an invasion. They would no doubt be highly effective. Again, however, the small number of missiles Taiwan possesses is a handicap.

In fact, the ROC navy would not be able to destroy a sufficient number of ships to ultimately stop the PRC navy. ROC naval forces, however, may compel the PRC to utilize a large number of its submarines in an invasion of Taiwan and divert its naval powers from other areas, which can be calculated in the deterrence equation.

The ROC air force has no bombers, and for that reason must be considered a purely defensive force. Its fighters could hit targets in the PRC and perhaps destroy some planes on the ground at the onset of a conflict. But this would not be crucial to the air war. Its combat aircraft, most of which are fighter-interceptors (nineteen) and fighters with ground attack capabilities (378), number only little more than 10 percent of those in the PRC air force. Taiwan's pilots are better trained and its planes are generally regarded as equal or better than those in the PRC air force. In past engagements the kill ratio favored Taiwan. This probably would be so in any future conflict. A serious problem for Taiwan, even in a limited engagement, would be refueling and pilot fatigue. The ultimate problem, however, is the PRC's numerical superiority in planes.

Taiwan's air power gives it a considerable measure of deterrence because the PRC would not want to commit a large portion of its aircraft to an invasion of Taiwan for fear of weakening its military posture vis-à-vis the Soviet Union or Vietnam. It would also be concerned about the monetary cost of lost planes.[14] In addition, air combat would quickly come to the attention of other concerned nations and the world community.

Taipei is currently very concerned about upgrading its fighter aircraft so as to maintain its present level of deterrence in the face of new and improved capabilities in the hands of the PRC. Of special worry is the fact that the United States has helped the PRC upgrade its F-8 fighter plane by recently selling Beijing $550 million in radar and avionics equipment. Meanwhile, Washington has not allowed Taiwan to buy a more sophisticated fighter plane, though the U.S. has permitted Taipei to buy military technology, some of which has probably given the ROC air force greater air-to-air missile capabilities.

The ROC air force has improved its antisubmarine warfare capabilities in recent years and this, it is assumed, adds to Taipei's overall deterrence capabilities. This advance was made possible largely by bringing on-line surveillance helicopters with sophisticated detection equipment.[15] It has also been aided by newly employed submarine detection equipment on ROC ships.

The main problem for Taipei in its efforts to maintain military preparedness has been the difficulty it has encountered in trying to purchase weapons from other countries. The United States has agreed (with Beijing) to reduce arms sales to Taiwan, though this promise has been recently defined so as not to include military and military-related technology. Taiwan has purchased two submarines from Holland, but because of pressure by the PRC on the government of Holland, there will probably be no more sales. Other European countries are unlikely to sell arms to Taiwan or are not considered by Taipei to be reliable sources of arms. Taiwan will not purchase weapons from Israel because of Taipei's close relations with Saudi Arabia and its oil dependence on the Arab countries.

South Africa and South Korea are possible sources of weapons, but they are generally not considered good options because Taiwan needs more sophisticated weapons than they can provide. Taiwan can build weapons itself, but this is costly and it is not feasible for Taiwan to build all of the weapons it needs.

Taiwan's Allies and Alliances

Although Taiwan has no formal defense alliances and is not considered an ally of any other nation, one cannot conclude that it is without any friends or "supporters" that will render it assistance in the event of a crisis or war. Nor should it be assumed that Taiwan is isolated, either militarily or politically.

The Republic of China was an ally of the United States and other Western nations during World War II. The "partnership" carried over after the war when the United States assisted the Nationalist Chinese in their struggle with the Communists. In 1949, when the Nationalists were defeated and fled to Taiwan, it was unclear whether or not the United States considered the alliance terminated.

In early 1950, when Secretary of State Dean Acheson stated publicly that Taiwan was not considered within America's "defense perimeter," it was assumed that any alliance relationship was canceled. However, a few months later the Korean War began. The United States immediately started supplying military assistance to Taiwan and continued to do so in ensuing years. Some assumed from this that an informal defense alliance or "relationship" existed. In any event, a formal treaty of defense was signed in 1954 as a consequence of the crisis engendered when Beijing laid siege to the Offshore Islands. Although the U.S.-ROC Mutual Defense Pact, as it was called, covered only Taiwan, the Pescadores, and other smaller islands near Taiwan (and excluded the Offshore Islands), an exchange of notes between Washington and Taipei recognized Nationalist China's "inherent right of self-defense" to "other territories."

The alliance was tested during the second Offshore Islands crisis in 1958. Though it appeared that the treaty was seen by the United States as a defense treaty and could not be used by Taipei to initiate hostilities against the PRC or as help in their effort to "liberate the mainland," U.S. actions in 1958 clearly enhanced the credibility of the defense relationship.[16] So did the subsequent absence of challenge to the islands by Beijing.

In 1968, the United States and the Soviet Union signed the now well-known Nuclear Non-Proliferation Treaty. Among other things, the treaty stated that both superpowers guaranteed nuclear protection to any non-nuclear nation threatened by a nuclear nation. If one assumes that the Republic of China was a legally constituted nation-state at that time (and it was recognized by a host of countries, including the United States, and was not only represented in the United Nations but was also a permanent member of the Security Council), this provision must have applied to it. That being the case, Moscow and Washington guaranteed Taiwan protection from the People's Republic of China, which in the meantime had gained nuclear status. Assuming that losing membership in the United Nations in 1971 and formal diplomatic recognition by the United States in 1979 did not affect Taiwan's nation-state status (It was never stated by any leader in the United States or the Soviet Union or any United Nations official that it did.) then it has had an alliance of sorts with both the United States and the Soviet Union that is applicable to the PRC's nuclear threat.

The credibility of either the Soviet Union or the United States may, of course, be questioned in this case. But neither has ever specifically repudiated any responsibility toward Taiwan under the treaty; neither has ever stated that Taiwan is not a nation or should not be afforded nuclear protection under the Nuclear Non-Proliferation Treaty because it is a province of the PRC (which the executive and legislative branches of government in the United States seem to disagree about in any case).

Taiwan may have still another indirect ally. In November 1969, President Richard Nixon and Prime Minister Sato of Japan met and signed a communiqué that discussed Japan's security concerns and its defense responsibilities in the Far East. This communiqué referred to Japan's "defense perimeter," which, it was stated, encompassed an area that included Taiwan. Assuming that Japan's "defense perimeter" designated an area of concern to both the United States and Japan and was "covered" by their alliance or relates to it, Taiwan is, by virtue of this inclusion in the area of Japan's responsibility, perhaps "allied" with Japan (as well as the United States). It is interesting to note that the so-called Nixon-Sato Communiqué has never been repudiated or in any way annulled by either side and that no leader in either nation has gone on record to deny the interpretation that it might put Taiwan in alliance with one or both countries.[17]

In January 1979, the Carter administration, after announcing its intention to establish diplomatic relations with the People's Republic of China, announced officially Washington's intention to cancel the U.S.-ROC Mutual Defense Treaty after one year. The treaty, in fact, was duly terminated January 1, 1980. This seemingly left Taipei without any formal ally and minus the protection of a superpower, and thus vulnerable to threat, intimidation, or even armed attack by the PRC. But President Carter's decision did not stand.

In April 1979, the U.S. Congress passed an act "to help maintain peace, security and stability in the Western Pacific. . . ." This act, called the Taiwan Relations Act (TRA), stated among other things that the "United States decision to establish diplomatic relations with the People's Republic of China rests upon the expectation that the future of Taiwan will be determined by peaceful means" and that it considers "any effort to determine the future of Taiwan by other than peaceful means, including by boycotts or embargoes, a threat to the peace and security of the Western Pacific and of grave concern to the United States." The TRA also, obviously with the previous statements in mind, promised Taiwan arms sales. Finally, the TRA stated that Congress finds the enactment of the act necessary "to maintaining the capability of the United States to resist any resort to force or other forms of coercion that would jeopardize the security, or the social or economic system, of the people of Taiwan."

Inasmuch as a congressional "act" has the legal authority of a treaty, and in view of the broader language (citing boycotts and embargoes that would jeopardize the security, or the social or economic system, of Taiwan), some have argued that Taiwan was offered a better security guarantee from the United States in the TRA than it had before in the form of the U.S.-ROC Mutual Defense Treaty.[18] Clearly the latter was not so broadly worded and could not be called into force because of a paper blockade or mere threat. Others have argued that the broad language might also be considered a weakness because it is too vague to mean anything. Still others have said that only time will tell.

A 1982 communiqué signed by Washington and Beijing, however, undermined the provision of the TRA promising weapons sales. Moreover, Congress did not act to protect the TRA. It indeed seemed that the TRA had been diluted or ignored. However, continued sales (albeit in gradually reduced amounts), and a refusal by the Reagan administration to include military technology in the promise to reduce sales, gives another impression. So did the fact that the United States has continued to refuse to pressure Taipei into negotiations with Beijing against its wishes, as did its policy of assuming Beijing has accepted a "peaceful settlement only" of the Taiwan issue and linking this to the communique.

Beyond what is stated in U.S. China policy speeches and documents, and communiqués between the United States and the PRC, it is necessary to note that any military action by Beijing against Taiwan would undermine the raison d'être of U.S.-PRC relations to many U.S. leaders and the American public. U.S.-PRC relations were founded to a large extent on a bipartisan perception in the United States that Beijing serves to help the United States counter the threat to peace in the region caused by the Soviet Union's rapid military buildup. The relationship also assumes the PRC to be a stabilizing force in world politics. Any action against Taiwan would change that view in the United States and as a consequence there would probably be a shift in U.S. China policy and likely considerable impetus to come to Taiwan's aid.

Moreover, there has been speculation to the effect that to prevent Taiwan from going nuclear, the United States has promised U.S. action in the event of an attack by the PRC. Considering the level of U.S. aid to Pakistan to prevent it from becoming a nuclear nation, such a promise to Taiwan seems reasonable. It also seems logical considering what a conflict in the Taiwan Strait would do to commerce in the region—especially to Japan's oil lifeline—and the loss of life it would cause.

In addition to possible U.S. guarantees that transcend U.S. policy as it is generally understood, there has been speculation over the years that there may be some secret defense agreements or informal understandings between Taipei and Moscow. PRC leaders have even said as much.[19] Moscow may have spread these reports in order to provoke Beijing or to divert attention away from their border problems. Nevertheless, there is good reason to believe that the Soviet Union favors that Taipei remaining sovereign and not becoming a part of the PRC, inasmuch as PRC jurisdiction over Taiwan might change the status of the Taiwan Strait, not to mention territorial claims in the South China Sea. Moscow clearly prefers to see the situation in both areas remain as it is.

Though rumors of a secret agreement between Taipei and Tokyo have not been heard, it is also reasonable to assume that Japan would prefer an independent or at least unincorporated Taiwan. This being the case, it can be expected that Tokyo would try to dissuade Beijing from taking military action against Taiwan. And while Japan at the present time cannot be expected or give Taiwan any guarantees thereby bolstering its security against the PRC, the fact that Japan is the PRC's largest trading partner and a major source of economic and capital investment means that Japan has some leverage over Beijing.

Taiwan's Economy and Its Security

Taiwan's economic growth over the past two decades ranks it the number one growth nation in the world. In fact, its economic "miracle" has pushed

The Taiwan Political Miracle

Taiwan into the category of "newly industrialized countries" and in some ways classifies it as a developed country. Per capita income is now more than $5,000 per year, which puts it in the developed nation category. Also, using the criteria of the number of telephones, televisions, and other such material goods, Taiwan is a developed country.[20]

By contrast, the PRC, notwithstanding its very impressive economic development in the past seven or eight years, is still among the poorest of the poor nations. Its per capita income is around $300 per year. It still has serious development problems and is constrained in its military spending as a result.

Taiwan's economic growth and the accompanying increases in the standard of living contribute indirectly to the nation's security by enhancing political stability and giving the impression of a foreign policy that regards peace as desirable in order to preserve the nation's material gains. In other words, Taiwan's economic success conveys the impression of a country seeking to preserve the status quo and avoid armed conflict—and indeed this is the case. This strengthens Taiwan's case that the PRC is an aggressor and helps win it international support and sympathy.

Taiwan's rapid economic growth also gives it an advantage in strengthening its security vis-à-vis the PRC. First, Taiwan can afford to spend more on defense if it wishes. In fact, its defense budget has increased annually for a number of years (while the PRC's has decreased or remained steady). This, increase however, does not give Taiwan a big edge against the PRC; in fact, it only helps marginally. It is certainly not enough to change the balance of power that clearly favors the PRC. But it means that Taipei does not have to worry that increased defense spending or the cost weapons development will damage its economy.

Second, Taiwan's successful economic growth has meant that its economy has made a transition from agriculture and labor-intensive production to capital- and knowledge-intensive production. Thus, Taiwan has been able to attract large amounts of foreign investment into its economy, and as a consequence there is a greater concern on the part of foreign countries (the most important being the United States and Japan) that Taiwan remain secure, sovereign, and non-Communist. Taipei, in fact, has intentionally accelerated foreign investment by making it attractive to invest in Taiwan while encouraging domestic investment to go elsewhere.[21]

Knowledge-intensive production has led to even more extensive ties with the United States and Japan and has facilitated the development of an arms industry in Taiwan. (This point will be discussed in further detail below.) It also makes Taiwan less vulnerable to economic competition from the PRC, a nation with a largely agricultural and labor-intensive economy.

Third, Taiwan's economy has been built on a free market and free and very extensive trade. Although trading makes Taiwan more vulnerable to a PRC quarantine or blockade, Taipei has reasoned that it is very vulnerable anyway and that extensive trade relations foster a security advantage by committing other countries to Taiwan. In other words, trading partners may help Taipei, at least indirectly, to counter a PRC blockade or trade war.

Taiwan's economic growth has, in addition, resulted in an integration of its economy with those of other Western countries. This means that technology transfers from Western countries, including military and military-related technology are easier and occur more naturally. It also translates into more joint ventures which are defense related. Taiwan's fledgling defense industries have certainly benefited recently from ties with weapons producing firms in the United States and elsewhere.

One particular aspect of Taiwan's technological progress (and its trade relationship with other countries) is its nuclear energy development. Taiwan is one of the most advanced nations in the world in terms of its use of nuclear energy. This makes Taiwan less vulnerable to a possible PRC interruption of its sources of energy, not to mention pressure on nations that supply Taiwan with petroleum. Similarly, it weakens the argument that Taipei should not discourage or ban trade ties with the PRC, since the latter exports petroleum that Taiwan needs. Finally, Taiwan's use of nuclear energy conveys the impression (which is partly an accurate observation) that Taiwan is a potential nuclear power. This factor makes it more difficult to ignore or isolate Taiwan or consider it unimportant in world affairs.

Taiwan's economic success has also produced a balance of trade surplus and as a consequence a large foreign trade reserves. In fact, Taiwan's foreign exchange holdings are one of the largest in the world. This makes it possible for Taiwan to buy sophisticated weapons, though Taipei has generally not been able to purchase what it wants as easily as other nations that have the money. This puts Taiwan in a position of needing to attract or make deals with arms producing companies that will put pressure on their governments to allow freer or better commercial relations with Taiwan.

Finally, both money and a more highly technical economy have made it possible for Taiwan to develop its own weapons, including a variety of very good missiles. It has enabled Taiwan to build a sophisticated air defense system and greater intelligence capabilities to compensate for the earlier loss of an intelligence network on the mainland. It is in these areas that Taipei has the most hope to maintain a sufficient level of capabilities vis-à-vis Beijing in the future.

Taiwan's Strategic Options: Possible Future Changes

It is unlikely that Taiwan will revise its thinking about who are its enemies and friends in either the near- or long-term future. Nor is it likely that it will drastically or fundamentally change its strategic thinking anytime soon. Both generally seem fixed for some time.

What then will Taiwan do in more specific terms? Taiwan's strategy in the military sense will remain overwhelmingly a defensive one, aimed at deterring an attack by the People's Republic of China. Taipei will endeavor to maintain a credible level of deterrence by making an attack on Taiwan costly to the PRC in terms of the loss of both weapons and manpower. It will do this by upgrading its military capabilities, particularly in air defense and anti-submarine warfare. It will also seek to increase its foreign trade in its own ships and thus develop a larger merchant fleet. This endeavor will lessen the threat of a paper blockade by Beijing. Taipei will no doubt continue to maintain a large army, though due to the need for labor in the civilian sector and Taiwan's narrowly defined defensive military posture, it may cut the manpower of its standing army while increasing its reserves (somewhat after the pattern of Israel).

Taipei will likely continue to try to maintain security and military ties with the United States, which holds the key to Taiwan's deterrence capabilities now and in the future. Taipei, to a considerable extent, relies on U.S. help to keep its defenses and will count on Washington in the event of a threat of PRC nuclear or all-out concerted conventional attack on Taiwan. This is also unlikely to change in the future.

Taipei probably will seek to build closer strategic ties with Japan in the future. Japan is assuming a bigger military role in the region wherein lies Taiwan's only enemy. Also, Japan's military strategy is very much like Taiwan's—heavily defense-oriented. Ties with Japan would help Taiwan strategically in terms of possible defense coordination and research in new defensive weapons. Taiwan's defense planners have expressed considerable interest in the fact that Japan has developed a more defined and sophisticated defense posture and has signed on the Strategic Defense Initiative. In the long run, SDI may offer something to Taiwan.

Taiwan has not expressed a greater interest in a strategic relationship with the Soviet Union. Taipei reckons that its ties with the United States, other Western countries, and Japan contradict strategic cooperation with the Soviet Union. This is particularly true in the context of its military buildup in the region and the threat that it poses to the United States and Japan.

Still, Taipei does not view the Soviet presence in the area, notably its naval presence, as a direct threat and probably will continue to view it as rendering Taipei certain advantages, particularly in offsetting PRC military power in the region. In particular, Taipei sees Soviet forces on the Sino-Soviet border as a signal that Beijing cannot divert much of its military power to the Taiwan Strait area. Ditto with Vietnam and the Soviet-Vietnam connection. However, Taipei knows it cannot influence Soviet strategic behavior and thus wants to avoid relying on the Kremlin. In short, the Soviet Union constitutes an option of last resort and a diversion or distraction for the PRC (and thereby an asset to Taipei), and Taipei need not, and, in fact, cannot, try to formalize this.

Taiwan's defense situation seems to constrain its strategic planning options. In some ways this is true. Taiwan is unlikely to go nuclear. It is probable that it will continue to cast some doubt in the minds of observers (probably intentionally) that it might have nuclear weapons or the desire and capability to build them. Uncertainty is something that is obviously to Taipei's advantage as long as it does not damage Taiwan's relations with its friends among Western bloc nations.

Though Taiwan's strategic planning cannot be very flexible because its defense posture is solely defensive and since it has a single and very formidable enemy and this situation is unlikely to change, Taipei does have some options (albeit they are seldom discussed). Taipei has control and apparent sovereignty over some territory in the South China Sea. In the event of a crisis it could, for example, offer to transfer this territory to Vietnam. Such an action would doubtless intensify already strained relations between Hanoi and Beijing (or in the event of better relations occurring between those two countries, could harm such relations). Taipei might also cause some difficulties for the Philippines, Japan, or Hong Kong if it wanted to demonstrate its ability to cause tension in the region and thereby prevent PRC threats from being seen as simply a "domestic" problem. It can and no doubt would also cause a refugee problem for Japan or the United States in the event Beijing seriously threatens Taiwan.

Taiwan's best option in coping with the PRC threat, however, is to demonstrate to the world, especially to the United States, that it is democratic and peace loving and that its population does not want to be ruled by Beijing. Taipei has been seeking the support of world public opinion and will no doubt continue to do so in the future. As the PRC becomes more dependent upon economic and other ties with the West as well as other nations in the world, it will become more vulnerable to global public opinion. So, too, international community support based on Taiwan's economic and political modernization and the situation of its being the underdog and the "victim" in its relationship with the

PRC is bound to increase. Taiwan's leaders thus perceive that time favors its claim to determine its own future.

Endnotes

1. See Akira Iriye, "Security and Stability in Northeast Asia: A Historical Overview," in Martin E. Weinstein, *Northeast Asian Security After Vietnam* (Urbana: University of Illinois Press, 1982), p. 17. The author argues that the decision to preserve the status quo in the region made China's unification a matter of danger.

2. See Thomas E. Stolper, *China, Taiwan, and the Offshore Islands* (Armonk, NY: M. E. Sharpe, Inc., 1985), for the argument that it was not the PRC's intention to take the Offshore Islands.

3. It was rumored that in the early 1960s Taipei's underground on the main-land was seriously damaged by the defection of one of its intelligence agents.

4. See John F. Copper, "Taiwan's Options," *Asian Affairs*, May-June 1979.

5. See John F. Copper, "Political Development in Taiwan," in Hungdah Chiu, ed., *China and the Taiwan Issue* (New York: Praeger, 1979). The author makes the argument that political modernization was accelerated in order to help cope with Taipei's deteriorated international position.

6. See Martin L. Lasater, *The Taiwan Issue: Sino-American Strategic Relations* (Boulder, CO: Westview Press, 1984), Chapter 7.

7. See ibid. Lasater discusses these issues and several others that follow.

8. See ibid. Also see Martin L. Lasater, *Taiwan: Facing Mounting Threats* (Washington, DC: The Heritage Foundation, 1987) for a revised and updated argument.

9. Lasater, *Taiwan: Facing Mounting Threats*, Chapter 2.

10. Ibid.

11. The following figures are taken from *The Military Balance, 1985-1986* (London: International Institute of Strategic Studies, 1985).

12. This is based on interviews I have had with defense planners in Taipei. Other scholars generally agree on the numbers.

13. See *The Military Balance, 1985–1986.*

14. This argument has been made cogently by A. James Gregor. See A. James Gregor and Maria Hsia Chiang, *The Iron Triangle: The U.S. Security Policy for Northeast Asia* (Stanford: Hoover Institution Press, 1984), Chapter 6.

15. For further details on recent acquisitions by the ROC, see John F. Copper, "Taiwan in 1986: Back on Top Again," *Asian Survey*, January 1987.

16. See A. Doak Barnett, *Communist China and Asia: A Challenge to American Policy* (New York: Random House, 1960), Chapter 13, for an early assessment of the threat in context of U.S.-ROC relations.

17. See Gregor and Chiang, *The Iron Triangle.* The authors note that in 1972, Japan-ese Foreign Minister Takeo Fukuda reassured the ROC ambassador that the "Taiwan clause" remained valid and that Sato himself later said that an attack on Taiwan would constitute a "threat to the peace and security of the Far East including Japan."

18. Senator Jacob Javits made this argument during congressional debate on the TRA. It has been argued by a number of observers since then, though it certainly depends on the TRA retaining an important place in U.S. China policy.

19. For an early assessment of Soviet relations with Taiwan, see John F. Copper, "The Future of Taiwan: An Analysis of Its Legal and Political Status," *Asian Quarterly*, No. 3, 1973. There has been less heard since about a possible Moscow-Taipei "deal," but there are occasional reports and rumors. Also see John W. Garver, *China's Decision for Rapprochement with the United States, 1968-1971* (Boulder, CO: Westview Press, 1982), p. 10. The author argues that fear of Soviet ties with Taiwan in large part motivated Beijing to seek better relations with the United States in the late 1960s.

20. See Copper, "Taiwan in 1986," for further details.

21. See John F. Copper, "Taiwan's Strategy and U.S. Recognition of China," *Orbis*, Summer 1977. One can argue that this remains true today even though Taiwan has huge foreign exchange reserves.

Chapter Nine
The Taiwan Relations Act:
A Ten-Year Record

In January 1979, both houses of Congress began work on legislation that would govern future U.S. relations with Taiwan. Two months later Congress passed the final product—the Taiwan Relations Act (TRA)—by a huge majority: 90 to 6 in the Senate and 345 to 55 in the House of Representatives. In April, President Carter signed the act into law.

This was the first time in U.S. history that Congress had enacted a law designed to define, govern, and oversee U.S. relations with a specific foreign country. The circumstances were unique. Relations with the Republic of China were officially terminated in 1978 when President Jimmy Carter signed the Normalization Agreement with the People's Republic of China, which required terminating formal diplomatic ties with Taipei. In the Normalization Agreement, President Carter made almost no provisions for U.S.-ROC relations after de-recognition. He either did not care, or perceived that this was something the legislative branch of government must and would do. The latter seems somewhat more probable. Carter later provided Congress with draft legislation, though it was clearly inadequate to serve the purpose of continuing meaningful relations with Taipei or ensuring that Taiwan remained secure and prosperous and that its people had the right to determine their own future.

Pundits have since argued that the TRA contradicts two previous State Department communiqués regarding U.S. relations with China. They also contend that there is a fundamental legal disagreement between the TRA and a communiqué signed after the Taiwan Relations Act went into force in August 1982. Most say that, this being so, the TRA takes precedence—because the it is law, whereas the communiqués are simply statements of policy, perhaps glor-ified press releases. Yet the media, the State Department, and White House officials often refer to all of the documents as if they were equal and in agreement (which they are not). Further complicating the situation, Beijing has made it clear that it does not like the TRA and would like to see it revoked and has adopted policies to challenge it. And it has found some support for its position among high officials in the United States.

After passage of the TRA and partly because of it, Beijing and Taipei engaged in a public relations struggle. Both made proposals to each other to resolve the two Chinas situation and to ostensibly bring about unification. Beijing offered what appeared to be reasonable proposals. But, since they required that Taipei give up its sovereignty, they were not, in fact, good offers. And one may doubt the sincerity of Taiwan's offers inasmuch as the population did not want unification (nor did the government), at least at that time and, most likely, in the foreseeable future, unless circumstances changed drastically. Thus, Taipei's proposals were more like counter-proposals broached to divert attention. They challenged Beijing to follow Taiwan's successful economic and political development model, which may make unification feasible (though leaders in Taipei knew this was unlikely to happen soon).

The future of the TRA in large measure depends upon Congress and the American public. But what happens to the TRA will also be influenced by political events in Taiwan. Taipei's response and counter-suggestions vis-à-vis Beijing are important. What Taiwan does in terms of continued economic and political development is also vital. Taiwan is now defined as the most successful nation in the world in economic development—as measured by growth in the gross national product over the past twenty years. Moreover, there seems little evidence that Taiwan's economy is going to falter. It may slow down a bit, but it will no doubt continue to provide for its 20 million residents a high and rising standard of living. Taiwan has also experienced rapid democratization. This has been less apparent, but in some ways it is more important than its economic development because it demonstrates that Taiwan is going in a different direction politically from China. That being the case, unification (assuming military force is not used against Taiwan) would seem unlikely at least in the near future and perhaps even in the long-term. Hence, the TRA will have relevance and importance for years to come.

The reasons the TRA became law in the United States, the debates at the time, its implementation and significance are the subject of this chapter. I shall examine its relationship to other documents (meaning the three communiqués) signed between Washington and Beijing, Beijing's efforts to undermine the TRA, the help it received in this endeavor from some Americans, Taipei's reactions, and the TRA's relevance in terms of political modernization and democracy in Taiwan and the "two China" situation. All of these factors affect the future of Taiwan.

Writing the Taiwan Relations Act

The United States maintained formal diplomatic relations with the Republic of China for several decades prior to 1978. It had granted diplomatic recognition to that government before the end of World War II and continued diplomatic ties even after the Communists captured the mainland part of China and established the People's Republic of China (PRC) there. Washington signed a number of treaties and agreements with Taipei, including the U.S.–Republic of China Defense Treaty, which went beyond most such agreements in terms of the breadth of U.S. commitments. The United States had considerable input, through both economic aid and advice, in the ROC's economic development success and in its political development and democratization.

President Richard Nixon in 1972 drastically altered Washington-Beijing relations, which had been bad since 1949. Strategic considerations weighed heavily on this decision. Nixon wanted out of the Vietnam War with honor. Beijing was involved in a serious conflict, some said a war, with the Soviet Union, and the United States was its only useful "ally." On this basis, the United States and the People's Republic of China sought to build a new relationship. Each needed the other to deal with the massive Soviet buildup in Asia and elsewhere. But Washington and Beijing had been enemies, and, to many in both countries, they still were. Relations had to be changed carefully.

This situation was reflected in the content of the Shanghai Communiqué signed at the end of the Nixon visit to mainland China in 1972. The two sides stated their disagreements up front. They also stated their points of agreement: about Soviet hegemony, a peaceful world, and so on. The "Taiwan issue" was the most intractable point of disagreement. Ambiguous language and incorrect translations, however, helped disguise their fundamentally different positions about Taiwan.

When Jimmy Carter became president, he repudiated Nixon's balance of power perspective of the world, his power politics (including the "China card"), and his "dishonesty in international affairs." Carter's view was of one world, without arms (or at least fewer), better relations with the Soviet Union, and better North-South relations. Soon, however, and after being rebuffed by the Kremlin and getting numerous doses of realism about world politics, Carter changed his view of the world dramatically.

In 1978, the State Department wanted ties with Beijing to enhance its role in policy making and give it more posts abroad. The National Security Council and the Defense Department were worried about the growing Soviet threat, and Carter's personal advisers were apprehensive about the president's chances of reelection. In other words, there was a strong impetus to make a "breakthrough" in relations with Beijing—namely, to establish formal diplomatic relations. The Panama Canal Treaty had passed by only one vote creating deep resentment and hard feeling. The SALT Treaty—President Carter's only arms control agreement—was failing. President Carter needed a foreign policy "victory."

Carter perceived that he could gain politically from establishing formal diplomatic relations with Beijing. But he also knew there would be opposition. In fact, Congress had passed a resolution saying that the president should first consult if he planned to abrogate a treaty (meaning the U.S.-ROC Defense Treaty). Congress also expressed an interest in having some input in any negotiations with Beijing or Taipei regarding recognition. Rather than deal with Congress or engage in open diplomacy, the president chose to proceed in secret. On December 15, 1978, to the surprise of the nation, he went on national television to announce that he had agreed to establish formal diplomatic ties with the People's Republic of China effective January 1.

Congress was on recess and could not react. When Congress did resume, one of its most important tasks was to write legislation to deal with the vacuum left in U.S. foreign relations, namely with Taiwan. The White House presented draft legislation, but, according to Congress, it was not well written and was highly inadequate. For the next two months, Congress, in a bipartisan effort, worked on the Taiwan Relations Act.

Congress penned a set of laws that treated "Taiwan" (the term used rather than "people of Taiwan," which the White House employed; neither used the "Republic of China." The act included provisions whereby Taipei could use U.S. courts and have diplomats in the United States (privileges reserved for sovereign nation-states). It also expressed specific concern for Taiwan's economic prosperity and pointedly sought to allow Taiwan access to U.S. arms so it could defend itself (against whom, it was not said, though it was obviously Beijing since Taiwan had no other enemy). Provisions in the act supported human rights and democracy in Taiwan, with the former linked to Taiwan's defense. Congressional oversight was also written into the law.

President Carter said that he would veto the bill if it violated the Normalization Agreement or any other agreement between Washington and Beijing. The TRA patently did. It treated Taiwan as a nation-state. In fact, it created two U.S. China policies: one made by the executive branch, one by the legislative branch. The latter did not regard Taiwan as a part of China, unless the population there wanted reunification. It saw relations with Taiwan as a matter of congressional concern. Nevertheless, in April, President Carter signed the bill and put the Taiwan Relations Act into force.

During the debate on the TRA, the White House and the State Department made few efforts to influence the course of debate or the final outcome. Both apparently perceived that this would be counterproductive. President Carter did not have a very good image in Congress or with the American people regarding foreign policy making. In fact, he was frequently criticized at this time for an incompetent foreign policy and specifically for signing the Normalization Agreement without really negotiating and for having been "taken to the cleaners" by Beijing. Some said he had political motives for signing the agreement. Moreover, much was said in the media at the time about disagreements among foreign policy making bodies of government, grandstanding by some of Carter's advisers, and his policy failures elsewhere.

Taipei reacted generally with approval when the TRA became law. Congress, to officials in Taiwan, had "repaired some of the damage." Taipei preferred to be called by its own designated name, the "Republic of China," not "Taiwan." But "Taiwan" was preferable to "the people of Taiwan"—which sounded as if there were no government. Its leaders could see that Congress and the American people favored Taiwan. They worried about continued economic ties and arms sales in the absence of formal diplomatic relations. The TRA resolved these issues.

Beijing reacted negatively to the TRA, but not very loudly at the time of the congressional debate. China and Vietnam went to war in February, and Deng Xiaoping was concerned about Soviet pressure and possible military actions against China. He needed U.S. support. Moreover, at this time, except for the war in Vietnam, domestic matters in the PRC had become more important than foreign policy issues. Deng gave economic growth a high priority and in that context good relations with the United States were essential. Thus, the TRA did not create immediate controversy or opposition on Beijing's side. That was left to subsequent months and years.

Beijing's Response to the TRA

In March, after the Sino-Vietnam War had become stalemated and it was clear that the Soviet Union would not intervene, Beijing launched a publicity campaign against the Taiwan Relations Act, repeatedly calling it an "unwarranted interference in China's internal affairs." In April, Deng Xiaoping told several U.S. senators that the TRA had "come close to nullifying" the normalization of relations. Behind the scenes, Beijing's diplomats complained to the Department of State, even suggesting that the TRA be abolished.

But Beijing's criticism in the end was muted. Deng had reason not to make trouble over the TRA. First, he did not want to give his opposition ammunition to use against him. He was using U.S. ties to strengthen his own power and as a means of promoting reform opposed by leftist party hard-liners. Second, after the Vietnam "war," Deng had other reasons to want to keep relations with the United States "on track." Especially important were American "aid" (Vice President Mondale had visited Beijing in mid-1979 and promised U.S. $2 million in American trade credits over five years) and technology transfers (in April 1980, the People's Republic of China was moved from the "Y" category, which included Warsaw Pact countries, to "P"—which entitled Beijing to purchase aircraft, communications equipment, and a number of other restricted goods from the United States). Afghanistan, especially after the Soviet invasion in December 1979 (which was seen as a threat in Beijing), was another factor.

Deng hence adopted a friendly approach toward Taipei. He offered trade and other links, including landing rights in Beijing and Shanghai, to Taipei. He even proposed that Taiwan could retain its own government and military in exchange for ceding sovereignty. In discussions with several U.S. Congressmen, Deng said that he would not use military force against Taiwan except: (1) if Taiwan refused indefinitely to negotiate, and (2) if there were Soviet interference in Taiwan.

During mid and late 1980, Beijing began to complain more loudly about the TRA. The PRC accused the United States of double dealing when President Carter resumed arms sales to Taipei (after a one-year moratorium following the establishment of diplomatic relations with Beijing) even though the president had little choice. Beijing expressed even greater displeasure some months later when Taipei's diplomats in the United States were accorded diplomatic immunity and when the sale of the FX, an advanced fighter plane to Taiwan was discussed. Beijing called the actions "reflective of a two-China policy."

Beijing in following months continued to complain about the FX, high-tech sales promised to Beijing, U.S. credits (which had been stalled), and an unfavorable trade balance with the United States. During this period, Beijing's hostility toward the TRA varied with its anxieties or displeasure on other matters. It also seemed to be a factor of Deng's domestic political problems. His opposition had grown and was quick to challenge him, especially on any matter of U.S. relations.

Beijing's displeasure with U.S. China policy increased in 1981. Deng's opponents on the Left (supporters of Mao, party hard-liners, and ideologues) and the media made frequent negative reference to the TRA and the Reagan administration's friendly gestures toward Taiwan. By 1982, the criticism got louder and relations between the two countries seemed to be on the verge of crisis. Beijing had earlier presented a "Nine-Point Proposal" to Taiwan to settle the issue of reunification, and Taipei had rebuffed it. And, though the proposal got considerable good press abroad, that did not quiet Deng's opponents. Also, Taipei was more clever in its answer than usual, offering reunification, but on Taiwan's terms. Taipei's response noted that it, Taiwan, was eminently more successful in both economic and political development than Beijing and that Sun's "Three Principles of the People" might fill the gap left by Deng and other leaders in Beijing who were abandoning communism and needed an appropriate model.

For Deng, pressure was building, even though in January President Reagan formally rejected the sale of the FX to Taiwan. In May, Vice President Bush visited Beijing and promised to get U.S. financial help and technology transfers "on track." It appears in retrospect that Deng's opposition had momentum. Party leftists harped about U.S. arms sales to Taiwan. Deng's opponents contended that U.S. actions in this realm were preventing unification and violated the Normalization Agreement. Deng, trying to ride the tide of Chinese nationalism while downgrading Communist ideology, however, was vulnerable. He thus sought a formal understanding with the United States on the issue of arms sales to Taiwan to answer his critics.

In August 1982, Washington and Beijing signed a communique saying the United States would reduce arms sales to Taiwan "with the eventual purpose of ending those sales completely." The Department of State, in particular Secretary of State Alexander Haig, pushed for the agreement, apparently to succor Deng. U.S. negotiators, knowing that what they were doing had no support at home, with the U.S. public, or in Congress and that the proposal violated the TRA, said they assumed that Beijing had promised a "peaceful solution only" to the Taiwan question in return. The next day, however, Deng (no doubt cognizant of his critics) said he had not made such a guarantee.

Thus, whether the agreement was to be taken seriously was thus a matter of conjecture. Clearly, the agreement contradicted the TRA's provision promising aid to Taiwan "sufficient to meet its defense needs." There were other problems and a lack of consensus on both sides.

Given the fact that a party congress was scheduled for the next month in Beijing and that Deng was under fire over his close relationship with Washington and his inability to resolve the Taiwan problem, he needed such an agreement to deal with his opposition. And President Reagan, upon the advice of Secretary of State Alexander Haig, gave it to him. While a policy of "equidistance" between the two superpowers was formulated at that party congress, presumably something much worse apparently might have happened. Or so argued the supporters of the August Communiqué. In any case, Washington-Beijing relations remained generally on track.

The arms sales "ban" was subsequently blurred or rendered meaningless. The United States factored inflation into the dollar amount of sales allowed to Taiwan, refrained from stating any specific termination date, and continued military technology transfers to Taiwan. Beijing subsequently complained about violations of the agreement, but these complaints were generally not very strident. Deng at least seemed to understand the advantages of ambiguity.

President Reagan traveled to mainland China in 1984. It was reported that only five minutes of a rather lengthy discussion with top Chinese leaders was about the Taiwan issue. Meanwhile, Beijing was put in "Group V" for U.S. exports of high-technology and military-related goods. U.S. oil companies were busy looking for offshore oil, the textile issue had been defused, and trade increased markedly. In addition, the Reagan administration was busy trying to cope with the growth of Soviet military power and in Asia gave clear signals of "hanging tough." All of this provided grist for Deng in convincing other Beijing leaders of the benefits of ties with the United States, and of the wisdom of not making an issue of the Taiwan problem. U.S. arms transfers to Beijing also weakened the argument often made by the military against Washington's right to sell arms to Taipei.

Beijing, however, continued to pursue its second strategy: making what appeared to be reasonable overtures to Taipei to negotiate the reunification of China. In 1984 (and after) when Beijing signed an agreement with Britain on the return of Hong Kong, Beijing brandished the term "one country, two systems." It promoted the reversion of Hong Kong as a model for the return of Taiwan. Subsequently, Beijing offered mail, trade, and other contacts with Taipei. Deng appeared to want to shift the focus of the debate about the "Taiwan issue" to his solution and away from the TRA.

Meanwhile, Beijing sought privately to enlist the support of a number of important U.S. leaders to help weaken provisions in the TRA and to pressure Taipei to the negotiation table. A number of past presidents, secretaries of state, and national security advisers joined what some called the "Kissinger Committee" or the "New China Lobby" to accomplish these goals. This group seemed to be waiting for an appropriate opportunity to gain access to the White House or Congress or to influence public opinion in the United States. Beijing also counted on the Department of State, which it assumed was almost always supportive of its views.

Taiwan's Response to the TRA

It would be an overstatement to say that Taiwan's democratization has been the result of the Taiwan Relations Act. Political modernization and democratization in Taiwan have been the products of its rapid economic growth, societal change that economic development has fostered, and a secure environment that has made political change easy. In addition, a democratic framework was long in place in the form of a constitution, while democracy had been practiced in local government for a number of years. Nevertheless, the TRA may be said to have been contributory.

Clearly, a "dual" U.S.-China policy, meaning one engineered by Congress that regarded Taiwan as a sovereign nation-state and a White House that did not, put pressure on Taipei. Taipei had to provide reasons for Congress to believe its Taiwan policy was correct and to continue to support Taiwan. Likewise, the fact that the TRA contained provisions expressing a concern for human rights and democratization in Taiwan helped. Ditto for congressional hearings focusing on these issues.

Also Taipei calculated that it had to respond to Beijing's overtures. The most effective way, it perceived, was to suggest that the matter should be decided democratically, since Taiwan was a democracy or was evolving toward it. In other words, the people of Taiwan should decide. Taipei similarly sought to appeal to the international community; vaunting its political development was the best means to do that (since its economic success story was already well known to most of the world).

Within months of President Carter's signing the TRA, Taipei held its first competitive national elections—in December 1980. A new election and recall law had been written. Independent politicians were allowed to organize (even though forming a new party remained illegal). The opposition ran as a group, known as the *tang wai* ("outside the Party"). They harshly criticized the ruling Nationalist Party and the government. To anyone who observed, it was an open, competitive, and free election—the first at the national level in Taiwan's history.

Subsequent elections of the same kind were held. In 1986, the ROC President announced an end to the ban on forming new parties. Soon after, the Democratic Progressive Party formed (from *tang wai* politicians, in large part) and began to campaign for the year-end national election. This election went down on record as the first two-party election in any Chinese nation or political entity (including the People's Republic of China, Hong Kong, or Singapore) and one of the first in any developing country that had no training in democracy from a colonial experience.

Meanwhile, the Nationalist Party became more representative of all segments of Taiwan's population. It ran as many as 90 percent Taiwanese candidates in some elections. Its recruitment favored Taiwanese more than they were a percentage of the population. Even its top decision-making body—the Central Standing Committee—became nearly half Taiwanese. Its links to government were broken, and ties to professional organizations, the business community, and intellectuals were strengthened. Its stated objectives of democratizing the country within the context of maintaining a secure and safe environment became widely accepted by the population.

In 1986, President Chiang Ching-kuo announced that martial law would be terminated. In July of the next year, that was done. Although martial law was not noticed by most citizens and ending it did not have majority public support, the move helped the democratization process psychologically. It also paved the way for a better and stronger legal system and government of law, not to mention wider public input into the decision-making process. Given the importance of abolishing martial law to Taiwan's image, especially because it reinforced the view that Taiwan was becoming a democracy, it was no coincidence that Beijing was not enthusiastic about the move.

Nor is it odd that Beijing criticized groups in Taiwan that talked of maintaining the status quo. Beijing sought to isolate Taiwan diplomatically. It did not want its case presented to the international community or even discussed by other countries. The PRC consequently tried to refute any suggestion that the TRA gives Taiwan a choice or implies that until that choice is made Taiwan possesses sovereignty.

In 1986, Taipei also announced that its citizens could travel to mainland China. It had heretofore encouraged foreigners to see both and make a judgment about how successful each had been. Now it decided to extend this policy to its own people. Many came back confirming that the People's Republic of China had been a failure. They took note of the contrast in standards of living, civil and political rights, and opportunity on the two sides of the Taiwan Strait.

In 1987, work was done on making the elective bodies of government in Taiwan representative of Taiwan and not all of China. During oversight hearings of the TRA, this change had been recommended. Critics had argued that Taiwan was less than free because the Legislative Yuan and the National Assembly claimed to represent all of China. This problem was being fixed—but in so doing it put Beijing on the defensive. In becoming democratic, Taiwan made the prospect of unification with China, at least on Beijing's terms, seem quite unreasonable.

The progress Taipei made in political development did not go unnoticed in the United States. Nor was it seen as unrelated to the Taiwan Relations Act. Congress applauded Taiwan's progress in human rights and democratization. It specifically praised the decision to abolish martial law. Recently it has supported other reforms, including efforts to make the elective bodies of government represent Taiwan only. The smooth transition to a Taiwan-born President has also been favorably received in the United States.

Events in Taiwan clearly justify continued U.S. support. They tell Congress that the Taiwan Relations Act should not be undermined or relegated to a status equal or subordinate to the communiqués, even if relations between Washington and Beijing are put at risk. The United States simply cannot abandon a nation that has been so successful in promoting economic development and democracy. Or at least this is the message Taiwan is sending to Congress and the American people.

Conclusions

The Taiwan Relations Act was written to fill a void in U.S foreign policy. After de-recognition, the United States had no guidelines or provisions for dealing with the Republic of China. Taipei was left in a delicate and unenviable situation. This was unique; the United States had never abandoned a friend and ally. Likewise, it had never espoused a policy that Taiwan belonged to the People's Republic of China. The Normalization Agreement thus said something quite new. Moreover, the American people and Congress disagreed, perceiving that the people of Taiwan should have a choice.

The Carter administration's actions had been in haste and with transparent political motives behind them. Alternatively, the administration ignored the problems it created because of not knowing how to deal with the situation. It was thus thrown in the lap of Congress, where Carter's advisers perhaps thought it should be anyway—or ultimately would be. That being the case, Congress acted, and in doing so, it restored to Taipei its sovereignty and nation-state status. Moreover, it guaranteed arms sales, and hence Taiwan's security, not only against military action but against boycotts. Finally, it demanded respect for human rights and democratization.

The Taiwan Relations Act, notwithstanding what many U.S. government officials have said, does not complement or support the Normalization Agreement and the other two communiqués. It contradicts them in many important ways. The Normalization Agreement and the communiqués view Taiwan as a part of the PRC. The Taiwan Relations Act does not.

Which view will prevail? The Taiwan Relations Act has legal status; the agreement and communiqués do not. The TRA is a law. The others are not. The Taiwan Relations Act is clearly superior in status. But, one must understand that Congress focuses most of its attention on issues of the day. It does not give priority to foreign policy issues. Consequently, the TRA is at a disadvantage in terms of Congress's disadvantage in foreign relations and the fact it may not be able to prevent the TRA from being ignored or diluted. It will have to be reminded and be vigilant if the Taiwan Relations Act is to prevail over the other documents in terms of setting the parameters for U.S policy toward Taiwan.

It is clearly Beijing's policy to oppose, weaken and marginalize the TRA and eventually cause it to be rescinded. Deng opposed the Taiwan Relations Act from the outset. He did not do so adamantly or very openly at first because he needed good relations with the United States. Subsequently, he changed his position. Partly, this was based on his view of Taiwan—that it is "lost territory." Partly, it resulted from pressure from the party Left, which made an issue of Taiwan to embarrass Deng. As a nationalist, he should be concerned about China's territory. His Taiwan policy suggested he was not. Deng had to be careful of appearing too friendly with the United States.

Beijing's strategy was to appear reasonable in offering Taipei conditions for unification. Deng seeks to give the impression that Taipei is stubborn and he is conciliatory. To some extent, this approach has worked. Deng has also sought the assistance of some noted Americans, some of whom have much at stake in keeping Washington-Beijing relations on track. Former President Nixon has a stake in terms of his reputation and the way future historians will treat his China policy. Thus it appears he was willing to help Beijing resolve the "Taiwan issue" to its satisfaction—even though he did not commit the United States to such a policy when he was president.

Taipei wishes to preserve the Taiwan Relations Act, even though some in Taiwan feel the act is demeaning because it does not make reference to or use the term "the Republic of China." Most realize that the TRA is beneficial and that preserving it is in Taipei's best interest. Indirectly, Taipei has supported it. Its leaders have endeavored to fulfill the TRA's call for improved human rights and democracy. And they have used it (both directly and indirectly) in parrying Beijing's offers for reunification.

The future of the Taiwan Relations Act will be determined by efforts by both Beijing and Taipei to respectively weaken and preserve it. It will also be influenced by similar efforts in the United States. And it will be affected by the international community and its support (or lack thereof) for Taipei. In terms of its foreign policy, America is in a dilemma. The United States has two China policies—one from Congress, one from the Department of State. The former is based on the TRA and favors Taipei. The latter is based on the communiqués and favors Beijing.

Chapter Ten
Taiwan and the New World Order

During the last five years, virtually all nations of the world have had to adjust to the demise of communism, the end of the Cold War, and the evolution of the bipolar system to another structure. The Republic of China (ROC), or the nation better known as Taiwan, is no exception. Taiwan's situation, however, was, and remains, very different in some important ways from that of most other countries of the world.

The Republic of China survived because of the Cold War. Had it not been for the conflict between communism and capitalism, Chiang Kai-shek's government and military, which relocated to Taiwan in 1949, would have been overwhelmed by Mao's forces that were poised to invade the island in 1950. The Korean War broke out at this juncture, greatly exacerbating the bipolar struggle. As a result, President Truman dispatched the Seventh fleet to the Taiwan Strait and saved Nationalist China.

Subsequently, Chiang's policy of "liberating the mainland" from communism reflected bipolarity and had resonance in the United States because of the bitterness over the "loss of China." Two confrontations in the 1950s with Beijing over the islands of Quemoy and Matsu made Taiwan a military focal point in the Cold War struggle. Taiwan thus remained a "front line" nation in the East-West conflict.

However, Washington took the position that, while it had to outface Mao, it also had to "leash" Chiang. Chiang subsequently bowed to U.S. pressure and declared that the recovery of the mainland would be 70 percent political (meaning, to many, the mission was being abandoned). In any event, in the new, stalemated Cold War, or loose bipolar system, Taiwan's leaders down-played their policy of liberating China and diverted their energies to economic development.

In the mid-1960s, Taiwan's economy took off. Economic success gave the government of Taiwan a mandate at home and a reputation abroad for improving the welfare of its citizens it never had before. But this was not enough to prevent

Taipei from losing the diplomatic war with Beijing as the bipolar world evolved into a multi-polar one in the 1970s. In 1971, the Republic of China left the United Nations after the General Assembly voted to grant the China seat to the People's Republic of China (PRC). Subsequently, a spate of nations moved their embassies from Taipei to Beijing thus tipping the balance in terms of diplomatic recognition. Taiwan had to adjust to a new "multipolar" international system, one that made China a major player and diminished Taiwan's importance.

When the United States switched sides diplomatically on January 1, 1979, Taipei suffered another blow, though the U.S. Congress subsequently passed the Taiwan Relations Act, which, from the perspective of U.S. policy at least, gave Taiwan back its sovereignty. In ensuing years, continued economic success made it possible for Taipei to sustain and even increase its commercial and other contacts with countries around the world. In addition, democratization won Taiwan kudos and global support to parry Beijing's unification proposals. Taiwan thus hung on.

By the time the old world order began to disintegrate in the late 1980s, Taipei had already adjusted several times to changes in the international order. As a result of its earlier adjustments, its policy makers were neither shocked nor overwhelmed by the sudden need to accommodate to new shifts in the global political system in 1989 and after. Furthermore, Taiwan was presented with some important new opportunities. Communism was no longer a barrier to Taiwan's foreign policy makers, who were seeking new nations with whom they could establish ties. After hard-line Communist leaders in Beijing massacred students in Tiananmen Square in June 1989, China's image in the West deteriorated dramatically. Taiwan, as a result, became viewed as the "good China." Beijing's primary enemy, the Soviet Union, disappeared from the scene, however, thereby enhancing the PRC's ability to threaten Taiwan militarily. Thus, in the security realm, Taiwan's situation was more perilous than it had been during Cold War.

Taiwan's effective adjustments to what might have been calamitous change are instructive. In fact, other nations may gain some insights about how to cope with the new world order from Taiwan's responses. Taipei's actions and policies also reveal much about the "China problem." In this chapter I will assess Taiwan's efforts past and present to adjust to a changing world order. Its policies are subsumed, for convenience, into four categories: (1) domestic, (2) foreign, (3) economic, and (4) strategic.

New Domestic Policies

In terms of its domestic politics, Taipei's responses to a new world order were conditioned by three decades of political modernization. Economic growth in the 1960s and 1970s pushed Taiwan to a stage of development such that the flow of information could not be impeded as it had been under an authoritarian system and rapid economic growth sustained. Economic prosperity also gave rise to a large middle class, and the nation's rapid urbanization spawned new political interest groups and ameliorated "ethnic" differences. In addition, Washington increasingly pressured Taiwan to live up to U.S. expectations regarding progress in civil and political rights. And, 50 million overseas Chinese expected democracy to develop in "Free China."

In the 1970s, political modernization advanced very fast following important internal government reforms. It continued to move forward in the early 1980s with two competitive national elections, followed by the nation's first two-party election in 1986. In 1987 martial law was ended. As democratization proceeded apace, Taipei began to see an opportunity: If Taiwan were a democracy, its leaders thought, how could the United States or the world community support China's efforts to annex Taiwan against its will?

In January 1988, President Chiang Ching-kuo died. His vice president, Lee Teng-hui, a native-born Taiwanese, became president and leader of the ruling KMT. President Lee signified an "end to Chinese history" in the sense that Taiwan's mainland-born leaders, who had put Taiwan at center stage in the bipolar struggle, no longer ruled the country. Within a year Lee engineered additional political reforms that included: (1) calling for the retirement of all "senior parliamentarians" (those delegates in Taiwan's three bodies of govern-ment who were elected when the government ruled all of China), (2) allowing Taiwan's citizens to visit China and PRC citizens to visit Taiwan, and (3) legalizing the formation of new political parties.

Notwithstanding the massacre of democracy advocates at Tiananmen Square in June 1989, Taiwan pushed reform, which was already on fast forward, even faster. It might have been otherwise. Taiwan's leaders perceived that the evolution of a new world order was irreversible: communism was dead (as was anti-communism); democracy was the wave of the future. Taiwan did not have to compete with China for popularity as it had, but it did have to adjust to a new global system.

In December 1989, Taiwan's ruling Nationalist Party oversaw Taiwan's most democratic election to date. During the campaign, the Democratic Progressive Party (DPP) called for reform with haste, citing the changes in Eastern

Europe as proof that democracy could not wait. They also advocated independence, saying that Taiwan did not want to be governed by the "butchers" in Beijing. They called for a two-party system in Taiwan. The DPP made unprecedented gains at the polls.

After this, Taiwan's government, meaning generally the KMT, since it was still the ruling party (notwithstanding a setback at the polls), stood firm when Beijing proposed party-to-party talks (not wanting to recognize the legitimacy of the government of the Republic of China by asking for government-to-government talks). KMT leaders replied, in a jujitsu fashion that exploited the opponent's weakness, that Taiwan no longer had a one-party system. They boasted of Taiwan's democratization. And they argued even more forcefully that the ROC's sovereignty (and thus its future vis-à-vis the PRC) should be decided democratically by the people of Taiwan.

In March 1990, 10,000 students met at the Chiang Kai-shek Memorial in downtown Taipei to protest the means of electing the president—by a National Assembly still representing districts in China. They also objected to the Temporary Provisions attached to the Constitution that allowed the government to delay granting important political and civil rights to its citizens because of the state of war with Beijing. President Lee met with student leaders and pledged to implement these reforms. Observers could not help but notice the difference between Lee's response and Premier Li Peng's reaction when students remonstrated in Beijing. Moreover, in little more than a year Lee fulfilled his promises. Meanwhile, the Legislative Yuan nullified Taiwan's sedition law which had defined discussion of Taiwan independence as an act of treason.

In the fall of 1990, the Legislative Yuan passed bills to create organizations to oversee increasing contacts with China. The Mainland Affairs Council and the semi-private Straits Exchange Foundation were set up. A National Unification Council was also established. In May, the National Assembly terminated the Temporary Provisions of the Constitution. Forthwith, President Lee ended the state of war with Beijing. Political reform in Taiwan was clearly being made with a changing world in mind. Taiwan's leaders realized that these global changes could bring Taiwan and China together or set them further apart. Taipei's strategy was to accommodate to a new democratic world. If Beijing could also adjust, the two governments might converge; if not, Taiwan would go its own way.

Preceding Taiwan's first non-supplemental election in December 1991 (an election for all seats in the National Assembly), the opposition Democratic Progressive Party made an independent Taiwan, or "Republic of Taiwan," a plank in its platform. The KMT condemned this proposal as not only illegal but also unrealistic in view of Taiwan's increasing economic ties with China. The KMT's view reflected a rational response to the new world order. The DPP's did not. China was a part of Taiwan's future—economically at least. Taiwan-China trade was increasing rapidly. Likewise for Taiwan's investments in the mainland. Tens of thousands of letters and telephone calls were going back and forth. The electorate agreed with the KMT and gave it an election victory, plus a democratic mandate it had never before enjoyed.

After the election, KMT leaders were confident. They revised the law to allow increased freedom of speech, making it no longer a crime to discuss either independence or communism. The infamous Black List was reduced from 282 to 5 names. The Taiwan Garrison Command, which had used censorship and other extra-constitutional means to maintain strict social order, was abolished. In April, the Legislative Yuan demanded, and got, the authority to veto government decisions involving new contacts with China.

In December 1992, Taiwan held an election for a new Legislative Yuan (the nation's lawmaking body). This was Taiwan's most important election to date. It represented both democratization and a breaking of links with China (because Taiwan-elected delegates replaced those that represented districts in China, and nearly two-thirds of the new elected legislators were Taiwanese). The DPP, arguing for self-determination and for a policy of globalism, as opposed to Taiwan becoming a part of a Greater China, "won" the election with a much-improved popular vote and a marked increase in its seats in the lawmaking body of government. The KMT had obviously overstated Taiwan's links to China.

Taipei proceeded to hold formal negotiations with Beijing, labeled the "Koo-Wang talks," in Singapore a few months later. Speculation arose that the talks would lead to eventual reunification of Taiwan with China. Others inter-preted the parlays to reflect Taipei's confidence that it could engage in formal public discussions with officials from Beijing and not endanger its sovereignty.

In August 1993, the KMT held its Fourteenth Party Congress. At this meeting the ruling party redefined itself as a democratic party instead of a revolutionary one. Internal reform made the KMT more democratic while giving elected officials a bigger, though not large enough according to many legislators, voice in party decision making.

By 1993, with a newly elected National Assembly and Legislative Yuan in place, the system and the ruling party having reformed, and opposition politics now a central part of the political process, one might say that Taiwan had fully democratized. To many observers, Taiwan was a model of political development. ROC leaders found this successful reform very advantageous in trying to win support from the inter-national community, which has been divided or apathetic about Taiwan's bid to decide its future as part of China or not. Rapid demo-cratization similarly, and perhaps more importantly, reflected the ability of Taiwan's leaders to adjust to profound systemic changes in inter-national politics both quickly and functionally.

A New Foreign Policy

Shifts in Taiwan's foreign policy have also been considerable, both before, but particularly after, the onset of the new world order. Again Taipei's decisions generally reflected accurate perceptions of the nation's predicament and functional responses.

In the late 1950s, Taipei, in response to the nuclear stalemate and U.S. prodding, softened its "return to the mainland" policy. In the 1960s, as Taiwan's domestic policy makers focused on economic growth, commercial ties with other countries increased. As a result, its Cold War, anti-Communist ideology diminished in importance. Following its expulsion from the United Nations in 1971, and in its wake the loss of diplomatic ties with many nations, the ROC adopted a new thrust in its foreign policy called "substantive diplomacy." Relations of substance, meaning primarily economic relations, were given more importance than formal diplomatic ties. In 1979, to adjust to the shock of U.S. de-recognition, Taipei broadened its substantive policy and displayed a willingness to carry on commercial, cultural, and other relations with nations having diplomatic ties with Beijing.

Come 1988, Taipei found it quite facile to accommodate to another new situation. Lee Teng-hui coined a new term, "pragmatic diplomacy," to describe policies designed to respond to reforms in China; the collapse of communism; and the demise of a bipolar, military power-based system. Taipei scrapped what was left of its anti-Communist foreign policy. It pursued economic and even political ties with the nations of Eastern Europe and the former Soviet Republics. It began to view China not so much as an enemy but more as an economic bloc partner.

At this juncture, Taiwan's leaders had already, for a year or two, perceived that the world was changing in fundamental ways. And they knew Taiwan had to adjust. By 1987, the ROC had begun allowing some of its citizens to visit the PRC. Trade via Hong Kong grew. Some contacts were subsequently made "formal" or legal. Taipei did not seek unification, but rather a rapprochement, with Beijing.

In June 1989, after Beijing employed brute military force against advocates of democracy in Tiananmen Square, Taipei did not respond by isolating China as did many Western countries. Why? Isolating any nation, but especially China, was not in consonance with the new world order. Taiwan's policy makers also perceived that reform in China would be put back on track. Communism was dead in China; its leaders were simply unwilling to admit it. Finally, Taipei calculated that the new world order's essential feature was economic blocs. China would be an essential part of an East Asian bloc. Or a "Greater China" bloc or sub-bloc could develop. In any case, Taipei and Beijing would likely be bloc partners.

For leaders in Taipei there was another factor weighing against eschewing contacts with China: the speed of political change in Taiwan. Democratization was pushing Taiwan quickly toward a future separate from China's. Separation or independence, however, translated into isolation (at least from an economic bloc that included China). It also threatened domestic political instability. Political separation, hence, needed to be balanced by increasing contacts with China. In October 1989, just four months after the Tiananmen massacre, a cabinet-level body, the Mainland Affairs Council, was set up to make rules, regulations, and laws to formalize ties with China.

There was intense debate in Taiwan's leadership circles about the nation's foreign policy at this time. Several schools of thought were expressed. All perceived, however, that economic influence would prevail in the new world order.

One group said Taiwan had to seek closer economic bonds with other East Asian countries (and indeed this was happening with, by 1993, half of Taiwan's trade and investment going to neighboring Asian countries). Its proponents argued that America and Europe were becoming increasingly protectionist and isolationist. A Pacific Rim bloc, led by Japan, would evolve. This bloc may or may not ultimately include China, they thought. (Most, however, thought it would). The Pacific Rim bloc, they asserted, would compete with the two other global economic blocs.

Another "school" spoke of a "Greater China" bloc made up of Taiwan, Hong Kong, Singapore, and the People's Republic of China. One prominent official in Taipei, reflecting a fairly widely held sentiment, opined that this group of Chinese "political entities" would make it possible to prevent Japanese economic domination or leadership in East Asia and thus a Japanese-led Pacific Rim economic bloc. Economic contacts with China were, of course, increasing rapidly. The "Greater China" view was opposed, however, by leaders in Taiwan who still feared Beijing and believed that communism was still alive and well in China.

Both views were offset, or complemented, by an internationalist view. Those of this persuasion argued that Taiwan's future was that of a unique global actor—like Switzerland. Switzerland was not a United Nations member; yet it was very international. It was a financial center. It was cosmopolitan. So, too, Taiwan. The ROC, they argued, should not be "tied down" to a bloc. The internationalist position was sufficiently strong to keep Taiwan in the Asian Development Bank, the Asian Pacific Economic Cooperation group, and Olympic competition, even though this required accepting such titles as "Chinese, Taipei" that were insulting to the ROC.

The intense debate among Taiwan's political leaders and academics stimulated public concern about Taiwan's role in a changing world order. As a result, foreign policy issues became a part of election politics. In the 1991 and 1992 elections, external issues played an unprecedented role. Admission to the General Agreement on Tariffs and Trade and participation in a "Greater China" bloc (which the conservative wing of the KMT advocated, getting rid of its anti-Communist ideology in so doing) or the North American Free Trade Association (which the DPP advocated) all became campaign issues.

In 1991, the Legislative Yuan passed a motion that Taipei should rejoin the United Nations, sending a message to the global community that Taiwan deserved a bigger say in international affairs. In 1992, that same body passed into law a "one China, two areas" formula to define Taiwan's relations with China. Meanwhile the Ministry of Foreign Affairs published a "White Paper" on Taiwan's foreign relations and foreign policy strategy signaling that Taiwan's foreign policy would be, henceforth, a democratically based one. An official, detailed statement of Taiwan's foreign policy had never been made public before. In April 1993, President Lee Teng-hui announced that Taipei would seek participation in the United Nations, setting a three-year deadline for making progress toward this objective. The Foreign Ministry subsequently made this a major goal of the nation's foreign policy. Taipei perceived that on moral grounds, because the U.N. should be a truly universal body, and in recognition of Taiwan's economic clout, it should not and could not be excluded.

Given the above, it became evident that Taiwan's foreign policy decision makers had engineered policies both to adjust to a new world order and exploit the opportunities it afforded. Taiwan needed to open up to China (but not allow its sovereignty to be threatened), think in terms of economic blocs, go global, and devise a foreign policy supported by the public. It did all of these.

New Economic Policies

Taiwan also adjusted its economy, economic growth plans, and more to changes in the global system. Before 1989, Taipei pursued global economic policies specifically designed to prevent it from being isolated. It established commercial contacts with other countries in lieu of diplomatic ties. With the onset of a new global order, changes in its economic policies revealed that Taipei not only anticipated the formation of economic blocs but also saw an increasing level of opportunity to use economic power to gain diplomatic advantage and international influence.

In fact, Taiwan appeared to anticipated a the new world order based on economic forces. In the mid- and late 1980s it acted to: (1) diversify trade while reducing the balance of payments surplus with the United States; (2) focus on East Asia in its investment and trade in recognition of the formation of global economic blocs; (3) encourage investment, trade, and other commercial relations virtually any-where, including with Communist countries; and (4) use economic clout to avoid diplomatic isolation and play a leadership role when possible in the international community.

Comprehending the pivotal role of the United States in the new world order, Taipei put renewed emphasis on good economic relations with Washington. Following tariff reduction policies launched in 1987 and other efforts to reduce its trade surplus with the United States in 1988, Taipei pursued still other measures in 1989 to obviate trade frictions. This included, among other things, importing U.S.-made products, even when more expensive and lower in quality, and providing subsidized loans to U.S. exporters of consumer and agricultural products.

As a result, exports to the United States declined from almost half of Taiwan's total exports, 47.7 percent in 1987, to less than 30 percent in 1991. Taiwan's trade surplus with the United States in the meantime fell from $18 billion in 1987 to less than $9 billion in 1992 and was projected to drop to $4 billion in 1994. Taipei thus avoided becoming the target of U.S. trade action. In fact, Taiwan won kudos in the U.S. for being a fair trader and a nation that pursued "friendly and stabilizing" economic policies. This favorable view of Taiwan in the U.S. no doubt helped Taipei win United States support to join or participate in various international financial organizations—including GATT.

Acutely aware of the development of global economic blocs, particularly a Pacific Rim bloc, Taipei put most of its foreign investment in Asia, with the lion's share going to Southeast Asia. By 1990, Taiwan was the second largest investing country in Southeast Asia, surpassed only by Japan, putting $3.2

billion into the region that year. By mid-1992 Taiwan had become the leading investor in Southeast Asia, its total exceeding $13 billion. By late 1993, the figure exceed $15.5 billion.

After Southeast Asia, China became the largest recipient of Taiwan's foreign investment. When China became internationally despised after the Tiananmen Massacre and many Western countries stopped investing in China, Taipei continued to transfer capital. Taiwan money became critical to China. By mid-1992 Taiwan's investment in China officially totaled more than $3 billion (but was obviously much more)—15 percent of the PRC's entire foreign investment using its official figures. In early 1994, Taipei reported that its total investment on the mainland exceeded $10 billion. Taiwan was buying leverage and playing bloc politics.

The United States ranked third. With growing protectionism in America and U.S. efforts to build a regional economic bloc in the form of the North American Free Trade Association (NAFTA), Taiwan wanted to ensure it would not be shut out. Taipei also viewed capital transfers to the United States as helping America at a time when it was suffering a shortage of capital, thereby winning points from Washington. Mexico was also singled out as a target for investment.

Fourth was Europe. As in the case of getting into the "U.S. bloc," Taipei channeled investment capital to several European countries to gain a foothold there before the final solidification of the European Economic Community. Taipei's decision makers foresaw a tripolar, economic-based world. Europe was the third pole.

Taipei's foreign investment engendered increased trade almost everywhere it went—as was intended. The largest increases were with the nations of Southeast Asia and China. By mid-1992, nearly one-third of Taiwan's exports went to Hong Kong (most of this being, in fact, indirect trade with China) and Association of Southeast Asian Nations (ASEAN) members. Trade with China alone reached $5.8 billion in 1991, $7 billion in 1992 and over $13 billion in 1993. By 1992, trade with China was nearly 5 percent of Taiwan's total (4.83 percent of total trade and 7.72 percent of exports). In some categories it was over 10 percent. In 1993, more than 16 percent of Taiwan's exports went to China and planners were saying that in 1994 Taiwan would sell more to China than to the United States.

Alarms went off in Taipei. Government officials had been saying for some time that 5 percent was a "safe figure," above which Taiwan might become vulnerable to trade pressure from Beijing. So the government "persuaded" Formosa Plastics, which was planning investments in China amounting to U.S.$6 billion, to build its plants in Taiwan instead. In 1992, the Bank of Taiwan decided not to loan money to local companies seeking to invest in China. Investments that went sour in China were widely publicized. In late 1993, the Security and Exchange Commission stopped Chun Yuan Steel from raising money on the stock exchange to finance a $10.7 billion project in China. In early 1994, Taipei announced a "Southbound Policy" to emphasize economic ties with Southeast Asian countries rather than China. Economic ties with China would continue to increase, but at a slower pace.

Earlier, in fact in the late 1980s, seeking to "balance" its economic relations with China and pursue a "global" economic strategy, Taiwan opened direct economic relations with the Soviet Union. With the breakup of the Soviet bloc, Taipei saw that it had even better opportunities to expand commercial contacts. Investment and trade relations subsequently increased with Russia and the former republics. Trade with Moscow grew an astounding tenfold in 1989. It continued to balloon—by 59 percent in 1990 and 90 percent in 1991. Taipei entered negotiations on buying natural resources and even on cooperation in aerospace and offered aid to Commonwealth of Independent States countries. A number responded with offers of informal diplomatic ties. Meanwhile, several East European countries signed economic and other agreements with Taipei.

Aware of the role economic power played in the new world order, in 1988 Taipei launched the International Economic Cooperation and Development Fund to provide aid to developing countries. Fund money was instrumental in Taipei establishing diplomatic relations with several Pacific Island and Caribbean countries. In mid-1992, this program helped persuade Niger to recognize Taipei and break with Beijing. It prompted a number of countries to upgrade relations, including the Philippines, several Eastern European countries, and some of the former Soviet republics. In June 1992, after Taipei offered Vietnam $30 million from the fund, Hanoi established trade offices in Taipei and signed an investment guarantee agreement.

Meanwhile, in January 1991, Taiwan's legislature approved a Six-Year Development Plan that allocated more than U.S. $300 billion for infrastructure and high-tech projects. Sixty percent, or U.S.$183 billion, was allocated to foreign contractors and suppliers. Taipei called for bids on a number of big projects, attracting large and politically influential foreign companies, notably from important nations. Observers said contracts given to French companies helped "encourage" the French government to later approve the sale of advanced fighter planes to Taiwan.

Taiwan also sought to use its financial clout to enlist support for joining various international organizations and to challenge Beijing's efforts to isolate

Taiwan. ROC leaders first targeted GATT, applying for membership in 1990. With the largest foreign exchange position in the world, Taiwan deserved in and said so—loudly at times. Its next objective, presumably easier to attain once it gained GATT membership, was to join the Organization for Economic Cooperation and Development (OECD). Policy makers in Taipei reasoned that Taiwan would benefit from being a part of this twenty-four member "club" of rich nations—six of which (Greece, Ireland, New Zealand, Spain, Portugal, and Turkey) had lower per capita incomes than Taiwan. With its trade exceeding that of more than half of OECD nations, and already in the economic assistance business, Taiwan's membership made sense. Because this organization was semi-official and high prestige, Beijing did want Taipei to join; but Beijing could hardly argue that it qualified to be in first. Taiwan's next targets would be the International Monetary Fund and the World Bank. Meanwhile, Taiwan became more active in the Asian Pacific Economic Cooperation (APEC) group and talked about becoming a "dialogue member" of the ASEAN.

With economic power becoming the main mode of influence in the new world order, Taiwan perceived that its path to global recognition and influence would be in large measure through bloc participation, economic globalization, selective foreign aid and foreign investment, and membership in global financial organizations. It seemed to be right.

New Security Policies

Taiwan's national security policy—unlike its domestic politics, foreign relations, and economic strategies—did not change dramatically with the arrival of a new world order. The reason for this is obvious: The new world order did not alter, in any positive way, Taiwan's threat situation. In fact, whereas it has been the grounds for perceiving a diminished threat of war by most countries, just the opposite was true for Taiwan.

The breakup of the Soviet Union, as noted earlier, eliminated Beijing's paramount adversary, allowing the PRC to divert its military forces to areas of the country other than the Sino-Soviet border and focus on other enemies—including Taiwan. Meanwhile, because of the economic travails in Russia and the former republics, China was suddenly able to purchase sophisticated weapons at bargain basement prices. Beijing bought SU-27s and MiG-29s—both much better planes than Taiwan's out-of-date F-5Es and F-104s and even better in many ways than its new Indigenous Defense Fighter, which was just coming off the assembly line. China also contemplated both buying and building aircraft carriers. This would make Taiwan vulnerable to air attack from other directions and certainly more susceptible to quarantine or blockade.

Second, because the People's Liberation Army had played a crucial role in suppressing the Democracy Movement in 1989, the Chinese military was rewarded with more money, more and better weapons, and increased political influence. Military spending in China increased more than 50 percent in the three years following the Tiananmen Massacre. This is how the PRC purchased the new weapons mentioned above. The PLA, which saw its political influence grow with its budget and as a result of continuing factionalism in the Chinese leadership, did not espouse a friendly attitude toward Taiwan.

Third, China has not abandoned communism. Beijing, in fact, feels surrounded and threatened by nations that "want to destroy China's political system." It thus espouses a hostile view of the world. Certainly Taiwan cannot expect Beijing, as long as it is at odds with much of the world, to consider Taiwan anything but a threat, especially given recent talk of independence, which is very provocative to Chinese leaders, and the fact that pro-democracy factions in China have proclaimed Taiwan a model.

Finally, Beijing seems determined to play a larger military role in the region, if not the world. Recent tensions in the South China Sea between China and Vietnam over offshore territorial claims attest to this. Also relevant is the fact that China appears to be in an arms race with Japan, the only other major nation in the world that is increasing its defense spending and a traditional rival for influence in Asia. The fact that Taiwan was once taken from China and made part of the Japanese Empire is certainly not forgotten by Chinese leaders in Beijing.

To decision makers in Taipei, the stark reality is that China is a military threat. If Beijing employed strategic weapons, or if it launched a full-scale assault on the island, Taiwan could not, without outside help, survive. This is as true now as it was during the Cold War. Hence, Taipei realizes it must increase its deterrence capabilities as China enhances its power projection abilities, while continuing to rely on U.S. security guarantees and the force of world public opinion.

Cognizant of its greater need for deterrence, Taipei, in 1989 and 1990, began arguing more forcefully its need for more advanced weapons. It asserted that the Taiwan Strait had not become a site of reduced tension because of the end of the Cold War; in fact, just the opposite. Taiwan's military leaders contended that the balance of power there was being upset and that if Taiwan were stronger, peace in the region would be more, not less, likely.

In early and mid-1992, it witnessed a payoff: Both France and the United States offered to sell Taiwan high grade jet fighter planes. Taipei was thus better able to maintain air superiority over and around the island, critical to its being able to use its antisubmarine warfare capabilities and/or stop a massive assault on the island by sea. Together with advances in its strategic industries and an enlarged merchant fleet, which might be used in the event Beijing were to intimidate foreign ships seeking to enter or leave Taiwan, these weapons will enable Taipei to deal more effectively with a quarantine or blockade.

Meanwhile, Taipei continues to entreat Chinese leaders in Beijing to renounce the use of force against Taiwan. Taiwan's policy makers, however, are sure that Beijing will never accede to this. They also realize that any promise not to use force is worth little or nothing (given the historical record of such promises) and may be a negative (in terms of lulling its own public into a sense of false security while engendering opposition to larger defense spending). Hence, Taipei is, in reality, aiming its charges against Beijing at the United States and the global community, which it sees as sympathetic.

Because it is essential to keep Washington's support to guarantee that the defense provisions in the Taiwan Relations Act are activated in the event of a crisis, Taipei has carefully avoided several strategic options it might otherwise employ. This helps further explain Taiwan's defense strategy. What are these options it has not exercised (and no doubt will not)?

One, Taipei has abandoned its nuclear weapons program—which it pursued to the point of near-development a few years ago. It has also stopped producing offensive missiles that might deliver nuclear warheads. Taipei calculates that it must preserve its good image in Washington and its worthiness of a U.S. rescue in the event its shores are assaulted. If and when an attack occurs, both public opinion in the United States and perceptions of Taiwan in the White House and the Congress will matter.

Two, Taiwan is not pursuing military cooperation with Moscow or Hanoi. While the Soviet, or now Russian, option may be little more than wishful thinking, it has been a possibility in the past and may be available again in the future. Certainly Moscow might be an alternative source of weapons. However, because of the importance of the United States, not to mention the fact that Russia is not considered reliable, Moscow is not considered a real choice in Taipei. Neither is a Vietnam option, though ties with Hanoi might also divert Beijing's attentions. Again, ROC leaders do not want to antagonize the United States, and a strategic relationship with Vietnam might do just that given the fact that Washington has not restored formal relations with Hanoi (notwithstanding the end of the U.S. embargo against Vietnam).

Three, strategic planners eschew the independence option, as they fear it would be the pretext for Beijing to use military force against the island. They reason that the United States will come to Taiwan's aid only if Taiwan is a victim of unprovoked aggression, meaning it does not challenge Beijing with a policy of separation. Thus Taiwan's military leaders have spoken of the "military imperative" for avoiding separation. They proclaim they do not want to go to war and do not feel they can be confident of Washington's help if Taiwan provokes Beijing by declaring independence. While military leaders cannot prevent opposition politicians from talking about independence or even from making it policy, they do offer a sobering message on the matter.

In contrast to these options not to be taken, Taipei has recently given serious consideration to a regional security organization. In September 1992, President Lee broached this idea and cited Taiwan's interest in participating. He even mentioned allocating funds for such an organization. Taipei is worried about the prospects of a U.S. military draw-down in Asia and hence seeks to promote a regional security solution that either includes China (to put collective pressure on Beijing to stop expanding its military power, especially in ways that threaten Taiwan) or excludes it (as a kind of collective defense measure).

Conclusions

In summation, Taiwan has had to respond to several major shifts in the international system over the past four plus decades. The ROC was a focal point in the East-West bipolar struggle of the old order and had to accommodate to policy shifts by the big powers, especially the United States, during that period. It adjusted to a kind of multipolar system in the 1970s and to a triangular relationship between Washington, Moscow, and Beijing that gave China a "swing" or special role. Recent adjustments to the new world order were not as difficult for Taipei as might otherwise have been the case because of its experience in adjusting to global systemic change.

In 1989, when sudden and unexpected changes occurred in the Soviet bloc signaling the end of the Cold War, democratization had already transformed Taiwan in the eyes of the world from an authoritarian dictatorship to a model of democratic political development. Taiwan, then in step with the global democratic wave, promoted even more reforms, boasted of the Taiwan experience, and made a bid for Taiwan's future being decided democratically.

Foreign policy shifts in 1989 and after mirrored an adroitness Taiwan had developed in adjusting to changes in the world in the late 1950s and 1960s and an ability to cope with diplomatic setbacks of the 1970s and 1980s. It also reflected an attitude of dealing with adversity. When the challenge of a new world order appeared, Taipei paid special attention to the United States in recognition of a post-cold war unipolar system with only one superpower—however temporary or tentative that might be. Taipei also began to think in terms of global blocs, and in particular a tripolar economic bloc-based world. It also increased its global perspective. It suffered humiliation because of its untidy position in the world (its sovereignty being challenged by a major world power); but it also took advantage of new opportunities. It brought foreign policy goals into tandem with domestic policy, or balanced the two. It based its external policy more on its financial power. Taiwan's foreign policy became, as it said, flexible, nonideological, and multidimensional. Never did Taiwan consider isolationism.

Taiwan's new economic policies, made to adjust to the reality of an economic power-based global system and three large, global blocs, consisted of a mixture of globalism, regional integration, and links with China to join a "Greater China" bloc. It also meant maintaining strong economic ties with the United States. Said one observer: "Taiwan is attempting to be a Switzerland, join Japan, buy the PRC and keep close economic ties with America all at the same time, and remain an economic development model for Third World countries." Taiwan saw that it could gain global influence from its economic clout. With the huge foreign exchange reserves, Taiwan became a capital exporter, and it picked targets. Finally, ROC leaders sought aggressively to join global financial organizations.

In the security realm Taiwan did not see an era of peace approaching as did most nations of the world. Instead it faced a threat similar to the one it faced in the days of a tight bipolar system. Taipei reacted by increasing its military deterrence. It also sought better relations with China, but it perceived it needed greater military strength to do this. Taiwan likewise pursued policies designed to: (1) keep its allies (particularly the United States), (2) win support from world public opinion, and (3) help build a global or regional collective security system to complement its deterrence strategy. It picked options that fit these objectives and rejected others.

In summation, Taiwan's place in world politics in the past was unique. This is even more true today. Taiwan has adjusted to global changes as no other nation has. It is doing it again. Democratization, flexible diplomacy, a combination of global and regional economic policies, and increased deterrence all seem different responses, yet they fit together. Taiwan's adjustments to the new world order have been well designed. If they continue to work, Taiwan will not only survive but may play a special role in the post-Cold War order.

Index

Infrastructure, 21, 25, 42, 147, 420, 559
Injuries, 204, 280, 355, 382, 429
Intellectuals, 128, 354, 365, 391-392, 545. See also Academics, Scholars.
Intelligence Bureau, 57, 85
International Monetary Fund, 560
Internationalism. See globalism.
Iran, 187
Ireland, 560
Iron Man of Asia, 210
Ishigaki City, 428
Islets, 454
Isolationism, 130, 311, 403, 488, 501, 512, 564
Israel, 16, 507, 525, 531
Italy, 509

Jails, 78, 86, 90, 93, 111, 136, 190, 192, 208-210, 213, 226, 247, 257, 324, 378. See also Prisons
Japan, 11-16, 20, 25, 29, 31, 34-35, 41-46, 50-51, 69, 72, 94, 108, 116, 122, 135, 142, 159, 162-163, 180, 217, 227, 229, 260, 263, 279, 323, 331, 336, 339, 350-351, 353, 364, 367-368, 374-375, 384-385, 396, 406, 414, 417, 420-423, 425-431, 435-436, 438-440, 442, 445-446, 448-452, 455, 457, 459, 465, 473, 492, 494, 516-518, 522, 526, 528-529, 531-532, 555, 558, 561, 564. See also Tokyo.
Japanese Current, 425-426
Japanese Defense Agency, 431
Japanese Empire, 438, 450-451, 561
Jaw Shao-kong, 163, 294-295, 298, 306, 325, 328, 330, 333. See also Chao Shao-kong.
Joint Commission on Rural Reconstruction (JCCR), 21

Jet Fighter Planes. See F-4, F-5, F-5e, F-8, Fighter-interceptors, FX, Indigenous Defense Fighter, Mig-29, Su-27, Warplanes
Jiang Zemin, 303
Jih Rong-ze, 328
Joint Chiefs of Staff, 415
Ju Gau-jeng, 251, 326-328. See also Rambo.
Judges, 21

Lawmaking. See Legislative Yuan, Legislature, Parliament.
Lawsuits, 323
Lawyers, 86, 89, 296, 392. See also Attorneys.
Lee Huan, 138, 142-143, 145, 166, 170
Lee Sen-fong, 294
Lee Teng-hui, 5, 49, 59, 62, 65, 80, 110, 126, 134, 139-141, 151, 161, 164, 259, 262, 271, 275, 282, 293, 296, 301, 321, 329-330, 360, 383, 393, 551, 554, 556
Leftists, 127, 338, 396, 541-542
Left-wing groups, 392
Legislation, 15, 35, 66, 89, 92-97, 116, 126, 171, 225, 227, 232, 238, 258, 312, 319-320, 351, 356, 363, 367, 389, 395, 406, 463-464, 468-469, 476-477, 481, 536, 539
Legislative Yuan, 7, 17-18, 24, 32, 66, 68, 70-71, 85, 89-91, 98, 110-113, 115-117, 124, 126, 139, 141, 144-146, 159-160, 162-163, 166-167, 169-171, 181-183, 185, 191, 193-195, 203, 205, 212, 215-216, 227-228, 236-239, 245-249, 255-258, 269, 272, 274, 279-280, 287, 291-292, 294-295, 298-299, 304-306, 308, 310-312, 319, 322, 324, 333, 335-336, 340, 357, 362-363, 365, 378, 380, 388-389, 392, 545, 552-

549, 554-555, 560-564. See also Army, Japanese Defense Agency, Joint Chiefs of Staff, Ministry of Defense, Navy, Pentagon, People's Republic of China Air Force, Republic of China Air Force Republic of China Army, Republic of China Navy, Seventh Fleet.
Militia, 523
Mines, 44-45, 48, 58, 78, 224, 523
Ming Dynasty, 426
Minister of Education, 442
Ministry of Cultural Affairs, 148
Ministry of Defense, 92
Ministry of Economic Affairs, 21
Ministry of Finance, 58
Ministry of Foreign Affairs, 233, 331, 483, 513, 556
Ministry of Interior, 227, 321, 390
Ministry of Justice, 169, 320
Minor Parties, 31, 183, 236, 270, 281-282, 287, 291, 308, 337, 387-396
Minority Groups, 423
Misconduct (of officials and politicians), 234, 320
Misgovernance, 60
Missiles, 444, 519-520, 522-524, 530, 562. See also Air-land-sea missile, Air-sea-ground missiles, Air-to-air missiles.
Missionaries, 351
Modernization (economic and political), 4, 6-7, 9-12, 15-17, 19, 22, 26, 34-35, 41-42, 46, 56, 63-64, 72, 81, 87, 96-97, 99, 109, 112, 114, 120, 124, 136, 147, 149, 179-180, 223, 238, 253, 260, 273-274, 288, 300, 349, 377, 439, 458, 489, 492, 495-498, 514, 532, 537, 544, 551
Monarchy, 134
Mondale, Walter, 91, 541
Mongolia. See Outer Mongolia.

Monopolies, 48, 58, 137-138, 148, 227, 232, 250, 361, 391
Monsoons, 425
Moralism, 424
Moscow, 77, 417-418, 422, 441-442, 448, 468, 473, 490, 493-496, 499-500, 502, 517, 526, 528, 559, 562-563. See also Kremlin, Soviet Union
Most Favored Nation, 474, 496
Motorcycles, 14
Mountains, 122
Multiparty System, 184, 256, 287, 308, 367-368, 373, 382, 385, 388
Multipolar System, 563
Municipalities, 273, 352
Murders, 47, 57, 213-214, 224, 247, 249, 322-323, 331. See also Killings.
M-14 (rifle), 416

NAFTA. See North American Free Trade Agreement.
National Assembly, 7, 17-18, 32, 66, 68, 70-71, 94, 110-112, 116-117, 124, 137, 159, 161-162, 166-167, 169, 181-182, 185, 191, 193-195, 203, 215, 225, 236-239, 246, 269-273, 277, 280, 282, 284-285, 293, 301, 310, 319, 335-336, 340, 356-357, 359, 362, 383, 388-389, 442, 545, 552-553
National Democratic Independent Political Alliance (NDIPA), 270, 277-278, 281, 283
National Defense, 23, 78, 89, 112, 146, 150, 299
National Defense Council, 78
National Health Insurance Plan, 330
National Political Council, 388
National Security, 44, 56, 59, 63, 69, 86, 89, 92, 94, 96-97, 113, 140, 225, 227, 230, 322, 363, 381, 403, 413, 468,

Villages, 77, 320, 331, 338
Violence, 22, 70, 125, 148, 181, 183,
    185, 187-188, 194, 204, 209,
    218, 228, 234-235, 249, 275,
    281, 285, 292, 308, 321-322,
    325, 329, 336, 353-355, 358,
    364, 378, 425-426, 458
Visas, 92, 247, 412, 440, 453
Vocational Assistance Commission,
    146
Voluntary Retirement of Senior
    Parliamentarians, 246
Vote Buying, 249, 287, 320-321, 337
Vote Getters, 213-214, 239, 257, 306-
    307
Voters, 20, 30-32, 48, 59, 61-62, 69,
    72, 94, 111, 115, 125, 180,
    182, 193, 196-199, 205, 208-
    210, 213-214, 223-224, 226,
    230-231, 234-235, 238-239,
    249, 252, 254-255, 258, 260,
    262-263, 270, 274-281, 285-
    287, 291-294, 296, 300, 302-
    304, 307-308, 310, 319, 321,
    326-327, 332, 334, 336-340,
    357, 363-364, 378, 383, 385,
    388-390, 392-393, 395, 455
Voting, 30-32, 60, 62, 71, 123, 139,
    165, 168, 190, 193-194, 199,
    205-206, 217, 240, 249, 251,
    262, 278-280, 282, 285-287,
    292, 304, 322, 325, 337-339,
    354, 390

Wages, 96, 135
Walkouts, 95
Wang Chien-shien, 295, 298, 306
Wang Hsi-ling, 57
Wang Sheng, 63
Wang Yi-hsiung, 365, 392
War, 4-5, 10, 16, 29, 34, 42, 46, 50,
    79, 85, 105, 108, 115-116,
    122, 135, 164, 180, 253-254,
    273, 307, 323, 327-328, 350,
    375, 393, 403, 406, 409,
    426-428, 441, 450-452, 454-

455, 457-458, 465-467, 469,
    479, 481, 485, 491-494, 498,
    502, 507, 509, 516-517, 519,
    521-525, 530, 538, 540-541,
    549-550, 552, 554, 560-561,
    563-564
Warfare, 63, 351, 375, 418, 473, 524,
    531, 562
Warheads, 444, 522, 562
Warlordism, 374
Warrants, 112
Warsaw Pact, 541
Warships, 430, 441
Washington, 67, 79, 88, 106-107, 114,
    129, 143, 151-152, 224, 227,
    246, 309, 323-324, 361, 403-
    405, 407, 409-412, 414-417,
    420-423, 427, 429-430, 432,
    435, 439-441, 446-447, 453,
    463-464, 466-467, 469-473,
    475-478, 481-482, 487-491,
    494-503, 517-518, 524-527,
    531, 537-539, 542-543, 546,
    549, 551, 557-558, 562-563.
    See also United States.
Washington-Beijing Relations. See
    Sino-American Relations.
Washington Post, 67, 88, 227, 361
Watergate, 467
Weather, 28, 61, 193, 213, 334
Wei Tao-ming, 428
West Germany, 435. See also Germany
Western Europe, 34, 42, 50, 79, 108,
    361, 448
Western Pacific, 527
Westerners, 11, 449
Westernization, 16, 197
Westinghouse, 444
White House, 114, 406, 416, 436, 440,
    463, 468, 474, 484, 492,
    499, 536, 539-540, 543-544,
    562
White Paper, 300, 556
Wine and Tobacco Monopoly, 48, 58
Wisdom Coalition, 294, 296
Wittfogel, Karl, 121

About the Author

John F. Copper is the Stanley J. Buckman Distinguished Professor of International Studies at Rhodes College in Memphis, Tennessee. He is the author of nineteen books on Chinese and Asian affairs, including seven books on Taiwan. His book *China's Global Role* (1980) won the Clarence Day Foundation Award for outstanding research and creativity. Professor Copper's most recent books are *China Diplomacy: The Washington-Taipei-Beijing Triangle* (1992); *Historical Dictionary of Taiwan* (1993); *Taiwan's 1991 and 1992 Non-Supplemental Elections* (1994); *Taiwan: Nation-State or Province?* second edition (1995).

Professor Copper has lived in Asia for thirteen years, including six years in Taiwan. He speaks Chinese.